Owning the Earth

BY THE SAME AUTHOR

Measuring America: How an Untamed Wilderness Shaped the United States and Fulfilled the Promise of Democracy

The Fabric of America: How Our Borders and Boundaries Shaped the Country and Forged Our National Identity

An Artist in Treason: The Extraordinary Double Life of General James Wilkinson

Why Spencer Perceval Had to Die: The Assassination of a British Prime Minister

The Code of Love

Wild People: Travels with Borneo's Headhunters

Unhusbanded: The Life of Charlotte Despard, Socialist, Suffragette and Sinn Feiner

The Black Watch: The History of the Royal Highland Regiment

OWNING THE EARTH

The Transforming History of Land Ownership

ANDRO LINKLATER

BLOOMSBURY
LONDON • NEW DELHI • NEW YORK • SYDNEY

First published in Great Britain 2014
First published in 2013 in the United States

Bloomsbury Publishing Plc
50 Bedford Square
London
WC1B 3DP

www.bloomsbury.com

Bloomsbury Publishing, London, New Delhi, New York and Sydney

A CIP catalogue record for this book is available from the British Library

ISBN 978 1 4088 1574 8

10 9 8 7 6 5 4 3 2 1

Typeset by Westchester Book Group
Printed and bound in Great Britain by CPI Group (UK) Ltd, Croydon CR0 4YY

MIX
Paper from responsible sources
FSC www.fsc.org FSC® C020471

For George Gibson
in friendship and gratitude

Table of Contents

THE WORLD'S GRASSLANDS

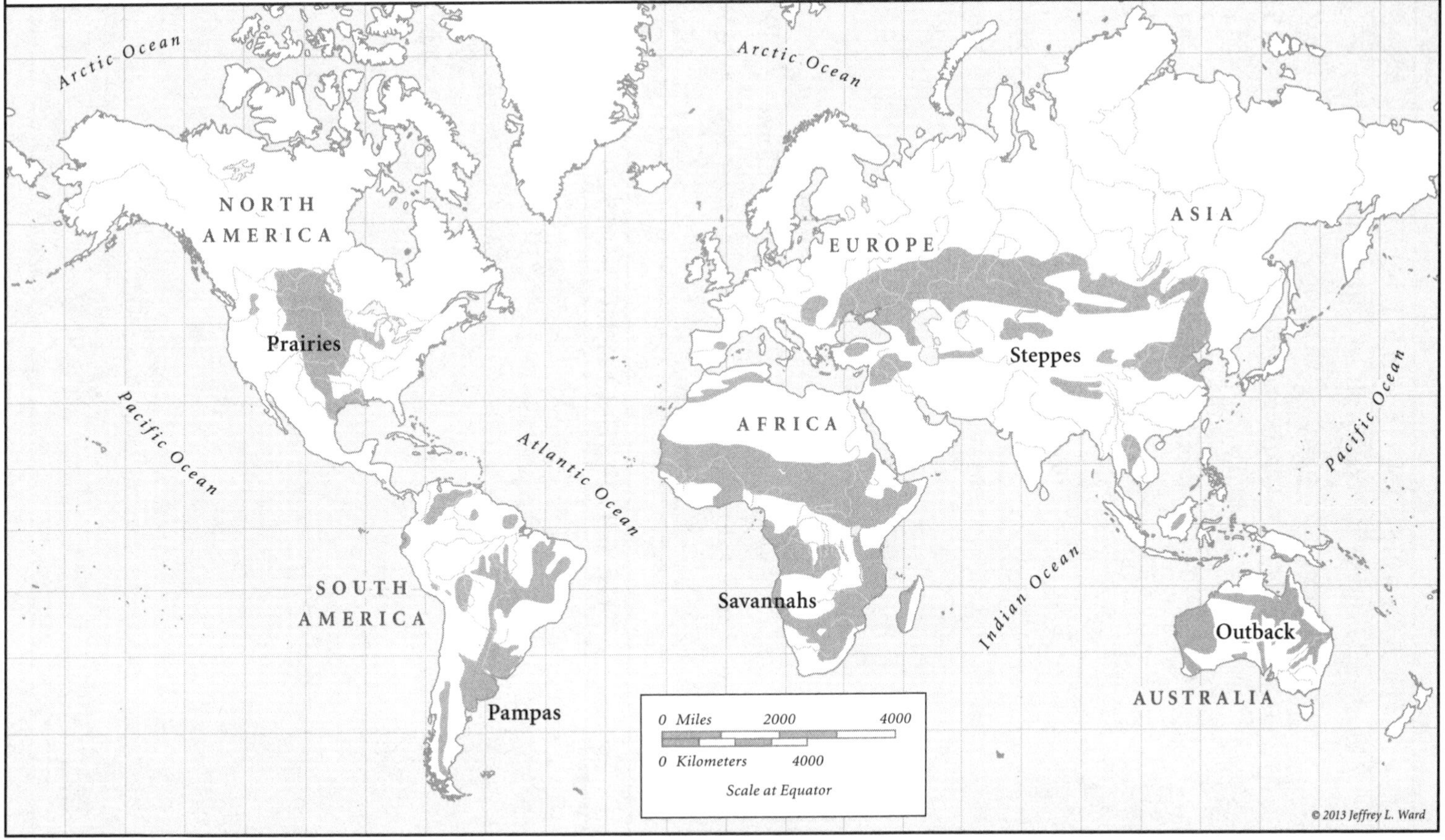

THE EXPANSION OF THE UNITED STATES

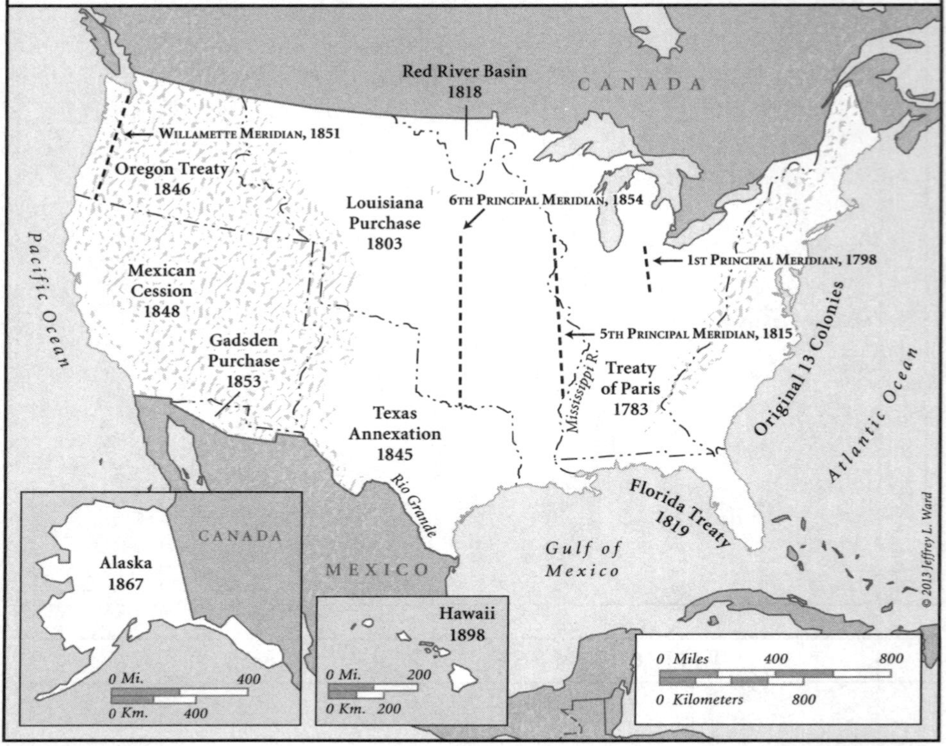
Red River Basin
1818
CANADA
Willamette Meridian, 1851
Oregon Treaty
1846
Louisiana
Purchase
1803
6th Principal Meridian, 1854
Pacific Ocean
Mexican
Cession
1848
1st Principal Meridian, 1798
Original 13 Colonies
Gadsden
Purchase
1853
5th Principal Meridian, 1815
Mississippi R.
Treaty
of Paris
1783
Atlantic Ocean
Texas
Annexation
1845
Rio Grande
Florida Treaty
1819
© 2013 Jeffrey L. Ward
CANADA
Alaska
1867
Gulf of
Mexico
MEXICO
Hawaii
1898
0 Mi. 400
0 Km. 400
0 Mi. 200
0 Km. 200
0 Miles 400 800
0 Kilometers 800

THE BRITISH EMPIRE c. 1920

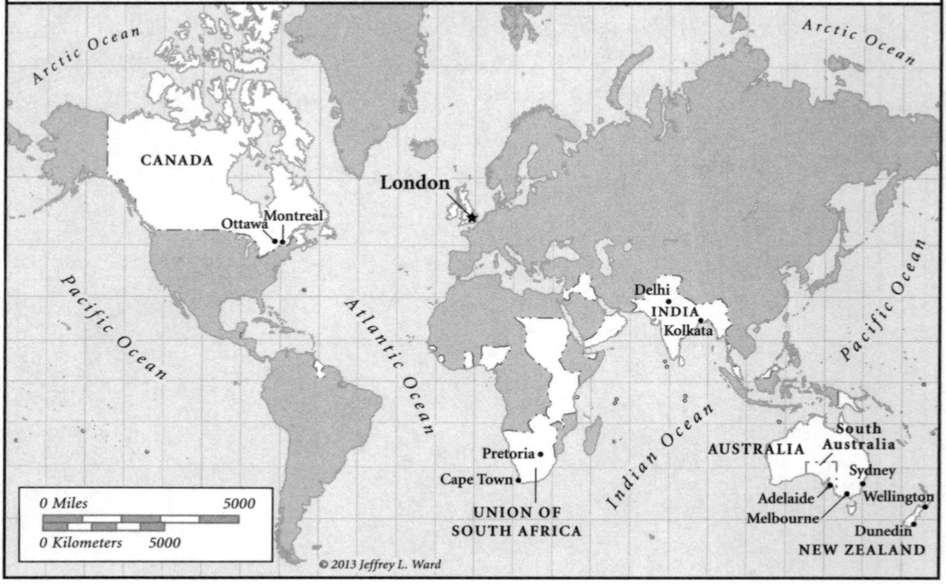
Arctic Ocean
Arctic Ocean
CANADA
London
Ottawa
Montreal
Pacific Ocean
Atlantic Ocean
Delhi
INDIA
Kolkata
Pacific Ocean
Indian Ocean
South
Australia
AUSTRALIA
Pretoria
Cape Town
UNION OF
SOUTH AFRICA
Sydney
Adelaide
Wellington
Melbourne
Dunedin
NEW ZEALAND
0 Miles 5000
0 Kilometers 5000
© 2013 Jeffrey L. Ward

THE RUSSIAN EMPIRE c. 1914
Arctic Ocean
Arctic Ocean
SIBERIA
Lena R.
Ob R.
Yenisey R.
St. Petersburg
VOLGA BASIN
Moscow
BLACK EARTH REGION
Volga R.
Voronezh
Amur R.
Beijing
CHINA
INDIA
Pacific Ocean
0 Miles 1000 2000
0 Kilometers 2000
© 2013 Jeffrey L. Ward

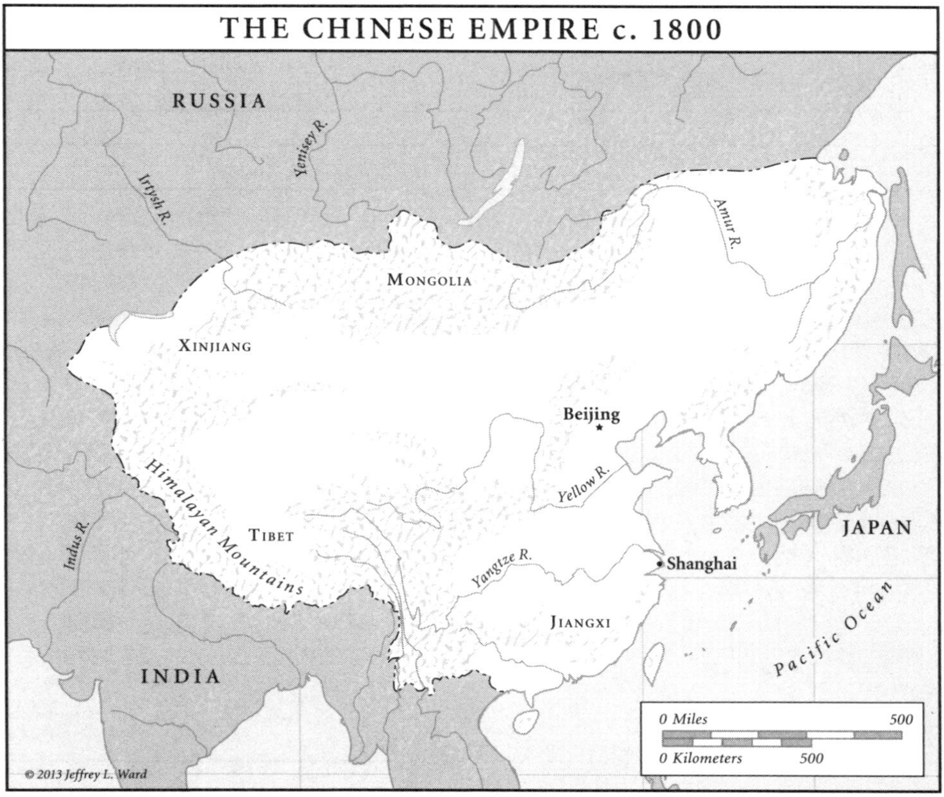
THE CHINESE EMPIRE c. 1800
RUSSIA
Yenisey R.
Irtysh R.
Amur R.
MONGOLIA
XINJIANG
Beijing
Yellow R.
Himalayan Mountains
TIBET
Indus R.
Yangtze R.
Shanghai
JAPAN
JIANGXI
Pacific Ocean
INDIA
0 Miles 500
0 Kilometers 500
© 2013 Jeffrey L. Ward

INTRODUCTION

THE BIRTH OF A REVOLUTION

ON SEPTEMBER 29, 1583, a storm of appalling violence swept across the eastern Atlantic. It caught the *Golden Hind* and the *Squirrel*, two ships led by Sir Humphrey Gilbert, a scientist and adventurer, as they returned to England from an expedition to plant the first English colony in North America. During the day, according to Captain Edward Hayes, master of the forty-ton *Golden Hind*, the waves were "breaking short and high, Pyramid-wise . . . men which all their lifetime had occupied the Sea never saw more outragious Seas." Amid this chaos of white water, Hayes could see downwind of him the ten-ton frigate, *Squirrel*, that carried Gilbert.

As he watched, a furious blast of the gale suddenly threw the *Squirrel* on her side. At once, the *Hind* bore down to offer what help she could. But miraculously the tiny vessel righted herself and, to Hayes's astonishment, Gilbert could be seen sitting in the stern, holding a book in his hand, and "giving forth signes of Joy." As the larger ship surged past, Hayes remembered, "[Gilbert] cried out unto us in the *Hind,* 'we are as neere to heaven by sea as by land'."

Nothing about the "valiant and learned" Gilbert was predictable. A character in perpetual conflict, he contrived to be a soldier and a mathematician, openly bisexual, cruel enough to decapitate his enemies after battle then line the path to his tent with their severed heads, creative enough to imagine the growth of a new world beyond the Atlantic, and forceful enough to push through his pioneering expedition without adequate funds or manpower. Perhaps the most striking testament to Gilbert's unorthodox character was his choice of a partner, Queen Elizabeth's astrologer, John Dee, known as the Great Magus.

Tall, bearded, and obsessed with numbers, Dee professed to communicate with the angels he saw in his crystal ball or scrying stone. Such was his authority as a student of the kabbalah and a reader of horoscopes, the young queen had timed her coronation in 1558 according to Dee's computation of the most auspicious moment for such an event. At his home in Mortlake, close to London, he boasted a fabulous library of six thousand books, the largest in England. Based on this formidable information he had provided charts for Gilbert that were as reliable as contemporary knowledge allowed, and he certainly had an inkling of the wealth waiting in America. In return for his assistance, he persuaded Gilbert to reward him with "5,000 akers of ye new conquest." While Gilbert adventured abroad, Dee had remained in Mortlake so that he could secretly study with his friend, Edward Kelley, how to transmute the base metal of lead into gold. But none of the Great Magus's esoteric arts possessed a power comparable to the magic that Gilbert carried to the newfound land beyond the Atlantic.

Its most obvious element was the wording of his royal charter. In response to Gilbert's proposal to explore "those large and ample countreys [that] extended Northward from the cape of Florida," Queen Elizabeth had given him permission to own "all the soyle of all such lands, countries, & territories so to be discovered . . . with full power to dispose thereof, & of every part thereof in fee simple or otherwise, according to the order of the laws of England." Among the many different ways of possessing the earth, fee simple was, and is, tantamount to outright ownership. Any part of North America from Florida to Newfoundland not already occupied by "any Christian prince or people" could become his property to be sold, rented, or mortgaged as though he were in England.

A further ritual was needed to convert the wilderness into property. The land had to be measured, mapped, and registered in the name of its owner. Thus when Gilbert sailed in June with a tiny fleet of five vessels, the crew included surveyors armed with measuring poles and compasses. Although one ship commanded by his half-brother, Sir Walter Raleigh, immediately turned back, the remainder took the route followed for more than a century by fishermen from France, Portugal, and England to the Grand Banks off Newfoundland.

On August 5, 1583, Gilbert arrived at Saint John's harbor to find almost forty fishing vessels already there, not only catching cod but drying and salting them onshore. Immediately the surveyors went to work, and, as Hayes put it, "did observe the elevation of the pole and drewe plats [plans] of the countrey exactly graded [to scale]." Before the end of the month, the first transactions had taken place, and parcels of land along the water's edge were being rented out to fishermen who until then had occupied them freely. "For which grounds" Hayes pointed out, "they did covenant to pay a certain rent and service." In return, Gilbert assured his tenants they now had the right to occupy their own particular spot from one year to the next.

On the face of it, Gilbert's behavior was absurd. For uncounted generations the granite hills overlooking the long, dog-leg inlet of Saint John's had been used by the Mi'kmaq people, who regarded it as their territory. The Basque fishermen who had discovered the sheltered haven perhaps before Columbus sailed to America in 1492 believed that they and any others who had the audacity to cross the ocean to fish for cod had earned the right to use the landing-grounds during the summer season. But that was as far as it went.

Yet now, under English law Sir Humphrey Gilbert asserted just such a right, and on that basis proposed to charge the fishermen rent for using a part of the wilderness for activities that they had always engaged in freely. For the first time, an idea that would revolutionize the structure of society and transform the way people thought about themselves had made itself known outside its homeland.

BIOLOGY UNDERPINS the pivotal influence that ownership of the earth exerts on human life. There are givens that remain as true for the nearly seven billion of us presently living here as they were for the five hundred million people scattered across the land in 1583. The body's core temperature must remain within a degree or two of 37 degrees Celsius or 98.6 degrees Fahrenheit. To maintain this temperature, an adult must consume a minimum of 1,800 calories a day, preferably 2,450 according to the Food and Agriculture Organization of the United Nations, and closer to 4,000 calories for the sort of labor demanded of the fishermen in Saint John's harbor. That adult must also be clothed and sheltered from the burning sun and freezing rain. Except for some coastal communities, the earth's population in every era has always depended on the land for at least 85 percent of the energy that keeps it alive, and for all its clothing and shelter.

This inescapable fact of life makes the challenge of caring for the nine billion inhabitants who will inhabit the earth in fifty years' time daunting. They must be fed, clothed, and housed on the produce of some forty-five million square kilometers of farmland, roughly eighteen million square miles. In optimum conditions, less than half of this area might be sufficient to produce the calories needed for survival. But the land must also produce biofuels, animal feed, minerals, timber, and cotton and other clothing fibers. At the same time, the soil degrades, cities spread, climate changes, and natural disasters such as droughts and floods, earthquakes and tsunamis, whittle away spare capacity to danger levels.

Any realistic scenario for 2050 has to consider how the earth will be owned.

In 2010, for the first time in human existence, more people lived in cities than in the country. But even in the sprawl of metal and plastic shacks that make up the slums of Kibera outside the Kenyan capital, Nairobi, or the intricate warren of dwellings that house a million people in the Dharavi slum in India's Mumbai, the same fundamentals hold good. The food and sometimes the clothing may be produced elsewhere, but occupancy of a room or a corrugated iron shack is the essential base every family needs for sleeping, eating, and working, so that it will be strong enough to produce whatever labor or goods are necessary to buy a bag of rice and a T-shirt. Laying claim to the ground in some form is an inescapable condition of human existence.

Yet it is never a purely economic relationship. In 1890, the pioneering psychologist William James speculated that the urge to possess was intrinsic to human nature. "We feel and act about certain things that are ours very much as we feel and act about ourselves," he wrote. "Our fame, our children, the work of our hands, may be as dear to us as our bodies are, and arouse the same feelings and the same acts of reprisal if attacked." It was not so much a materialist or acquisitive desire as an elemental urge for attachment, a "blind impulse" as he put it, that embraced both people and objects. Everything that could have the adjective "my" in front of it—parents, spouse and children, clothes, jewelry, and home—strengthened the inner sense of identity by offering external evidence of who a person really was. And, James added, "An equally instinctive impulse drives us to collect property; and the collections thus made become, with different degrees of intimacy, parts of our empirical selves."

Whether we live in a slum, a town house, or a castle, that possessive need touches each of us, not just economically but through the emotional pull that the locality called home exercises upon our head and heart.

"This was the room I had to live in," mused Philip Marlowe in *The Big Sleep*. "It was all I had in the way of a home. It was everything that was mine, that had any association for me, any past, anything that took the place of family. Not much; a few books, pictures, radio, chessmen, old letters, stuff like that. Nothing. Such as they were they had all my memories." For Marlowe, Raymond Chandler's hardbitten private eye, the room was his backstory, its spareness a guarantee that, however flawed, he was ultimately incorruptible. The space we occupy always has that double function, a carapace that is intended to protect us and a canvas where we paint our inner secrets. Few things in our lives affect us more directly and persistently.

MOST INHABITANTS of the Western world live in a private property society and are consequently prejudiced in its favor. But across the globe people have evolved a myriad means of owning the places they live in, and, as Rudyard Kipling said of competing tribal myths, "Every-single-one-of-them-is-right!" The differences affect the way we look at ourselves and the world.

As late as 1800, much of the world's grassland—the North American prairies, the South American pampas, the Australian outback, the African savannah—was still communally owned by indigenous peoples. The most extensive single pattern of land ownership was the feudal monstrosity of the serf estate that reached with the Russian Empire from the Baltic to the Pacific. The majority of the world's population, however, understood land ownership to take various forms of peasant farming. In much of Europe, in India, and in China, the most populous and powerful nation in the world until the late eighteenth century, peasants worked the ground and owned its produce, but ownership of each small plot was shared, with a family or a clan, with a local potentate, or with the monarch. And in the wide swath of Islamic states from North Africa to Java, peasants worked, landlords possessed, but ultimately the earth was deemed to belong to its creator.

The disruption of this pattern is the great revolution of the last two hundred years. The idea of individual, exclusive ownership, not just of what can be carried or occupied, but of the immovable, near-eternal earth, has proved to be the most destructive and creative cultural force in written history. It has eliminated ancient civilizations wherever it has encountered them, and displaced entire peoples from their homelands, but it has also spread an undreamed-of degree of personal freedom and protected it with democratic institutions wherever it has taken hold.

All this potential was contained in the magic that Sir Humphrey Gilbert took with him to Newfoundland. His original intention had been to extend his ownership over more land a thousand miles to the southwest around what is now Rhode Island, but one of his vessels had to be sent home early, and another was driven ashore in a gale. With only the *Golden Hind* and the *Squirrel* left, he decided to return to England for the winter. Nevertheless, the potential for profit in America convinced "the General," as he was known, that Queen Elizabeth would finance his next voyage there to the tune of ten thousand pounds. Perhaps it was this thought that kept his spirits high even when the storm almost capsized the *Squirrel* as they approached the English Channel in the fall of 1583.

Several times the *Golden Hind* sailed close to check that all was well on the smaller boat. On each occasion, Gilbert cheerfully waved his book and shouted his belief that heaven was as close to the ocean as to the land. Some have conjectured that he must have been reading Sir Thomas More's *Utopia*, which contains a sentence with a similar phrase, the inference being that this was his blueprint for an ideal community to be founded in America. But *Utopia* contained a savage attack on the destructive effects of private property. More probably, Gilbert was immersed in *General and Rare Memorials Pertayning to the Perfect Arte of Navigation* by his partner, John Dee. This book was devoted to the magus's vision of an "incomparable Brytish Impire" that the future would bring.

Whatever prompted Dee's vision, his scrying glass or simply Gilbert's manic ambition, it was undoubtedly prophetic. According to the *Memorials*, the empire would be spread across the seas by a mighty navy. Implicitly, as this British Empire expanded, it would carry with it Gilbert's wild idea that land could be owned as private property around the world.

The general, however, was not destined to live long enough to test the accuracy of Dee's foresight. As night fell, the *Squirrel* hoisted two lanterns so that the *Golden Hind* could follow her through the raging seas. But soon after midnight, wrote Captain Hayes, "suddenly her lights were out, whereof as it were in a moment we lost the sight, and withall our watch cryed, the Generall was cast away, which was so true. For in that moment the Frigat was devoured and swallowed up of the Sea."

Section One

A NEW WAY OF OWNING THE EARTH

Chapter One

The Concept

I live in a fifteenth-century farmhouse that boasts a cat's slide roof, a chimney stack leaning like the tower of Pisa, and a living-room whose ceiling is supported by an immense wooden beam low enough to stun anyone taller than a jockey. In other words, it looks like the quintessential English country cottage. But quaint though they now seem, those three elements—the roof, the chimney and the beam—are evidence of a revolution in human behavior. Looking at them, I can be as sure as a detective surveying a murder scene that almost exactly five hundred years ago, my predecessor in the house was infected by an idea that had never existed before. It changed him so radically that he altered the shape of the entire building so that it would reflect the new way that he thought about himself and the world around him.

Built of clay, lime, and horsehair to bind the materials together, the house had originally consisted of a single space like a medieval hall, with a fire burning in the middle of the earth floor whose smoke drifted up to the beams supporting the roof. One end would have been allocated to sleeping and storage. Until about 1530, the farmer and his wife used to eat, cook, spin wool, churn butter, shelter lambs, hire labor, and meet neighbors in the hall, and on a freezing winter's night they would even bed down close to the warmth of the fire.

All that way of life disappeared within a generation. The farmer was not alone. Just sixty miles away in the Essex village of Radwinter, the Reverend William Harrison began collecting the reminiscences of elderly neighbors during the 1570s for his *Description of Britain and England.* He noted one thing in particular that the old men in the village thought to be "marvellously altered in England within their sound remembrance . . . the multitude of chimneys lately erected, whereas in their young days there were not above two or three if so many, but each [person] made his fire against a reredos [the back wall of an open hearth] in the hall, where he dined and dressed [cooked] his meat."

The chimneys were the most obvious symptom of the contagion. In the common space inside the house, each infected farmer constructed a large fireplace against one of the sidewalls with a tall chimney stack outside to carry away the smoke. Then he extended the roof almost to the ground behind the back of the fireplace to keep in the heat. The result was a long expanse of tiles, colloquially known as a "cat's slide roof" presumably because it would allow any cat foolish enough to fall out of a nearby tree to skid harmlessly to earth.

Now cooking was done on a spit over the fireplace and in a brick oven next to the fire on one side of the hall, while food was eaten at a table on the other side. But the hall was no longer one space. The storage area was walled off into a separate room. The final, vital part of the transformation was the huge black beam that my revolutionary predecessor installed in the ceiling of what is now the living room of this farmhouse. The sixty-foot length of oak was put in to support the floorboards of the upper rooms where the newfangled bedchamber was to be situated so that he and his wife could sleep alone. By the time he had finished, the common space inside his home, like the homes of all those sixteenth-century yeoman farmers, was divided into individual, enclosed rooms for eating, sleeping, and other, more private activities.

For almost a century, a similar impulse had driven powerful aristocrats and wealthy city dwellers in Amsterdam, Florence, and London to build new houses that were divided up in this way. Separate rooms, beautiful furnishings, and effective heating were expensive. Even in the opulent Venetian republic, Andrea Palladio's fame as an architect in the sixteenth century would rest on the relatively moderate cost of his private-roomed villas with their imposing facades. But these English yeomen farmers were not in that league. They were too poor and obscure for their names to linger in history. The only record we have of them is the shape they gave to their homes. Yet their changes betray the same self-assertive desire for privacy and comfort.

In Essex, the Reverend Harrison noted that next to chimneys the two biggest changes his ancient villagers had seen were the introduction of pewter plates to put on the table in the new dining area instead of wooden platters, and the exquisite comfort of sleeping on feather beds in the bedroom rather than on straw mattresses. For generations to come, peasant farmers in Europe would continue to live in single-roomed houses with earth floors and no chimney. In the sixteenth century a French attorney, Noël du Fail, described the way that peasants in western France used to share the muddy space with cows and sheep on either side, furnish it with a straw bed, a rough table, and rickety chairs, decorate the walls with ploughs, billhooks, and sickles, and heat the room with a smoky fire in the center. According to the nineteenth-century memoir of the Polish farmer Jan Slomka, peasants in eastern Europe were living in almost exactly the same conditions. But in the 1530s, their counterparts in southeast England were caught by a mad compulsion that drove them to risk ruining themselves in order to enjoy a home that was specialized, enclosed, and self-indulgently comfortable.

The revolutionary idea that transformed the way they thought about themselves now seems simple: that one person could own part of the earth exclusively. Its connection to the birth of a new mind-set in the early 1500s is more complex, if only because the concept of owning the large, immovable earth is now so integral to our values and those of the society in which we live.

In 2008, at the edge of her property on an island in Puget Sound in the state of Washington, Pam Kohler, mother of Colton Harris-Moore, notorious as the "Barefoot Bandit" for his shoeless theft of planes and boats, nailed up a handpainted notice on a tree on the boundary of her land conveying a concept of property so exclusive it claimed for the individual owner the right to kill anyone who stepped on it without permission: "If you go past this sign you will be shot"—and, according to a neighbor, "She shoots." That same year in Wärmland, a province of beautiful valleys in western Sweden, I happened to be with dairy farmer Kristina Andersson when she came upon a stranger's tent that had been pitched without her knowledge by the river that flows through her meadow. Ms. Andersson shrugged and with a single word, *Allemansrätten*, acknowledged the ancient right of Swedes to roam and even camp overnight where they please, regardless of who owns the land.

In the 1980s, the planning committee of a kibbutz near Acre in northern Israel was forced to deal with another way of owning the earth as they discussed a proposal to expand their avocado groves. One important consideration was the possibility that they might lose the avocado trees since the kibbutz land, like 90 percent of Israel's territory, was actually owned by the state, and their lease was due to run out in 1997. During that decade, I lived for a period in the mountainous jungle of Sarawak in Borneo with the indigenous Iban whose use of the land was even further removed from personal ownership. Every year, they would clear a few acres of forest to plant rice, but before they laid an ax to a tree they offered a lavish sacrifice of rice, eggs, and tobacco to Singalang Burong, the god of the earth, to Pulang Gana, the god of the harvest, and to each of the other spirits who actually possessed the land, and whose goodwill was necessary if humans were to make successful use of it.

It is only the outsider who finds anything strange in these ways of owning the earth. To those on the inside, the form of ownership will always seem normal because of the insidious way it shapes the owner's outlook. It is difficult if not impossible to retain Swedish values for long in California, or to take Singalang Burong to Israel. Living in a private property society encourages a primacy of self quite different to the clan values prized in Ghana, the family priorities promoted in Japan, and the communal discipline advocated in China.

"If a man owns a little property that property is him," John Steinbeck wrote of the dust bowl farmer of Oklahoma in the 1930s, "it's part of him and it's like him . . . and in some way he's bigger because he owns it." Because this possession is also our home, it plays intimately upon our happiness and security, and often enough on our discontent and anxiety. As the twenty-first-century English writer Bel Mooney wrote of her own home, "when you enter my home, you are walking into the pathways of my mind and my heart." Yet it can never be an entirely private relationship. This form of property is like no other.

In a campaign speech in 1906, Winston Churchill explained the essential difference in a fine, rolling phrase: "Land, which is a necessity of all human existence, which is the original source of all wealth, which is strictly limited in extent, which is fixed in geographical position—land, I say, differs from all other forms of property in these primary and fundamental conditions." Consequently, unlike a hoe or an iPad which can be carried, is available by the million and so can be owned without depriving anyone else of its benefits, the way you own the earth requires the agreement of your neighbors, the society you live in, and the government of your country. In a very fundamental way, it is the glue that holds a community together.

And every society agrees that it cannot in fact be owned.

All formal laws and informal customs, such as the Iban *adat*, that have the force of law treat land ownership in terms of rights to its exploitation rather than possession of the ground itself. At one end of the scale, the property might be limited to nothing more than a season's right to grow crops or pasture cattle. But at the other end, the bundle of rights to "real property" or "real estate," its designation under common law, or to "immovable property" under Roman law, might include the right to raise cattle and crops, and to hunt any wild creature that steps inside the boundary, as well as the right to mine beneath the ground, to take the light above it, and to construct as many homes and factories on it as public health and safety will permit, together with the right to sell, mortgage, and pass the ownership on to the next generation.

But the idea that burst upon my predecessor in this farm five centuries ago, and that Sir Humphrey Gilbert would soon afterwards attempt to introduce to the New World, was that these rights could be owned individually. It engendered a unique set of values promoting a sense of greed and selfishness at variance with the essential belief that people everywhere had always held about owning rights to the earth, that they were subject to duties and obligations to gods and monarchs, and to families, clans, and communities.

FROM MY STUDY, I can see on the grassy hillside the remnants of the first step in the revolution. Across the slopes my predecessor planted hedges that divided off the higher pasture where he lived from the meadows in the valley bottom. The hedges have left ridges that mark out what were once small fields, measuring more or less five acres on either side of a deep ditch dug to drain the yellow clay soil. He must have enclosed the land before he changed the house, because it was the sheep grazing inside the hedges that paid for the chimney and the new rooms.

From about 1450 wool prices rose across Europe almost without interruption until the 1530s, driven by the clothing needs of a rapidly growing population. France's eight million inhabitants in 1420 had virtually doubled by 1500, and the rate of growth in Spain and Germany was not far behind. Apart from luxurious trimmings of silk, linen, and cotton lace, and the sturdy protection of leather coats and fur hats, they dressed entirely in wool. Just across the sea from southeast England lay Antwerp, the cloth-making capital of fifteenth-century Europe, and to the north and south of it the Elbe and Rhine river systems that carried goods into the heart of Europe. It was a perfect match.

Silver flowing from newly opened mines in southern Germany, soon to be supplemented by a flood from Spanish possessions in America, helped grow the trade, and owners of large pastures in England could become rich. Even tenant farmers like the Reverend Harrison's informants and my predecessor made more money in the 1500s than they or their parents ever had before. They boasted of being rich enough to pay the landlord six or seven years' rent, cash down, with enough left over to buy a shelf of pewter plates, "three or four feather beds, so many coverlids and carpets of tapestry, a silver salt, a bowl for wine, and a dozen of spoons to furnish up the suit."

They certainly earned enough to afford the cost of dividing up the inside of their homes. But to make enclosure work, it was necessary first to amalgamate strips of arable land or take over part of the shared grazing to make a compact parcel, a process known as "engrossment." Logical though it might seem, the process would split asunder the principle of mutual obligation implicit in land use around the world. Until about 1500, England's population hardly numbered more than two million, and there was enough underused and empty land to make engrossment possible without too great an impact on other people. But wherever sheep were kept, in small flocks or large, the compacted land was soon enclosed with hedges, ditches, or stone walls.

The most immediate goal was simply to improve the grazing. Keeping sheep within one area concentrated deposits of their manure containing nitrogen and ammonia and thus gradually helped to enrich the soil. The results were so unmistakable that by the sixteenth century the two words "manure" and "improvement" had become interchangeable. "The word of God," declared a Calvinist tract of 1561, "if it light upon a soul manured with the hand of the heavenly spirit, it will bee most fruitful."

Enclosed fields also allowed good, carefully tended sheep to be kept separate from the common flocks where neglected animals encouraged the spread of various deadly diseases, known collectively as murrain. The physical fact of these boundaries introduced an insidious new element into the feudal system. The grazing, once shared with others belonging to the same manor, was now private and enclosed. In place of the scattered strips that grew wheat and rye and cabbage, there were compact fields, physically identified by their boundaries and seen to belong to the farmer. They were his to use, to improve, and to profit from by employing his enterprise and industry in whatever way he chose.

It fostered an outlook that would spell the death of feudalism. The motive that drove my predecessor to plant hedges and dig ditches was simply the desire for profit. "The poor man who is monarch of but one enclosed acre," the assiduous seventeenth-century observer Thomas Fuller commented, "will receive more profit from it than from his share of many acres in common with others."

The economics could be understood by anyone. Under the old feudal system, a manor might support a small army of laborers who ploughed, sowed, and harvested crops on open land and looked after herds of sheep, cattle, and pigs on the common pasture and woodland. But when the same land was converted to grass and divided into fields where sheep might be left safely, it could be run with just a few shepherds. "The latter way the landlord may perhaps have double the rent [return] he had before," explained the seventeenth-century historian Robert Thoroton. "The reason whereof is that in pasture he hath the whole profit, there being required neither men nor charge [expense] worth speaking of."

Close to William Harrison's parish, the manor of Earls Colne kept records of its court proceedings stretching back to the year 1200. From the endless disputes that fill the pages for more than three centuries comes a picture of life before the land revolution. A few cases involved such everyday matters as the fine of three pennies imposed in 1489 on Thomas Mannying, a candlemaker, for "taking excessive profits," a similar penalty on two "tasters of ale [who] have badly executed the office," and on Joan Payn, "a common scold [for] disturbing our lord the king's peace and her neighbours," but nearly all the other disputes concerned the land rights to woods, meadows, and fields that had been awarded, lost, sold, inherited, and forfeited, and the rent and obligations that went with them. It was clear that the lord of Earls Colne wanted as many people as possible on the manor because each of them was liable for a wide range of dues, not just for rent, but for inheriting and exchanging their strips of land, for borrowing seed, for use of tools, for credit, and for protection in the manor court against other peasants and the outside world.

The cases were settled according to long-accepted customs and inherited rights whose guiding purpose was one of mutual obligation. The lord of the manor might be both judge and prosecutor, but he in turn was subject to written and unwritten constraints in his behavior toward his tenants. And so the records not only provide an account of fines assessed and dues exacted, but also of rents postponed and gifts made to the sick and needy, usually accompanied by the phrase "according to the custom of the said manor." And in really difficult cases, the lord was expected to provide the equivalent of social security, the suspension of rent due from an elderly widow, or the allocation of an added share of grazing for a young family with an extra mouth to feed.

Consequently, the manor lay at the heart of classic feudal land ownership. My sixteenth-century predecessor lived on the Penshurst manor, one of a dozen belonging to the archbishop of Canterbury. Physically Penshurst consisted of the archbishop's private landholding, his "demesne land," and the remainder of the estate—the "tenements"—divided between tenants, including my predecessor, who had written agreements to work the land, and villeins and cottagers who usually had no better right to their strips of land than long-established custom and the labor they contributed to farming the archbishop's demesne. Grazing rights on the common pasture were held in the same variety of written and traditional forms. But the idea of the manor as a social contract was more important than its physical form.

Dismissed today as old-fashioned and exploitative, the feudal relationship not only persisted throughout most of European history, but could be found across most of the world in the form of a contractual understanding between the owner and the worker of the soil. As late as 1970, a landlord in the Mekong delta in South Vietnam was asked about his relationship with his peasant tenant, and his answer described a feudal set of obligations: "When the tenant's father dies," he said, "it is the duty of the landlord to give money to the tenant for the funeral; if his wife is pregnant, the landlord gives money for the birth; if he is in financial ruin, the landlord gives assistance; therefore, the tenant has to behave as an inferior member of the extended family."

The English used an even closer analogy, comparing a manor to a human being where, as John Norden, a sixteenth-century surveyor, put it, "the tenants are the members [limbs], the land the body, and the lord the head." It was inconceivable that the head would want to have the limbs hacked off in order to monopolize the body. But in the early sixteenth century, that was what happened. Driven by the prospect of wool profits, landowners and some tenants competed to take exclusive control of the ground, clearing away if need be those without secure title to their strips of earth.

THE EASIEST TO MOVE were families who lacked a written tenancy agreement or an entry copied into the manor records showing their right to use the land. In a single day in 1567, Sir Thomas Gray of Chillingham in the north of England cleared off his manor no fewer than 340 people, villeins, cottagers, and laborers whose right to work their plots of land existed simply by tradition. Whole villages and townships were soon emptied—in Shakespeare's county of Warwickshire alone, sixty-one villages were wiped out before the year 1500.

It was harder to shift tenants with written leases, but a greedy landlord could achieve the same result over time by doubling the rents and dues. So widespread was the practice that the new Church of England brought into existence by Henry VIII in 1531 found it necessary to have a special prayer directed at landlords read out in church: "The earth O Lord is thine and all that is contained therein; we heartily pray thee to send thy Holy Spirit into the hearts of them that possess the grounds, pastures, and dwelling places of the earth that they, remembering themselves to be Thy tenants, may not rack and stretch out the rents of their houses and lands, nor yet take unreasonable fines and incomes after the manner of covetous worldlings, but so let them out to others that the inhabitants thereof may both be able to pay the rents, and also honestly to live to nourish their families and to relieve the poor."

In *Utopia*, written in 1516, the Roman Catholic Sir Thomas More, himself a considerable landowner and soon to be lord chancellor, damned the powerful magnates who "enclose all in pasture; they throw down houses; they plucke downe townes [villages]; and leave nothing standynge, but only the church, to make of it a shepehouse . . . The rich men not only by private fraud, but also by common laws, do every day pluck and snatch away from the poor some part of their daily living . . . I can perceive nothing but a certain conspiracy of rich men procuring their own commodities under the name and title of the commonwealth." From the other end of the religious spectrum, the radical Protestant preacher Thomas Becon gave vent to a similar fury. "Do not these ryche worldlynges defraude the pore man of his bread," he thundered, "and suffer townes so to decay that the pore hath not what to eat, nor yet where to dwell? What other are they, then, but very manslears [manslayers]?"

Up to the 1530s the land revolution had affected at most 5 percent of the country, but the very intensity of language indicated how shocking the new movement was to people accustomed to the crowded, intricately linked obligations that held the manor together. Clearing people off the land to suit one person's interests was unprecedented. When an Oxford college first proposed engrossing its multioccupied feudal land and renting it out as a single farm, the local priest wrote in bewilderment, "Aftur my sympull reson, it is mor meritory [meritorious] to support and succur a comynte [community] then one man . . . and the pore and the innocent for [instead of] a gentylman."

Yet that was the very point of the revolution, to allow one person to profit from the land, regardless of the consequences to the community. The whole basis of land ownership up to that moment—mutual obligation, recognition of custom and tradition, and the encompassing sense of justice that tied all to the same set of values—became irrelevant. Compounding people's anxiety, the accepted religion, Catholicism, was challenged by Protestant doctrine, and inflation had quadrupled the cost of living.

In the early twentieth century, Max Weber, one of founders of modern sociology, would suggest in *The Protestant Ethic and the Spirit of Capitalism* that profit-driven enterprise sprang out of the individualized tenets of the Protestant Reformation. But in England Weber's dating is wrong. The land revolution had acquired enough headway by 1489 for king Henry VII to push through an act entitled Agaynst the Pulling Doun of Touns [Towns] designed to stop engrossment. Not until 1531 did his son, Henry VIII, proclaim himself head of the Church of England, and it did not become a fully Protestant church until after his death in 1547. It would be more accurate to say that individual property owners were naturally drawn to a faith that gave priority to individual conscience.

Two great revolts shook the stability of England at the time—the Pilgrimage of Grace in 1536 and Robert Kett's rebellion in 1549—and in each protests against enclosure were mixed inextricably with protests against religious and economic change. The rebels' demands to have hedges torn down and Catholicism restored were encapsulated in Kett's pleas to the king to turn back the clock to 1485, "the first year of king Henry the VII," before the revolution had started. But not even the king could resist the momentum for enclosing land.

The royal government had enacted at least nine statutes, issued many royal proclamations, and set up three government commissions, all designed to prevent ploughland from being turned to pasture, the countryside being depopulated, and the highways being thronged by an army of homeless "rogues and vagabonds" who had been dispossessed of their land. For two decades after 1517, the royal courts fined or imprisoned those who broke the law against enclosing land, including no fewer than 264 peers, bishops, and knights. But repeatedly, the new, property-owning members of the House of Commons watered down government proposals. When yet another royal bill against enclosure was presented to Parliament in 1547, the Commons flatly rejected it, making clear that the royal government's cause was lost.

The parliamentary battle was in a way the most significant result of the land revolution. Politics had traditionally taken place in the king's council where the great nobles and the City of London's leading merchants had argued with the king's servants, his chancellor, his chief justice, and the keeper of the royal purse. But the new property owners sought to protect their interests in the House of Commons where landowners outnumbered courtiers.

One of the earliest symptoms of their growing influence came in a prolonged battle over the tax-avoidance trusts they set up, or "uses" in sixteenth-century language, to own their new properties. When Lord Dacre, who owned estates worth £1,000 a year, died in 1533, the "use" that he had created allowed the land to pass on to the next generation without any dues being paid. An irate Henry VIII estimated that "uses" cost him two thirds of the revenues he should have collected, and he sued in his own law courts to get the money back. But using their power in the House of Commons, landowners created a new statute that overturned the law court's decision. In 1535, at the end of a two-year battle, the king was forced to accept a compromise that favored the new property owners.

So obscure as barely to merit a footnote in most history books, that parliamentary struggle should be famous. It represented the moment when one vital feature of the private property society became established, the landowners' use of political power to protect their own interests against the royal executive. Ironically, the thwarted king's next attempt to find an alternative source of revenue tipped the balance of the land revolution irremediably in favor of the new owners.

In the course of four centuries, England's monasteries had acquired more than two million acres of farmland, almost 20 percent of the total cultivated in England at that time, including some of the most fertile and valuable manors in the kingdom. Throughout Europe, the Protestant Reformation had brought into the open rumors of the luxury and decadence of monastic life, and when Henry VIII had made himself head of the church in England in 1531, the monasteries naturally attracted his scrutiny as well. A rigorous inspection, the *Valor Ecclesiasticus*, carried out in 1535 by his new lord chancellor, Thomas Cromwell, revealed the extent of their wealth, and a less reliable investigation confirmed popular rumors about the immoral behavior of monks and nuns. On these grounds the king ordered the monasteries to surrender their lands and buildings. By 1540, this immense estate, worth about £150,000 a year, had fallen into the king's hands. To pay for his navy and his foreign wars, Henry VIII sold off half of it within seven years, raising more than £1,400,000.

The opportunities presented by the former monastic estates were obvious to anyone interested in the profits of wool production. They had been worked conservatively, with few hedges planted and many laborers employed. Enclosed, manured, and cleared of unnecessary occupants, they could only appreciate in value. For good reason, aristocrats with influence at court were at the head of the queue to buy monastic land. Among them was the de Vere family, owners of Earl Colne, who snapped up the neighboring land that belonged to Colne Priory. Unfortunately for many of these early owners, their purchase coincided with a collapse in the wool market in the 1540s, the first in close to a century, and since it was impossible to be a courtier and farm profitably when prices were falling, many were forced to sell. Prominent among them was Edward de Vere, earl of Oxford, who put Colne Priory up for sale rather than allow himself to be distracted from the theater, where he acted as patron to William Shakespeare, and by some accounts wrote his plays. As the sardonic Thomas Tusser put it in a famous piece of sixteenth-century verse:

When gentles go walking
With hawks on their hand,
Good husbands [farmers] with grazing
Do purchase their land.

Thus, within two generations a high proportion of England's most productive land was bought and sold twice over, and its eventual destination was not the ancient nobility, but people with cash—London merchants, careful farmers, government officials, even tenants on fixed rents—anyone looking for a secure investment.

The pattern was set by Henry VIII's lord chancellor, Thomas Cromwell, himself. In three frenzied years, from 1537 to 1539, he bought almost twenty properties in the southeast of England at a cost of £38,000, then sold most of them again for a total profit of more than £4,000. When Cromwell was arrested in 1540, he was found to have £7,000 in cash in his house, largely earned from property deals. His example was copied by a multitude of "Merchant Adventurers, Clothmakers, Goldsmiths, Butchers, Tanners, and other Artificers," until in 1550 the popular preacher Thomas Lever was driven to deliver a bitter denunciation of "the merchants of London" who "bie [buy] fermes out of the handes of worshypfull gentlemen, honeste yeomen, and pore laborynge husbandes [farmers]."

But the profit to be made from the rising value of land was irresistible. When the mighty abbey of Tewkesbury lost its lands near the south coast, a wealthy London cloth merchant, Sir Robert Palmer, bought three of its manors in 1540 for £1,255, and immediately cleared off villeins and cottagers. Then he turned on the tenants, harrassing them and even breaking into their homes. "Jesu, sir, in the name of God what mean you thus extremely to handle us poor people?" Margaret Bennet, wife of one of the tenants, demanded when Palmer kicked in her door.

"Do ye not know that the King's grace hath put down all the houses of monks, friars and nuns?" Palmer retorted. "Therefore now is the time come that we gentlemen will pull down the houses of such poor knaves as ye be."

As it happened, this flouting of the anti-enclosure laws was deemed too flagrant, and the king's Star Chamber court found Palmer guilty of trespass. But it was only a brief setback. Over time his family gradually winkled out all the tenants, and when the Palmers decided to sell just one of the three manors in 1604, the price was £4,600, a profit of more than 1,000 percent.

The financial gains to be made from displacing older rights to ownership of the earth ensured that Palmer was neither the first nor the most brutal creator of new facts on the ground. So many peasants were driven off the manors that once supported them, they were deemed a menace to England's emergent property-owning society. New legislation condemned homeless people without means of support as "rogues and vagabonds" who were liable to branding with a red-hot iron if found begging in the highway.

Yet by the 1580s, this new, selfish form of ownership had begun to pay a dividend that enriched more than the owners themselves. In the old, feudal model, the manor's population grew enough food to feed themselves and only sold what was left over. And to make best use of communal labor, everyone needed to follow the same agricultural calendar, so that families could help one another sow, weed, and harvest, and when the grain had been gathered in, the animals could be turned out onto the unfenced stubble. But the new farms did not live off their produce. They aimed to sell their major crop in order to earn the money they needed for food and sustenance. With landlords pressing to increase rents and tenants eager to improve their margins, each individual had to find ways of making the land more profitable.

Roger Harlakenden, the new owner of Colne Priory, not only raised sheep, but began to make the wool into cloth on his own estate by employing landless laborers who, he explained, "have of a long time been set on work by spinning wool." Other landowners specialized in breeding larger cattle as well as heavier horses and meatier rabbits. Arable farms increasingly abandoned the medieval two-field rotation of crops, where one half of the land was left fallow each year, adopting instead a three-field pattern where peas or beans followed a cereal crop, and only a third of the land lay fallow. Not all arable farmers bothered to enclose their fields, even in the productive midlands of England, but none could escape the pressures of inflation, high interest rates, and the need for a profit. They manured more heavily, planted and weeded more carefully, and the most progressive followed the advanced, intensive farming used in the Netherlands, growing turnips for winter feed, and sowing nitrogen-fixing clover on the fallow ground—"there can be no better fodder devised for cattell", declared Barnaby Googe in his *Foure Bookes of Husbandry* published in 1577.

The farms themselves grew bigger, around fifty acres for arable land and eighty acres for pasture, compared with barely five acres of strips that had been the average before the revolution. The sheer speed of change, in horticulture as well as agriculture, drove the poet George Puttenham to warn in 1589 against experiments that made "the white rose redde, yellow, or carnation, a bitter melon sweete, or sweete apple soure, a plumme or cherrie without a stone, a pear without core or kernell, [and] a goord or coucumber like to a home."

The consequences were unmistakable. In the course of the century, England's population had almost doubled from just over two million in 1500 to well over four million, a situation that should have led to food shortages and higher prices. Instead, increasing yields from the land not only led to a fall in prices but, according to William Harrison, an improvement in the general diet. "White meats—milk, butter, and cheese (which were never so dear as in my time [the past], and wont to be accounted of as one of the chief stays throughout the island)—are now reputed as food appertinent only to the inferior sort," he noted in the 1570s, "whilst such as are more wealthy do feed upon the flesh of all kinds of cattle [livestock] accustomed to be eaten."

For the first time in European history, a society was about to escape the choke on population growth that was created by subsistence farming. Harrison was clear about the reason. By the last quarter of the century, "the soil had growne to be more fruitful, and the countryman more painful [painstaking], more careful, and more skillful for recompense of gain."

My predecessor in the farmhouse never did well enough from the land revolution to make a will or leave any record of his identity. His rights as a tenant gave him a property in the land and the opportunity to earn enough to transform his house and enjoy pewter plates on the table and a feather mattress on the bed. But either he was not ruthless enough in enclosing more fields—I hope so—or he may have been hit by the fall in wool prices in the middle of the sixteenth century. Had he been more driven or efficient, he would have prospered, because prices soon recovered, and other, larger estates nearby prospered. But the horribly skewed door he installed in the living room, more diamond than rectangle, and the dangerously leaning chimney suggest a man who was more excited by the idea of innovation than by the need to master its technical challenges. Perhaps it was just as well. Had he made money, he would surely have built a large mansion befitting his status. The old farmhouse would have been torn down, and with it would have gone its ramshackle evidence of the first, startling arrival of the modern world.

Chapter Two

The Rights and Politics of Owning the Earth

THE 102 PILGRIMS who in 1620 sailed across the Atlantic on the *Mayflower* to the New World were destined to be communists. Under the terms of their agreement with the Plymouth company that backed their settlement, they were to work communally for the first seven years, "during which time, all profits & benifits that are gott by trade, traffick, trucking, working, fishing or any other means . . . remaine still in ye comone stock." After that time the proceeds would be shared with the investors in England. The arrangement was particularly welcome to the tightly knit core of migrants united by the common experience of persecution by the Church of England who had been living for more than a decade as religious refugees in the Dutch university town of Leiden. Their chief spokesman, Robert Cushman, condemned personal greed as ungodly, and pointed to the better example of the early Christian societies where property had been held "in common."

Arriving late in the year, they spent most of the first bitter winter living aboard ship, but when the fifty-three hardy souls who survived the horrific epidemic of disease that raged through the *Mayflower* dragged their weary bodies onshore in the springtime, the hard business of farming for the common good aroused little enthusiasm. "The young men, that were most able and fit for labour and service, did repine that they should spend their time and strength to work for other men's wives and children without any recompense," William Bradford, their future governor, wrote. Only repeated whipping kept them at work. A rift opened between those who "thought [it] injustice" that a hard worker should receive no more food than a feeble one, and those like Cushman who denounced anyone who worshipped the "belly-god" of selfishness instead of seeking "the good, the wealthe, the profit, of others."

This was not a problem anticipated by the merchants of London and Plymouth who invested in the company. They had expected the settlement to operate as a trading post, acquiring salt cod and beaver skins for sale in Britain. The desire for religious freedom was what drove the tiny band of separatist Puritans to accept the contract to be shipped across the Atlantic. Neither side thought the ownership of land to be of any importance. And certainly it was never supposed that the contagion of private property might enter the New World with them.

Beset by quarrels and threatened by starvation, the colony struggled on until the spring of 1623. With a new planting season at hand, the majority decided that, on the basis of the compact signed onboard the *Mayflower* to "combine ourselves together into a Civil Body Politic, for our better ordering and preservation," they had authority to change the company rules. They persuaded the governor that "they should set corn every man for his own particular, and in that regard trust to themselves. And so," Bradford noted in his history of the Plymouth colony, "assigned to every family a parcel of land according to the proportion of their number . . . This had very good success for it made all hands very industrious." Smaller matters had been debated and resolved before, but that this, the first major democratic decision taken on American soil, should have been in favor of individual ownership carried a symbolism that echoes down the centuries.

The failed experiment in communal ownership convinced Bradford that it was contrary to human nature. To believe that "the taking away of property" would lead to happiness was to imagine oneself to be "wiser than God," he concluded. Yet the new regime came at a cost. "And no man now thought he could live except he had catle and a great deale of ground to keep them all," Bradford observed sadly, "all striving to increase their stocks. By which means they were scatered all over the bay quickly and the towne in which they lived compactly till now was left very thinne . . ."

AMONG MANY SETTLED ANIMIST CULTURES, including the Wampanaog people on whose land the Pilgrims had come to live, parcels of ground could be used and occupied by individual families, even passed on to the next generation, often from mothers to daughters, but exclusive ownership of what was regarded as the fundamental life source was impossible.

Massasoit, a Wampanaog leader who befriended later settlers, used an analogy common in such cultures to explain the relationship: "The land is our mother," he said, "nourishing all her children, beasts, birds, fish, and all men. The woods, the streams, everything on it belongs to everybody and is for the use of all. How can one man say it belongs only to him?"

A similar belief that people could use but not possess the earth held good under Judaic law, springing from Yahweh's commandment in the book of Leviticus that "the land is mine" and that mortals, as mere "strangers and sojourners," were unable to own it. Islam adopted the same view, incorporating it into sharia law. Even in cultures where land could be owned in secular terms, it belonged to the human ruler, the monarch, emperor, or khan, who represented divine power on earth. In the earliest surviving codification of laws, dating from the second millennium BC, the Babylonian king Hammurabi traced the roots of his sovereignty to Baal, "the lord of heaven and earth who decreed the fate of the land." And the laws made it plain that just as Hammurabi owed his possession of Babylon to his devotion to Baal, so his subjects might use the land in return for service to the king. From the third century BC, when Chinese emperors began to assume the title of the "Son of Heaven," they too acted as intermediaries between the spiritual and and material worlds, claiming the mandate of heaven to rule China, and allocating its territory to their nobles in exchange for military and governmental services that forwarded their divine mission. In similar fashion, the feudal system in Christian Europe understood the contract between lord and tenant to be part of a chain of mutual obligation leading through the chief barons to the king, who granted them use of the territory he ruled by the grace of God.

Thus a relationship with the earth that began as a spiritual connection ended as a contract on which constitutional authority ultimately rested. Ordinary Englishmen wishing to claim individually owned land in the New World were engaged in a dangerous activity.

TEN YEARS LATER, the experience of the Plymouth colony played heavily on the minds of the seven hundred Puritans who assembled in Southampton in March 1630 to take ship to Massachusetts Bay. Many, including their governor, John Winthrop, had left comfortable homes that were furnished with fireplaces and private bedrooms and surrounded by enclosed fields. Indeed, one of Winthrop's close companions even lived in a house with a cat's slide roof, side chimney, and low beam. They had had two years to prepare, and were under no illusions about the hard conditions ahead. "Plantations are for young men that can endure all pains and hunger," a friend had warned the forty-year-old Winthrop. "To adventure your whole family upon so many manifest uncertainties standeth not with your wisdom and long experience."

The original Pilgrims had had nothing to lose, but this second wave were giving up security and worldly achievement. They had a pressing need to know that braving the dangers and harsh climate would not only win them the freedom to worship as Puritans, but to live in a new English society where land could be individually owned. The question was whether a concept recognized by English common law could exist in the American wilderness.

To reassure them, Winthrop put forward a revolutionary proposal, usually ascribed to John Locke half a century later. In a pamphlet published in 1629, he argued that private ownership of the earth did not depend upon the law, but was created by human toil. He constructed this novel explanation by weaving together Puritan doctrine and the pragmatic outlook of the enclosers. "God has given to the sonnes of men a double right to the earth," Winthrop declared, "a naturall right, and a Civill Right." The natural right to land was established by use and occupancy, and Winthrop was merely echoing the accepted view put forward by the Dutch jurist Hugo Grotius when he declared that land "which lies common, and hath never beene replenished or subdued is free to any that possesse and improve it." That natural right to occupy empty land grew ultimately from God's injunction in the book of Genesis, "Increase & multiply, replenish the earth & subdue it."

But Grotius had nothing to say about the purely English civil or legal right to own land as private property. Winthrop was breaking new ground when he asserted that such a right came about when men "appropriated certaine parcells of Grownde by inclosing and peculiar manuerance [individual manuring or improvement], and this in time gatte them a Civill right."

It must have seemed a convincing argument to readers who had heard from their grandparents firsthand accounts of the way enclosure had enabled common ground to be converted into legally recognized property. And few would have quarreled with Winthrop's conclusion: "As for the Natives of New England they inclose noe land neither have any settled habitation nor any tame cattle to improve the land by, & soe have noe other but a naturall right to those countries. Soe as if we leave them sufficient for their use wee may lawfully take the rest, ther being more than enough for them & us."

Yet because Puritans were guided by conscience in such matters, they sought their ultimate authority not in the law but in the Bible. As they waited in Southampton before sailing to America, they heard a sermon from the Reverend John Cotton that gave private property the biblical backing they needed to hear.

Cotton's sermon, entitled "God's Promise to his Plantation," was based on a passage in the book of Genesis about Abraham's search for a place to settle among the Philistines. When he was prevented from using a well he had dug in the dry land of Beersheba, Abraham appealed to the Philistine king, Abimelech, claiming that he had the right to draw water because he was the person who had sunk the well. In Cotton's sermon, however, Abraham also made a specific claim of individual ownership, based on "his owne industry and culture in digging the well." And, rather than simply accepting Abraham's oath that he was telling the truth, as the Bible recounted, the Philistine Abimelech, by Cotton's account, responded forcefully, "admitteth it as a Principle in Nature, That in a vacant soyle, hee that taketh possession of it, and bestoweth culture and husbandry upon it, his Right it is." In other words, there was biblical evidence to reassure the new Americans that their right to individually owned, landed property depended on their own efforts in improving the ground, and not on English law.

While they waited for favorable winds, the same audience was told by Winthrop that the eyes of the world were upon them, and they should regard their settlement as an example to all those who desired freedom. They would be, he said, "a city upon a hill." Three hundred years later, his is the talk that history remembers, but at the time it quickly slipped into obscurity. It was Cotton's sermon on the natural right to individually owned property that was published and treasured by those about to sail for Massachusetts Bay.

Among the rest of Britain's burgeoning number of Atlantic colonies—by the end of the seventeenth century there were seventeen from Nova Scotia to Barbados—the question of how property came into being hardly arose. The West Indies colonies were easily the most important in terms of profitability and migration, thanks to the production of sugar. The almost industrial process of growing tall-stemmed sugarcane, then extracting its juice to be boiled and crystalized into dried sugar and rum, ensured that landowners were also employers in charge of a manufacturing hierarchy of white overseers and indentured servants and a growing number of enslaved Africans. In 1650, there were forty-four thousand British colonists in the West Indies, more than in all eight colonies on the North American mainland.

Possession of the earth, in both America and the Caribbean, was deemed to be derived from the royal charter that granted the territory to a company or to a powerful proprietor, such as the Earl of Carlisle, who was given Barbados in 1627. Every charter detailed how the land was to be owned and administered, and ended with a striking phrase explaining that the monarch had made this happen by "our especiall grace, certain knowledge, and mere motion." In other words, the king's royal power, backed by "divine grace," as the charter also specified, was the ultimate authority that enabled colonists to claim that particular bit of the earth's surface as their property. This happened, as it were, with a mere wave of the regal hand. Real estate was, literally and legally, royal estate.

Against this background, the peculiarity of the New Englanders in seeking some deeper source of legitimacy drew mockery, not least from Captain John Smith in his *Advertisements for the Inexperienced Planters of New England*, published in 1631: "Many good, religious, devout men have made it a great question, as a matter in conscience, by what warrant they might go and possess those countries which are none of theirs but the poor savages'." Drawing on his own experience as governor of Virginia, where he had negotiated the colonists' acquisition of land from the Powhatan confederacy of native Americans, Smith casually dismissed the Puritans' doubts. America had enough space for everyone, whether native or newcomer, and so under international law as outlined by Grotius they were allowed to take possession of what was essentially unoccupied ground. "If this be not a sufficient reason for such tender consciences," he added off-handedly, "for a copper knife and a few toys as beads and hatchets, they [the native inhabitants] will sell you a whole country; and for a small matter their houses and the ground they dwell upon."

Smith's scoffing at the Puritans' search for biblical authority missed its subversive implications. If property was created by individual effort, and not just by the king's "mere motion," then there was another authority in the land whose power rivaled that of the royal prerogative. And it was one that everyone possessed. In which case, an awkward question arose: Where did ultimate authority lie? With the people or with the crown?

* * *

SUCH A QUESTION could only have arisen under English common law. In Europe, medieval legal structures grew out of Roman law whose goal, in the words of its sixth-century codifier, Emperor Justinian, "is the constant and perpetual wish to render to everyone his due." These dues were based on mutual obligation, and the best example of how this worked was always taken to be the family. Thus parents had a duty to guard their children, an obligation matched by the children's duty to obey their parents. And while a wife and children were subject to the authority of their husband and father, their obedience gave them inextinguishable rights to a share in his property.

The same principle applied where land was concerned. Roman law held that it had to have a lord who was obliged to guard it, as a father guarded his family, on behalf of his sovereign. In return he could expect to be obeyed by those who lived there and to enjoy their services. This was the matrix of the feudal system. Crucially, these rights of property went with the land rather than existing separately. Should an estate be confiscated, or its inheritance be disputed, the contract of mutual obligation disappeared, and with it the rights of ownership.

The English idea of property evolved separately because the laws of ownership became a battleground for supremacy between the crown and the chief barons of England. The beginning of the war dated back to the twelfth century, when King Henry II started to use "common law," meaning applicable in the same way to everyone, to undermine the power of the barons' manor courts. Royal judges were sent out on tour to every part of the kingdom with the power to enforce the common law and the statutes that had been enacted by the king's council in London. The goal of these judges "on assize," as it was termed, was to ensure that royal justice overruled the permanent local justice administered by the manor.

For four centuries a thunderous drumroll of royal statutes, edicts, and legislation, many with Latin and Norman French names, created rights for tenants that the king's judges were expected to impose against the wishes of feudal lords: *Novel disseisin* enabled tenants to appeal to a royal judge against unjust eviction; *Mort d'Ancestor* acknowledged their right to inherit on the death of a relative; *Quia Emptores* permitted them to sell inherited land; a writ of ejectment prevented the landlord from coming on to the tenant's land. By the early thirteenth century manor courts were also forced to accept the tenants' right to trial by jury in the king's court, and to issue a writ of habeas corpus guaranteeing them the freedom to appear there in person. But in 1215, twenty-five mighty barons turned the royal strategy on its head by forcing King John to sign the great charter, known as Magna Carta, limiting the king's own misuse of feudal power. Effectively it gave the barons, together with all freeholders of land, the right to claim the protection of the common law against the king, just as it protected their tenants against them. "No Freeman shall be taken or imprisoned," ran the critical clause, "or be disseised of his Freehold, or Liberties, or free Customs, or be outlawed, or exiled, or any other wise destroyed; nor will We not pass upon him, nor condemn him, but by lawful judgment of his Peers, or by the Law of the land."

There was nothing about mutual obligation in Magna Carta. These were absolute rights invested in the owner of freehold land

In sharp contrast to Roman law, and for that matter to the civil obligations of landowners under Chinese and Islamic custom, the version that evolved under English common law had no counterbalance. Far from subjecting rights of individual ownership to those of social obligation, throughout the sixteenth century the law heaped civil liberties, political power, and legal protection upon the freeholder at the expense of everyone else. "Day labourers, poor husbandmen, yea merchants or retailers which have no free land," the leading Elizabethan lawyer Sir Thomas Smith wrote in the 1560s, "have no voice nor authority in our commonwealth, and no account is made of them, but only to be ruled."

Such an approach ran counter to all civilized norms because it was so unbalanced. Throughout the development of human society, laws that defined what belongs to one person and not to another, were complemented by rules and customs that regulated greed. Thus the Judaic commandment "Thou shalt not steal" was accompanied by the injunction "Thou shalt not covet thy neighbor's goods." The very source of European law could be found, according to Demosthenes, in the outrage felt by the sixth century BC Athenian law-giver, Solon, at the avarice of the powerful, eager to "Indulge their lustful appetite of gain." In the *Republic*, Plato demonstrated that unless kept in check by law the greedy part of the soul, *to epithumetikon*, will "enslave and rule over the classes it is not fitted to rule." On the other side of the world, the central theme of the sixth century BC *Analects* of Confucius was the belief that social harmony could be achieved only if all people, governors and governed, subscribed to firm rules of conduct that inhibited selfish behavior. And the Hindu emphasis on socially moderated behavior had its roots in the second century BC

Bhagavad-Gita's warning against greed as one of the three self-centered gates to hell that, together with lust and anger, were "so destructive to the embodied self they must be abandoned."

Yet if Winthrop and Cotton were right, and individual effort gave a natural right to property, the common law envisioned no check on the liberties and rights that the individual owner would then enjoy. The lack of limits betokened a freedom from social constraint that had never been acceptable before. By all the civilized norms that existed in the history of human society, a monster had been born.

THE BIRTH of this changeling was largely hidden behind the clutter of feudal customs that continued to surround private property transactions into the eighteenth century. But in every country where the concept of individually owned landed property has taken hold, one unmistakable indicator of its arrival has been provided by a change in the way land is measured.

On May 1, 1602, William Shakespeare paid William Combe the handsome price of £320 for four yardlands of arable land and twenty acres more of meadow in Old Stratford. A yardland was a feudal unit representing an area large enough to support a family. As a result, a yardland of good arable soil, like the Old Stratford ground, covered about twenty-five acres, as opposed to a yardland of rough pasture which could have been more than forty acres. The difference depended, Robert Thoroton pointed out, on "the lightness or stiffness of the Soil [and so] could not be equal in all Places."

In a localized, peasant economy where the earth was valued primarily for its ability to support people, measurements that varied according to the fertility of the soil provided the most useful indication of what a farmer needed to know. Around the world, the amount of seed that had to be sown to feed a family from the harvest provided a basic, and perhaps primeval, unit of measurement of the earth. Even in the twentieth century, fields in Guangdong Province next to Hong Kong continued to be measured in *dou*, roughly equivalent to a quarter of a bushel of rice, while up to the mid-nineteenth century land in New Mexico was computed by the *fanega*, approximately two bushels of wheat. Similar variable measures were used throughout feudal Europe—as late as 1789 the local council in Bourges in northern France declared that the *seterée*, based on a *setier*, or half-bushel of seed, "is the only measure known in this canton. It is larger or smaller depending on the quality of soil."

But in a market involving buyers with no local knowledge, an objective, unchanging quality such as area allowed strangers to compare the value of different commodities. Thus one unmistakable indicator that a true market in land had developed was the appearance of exact, invariable measurements in place of local, organic units. Significantly, Shakespeare's land at Old Stratford was also measured out as 107 acres, the amount registered by the courts.

The need for accurate measurement was met by a new breed of surveyor, not the old feudal "overseer" who ensured that rents were in line with the productivity of the land, but "measurers" equipped with instruments akin to theodolites and compasses, and employing mathematical innovations such as trigonometry. The modern, definitive *Dictionary of Land Surveyors and Local Mapmakers of Great Britain and Ireland* dates the beginning of the trade to 1530, and identifies by name 235 surveyors of the new kind at work in the last half of the sixteenth century. In the early seventeenth century, the mathematical inventor Thomas Gunter provided them with what would become the surveyor's definitive tool, a twenty-two-yard chain divided into one hundred links, an instrument perfectly suited to the measurement of traditional, four-based measurements such as the 4,840-square-yard acre, and the 640-acre-square mile. That the archaic chain should now be enshrined as a unit of measurement in the areas of almost every major city founded in the nineteenth century in the United States, Canada, Australia, New Zealand, and South Africa—streets one and half chains, or ninety-nine feet, broad, blocks of five acres, eight chains long by five broad, and public squares of ten acres, eight by ten chains—indicates the symbiotic nature of its relationship to the spread of private property.

As surveyors gave shape to property, a subtle change in mortgage law allowed it to be translated into financial muscle. In its old use, a mortgage meant "dead pledge," signifying that a borrower automatically forfeited his land if he failed to repay the money in full on the specified date. As Sir Thomas Lyttleton, the leading legal authority of the sixteenth century, put it, "If he [the borrower] doth not pay, then the land which is put in pledge upon condition for the payment of the money, is taken from him for ever, and so is dead to him." The forfeiture of an entire property as a penalty for failing to repay every penny that had been borrowed naturally struck the new landowners as inequitable. In response to their growing political influence, sympathetic judges began to interpret the law so that failure to repay the debt at the required date did not totally extinguish an owner's title to the land. Instead, under the principle known as "the equity of redemption," the courts ruled that so long as a borrower paid off the mortgage, even years late, he could reclaim his property.

Modern mortgage law grew out of this interpretation, but so too did modern finance. To regain his money, the lender now had to get a writ to foreclose, forcing the borrower to sell the land. Once the debt was paid, however, the remainder of the proceeds belonged to the former landowner. This was his equity in the land. As the new idea took hold during the seventeenth century, equity, meaning fairness, would gradually morph into equity, meaning capital.

THE POWER THAT TRANSLATED the wish to own land individually into a legal reality could hardly have been less substantial. It is neatly summarized in a throwaway aside uttered by Hamlet as he gazes down at the gravedigger disinterring a skull that will turn out to be Yorick's. Musing on the absurdity of a mere mortal presuming to own the earth that will shortly swallow him up, the moody Dane remarks, "This fellow might be in's time a great buyer of land, with his statutes, his recognizances, his fines, his double vouchers, his recoveries: is this the fine of his fines, and the recovery of his recoveries, to have his fine pate full of fine dirt?"

As one of the most famous beneficiaries of England's land revolution, William Shakespeare knew whereof he wrote. Hamlet's list includes four centuries of statute law, evidence of the buyer's financial resources in the form of recognizances, records of the fines or fees he had to pay for transfer of ownership, invoices or vouchers in duplicate of the purchase price, and receipts or recoveries for the deposit he had put down. Missing from the recital is the deed of sale registered with the Court of Common Pleas, and the complications of surveys, mortgages, and conveyancing that had grown since the 1540s. But this was the hidden weapon of private property, paper. Everything was written down. The title deeds described how the property had been created and come into the owner's hands, and any incursion upon it brought the whole panoply of the law against the perpetrator. Paper recruited the power of government to the side of the property owner.

The decisive shift occurred during the parliamentary struggle of the 1530s and 1540s between the king and the upstart, property-acquiring members of the House of Commons. Despite exercising greater personal power than any other monarch in British history, Henry VIII was forced to negotiate to obtain the Commons' consent to taxes to fund his insatiable taste for military spending.

"If you will not take some reasonable end now when it is offered," the king threatened, "I will search out the extremity of the law, and then I will not offer you so much again." But "the frowarde and wilfull" members of Parliament, as a contemporary reported, "woulde neither consent to the byll [to increase the royal revenue] . . . nor yet agree to no reasonable qualificacion of the same."

By the 1540s they had forced the monarchy to accept crucial changes to property law, affecting wills, mortgages, inheritance, and conveyancing. The guiding principle of the new laws was to make it simpler for two individuals to negotiate the exchange of a property, by purchase or inheritance, without interference by lord or monarch. The result was to erode and largely destroy the core of the contractual structure of feudalism, leaving in its place a system of rights.

To explain the new rules, a raft of manuals on property law began to appear. It was important to know what was happening, Thomas Phayer pointed out in *The New Boke of Presidents* [Precedents] published in 1543, because "without [these] thynges there can no tytle lawfully be claymed, no landes nor houses purchased."

Each of these incremental changes helped give the monster of private property its shape. But the most dramatic indication of its break with past standards of fairness and mutual obligation came with the law of "couverture" enacted in 1542. This obliterated the right of a wife to a "reasonable part" of the family property that had been enshrined in Roman law and feudal practice, and transferred everything she owned to her husband's name. In the bleak words of the great legal authority William Blackstone, the law of couverture meant that "the very being or legal existence of the woman is suspended during the marriage, or at least is incorporated and consolidated into that of the husband: under whose wing, protection, and cover, she performs every thing."

In *The Merchant of Venice*, written in the 1590s, Portia dresses the idea in more romantic guise when she promises herself to Bassanio:

Myself and what is mine to you and yours
Is now converted. But now I was the lord
Of this fair mansion, master of my servants,
Queen o'er myself; and even now, but now,

This house, these servants, and this same myself
Are yours, my lord's. I give them with this ring.

In practice, resourceful wives often found a way around the couverture law by insisting on a prenuptial or "church-door" agreement guaranteeing some control over their share of the property. But in disposing of his own property, William Shakespeare illustrated how the land revolution inexorably pushed women to the margin. The family share guaranteed under Roman law played no part in his plans. Only one person would inherit his land. Having lost his son, Hamnet, Shakespeare willed his many properties to his daughter Susanna, but detailed minutely who would inherit them from her. After her death, they were to go "to the first sonne of her bodie lawfullie yssueing, and to the heires males of the bodie of the saied first sonne lawfullie yssueinge." In case there was a problem, the land would go to her second, or third, or fourth, or even to her seventh son, and after his unborn grandson's death, William Shakespeare specified that it would pass to that distant descendant's first, second, or even seventh son. Women played no part in that uncertain future.

Step by step, the political influence of the new landowners had succeeded in creating a monopoly. This was what was contained in Hamlet's mordant list of documents. The traditional rights of villeins and laborers were overturned. The claims of the feudal superior, whether lord or king, were frozen out. The needs of wives and children were subsumed. All those who might have challenged the solitary male owner's right to exclusive possession of the land were sidelined.

In 1450 about 60 percent of the twelve million acres of farmland in England had been held by the crown, by the church, and by some thirty dukes, earls, and barons. By 1700, the nobility, church, and crown together owned less than 30 percent of the cultivated land. Almost three quarters of what had grown to be fourteen million acres of farmland now belonged to the heads of more than two hundred thousand families of gentry, yeomen, and tenant farmers with land worth more than forty shillings a year in rent. And perhaps 150,000 more families rented less valuable properties. Out of a population that had increased to almost five million in 1700, about two million had an interest in landed property.

Not only did the adult males of some two hundred thousand landowning families vote for the members of Parliament, they provided the magistrates who enforced Parliament's laws, and the officers of the cavalry that ensured compliance with the magistrates' orders. Statutes intended to protect a tenant's rights, such as *novel disseisin* or *quia emptores*, had become part of a property owner's defense against the king's exactions. The common law's writ of ejectment originally used to keep feudal landlords from invading their tenants' land was now employed to keep trespassers off private property. The hedges that anti-enclosure legislation had repeatedly ordered to be torn down had become sacrosanct, boundaries that no poacher or paperless claimant, nor even a royal writ, could cross without the owner's permission.

The priorities of the land revolution fostered a change of temper in England's growing population. It is possible to see the new spirit in the sheer verve of the Elizabethan age, from the freebooting exploits of Sir Francis Drake and Sir John Hawkins pirating away Spanish treasure to the flowering of English poetry and above all in the drama of William Shakespeare.

What seems perpetually modern in Shakespeare's drama is the consciousness of an individual self, heard most clearly in Hamlet's doubts and inner turmoil, but traceable from the farcical confusion of identities in *The Comedy of Errors* through the spectacular gore of *Titus Andronicus* to the great tragedies of *King Lear* and *Macbeth.* Consistently his protagonists, from vendetta-entrapped Romeo to racially snared Othello, struggle to escape an enveloping past and achieve a goal of personal autonomy. "Men are at some time masters of their fate," Cassius asserts in *Julius Caesar.* "The fault, dear Brutus, lies not in our stars, but in ourselves that we are underlings."

The erosion of old communal values also triggered unmistakable anxiety about the materialist outlook of the new order. It was most evident in the rising popularity of Puritanism. Appalled by the lack of social conscience in the new age, Thomas Becon, one of the founders of Puritanism and no friend of Catholicism, declared that the selfish behavior of property speculators who bought monastic lands made even the corrupt old monasteries look good: "They [the new owners] abhorre the names of Monkes, Friars, Chanons, Nounes [nuns], etc., but their goods they gredely gripe [grasp]. And yet where the [monastery] cloysters kept hospitality, let out their fermes at a reasonable pryce, noryshed scholes, brought up youths in good letters, they [the new owners] doe none of all these thinges."

Hostility was not confined to the Puritans. In 1597, the self-centered indulgence of the day drew a reprimand from the highest power in government, Queen Elizabeth's Privy Council. In a royal proclamation, the children of the land revolution were condemned for their "lack of hospitality" caused by "the immeasurable charges and expenses which they are put to in superfluous appareling of their wives, children and families."

Even in Shakespeare's plays, the struggle for autonomy is fraught with anxiety. Once selfishness takes over, says the Earl of Gloucester in *King Lear,* it destroys every emotion holding families and communities together: "Love cools, friendship falls off, brothers divide. In cities, mutinies; in countries, discord; in palaces, treason; and the bond crack'd 'twixt son and father." The unease is even more apparent in the dramas of inheritance such as *Hamlet, King Lear, Henry IV,* and *Richard III,* where a new order is about to displace the old. But it is in *Troilus and Cressida* when Ulysses rails against the self-centered behavior of the Greeks at the battle of Troy that Shakespeare expresses best his contemporaries' deep-seated apprehension about the ravening world where "insaciable gredyness of mynde," as an antiproperty pamphlet put it, has been unleashed:

. . . the rude son should strike his father dead:
Force should be right; or rather right and wrong,
Between whose endless jar justice resides,
Should lose their names, and so should justice too.
Then every thing includes itself in power,
Power into will, will into appetite;
And appetite, an universal wolf . . .

Yet there was no going back. The individualized ethos of the property owner influenced government, the law, and everyday life. And in Shakespeare's drama can be sensed a psychological development that no previous society had experienced. Allowing greed to be unconstrained by law had forced its battle with moderation to become internalized. The beginnings of a modern sensibility had begun to emerge.

Chapter Three

The Rights of Private Property

On April Fools' Day 1649, Gerrard Winstanley, a bankrupted cloth merchant, led a score of likeminded souls out on to the wooded slopes of Saint George's Hill in Surrey, about twenty miles west of London, and began to clear the ground. Their action in digging up the earth gained them their nickname, the Diggers, but their purpose had a wider significance than merely preparing the earth for cultivation. The soil on the hill was acidic and incapable of supporting much other than thin grass, heather, and fir trees, and today the slopes are home to one of the most expensive and exclusive golf-centered building developments in England. Such a fate could not have been further from the Diggers' intentions. They planted subsistence food, beans, barley, and roots, but what they really intended to grow was a new, egalitarian society.

"[T]he earth was not made purposely for you, to be Lords of it, and we to be your Slaves, Servants, and Beggers," Winstanley wrote in a pamphlet addressed to the property-owning gentry, "but it was made to be a common Livelihood to all, without respect of persons: And that your buying and selling of Land, and the Fruits of it, one to another, is the cursed thing." In place of that unequal society, the Diggers wanted to re-create the communal living of the early Christians when, as the Acts of the Apostles recorded, "All who believed were together and had all things in common." The basis of this new society was communal ownership of the land: "For the Earth, with all her Fruits of Corn, Cattle, and such like," wrote Winstanley, "was made to be a common Store-house of Livelihood to all Mankinde." They were not concerned with politics, because they believed "we shall need neither [magistrates] nor [laws] in that nature of Government; for as our Land is common, so our Cattell is to be common, and are not to be bought and sold among us . . . and we shall not arrest one another."

There was nothing new about trying to alter a society's values by changing the way that its land was owned. In Europe, similar attempts went back at least to 133 BC when the populist tribune, Tiberius Gracchus, set out to restore the Roman republic to its original egalitarian state by appropriating land from the wealthy and redistributing it to poorer citizens. Seen through the angry eyes of the Diggers, the feudal system of government had been another such experiment, because William the Conqueror's seizure of once freely occupied English land in 1066 created a society in which everyone from duke to peasant became dependent on the king as owner of the earth. "Surely he took freedom from every one," Winstanley declared, "and became the disposer both of inclosures and commons."

The scattering of hastily erected Digger cabins on Saint George's Hill stands out from earlier experiments, however, for being the first attempt in a long line that stretches into the twenty-first century to try to find an alternative to, in Winstanley's phrase, "that disturbing devil, called *Particular propriety* [private property]." None of the various Digger encampments lasted more than a year. They suffered physical intimidation by neighboring landowners, and as a group they clearly failed to deal with the tensions of communal ownership. Nevertheless, their experiment has had a long line of successors, from Jean-Jacques Rousseau by way of Vladimir Lenin to the Prachandra Path adopted by contemporary Nepal's Maoist Communists. Nearly all have followed Winstanley's line of argument: that private property is fundamentally unjust, being based on violence and inequality, and that an egalitarian society can be created by redistributing land as communal property. Making such a society work, however, has always proved exceptionally difficult.

At one period of my life, I believed passionately in Winstanley's egalitarian ideals, and lived for longer than was sensible on communes in the United States and Europe, farming unproductive, steeply sloping fields locked away in the mountains, unwanted by their original owner. The experience offered a salutary lesson in understanding how ownership of the earth shapes the way society is organized.

The most attractive qualities of a primitive commune, sharing the labor and the rewards, turned out to be its most destructive. It was not the group but an individual who actually plowed the field, dug the ditch, milked the goats, and made the granola. Over time, it became obvious that some performed these tasks better, or more slowly, or more lazily, than others, and so the tasks either had to be organized with rigid efficiency to spread the burden fairly, or the sort of dissensions that plagued the Plymouth colony boiled up and tore the community apart. On that very basic level, it was clear that Winstanley was wrong. Far from being able to dispense with government, equal ownership entailed a surprising intensity of organization and policing of personal foibles.

However, communal ownership was not the only way to deal with the inequalities of property. Winstanley's experiment took place during a brief break in the ruinous civil war that wracked England, Scotland, and Ireland from 1642 to 1651 and took the lives of as many as one million of their eight million inhabitants. In the horror of those events, whole countrysides were emptied, and more than one million English acres and most of Ireland's farmland changed hands.

When parliamentarian forces routed the royalist army in the summer of 1647 and King Charles I was deposed, all three kingdoms were left without a legitimate government. In their crude attempt to create a new, more equal kind of society, the Diggers attempted to extinguish the monster of private property, but in the last months of 1647 a more sophisticated plan for a fairer society was discussed by the most powerful people in the country. In their debates, which took place in the village of Putney, just outside London, the monster was not only assigned a central role in constitutional government, but even talked of as the starting point of genuine democracy.

MANY ANTAGONISMS, religious, economic, and social, contributed to the conflict that broke out between crown and Parliament in 1642. But all of them led back to a fundamental dispute about sovereignty. Did it ultimately lie with the monarch, who, as Charles's father, King James I, had claimed was "the supremest thing on earth, for kings are not only God's lieutenants on earth, but even by God himself they are called gods," or should it somehow be exercised by the representatives of the freeholders and merchants whose wealth paid for the government of the country?

Taxation was the trigger that turned argument to fighting. Using their political stronghold in the House of Commons in the 1540s, the landowning gentry had claimed new privileges for property owners, encapsulated in the 1628 Petition of Right that stated as a principle that there should be no taxation without representation and no imprisonment except by process of law. To avoid giving his consent, King Charles I had attempted to rule without Parliament, raising money by various methods that included imposing a massive total of £50,000 in fines for illegal enclosure, the last attempt to turn back the irresistible tide. When debt finally drove Charles to recall Parliament, he was confronted by a House of Commons intent on punishing his advisors before voting on taxes, and when royal troops tried to force them to vote, violence ensued.

For the royalists, a monarchy provided the only form of legitimate government, but in October 1647 the parliamentarians were confronted by the urgent need to find an alternative when the first phase of hostilities ended with victory and the capture of the king. Their most powerful leader, a plainspoken, middle-aged landowner with a prominent wart on his square chin, epitomized their indecision about what form the government should take. "I can tell you, Sirs, what I would not have," Oliver Cromwell confessed, "though I cannot what I would."

Cromwell's dominance rested mostly on his command of the Ironsides, Parliament's fiercely disciplined cavalry, but partly on his own unshakeable personality. He was a reborn Puritan, once "the chief of sinners" who had seen the light and now consulted his conscience to discover what course Providence required him to follow. "If here I may serve my God," he wrote on the eve of a battle in 1645, "either by my doing or by my suffering, I shall be most glad." But, coming from a family that was related to Thomas Cromwell and had grown rich on monastic land, he was also the quintessential property owner, committed to the preservation of its rights against royal depredation. "I was by birth a gentleman, living neither in any considerable heights, nor yet in any obscurity," he admitted. But the family fortunes had declined despite his efforts, and his slightly shabby appearance was caught in the description of him in Parliament wearing a plain woollen suit and linen shirt, its collar "spotted with blood."

Cromwell's inclination was to support the Presbyterian "grandees" on Parliament's side, made up of lawyers, merchants, and senior military officers who believed that the monarchy had to remain, but in future should be controlled by the legislature. During the war, however, the parliamentary cause had sprouted another, radical wing, the Puritan-influenced Independents who wished the monarch to be stripped of all power. Among them a group of pamphleteers and junior officers calling themselves Levellers had started to ask a question that could not have been put into words before: if kings were not divinely appointed, if they could be defied, fought against, and chased all over the country, where did sovereignty actually come from?

To resolve their differences, Cromwell summoned the Levellers' representatives in November 1647 to an army council meeting in Putney. Five cavalry regiments elected representatives, known as "the agitators," to make their case, while Cromwell and his advocate and son-in-law, General Henry Ireton, appeared in person. On the face of it, there was not much to choose between the Cromwellian agenda, "The Heads of Proposals," and the Levellers' "Agreement of the People"—parliaments elected every two years, religious toleration for everyone and the king's executive power either minimized or shared with a council of state answerable to Parliament—but they disagreed fundamentally about who could vote in these elections. Take away some of the king's sovereign power, and it must evidently come to rest with the people who elected the new powerful legislature.

To Ireton, speaking for Cromwell, it was obvious therefore that voting could only be exercised by those with "a permanent fixed interest in this kingdom," meaning landowners or tenants paying at least two pounds a year in rent, and wealthy merchants. Without property, there could be no rights. That was what most respectable people in England had believed before the war. "He that hath no property in his goods" a member of Parliament had said bluntly in 1624, "is not free." The liberties enshrined in the common law and in statutes from Magna Carta onwards—freedom from taxation without representation, recourse to the supreme authority of the legal system, the necessity of trial by jury, the existence of habeas corpus—had all emerged from the landowners' basic need for security of tenure. Freedom was a privilege and, as the moderate and thoughtful Presbyterian Richard Baxter put it, lack of property was bound to "keep men out of freedom in the commonwealth."

Once blood had been shed, however, it brought in a wider issue than property rights. In forthright language, Colonel William Rainborough, the Levellers' chief speaker at Putney, pointed out that the rank and file in the army were not fighting for property rights but "for the liberties of the people of England." Thus when it came to voting, "I think that the poorest he that is in England hath a life to live as the greatest . . . and I do think that the poorest man in England is not at all bound in a strict sense to that government that he hath not had a voice to put himself under." In short, anyone could vote. "I do verily believe," he declared, "that there is no man but will say that the foundation of all law lies in the people."

The Levellers' proposal brought into the political arena an idea that until then had been confined to religon, that of human equality. Such a concept came more easily to Puritans, who believed that all souls were equal in the sight of God, than to Presbyterians, who held that only a minority of souls belonged to the elect destined for paradise. "Error No. 52," the Presbyterian preacher Thomas Edwards wrote in a long list of the Levellers' mistaken beliefs, "By natural birth all men are equally and alike born to like property, liberty and freedom."

For property owners, there could be no question of giving the king's sovereign power to landless voters who, in Cromwell's dismissive words, "have no interest but the interest of breathing." Representatives of the unpropertied might legislate against property, the very bulwark of individual freedom, and Ireton's outrage at Rainborough's proposal is apparent even through the muffled, occasionally confusing transcript of the debate. "Give me leave to tell you, that if you make this the rule," he exclaimed, "I think you must fly for refuge to an absolute natural right, and you must deny all civil rights." If people could lay claim to "natural rights" of freedom and voting, Ireton spluttered, they would go on to make other unreasonable claims, saying "this is so just, this is so due, this is so right to them."

In fact the Levellers did not believe that every male could vote—they would have excluded beggars and servants who might too easily be bribed—and their purpose in arguing for a near-universal male franchise was actually to strengthen the authority of government. To Ireton's persistent assertion that the Levellers' program would destroy the constitution, Rainborough replied in irritation, "I wish you would not make the world believe that we are for anarchy." Rainborough was dogged and courageous, unintimidated by the senior rank of his opponents, and his arguments contain the central belief of modern democracy, that the authority of government, its sovereign power, is derived from the assent of all the people, regardless of the property they possess. But the Levellers made a still more audacious claim.

One year earlier, in 1646, the savage satirist and pamphleteer Richard Overton had carved out of the concept of property-based individual freedom a principle that had never before been voiced. From confinement in the fortress-like prison of Newgate, opposite the royal courts of justice in London, he fired off what he called "An arrow against all tyrants and tyranny, shot from the prison of Newgate into the prerogative bowels of the arbitrary House of Lords, and all other usurpers and tyrants whatsoever."

The arrow's message was that everyone was born with equal rights, and it began with a declaration startlingly modern in its egotism: "To every individual in nature is given an individual property by nature, not to be invaded or usurped by any. For every one, as he is himself, so he has a self-propriety [property in himself], else could he not be himself; and of this no second [person] may presume to deprive any of, without manifest violation and affront to the very principles of nature and of the rules of equity and justice between man and man."

What is remarkable about Overton's arrow is that it uses the central concept of the land revolution to claim universal rights that until then had been thought of as privileges restricted to property. "No man has power over my rights and liberties, and I over no man's . . . For by natural birth all men are equally and alike born to like propriety [property], liberty and freedom; and as we are delivered of God by the hand of nature into this world, every one with a natural, innate freedom and propriety—as it were writ in the table of every man's heart, never to be obliterated."

Although little is known of Overton's early life, several of his pamphlets are written in the form of plays, and good evidence suggests that he was a onetime actor in the company attached to London's Fortune Theater. That background would have immersed him in Shakespeare's plays, and the individualized struggle of his characters to assert what was authentically theirs against the grip of the past. It would also explain the punchy style of his writing. But Overton's fearlessness was his own. Better than most, he understood the cold, murderous insistence on having his way that underlay Cromwell's religiosity, and he did not hesitate to depict the general as the sort of treacherous assassin popular in Jacobean drama and familiar to play-goers of the period. "You shall scarce speak to Cromwell about anything," Overton wrote, "but he will lay his hand on his breast, elevate his eyes, and call God to record, he will weep, howl and repent, even while he doth smite you under the first rib." The accuracy of that murderous characterization would soon be revealed.

Cromwell's supporters had Overton condemned for treason after he had issued yet more pamphlets calling for greater democracy and wider freedom. Although he escaped execution, other Levellers who adopted his views were less lucky. The Putney debates broke up with no agreement.

Two years later, however, a troop of Ironsides wearing the Levellers' green ribbons were imprisoned by Cromwell's troops in the church at Burford, a market town near Oxford, and accused of mutiny.

A relic of their captivity can still be seen in the unsteady letters carved into the church's lead font, "Antony Sedley prisner 1649." One by one, their ringleaders were led out and shot, among them Corporal Perkins, and this account of his courage might serve as an epitaph for the first doomed attempt to establish the foundation of modern democracy: "The place of death and sight of his Executioners was so far from altering his countenance or danting his spirit that he seemed to smile upon both, and accompt it a great mercy that he was to die for this 'quarrel'; and casting his eyes up to his Father and afterwards to his fellow-prisoners (who stood upon the [church roof] to see the execution) set his back against the wall, and bad [told] the Executioners shoot; and so died gallantly, as he had lived religiously."

Four years later, having established complete control of the army, Cromwell had himself sworn in as Lord Protector, and ruled until his death as a deeply religious, unmistakably military, and instinctively property-supporting dictator.

The Lord Protector's rule was just what the most influential political commentator of the day felt the nation required. Thomas Hobbes believed the concept of natural rights to be wrong and pernicious. He had spent much of his exceptionally long life considering the state of nature, and had come to share Winstanley's belief that property was an artificial concept kept in place by the violence of government and the fear of the governed. Unlike the Diggers, however, Hobbes believed that guaranteeing the security of private property was the only way of leading mankind out of the dark shadows of its depraved nature into the sunlit uplands of civilized society.

Two qualities were at war in Hobbes's character, timidity and aggression. Born in 1588, the year a Spanish armada sailed to conquer England, he himself attributed his phobic fear of physical violence to his mother's "Dread of the Spanish invasion" at the time of his birth. His rages were equally marked. "If any one objected to his Dictates," a contemporary remarked of Thomas Hobbes, "he would leave the Company in a passion, saying, his business was to Teach, not Dispute." Both traits marked his philosophy.

At the age of fourteen the boy was a good enough scholar to be admitted to Oxford University, and his exceptional learning led to his appointment soon after graduation to be tutor to the future Earl of Devonshire, and later to his son. These positions he held almost continuously until his death in 1679 at the age of ninety-one.

What is striking about *Leviathan*, Hobbes's magnum opus, published in 1651, was that he only came to the political discussion after a prolonged dissection of human nature. Having laid bare what he called "the characters of man's heart, blotted and confounded as they are with dissembling, lying, counterfeiting," he concluded that people were driven by passions, "appetite, desire, love, aversion, hate, joy, and grief," and these in turn were manifestations of two fundamentally selfish impulses, greed and fear, that could never be satisfied or dispelled. "I put for a general inclination of all mankind, a perpetual and restless desire of power after power, that ceaseth only in death . . . because he cannot assure the power and means to live well which he hath present, without the acquisition of more." In a state of nature, therefore, the passions remained uncontrolled, leading inevitably to tensions, aggravation, and violence. In the book's best-known sentence, he bleakly described the consequence. There would be "no arts; no letters; no society; and which is worst of all, continual fear and danger of violent death; and the life of man, solitary, poor, nasty, brutish, and short."

As though General Ireton were dictating at his elbow, Hobbes poured scorn on the idea that property, or any form of ordered society, could exist without government: "Where there is no common power, there is no law; where no law, no injustice . . . no propriety, no dominion, no mine and thine distinct; but only that to be every man's that he can get, and for so long as he can keep it . . . in such a condition every man has a right to every thing." The theory proposed by Cotton and Overton shrivelled in the face of Hobbes's logic.

Significantly, this unflattering portrait of humanity was taken from an earlier book, *De Corpore*, written in the 1630s, long before civil war broke out, when the royal government was making its final, doomed attempt to limit the power of the property-making gentry. Hobbes was already middle-aged by then, having grown up in the generation of Shakespeare's children, and it was evident that something had changed in people's outlook. The unease about separating the self from the past that shadowed Shakespeare's drama had gone. The unease that Hobbes expressed, and was evidently shared by his wide public, concerned the children and grandchildren of those who had done well out of the Tudor land grab and knew no restraints on their behavior.

Hobbes believed in science, not democracy. On his tours of Europe as tutor to the Earl of Devonshire, he had met Galileo and become a friend and later close enemy of the French mathematician René Descartes. In England, he acted as note-taker to Francis Bacon, pioneer of experimental science, and was friendly with many of the early scientists who later formed the Royal Society, including William Harvey, discoverer of the circulation of the blood. Next to politics, most of his time was spent trying to solve the impossible mathematical problem of squaring the circle. And *Leviathan* is in large part a scientific attempt to describe a system of government that would make sense of the balkiness of human nature. In Hobbesian philosophy, people behaved like the elements in a chemical experiment, reacting to the introduction of outside agents like danger and opportunity according to patterns determined by their innate passions, appetites, and trepidations.

According to Hobbes, however, government of some kind could be expected to emerge spontaneously from this chemical soup. The one force greater than the individual's greed to acquire more of everything was the individual's fear of being destroyed by the violence of everyone else's greed. Love of life, one of the driving passions, impelled people to use their reason and see that some sacrifices were worth making for greater security. This gave rise to what Hobbes called "the first and fundamental law of nature, which is: to seek peace and follow it." The same law of nature also drove people to desire other qualities impossible in the violent brutish world, such as justice and mercy, "and in sum, doing to others as we would be done to."

So, despite themselves, people would prefer to exchange their natural right to everything for the civil rights that a state guaranteed, and especially for those laws "by which [a person] acquireth and holdeth a propriety in land or goods, and a right or liberty of action." But because these goals were "contrary to our natural passions, that carry us to partiality, pride, revenge, and the like," it was necessary to have "the terror of some power to cause them to be observed." Step by step, each individual would be driven to the point where he turned to his neighbor and said, "I authorise and give up my right of governing myself to this man [Leviathan], or to this assembly of men, on this condition: that thou give up thy right to him, and authorise all his actions in like manner." Thus, self-interest would end in stable, albeit dictatorial, government.

Hobbes's argument extended over several hundred pages, but its conclusion was conveyed by the magnificent engraving on the book's cover.

In the foreground stood a prosperous walled city with fine houses and a sumptuous cathedral, while behind it villages nestled in a peaceful countryside crossed by neat hedgerows, and sailing barges waited on the river to take produce down to a thriving port. Towering over this scene of peace and prosperity was the crowned figure of Leviathan, a sword in one hand, a bishop's crozier in the other. Leviathan represented the commonwealth or state that would cause the law of nature to be observed, and his torso and limbs were composed of hundreds of tiny men and women gazing up at his face in devotion. On each side of the book's title a column of panels illustrated the powers that the state had tamed: to the left, castles, cannons, clashing armies, and warfare, to the right, cathedrals, argument, and disputatious prelates.

DURING THE LAST YEARS of the twentieth century, a long swath of Arab states from Algeria to Yemen experienced something close to the desperation that Hobbes imagined occurring in a state of nature. More than 150,000 people lost their lives in Algeria, tens of thousands of them murdered by having their throats slashed, and the frenzy only ceased with the installation of Abdelaziz Bouteflika as its "strong man" ruler. For the inhabitants of Egypt, Libya, Saudi Arabia, and Yemen, security without political freedom was preferable to such chaos. In 1991, Somalia lost its Leviathan, the longtime dictator Siad Barre, and fell into a cycle of civil war, foreign invasion, and famine that indeed rendered most people's existence solitary, poor, nasty, brutish, and short.

However, the behavior of these autocratic rulers illustrated the drawback to the Hobbesian solution to civil chaos. If property only survives thanks to Leviathan's protection, it will always be in danger of being appropriated and redistributed to the advantage of Leviathan's family and cronies. Until the "Arab Spring" of 2011, the mass of people living under this sort of rule had to purchase protection for their lands, shops, and businesses by paying bribes and other favors to the rulers' families and associates who became bloated with wealth. The death of a Tunisian fruitseller, Muhammad Bouazizi, who set himself on fire rather than endure more of the regime's harassment and humiliation, encapsulated the despair that a Leviathan government engenders.

Even to Hobbes's contemporaries, the danger of a corrupt and bullying ruler was obvious. Despite the risk of offending Cromwell, criticism of *Leviathan* centered on this outcome. Yet it was not clear whether a more attractive form of non-monarchical government existed. To a country still recovering from civil war, peace and security were too valuable to be lightly discarded. One way through this apparently insoluble dilemma was suggested by the most eccentric of Hobbes's critics.

In 1656, James Harrington published a highly individual history of English politics entitled *Oceana*. His purpose was twofold: partly to correct Hobbes but mostly to explain how the cataclysm of the civil war could have occurred. Looking back at the history of the previous two centuries, he became convinced that property explained it all. He took for granted that its owners would be selfish in pursuit of their own interests. What intrigued him was the way that this shaped a country's government.

A polyglot intellectual, and the spoiled darling of his family, Harrington supported Parliament in theory, but the execution of Charles I in 1649, which he personally witnessed, so shocked him that it caused what appears to have been a nervous breakdown. *Oceana* was begun a few years later, and, although written as a kind of fairy tale, remains remarkable as the first attempt to analyze political events in terms of economic forces.

Harrington's theory depended on a simple observation: the shape of government was bound to reflect the way the earth was owned because in the last resort, those who controlled most property could sustain the largest number of soldiers. "An army is a beast that hath a great belly and must be fed," he pointed out, followed by the observation that "he that has the land can feed the soldiers." Harrington's conclusion was contained in a single sentence: "Such . . . as is the proportion or balance of . . . property in land, such is the nature of empire [government]." Where one man was "sole landlord" of an entire country, "his empire is absolute monarchy"; where the ground was in the hands of only a few, the government was an aristocracy; and where many owned it, as in England, "the empire is a commonwealth." A century later, the founders of the American republic read Harrington with particular attention, and John Adams summed up his philosophy in a pithy phrase, "Power follows property."

Where a government did not reflect this underlying reality, there was bound to be conflict ending in an explosion. Absolute monarchs, such as the Bourbons in France and the Hapsburgs in Spain, who owned their nation's territory, had to prevent any attempt by the people to widen their share of the land. Conversely, where people won land for themselves—here Harrington pointed to the Dutch winning independence from the Spaniards, and the Swiss from the Austrian Hapsburgs—the explosion went off under the foreign monarchs. "Where are the estates, or the power of the people in France?—blown up," Harrington wrote gleefully.

"Where is that of the people in Arragon, and the rest of the Spanish kingdoms?—blown up. On the other side, where is the King of Spain's power in Holland?—blown up. Where is that of the Austrian princes in Switzerland?—blown up."

The cause of the civil war in England, according to *Oceana*, could be traced directly back to Henry VIII's disposal of monastic estates in the 1540s. It put land in the hands of so many people, "that the balance of the commonwealth was too apparently in the popular party." The explosive pressure of that imbalance had to be relieved. If "their kings did not first blow up them," meaning the landowners, the owners would have no choice but to destroy royal government. "Rights" played no part in Harrington's thesis. The drive toward democracy was not about personal freedom, it was about the distribution of power based on property.

IN EFFECT, *Oceana* vindicated the belief held by Winstanley and the Diggers that the way the land was owned did shape society and government. However crude, Harrington's economic model suggested a mechanism to explain why property should have such far-reaching effects. And so long as land remained the prime source of wealth and income, its assumption that landowners were bound to want political power offered a surprisingly far-reaching approach to the analysis of a country's social and governing structure. Late into the twentieth century, United States foreign policy continued to provide practical vindication of Harrington's thesis. "When you answer the question, 'Who really owns the soil?'," wrote George McBride, a pioneer of the Green Revolution in Mexico, "you lay bare the very foundations upon which its society is based, and reveal the fundamental character of many of its institutions."

The answer led the Soviet Union to break up privately owned farms and establish collectives on state-owned land in the 1930s, and drove the United States in the 1940s to promote democracy in Japan by forcibly destroying "the undemocratic land tenure system" and redistributing it to owner-occupiers. "We believe in the family-size farm," President Harry S. Truman declared in 1950. "That is the basis of our agriculture and has strongly influenced our form of government." Throughout the Cold War, the struggle between capitalism and Communism in Asia, Latin America, and the Middle East was shaped by the Harringtonian belief that once land was either privately owned or state-owned, the politics would follow suit.

Harrington, however, took his pioneering analysis no further. Instead, with obsessive, almost autistic attention to detail, he devoted himself to creating a blueprint for his ideal commonwealth, with every inch of land surveyed, mapped, and measured to become property, and elaborate rules set in place to keep its government honest.

To prevent any one individual acquiring too much power, he proposed limiting the amount of landed property each person could acquire, and to avoid corruption in government, members of both the legislature and the executive were to be "rotated," that is elected by ballot for a set term, usually of three years. Ideas such as these appealed strongly to the scientific, rationalist people who dissected dead bodies and examined the shadows on the moon through a telescope. When Harrington founded the "Rota club" in the late 1650s to promote his ideas, its membership included people such as William Harvey and the architect Christopher Wren.

In his remarkable, though almost unreadable, study of how a democracy could come into being, Harrington offered a corrective to Hobbes's fearful view of the greediness of the land revolution's beneficiaries. Although his model of government formation was drawn from the same period of English history, *Oceana* showed in effect what might happen after *Leviathan*. With security, Leviathan's subjects would grow wealthier, and sooner or later seek power to protect their property against the depredations of the ruler. One side or the other would then be blown up. Missing from Harrington's truncated analysis, however, was the volatile substance that led to the explosion.

THE CATALYST was to be found in the claim of the English Levellers to a universal right to freedom and property. Because it sprang, as Overton put it, from "the rules of equity and justice between man and man," this right existed in nature, before monarchs and laws existed. A "civil" right, created by the law, could be legally removed by the law. But a "natural" right, while it might be temporarily obliterated, could never be destroyed. In other words, the protection the common law gave to individual ownership merely enshrined a preexisting right. As one of the Leveller agitators at Putney put it, "Really properties are the foundations of constitutions, and not constitutions of property. For if so be there were no constitutions, yet the law of nature does give a principle for every man to have a property." Thus King Charles's attempt at autocratic rule was not only illegal, it ran counter to natural justice, and justified his overthrow and execution.

* * *

HAD THESE ARGUMENTS about "natural rights" to freedom and voting been confined to a powerful elite, their significance would have been diminished. But amongst the Puritan-influenced, private-propertied English, the capacity to read their Bible and their title deeds gave their own language both spiritual and political authority. As a result, Leveller pamphlets, like those of their mainstream critics, together with *Leviathan*, *Oceana*, and other books in the same vein, were not only written in the vernacular, but widely read by landowners and by those accustomed to seeking biblical texts to buttress the dictates of conscience.

Elsewhere in the world, the language of power divided government from the governed. In China, Mandarin was spoken and written only by the ruling elite who made up the imperial bureaucracy, and on the continent of Europe the majority of people communicated in local dialects—as late as 1794, according to Abbé Grégoire, barely a quarter of France's inhabitants understood French—while law courts and universities used Latin. Consequently the flood of treatises on natural law published in seventeenth-century Europe, such as Francisco Suárez's *De Legibus*, Hugo Grotius's *De Jure Belli ac Pacis*, and Samuel Pufendorf's *De jure naturae et gentium*, were composed for a privileged class of lawyers, academics, and administrators.

This restricted audience dictated the nature of their discussion of natural rights. Framed in relation to abstract principles derived from familiar church authorities and Latin and Greek texts, personal freedom was defined in the familiar negative sense of not having the status of a slave, while the political freedom to resist a lawful ruler was equally constrained. However unjust a sovereign's actions, rebellion was akin to children killing their father, an unnatural crime wrong in itself and liable to produce, as Grotius put it, "a turbulent state of affairs, which no sober minded people ever wished to experience." Protestant and Catholic alike shared the belief of Saint Thomas Aquinas, the medieval church's great lawyer, that only a direct threat to personal safety justified resistance to a king.

By contrast, the Putney debates and scores of Leveller-inspired pamphlets not only imagined the possibility of the king being subject to the will of the people, but made the breathtaking claim that every free person was entitled to the unique array of privileges won by property owners—freedom from arbitrary arrest, protection of the law's due process, the right to trial by jury, and other defenses against the king's power—and a right to vote and thus participate in government.

So long as Puritanism, and with it the primacy given to individual conscience, carried political influence, the possibility that these individual rights might be universal remained in existence. But, as the landowners monopolized power and entrenched their privileges after 1653, the balance of opinion would tip away from the Levellers and toward Cromwell, so that by the end of the century English freedom was once more seen to be a privilege of property. But the revolutionary thought that Overton had put into print and the green-ribboned Levellers had fought for, that by natural justice such rights belonged to all, was not extinguished. On the other side of the Atlantic, it would not only burst into life but shape the constitution of a new nation.

Chapter Four

The Two Capitalisms

Drawing up his will in 1685, William Petty felt it necessary to begin by disclosing the precocious intelligence that had made him famous: "In the first place I declare and affirm that at the full age of fifteen years, I had obtained the Latin, Greek and French tongues, the whole body of common arithmetick, the practical geometry and astronomy, conducing to navigation, dialling [surveying], etc., with the knowledge of several mathematical trades."

At the time of writing, he was sixty-two years old, and in poor health with less than two years to live, yet for all his pride in past achievements—his professorship of anatomy at Oxford University, his readership in music at Gresham College, London, the annual income of £15,000 he earned from his investments in Ireland—it was still the future that most concerned him: "I intend to attend the improvement of my lands in Ireland, and to get in the many debts owing unto me, and to promote the trade of iron, lead, marble, fish and timber whereof my estate is capable: and as for studies and experiments, I think now to confine the same to the anatomy of the people and political arithmetic, as also to the improvement of ships, land carriages, guns and pumps, as of most use to mankind."

A portrait painted at the height of Petty's success shows him, full lipped and double chinned, gazing out with an expression of lazy arrogance from beneath half-closed eyes. It is not difficult to guess at the piercing intellect that drove his enemies to frustration and even thoughts of murder. To his friends, however, he was a generous, witty companion. "His eyes were a kind of goose-grey, very short sighted and as to aspect beautiful," wrote his friend John Aubrey, the Oxford antiquarian. "They promised sweetness of nature and they did not deceive, for he was a marvellous good natured person."

Out of his fertile mind came plans for mass-produced clocks, improved "Chariotts, new riggs for shipps, a Wheele for one to run races in," and a "double-bottomed ship," the first working catamaran in Europe. But he preferred to think of himself as a scientist, following the principles of practical experimentation laid down by Francis Bacon, and in 1660 he became a founding member of the Royal Society, Europe's oldest scientific body. On scientific grounds, he deliberately chose "to express my self in terms of Number, Weight, or Measure; to use only Arguments of Sense, and to consider only such Causes, as have visible Foundations in Nature." This method gave birth to what he thought of as his greatest achievement, "political arithmetic," a combination of statistics and economics.

As a statistician, Petty revealed himself to be imaginative though over-adventurous in his use of information. Using tax returns, housing construction figures, and the newly published data of births and deaths collected from parish registers, he extrapolated wildly to estimate the population of London, then less than half a million, to be somewhere between six hundred thousand and more than seven hundred thousand, and for England, a figure in excess of seven million, about one third more than the real total.

As an economist, however, he came close to genius. In all his writing, but especially in three essays written between 1662 and 1682, *A Treatise on Taxes and Contributions*, *Verbum Sapienti*, and *Quantulumcunque concerning money*, he showed an almost intuitive understanding of the connections between inflation and money supply, taxation and rates of interest, international trade and foreign exchange markets, and the availability of credit and the velocity at which money circulated. There was no overarching theoretical explanation, merely a series of practical examples to illustrate how things worked. In other words, he was describing an already existing capitalist economy. And compared to the static mercantile model of the time that pictured economies as closed systems designed to accumulate money, his ideas are startling in their scope and assurance.

The son of a village clothier, Petty owed his wealth and his knighthood to nothing but his own energy and talent. He paid for his education and an apprenticeship as a mariner by gambling and writing letters for the illiterate. His cleverness was so intolerable, however, that on his first voyage his fellow sailors dumped him on shore in Normandy after he broke a leg. Characteristically, Petty made the most of the opportunity to learn French, math, and logic at the nearest Jesuit college, then trained in medicine at Amsterdam and Paris.

His unique combination of drive and intelligence first became widely known in 1650 when the body of Ann Green was brought to him as professor of anatomy at the University of Oxford. She had been hanged for the murder of her newborn baby, a crime she denied vehemently, claiming that the child was stillborn. After dangling from the rope for fifteen minutes where it was noted "divers friends of hers and standers by . . . hung with their whole weight upon her" to hasten her death, she was cut down and taken to be dissected in the interests of science. But, as Petty inspected the corpse, he heard a rattle in her throat. Although the body was cold and the muscles rigid with the agony of strangulation, he "wrenched open her teeth which were fast sett and put in some strong waters." Her choking and coughing showed there was still life present. Immediately he set out to resuscitate her, massaging her feet and clenched hands, taking blood, giving an enema to set her intestines working, and, as she began to show signs of revival, putting her to bed with another woman to keep her warm.

Within a week Petty's treatment restored Ann Green to full health—she would live another twenty years, get married and have three children—and his success caused a sensation. Reprinted in numerous pamphlets, the meticulous record he kept of remedies, their effectiveness, and his patient's response, earned him a reputation that, as he liked to boast, could have made him a fashionable doctor. Instead he chose to accept the post of physician-general to the army that Cromwell sent to Ireland in 1652. It was a shrewd decision. Following in the army's bloodstained wake, Petty would survey all of Ireland, acquire huge estates, and make his fortune.

PETTY'S POLITICAL ARITHMETIC was not conceived in a vacuum. Many of his examples were drawn from Holland's sophisticated banking and stock exchange structure that enabled it to finance a gigantic trade with the Far East and establish trading settlements in South Africa, Connecticut, and New Amsterdam on the Hudson River. He was aware also of the economic policies of Louis XIV's chief minister, Jean-Baptiste Colbert. But while Colbert was a mercantilist trying to trap money inside France, and even the Dutch economy was based on the monopolistic trading pattern of medieval Venice and Renaissance Florence, Petty developed into a relentless free trader, dedicated to the principles of unfettered competition and to the operation of what Adam Smith would a hundred years later call "the marketplace" to determine prices, exchange rates, and the efficiency of production.

At the heart of Petty's work were two complementary ideas: land had to be treated as capital, and only labor could release its value. The relationship was like sex, "labour is the father and active principle of wealth, as lands are the mother." To make the most of England's land and labor, he suggested three basic principles drawn from Dutch experience. The significance of Petty's proposals, put forward mostly in the 1660s, is that they delineate the precise point at which capitalism and private property can be seen to have merged.

The first, perhaps unexpectedly, was to allow "liberty of conscience" to everyone, whether Puritan, Catholic, or Jew. Petty's reasons were both social and economic. The sort of people who challenged orthodox religion were "for the most part, thinking, sober, and patient Men" and therefore useful to society, but they also conferred a competitive advantage because any economy would benefit from the ideas of ambitious outsiders who took a different view of the world from "men of extreme Wealth and Power." His second and third ingredients were, however, purely economic.

To demonstrate how to make full use of the potential wealth in land, Petty made a distinction between viewing it simply as a static resource—England's fourteen million farmable acres had a sale price of £144 million by his estimate—and treating it as capital. In the latter state, once its value was released by labor, it created multiple benefits. The wages it paid sustained families, the profits it generated created further investment, and the taxes on its operations financed government. Assessing these variables, Petty estimated that the capital value of England's acres amounted to £417 million, almost three times the resale value. That sum could be increased still further, he suggested, by fairer taxation, more efficient agricultural production, and the establishment of a land registry to remove any possibility of doubt about the title to a property, "for there can be no incouragement to Industry, where there is no assurance of what shall be gotten by it."

Once land was viewed as capital, however, an adequate supply of money became essential for its full value to be realized. Anticipating Milton Friedman's monetarist approach to the same subject, Petty declared, "For Money is but the Fat of the Body-Politick, whereof too much doth often hinder its agility, as too little makes it sick . . . so doth Money in the State quicken its Action." The kingdom possessed only six million pounds in gold and silver, by his estimate, and two thirds of that total was saved by tenants simply to pay rent on land. There was, as a result, too little money being invested in the improvement of fields, animals, and crops, in transport and accessibility to markets. The knock-on effect was to diminish returns that could be earned in the form of profits, wages, and taxes, as well as in the increased value of the land itself. Petty's final ingredient, therefore, was a national bank, "the use whereof is to encrease Money, or rather to make a small sum equivalent in Trade to a greater." A reputable bank could make available credit worth double the amount of cash in its vaults, and adjust the flow to what was needed to keep the market stable. "Money," he concluded, "is the best rule of commerce."

The lack was made good in 1694, when William Paterson founded the Bank of England with the power to issue paper notes backed by £1.2 million in cash subscribed by wealthy investors. Its lending power effectively increased the money supply—the "Fat of the Body-Politick"—by almost one third, boosting the economy at a time when the rest of Europe was in economic recession. By no coincidence, Paterson's well-stocked library contained all Petty's published work, including two copies of his *Political Arithmetic.*

In practice as well as theory, William Petty was the complete capitalist. At the age of twenty-nine, while still acting as physician-general to Cromwell's army, he won the contract to survey and map Ireland, except for the western province of Connacht and some areas already mapped. In the face of stiff competition, he undertook to complete the gigantic task in the space of thirteen months for a price barely half that of other bidders. His method was surprisingly modern. He created an assembly-line that divided up each aspect of the process into simple repeatable tasks, and a management team to run the organization.

The equipment required by the surveyors consisted of a chain measuring two Irish perches (approximately forty-two feet) and a basic compass known as a circumferentor. To produce these, Petty appointed one specialist firm of wiremakers to manufacture a thousand identical chains, a watchmaker to provide a thousand magnetized needles for the compass, a carpenter to make a thousand boxes for the compass, a craftsman "of a more versatile head and hand" to assemble these components into a thousand surveyors' compasses, a pipemaker to produce three thousand metal legs for the tripods to support them, and a stationer to run off a thousand identical ruled notebooks. To act as surveyors, he hired from the army a thousand soldiers who were "headfull [heedful] and steddy minded though not of the nimblest witts" but able to read and write, and forty clerks working in Dublin to transcribe their data, and map them to scale. Finally he personally selected "a few of the most astute and sagacious persons" to oversee the quality of the work and eliminate inaccuracies.

The clerks' duties, known as "laying down" the information, gave the entire project its name, the Down Survey. It was completed on time, under budget, with an 87 percent accuracy reckoned by modern standards, and at huge profit to its organizer, who made almost £10,000 in fees and bonuses directly from the operation, and was later awarded fifteen thousand acres to cover additional expenses. By his own account, he had been worth just £500 before he began the survey.

For understandable reasons, Petty believed strongly that his assembly line would bring similar benefits to manufacturing. The division of labor had this overwhelming advantage, he explained, "the work of each artisan will be simple and easy . . . In the making of a watch, [for example], if one man shall make the wheels, another the spring, another shall engrave the dial-plate, and another shall make the cases, then the watch will be better and cheaper, than if the whole work be put upon any one man." In 1776 Adam Smith would advocate similar specialization of labor with his famous example of the pin-maker's trade, but 120 years earlier Petty had shown how the process could be applied to a far more complex operation.

Since labor was what released the value in capital, Petty also assumed that for entirely materialistic reasons a strong government would look after its citizens' health and education, if only to ensure that its resources were exploited to the full. Although England's workers only spent seven pounds a year per person, each one by Petty's reckoning had a capital value of sixty-nine pounds when fully employed, making it worth spending ten pounds or more a year to provide him or her with work and schooling. Even his whirring brain could never have imagined how profoundly the addition of steam-power would change that calculation.

The rural economy that Petty described had already diverged from the largely peasant structure of northern Europe. The farms were bigger; by the end of the seventeenth century most measured more than fifty acres and were growing larger, compared to average sizes around Paris of less than ten acres, and growing smaller through subdivision.

The purpose of English farming had also fundamentally changed. The self-sufficient goal of peasant agriculture remained as it was in the first century AD when the Roman farming authority, Lucius Columella, declared, "He is a bad farmer who buys what he can get his land to supply." Peasant markets were devoted to exchange and barter, and even when farmers sold their produce for money, it was only the surplus after their own needs had been met that went on sale. The capitalist agriculture that Petty described, however, was aimed at selling a commodity, be it corn, wool, or beef, and using the proceeds to buy labor, food, transport, and improved breeds of animals or strains of cereal. Consequently its goal was to make a profit, and since the weather rendered farming a gamble—especially during the "Little Ice Age" of lower temperatures that reached its nadir in the 1680s—it needed credit.

Throughout Petty's writings, it is clear from his ready calculation of the interest rates to be charged for loans and mortgages secured against the value of land that a thriving if unofficial banking system existed in both England and Ireland to supply funds on credit to landowners. In a classic definition, Petty described interest as "A Reward for forbearing the use of your own Money for a Term of Time," but the size of the reward was one that only the market could determine. The rate might go as high as a wholly illegal 100 percent in risky deals—a sixteenth-century statute set 12 percent as the legal maximum—but he was certain no government could hope to regulate interest rates any more than it could control prices or exchange rates.

Yet, the most important ingredient in Petty's restless reckoning of the value of privately owned land was the inexorable way that, as he put it in *Political Arithmetick,* "the Rent [profit] of Land is advanced by reason of Multitude of People." In a sense it was obvious that the demand from a growing population would push up land values, and that "Land of the same quantity and quality in England, [should be] generally worth four or five times as much as in Ireland, and but one quarter of what it is worth in Holland; because England is four or five times better Peopled than Ireland, and but a quarter so well as Holland." But this would turn out to be the secret weapon that made exclusive, private property the most dynamic way of owning the earth. All things being equal, exclusive possession guaranteed that the demand from a growing population would increase the capital value of a landowner's property. So convinced was Petty of its national importance that he contemplated bringing back the entire population of British colonists from America to their homeland so that "the Rents of Lands shall rise by this closer cohabitation of People."

The effect that a growing population had on increasing the value of land was to become the fundamental driving force that powered the expansion of private property economies. Its earliest impact came in 1660 when the monarchy was restored and King Charles II came to the throne. A succession of royal favorites, among them the Penn family, George Carteret and John Berkeley were recompensed for their loyalty while the king was in exile by being awarded land in the New World, covering much of the colonies of Pennsylvania, Carolina, and New Jersey. At the time, American land was so cheap, existing colonies like Virginia still gave a free "headright" of one hundred acres to any adults who paid their own passage. The new proprietors, however, all intended to make a profit from their territories, both by selling farms to new settlers and from the increased value of their own holdings as immigrants to the New World drove up the price of land. Unlike the New England colonies, the policy of proprietors from 1665, soon followed by the authorities of existing colonies, was to entice potential land buyers by offering lists of concessions that guaranteed them surveyed properties, security of tenure, and even representation in colonial assemblies. The success of this strategy quickly became evident.

In 1699 Virginia's growing population enabled the colonial government to abolish the free award of land and to start selling it at five shillings for fifty acres. Six years later, demand was so brisk that the colony's first historian, Robert Beverley, described his countrymen as "not minding anything but to be masters of great tracts of land," and the seventeen-year-old George Washington solemnly noted in 1748 that the wealthiest Virginians made their money "by taking up & purchasing at very low rates the rich back Lands which were thought nothing of in those days, but are now the most valuable Lands we possess." By the second half of the eighteenth century, Benjamin Franklin could unblushingly emphasize that no effort was required to make money in this way, and that he had personally known of "several instances of large tracts of land bought on what was then the frontier of Pennsylvania, for ten pounds per hundred acres, which after 20 years when the settlements had been extended far beyond them, sold readily without any improvement made upon them for three pounds per acre."

Driven by this new dynamic motive and buoyed by an equity in their land that grew as the population overcame the losses of the civil war, farmers in the private property economy of Britain's multiple kingdoms increased the productivity of their land even faster than the demand. Wheat yields were rising from the medieval standard of around ten bushels per acre toward the eighteenth-century level of twenty-five bushels, consistently about three bushels more per acre than in France.

While French peasants relied on cereals generally eaten as gruel—flavored with onions, carrots, and cabbage—for 95 percent of their nourishment, and supplemented only infrequently by milk, cheese, and an occasional egg, English workers usually added mutton, bacon, or cheese to a diet that consisted largely of cabbage, turnip, bread, and boiled potatoes. Even the families of laborers owned chairs, saucepans, earthernware plates, and knives—items often absent from peasant homes in western France—and the wills of slightly richer tradesmen itemized the books, clocks, and mirrors they left to their successors. By the early eighteenth century, military records showed that the average height of English army recruits was around five feet six inches (169 centimeters), three inches taller than their French equivalents.

More and more workers lived in towns rather than in the country—London's population had jumped from fifty-five thousand at the start of the land revolution to 475,000 in 1670—but wages rose strongly from the middle of the seventeenth century, at a time when they were falling in southern Europe. The wool economy had changed radically from simply producing the raw materials for Flemish weavers, to finishing, spinning, knitting, and weaving both a finer cloth for the Mediterranean market, and heavier broadcloth for northern Europe. Raw wool, worth around two million pounds a year, earned more than eight million pounds a year as cloth, and its production employed almost one in five of the workforce in the mid-seventeenth century. And almost uniquely among European nations, England charged no internal taxes on the movement of agricultural produce from the country to the town.

"The working manufacturing people of England eat the fat, and drink the sweet, live better, and fare better, than the working poor of any other nation in Europe," declared Daniel Defoe in 1726. "They make better wages of their work, and spend more of the money upon their backs and bellies, than in any other country."

The significance of this widening divergence has provoked furious debate amongst historians and economists attempting to explain why it happened. The emphasis used to be placed on enclosures as the spur to more efficient farming until research showed that open fields in England and France had also increased yields of cereals in the seventeenth century.

More recently the growth of representative government and the rule of law have been picked out as vital in guaranteeing social stability and encouraging investment. But in Poland, sixteenth-century landowners elected the members of the Sejm, or parliament, while in France the law guaranteed peasants a security of tenure that was virtually unbreakable. Yet neither country experienced an agricultural revolution in the seventeenth century.

Today, economists argue for the influence of trade and of urban merchants from London who bought land as vital in fostering a businesslike outlook. They cite the nineteenth-century German economist Heinrich von Thünen, who identified proximity to cities, both as markets and suppliers of capital for investment, as the crucial factor in transforming farmers from feudal to capitalist producers. But this theory, like its predecessors, overlooks one critical detail, the actual way that land was owned. As a result it fails to explain why only in England and North America did seventeenth-century land become capital. More seriously, it ignores the vital contribution that land ownership made to the development of free-enterprise capitalism. It was not a mistake that Adam Smith, its first and greatest theorist, ever made.

When he considered how the free-market economy came into existence, Smith took it to be almost a freak of circumstance. In most of Europe, the feudal system had prevented a market in land developing, and consequently money had been invested in trade and manufacturing, where the profits were greatest. England, however, had geography, "natural fertility of the soil . . . [and] the great extent of the sea-coast in proportion to that of the whole country, and of the many navigable rivers which run through it, and afford the conveniency of water carriage to some of the most inland parts of it." So the movement of food from country to town, and the trade in wool to Europe's growing market, could flourish.

Uniquely then, England had favored agriculture. It had forbidden imports of cattle, and put high duties on imports of wheat—measures that Smith disapproved of and thought ineffective—but it also guaranteed individual ownership of land: "What is of much more importance than all of them, the yeomanry of England are rendered as secure, as independent, and as respectable as law can make them." This was the achievement of the common law, and especially the writ of ejectment that allowed an owner to establish a monopoly on the use of his property. It made an investment in land secure.

Private property had allowed about 350,000 capitalist enterprises to come into existence, fated to compete against each other in the supply of food and clothing. "A revolution of the greatest importance to the publick happiness," Smith concluded, "was in this manner brought about by two different orders of people [existing landowners and merchants investing in land], who had not the least intention to serve the publick."

THE PRIVATE PROPERTY SYSTEM was not the first appearance of capitalism. In Europe, the trading economies of thirteenth-century and fifteenth-century Venice and Genoa undoubtedly qualified in financial terms. That is, they raised capital by public subscription, invested it in ships and commodities, and paid dividends from the profits. At the heart of the system was the security offered by the borrower's capacity to repay. Borrowing against the future was always risky, but nothing reduced risk more effectively than owning a monopoly on an assured source of income.

The classic example was Florence in the fourteenth century, a period when the city needed to borrow money from its citizens to pay for the professional soldiers or *condottiere* who fought its wars against Milanese enemies. In an early form of the bond market, the city authorities exacted interest-bearing loans, offering as security the future revenue from taxes and excise duties that only the city could levy. Acting as both politicians and financiers, the Medici family ensured that the city allocated enough from its monopolized income to pay lenders before anyone else, and the confidence that ensued from the family's dual role kept interest rates low. As the economic historian Niall Ferguson put it, "This oligarchical power structure gave the bond market a firm political foundation."

In the early seventeenth century, the seven United Provinces of the Netherlands (roughly today's Belgium and Netherlands) boasted the most advanced capitalist economy in Europe, with the largest stock market, the highest per capita income, the finest houses—"In all Europe," a contemporary English commentator, Bernard de Mandeville, asserted, "you shall find no private buildings so sumptuously magnificent as the merchants' and other gentlemen's houses are in Amsterdam"—and a merchant fleet equal in size to those of England, France, Spain, and Portugal combined.

All this was built on a dynamic trade economy based largely on fishing and the import of spices, silk, and china from the Far East. In 1602, the inner circle of bankers, traders, and guild masters in six of these cities used their political clout to create the United East India Company, in

Dutch *Vereenigde Oost-Indische Compagnie* or VOC, by amalgamating those companies trading with the Orient and especially the spice islands of modern Indonesia. The behemoth that was set up, eight times larger than the English East India Company founded in London two years earlier in 1600, transformed the financial and corporate environment. Its funding brought into existence such innovations as the public sale of shares, the concept of the joint stock company where the owners' liability for debt was limited to their shareholding, the issue of bonds backed by future earnings, a stock exchange for trading the company's shares, and a board of directors responsible to the shareholders for running the enterprise.

The phenomenal wealth generated by the VOC—for two centuries its dividends averaged almost 20 percent—lifted the development of commercial capitalism to a new level, but the company was not designed for free enterprise. Not only did the States-General, the Netherlands federal parliament, guarantee the VOC a monopoly of trade with the east for twenty-one years, it enforced restrictions on competition to the point of forbidding any Dutch ship to enter either the Indian or the Pacific Oceans, by sailing around the Cape of Good Hope or through the Straits of Magellan at Cape Horn, without its permission. To recycle the profits from this immense monopoly, and from other smaller trading companies, Amsterdam bankers and politicians generated a range of financial and fiscal instruments, including government bonds, annuities or *rentes*, and debentures, that reduced the cost of government borrowing to just 4 percent. Nevertheless, the basic structure of this complex financial market was what the socialist historian Eric Hobsbawm described as "a feudal business economy."

The London trading monopolies operated in the same way. The East India Company obtained a monopoly from the crown for trade in spices from India and the Far East; the Greenland Company obtained a monopoly from the crown for trade in whales from the Arctic; the Muscovy Company obtained a monopoly from the crown for trade in furs and tallow from Russia; the Levant Company obtained a monopoly from the crown for trade in spices from the Middle East; and the Royal African Company obtained a monopoly from the crown for trade in slaves from Africa. None of these capitalists wanted competition. It was wasteful, inefficient, and made raising money more expensive. Unregulated competition, the Levant Company told England's Privy Council in 1588, "will not only discourage us and others in like respect hereafter to attempt and go on with like charges and discoveries, but be utterly discouraged to enter into any new charge [expense]."

HAD LONDON'S MERCHANTS dominated politics in England as completely as the Dutch burghers did that of the Netherlands, they would have evolved the same kind of capitalism. The difference was the land revolution. Its vital role in England was made plain by the inadequate part it played in the Netherlands.

A truncated version of the English model did in fact emerge in the Netherlands' two northern provinces of Friesland and Groningen. There, most families owned their farms outright; mortgage law treated coastal land newly reclaimed from the sea as a commodity providing an investment opportunity for urban merchants; and crops and livestock were raised for market rather than subsistence. The property-owning jonkers, widely caricatured with gin-inflamed red noses and a prickly snobbishness about their supposedly noble ancestry, bore a distinct resemblance to the gentry in England, and exercised a similar degree of influence in the provincial assembly. But these two provinces were the most poverty-stricken in the Netherlands, and beyond their borders the political influence of landed property was negligible.

In the other five provinces, the most valuable property was the directly possessed, urban variety, not land but a house, its furniture, paintings, jewelry, and other valuables, and the less tangible ownership of shares in a fishing vessel or a trading enterprise. The states—the governing assembly of each province—were dominated by the cities' representatives, prosperous, black-clad burghers whose goal was to safeguard the financial and commercial interests that made this kind of property possible. So intimate were the ties between commerce and politics in cities like Amsterdam, Rotterdam, and Delft, that an oligarchy of wealthy families was able to coordinate government policies and trading goals to create the most favorable conditions for their investments.

The difference between Dutch and English attitudes to the ownership of land, and thus to the shape of government and society, became obvious when each was exported across the ocean. The string of VOC trading posts stretched from South Africa to the coasts of India, on to Sumatra and Java in the South Pacific, and as far north as Japan. In all these places Dutch settlers possessed land, but they did so under the near-feudal terms of the VOC's monopoly that required them to provide food and manpower in return for their holdings. In 1621, the Dutch West India Company

(WIC) was formed to trade with the Americas, and its monopoly was so sweeping that the very cabbages grown outside its trading-post of New Amsterdam on Manhattan Island belonged to the company. In 1629, when competition from the English colonists in North America forced the WIC to offer land rights to the colonists of New Amsterdam, it did so within a feudal structure proposed by Kilijaen van Rensselaer from the inland province of Gelderland.

The WIC's "Charter of Freedoms and Exemptions" allowed any magnate or *patroon* who undertook to transport fifty colonists to New Amsterdam the right to own "as a perpetual fiefdom" a gigantic manorial estate along the Hudson or Connecticut Rivers. The greatest of these *patroons*, Van Rensselaer acquired seven hundred thousand acres, including the present county of Albany in upstate New York, while another, Cornelis Melyn, was granted Staten Island. Their tenants swore an oath of allegiance to the *patroon* and expected to have disputes and infractions of the law tried in the *patroon's* manor court. These were conditions that William the Conqueror, creator of feudal England, would instantly have recognized, but not even he had presumed to grant such large fiefdoms to his chain-mailed barons.

It was for this mercantile audience that Hugo Grotius wrote when he insisted in *Mare Liberum* that the seas were open to everyone, and in *De Jure Belli ac Pacis* that justice and mutuality governed the conduct of nations even when caught in the horrors of war. Personal liberty was not Grotius's concern. Although he believed that people agreed to be governed, it was a one-sided, irrevocable agreement to give up all personal rights. Citing Aristotle as his authority, Grotius declared, "It is permitted to every man to enslave himself."

This was not an academic point. It went to the heart of the difference between the two capitalisms. Parliament, Puritanism, and the common law had created a unique monopoly by which one man owned outright part of the earth. When Gregory King made the first attempt to tabulate the occupations of people in England in 1688, he reckoned that of 1.3 million families, the head of 350,000, or 25 percent, of them were tenant farmers, freeholders, or landowning aristocrats. Each had to compete for markets in the supply of food and clothing. For a Cromwell fighting for property rights, a Leveller demanding equal rights, a Harrington analyzing constitutions, a Petty computing economics, everything came back to that individual owner. The type of capitalism, of government, and of social justice all bore the stamp of private landed property.

By contrast, Grotius argued that in its own interest, any government, monarchical or democratic, would establish law, keep the peace, and enforce contracts. That, as the examples of Venice, Florence, and the Netherlands demonstrated, was all that the financial and commercial markets needed. If a Grotius government failed, there was no mechanism for replacing it, because the governed had no rights except those that came from the state. Quite specifically Grotius rejected the idea that "sovereignty resides in the people, so that it is permissible for the people to restrain and punish kings whenever they make a bad use of their power."

To confuse mercantile capitalism with its free-market equivalent is to miss the most important element in the system that William Petty was describing. As the modern examples of China, Russia, and half a dozen other state-managed economies make glaringly obvious, capitalism of the mercantile kind can flourish with no need of democracy.

In 1763, Adam Smith arrived in Paris with a towering reputation as the author of the *Theory of Moral Sentiments*. Any believer in Hobbes's view of humanity's inescapable selfishness would have found much to criticize in his book, for Smith depicted people as naturally sociable. "How selfish soever man may be supposed," he declared in the first sentence, "there are evidently some principles in his nature, which interest him in the fortune of others, and render their happiness necessary to him, though he derives nothing from it."

This insight into the innate sociability of human nature was the contribution of the Scottish Enlightenment, and gave rise to their distinctive political philosophy. Thinkers like Glasgow University's Francis Hutcheson held that responsible people were guided by the pleasure of social approval and the pain of social condemnation, and so needed no government beyond what would safeguard their property and their right to life and personal liberty. The rule of thumb for deciding political questions was succinctly summed up in Hutcheson's phrase, "That action is best which procures the greatest happiness for the greatest numbers."

Although unmistakably a product of Scotland's culture, the awkward composition of Adam Smith's character—an extreme personal sensitivity that grew from a sense of his physical unattractiveness conflicting with insatiable conviviality and an incurable interest in the way the world worked—ensured that his conclusions were purely his own. For understandable reasons, self-consciousness of a marked, almost adolescent kind played a significant role in his picture of human nature. In Smith's view, the sociability of human nature sprang not just from an innate sympathy for other people's feelings, but also from a selfish desire to gain an objective view of "our own sentiments and motives." The only way to do this was "by endeavouring to view them with the eyes of other people, or as other people are likely to view them."

With the sweep of imagination that gave lasting value to his ideas, Smith lifted this oscillation between altruism and selfishness into a universal context, quoting with approval the Stoics' belief that "the vices and follies of mankind were as necessary [to the overall happiness of the world] . . . as their wisdom and virtues." From this he derived the argument that people could not help contributing to the greater good even at their most selfish, because they "are led by an invisible hand . . . and thus without intending it, without knowing it, advance the interest of the society." What Smith emphasized in *The Theory of Moral Sentiments* was that the "invisible hand" grew out of an awareness of other people's opinions, and the desire for general happiness. It could not operate in a moral vacuum. "Justice is the main pillar that upholds the whole edifice," he insisted. "If it is removed, the great, the immense fabric of human society . . . must in a moment crumble into atoms."

Even before his visit to Paris, Smith had begun to apply the ideas in the *Theory* to the study of what he called "political economy." But one vital element was added during his time in the French capital. From his encounters with Dr. François Quesnay, founder of the fashionable school of economists known as the *physiocrates*, he became aware that, as he put it, "The different progress of opulence has . . . given occasion to two different systems of political economy with regard to enriching the people." In other words, two distinct kinds of capitalism had come into existence.

The younger, passionately supported by the *physiocrates*, was based on agriculture, and was directly opposed to the older, mercantile capitalism, that had developed around the exchange of goods. It was the controlled structure of mercantile capitalism that the *physiocrates* opposed. In its place they championed a form of agricultural enterprise where prices were fixed by supply and demand with no distortion from monopolies, dues, subsidies, and tariffs. Such a form did not exist in France, but they had found the model for it in a book published in 1732, *Essai sur la nature du commerce en général*, by the Irish-born, Paris-based economist Richard Cantillon. Its first two sentences were lifted straight from William Petty: "Land is the source or material from whence all wealth is produced. Human labour is the form which produces it." In other words, the *physiocrates'* economic model was based on conditions in seventeenth-century England.

Whereas Petty's observations were scattered piecemeal through a variety of pamphlets written for different purposes, Cantillon set out to analyze in a single, closely argued volume how wealth was created. Taking the operation of a food market as one paradigm example, his *Essai* followed the flow of silver, the basic currency of the day, into and out of the market; from the housewife to the farmer as payment for butter; from the farmer who pastured the cattle to the landlord as rent; from the landlord who owned the land to servants and workmen as wages; and from each of those back to the market where food was sold. What makes Cantillon's work exceptional is his sophisticated analysis of the way money circulates in these different forms of wages, rents, and profits, and the influence that inflation, consumer confidence, availability of credit, and the level of interest rates exert on the operation of a market. Cantillon explained that these factors applied to both mercantile and private property economies. In his conclusion, however, the difference between the two became clear.

Compared to the general increase in prosperity that might be expected from agricultural capitalism, the *Essai* explained that mercantile capitalism served to enrich the powerful few who supervised a country's financial institutions. Within cities they controlled wages and the supply of labor through craftsmen's guilds, and nationally they limited the scope of competition through the imposition of duties and the creation of monopolies. Strangled by the restrictive practices of the guilds that monopolized the building and textile trades, once thriving cities like Leiden, Rouen, and Cologne actually lost population in the eighteenth century as prices rose and output declined. Even in the Prussian capital of Berlin, where government and a well-financed military training center guaranteed employment, the power of the guilds condemned one third of the population to unemployment or at best casual labor.

The *physiocrates* never quite grasped the monetarist aspects of Cantillon's masterpiece. What they held on to, however, was the preeminent importance of agriculture—"*La terre est l'unique source des richesses,*" their founder, Dr. François Quesnay, flatly asserted—and the consequent need to reward the efficient farmer. Their solution was to sweep away the plethora of feudal restrictions that still existed in France—about where corn could be milled, flour sold, animals marketed—then replace the myriad of charges and fees on the transport of produce with a single tax on the profits of landowners. Once markets operated freely, the economy would regulate itself. The application of laissez-faire economics, the first use of the term, would also remove any need for government intervention in the economy, as Quesnay frequently declared, not least in a conversation with Louis XV's heir. Hearing the young prince complain of the burden of responsibility he would carry as king, the doctor replied dismissively, "I do not see that it is so troublesome." Irritated, the prince demanded, "Then what would you do if you were king?" Quesnay's reply was the classic *physiocrate* description of government's role: "Nothing."

ADAM SMITH OWED THE THEORY of laissez-faire economics to the *physiocrates*, and he owed some at least of his understanding about the behavior of money to Cantillon. But *The Wealth of Nations* was more than the sum of its parts. It extended the market-driven motivations of capitalist agriculture to industry and trade, and yoked them to the financial systems of mercantile capitalism. And it based its analysis of the wealth-producing capacity of free-market economics on the pragmatic reality that human nature is encouraged by the prospect of profit and discouraged by the experience of injustice.

The Wealth of Nations was not published until 1776, seventeen years after *The Theory of Moral Sentiments*, but the sociability of the *Theory* provided its essential springboard, just as Hobbes's delineation of insatiable greed was the necessary starting point of *Leviathan*. From its first publication, Smith's startling insights, not least about the way that selfishness acted for the public good—"It is not from the benevolence of the butcher, the brewer, or the baker, that we expect our dinner, but from their regard to their own interest"—guaranteed the success of *The Wealth of Nations.* The first edition sold out in six months, another four followed in his lifetime, and it has served as the bible of free-market capitalism ever since.

Its unique quality lies in its depiction of the market-led economy as an unstable machine constantly adjusting itself in the effort to achieve an impossible equilibrium. A shortage of supply, for example, should result in higher prices that encourage greater produce and reduce demand; exchange rates ought to adjust to equalize the value of two different currencies; and cheaper production through division of labor will create increased market share until canceled out by rising wages and costs of distribution. This was the "invisible hand" at work, which led to growing prosperity so long as individuals were left free to pursue their own interests with the chance to maximize their gains and minimize their losses. There was, however, the same caveat as in the *Theory*, that the self-righting capacity of the hand only operated in the context of a concern for the general welfare.

Without it, the market needed supervision, otherwise the more powerful participants would choke the weaker by rigging its operation in their favor. The most important role of a free-market government was, therefore, to provide "that equal and impartial administration of justice which renders the rights of the meanest subject respectable to the greatest, and which, by securing to every man the fruits of his own industry, gives the greatest and most effectual encouragement to every sort of industry."

NEVERTHELESS, this extraordinary analysis of free-market capitalism grew out of what seems today like a glaring anomaly at the heart of his work. The precepts of *The Wealth of Nations* are usually cited in relation to the operation of financial markets and of industrial production, but its core is William Petty's rural capitalism, as theorized by Cantillon and adapted by the *physiocrates*. It appears in Smith's repeated assertion that "land and labour" represent a nation's "real wealth." Unlike his French tutors, Smith did not believe the earnings of industry and commerce to be "altogether barren and unproductive," but the need for food put agriculture at the center of the economic engine. The title of his final chapter in Book One makes the point bluntly: "the Produce of Land [is] either the sole or the principal Source of the Revenue and Wealth of every Country."

Such an assumption might just have been acceptable in Petty's seventeenth-century England, but in broad terms it made no sense applied to a Britain already in the early stages of the Industrial Revolution and enjoying a booming trade with colonies in the West Indies and North America. How could such a basic error have occurred? It might be argued that in the context of the time, it did not distort Smith's argument. Land remained the most widely held form of equity, the dominant supplier of working energy in the form of water, and the most important single source of income. But Smith meant what he said. The wealth of nations came from free-market capitalism, and in 1776 the only free-market to be found was in the produce of the land.

Nowhere in Marxist writing are there fiercer attacks on the monopolistic tendency of mercantile capitalism than in *The Wealth of Nations.* For Smith, free-markets could only ever be at bitter war with its older sibling. "But the mean rapacity, the monopolizing spirit of merchants and manufacturers, who neither are, nor ought to be the rulers of mankind," he wrote, "though it cannot perhaps be corrected, may very easily be prevented from disturbing the tranquillity of any body but themselves." And the way to prevent it was to ensure that government set the conditions for free-markets to operate, and prevent the evil genius of mercantilism sliding toward monopoly.

Chapter Five

The Morality of Property

The gigantic landmass that barred the Europeans' westward route to the South Seas forced them to deal with the unexpected challenge of organizing its possession. For obvious reasons, all of the newcomers attempted to impose a system based on the one they knew at home. But the sheer expanse of territory and the exuberance of wealth that fell into their hands defeated their best intentions. Each of the European powers who colonized the New World, from the Spaniards in Mexico and the Portuguese in Brazil down to the Swedes in Delaware and the Danes in the Caribbean, suffered the same fate. As though it were a giant distorting mirror, the Americas reflected an image of European land ownership, but one pulled out of proportion and sprouting strange protuberances unknown in the Old World.

Its extravagant fertility can be sensed in the language used by the English when they arrived: "the millionous multitudes" of seabirds, the "huge flights of wild Turkies," "such infinite Herds of Deare," "innumerable of Pines, tall and good for boards or masts," and forests of oaks with "great Bodies tall and streight from 60 to 80 foot, before there be any Boughs in height," all of it fed by soil that was "like to manure" so that "we cannot sett downe a foot, but tread on Strawberries, raspires, fallen mulberrie vines, acchorns, walnutts, saxafras etc."

But soon after that first rapture came a sharp consideration of the profit it represented. "The mildnesse of the aire, the fertilitie of the soile, and the situation of the rivers," Captain John Smith wrote of Virginia in 1624, "are so propitious to the nature and use of man as no place is more convenient for pleasure, profit, and mans sustenance." Ten years later, the

Jesuit priest Andrew White felt a similar stab of greedy delight in the richness of Maryland's untouched country: "the place abounds," he wrote, "not alone with profit, but also with pleasure." And in 1654, Francis Yeardley, exploring south into Carolina, found "a most fertile, gallant, rich soil, flourishing in all the abundance of nature, especially in the rich mulberry and vine, a serene air, and temperate clime." Admiration immediately prompted him to buy the entire territory for £200 from the native inhabitants, "and so the Indians totally left the lands and rivers to us, retiring to a new habitation."

In New Spain, Hernán Cortes had felt the same gluttonous shiver as he contemplated the city of Tenochtitlán in 1521, capital of Moctezuma's Aztec Empire, containing wealth and art beyond imagination, criss-crossed by canals and avenues and studded with public squares and thriving markets. "There is one square," he wrote to his king, Charles V, "twice as large as that of the city of Salamanca, surrounded by porticoes, where are daily assembled more than sixty thousand souls, engaged in buying and selling; and where are found all kinds of merchandise that the world affords, embracing the necessaries of life, as for instance articles of food, as well as jewels of gold and silver, lead, brass, copper, tin, precious stones, bones, shells, snails, and feathers . . . what can be more wonderful than that a barbarous monarch, as [Moctezuma] is, should have every object found in his dominions imitated in gold, silver, precious stones, and feathers; the gold and silver being wrought so naturally as not to be surpassed by any smith in the world."

In Canada, Samuel de Champlain, exploring the land on behalf of his patron, Pierre de Mons, noted acquisitively that islands in the lake now named for him contained "very fine woods and meadows, with abundance of fowl and such animals of the chase as stags, fallow-deer, fawns, roe-bucks, bears, and others, which go from the main land to these islands. We captured a large number of these animals. There are also many beavers, not only in this river, but also in numerous other little ones that flow into it." The fact that Champlain's sponsor expected to make his profits from fur rather than land or gold explained the difference in emphasis. Already, Champlain assured him in 1608, he had set up a trading system by which the native inhabitants close to Quebec contacted others living deep in the interior and exchanged "the merchandise we give them for their furs, such as beaver, marten, lynx, and otter, which are found there in large numbers, and which they then carry to our vessels."

Each of these accounts was written at least partly as a prospectus, emphasizing the riches in order to encourage backers to commit more resources to their exploitation. Cortes concentrated on the gold, primarily to distract royal attention from his mutinous conduct in attacking the Aztecs, but also because he could not own any of the territory. When his small army captured Tenochtitlan that year, it took possession of Moctezuma's empire, following a pattern that had been developed by the Spanish crown during the long campaign to recapture Spain from the Muslims. Ownership of the retaken ground belonged to the crown, but the adventurer who drove out the Muslims from a particular area was entrusted—*encomendado*—with the use of the inhabitants to farm it and extract its minerals. The young gentlemen *hidalgos* who followed Cortes to seek their fortune in New Spain did so knowing that, in strict legal terms, all they could own was the produce of the earth and the labor of the Indians—a reality encapsulated in the aphorism they coined, *sin indios non hay Indias* ("without Indians, there's no Indies"), meaning that without their ownership of the people, the rich land was worthless.

France's empire offered its settlers, the *habitants*, even less scope for ownership. Pierre de Mons had been granted a monopoly in the fur trade, and French colonists living close to the fortified trading post Champlain founded at Quebec were expected merely "to dwell there, and to trade with the savage inhabitants of the said places." Quite simply, it was impossible for the French *habitants* of Canada, as it was the Spanish *conquistadores* or the ordinary Dutch settlers who arrived at the same time in the Hudson valley, to own the land in the way that the English did. The culture did not exist for such an eventuality. But even the English found it difficult to adapt their ideas of property to the vast land before them.

IN THE GIANT AMERICAN MIRROR, one aspect of English land ownership, almost obscured in the original, stood out sharply. It sprang into prominence as a result of a bad-tempered spat that erupted in 1674 between the Lords Proprietors of Carolina and the villainous figure of Sir John Yeamans, widely suspected of poisoning his best friend in order to marry his widow, and largely responsible for introducing slavery to Barbados by importing hundreds of captured Africans to work on his sugar plantations on the island. Despite his sinister background, the wealthy Yeamans carried influence among his fellow planters in the West Indies, and the Lords Proprietors had gone to great lengths to persuade him to settle in their new colony.

They had secured him his title (he had been plain Mr. Yeamans until

1665) and in 1669 drawn up a constitution—the Fundamental Constitution of Carolina—that was shaped to appeal to him in particular and in general to "the adventurers of the Island of Barbadoes" and other British colonies in the West Indies. The West Indian sugar planters stood at the pinnacle of a highly stratified society built on slave and indentured labor with clearly defined grades of social class dividing rich from poor. The Fundamental Constitution envisioned Carolina becoming an equally hierarchical society where slavery was legal and rank and power were based solely on land ownership. In each county, 40 percent of the territory was to be set aside for the Lords Proprietors and an instant nobility of landgraves and caciques. The remainder was available for sale at three pounds per acre; the owner of twelve thousand acres became a baron with powers over local government; three thousand acres made the purchaser a manor lord with powers of administering justice; and a mere fifty acres qualified the owner to vote.

As a real estate advertisement, the constitution did its work. From the 1670s to the 1690s more than half of Carolina's colonists came from Barbados, and many more, "a hodge-podge" by contemporary accounts, arrived from other West Indian islands, Jamaica, Saint Kitts, and Montserrat. Prominent among them was Sir John Yeamans, who arrived in 1673 and was appointed governor the following year.

Carolina was not exceptional in offering such inducements to would-be immigrants. Soon after they had received their royal charters, the proprietors of New Jersey and Pennsylvania had both issued a list of concessions "to the Adventurers and all such as shall settle there." The concessions were in effect advertisements designed to attract new settlers. Two items appeared on each list, clear ownership of land and political representation.

One of the most important promises made was the assurance that the land would be surveyed and registered and, as the Carolina Lords Proprietors put it, "to avoid deceits and lawsuits [the register] shall record and enter all graunts of land from the Lords to the planters; and all conveyances of Land, Howse or Howses from man to man." The Calvert family, owners of the old established province of Maryland, followed suit, promising in their 1718 constitution to divide the territory into counties, and appoint no fewer than nine public surveyors for each county, as well as an efficient form of land registration. Finally, because as Petty had explained, land needed labor to release its value, the concessions also offered a free headright grant of land, up to 150 acres, either to heads of families, or to every adult, who paid their own passage to the new colonies.

Such inducements had a powerful effect. By 1751 the population of Britain's North American colonies had risen to more than one million, far outstripping the fifty-two thousand colonists in New France, and more or less equalling the Spanish-descended population that had begun to arrive in New Spain a century before the first English settlers in Virginia.

Both the royal charters and the lords proprietors' concessions also outlined the political consequence that went with property. To ensure that their interests would be safeguarded, once the adventurers had transformed themselves into landowners and thus qualified as "freemen," they would be eligible to vote for a representative in the provincial assembly, or, in the sales pitch made by William Penn, "to chuse out of themselves seventy-two persons of most note for their wisdom, virtue and ability . . . [to] act as the provincial Council."

To their bewilderment, all the proprietors, even the Penn family who offered the most generous concessions, found themselves subjected to a barrage of criticism and occasionally violent attack from the settlers. By the mid-eighteenth century, the crown had been forced to take direct control of all the embattled proprietors' colonies. In every conflict, one vital question was posed: Who in fact owned the American land? The proprietors who had received it by the power of the king's "mere motion" and the "divine grace" that had seated him on the throne, or the settlers who had worked, improved, and defended the soil? Nowhere was the question posed more abrasively than in Carolina, a gigantic province taking in the modern states of North and South Carolina and most of Georgia. And since the experience fed directly into the thinking of the secretary of the Lords Proprietors of Carolina, John Locke, nowhere was there a more interesting answer given.

The relationship of the six Carolina proprietors with the egregious Yeamans was summed up in an angry letter written on their behalf by Locke in 1674 in response to Yeamans's demand for more tools, more cattle, and more plants to help him and his fellow colonists make a living from the land. Angrily, Locke pointed out that the proprietors had already spent "several thousand pounds" in assistance, and instead of thanks from Yeamans, there had been "complaints made and reproaches insinuated." Dismissing his request for more help, Locke wrote "it must be a bad soil that would not maintain industrious people, or the Lords Proprietors must be very silly that would maintain the idle."

But other discontented colonists soon joined Yeamans at his palatial mansion at Goose Creek and added their own complaints. They included settlers annoyed by the dues they were forced to pay on their land, such as the annual quit-rent to the proprietors; devout Anglicans irritated by the policy of religious tolerance that gave equal rights to Jews and Quakers; fur traders infuriated by the proprietors' insistence that they alone had the right to buy pelts from Native Americans; and slave owners chafing against the proprietors' refusal to allow raids on the Spaniards who harbored runaway slaves in Florida.

There was a pattern to this apparently incoherent range of discontents. And despite the tone of his letter, Locke showed that he understood its cause when he came to write the work for which he is now best known, *Two Treatises on Government*. From the start, it betrays his long experience, from 1669 to 1675, of dealing with the correspondence and negotiations with the recalcitrant settlers of Carolina. Thus in imagining the earliest state of nature before there was government, the picture he painted was not of Hobbes's brutish savagery, but of limitless possibility where people lived in perfect freedom surrounded by empty land. "In the beginning," he wrote simply, "all the world was America." It was from this unconstrained state, he argued, that private property spontaneously, naturally, and inevitably occurred. For more than three centuries, his thesis has shaped democratic thought in private property societies. Yet, even today, the explosive quality of his argument is only half-understood.

As a student, Locke was known as "a man of turbulent spirit, clamorous and never contented," but as he grew older, any public display of this rebellious passion was hidden by an austere demeanor and a narrow, unrevealing, hatchet-nosed face, as sharp as a ship's prow. "I believe there is not in the world such a master of taciturnity and passion," one of his Oxford colleagues declared, and Locke himself alluded to the effort it cost, declaring that the guiding principle "of all Vertue and Excellency lies in a power of denying our selves the satisfaction of our own Desires, where Reason does not authorize them."

His well-camouflaged radicalism makes the revolutionary nature of his argument—that people, not laws, created property—less surprising. Indeed, the timing of the first *Treatise*'s composition in 1681, when Locke's employer, Lord Shaftesbury, was suspected of planning a coup to overthrow the increasingly dictatorial and Catholic rule of King Charles II, suggests that its real purpose might have been aimed at justifying popular sovereignty. In outline, Locke was harking back to Winthrop's old Puritan thesis that labor itself created privately owned property independently of the common law. Unlike the Puritans, however, Locke turned not to biblical precedent but to Overton's subversive Leveller idea that everyone naturally owned his or her own person, with its rights to life and liberty.

Like the politics of Hobbes and Smith, Locke's *Treatises* make most sense in relation to his ideas about human nature. In his own lifetime, Locke was better known for his four-volume *Essay Concerning Human Understanding*, which depicted the personality as an individualized organism, born a separate blank receptacle for experience, but growing in such complexity and richness of thought from youth to age as to be barely recognizable as the same person. What connected the child with the adult, Locke concluded, was the sense of identity that came from consciousness, particularly the consciousness of being a separate self. "Consciousness always accompanies thinking, and 'tis that that makes everyone to be, what he calls self; and thereby distinguishes himself from other thinking beings . . . it is by the consciousness it has of its previous Thoughts and Actions, that it is self to its self now; and so will be the same self as far as the same consciousness can extend to actions past or to come."

This extraordinarily modern focus on personal self-awareness only made sense to a readership familiar with Hobbes's greedy individualism, and the unique social importance attached to privately owned property. Even in the advanced society of the Netherlands, it would have been impossible for Locke's contemporary, Baruch Spinoza, perhaps the supreme philosopher of the seventeenth century, to write baldly as Locke did in the *Essay*, "Self depends on consciousness." People in Spinoza's philosophy were not alienated, autonomous psyches, but part of the natural world and subject to its universal, rational laws.

Consequently, when Locke wrote about the origins of popular sovereignty, his explanation centered on individual action. In the bounteous, unlimited America that existed before government, the land and everything that it produced was held in common ownership. By working a parcel of the earth and improving it, however, a person separated it from what had been shared and thereby acquired exclusive ownership. "Though the earth, and all inferior creatures, be common to all men, yet every man has a property in his own person; this no body has any right to but himself. The labour of his body, and the work of his hands, we may say, are properly his. Whatsoever then he removes out of the state that nature hath provided, and left it in, he hath mixed his labour with, and joined to it something that is his own, and thereby makes it his property."

Although often overlooked, it was essential to Locke's reasoning that such self-ownership had a divine origin. The act of creation made each person God's property, and the same creative process enabled people to own the earth they had cultivated, in the way that a craftsman owned what he had created. But wealthy individuals could also purchase the property-making powers of others, much as they would when commissioning a craftsman to make an object for them: "the Turfs my Servant has cut; and the Ore I have digg'd in any place where I have a right to them in common with others, become my Property."

The inequality that resulted made it more difficult to secure property, and so people were forced to accept that it was better to give up some of their unconstrained freedom in order to protect what they owned: "The great and *chief end* therefore, of Mens uniting into Commonwealths, and putting themselves under Government, *is the Preservation of their Property*." This is the classic formulation of the argument that sovereignty in a democratic state lies ultimately with the people. In a state of freedom, autonomous individuals agree with one another to give up some of their natural liberty in order to preserve what they already own.

It is not difficult to discern the influence of Locke's American experience in his depiction of the contractual nature of government. However hostile he might have been as secretary to the Lords Proprietors of Carolina, by the time he came to write the *Treatises*, it was evident that Locke understood the conflict with the settlers to have arisen from their different understanding of what constituted ownership.

The settlers' natural rights of ownership came from their daily labor in clearing the ground of its giant trees, of planting rice and herding cattle, and of dealing with the emergency demands of floods, hurricanes, and wars against Native Americans and Spanish marauders. Underlying their complaints was the basic assumption of a contract between two equal parties: if the settlers were to be governed by the Lords Proprietors, they must receive protection for their property. Sustained by their legal rights, the proprietors saw the matter differently: the settlers were tenants who should be expected to make their living from the land, and to pay the proprietors for its use. This attitude soon turned even the proprietors' handpicked supporters against them, prompting the accusation that, "like a Landlord to his Tenant, they [the proprietors] have their Eyes [only] upon the Rent." A sullen stand-off developed that continued long after the death of Yeamans in 1674 and Locke's departure from his post the following year. The dispute was not resolved until the next generation of settlers took more assertive action in the eighteenth century.

When the *Treatises* first came to prominence more than fifty years after they were published, British commentators shifted Locke's emphasis away from the contractual nature of government toward the sacredness of property. In his *Commentaries on the Laws of England*, published in 1765, William Blackstone cited Locke in support of his theory that individually owned property constituted one of three natural rights "which every man is entitled to enjoy, whether out of society or in it . . . the right of personal security, the right of personal liberty, and the right of personal property." Although the mixing-labor theory could justify the creation of any kind of ownership—where wives and children were expected to work alongside fathers in the fields, for example, it would logically support a concept of family possession—Blackstone insisted that it created only a monopolized ownership. In short, natural rights and the common law were at one in privileging "the sole and despotic dominion" of the land, as Blackstone put it, of one man. And it was a right that no government could challenge: "So great moreover is the regard of the law for private property, that it will not authorize the least violation of it; no, not even for the general good of the whole community."

It followed that without the assent of the property owner, any form of taxation was oppressive and should be resisted as an attack not just on his possessions, but his standing as a free person. "If taxes are laid upon us in any shape, without our having a legal representation where they are laid," Samuel Adams demanded in 1764, "are we not reduced from the character of free subjects to the miserable state of tributary slaves?" Locke's contractual theory of government thus became the intellectual fulcrum for American resistance to British taxation, and his forecast that free people were justified in rebellion if subjected to "a long train of abuses, prevarications and artifices all tending the same way" made its way almost unaltered into the Declaration of Independence.

In 1973, the economist Robert Nozick developed this argument to build the dazzling libertarian vision of a minimal government whose sole purpose was to protect property and, stripped of power, to raise taxes or take action beyond what was necessary to achieve that goal. Echoing Blackstone, he argued that property "to which . . . people are entitled may not be seized, even to provide equality of opportunity for others." The idea that any increase of government diminished individual liberty by threatening the primacy of property rights acquired such popular appeal by the end of the twentieth century that it became a sort of orthodoxy. Yet in that form, the argument lost sight both of Locke's thesis and the moral force that gave it such power.

THE ARGUMENT for popular sovereignty that is actually put forward in the *Treatises* is grounded in an infinitely grander vision than title to a parcel of land. Quite explicitly Locke sets out to show that democracy grows out of a sense of fairness common to all individuals. This is "the law of nature" that exists when people live in a state of total freedom. Reason reveals to each of them that "no one ought to harm another in his Life, Health, Liberty of Possessions." As self-conscious individuals, people cannot help making things that belong to them, but these things, land included, can only become exclusive property "where there is enough, and as good left in common for others."

By this reasoning, the long list of dispossessed—women, villeins, Irish, and Native Americans among them—might seem to render the selfish monster of private property illegitimate from the start. But Locke was concerned with every claim to possession, theirs included. What he described was a dynamic process rather than a static situation.

From the first chapter of the first *Treatise*, he is clear that the right to own exclusively what you have made comes out of a sense of justice, because justice demands that the craftsman and laborer has a right to own what he or she has created. But justice cuts both ways, and automatically gives rise to other rights: "As Justice gives every Man a Title to the product of his honest Industry, and the fair Acquisitions of his Ancestors descended to him; so Charity gives every Man a Title to so much of another's Plenty, as will keep him from extream want, where he has no means to subsist otherwise."

That justice rather than labor-mixing should be the real basis of Locke's argument for a natural right to private property is what makes him revolutionary. The difference is crucial. By its nature fairness is all-inclusive and applicable equally to everyone. Otherwise it becomes its opposite. The moral authority that fairness gives to private property is what allows the institution to exist independently of law and government. To lose sight of that universal morality must lead to property having another, man-made basis, one that logically could be destroyed by man.

But repeatedly, and in the starkest terms, Locke set out the consequences of fairness. "[N]o man could ever have a just power over the life of another, by right of property in land or possessions, since it would always be a sin in any man of estate to let his brother perish for want of affording him relief out of his plenty . . . God the lord and father of all has given no one of his children such a property in his peculiar portion of the things of this world but that he has given his needy brother a right to the surplusage of his goods."

To the next generation, living in a world populated by nine billion humans, the awkward implications of Locke's premise will be an everyday reality. It is increasingly common already to defend the existence of private property and its inevitable inequalities on the utilitarian grounds of its incentive to greater productivity. But productivity is a shallow foundation for such a great edifice.

The democracy that Locke discerned in the 1680s was grounded in the moral principle that underpinned both property and popular government. And the dynamic forces it incorporated would ultimately enable the dispossessed to regain the rights they had lost.

NEVERTHELESS, by the early years of the eighteenth century, Locke's criterion that private property could only be justified "where there is enough, and as good left in common for others" appeared close to impracticable even in the vast expanses of America. That was made obvious by the stiffening resistance of Native Americans to the land hunger of the new immigrants, and in Carolina, a bloody war would shortly consign the native Yamassee to the long line of the despoiled. Yet despite the carnage inflicted by individual ownership of land, it was apparent that the system also contained a mechanism of restitution.

From its birth in sixteenth-century England, the acquirers of private landed property found it necessary to take account of those they had dispossessed. A series of measures beginning in 1536 and culminating in the 1601 Poor Law Act imposed local taxes on "every occupier of lands" to provide welfare relief for the "lame, impotent, poor, old, blind and such other among them being poor and not able to work" who had been deprived of support following the abolition of the manors and the monasteries. The poor law tax was imposed by the representatives of the landed gentry and, until the early 1800s, the cost of this system of welfare—it gradually rose from 1 to 2 percent of GDP compared to almost 5 percent levied in advanced economies today—was borne solely by landowners.

The debates that accompanied a torrent of legislation averaging almost two bills a decade during this period revealed that their motives swung constantly between self-interest—to preserve social order—and genuine social concern. But the roots of these conflicting motives ran deeper than mere politics.

In 2003, Sarah Brosnan, a young psychology professor at Emory University, conducted an experiment with five capuchin monkeys who were paired up and trained to return a token in order to receive a reward of cucumber slices. When the exchange was then skewed so that one of the pair was offered a more desirable reward in the form of grapes, the other would frequently refuse to participate, often throwing away either the token or the cucumber. Such irrational behavior—effectively denying oneself nourishment—clearly had some deep-rooted cause. Brosnan and her colleague, primatologist Fran de Waal, concluded that it pointed toward "an early evolutionary origin of inequity aversion." The finding sparked a furious debate that revolved around the possible effect of what was quickly dubbed a "fairness gene."

Much of the argument about Brosnan and de Waal's findings as well as the results of other experiments arose from the difficulty of defining what a sense of fairness, or "inequity aversion," entailed: did it mean expecting to share a reward equally, or simply hoping to receive a small part of the reward given to another, or even forgoing all reward so that another, more deserving (in primate terms, higher-ranking) participant could benefit? Yet unmistakably, the subjects' behavior changed in reaction to a perceived disparity of reward; as one otherwise skeptical researcher put it, "seeing another individual receive high-quality food creates the expectation to receive the same food."

Human experiments involving games such as Prisoner's Dilemma (two prisoners each with the choice of staying silent or betraying the other) and the Ultimatum Game (sharing out of money so that each of two players is satisfied) gave rise to equally irrational behavior. Alongside the understandable selfishness of homo economicus who could be expected to maximize his own gain ran an equally deep-seated sense of injustice, so strong it could operate against the best interests of the individual. Thus in the Ultimatum Game, where one person was given one hundred dollars with the proviso that the money had to be shared with a second person or it would be lost, the second person, who theoretically should have been happy to receive any share because it represented pure gain, was almost always ready to refuse a sum less than what he or she considered a fair share (usually somewhere between twenty and fifty dollars), even though it deprived both participants of any gain.

As in primate experiments, the conclusions were blurred by semantics—did apparently altruistic behavior really conceal a deeper selfishness?—but what could not be overlooked was the visceral response to perceived unfairness. Indeed, medical research suggested that the response began with the release of a hormone, cortisol, associated with tension; its opposite, oxytocin, generated most powerfully in recovery after childbirth, was similarly associated with the generous impulses of sharing. Although the action of a single hormone is invariably mediated through other endocrinal responses, making it impossible to ascribe behavior directly to its effects, the release of cortisol in these situations underlined the profound nature of the response to injustice. Taken in conjunction with the equally automatic release of oxytocin, these findings demonstrated how intrinsic to human nature are the contrary impulses of selfishness and fairness.

In a sense, all social history reveals the interplay of these two drives. What was particularly intriguing about their role in the private property societies taking shape on either side of the Atlantic was not so much the primacy accorded to selfish behavior as the factors that gave an almost equal weight to the impulse toward fairness. Significantly, both Locke and Adam Smith held the latter quality to be vital both to property and to free-market economics.

In its most efficient form, Smith argued, a free-market economy showed how "the obvious and simple system of natural liberty establishes itself of its own accord. Every man, as long as he does not violate the laws of justice, is left perfectly free to pursue his own interest his own way, and to bring both his industry and capital into competition with those of any other man, or order of men."

His phrase "the laws of justice" pointed to the principle that Locke identified as the basis of property. Freedom exercised at the expense of someone else's liberty became a form of tyranny. It had to be equal and inclusive. Consequently it was fundamental to Smith's description of the free-market system that everyone, rich and poor, should have an equal opportunity to profit from their labor. Because there was no mechanism more effective in regulating wages and prices than the "invisible hand" of the free-market, it was incumbent on government to maintain open and equal access to it. Morality and efficiency coincided.

The same reasoning required the laws of justice to underpin the system of private property. Perhaps surprisingly, the strongest modern advocate of this approach was the libertarian Robert Nozick. Holders of property were "entitled" to claim what amounted to a natural right to ownership, he proposed, when three principles of justice were observed: the property had to have been justly acquired by the original holder and justly transferred to the present owner, and any injustice in these processes had to be made good by a policy of "rectification." Both Nozick's supporters and his critics tended to overlook the degree of government intervention entailed by this last requirement, but his rationale for believing that justice had to provide the foundation of a private property society hardly differed from that of Adam Smith: crudely put, the system would work better, offer more freedom, and require less adjustment if everyone, propertied and unpropertied, believed its rewards and penalties to be distributed fairly. The paradoxical outcome was that the most selfish system of ownership had an altruistic motive for promoting fairness even at the expense of its immediate self-interest.

The mechanism by which this took place was provided by the recognition of rights. And the achievement of the dispossessed in using that mechanism to regain or at least compensate for what was taken from them constituted a major part of the history of private property societies.

In March 1656, more than 350 years of institutional intolerance were swept aside in England when twenty-five Jewish families living in disguise in London were formally given permission to live and worship freely. The decision overturned a royal edict issued in 1290 by King Edward I that expelled all Jews from England—the first such action by a European ruler—and declared any who remained in the country to be outlaws whose goods were forfeited to the crown. By the seventeenth century, however, the example of the Netherlands, where Jewish merchants made a vital contribution to the growth of the country's international trade, had shown that, as William Petty argued, an open society benefited by attracting such enterprising outsiders.

Out of a curious mixture of pragmatic belief in the importance of encouraging trade and millenarian faith that the Jews needed to be converted before Christ could return, England's enigmatic Lord Protector, Oliver Cromwell, wanted to have the royal ban abolished and Jews permitted to live freely in England. Privately he gave the London Jews permission to stay in the country, and he had the 1290 edict of expulsion abolished on the grounds that it did not have parliamentary approval. But even his near-dictatorial power could not persuade either Parliament or a special conference of leading clergy and lawyers to overcome their unshakable prejudice and allow the Jews a public right to residence and freedom of worship. To the Puritans, they were "as full of blasphemy as any under the sun," while the anti-Semitic feeling among London merchants surfaced in a letter written by one to a friend in Amsterdam in which he commented, "touching Judaism, some corners of our city smell as rank of it as doth yours there."

Yet where Cromwell was powerless, the law of property provided the necessary lever. The London Jews had passed themselves off as Spanish merchants, a disguise that fell apart when war against Spain was declared in 1655. Taking advantage of the outbreak of hostilities, a rival had the goods of the counterfeit Spaniards confiscated as enemy spoil. But one victim, Antonio Robles, publicly declared, "I am a Portuguese Jew," and as a legal resident petitioned the Council of State to have his property restored. Ignoring his status as a Jew, the Council declared that since he was a property owner, he enjoyed the full protection of the law, and that his goods must be immediately returned. By itself that decision was sufficient to overturn almost four centuries of legal discrimination, and with Cromwell's written permission to worship freely and bury their dead in a separate burial ground, England became a more or less safe haven for Jews from all over Europe. Prejudice remained, but the common law's protection of property rights also ensured their legal protection.

Other legal outcasts—unpropertied males, women, and displaced indigenous races—would follow a similar if more prolonged and complex course in securing legal and political rights equivalent to those of a white, Protestant, propertied male. The process could only begin once the group had the legal capacity to own property, a privilege specifically denied to slaves and married women until the nineteenth century. But time and again, where ownership of land was secured, the disadvantaged group was able to lever property into civil rights.

One early example led to the resolution of the stand-off between Carolina's proprietors and settlers. In the wake of a drawn-out war with the native Yamassee inhabitants that by 1717 had devastated half the province and left debts of £235,000, the settlers' anger exploded at the failure of the Lords Proprietors to protect them from their enemies. Although still treated as tenants subject to the owner's dictates, their representatives in the provincial assembly now declared that they were "unanimously of Opinion they would have no Proprietors' Government." On December 21, 1719, they mustered the militia, armed with muskets, in the main square in Charleston, and forcibly replaced the Lords Proprietors' governor with their own man, James Moore Jr., who had previously led them in wars against the Indians and Spaniards. The success of the coup went beyond the physical seizure of power. Even London recognized that the settlers' right to have their property protected had been ignored by the proprietors, invalidating the latter's legal claim to govern them. Their charter was revoked in 1729, putting the colony under direct royal control, a change that embodied the settlers' status as colonists rather than tenants. Barely fifty years later, those colonists would again assert their rights as property owners, this time against the exercise of royal power, and eventually establish an understanding of liberty beyond any that property alone had made possible.

Despite itself, the privileged, selfish system of private property proved to have a mechanism for openness and equality built into it. Antonio Robles had demonstrated that the laws that created a monopoly of rights in a male property owner had to apply to everyone who enjoyed that status. And the prize for those able to use the mechanism was the enjoyment of a legally protected liberty that was independent of government because it originated in human existence.

Section Two

THE ALTERNATIVES TO PRIVATE PROPERTY

Chapter Six

What Came Before

Seen from the high-definition cameras in the satellites used by Google Earth, the mountains of Sarawak that sprawl across the northern third of the island of Borneo make a lumpy, chaotic jumble. It is easy to understand why the indigenous inhabitants used to believe the land was formed when its creator idly crumpled it up like paper and dropped it into the ocean. What the cameras cannot show is that the gigantic range was until the 1980s still shrouded by dense tropical forest almost down to the coastal plain. When I went there in 1982, the trees covered more than 70 percent of Sarawak, providing a habitat for orangutans and proboscis monkeys, and a home for more than 150,000 native inhabitants, among them as many as 100,000 Iban.

The Iban were admired for their enterprise and good looks, and notorious for having been headhunters. The shock of waking up in the dark light of predawn on my first morning in an Iban longhouse deep in the jungle remains vivid: hanging a few feet above me were what looked first like three globes, then hollow soccer balls, a few blinks more and they became ivory carvings, then finally unmistakably three human skulls.

Although the practice was supposed to have ended early in the twentieth century, Japanese soldiers became a target in the Second World War, and in the 1960s, when Communist insurgents from Indonesia crossed the border, Iban scouts working with British Special Forces repeatedly took the heads of enemies they killed. Their motive was simple: a severed head possessed incredible sex appeal. It gave any headhunter such potent celebrity, every woman desired him—in 1945 a Sarawak newspaper commented disapprovingly on the way "the girls change into little furies of excitement when a fresh [Japanese] head is brought in"—and even more importantly the earth itself responded by producing richer crops.

Iban legends explained why fertility was associated with a severed head. Epic songs chanted by professional bards—I heard one that lasted for three days and two nights—described in mythic terms how the Iban and their gods invaded Sarawak, coming down its main rivers in the early nineteenth century. By killing the existing inhabitants, the Kayan and Kenyah, the Iban were able to acquire more land, grow more rice, and breed more children. Thus decapitation, harvests, and pregnancy became synonyms for each other, and a verse that apparently told of successful head-taking—

Behold brains ooze out along with layers of fat,
Behold lumps of flesh are strewn on the mat,
Behold hair from human heads is scattered everywhere—

could also serve as a metaphor for a bumper crop of rice.

Apart from the gory details, Iban epic verse, and indeed the ordinary tales told by storytellers to fill the dark hours before sleep, were notable for one particular feature they shared with legends from other preliterate societies. Whether describing journeys, as in Homer's *Odyssey*, or the sort of territorial conflicts that ran through the fabulous twelfth-century Irish epic, the *Taín Bó Cuaílnge*, or the coming of social order like the Ojibwe myths about Hiawatha collected by Henry Schoolcraft in the nineteenth century, these originally oral compositions always weave the naming of specific places into the unfolding tale. Today the stories attract the most interest, rather than the geography they contain. But watching the immediate, lively reaction of Iban listeners to the names of mountains and rivers familiar to them as they heard how gods and heroes of the past traveled through Sarawak, it was plain that place and myth were inextricably entwined.

The best-known contemporary examples of this intense relationship between preliterate people and land naming are the creation songs of Australian Aboriginals. In their public form, they tell how different places, animals, and tribes received their names during the Dreaming at the beginning of time. Each feature of the local landscape is identified with a feat of myth or magic in the songs. The origin of the tribe is described and how its people came to be related to one of the totem creatures, from ants to emus, living in that particular part of the country. The private version for initiates is so minutely related to the landscape that, allegedly, dream songs can guide the singer from northern Australia through the dry interior to its southern coast three thousand miles away. The continent is supposed to be checkered with such songlines.

The association between naming and owning was critical in a famous legal victory won by Eddie Mabo, a Torres Straits Islander, in 1992, against the Australian govenment over ownership of his people's traditional homeland. Part of his evidence consisted of the relation of people and land contained in the Islanders' mythic songs, and the customs that they enjoined upon people living there. In a watershed decision in Australian Aboriginal land rights, the judge accepted this oral tradition as an indication that Mabo's people had a form of property in the lands they had traditionally occupied. The judgment appeared to undermine the common law rights of Australia's stock farmers to almost half their land, and the political backlash led to legislation overturning the ruling. Nevertheless, the principle that these epic legends incorporate a sense of ownership remains intact in other common law jurisdictions. In 2007, the Supreme Court of British Columbia delivered judgment in favor of the land claims of a hunting group in British Columbia largely on the basis of what the judge called "verbal messages from the past beyond the present generation." In so doing, they shed a light on the relationship between preliterate cultures and the ground on which they lived.

UNTIL THE MIDDLE of the seventeenth century, the Irish could look down the green Shannon valley or across to the bare mountains of Connacht and read their features as a record of their past and their imagination. As in Sarawak and Australia, songs and poems of immense length chanted by professional bards told how these names arose. Surveying the fragments that survive in early Irish ballads and legends, the twentieth-century poet Thomas Kinsella was struck by "the continuing preoccupation [with place naming] of early and medieval Irish literature." And he himself provided an electrifying example in his translation of the *Taín Bó Cuaílnge*.

Compiled in the twelfth century from earlier sources, the poem ostensibly tells the story of a cattle raid by Ulster's warrior chief, Cuchulainn, against his neighbors. But its narrative is woven intricately around Ireland's topography. Even the blood-boltered battle between two bulls that provides the climax of the *Táin* merely serves as a device to tell how different towns and rivers were named. "At that, the dun-colored bull [the *Donn Cuailnge*] jerked back his hoof. His leg broke, but the other bull's horn was sent flying to the mountain nearby. It is called Sliab nA-darca, the Mountain of the Horn [in modern County Offaly], ever since. Then the bulls fought each other for a long time. Night fell upon the men of Ireland and they could only hear the uproar and fury in the darkness."

The background to this mythic duel was a rapid growth in population and the emergence of a few dominant clans or septs in the ninth and tenth centuries, whose wealth was counted in cattle. Until then, according to the *Senchus Mor* or Great Book of the Law, the source-book for Brehon lawyers, also compiled in the twelfth century, no boundaries had been necessary: "there was not ditch, nor fence, nor stonewall round land . . . but [only] smooth fields." Thus as the bulls battled across northern Ireland, they not only baptized mountains, rivers, valleys, lakes, and fields with blood and guts, but allowed the bard to claim these features for his audience. When the victorious bull tosses the loser's loins into a river-crossing, the *Taín* declares "that is how the place was named Ath Luain, the Ford of the Loins [modern Athlone] . . . He [the bull] drank again at Tromma where [the loser's] liver fell from his two horns—from which comes the name Tromma, or liver." The gothic violence of these stories made them memorable, and with their help the entire country became a mnemonic that enabled a people to recall who they were and how the land came to be theirs.

The colonists in Massachusetts Bay discovered a similar characteristic among the remnants of the Wampanaog living there. Every place was named, and simply to say the name united the speaker to the place. The trait caught the attention of Edward Winslow, author of the 1624 *Good Newes from New England*, who learned the language of the Wampanaog and became the trusted friend of their *sachem*, or leader, Massasoit. Hills and streams were identified by their association with past events such as a battle or a famous hunt, and so important was this geographical reminder that where something extraordinary had occurred and no physical feature was prominent, the Wampanaog would commemorate the event by digging a round hole nearby so that later it would jog their memory. The holes were maintained and kept free of undergrowth, Winslow explained, because they served as "Records and Chronicles . . . by which means many things of great Antiquity are fresh in memory."

In Virginia, John Lederer recorded a different kind of memory aid that the Chesapeake Bay Indians built into the landscape. "Where a Battel has been fought, or a Colony seated" he wrote in 1672, "they raise a small Pyramid of these stones, consisting of the number slain or transplanted." According to the book of Joshua, the very same kind of reminder was used by the Israelites. Having escaped from Egypt and after forty years' nomadic wandering in the desert, they crossed the Jordan in the first step toward acquiring the land of Canaan for themselves. As they went over the river, each of the twelve tribes took a stone, and "those twelve stones which they took out of Jordan, did Joshua pitch in Gilgal. And he spake unto the children of Israel, saying, When your children shall ask their father in time to come, saying, What mean these stones? Then ye shall let your children know, saying, Israel came over this Jordan on dry land."

The oral origin of these earliest books of the Old Testament is evident in the way the book of Joshua describes how the Israelites smote, slew, and massacred the original occupants of Canaan, such as the Amorites, Hittites, Jebusites, and others. In the repetitious phrasing characteristic of oral epics in particular and folk ballads in general, what must once have been a chant or song describes their fate: "And that day Joshua took Makkedah, and smote it with the edge of the sword, and the king thereof he utterly destroyed, them, and all the souls that were therein; he let none remain." No fewer than thirty-one cities are attacked, each one is named, and each falls to Joshua in the same way: "he smote it with the edge of the sword, and all the souls that were therein; he let none remain."

In reality, as is apparent elsewhere in the text, supposedly slain Canaanites survived in large enough numbers to fight and marry generations of Israelites. Nevertheless, there was a point to this mythic extermination, just as there was to the Iban's headhunting epics: the elimination of the original occupants showed that the victorious newcomers had the right to take possession of the land. And when Joshua divides up the country between the tribes of Israel, the boundaries are denoted in a long list of place names, liberally spattered with gory details to fix them in memory. With the bloodthirsty book of Joshua as his guide, an Israelite bard might have sung himself from the Jordan to the Mediterranean.

In his poem "The Gift Outright," Robert Frost wrote of the way the land of the United States made its colonial settlers American. It did so by possession, both in the sense of being owned by them, but more powerfully by possessing them when they gave their lives for it. Imagining the unexplored West, Frost described it as "still unstoried, artless, unenhanced," adjectives that ignored the intensity of myth, magic, and memory woven round the land by the Iroquois, the Mi'kmaq, or the Ojibwe.

Nevertheless, it remains true that through stories, arts, and improvements the earth does come to inhabit its inhabitants, newcomers and natives alike. For preliterate people, however, undistracted by documents and artificial records, the land *was* the story.

In the 1980s, the traditional Iban living high in the mountains where the rivers of Sarawak have their source still practiced what anthropologists call "slash-and-burn" agriculture, clearing a few acres of forest each year to plant rice, then moving on. But they too had a clear sense of ownership. In the longhouse where I stayed near the head of the Bangkit River, the seventeen different families spent hours animatedly discussing where each intended to clear the trees for next season's rice. Twelve years had passed since they last farmed in that area, and secondary jungle had obliterated their fields, but *adat* or customary law held that those who wanted to use the same land as before had prior rights to do so.

Adat had one goal above all others, the maintenance of social harmony within the contiguous line of dwellings that made up a longhouse. It was made up of tradition, myths, religion, and the results of augury by dreams and such natural events as the flight of a bird or the call of a deer. The Iban were notable for their drive and enterprise, and the purpose of *adat* was not to eliminate personal ambition but to accommodate it.

The clearest example of the way this worked was when Langga, the forceful, powerfully built, thirty-year-old headman of the longhouse, decided to cultivate an untouched section of virgin forest where the trees would be harder to fell, but the soil would be more productive. To establish a claim to new ground, he needed the acceptance of both the longhouse and the jungle itself. Although they did not oppose him, the other families felt he was taking an unnecessary risk for which they feared, and some half-hoped, he might be punished by the spirits of the jungle. Aware of their attitude, Langga made it clear that he did not welcome my alien presence when he went to claim his new farm, but I was determined to witness what was by then a rare event. As it turned out, we were both rewarded.

Once Langga had marked off the land he proposed to clear, setting his family's whetstones at the center and their boundary sticks at the perimeter, he arranged on the bare forest floor separate offerings of rice, eggs, and tobacco to Singalang Burong, the god of the earth who actually possessed it, and to Pulang Gana, the god of the harvest who oversaw its produce. Then under the heavy jungle canopy, he began to call for Singalang Burong's blessing on his endeavors, and as he did so, a finger-thick, diamond-patterned snake detached itself from a branch and slithered toward the food, its blunt head weaving back and forth. Such an exceptional sign could not be ignored. Immediately Langga switched from invoking the god's assistance to speaking on behalf of the god to announce that he had sent a messenger to bless his farm. "You will gain great wealth," said the god, speaking in Langga's voice but with extraordinary fierceness and excitement, "and you will be known through the land." Whatever anxieties he might have had were swept aside by this wave of pride and confidence.

Social harmony was one thing, the desire to be extraordinary was another. And Iban *adat* always recognized both. Precepts designed to promote a harmonious society went into abeyance when someone experienced a favorable omen, had an auspicious dream, or best of all came home with a severed head. The Iban were not alone in their need to reconcile these conflicting priorities. It was central to the rules of land ownership in widely different peasant societies around the world.

FOLLOWING THE PUBLICATION of the first volume of *Capital* in 1867, Karl Marx turned his attention to this very question, the way that land was owned in early societies. He wanted to show that before feudalism was imposed the land was communally owned. Restricted to London by poverty and the discomfort of boils on his bottom, he commissioned his friend, the wealthy industrialist Friederich Engels, known as "dear Fred," to investigate records of Ireland's medieval Brehon laws held in Manchester's public libraries in northwestern England. In November 1869, Fred wrote excitedly to Marx, "The tracts show clearly that, in Anno 1600 common ownership of land still existed in full force."

Engels based this conclusion on the research of Sir John Davies, the English poet and attorney-general who supervised the first mass introduction of private ownership of land to Ireland in the early seventeenth century. In the five previous centuries, since Norman knights first crossed from England to invade Ireland, successive waves of English incomers had been absorbed into Irish society. The children of foreigners like the Fitzgeralds and Butlers grew up speaking Gaelic and grafted their ideas of feudal tenure onto the tribal ownership of land inherent in traditional Brehon law. Thus territory nominally held by a sept or clan such as the O'Neills in Ulster and the O'Connors around Dublin was divided into strips of land that were allocated to families within the sept according to their importance and the service they rendered. Beginning in the 1560s, however, this feudalized sept-owning structure was broken apart by the arrival of a new breed of Protestant, individual-owning English invader. The lands confiscated from the sept chiefs in Munster, Dublin, and Ulster were designated "plantations" and leased out to English and Scottish colonists who held them under English common law. It was this stage in 1603 that Davies described in his report on traditional land holdings in Ireland.

The discovery that Brehon law was apparently concerned with communal ownership inspired Marx to further research, and his "Ethnographic Notes" are filled with crosscultural comparisons with Indian, Scottish, and above all Irish landowning customs. Around the world, he found similar tendencies toward community-controlled use of the land. Through customary law, village councils, or group pressure, these societies felt able to impose rules for use of the land on the families or individuals who worked the soil. Some rules, such as limiting the number of animals that could graze common pastures, were designed to prevent its despoliation, but the most important had another purpose. The strips of arable land where wheat and corn were grown, and the pasture meadows where hay was made, and the areas of woodland where they took timber and fruit, all these were to be redistributed every few years so that each family got a fair chance to enjoy the best and worst land.

To Marx's eye, the material not only revealed how widespread these egalitarian values were among early cultures, but how over time they were undermined to benefit the more powerful members of society. In Scotland whole clans were enslaved to serve more powerful neighbors; jumped-up Irish cattle ranchers, known as Bo-Aire or "cow lords," grew rich "through obtaining the use of large portions of tribe-land"; low-caste Indian farmers were evicted from their land by powerful Brahmins. His prejudice was encouraged by reading *Ancient Society*, the groundbreaking study of Native American culture by the anthropologist Lewis Morgan.

Bewitched by Charles Darwin's theory of evolution presented in *The Origin of Species* in 1859, Morgan argued that all societies evolve through different stages of complexity, from savagery through barbarism to civilization. Beginning with a time when people lived in a kind of communal soup sharing land, sex, children, and goods, he theorized that first matrilinear tribal patterns emerged, then patriarchal family distinctions with an accompanying change in ownership of land toward feudal ownership.

It was a thesis that Marx embraced wholeheartedly since it apparently showed communal ownership to have been a natural state overthrown in the interests of the most powerful.

Perhaps deliberately as the most secular of Jews, Marx did not include in his research the well-recorded efforts of the Israelites to construct an egalitarian state three thousand years ago. Once they had crossed the Jordan into Canaan, the land whose boundaries had been so minutely described in the book of Joshua was shared out among the families of each tribe. But, as the book of Leviticus made clear, it was understood that after time an individual might have "waxen poor, and [have] sold away some of his possession." Nevertheless, because the earth itself belonged to Yahweh, such deals were not final—"The land shall not be sold for ever: for the land is mine, for ye are strangers and sojourners with me." And after forty-nine years the law stipulated that all debts and sales of land were to be canceled and the right to work the ground returned to the original owners. In this way the frontierland conditions that existed at the time of conquest would also be restored.

Despite the obvious difficulties involved, the jubilee, as Leviticus described it, may have been observed in some form for several centuries after the settlement of the Israelites in about 1400 BC. The Jews' commitment to equality must have marked out their society among the hierarchical kingdoms of the Middle East more distinctly even than their diet or often-wavering faith. Instead of reverence for kings, their social duty was to care for orphans and widows, and in the words of their most ancient writings, the Psalms, to "raise the poor from the dust, and lift the needy from the ash-heap." But as the formerly desert people transformed themselves into settled farmers, the jubilee fell out of favor. Without redistribution, the most efficient cultivators were not only able to add to their holdings of vineyards, olive groves, pastures, and animals, but could pass them on to the next generation, consolidating their prosperity and social status.

According to the later prophets, the cause of Israel's woes lay in its abandonment of the old egalitarian principles concerning use of the land, both the jubilee and a requirement that every seventh year the soil be left fallow for a year. When the Jews were conquered and sent to Babylon in 605 BC, Jeremiah predicted an exile of seventy years to make up for the seventy fallow sabbaths they had failed to observe, a timespan equivalent to 490 years. During the absence of the Jews from the territory they had once occupied, the soil so greedily accumulated resumed its god-owned status. "The land enjoyed its sabbath rests," the book of Chronicles recorded; "all the time of its desolation it rested, until the seventy years were completed in fulfilment of the word of the Lord spoken by Jeremiah."

The Russian Empire offered Marx a more appealing illustration of this ingrained urge to use the land fairly. Although serfdom existed in Russia until 1865, and nearly all the land was owned by the tsar and his nobles, more than half of it was actually administered by the *mir* or village commune to which all peasants belonged. Conditions varied hugely from the frozen forests of the north, where serfdom barely existed, to the rich black soil in the Volga and Dnieper valleys, but everywhere the power of the *mir* was such that, like the Irish sept, it could redistribute land not just to meet the needs of families as they grew larger or smaller, but to preserve equality, to ensure that no single family could monopolize the best soil to the detriment of others.

The evidence of communal ownership of land administered by communal government for egalitarian purposes led Marx to a momentous ideological decision in the last year of his life. After a career devoted to mapping out the iron law of economic evolution by which feudalism developed into industrialized capitalism, and capitalism inevitably collapsed through overproduction into socialist revolution leading to the establishment of the proletarian state, he decided that a country might be able to short-circuit the entire process and jump straight from communal land ownership to revolution. In the preface to the Russian translation of the *Communist Manifesto*, published in 1882, he wrote, "If the Russian Revolution becomes the signal for a proletarian revolution in the West, so that both complement each other, the present Russian common ownership of land may serve as the starting point for a communist development." This single sentence was to reverberate through history. From Marx's guarded assurance that Communism might come about before the rural economy of Russia had been industrialized, Vladimir Ilyich Lenin drew the assurance he needed to plan both the 1917 revolution and the collectivization of Soviet agriculture, events that would set the world's agenda for the second half of the twentieth century.

By a double irony, however, it is apparent, even from the data that Marx himself collected, that his evolutionary interpretation is simply wrong. What his research revealed, and modern anthropology confirms, was not a chronological development, with the equitable distribution of land progressively destroyed by selfish family ambition, but an uneasy equilibrium that occurred in a variety of forms in different countries, sometimes lasting for centuries.

Running through Brehon law, for example, was the assumption that some families would always try to escape redistribution, that if successful they could accumulate wealth both by employing *fuidhir*, or landless workers, and by making vassals of freemen by lending them cattle, and that over generations, if they could hold onto their land and their stock, a once-poor family might rise to provide the chief of the sept. The remit of Brehon lawyers was not to prevent this, but to ensure that it happened justly. As late as the eighteenth century, almost a thousand years after Irish families first began to enclose land as their own according to the *Senchus Mor*, a visitor to Westmeath near Dublin still found strips of ground being redistributed among different families: "The utmost care was taken by joining together in one share, plots good and bad from different quarters of the field, that the shares might be of exactly the same value."

Marx himself noted that in his own day *Allmenden* or commons regulations still dictated the periodic reallocation of communal land in German cantons in Switzerland on grounds of need and fairness, even though peasants there had also owned the right to inherit and pass on use of their land for more than two hundred years. And in the Russian Empire, the *mir's* policy of egalitarian redistribution took place against the constant pressure of ambitious serfs to negotiate better terms of service for the use of their horses and plows, and to acquire skills such as carpentry that could be sold for cash. Known pejoratively as iron fists or *kulaki*, successful serfs could employ poorer neighbors to fulfil their labor duties, while they earned more money for themselves to the point where the wealthiest were often richer than the poorest nobles. These twin tendencies survived centuries of serfdom, the shock of emancipation in 1865, and a few decades of private property, until the *mir* itself was wiped out, with tragic irony, by Lenin's collectivization of Russia's farms.

Among the Wampanaog, who not only hunted and fished but raised corn, squash, and beans, Edward Winslow insisted "Every *Sachem* knoweth how far the bounds and limits of his own Country extendeth, and that is his own proper inheritance; out of that if any of his men desire land to set their corn, he giveth them as much as they can use, and sets them their bounds." Since hunters also gave the *sachem* a portion of any deer they killed within those bounds, he clearly exercised some degree of overall ownership. But the families to whom he granted use of the land evidently also understood that they owned that use.

Roger Williams, perhaps the best educated of the New England colonists, who became fluent in the languages of both the Wampanaog and their more powerful neighbors the Narragansett, believed their property rights were clear enough to be recognized under English common law. "The Natives are very exact and punctuall in the bounds of their Lands," he wrote in *A Key to the Languages of America*. "And I have knowne them make bargaine and sale amongst themselves for a small piece, or quantity of Ground."

Modern anthropology confirms the intricate and infinitely variable forms of family ownership of homes and of the ground nearest them within a generally communal structure of possession. It is possible that even the five-thousand-year-old clay boundary markers from Lagash in Mesopotamia that are some of humanity's oldest inscribed records may delineate family farms rather than tribal territories. And, Jeremiah notwithstanding, both observance and neglect of the fallow sabbath and the jubilee forgiveness almost certainly coexisted in Israel for centuries before the Babylonian captivity.

HOWEVER, any form of communal land ownership requires a governing organization that operates with general consent if it is to hold the balance between personal and common interests. This remains true today. Where pasture rights are still held in common, as in crofting communities in the Scottish Highlands, the decisions of the grazing council will bind its members not only to the number of animals, but to the dates when they can be put out to grass and taken in. And in cities, the most maverick condominium owner buys into the belief that on matters such as redecoration of the building or use of the common entrance space, individual preferences must give way to the majority choice of a committee.

This was the function provided in various forms by the tribal sanhedrins of the Israelites, the manor courts of feudal England, the *fine*, or council, of the sept in Ireland, the *mir* in imperial Russia, the *sachem's* meetings among the Narragansett and other Native Americans, and the longhouse discussions of the Iban. Land was not their only concern, but the earth's role as the source of food and culture gave such questions a central, even spiritual, importance. The communal resolution of disputes over the use, transfer, and inheritance of land involved relationships with family, neighbors, and outsiders, matters that might be considered personal in a private property society. But the need for social cohesion gave the communal decision even on intimate matters such as religious belief or the marriage of children a sanction of formidable weight—exclusion from the community's affairs. Even when no formal organization was involved, social ostracism was always a powerful weapon in a rural community, as was demonstrated in Ireland in 1880 when Captain Charles Boycott, a bullying landlord's agent, was reduced to impotency by the refusal of the community even to talk to him. Few things divide the modern private world more completely from the past than the collegiate nature of tribal and peasant life.

The strength of this culture came from the involvement of each participant in decisions that affected everyone. Hence the long list of Wampanaog and Narragansett names that were added to deeds of sale of tribal land when the British government made formal purchase of land from the Indians mandatory in New England after 1662. But the reverse held equally true, that in the face of really determined opposition, important decisions were often deferred. As Roger Williams noted before the Wampanaog were wiped out, "The *sachims* . . . will not conclude of ought [agree to anything] that concerns all, either Lawes, or Subsidies, or warres, unto which people are averse, or by gentle perswasion cannot be brought."

This was and is the Achilles' heel of communal land ownership. The need for social cohesion made the response to change slow and disjointed. But as Marx repeatedly discovered in his research, it also rendered them vulnerable to manipulation in favor of the most powerful because membership of the ruling bodies was usually earned through social seniority or wealth. Above all, communal systems were almost defenseless against the individualized challenge of private property. The ability of paper-based structures of private property to harness the legal resources of an entire society, to direct them at a particular parcel of ground, and to offer financial rewards for success simply overwhelmed the oral, local, and conservative systems of communal land ownership that stood in their way.

IN THE LATE TWENTIETH CENTURY, terrorist warnings from paramilitaries of the Provisional Irish Republican Army in northern Ireland that a bomb had been planted were usually authenticated with the pseudonym "P. O'Neill." This brief signature had an ancient history. It referred back to the Irish uprising that began on October 23, 1641, with a massacre of Protestant settlers initiated by Phelim O'Neill. The date was significant because the killings marked a watershed in Ireland's history.

Unlike the previous five hundred years of English incursion into Irish affairs, the spread of plantations owned as private, inheritable property posed a threat to the very identity of traditional Ireland. The effects were felt most acutely in the O'Neills' territory of Ulster where areas of woodland once available for distribution to landless O'Neills were being claimed as private property not just by incoming settlers but by powerful leaders in the sept. The change was exacerbated by the policy of the London government, which attempted to win over potential troublemakers by confiscating communal land then returning it as personal property to the chieftain, Earl Hugh, and his relatives. When the earl and two other Ulster magnates fled in 1607, the old Brehon structure, already undermined, fell apart. Local territorial enmities sparked the 1641 rebellion as much as fear that more Protestants would shortly swell the existing plantations in Ulster and Munster.

Once the rebellion broke out, however, the killing of as many as four thousand men, women, and children of the forty thousand Protestants in the province provoked immediate retaliation against Catholics. During the next decade, atrocities on both sides left Ulster so devastated that Owen Roe O'Neill, a Catholic general, declared that it "not only looks like a desert, but like hell." In 1649, the carnage reached a climax with the invasion of Oliver Cromwell's army, and in the next four years the ruthless slaughter of any who resisted his forces added an estimated 167,000 victims to the toll. In the wake of the rebellion, Cromwell's government imposed both Protestantism and private property on Ireland.

Not only was the estate of every rebel automatically forfeited, but all Catholics, and any Protestants who had not actively demonstrated loyalty to the London government, were ordered to leave their lands and relocate west of the Shannon River, the boundary that divided the province of Connacht from the rest of Ireland. Those who failed to obey were to be hanged, the choice summed up in the savage phrase that they could go "to hell or Connacht." Although many Catholics stayed where they were, from Ulster in the north to Munster in the south, a great swath of the country was emptied of its traditional owners.

Eighty thousand of them trailed westward, crowds of refugees clutching passports and certificates that entitled them to a smallholding in Connacht. The odd scrap of paper that still survives gives individuality to the mass of wretchednes: "Ignatius Stacpole of Limerick, orphant [orphaned], aged eleven years, flaxen haire, full face, low stature; Katherine Stacpole, orphant, sister to the said Ignatius, aged eight years, flaxen haire, full face;

having no substance to relieve themselves." In their wake came William Petty's army of surveyors, measuring out the devastated land to be owned as private property.

In 1641, the population of Ireland was thought to number about two million. Twenty years later it had been reduced by between three hundred thousand and, William Petty's estimate, six hundred thousand people. Traveling through the heart of Ireland in 1653, Colonel Richard Lawrence, an English officer, declared that "a man might travel twenty or thirty miles and see not a living creature, either man, beast or bird." Not even the famine years of the 1840s caused a greater proportionate loss of life.

About ten thousand colonists from Britain settled in Ireland. Some, like Petty himself, who acquired thirty thousand acres, became great landowners, and their descendants constituted the Protestant aristocracy known as the Ascendancy. Others, especially the soldiers, received nothing more than a smallholding and were gradually absorbed into the surviving Irish society. In both cases, however, they held their land under English common law that recognized a single owner whose exclusive rights would be enforced by the magistrate and, if need be, by the army.

With communal ownership disappeared the bardic schools and the land-reading Brehon law and the power of the sept. Before 1641, Catholics had owned almost two thirds of the land in Ireland, but 90 percent was in the hands of Protestants by 1659. The revolution was complete. Or appeared to be.

Anti-Catholic legislation ensured that Protestant landowners controlled the administration of government in Ireland, enforcing the law, raising taxes, and securing the peace. But they had no political power. As Petty himself objected, the Irish government was controlled from London where English landowners could directly affect its policy. Without political control to protect their property, Irish property owners could not realize the full capital value of their land or secure freedom to export their products to England. "And why should Men endeavour to get Estates, where the Legislative Power is not agreed upon; and where Tricks and Words destroy natural Right and Property?" Petty demanded. "And how should Merchants have Stock, since Trade is prohibited and fetter'd by the Statutes of England?"

By the end of the century, a more benign regime had enabled many Catholics to recover their farms, the population had bounced back to more than two million, and an uneasy peace had descended. According to Harrington's law, political power in Ireland should have followed property, but so long as London controlled Irish affairs that necessary next step could not be taken. The religious apartheid imposed by British colonial policy provided the flashpoint of tensions, but, as the nineteenth-century famine would make tragically obvious, ownership of the land was the key to Ireland's destiny.

FROM A GLOBAL STANDPOINT, the Irish settlement had a significance that stretched far beyond Britain and Ireland. It proved to be the blueprint for a way of owning the earth that, with some significant variations, would eventually displace millions of people and overwhelm hundreds of indigenous cultures from Newfoundland to New Zealand.

It is possible to regard this cataclysmic change simply as a matter of realpolitik. The land revolution that linked property interests to capital creation brought into being a modern system which archaic societies organized on half-feudal, half-tribal lines were powerless to resist. The disparity was apparent in Ireland where Cromwell and Ireton could keep a professional army in the field for four years and finance the ten-million-pound cost of the campaign with London loans, fully covered by the sale of Irish land. The history of the next two centuries would make it universally obvious that a private property society could harness resources that were not available to societies organized in other ways.

Alternatively, it could be argued on utilitarian grounds that the unhappiness of several million people should be set against the billion or more living happily on the ground once occupied by the victims, with greater freedom from want and suffering than the original inhabitants.

However, these responses are rendered inadequate by Locke's argument that the right to an exclusive, individual ownership of land was a matter of justice that applied equally to those deprived of their land. The violence of expelling indigenous people and taking the territory that gave them identity as well as feeding them was an injustice that should invalidate the moral argument for private property.

Yet human existence has a moral value, and both the sustenance of the extra lives and the improvement of their quality that were made possible by the change in the way the earth has been owned must be entered into the balance. Throughout their history, too, the inhabitants of private property societies have claimed for themselves a degree of individual freedom unknown in other societies, and measured by our cultural yardstick, that moral autonomy has undoubted value. To the extent that the dispossessed have been able to claim a similar freedom by regaining or being compensated for what they have lost, that also meets Locke's criterion.

The balance can never be finally struck because a changing present must always be weighed against an unchanging past. But, as even the libertarian Robert Nozick acknowledged, the need to find a moral basis for private property, and indeed for any other society, requires its history to be faced, and an argument made to justify the facts that have been created on the ground. Without that moral basis, a private property society is inherently unstable. The earliest illustration came from Ireland's history. The latest can be seen in Sarawak.

THE SITE OF LANGGA'S FARM some thirty years after he had been promised wealth and fame provides firsthand evidence of the result of a private property invasion. Most of that primary forest, where trees grew to the height of a cathedral, creating a home for the orangutan, the hornbill, and the Iban, had gone. In its place the sun beat down on scrubby grass, a few spindly trunks of secondary woodland, and down the valley, the long succulent green rows of a palm oil plantation. A way of life that depended on divining dreams, reading the omens, and recalling how the Iban came to inhabit their land had become a tourist attraction. If Langga's name was known, it was because it had been attached to a vacationer's version of the traditional longhouses that once lined the Bangkit River.

In less than a generation, one of the most rapid land revolutions in history has transformed Sarawak. Under the guidance of Abdul Taib Mahmud, who from 1981 served for thirty years simultaneously as the Malaysian state's chief minister, finance minister, minister of planning and natural resources, and, until 2008, chairman of the Sarawak Timber Industry Development Corporation, the trees have been changed into almost half a billion cubic meters of plywood and other lumber products, a million hectares of forest have been converted into monoculture plantations growing palm oil trees, and the gigantic Bakun hydro-electric dam, the second largest in the world, will shortly drown another seven hundred square kilometers of forest, home to seven thousand indigenous Penang, Kayan, and Kenyah people, in order to provide electricity for aluminum smelters along the coast a hundred miles away.

In a peculiarly twentieth-century fashion, Taib translated political power into property—using his party's control of the state government to secure ownership of the land itself. Government organizations took over national interests in the territory, overriding where necessary the Native Customary Rights that recognized possession by indigenous peoples, and then sold off its products, predominantly timber, oil, and natural gas, to gigantic corporations, at least four of which, according to a Bloomberg News report in 2009 "have ties to Taib or his family." Perhaps the most significant single measure taken by Taib's government in pushing through these sales was the decision to make surveying a government monopoly, so that any property maps drawn up by the Iban and other forest dwellers would be rendered illegal.

Unmistakable material gains have come from destroying the old way of life and privatizing public resources—living standards for most people in Sarawak have improved dramatically, the state's economy has grown by an average of 6 percent a year for almost twenty years, and the center of the sleepy capital of Kuching has been transformed by towering concrete citadels, housing international corporations and hotels, that soar above the old fish market. But economic prosperity cannot disguise the political fragility of a system built on a family's monopoly of power.

Missing from the privatization of Sarawak, as it was from the settlement of Ireland, is the awkward element of social justice that holds a society together. The destitution suffered by formerly land-rich, indigenous communities like the Iban compared to the fabulous wealth of Taib's friends and relatives—four Sarawak billionaires appear on the latest *Forbes* rich list—is as manifestly unjust as the exile of Irish landowners to enrich William Petty and his friends. Yet in his criticism of the injustice of English government, Petty showed that he at least half-grasped the concrete importance of what was absent. The connection between social equity and political stability was supplied by his friend James Harrington.

The precedents of Anastasio Somoza's dynasty in Nicaragua and Ferdinand Marcos's regime in the Philippines illustrate what happens to a private property system when a family attempts to monopolize its resources. In Harrington's terms, it must fail because too many competing property interests are created for one family to control, however extended its network of cronies.

Ultimately Sarawak's new property owners are bound to demand a share of the political power monopolized by the Taib clan to protect their own interests. The uncertainties created by resistance to their demands will erode the security that international trade and the financial industry prize, raising the cost of doing business and diminishing profits. At some point, the resentment of the many despoiled have-nots will coincide with the ambitions of a sufficiently large number of have-not-enoughs to create a more or less viable democratic uprising. One more oligarchy attempting to govern a multiplicity of property owners will then be blown up.

Chapter Seven

The Peasants

In the summer of 1583, Queen Elizabeth's astrologer, John Dee, received a visit that testified to his towering reputation for learning. As he recorded in his journal, Prince Albertus Laski, one of the mightiest nobles in Poland-Lithuania, itself the greatest kingdom in Europe, arrived with loud fanfare at Dee's house besides the river Thames: "he was rowed by the Quene's men," the magus noted with pride, "he had the barge covered with the Quene's cloth, the Quene's trumpeters, &c. He cam of purpose to do me honor, for which God be praysed!"

It was one of the last truly happy entries in Dee's journal. He was still waiting for Sir Humphrey Gilbert's return from America, unaware that in the very week of Laski's arrival his partner had drowned in the Bay of Biscay. Meanwhile his book buying had landed him in such dire poverty he needed a patron, and he eagerly accepted the Polish prince's offer of a position in his household. The relationship would involve Dee in a folly that would tarnish his reputation down the centuries.

The Polish commonwealth stretched from Lithuania in the north to Prussia in the west and Ukraine in the south, making it the largest country in Europe. Its military strength was in proportion. No fewer than seventy-five Muslim attacks had been repelled by Poland's armies between 1474 and 1569, earning the country the title of "the Christian bulwark" of Europe. And Prince Laski, in the words of Lord Burleigh, Queen Elizabeth's chancellor, was "a personage of great estimation, few exceed him in sovereignty and power." As one of the foremost members of the *szlachta* or nobility, he had not only been influential in the election of Poland's new king, Stefan Bátory, in 1576, but thanks to the country's system of electoral monarchy, was seen as a potential future king himself.

In England, anyone who possessed land and political influence on such a scale would be dripping with cash. And when Laski recruited Dee and his Irish associate, Edward Kelley, into his service, the magus felt his future had been secured. But the once-feudal economy of the eastern European plain had developed along a different path from England's. Prince Laski's extensive estates near Lodz were worked with serf labor.

On the face of it, there seemed little reason why private property should not have emerged in Poland. Like their English counterparts, Polish landowners enclosed common land, squeezed out smaller freeholders, and regarded their estates as private possessions to be passed on to the next generation free of feudal dues. A solid trade in wheat and rye, more than eighty thousand tons a year at its peak in the sixteenth century, sent down the Vistula River for export through Danzig, might have provided the same impetus to treat the earth as a private source of wealth as the wool trade did in England.

The financial sophistication to back such a transformation could have come from Danzig, now Gdansk, a city port with a mercantile structure as advanced as London's, and sufficient wealth to put an army of five thousand mercenaries in the field. The Jews who had been expelled from Spain in the fifteenth century had dispersed beyond Amsterdam to Poland, promoting international trade and financial links to the outside world. Under the liberal constitution of 1505, the *szlachta* elected the monarch and members of the Sejm, or parliament, thus giving landowners enough political influence in government to enact the measures that would give them property in their estates. The legal system guaranteed individual freedoms, including a degree of religious tolerance that made Poland the first country in the world to deem anti-Semitism a crime. Poland's Renaissance culture fostered the heliocentric discoveries of Nicholas Copernicus, the art of Hans Dürer, and the Protestant theology of Jan Laski, the prince's cousin and a friend of Erasmus.

Hanging in the National Gallery in Washington, Rembrandt's *Portrait of a Polish Nobleman*, painted in 1637, gives a glimpse of what it meant to be a member of the *szlachta*. The model may be Rembrandt himself, but the flamboyant Asiatic garb, the sable fur flung round the shoulders, the pearl earring dangling from the fleshy ear, and the winged mustache spreading luxuriantly beneath the bulbous nose, all suggest the extravagant freedom that was encapsulated in the gentlemanly code known as "Sarmatism" that governed the nobility's conduct. Within their own caste, every member of the *szlachta*, however needy, was assumed to be equal, and united in gallantry, independence of mind, and generosity of behavior. But the extravagance of Sarmatian values was not reflected in the economy. While the harvest produced money, there was, as Dee's journal makes clear, none in the land itself. Although he and Kelley were living on Laski's enormous estate, or *folwark*, near Lodz, worked by over a hundred serfs, there was barely enough silver and gold to pay the prince's two new advisors.

During the very period that England's landowners were transforming land from a feudal possession into capital and relying on paid labor to exploit its value, their Polish counterparts were going in the opposite direction, converting feudal dues to forced labor, pushing peasants into serfdom, and enshrining land as the symbol of nobility. The basic division of a feudal estate, between demesne land belonging directly to the lord and the tenements that were worked by peasants in return for dues to the lord, was carried over into serfdom. But in contrast to the relative freedom of a peasant, a serf in eastern Europe was unable to move from the estate where he or she was born.

THE BIRTH OF THIS MODEL of land ownership took place during the fifteenth century conflict between king and noble landowners. Like every other European country, Poland's feudal system was shaken by the inrush of silver, first a stream from southern German mines then a flood from Spanish America, giving rise to decades of inflation. Across the continent, the era of the self-financed army sustained by feudal dues came to an end, its demise accelerated by the new and dramatic cost of supplying heavy artillery and portable firearms such as the arquebus and musket. By the end of the sixteenth century, the price of waging war had made national taxation a central strategic concern, and the Europe-wide struggle between monarchs and their most powerful subjects for control of the land's revenues reflected its importance as the primary source of wealth and income. Only the commercially successful Netherlands and the silver-enriched Spanish Habsburgs were exempt. Elsewhere on the continent, the struggle tilted in favor of kings, emperors, and single rulers, but in Poland the outright winners were the *szlachta*.

From the early fifteenth century, the commonwealth of Poland-Lithuania—the two countries were united in 1446—not only waged a prolonged war in the south with Islam, in the shape of the Ottoman Empire and later the Crimean Tatars, but mounted repeated campaigns in the north against Prussia, Russia, and Sweden. Although Polish armies employed mercenaries, its powerful cavalry, whose reputation reached from Istanbul to Paris, was supplied and led by the nobility. Initially, the cost of each armored knight was, in theory, covered by the revenues and services from each feudal estate, while the army's other needs were met by taxation and the resources of royal lands. But under the strain of the incessant demand for men and military resources, the structure buckled. To persuade the *szlachta* to neglect their fields and forests for lengthening periods of warfare, Poland's kings were forced to cede an ever-growing list of concessions.

Some of the nobility's gains resembled those later won by England's landed gentry—the elected Sejm, to represent their interests; a guarantee that the king would secure the approval of the Sejm before raising taxes or going to war; an unequivocal declaration that should the king break any of these agreements, the *szlachta* would have the freedom to rebel. But there were some still unknown to a private property society. The most astonishing was the agreement made under the liberal constitution of 1505 that kings should be elected by the nobility.

Given these ingredients, there might seem little reason why private property should not have emerged in Poland. Like their English counterparts, Polish landowners regarded their estates as private possessions to be passed on to the next generation free of feudal dues. The crucial difference were two measures that affected ownership of the broad, flat grasslands that provided nearly all Poland's exports and the bulk of her wealth. In 1496 the Piotrków Privilege, extracted from the king shortly before the outbreak of a fresh campaign against the Ottoman Empire, conferred on the *szlachta* the power of preventing any of their peasants from leaving their estates, and at the same time it prohibited city merchants, a class that was not liable for military service, from buying land "because they have no part in the general levy." The short-term purpose of these privileges was to reward Poland's noble commanders by restricting the privilege of owning land to them, and to reassure them that during their absence on service the workforce could not be enticed away from their estate. The long-term consequence was the creation of the serf economy.

Once a peasant's movements were restricted to the estate on which he was born, he and his family could no longer escape their feudal lord's demands. As peasants, they continued to own the use of farms, large enough sometimes to employ laborers themselves, and to have teams of horses and oxen to work the soil, and in exchange they still gave their labor to the noble landowner. But, like slavery, the new institution soon altered every aspect of social life.

Within an estate's boundaries, peasant life was organized tightly around the provision of forced labor—*Robot* in German—primarily for the cultivation of the noble's private land, but also for road building or military service, and only when these obligations had been fulfilled could serfs work on their own strips of land. In order to keep the entire family on the estate, landowners put in place a continually growing list of regulations, that "Peasants . . . must not give their daughters in marriage within other jurisdictions"; that without permission children were forbidden to "rent their working strength out to others"; that unless the widow of a deceased plowman "remarries within a year," she would be evicted; and that "since the land is the lord's property, none of his subjects has the right . . . to share it among his relatives."

Even after serfdom had been abolished, it left a nightmare memory that a nineteenth-century teacher, Jan Slomka of Dzikow in southeast Poland, found to be still vivid when he talked to former serfs in the area. "As the folk who knew this system and remembered it used to tell of it," he recounted, "no worse punishment could be found for men and women than serfdom." As late as the 1800s, a serf's home might be no better than a single-roomed cottage with an earth floor, sheepskins for bedding, and a central fire that had no chimney. Until his family had fulfilled their quota of *Robot*, the overseer was liable to burst into their cottage, throw a bucket of water on the fire, or tear the door off its hinges and drive them out to work. "The lord of the manor was owner of everything," Slomka concluded. "His was both land and water, yes even the wind; since only he was allowed to build a wind-mill to grind corn. Only when all his compulsory dues were completed could the peasant sing the old song: 'I'm not afraid the landlord will molest me, My dues are done, I'll set me home and rest me!' "

As Polish landowners tightened their grip in the sixteenth century, they absorbed smaller estates and unoccupied territory until the possessions of the greatest nobility resembled *latifundia*, the term employed during the Roman Empire to describe the gigantic spreads amounting to petty kingdoms accumulated by its most powerful citizens. The Polish word was *folwark*, and the power of *folwark* courts to enforce regulations reduced the already limited freedom of peasants to the constricted condition of serfs. Their one weapon was to perform their *Robot* more slowly, but the *szlachta* retaliated by marking out the area of aristocratic fields and the length of public roads with their own measuring rods, which grew longer until what had been a day's work in the 1500s took a day and half to complete in the 1600s. Meanwhile the serfs' own fields were measured, as one petition to the Sejm put it, "with a very small rod which reduced [our land] so badly that we no longer know what to do, and how to support ourselves."

In the fifteenth century, the historian Jan Dlugosz penned a notable sketch of the characteristics of his countrymen: "the Polish gentry are eager for glory, keen on the spoils of war, contemptuous of danger and death, inconstant in their promises, hard on their subjects and people of the lower orders . . . courteous to foreigners and guests, [and] lavish in hospitality."

Since disputes were ultimately resolved by the landowner's overseer, with refractions punished by the manor court, serfs had little hope of redress. Nevertheless, as at least one *folwark* regulation suggested, they still refused to labor for their masters with any enthusiasm. "In order to encourage people to work in a perfect fashion," ran one decree issued by a nobleman with an estate near the Baltic coast, "I have decided that the son or the son-in-law (preferably the son) will inherit [the right to work the farm] from the deceased parent if . . . either is capable of replacing the father." Presumably this privilege must have served as an incentive, but one so easily given could be taken away with as little difficulty.

BY PREVENTING OWNERSHIP from passing outside the nobility, however, the Piotrków Privilege inadvertently made it impossible to use the land as security to raise loans from the wealthy city burghers of Krakow or Danzig. There could be no equity in *szlachta* property, no competition to improve its fertility, no cash in the employment of its workers. While in town, Laski and his like had access to silver and gold, but on their estates they were persistently short of cash.

It was the desperate need for money that led John Dee astray. He allowed himself to believe the claim of his colleague Edward Kelley that the angel Uriel had shown him how to concoct a chemical that would turn base metals to gold. This may have been what really interested Prince Laski, rather than the magus's extensive learning. But when Kelley refused to repeat the experiment, the two alchemists were allowed to leave for the more promising surroundings of the court of the Holy Roman

Emperor, Rudolph II, in Prague. Under pressure to produce results, Kelley claimed in 1586 to have performed the experiment again, and in his diary Dee solemnly recorded the result in the Latin he used for esoteric events: "*et producta est optimi auri oz. fere*" ("and [it] produced almost an ounce of finest gold"). For a period, their stock soared, and Kelley seized the chance to acquire another powerful patron. But among less credulous courtiers, Dee's reputation was sullied, and his inability to find a patron himself forced him to struggle back to the safety of London in 1589, where he found his library ransacked and a life of poverty awaiting him.

IN EFFECT, serfdom was a command structure, shaped by the demands of war and the relative emptiness of the war-torn grasslands of eastern Europe. In the late fifteenth century, the system spread to the Austrian Empire then engaged in its own long life-or-death struggle with the Ottoman Empire, and it was introduced by the Poles to the duchy of Prussia in 1525 when the duchy was still ruled by the military order of Teutonic Knights. Serfdom's most significant convert, however, was Poland's old enemy, Russia, and it took root during the 1550s while Russia was fighting for survival against repeated invasions by the Tatar khans of the Crimea and the Volga basin.

The obvious inefficiencies of serfdom's micromanagement, quite apart from the injustice of reducing more than two thirds of the population to such a servile state, ought to have made the serf economy uncompetitive from the start. Yet for more than two centuries, it turned out to be a far more dynamic way of owning the earth than private property. The great serf empires of Austria and Russia would spread faster and further until in 1789 they enveloped all of central and eastern Europe, from Vienna to the Urals, while private landed property was still confined to the islands of Britain and Ireland and a thinly populated coastal region in North America.

Warfare provided the ultimate test of an economy's efficiency, and judged by that ruthless yardstick, the source of serfdom's energy becomes obvious.

THE GREAT RIVAL OF POLAND, as of the other serf economies of Russia and Austria, was the Ottoman Empire. So potent were its armed forces that in the middle of the sixteenth century, its sultan, Süleyman the Magnificent, could claim to be the most powerful ruler in Europe, outranking the Polish king, Sigismund II, and the Spanish Habsburg emperor, Philip II.

Habsburg possessions stretched from Spain through the Netherlands and Burgundy into Italy, but Süleyman held the Balkans, Greece, Romania, and most of Hungary and Austria, as far north as Vienna in the heart of Europe, and his navies enveloped Italy and threatened the southern coast of Spain. The Atlantic Ocean divided the Spanish Habsburg possessions in Europe from their American empire, but the sliver of the Hellespont, less than a mile across, was all that separated Suleiman's European domain from the rest of the Ottoman Empire stretching through Turkey and the Middle East into North Africa and as far east as the Persian Gulf.

The empire had its roots in the nomadic Turkic people of central Asia who had swirled westward with the Mongol invasions in the thirteenth century and established themselves in what is now known as the Middle East. The cutting edge of Ottoman armies was delivered by its fearsome horse-mounted archers, known usually as *sipahis*, or sometimes as *timariots*, from the landholding or *timar* that fed and supplied them with their mounts and arms. Adopting the tactic of the Mongol horsemen who were their forebears, the *sipahis* shot arrows at the gallop, outflanking enemy formations by their speed of movement. They were recruited only from Muslim landholders. At the height of his power in the 1560s, Süleyman the Magnificent could rely on the *timar* system to finance the deployment of eighty-seven thousand *sipahi* cavalry.

Although an Ottoman cavalryman held his *timar* directly from the sultan in return for service in war—much as a Christian feudal knight held his land from the king—it could never be a purely military relationship. A fundamental concept of sharia law, the basis of the empire's legal system, was that the earth belonged to God—"Unto Allah belongeth whatsoever is in the heavens and whatsoever is in the earth," the Koran states explicitly. Thus, Süleyman the Magnificent, in common with all Ottoman rulers, possessed the soil simply as God's agent, the leader of the Muslims, *Amir-al-Muslimin*.

Land, in other words, was the currency paid to those who served the empire, and thereby advanced Islam. Holders of *timar* land not only fought, but were responsible for gathering taxes and providing local justice and administration, while alongside them the holders of religious land, the *waqf*, a category comprizing almost one fifth of the empire's territory, were expected to build schools and hospitals. In theory at least, the holders of Ottoman soil could neither inherit it nor lease it to someone else. As in Poland, however, the strains of war had begun to distort this formal structure, and as a European power, the Ottoman Empire could not escape the destructive effects of silver inflation. In the course of the sixteenth century, the cost of equipping a *sipahi* soared, while the value of revenues from *timar* land remained fixed.

Next to his military achievements, Süleyman's magnificence lay in his legal reforms, and especially the framework of land law that he laid over the patchwork quilt of imperial land ownership. It remained in force for three hundred years. And in European terms it represented a preemptive strike to establish imperial control of the land's resources. The main purpose of the changes was to increase revenues for the state, and so it made the use of land dependent on payment of taxes and dues. Cadastral surveys—to map the ownership of land—were ordered throughout the empire in order to register its main categories—*miri* or state land, including the *timariot*; *waqf* or religious land; and *mülk* or private land, including small allotments and large tracts of reclaimed land.

A strongly centralized bureaucracy in Istanbul, headed by the Grand Vizier, used the information to impose imperial taxes that were levied through provincial governors. Throughout Süleyman's reign these produced a treasury surplus that amounted to 71 million *akçer* (very approximately twelve million dollars) in 1528. Measured by the crude but unforgiving test of war, his revenue permitted him to raise an army of up to one hundred thousand warriors in the west, strong enough to force the Hapbsburg Austrians to cede control of Hungary, while a smaller force in the east captured Baghdad from the Persians and took possession of the Persian Gulf.

A century later, the French traveler Jean de Thévenot testified to the lasting effects of Süleyman's reforms, writing of the empire's "strong agricultural base . . . the well being of the peasantry, the abundance of staple foods, and the pre-eminence of organization in Süleyman's government." But the appearance was deceptive. By then his successors were losing control of the land, and in 1670 the treasury would be in deficit by forty-four million *akçer* or about seven million dollars.

In part the loss of control was due to the localized structure of Sunni Islam—the version favored by Ottoman sultans—that fragmented the general tenets of Süleyman's reforms into hundreds of regional variations. The eternal conflicts arising over land's inheritance, use, and taxation were adjudicated, in the last resort, by an imam who made reference to the two highest authorities on the subject, the Koran and the *sunna*, the nonsacred sayings and actions of Muhammad, but was free to interpret these in the light of one of four established bodies of legal opinion, and adapt his interpretations to take account of local custom and geography. Ottoman land law was anything but common, and Süleyman's own creation of the *millet*, a separate administrative system for each religion, Muslim, Jew, and Christian, added to the complexity.

Disputes about land, its taxation, and its revenues, lay at the heart of nearly every one of the increasingly ferocious revolts that shook the empire after Süleyman the Magnificent's death in 1566. Significantly, the most serious uprisings, at the end of the sixteenth century, and again in 1622 and 1657, occurred in the very heartland of the empire, the Anatolian Peninsula, and involved the disaffected *sipahi* cavalry. Caught between the growing expense of military service and the fixed revenue from *timariot* estates, the class that had been the backbone of the empire turned in on itself and abandoned its military duties. Increasingly *sipahis* took to treating the *timariot* as property that was theirs to occupy even when they no longer went to war, and might in time be passed on to their offspring. By 1630, Süleyman's successors could expect barely eight thousand *sipahis* to take to the field. "Most of the feudal lords today release themselves from their military obligations," the treasurer of sultan Ahmad I complained at that time, "so that on campaign where military service is required, from ten timars not a man will turn up."

It was possible to see what was happening from an otherwise minor skirmish that took place between several squadrons of Polish hussars and Ottoman *sipahis* on September 7, 1621. In the course of a long, bitterly fought siege of the Polish-occupied fortress of Khotyn situated in the frontier region of Moldavia, a force of Ottoman infantry, the elite janissaries, guarded on the flanks by a screen of *sipahi* horsemen, broke through the outer defenses of the Polish line. At the critical moment, the defenders' commander, Jan Karol Chodkiewicz, let loose an onslaught of about six hundred heavily armed hussars. In a devastating charge, the Polish riders cut through the Turkish cavalry, sabered the infantry, then, sweeping away the last of the horsemen, drove into the advanced camp of the enemy, killing almost five hundred men. For the besieged Poles, the sight of the irresistible power of their cavalry restored flagging morale, and they continued to hold out until the first winter snow forced the Ottoman army to lift their siege and retreat to Istanbul.

Although the subsequent treaty left both sides claiming victory, a watershed had been reached. On his return, Osman II, the young Ottoman ruler, was assassinated by his janissaries, and his successor faced both rebellion and the need to find a substitute for the once-famed *sipahis*. For the Polish nobility, the triumphant cavalry charge and the Turkish retreat vindicated their monopoly on the possession of the land and its revenues. While the Ottoman sultans attempted to impose central bureaucratic control over distant landholders, the *szlachta* policed themselves and could direct the country's resources where they were most needed. They kept government both small and immediately under their control but, as it must have seemed to them in 1621, strong enough to see off their enemies.

In the course of the seventeenth century, the *szlachta* used their hold on power to extend their privileges, permanently ensuring that taxation fell on their serfs and the urban population and persistently voting in weak kings who would not challenge aristocratic rule. Notoriously, they created the "*liberum veto,*" a nuclear option that allowed a single negative vote by one representative in the Sejm to defeat any legislative proposal however great the majority that supported it. Quite suddenly this concentration of power, once a source of strength, became toxic.

In 1648, the *szlachta* in southern Poland attempted to extend serfdom into estates they held in Ukraine, provoking a Cossack revolt that soon brought in Russia. Poland was now encircled by enemies, from Sweden in the north to Ukraine and Islam in the south, from Russia in the east to Prussia in the west. Prevented by the *szlachta* from raising adequate taxation to cover the military budget, the government of what had been the most powerful country in Europe a generation earlier was effectively bankrupt by the second half of the seventeenth century.

Nevertheless, as late as 1683, the Polish cavalry were able to offer one final and decisive display of military muscle. In that year, an Ottoman army, made up largely of professional janissaries and Muslim Tatar cavalry from the Crimea, invaded Austria and were not stopped until they reached the gates of Vienna. For most of one day, September 12, a mighty infantry battle raged in front of the city until in the evening, Jan Sobieski, king of Poland, led some twenty thousand horsemen of many nationalities, including the famous Polish hussars, in what is often described as the largest cavalry charge in history against the weary Ottoman troops. A few thousand *sipahis* were brushed aside, the Tatar cavalry melted away, and Sobieski's charging horsemen destroyed the army of an empire that had threatened to overwhelm eastern Europe for 250 years.

In 1786 James Madison examined Poland's elected kingship as a possible model for the United States constitution. By then the country was close to final dismemberment by its serf-owning neighbors, Russia, Prussia, and Austria, and Madison concluded that the fatal flaw lay in its form of government. This left "the Chief Magistrate," or executive arm, too weak to resist a landowning legislature that had pushed its monopoly of power to the point of allowing a single member to veto the executive's policy. As a result, Poland's very existence was about to be sacrificed to the interests of one small power bloc. In his recommendation that the president have an electoral mandate separate from Congress, and independent powers in foreign and military policy, Madison was determined that the United States would not make the same mistake.

There was no possibility that the United States would look to the declining Ottoman Empire for any examples in democracy. Denuded of self-supporting soldiers and tax-gatherers, eighteenth-century sultans were forced to rely on a central bureaucracy backed by the professional janissaries, who acted as both police force and infantry. Tax gathering was farmed out for a percentage of the revenue to private contractors, while provincial governors were expected to administer their regions from their own resources. In the west, it had become a byword for tyranny.

Nevertheless, by changing Ottoman land ownership, Süleyman the Magnificent's laws transformed Ottoman society. Legislation linking tax payment to land possession accelerated the process by which the tax-gathering *sipahis* came to regard themselves as owners who could inherit the land rather than office holders. Marking the change, the land in their possession was increasingly described as a *çiftlik*, a name that referred to the size of the estate.

In the Balkans and southern Europe generally, a *çiftlik* looked like a serf estate, with peasants forbidden to move and subjected to an ever-growing weight of labor dues by a superior who was both government official and feudal lord. In the Middle East and North Africa, however, sharia law's emphasis on the priority of supporting members of the family tended to give the peasants on a *çiftlik* a closer resemblance to members of a clan who acknowledged the owner as their chief. Except in the immediate vicinity of cities such as Cairo and Damascus and trading ports such as Izmir and Alexandria, where commercial farms supplied food for urban consumers, agriculture aimed at peasant self-sufficiency rather than capitalist profit making.

Yet, compared to the peasant monarchies of Europe, the Ottoman Empire had a lesson to teach. The wide range of land holdings allowed an equally wide variety of societies to flourish, from the desert tribes of Iraq to the typical peasant villages of Anatolia, and this multiplicity encouraged the growth of a degree of religious toleration within the millet system that was otherwise absent from the continent of Europe.

THE OWNERSHIP OF LAND never exacted a greater toll than during the Thirty Years War that pitted Catholic against Protestant in Europe between 1618 and 1638. Up to one third of the German-speaking population died from internecine slaughter and miserable deprivation. Superficially, the conflict was triggered by the reluctance of newly Protestant states to hand back to the Catholic authorities church lands they had confiscated at the time of their conversion. But this concealed the deeper struggle of peasants who actually worked the soil to retain a degree of freedom from feudal lords intent on squeezing them into serfdom on the Polish model. In both cases, however, these rulers were driven by the same imperative to gain greater control of the land and its revenues during a period of inflation and mounting military expenditure.

Like their eastern counterparts, feudal landlords further west had attempted to coerce smaller freehold peasants into providing forced labor, to broaden the services demanded of existing tenants, and to claim common grazing and woodland as their own. Unlike the serfs to the east, however, peasants in every country from Hungary to England resisted. In western and southern Germany especially, they rose up in a bloody rebellion in 1525.

For most peasants, the church was the forum where their labor was given a moral context. Since few of their rights were written down, they needed the church's authority to reinforce what tradition and their own fierce sense of justice suggested was right. Consequently, they grasped at the anti-authoritarian language of Martin Luther's Protestantism to give voice to their revolutionary impulses. First among the demands made by a meeting of Black Forest peasants in 1525 was an insistence on having their own preachers rather than those imposed on them by feudal superiors, and close behind came the declaration that "it is devised by the scripture, that we are and that we want to be free."

The freedom they had in mind entailed an end to the feudal burdens and taxes that so constricted their lives. Unfortunately for their hopes, Luther was determined to support the princes, electors, dukes, and landgraves who had converted to Protestantism, and he defended their cause in a vicious pamphlet entitled "Against the Murderous, Thieving Hordes of Peasants." It was left to Thomas Müntzer, a former student of Luther turned Anabaptist preacher, to give a lead. Quoting Christ's words "I came not to bring peace but a sword," he preached a social and spiritual crusade against all authority beyond individual conscience, and against any form of property except what people needed for their shelter and nourishment.

The decisive clash between peasant and lord took place on May 15, 1525, outside the central German town of Frankenhausen where the Landgrave Philip of Hesse lined up his well-trained army of mercenaries against the eight thousand peasants assembled by Thomas Müntzer. When the landgrave sent them an order to lay down their arms and surrender, Müntzer gave voice to the egalitarian Christian impulse that drove his footsoldiers: "Say, you wretched, shabby bag of worms! who made you a prince over the people whom God has purchased with his precious blood?"

Before nightfall, the rebels were destroyed, Müntzer was about to be tortured to death, and as a class peasants would sink below the historical radar, becoming a byword among urban commentators for their secrecy, superstition, and conservatism. Yet through the growing religious turbulence and land grabbing of the next century, a consistent pattern emerges of peasant resistance to encroachment by lords and rulers on their land and their liberty. From the river Elbe to the Atlantic, the same grinding battle pitted landlord against peasant. In the poor valleys of Burgundy, farmers struggled relentlessly against their lords' attempts to prevent them marrying outside the estate, a restriction that would have taken them toward serfdom, while the nobles whose sheep grazed the mountainsides of Saxony did their best to stop peasants erecting fences to protect their crops from the animals.

Usually the conflict was resolved peacefully—in France the advocate Sébastien Rouilliard won a notable legal case in 1582 against a landlord attempting to impose on his tenants longer hours of forced labor, hailing it as a victory for "*la liberté publique*"—but very often the antagonism spilled over into violence. In France, resistance to the imposition of fresh dues triggered so many peasant revolts that Marc Bloch, the foremost twentieth-century authority on feudal France, deemed them "as natural to the seigneurial regime as strikes are to large-scale capitalism." Further east, in the myriad of tiny German-speaking states in the Holy Roman Empire, where landlord and ruler tended to be the same person, peasant anger over matters of land and liberty quickly became caught up in the religious conflict that pitted one ruler against another.

During the Thirty Years War, differences between secular and religious causes were soon drowned in blood, but from 1648, when disputes could again be settled peacefully, the law courts of a major state such as Saxony became clogged with cases of peasants attempting to protect traditional freedoms against landlord encroachment. Owning the earth in any form was inextricably linked to liberty.

The outcome of this prolonged struggle for power over the land left Europe divided roughly between the serf east and the peasant west along a line customarily taken to be the river Elbe that flows from the Czechoslovak mountains northwest to the German port of Hamburg on the North Sea. No ruler survived the crisis of the seventeenth century without control of the land's resources, either directly or through the nobility, but unlike the east, where monarchs allied themselves to aristocratic landlords against those who worked the soil, royal government in France and the Rhineland gave a more sympathetic hearing to peasant demands. Free from the threat of Islamic invasion—France even formed alliances with the Ottoman Empire against its enemies in Spain and Austria—these rulers had little reason to placate noble landlords. From the last half of the seventeenth century, their law courts increasingly upheld peasant freedoms against the claims of a potentially divisive aristocracy, and society was sufficiently open for wealthy urban merchants to be allowed to become seigneurs and buy the estates of impoverished landlords.

Even in the west, the earth continued to be held by a feudal lord, but his ownership extended no further—in German terms it was simply *Grundsherrschaft* (ground ownership), as opposed to the *Gutsherrscaft* or manorial ownership practiced by serf societies. Peasants would be charged rent or labor for the use of the landlord's earth, for the right to inherit or transfer its use, and, as their feudal superior, he would require them to pay to have their corn ground in his mill, their cows inseminated by his bull, and their produce weighed and measured with his scales and containers. But in return a feudal lord provided justice, law, and order, and his decisions either conformed to traditional practice or could be appealed to the royal courts.

Out of it came a wary equilibrium that allowed peasants across much of France and the Rhineland to enjoy something close to a guaranteed tenure of the land they worked. They responded by increasing crop production or, in the south, by diversifying into cash crops like vines grown on soil unfit for other purposes, or by cultivating chestnuts and mulberries for feeding pigs and silkworms, respectively. Compared to the serf economies of eastern Europe and the sharecropping regions of Italy and Spain, where productivity per head was no higher in 1700 than in 1600, the output of French peasant farmers grew by almost 8 percent between 1650 and 1750, roughly in line with what was happening across the Channel. *La liberté publique* evidently paid dividends. Even more astonishing was the expertise of peasant farming in the Rhineland. During the eighteenth century, emigrants from the Palatinate and Hesse regions would travel to farm in the capitalist surroundings of Pennsylvania and the serf economy of the Volga basin, and in both places their methods would become a byword for efficiency and high production.

The difference between peasant Europe and capitalist Britain was not one of production but of ownership. While the common law concentrated ownership of land and produce in one person, peasant ownership was always held by the family, and however clearly its use belonged to the peasant, the land itself ultimately belonged to a lord. This divided ownership gave peasant society a particular quality that prized endurance over enterprise.

A peasant could not conceive, as Shakespeare did, that all his land would pass intact to one male heir at the expense of others. As Alexander Chayanov, the leading twentieth-century authority on the nature of the peasant economy, pointed out, in the struggle to survive, members of a peasant family were prepared to accept such tiny rewards for their unremitting labor that it amounted to "self-exploitation." The sheer hard work fostered an outlook that was crippling compared to the capitalist model. Chayanov's extensive research in both tsarist and Soviet Russia showed that peasants had no incentive to produce a surplus beyond what they needed to meet the needs of their family. Thus a peasant economy would always tend toward subsistence farming rather than profit and growth. The increase in productivity achieved by French peasants was driven by the growth of population and the burden of higher taxes that Louis XIV's glittering, expensive reign imposed. There was no gain to the peasants themselves. Indeed the demand for land from a growing population in the eighteenth century undermined the little liberty they had won for themselves.

Peasant families were large because many children lightened the burden of peasant work, but it was axiomatic that when grown they had to be provided for, and their children too. During the century up to 1750, when the average size of an arable British farm was growing from fifty to eighty acres, the land around Paris known as the Île-de-France was being subdivided into ever-smaller holdings until 90 percent of them measured less than seven acres. Each intensively worked acre was more productive than its British equivalent, but after all the mouths had been fed, it earned an infinitely smaller surplus.

Across western Europe, landowners reasserted their powers as the population grew, using the courts to enforce old, income-generating privileges like mandatory use of the landlord's mill and payment of inheritance fees. By 1789, France's population numbered twenty-seven million, twenty million of whom were peasants caught in a relentless cycle of labor to wring a living from the earth. The margin between success and failure grew too small for experimentation, too uncertain for optimism, too dependent on communal efforts for individualism. "Don't run away from anything" was the old peasant maxim, "but don't do anything." Survival rather than progress was the goal.

For most of history, most people have viewed their pasts and their futures as peasants. No other system of land ownership is so stable and widespread. Various forms of it have appeared in China, India, Latin America, and much of the Middle East. It allows governments to collect taxes and enforce order through landlords without paying them. Landlords receive money for no work, and peasants have the benefit of the land without needing to find the capital to buy it. And so empires have survived for centuries on peasant economies. Entire societies have been fed by peasant labor. Armies and religions have filled their ranks with peasants. Whole cultures of farming, of weaving and knitting, of cooking, preserving and fermenting, of storytelling and music-making, have grown out of the peasant family's struggle to keep body and mind alive in hard times. What the skeleton is to anatomy, the peasant is to history, its essential, hidden support.

THE EIGHTEENTH CENTURY would demonstrate that each of these three ways of owning the land—serfdom, peasantry, and private property—had a distinct social and political outcome, and the differences were exaggerated by a unique concept enshrined in the Peace of Westphalia that ended the religious bloodletting. It was summed up in the phrase *Cujus regio, eius religio*, literally "whose kingdom, his religion," meaning that within a state's boundaries a ruler's authority ranked above any external power. To later generations, this pragmatic phrase crystallized the concept of the nation-state, although it would be more accurate to call it "the territorial state."

It became obvious, for example, that the ability of rulers to gain control of revenues from within the physical boundaries of their realms gave the most successful a head start over their rivals. They could finance the manufacture of expensive armaments—everything from artillery to battleships—and encourage the growth of science and the manufacture of scientific instruments through awards, such as Britain's £20,000 prize for a method of working out longitude, and by government contracts for mapping and exploration, as Louis XV did with the Cassini family of cartographers.

By this test, the states of northwestern Europe performed well. In the mid-eighteenth century, the French government, with twenty-seven million inhabitants and a gross national product of £160 million raised more than sixteen million pounds in taxes. To put that achievement in perspective, the imperial government of Manchu China, the wealthiest peasant-based economy of the period, raised only twenty-six million pounds from a population ten times as large. The point at which the economies of China, the world's largest economy in the eighteenth century, and northwestern Europe began to diverge was heralded by the superior efficiency of territorial states in taxing their rural economies.

Within Europe itself, the nationalist wars that characterized the eighteenth century offered a test of the effectiveness of each form of land ownership. Flexing its peasant muscles, Bourbon France first drained then defeated the serf power of Habsburg Austria that had dominated Europe in the sixteenth and seventeenth centuries. But increasingly it also locked horns with Britain's private property economy in a series of expensive wars that tested both models to the limit. Given the disparity in population—with barely seven million inhabitants, Britain was less than a third of France's size—the outcome should not have been in doubt. But the British government managed to squeeze more than twice as much revenue from each one of its citizens, giving it resources almost on a level with those of its great rival.

Paradoxical though it might seem, a legislature representing the nation's wealth producers was ready to tax them at a much higher rate than France's government. "Having seen the extraordinary [taxes] which the subjects have to pay in England," a French diplomat commented in 1708, "it has to be said that one is very lucky to be in France." Not only did Parliament in London tax land and personal property, it assessed and raised the money directly rather than farming the process out to private contractors as the French government did with the *Ferme Générale*. To the "country gentlemen" in the House of Commons who represented landed wealth there was no paradox. They were ready to pay for Britain's wars—more than a hundred during the century—because they believed them to be not only in the national interest but necessary to protect the particular kind of freedom that went with private property.

By the time the Bourbon economy began to implode in 1789, the country gentlemen's belief had helped win an empire in India and the West Indies, and both win and lose another in North America. Yet these acquisitions were dwarfed by those made by Europe's least efficient form of land ownership. If war was indeed the ultimate test, Russia had apparently found the key to making serfdom work.

Chapter Eight

Autocratic Ownership

At about eleven p.m. on one freezing night in February 1947, the great film director Sergei Eisenstein was summoned peremptorily to join his producer at the Kremlin for a meeting with the general secretary of the Communist Party, Joseph Stalin. Eisenstein had just completed the second part of his movie, *Ivan the Terrible*, and the rough cut had been shown to senior members of the party for their approval. The reason for the meeting was made clear by Stalin's first question to the director: "Have you studied history?" When Eisenstein answered "More or less," Stalin echoed his words sarcastically, "More or less? I am also a little familiar with history . . . Your tsar has come out as being indecisive, he resembles Hamlet. Everybody prompts him as to what is to be done, and he himself does not take any decision . . . By showing Ivan the Terrible in this manner you have committed a deviation and a mistake."

What followed must have been one of the most terrifying lessons ever given in Russian history. It lasted for more than an hour, with both teacher and student aware that any failure to pay attention would be rewarded by a bullet in the back of the student's skull. The lesson that Stalin intended Eisenstein to learn was that the goals and methods of Ivan's rule in the sixteenth century still applied in the twentieth, when the Soviet Union, successor to the Russian Empire, occupied one third of the earth's surface. "Tsar Ivan was a great and a wise ruler," Stalin declared firmly, "he looked at things from the national point of view and did not allow foreigners into his country, he barricaded the country from the entry of foreign influence."

It was in the spring of 1565 that Tsar Ivan IV, the Great or the Terrible, began to impose his nationalist will upon a state that had been the duchy of Muscovy but was in the process of becoming Russia. After eighteen years as tsar, most of its territory was still possessed by the mighty, semi-independent barons known as the *boyars*. The second part of Eisenstein's film began with Ivan's dramatic announcement that he intended to abdicate as tsar and create a separate kingdom or *oprichnina*, where he would exercise absolute power. The region included most of northern Muscovy, center of the lucrative fur trade that provided much of the tsar's revenues. The remainder, the *zemshchina*, was left under the control of the *boyars*.

Part 1 of *Ivan the Terrible* had covered the heroic period when the young Ivan, barely twenty years old, launched a series of campaigns against the khans of the Golden Horde, the powerful remnants of Mongol armies to whom Muscovy had paid tribute for generations. Supporting the Russian cavalry, his army's main attack force, was a new corps of professional musketeers, the *strel'tsy*, that the tsar himself had created. Using their firepower, a novel weapon to Tatar horsemen, Ivan's armies drove back the enemy, bringing the province of Astrakhan under Russian control, and giving them a first foothold in the gigantic Volga river basin that lies between Moscow and the Urals. To commemorate his success, Ivan constructed within the walls of the Kremlin, Moscow's inner citadel, the magnificent cathedral of Saint Basil, with its eye-catching, blue and green gilded onion dome spires.

But the tsar's greater achievement was less visible, the foundation of a central administration to run Russia's growing state. Although often haphazard and disjointed, the shape of his reforms was clear: to displace the old, feudal power of the *boyars*. The jurisdiction of their manorial courts was challenged by a new, tsarist law code, issued in 1550, that created a structure of regional councils, *zemskiy*, to administer justice and raise taxes. Significantly, they reported directly to Moscow rather than to the provincial *boyar* governor.

Underpinning this shift in power was a shift in land ownership from feudal to bureaucratic. Service in the tsar's government was rewarded with land. A thousand estates close to Moscow were, nominally at least, allocated to officials concerned with civil affairs, taxation, justice, and the royal court, while on the expanding borders many more were awarded to those who rendered military service. By regulations brought into force in 1556, for every four hundred acres, military landowners had to supply one cavalryman "on a horse with complete equipment, and for a long march he must have two horses." Under the tsar's direct control was the

Pomyestny Prikaz, or Estate Office, which was responsible for distributing this land and ensuring that the *pomeshchiki*, or landholders, provided the service required of them, both civil and military.

The dry administrative detail of Ivan's reforms muffled the murderous threat this growing structure posed to the *boyars*. What had begun as a question of government became personal when Ivan IV's uncertain psychological state was shaken by the death of his first wife, Anastasia Romanovna, in 1560, due to poison, it was whispered, administered by the *boyars*. The second part of Eisenstein's film revealed how Ivan launched his attack.

THE SHORT-TERM REASON for the tsar's decision to abdicate in 1565 and take absolute control of the *oprichnina* was his determination to weed out dissidents suspected of collaborating with Russia's powerful neighbor to the west, the great commonwealth of Poland-Lithuania. Strategically, however, the goal was to create a core of total unity centered on Ivan himself. But the methods, as described by Heinrich von Staden, a German adventurer who had joined the tsar's entourage, point also to a tortured mind. The landowners living in the *oprichnina* "took an oath not to have anything to do with the *zemskie* people [i.e. those living in the *zemshchina*] or form any friendships with them. Those in the *oprichnina* also had to wear black clothes and hats; and in their quivers, where they put their arrows, they carried some kind of brushes or brooms tied on the ends of sticks. The *oprichniki* were recognized in this way."

Eisenstein's depiction of the *oprichniki* in tall black cowls was another irritation to Stalin, who thought they looked "like the Ku-Klux-Klan." As part of the history lesson, he emphasized that these black-clad figures, often professional soldiers, *strel'tsy*, and cavalrymen, were "a progressive army" because they enforced the absolute power that could alone unite Russia. Their brooms symbolized Ivan's determination to sweep Muscovy clean of its enemies, and the appearance of the *oprichniki* in a neighborhood was as terrifying to the inhabitants as the nighttime hammering on the door by Stalin's secret police in the Soviet Union four centuries later.

"A person from the *oprichnina* could accuse someone from the *zemshchina* of owing him a sum of money," von Staden wrote. "And even if the *oprichnik* had never known nor seen the accused from the *zemshchina*, the latter had to pay him immediately or he was publicly beaten in the marketplace with *knouts* or cudgels every day until he paid. No one was spared in this, neither clerics nor laymen. The *oprichniki* did a number of indescribable things to the *zemskie* people to get all their money and property."

The purpose of the terror was not just to cow opponents, but to ensure that land, the source of imperial service, was held only by those loyal to the regime. Consequently, the estates of anyone suspected of collaboration with Poland were confiscated on behalf of the tsar, and transferred to the loyal *oprichniki*.

But the campaign of terror soon extended to anyone opposed to the tsar's policies. In 1570 Ivan accused the inhabitants of Veliky Novgorod, the oldest and most cultured city in Muscovy, of maintaining links with Poland. Between three thousand and fifteen thousand citizens were tortured and murdered, many under the tsar's personal supervision. Soon the *oprichniki* were running out of control. During Ivan's periodic, Hamlet-like fits of remorse when he retreated to pray for forgiveness, they took to murdering and terrorizing at random in an orgy of fear and greed.

Seven years after it began, the terror was brought to an abrupt halt. In 1571 the southern Tatars living in the Crimea and along the Black Sea took advantage of the devastation to invade and burn Moscow. Shocked, Ivan turned against the *oprichniki*, fining and executing them for crimes he had earlier approved. Yet, once he had resumed his authority in 1572 as tsar of all Russia, it became apparent that the terror had succeeded in its purpose and eliminated almost all rivals to his power. His bureaucratic structure was still in place, his reconstituted army inflicted defeat on the Tatars the following year, and only a few *boyar* families retained any independence. Most significantly, the church, the one remaining institution that could challenge the state, was forbidden in 1580 to acquire more land, leaving Ivan and his successors to claim as their own personal territory every crumb of earth the Russian Empire would acquire between the Baltic and the Pacific over the next 337 years. By uniting all its territory in their possession, the tsars united Russia.

Summing up his history lesson, Stalin pointed out that the founder of the Russian Empire and the founder of the Soviet Union had followed exactly the same policy. "Ivan the Terrible was first," Stalin pronounced, "Lenin was the second." To his credit, Eisenstein made only a grudging apology for having failed to appreciate the similarities, but his terrified producer grovelled, promising to change everything if they could be allowed to learn from their mistakes. Seemingly appeased, Stalin allowed the filmmakers to leave soon after midnight.

The one criticism that Stalin made of Ivan IV was his failure to be ruthless enough. After the tsar's death in 1584, the remaining *boyars* fought among themselves for supremacy, a period known as "the time of troubles," leaving Muscovy so vulnerable that in 1612 a Polish army occupied Moscow for twelve months. "He did not completely finish off the five big feudal families," Stalin complained. "If he had destroyed these five families then there would not have been the Time of Troubles. If Ivan the Terrible executed someone then he repented and prayed for a long time. God disturbed him on these matters . . . It was necessary to be [more] decisive."

Demonstrating his familiarity with history, Stalin showed no mercy when his own *oprichniki*, the NKVD secret police, purged his supposed enemies in the 1930s. Where Ivan killed his thousands, Stalin exterminated his millions. As Anna Akhmatova wrote in the opening lines of *Requiem*,

In those years only the dead smiled,
Glad to be at rest . . .

Among those executed on Stalin's orders were almost half a million *kulaki*, rich peasants and smallholders, who mistakenly assumed they had rights to the soil they farmed. A greater knowledge of history would have told them that with ownership of the earth came a claim to power. By definition, an autocratic government had to possess all the land. Stalin's Communist Party was no more prepared to let ownership pass into the hands of peasants than Ivan the Terrible had been to leave it with the *boyars*.

Each of the three tsars who have had the accolade "the Great" added to their names—Ivan, Peter, and Catherine—put the distribution of land at the heart of their policy of government. None did so to more dramatic effect than Peter in 1722. As part of his violent campaign to wrench Russia into becoming a Western power, he had already founded a new capital, Saint Petersburg, on the banks of the Baltic, imported Dutch, German, and British merchants and craftsmen to modernize industry and production methods, and put swingeing taxes on Russian smocks and beards in order to force changes in dress and appearance. As a clean-shaven youth with dark wavy hair, Peter himself had resembled a Western romantic hero, but now in his fifties his face was deeply lined and his determination to drag his country into the current of European affairs had grown ruthless. He had executed by the thousands any who resisted him, and flogged to death his own son, Alexis, in rage at his disobedience.

The land autocracy that the Romanov dynasty had inherited from Ivan the Great had not only grown in size as the empire expanded, but changed in nature. In less than a century, estates originally tied to imperial service had come to be treated as family possessions that could be inherited, leased, and exchanged. In 1649, an attempt had been made to reverse the trend. A great compilation of laws known as the *Ulozhenie* specified that whoever had the privilege of holding *pomeshchik* land must also pay the taxes and provide the military or civil service associated with it. Yet, by the time Peter the Great took power in 1682, the ineffectiveness of the law could no longer be disguised. It was hardly possible to tell a *pomeshchik* property from those of the greatest nobility, who enjoyed right of inheritance in return for their hereditary duty of serving the tsar at court. Taxes that should have come to the central treasury were diverted to *pomeshchik* pockets, and their growing local authority began to endanger the national unity that Ivan's land monopoly was designed to sustain.

Root and branch, Peter set out to restore the old system of government, locking the whole of Russian society, except for merchants and city dwellers, less than 10 percent of the population, into a new structure that matched government service exactly to the allocation of land. In 1722, he created a "Table of Ranks" placing everyone employed by the government in one of fourteen ranks, from general to junior lieutenant in the army, and from imperial minister to lowly registrar in the civil service. At each level, service merited the award of an estate. More importantly, the privilege of owning serfs, the essential means of making an estate profitable, was restricted to those holding a high rank.

In place of the old *Pomyestny Prikaz*, or Estate Office, the tsar appointed a College of Heralds, whose chief executive, the Master, had absolute power to supervise the elaborate uniforms that marked each rank of nobility, the progression from white pants to black, from red ribbons to blue, from white epaulettes to gold. Dress was one thing, but the Master also kept the records that showed what estates each nobleman held, and what duties were expected in exchange. Thus as a reward for promotion to vice-admiral, Adam Weid was given an estate of 188 serf households in Finland, which the Master duly clawed back after his death. On his appointment as chief judge, Andrei Matveev received a large property of

132 serf households, but rather close to the Swedish border, and when a treaty alteration placed the land within Sweden, the Master allocated a smaller but safer estate of eighty-two serf households, that reverted to the tsar on Matveev's death in 1728.

That was how the system was supposed to work, and it demonstrates the profoundly contradictory nature of Peter the Great's reforms. To make Russia modern, he saddled it with an administrative system akin to those of Ivan the Terrible and Süleyman the Magnificent. His insistence that possession of land should be linked to government service was not just a disastrous attempt to turn back the clock, it flew in the face of human nature by denying the possibility of even family possession of land. In the rest of eighteenth-century Asia, the Ottoman Empire and the great powers of China and Mogul India espoused various forms of peasant ownership that gave some security of tenure to most landowners and guarantees of use to most tillers of the soil. The majority of owners and users could also hope to pass on, albeit at some cost, what they possessed to the next generation. In those places, as in the peasant kingdoms of western Europe, the sense of security was accompanied by agricultural improvements that led to increasing yields in crops and livestock. No similar trend emerged in Russia until Peter's reforms were pushed aside.

Nevertheless, a land-based autocracy remained the template for the Russian Empire as it spread across Asia with a speed unequaled by any private property society. Ideologically, the conquest of new lands was seen as a spiritual crusade against Muslims and other "enemies of the Holy Cross." And the tsars' absolute authority over their new territories was explicit in their official title, "By the grace of God Emperor and Autocrat of All the Russias." It was this divinely authorized command structure that exploded out of eastern Europe and into Asia.

During the three centuries of Romanov rule, the empire swallowed up an average of almost thirty thousand square miles of new territory every year. From its Muscovite enclave largely covered by conifer forests, it had already broken out in the sixteenth century north to Finland, and eastward across the forest and swampland of the Siberian *taiga*. This frozen expanse was home to such a cornucopia of fur-bearing animals that by 1650, when the first traders had already reached the Pacific, one third of the imperial revenues came from the sale of sable, black fox, and ermine. As France's missionaries and *coureurs de bois* would do in North America, Russians claimed a sparsely populated land but did not settle it. The real imperial thrust of the seventeenth and early eighteenth centuries was to the southeast through a warmer country thick with birch, oak, and maple, increasingly broken in the east by the grasslands of the Volga river basin, and suddenly opening out in the south toward the Black Sea into the vast ocean of the steppes.

As early as the 1640s the Russians began to face a colonial challenge Americans would not encounter until the nineteenth century, how to organize the possession of grasslands taken from their indigenous occupants. Just as the American way of converting the prairies into property would leave an indelible imprint on United States society, so the Russian method of imposing their ownership of the steppes profoundly affected the outlook and structure of the Romanov Empire. And at almost the same time in the 1890s, as Frederick Jackson Turner was selecting the frontier experience of the United States in its westward expansion as "the crucible [where] the immigrants were Americanized," his Russian contemporary, Vasily Klyuchevsky, was insisting that the colonization of Asia was "the fundamental factor" in Russian history.

At first the open country beyond the trees was simply called "the field" or *polye*, but quite soon people started using the word *steppe*, which dictionaries defined as an area that was grassy, treeless, and, despite the presence of several million nomadic Cossacks, Bashkirs, and Kalmyks, empty. Thus the Russians, like the Spanish, French, and British in the New World, could see nothing to stop them planting their own society in a land that stretched for more than a thousand miles to the Urals.

The first impression created by the richness of the steppe was of wonder, not unlike the feeling of early settlers in America. "Nothing in nature could be finer," wrote Nikolai Gogol in *Taras Bulba*. "The whole surface resembled a golden-green ocean, upon which were sprinkled millions of different flowers. Through the tall, slender stems of the grass peeped light-blue, dark-blue, and lilac star-thistles; the yellow broom thrust up its pyramidal head; the parasol-shaped white flower of the false flax shimmered on high . . . The air was filled with the notes of a thousand different birds. Oh, steppes, how beautiful you are!" The same vision of Eden-like exuberance struck John Perry, a British engineer employed by Peter the Great to construct a canal in the Volga valley. "The tulips, roses, lilies of the valley, pinks, sweet williams, and several other flowers and herbs spring up like a garden," he declared. "Asparagus, the best I ever eat, grows so thick, that you may in some places mow it down, and the common grass in the meadows is up to the horse's belly. Liquorish, almonds, and cherries, the fields are cover'd with." The luxuriant grasses fed herds of wild animals, deer, elk, boar, and a breed of sheep that the gourmandizing Perry insisted "eat tenderer, and was much preferable to common mutton."

Whereas American settlers immediately saw the prairies as potential property—John Quincy Adams compared their eagerness to acquire western land to "the thirst of a tiger for blood"—the Russians responded to the steppes in military terms. The grasslands were where the Tatar hordes came from, and the empire advanced into them behind lines of defensive fortifications under the command of a military officer.

During the seventeenth century, when Russia was expanding down the Don River toward the Black Sea, one major line running across the steppes was centered on the fortress of Voronezh, built at a strategic point high on wooded bluffs overlooking the river. The land along the line was allocated by the fort's commander to frontier militia farmers, the *ornodvortsy*, a motley group including army veterans, Cossacks, a scattering of aristocratic adventurers, and even escaped serfs. They kept a few horses, cattle, and pigs, grew enough wheat and vegetables to feed themselves, and traded iron tools with the native inhabitants for furs, hides, and beeswax. Nominally, they were under the command of the senior officer in Voronezh, and were required to defend the earthworks and fortified posts of the line against Tatar or Cossack attack, and if need be to aid the garrison in Voronezh itself.

The horse-riding Cossacks provided a vital but unreliable element in this first phase of settlement. Clustered in loose alliances along the rivers that fed the Black Sea and the Volga, they were the definitive frontier people, half-nomadic and half-settled, many of them runaway serfs, linked to Russia by their Christianity, but too free to accept its absolute government. They rendered invaluable service as scouts and outriders of the regular military, but, as was made dangerously obvious in 1670, when resentment at Russian demands provoked the Cossacks to rise in a furious rebellion led by Stenka Razin, their loyalty could not be relied upon. Their faces, decorated by the extravagant beards and mustaches that Peter the Great would ban, proclaimed their independence.

The ineffectiveness of the frontier militia in the face of Razin's failed revolt led to the next stage in the development of the frontier, the introduction of regular troops. Where Voronezh was concerned, this meant the arrival of the Ostrogozhsk regiment numbering about twelve hundred professional soldiers, sent to beef up security. Counting families and servants, almost six thousand new inhabitants had to be settled in the Voronezh area, transforming its nature. It now began to resemble the land-based autocracy of old Russia. Many of the militia farmers found their smallholdings incorporated into larger estates allocated to officers and civilian administrators in return for their service. The tsar personally awarded the regiment's colonel a large parcel of land a short distance down the Don River, while new farms close to the fort were carved out for the families of the regiment's regular soldiers.

Then in 1695, Peter the Great arrived in person with fifty thousand troops and five thousand shipwrights and laborers to build a navy to attack the Ottoman Empire. During this third phase of imperial settlement the critical element in Russia's command society took shape. The tsar awarded most of the fertile black earth in the region to his nobility—one general, Mikhail Tchertkov, acquired almost half a million acres—on condition they settled privately owned serfs on the new land.

Serfdom had come to Russia from Poland, but with one crucial difference. Instead of being the creation of the nobility, it served the interests of a single autocratic ruler. Like other aspects of Russian society, the seeds of serfdom had been sown in the course of Ivan the Terrible's reign. During the *oprichnina*, thousands of peasants had fled from the nightmare into the northern forests or south to join Cossack societies living beyond the woodland in the open steppes. *Oprichniki* who were awarded confiscated estates found them denuded of workers and rendered unproductive. To prevent this from happening, harsh punishments were decreed for peasants who left their estates.

The Romanov tsars went further, forbidding peasant children from moving away or from marrying anyone outside the estate on which they worked, so that *pomeshchiki* serving as military officers in the field against Tatars and Poles could be sure that their lands would still be worked in their absence. In 1649 all these laws were amalgamated in Chapter XI of the Russian legal code, the *Ulozhenie*, formally making serfdom a permanent, inheritable condition. From then on, serfs could never legally escape the estate on which they lived, nor could their children, except with the owner's permission.

By the early eighteenth century, two thirds of the thirteen million inhabitants of Russia were serfs, with over half belonging to the nobility and the remainder to the church and the state, meaning the tsar. Nineteenth-century commentators would compare their status to slavery, but unlike slaves, serfs were at least free to marry, and to live as a family. Indeed, many of the 2.5 million state serfs living on state land enjoyed a range of liberties, including the right to earn an independent living from such skills as carpentry and ironwork. They might have been regarded as free peasants, except that they still fell under the tsar's direct control. In 1701, for instance, Peter the Great arbitrarily ordered more than a thousand state peasant families to move from northern Russia and settle near Voronezh, while fourteen hundred state carpenters who had been sent to work in Voronezh were instead suddenly dispatched to Saint Petersburg, more than six hundred miles away.

The worst conditions, however, were suffered by serfs tied to private estates who were liable to forced labor for up to six days a week. Any disputes were settled in their owners' courts, and infringements punished by use of a leather-thonged whip, or *knout*, wielded by the owner's overseer. Early in his reign, Peter the Great had found it necessary to criticize landowners for "beating and tormenting [serfs] so that they run away" and had passed a law banning them from selling serfs to new owners singly rather than by families.

So vital was serfdom to Russia's mainly rural economy that estates were measured not by size, but by the number of "souls" or serfs they supported. It was reckoned that the labor of a hundred souls was needed to let an aristocratic family live comfortably, but most of the lesser nobility on the Table of Ranks possessed fewer than twenty serfs. Out in the provinces, there were even noblemen dressed in woollen smocks and felt boots who were no wealthier than their richest serfs. At the other end of the scale, more than three million of Russia's serfs belonged to a tiny elite, mostly of the old court nobility, each of whom owned at least one thousand souls.

Even among this group, however, none could compete with the holdings of the richest man in eighteenth century Russia, Count Pyotr Sheremetev, whose inherited property, coupled with the tsar's awards for service as Marshal of the Nobility, amounted to more than 1.5 million acres with two hundred thousand serf households, comprising more than one million souls. A small army of 340 servants staffed his palace in Saint Petersburg, almost twenty times as many as England's richest nobleman, the Duke of Devonshire, employed in the ducal mansion of Chatsworth. Serfs not only worked the land, they acted as carpenters, painters, builders, or, in the case of the beautiful Praskovya Kuznetsova, as an opera singer, mistress, and eventually wife of Count Nikolai Sheremetev, Pyotr's son.

Yet, unnoticed by tsarist rule, the serfs created an institution that came to be seen as the embodiment of the Russian spirit. Although serfs could not own the soil, part of each estate—approximately a quarter in the black earth region, but more than half in the less productive north—had to be set aside for their sustenance. The owner's steward was responsible for the organization of labor on the manorial land, but the serfs arranged their own lives and the distribution of the land they occupied through the commune, known formally as the *obshchina*, and more colloquially as the *mir*.

Each family had its own dwelling and garden, but the number of strips of land that it could farm and their location, together with the quantity of sheep and cattle it could graze on the common pasture, were decided by the *mir*. And in the interests of fairness, the *mir* periodically redistributed both land and grazing rights. It specified the amount of tax each person would pay, and because the three-year rotation of crops required one field in three to be left fallow with the other two given over to grazing or cereals, the *mir* also selected the type of crops to be grown, and the dates for sowing, harvesting, and ploughing, or for turning out the cattle in spring.

Thus, paradoxically, the autocracy of tsarist rule made possible for most Russians the communal life that Winstanley and the democratic Levellers had dreamed of. In the nineteenth century, the institution of the *mir*, with its apparent equality of ownership, would enter the Russian imagination as the embodiment of a national ideal, a property myth as powerful as the Englishman's vision of his home as a castle.

In 1790, while Enlightenment believers from Philadelphia to Saint Petersburg were still buzzing with news of the fall of the Bastille and the collapse of feudalism in France, Alexander Radischchev, an earnest, twenty-one-year-old advocate of rationalist politics, published a fictionalized account of serf life entitled *A Journey from St Petersburg to Moscow*. One of his stops on the journey was at the city of Novgorod, whose inhabitants had been massacred in 1570 by Ivan the Terrible. Radischev made the mistake of associating the serfs' wretched lives with the land autocracy that Ivan founded. Both institutions, he pointed out, demanded an unquestioning obedience that excluded more rational and progressive policies—"Russians," Radischev observed in a phrase that became famous, "grow to love their bonds." It was an acute analysis, but his logical conclusion that tsarist government needed reform could not have been more subversive.

In the margins of her copy of Radischev's *Journey*, Catherine the Great scribbled an angry defense of Ivan's policy, and promptly had the author exiled to Siberia where his health was ruined. Broken by the experience, Radischev later committed suicide. Once an enthusiast for Enlightenment values, Catherine had become converted since taking power in the 1760s to an equally determined belief in the virtues of despotism. Explaining why Radischev was wrong and she was right, the empress wrote vigorously, "[T}he sovereign is absolute, for no authority but the power centered in his single person can act with the vigour proportionate to the extent of such a vast dominion. All other forms of government whatsoever would not only be prejudicial to Russia but would provoke its entire ruin."

Nevertheless, it was impossible to ignore the problems of despotism. Quite apart from the immorality of reducing most of the population to a near slave-like condition, autocracy had consequences that choked the economy of the Russian empire even as it spread to become the largest territorial unit on earth. With all the resources of the empire available to it, the imperial army possessed a cutting edge that overwhelmed any resistance from Cossacks and nomadic Kalmycks and Uzbekhs who lived beyond the Volga. Even against the fading might of the Ottoman Empire, Russian forces established superiority on land and sea. But the society imposed behind the frontier was dysfunctional.

To FOREIGN OBSERVERS, the lack of interest that Russian aristocrats showed in their estates was shocking. Instead of improving the soil, they were content to live off the forced labor that came with the land, or to commute it to cash rents, and accepted the discomforts of living in houses built of logs and split greenwood planks. "The nobility is not identified with the soil as in the rest of Europe, nor with the region in which it resides," a French diplomat complained. "The wooden house, so often burned down, so quickly worm-eaten, so easy to transport or to reconstruct, is a meet emblem of Russian life." Long after Essex farmers had learned to snuggle into feather beds, an envoy from the Duke of Holstein noted that Russian lords "lie on benches covered with cushions, straw, mats or clothes; in winter they sleep on flat-topped stoves."

The French-speaking, European-minded ministers and courtiers in Saint Petersburg termed this disconnected state of mind "Asiatic." According to Nikolai Gogol, the characteristics of the Asiatic temperament were "indifference, naivety and cunning, an intense activity [followed by] the greatest laziness and indulgence." Those worst afflicted were the great mass of landowners who never attended court, but lived on their estates, supposedly acting as the government's tax gatherers and law enforcers in the provinces.

In 1859, the lassitude of the minor nobility was fictionalized in Ivan Goncharov's novel *Oblomov*, whose protagonist lounges all day on a couch wearing an "oriental dressing-gown" and daydreaming in a state of "Asiatic immobility" of all the deeds he will never undertake. The term "Oblomovism" was immediately adopted into the language, but the state of mind it described had existed for generations. A century earlier, the need to overcome this Asiatic indifference had become a constant theme in the documents generated by Catherine's growing horde of bureaucrats once they started to report on the state of New Russia.

Increasingly, the lazy aristocrats were bypassed by Catherine's new centrally organized professional administrators. But the attention of these professionals was soon also attracted to the lack of enterprise shown by the state peasants sent to settle on the frontier. Instead of exploiting the natural fertility of the soil, they seemed content to do no more than the minimum amount of labor needed to keep themselves alive. Like the original militia-farmers, they kept a few animals and grew some wheat, and did nothing to improve homes that were often no more than a one-roomed, chimneyless, earth-floored cottage. The files bulged with reports of settlers "living in dugouts," of their "extreme immiseration," and their need for "material and technical assistance." In 1806, after three thousand peasant settlers had almost starved to death on the rich soils of New Russia, the minister responsible decided the government had to intervene "to put an end to the tragedies and deprivations that so often accompany the peasants' thoughtless acts."

Their failings were spectacularly obvious when compared to the energy and drive shown by the colony of twenty-three thousand German Mennonites who migrated to the Volga valley in 1763 at the invitation of Catherine the Great. Like their fellow emigrants to Pennsylvania, the Germans were skilled and successful farmers who grew rye as well as wheat, alternated cereal crops with roots and clover, and employed teams of powerful horses rather than a few plodding oxen to pull their iron-tipped plows through the matted, black earth. Within a generation, they created a mini-Pennyslvania of neat fields, red barns, and white, clapboard houses beside the Volga.

"Why I asked myself would our peasants not want to imitate these settlers?" demanded Judge Pavel Sumarokov after touring the Volga valley in 1803. "Why would they not prefer profit and tranquillity to filth and disorder? Would it not be better for them to live in airy and sunny rooms rather than to suffocate in smoke, breathe foul air, and share their dwellings with cattle?"

The answer went to the heart of Russia's land-autocracy. So far as it was possible for people who were not high-ranking nobles, the Germans could own the land. They were permitted to inherit the fields they cultivated, and, with local variations decided by each settlement, they could buy and sell the ground they had improved. Only the rough pasture, woods, and waterholes were owned in common. For some critics, their productivity seemed to be simply a matter of culture—"the Germans are like willow twigs," one Russian commented dismissively, "stick them in any kind of soil and they grow immediately"—but the willingness of free Ukrainian peasants and even some Cossacks to learn German skills, and the reluctance of Russian serfs to imitate them, pointed to a different reason.

The state peasants and privately owned serfs who actually worked the soil were not only denied any incentive, they were required to pay an arbitrarily assessed poll tax from which the nobility were exempt. In his memoir of his service under Peter the Great, John Perry pointed out the consequence: "the common people have but very little heart or desire to any industry farther than necessity drives them. For if at any time by their ingenuity and endeavours they do get money, it cannot rightly be said they can call it their own; But with submission they say, All that they have belongs to God and the Czar: Nor do they dare to appear as if they had any riches, in their apparel, or in their houses, it being counted the best way to seem poor, lest there should be any notice taken of them that they have money; and they are troubled and harrass'd till they must part with it, and always be making bribes and presents to be at rest; of which there are ten thousand instances. So that everywhere as you travel through the villages in Russia, for this reason you will see the general part of the common people idle in the streets."

JUST BEHIND THE FRONTIER was where the weakness of the empire's command system became most obvious. It was easy to order the construction of a fort, the deployment of a regiment, or the movement of peasants so that the empire could spread more widely. The structure of serfdom should have made it equally simple to have the newly conquered areas colonized in "the state's interest," as Catherine the Great put it. But a quarter of the families forcibly moved to Belgorod near the Ukraine in the fall of 1647 had left by the end of December that same year, and of the 1,021 families settled in the region of Voronezh itself in 1701 by Peter the Great, only 159 were still there three years later. Where they had gone is not known, but a 1685 petition from a group of nobles awarded estates close to the frontier indicated the escape route chosen by private serfs. The runaways had gone to join the semi-nomadic Cossacks living beyond the frontier, the nobles complained, "and after spending a short time on the Cossack settlements, they return to . . . the villages of their fellows and kinsmen," where they could then pretend to be free peasants or militia farmers.

In the confusion of frontier conditions, it had always been relatively simple to enter a Cossack camp and enlist in the ranks of a local commander. Those who wanted could later return from beyond the border to claim land on the defensive line as farmers, hiding their previous identities behind a mustache and frontier manners. Blurring the distinctions still further, the predominantly male Russian frontier dwellers frequently married or concubined into native Kalmyck and Bashkir families, dressed in Cossack boots and baggy pants, ate the Tatar specialty, mutton-fat stews, and drank the Bashkir liquor of choice, *kumiss* or fermented mares' milk. And most forts also acted as a trading post for fur trappers, horse breeders, and nomadic herders, some of whose Cossack and Bashkiri relatives might be serving in the garrison.

As the frontier moved on, escaped serfs had further to go, but the process could be seen continuing with the foundation in 1734 of the great military outpost of Orenburg eight hundred miles to the east on one of the Volga's tributaries close to the Urals. Situated in the middle of the grazing territory of the Bashkir nomads, it was intended to control their movements and introduce settlers into the heart of their country.

To those trapped in the serf economy, however, the chance of freedom offered by the frontier was irresistible. During the eighteenth century, the stream of runaways and other illegal migrants grew to levels that caused serious concern to serf owners and the government in Saint Petersburg. Indeed, the scale of unauthorized migration to frontier regions became so large from 1741 to 1797, when the population of the steppes grew by approximately half a million new inhabitants, that the system of governmental direction was evidently close to breaking down. No fewer than forty-seven thousand migrants were estimated to have crossed the border into the province of Orenburg without authorization in just eight years between 1754 and 1762.

In 1773, the pressure of official and unofficial incursions on nomadic land prompted the last great frontier rebellion led by the Don Cossack, Yemelyan Pugachev, against incomers who wanted to take the "rivers, seas, steppes and lands" from their free, bearded occupants. Pugachev's rebellion ended with the capture of its leader in 1775, but at its height the entire Volga basin had risen up in revolt against tsarist rule. Once the leader was safely executed, Catherine the Great's government adopted a new policy aimed at making despotism more efficient.

In 1775, the entire empire, from Ukraine throughout the Volga basin right up to the Urals, an area increasingly known as New Russia, was reorganized so that it had the same administrative structure as Old Russia. Voronezh and Orenburg, and a score of other military fortresses, became provincial capitals with governors, administrative councils, and law courts. Teams of civilian mapmakers, tax collectors, and judges were sent out to New Russia. And a blizzard of decrees from the government in Saint Petersburg ordered governors to survey their provinces, identify empty areas, and settle peasants sent by imperial order from overcrowded parts of Russia. In 1776, one such order required two thousand "economic peasants from areas with land shortage" to move south to the Lower Volga, close to the Caspian Sea, an area whose original Cossack inhabitants had themselves just been ordered to settle still further south in the Caucasus.

Meanwhile, controls on serfs, whose runaways were the lifeblood of the Cossacks, became progressively harsher. Private owners imposed ferocious punishments on any they even suspected of plotting an escape, not merely flogging them but forcibly enlisting them in the army, or selling them into exile in the frozen north. Sixty years after Peter the Great had criticized landowners for their inhumane treatment of serfs, Catherine II gave the gentry and nobility freedom to punish them in any fashion short of murder, to exile them to Siberia and to buy and sell them individually as chattel goods. Adding to the sum of serf misery, she arbitrarily transferred more than one million peasants from state lands where they lived in relative liberty to the near slavery of private ownership.

When William Richardson, a visitor from Scotland, arrived in Moscow in the 1770s, he was appalled to discover how completely serfs were at the mercy of their owner's whims. One eighty-year-old aristocrat, Pyotr Koshkarov, was notorious for surrounding his bed with pretty serf-girls who read him stories, slept on the floor, and were whipped in the morning if they did not satisfy him. Richardson himself cited the example of a Muscovite noblewoman who amused herself by setting her attack dogs on serfs. "The peasants in Russia," he concluded, ". . . are in a state of abject slavery; and are reckoned the property of the nobles to whom they belong as much as their dogs or horses."

CATHERINE THE GREAT'S ATTEMPT to reform the serf economy through a professional bureaucracy without ties to the land marked the abandonment of the old policies of her two "Great" predecessors, Ivan and Peter. Many of her provincial governors were still drawn from the ranks of serf owners, and the new administrative class could barely function without their complicity, but a gap had opened between tsarist government and those who controlled the earth's revenues. Autocratic power would be exercised not through the award and confiscation of estates, but by the promise of higher rank and state contracts, and the threat of prison or Siberian exile. Yet, if landholders were no longer the direct servants of the tsar, it was not immediately clear what they were.

The answer came from an innovation that first arrived almost imperceptibly in 1734. The dumpy, unpredictable empress, Anna, first of three remarkably forceful women rulers, gave an estate to her favorite, Count Petr Saltykov, for his "eternal and hereditary possession," or *vechnoe i potomstvennoe vladenie*. That precedent was soon followed by other grants and sales of land under the same provisions. By the time Catherine II succeeded her murdered husband in 1762, land in New Russia was more often sold to the nobility under the *vechnoe i potomstvennoe vladenie* formula than granted to them. Land that could be inherited legally by its holder no longer belonged to the state. In 1785 Catherine went further. To cement her support among the aristocracy who had once doubted her fitness to govern, she abolished the formal requirement that they should undertake imperial service in return for holding their estates. A form of property rights had been recognized.

Some effects began to occur during her lifetime. One early consequence was the foundation of the State Loans Bank, or *Gosudarstvennyi Zaemnyi Bank*, barely a year later. So long as ownership of serfs was restricted to nobility, land itself had little value, but the bank did allow aristocrats to mortgage their serfs for up to forty rubles each, creating an instant source of capital. The first signs of a market in aristocratic estates began to develop among the nobility, and the Free Economic Society, once a fringe organization, became an influential source of advice on how to increase yields and profits. Among the topics debated by the society was whether some property rights should be extended to peasants. Naturally the proposition was defeated, but that it should even have been considered was evidence of a new way of thinking.

Nobility with rights of hereditary disposition increasingly invested in their New Russian estates, building plants to process sugar beet for the sweet-toothed west, and growing flax to make canvas for the huge merchant fleets of both Europe and the United States. And the smartest of the aristocracy, ancient families such as the Timoshevs and Manshurovs, sent representatives to buy up cheap land in Orenburg directly from the Bashkirs.

What was recognizably a form of rural capitalism began to take root in Catherine the Great's Russia. According to the iron law of property, its new owners were bound to seek the political power necessary to protect their interests, but, as the empress had made clear, the absolutist ideals of the tsars had not altered. The conflict would lead, if James Harrington, the seventeenth-century author of *Oceana*, was correct, to either the new or the old owners of the land being blown up. The remaining history of the Romanovs did indeed resound to muffled and sometimes deafening explosions: in the mordant words of one nineteenth-century Russian, "Every country has its own constitution; ours is absolutism moderated by assassination."

Chapter Nine

The Equilibrium of Land Ownership

In 1948, an American farmer, William Hinton, went to live and work in a village called Long Bow, or, in Chinese, *Zuangzuangcun*, in the Shanxi province of China, about four hundred miles southwest of Beijing. It was a momentous time. After more than two thousand years, the oldest system of land ownership in the world was about to end. The Communist Party called it "feudal" referring to the privileges enjoyed by the owners of the soil, and the obligations heaped on the peasants who worked it. But the term was inaccurate. To most Western eyes, what China enjoyed was something like private property. But its roots were more ancient, and it had evolved in a way that created lords and peasants rather than capitalist landowners.

To the Communists, locked in a civil war with the Kuomintang of Chiang Kai-shek, the difference was immaterial. Article One of the Draft Land Law published on December 27, 1947, had spelled out the party's intention in plain language: "The agrarian system of feudal and semi-feudal exploitation is abolished. The agrarian system of 'land to the tiller' is to be realized." In case any doubts remained, Article Two rubbed the message in: "Land ownership rights of all landlords are abolished."

The word used for this dramatic upheaval was *fanshen*, meaning "turn over," and Hinton chose it as the title of his account of what happened. Setting the scene for his American readers, he tried to convey the immensity of the Asian landscape, stretching for almost five thousand miles from the China Sea to the Urals, and from the frozen wastes above the Arctic Circle southward through the short-grass steppes and across the vastness of the Gobi and Taklamakan Deserts into the atmosphere-piercing ranges of Tibet and Nepal. Frost still gripped the plains after the longest day of summer had passed, and the continental earth still pumped its warmth into the naked skies when winter returned. "This ancient lag, this ever-recurring cosmic overlap of heat and cold, cold and heat, brings a violence to the climate of all North China that is incalculable in its effect," Hinton wrote. "From February to June cold winds blow from Mongolia outward toward the sea, gripping all the land from the Yangstze to the Amur [Rivers] in drought. Then, after weeks of hot and pregnant calm, the skies reverse themselves. Fierce torrential rains sweep in from the Pacific, flash floods carve up the earthen hills of [Shanxi] and [Shaanxi] [provinces in central China], swell the rivers with mud-clogged water, and inundate the flat plains bordering the sea."

Repeatedly flooded and enriched with silt, the fertile flatlands close to China's rivers, and especially those around the deltas of the Yellow, the Yangtze, and the Pearl Rivers, became the birthplace of the first Chinese dynasties in the first millennium BC. Two earlier civilizations, Egypt in the third millennium BC, and Babylon a thousand years later, had also grown up in similar riverside conditions. The concentration of people made possible by the ground's fertility, and the need to organize communal projects such as irrigation channels and tall, protective dykes, encouraged the growth of formal government. But while the Egyptian pharaohs and the Babylonian kingdom belong to history, China has survived conquest, rebellion, and more than 150 years of humiliation by the technologically superior powers of the West.

Two competing needs, to maintain harmony within its enormous population and to keep control of it, have guided the policies of China's different governments. In dull times, the two needs are in equilibrium, but when they are in conflict, the times grow interesting. Even today, with the second largest manufacturing and trading economy in history, China's politics and administration are still shaped by the same goals. And central to the values of the Communist Party, as it was to those of its predecessor, the Qing Dynasty, is the belief that ownership of the earth is the key to achieving harmony without losing control.

The Qing Dynasty had collapsed in 1911 because of its inability to keep those imperatives in balance. A generation of intermittent civil war followed, exacerbated by Japan's invasion of Manchuria and northern China, and ended in the victory of Mao Zhedong's Red Army over Kuomintang forces led by Chiang Kai-Shek in 1949. The abolition of private property rights lay at the heart of the new regime. In Mao's words, Chinese history was to be understood in terms of ownership of the earth.

"Under the bondage of feudalism [peasants] had no freedom of person," he wrote in 1938. "The landlord had the right to beat, abuse or even kill them at will, and they had no political rights whatsoever. The extreme poverty and backwardness of the peasants, resulting from ruthless landlord exploitation and oppression, is the basic reason why Chinese society remained at the same stage of socio-economic development for several thousand years." It followed, therefore, that the creation of a new society depended upon the creation of a new way of owning the earth. When the idealistic Hinton arrived in Long Bow, it was to discover that this historic change was already taking place. The oppressed condition of peasants in the village seemed in itself enough to justify the revolution.

After three thousand years of civilization, most peasants still lived in homes built of yellow mud and adobe, hardly better than the hovels of seventeenth-century Russian serfs—earthern-floored, heated by an open-fire stove, and consisting of little more than a single space, divided by partitions or curtains into three sections for sleeping, eating, and a public area where the ancestral shrine was kept. In the first house Hinton visited, he found a garlic-chewing peasant, Wang Wenping, living in a single room with no door and no glass in the windows, only torn paper. Despite a revolution in agriculture and crop production that had taken place in China a thousand years before, Wang himself still relied on an iron hoe to cultivate a plot of land less than three acres in area, growing wheat, millet, and maize. He and other villagers lived so close to the breadline that their habitual greeting was not "How are you?" but "Have you eaten?" Yet Wang was not the poorest in the village. About a third of the families had no land and survived for most of the year on a diet of millet porridge, pickled turnip, and whatever edible herbs they could find growing wild on the hillside. "To live without land," Hinton concluded, "was to live in a state of constant disaster."

The exceptions were a few peasants rich enough to employ others to help them work their tiny farms, and a ruling elite of landlords who did no work, leaving it entirely to hired labor. Even the wealthiest man in the village, Sheng Ching-ho, owned only twenty-three acres, but the surplus food and wealth his land produced paid for a home fifteen sections wide and made of expensive gray brick. More importantly, the prestige attached to the possession of so many fields also made him the village headman, tax collector, and local judge, earning enough cash from these activities to become chief banker, lending money to poorer peasants at rates of interest up to 50 percent per month.

Since the only worthwhile security the Long Bow peasants could offer were their crops and their labor, failure to repay loans locked many poorer families into long periods of dependency on moneylenders and led some to sell their children into virtual slavery to pay their debts. Their servile condition was enforced by physical beatings and flogging. There was no capital available for investment to improve the land, to expand the local inn, or to increase production of iron from the nearest foundry. In the absence of banks or any more secure repository, Sheng buried his surplus of silver dollars in the earth beneath his courtyard.

The state of Long Bow in 1948, however, illustrated a historical mystery. In the eighteenth century, the well-informed Adam Smith could confidently declare, "China has long been one of the richest, that is, one of the most fertile, best cultivated, most industrious and most populous countries in the world." Even allowing for distortions in converting traditional measures such as the *shi* (roughly two bushels) and the *mu* (about one sixth of an acre) to their English equivalents, it has been estimated that in 1800 a well-farmed wheat field in northern China might yield close to thirty bushels an acre compared to the twenty-five bushels expected from a good English field. The energy yields from China's rice paddy fields, although worked only by hand, were greater than those from English wheat fields that had been fertilized, deep-plowed, and harvested according to the best scientific practice. More than a century after the land revolution in England, the growth in productivity that it triggered had still not enabled its farmers to catch up with the yields achieved by Chinese peasants.

Yet, in the twentieth century, long after the West had escaped the threat of famine, the chronic poverty of China's peasants brought them so close to starvation that the British historian R. H. Tawney compared them to "a man standing permanently up to the neck in water so that even a ripple is enough to drown him." The gap that opened up between China and the West in those two hundred years is often referred to by historians as the "great divergence." In the West, it has been blamed variously on China's failings, in technology, in economics, in politics, even in individual psychology. However, the Communist Party still adheres to Mao's explanation that it was caused by the feudal exploitation of peasants by brutal landlords coupled with foreign domination in the nineteenth century.

* * *

In 1758, an urgent report was sent from the northwestern province of Gansu to the Qianlong emperor in Beijing. Starving peasants had rioted, assaulted state guards, and broken into the imperial granaries to steal grain. This was more than crime, it came close to rebellion, and the provincial governor advocated harsh punishment. The empeoror's severity toward his enemies was legendary. In a campaign twenty years earlier against the powerful Dzungar nomads in central Asia who controlled the Silk Route connecting China and Europe, Qianlong had not only defeated a potent threat but, in an act of genocide, virtually exterminated the Dzunghars by slaughtering close to one million of them. In nine other military campaigns against Tibetans, Taiwanese, and descendants of the Golden Horde, the Qianlong emperor had never been less than ruthless when confronted by opposition.

Yet, presented with evidence of the peasants' assault on imperial property, he responded by warning Gansu's governor not to "punish the people as thieves. If crowds consist of truly famine-stricken people who plunder for food, and if they do not have weapons, and their numbers are small, governors should be lenient according to the situation." Then he ordered the extensive imperial bureaucracy into action. Messengers were dispatched to the neighboring province of Shanxi, requiring its government-controlled granaries to send wheat to Gansu, while the southern province of Sichuan was commanded to send surplus cereals to resupply Shanxi, and Sichuan's neighbors were told to reduce their own consumption so that they too could help if called upon.

This was how imperial rule was supposed to work. The emperor cared for the people as though they were his children, and they obeyed him as though he were their father. Mutual obligation was in effect a cosmic law, connecting heaven and earth, greatest and lowest, and its purpose was the promotion of social harmony. The most compelling description of this unifying principle had been given by the sixth century BC ethical master K'ong, better known in the West as Confucius, the Latin name given him by the Jesuits. It was not by chance that in Confucian texts the character representing "harmony" was made up of two parts, "grain" and "mouth"—without an adequate supply of food, harmony was impossible. Indeed the very mandate from heaven, the moral authority that gave an emperor sovereignty over his subjects, depended on his ability to preserve harmony. As generations of Confucian scholars pointed out, hunger was so destructive of harmony that its existence suggested the emperor had lost the trust of heaven. When the failure of the monsoon devastated food supplies in 1744, Qianlong himself had not only prayed for rain but publicly fasted in order to regain "the grace of Heaven" and restore the harmony that had been lost.

The need for maintaining harmony was inculcated among the mighty army of scholar-bureaucrats who administered China's vast landmass and its millions of inhabitants. Their ethos was based squarely on *The Analects of Confucius*. At each stage of their careers, they had to demonstrate their mastery of Confucian teaching in order to pass the demanding examinations required of every office-holder. The lowest county administrators, numbering more than one hundred thousand in the sixteenth century, needed only to memorize the major texts for their *sheng-yuan* degree, but increasingly sophisticated interpretation was required through the next eight higher levels ending with the palace exam, the *jinshi*, that guaranteed the highest offices in the imperial service to successful candidates. This topmost elite of mandarins rarely numbered more than four thousand.

Confucian principles placed the use of land at the heart of society's structure. Although the highest social class was reserved for scholars (who were also government officials), they almost invariably came from landowning families, and immediately below them came food-producing farmers, leaving craftsmen and merchants to fill the two lowest ranks. During most of the Ming Dynasty, the last native Chinese rulers who held power from 1368 to 1644, the structure of society and government was provided by that inherited hierarchy.

In the 1480s, however, a wave of inflation caused by uncontrolled printing of paper money began to undermine the existing order. The incomes of old-established families dependent on fixed rentals were progressively reduced, and at the same time the despised merchant class began to benefit from a rapidly increasing trade as European vessels found new routes to the east. Silver originally mined in Bolivia and shipped to Cadiz was exchanged by Portuguese and later Dutch shippers for Chinese silk and porcelain. In modern Indonesia and along the coasts of the China Sea, the massive purchases of spices by the newcomers kick-started a general trade within the Far East that enriched the merchants of Canton and Shanghai still further. In the last century of the Ming dynasty, up to 1644, almost seventy-five hundred tons of silver flowed into China, not only from Europe but from the rising trade economy of Japan.

The surge of precious metal completed the destruction of the old order, with inflation tripling once more in the second half of the sixteenth century. The standby form of cash, strings of copper coins, was valued in terms of the silver tael, roughly equivalent in weight and value to a silver dollar. Taxes, once assessed in *shih*, the weight of cereals, now had to be paid in silver. No class had better access to this new currency than merchants, who upset the higher echelons of society with a restless ambition at odds with the unflappable calm of the mandarin class. "People pursue what is profitable to them," complained the sixteenth-century scholar Zhang Han, "and with profit in mind they will go up against disaster [i.e., take risks]. They gallop in pursuit of it day and night, never satisfied with what they have, though it wears down their spirits and exhausts them physically."

In a social upheaval as dramatic as the private property revolution in England, Chinese merchants, flush with silver, began to buy land, once the preserve of the aristocracy. It was an investment, but the return was not measured in cash. British officials examining property documents in nineteenth-century Hong Kong, formerly part of Guangzhou Province, concluded from records going back to the sixteenth century that "Land according to Chinese tenure is held as freehold." In other words, China had the potential to be a private property economy. There was a crucial difference from Anglo-Saxon property, however.

Although owned outright, the land was not an exclusive, individualized possession, as recognized by English common law, but a family asset that existed to sustain the household. Since the owner also faced a direct legal obligation to pay the land tax that provided two thirds of the imperial revenues, it might seem surprising that anyone should have wanted to invest in land. Yet, during the sixteenth century, under the Ming Dynasty, government officials and city merchants in China began to behave like their English counterparts and put their savings into owning the earth.

What motivated them was the Confucian ethos that placed family loyalties at the center of private and public conduct. No more effective means of meeting family obligations existed than owning land, the basic source of sustenance where children, cousins, and distant kindred could all work and feed themselves. When the land passed to the next generation, the same values required it to be divided equally among the male children. Should it have to be sold, the new owners were supposed to come from within the wider clan or the immediate community, whose members were expected to provide shelter and employment for the family. Although not directly stated as legal requirements, these moral obligations had the force of civil law, and were interpreted as such by the Confucian-trained officials who adjudicated in cases of dispute. In other words, ownership of land came burdened with duties. It was the reverse of the English belief that attached rights to property.

Nevertheless, in Confucian terms, land proved to be a sound investment for its wave of new owners. Nationally, the inferior status of merchants merged into the superior class of landowners, and within each clan the prestige of the owner soared, and his dependents did well. In about 1600, a landless laborer employed on a clan farm in the rich Yangtze delta earned almost 20 percent more than his equivalent in England, and up to twice as much as farm workers in Mediterranean parts of Europe. A peasant family in the same fertile area, owning an average-sized farm of fifteen *mu* (roughly 2.5 acres) could make as much as the tenant farmers of a hundred acres in Essex. Adding in the earnings made by their wives from cotton spinning and silk weaving, the rural population along the rivers and coasts of China made a better living in 1600 than any other in the world, with the possible exception of the newly liberated peasants in the Ganges valley of Mogul-ruled India. Food production in coastal regions increased, and with it came a rapid growth in the population, from about fifty million in 1500 to one hundred million by the mid-seventeenth century.

The exploding population growth placed enormous strain on both the framework of government and the supply of land. In the country's vulnerable northern and eastern provinces, there was a marked incidence of famine, undermining the Ming Dynasty's mandate of heaven. At the same time, existing landowners found their dominance of China's bureaucracy challenged by the children of rich merchants who began to study for and pass in large numbers the exams that qualified them to hold official positions. To the anguish of conservatives, social mobility began to overwhelm the old order, and writers like the sixteenth-century essayist Kuei Yu-kuang lamented the vulgarization of society that occurred when the traditional "distinctions between scholars, peasants, and merchants became blurred."

The merchants' sudden interest in government appears to have been sparked by the sort of motive that impelled the subjects of King Henry VIII to seek representation in the House of Commons—as new landowners they needed political power to safeguard their interests. In China, such power was represented by the gigantic bureaucratic system that raised taxes and enforced the laws and the emperor's instructions.

Worse still for traditional Confucianists, even their foundation belief that mastery of the ancient texts was the ultimate source of knowledge came under challenge. The most influential exponent of Confucian studies in the sixteenth century, Wang Yangming, argued that book-learning was not enough: true wisdom emerged from the experience of individual action. The new teaching viewed merit as individual, almost democratic, not a matter of hierarchy. "There is the sage in everyone," wrote Wang. "Only one who has not enough self-confidence buries his own chance." Self-confidence was not a quality lacking in the upstart gentry.

To protect their own interests, the old Ming aristocracy tried to restrict the number of passes in official exams to a fixed quota and refined to a fiendish level the requirements of the "eight-legged essay" that was mandatory for higher-grade mandarins. But resistance cracked in the late sixteenth century when provincial governors on the northern frontier, desperate for cereals to feed their troops, began offering degrees for sale in return for food. Thousands of wealthy merchants-turned-landowners, especially from further south around the Yangtze delta, took advantage of the opportunity and shipped rice and wheat north in exchange for a *sheng-yuan* qualification and the chance to put a clever child in charge of local administration. Once a family had a foot on the ladder, it became easier to progress further. In the southern province of Fukien, just 3 percent of the top provincial officials came from the merchant class at the start of the sixteenth century, but almost a quarter by the end.

As in England, increasing control of the bureaucracy allowed the upstart gentry to frustrate the government's desire to impose new taxes. In wealthy Anhui Province, close to the Yangtze delta, for example, the once-powerful bureaucrat Yao Wen-jan, a descendant of merchants, was notorious for spending his retirement in the mid-seventeenth century "interfering in matters of local administration" and blocking imperial attempts to conduct a new land survey of the province in order to increase the taxes and labor services payable by its merchant landowners. During the long Ming Dynasty, when the population had grown by as much as a quarter, and the area of cultivated land by almost one third, the revenue from the land tax remained what it had been in 1385.

In their attempt to maintain control over an increasingly turbulent empire, the Ming emperors were forced to find alternative levers of power. In the sixteenth century, the palace eunuchs who ran the imperial household were given a wider role. Armed with sweeping executive powers, including that of capital punishment, eunuchs were sent into the countryside to supervise provincial officials, raise new taxes, and organize imperial projects such as silk and salt production. In effect, a parallel government had come into existence.

Despite the obvious differences in culture and scale, the financial battle that developed between the Ming Dynasty and its landowners shared one fundamental consequence with the confrontation between king and property owners in England. Step by step, a dispute over taxation drove the children of China's new gentry to challenge the emperor as the ultimate sovereign power. Provincial hostility developed into civil war during the 1620s and 1630s, with a number of provinces asserting their complete independence from the Ming government in Beijing. Amid the turmoil, the province of Jianxi in the Yangtze delta, later the site of the first area of Communist rule, offered a glimpse of how things might have developed.

It was there that Wang Yangming's interpretation of Confucianism had taken deepest root. The T'ai-chou school that embodied his optimistic, self-assertive teaching attracted not just middle-class landowners and merchants, but craftsmen such as potters, brick burners, and stone-masons, as well as thousands of peasants. When they went to war, they fought both for independence and for a recognizably democratic agenda. The banners of the poorest of them were torn cotton pants, their weapons, sharpened hoes, and they called themselves the "Levelling Kings." Their proclamations demanded the "levelling [of] the distinction between masters and serfs, titled and mean, rich and poor." Two years before Richard Overton fired his arrow into the bowels of the House of Lords, a band of Levelling Kings broke into the home of an important official and ordered "the master to kneel, [saying] 'We are all of us equally men. What right had you to call us serfs.' "

Predictably, the delta landowners were as outraged by this presumptuous assertion as Cromwell and Ireton were at Putney. But at the end of the Ming Dynasty something like the language of rights was in the air, and the landowners themselves were seeking political power to protect their property. Instead of political reform, however, the civil war paved the way for a foreign coup d'état that reimposed the old system more vigorously than before.

Denuded of resources and unable to pay or feed his troops—desertion reduced some units to just 10 percent of their original strength—the last Ming emperor lost control of the army. In 1644 invaders from Manchuria seized control of an almost undefended Beijing. The mutiny that might have changed everything was not defeated, merely frozen.

* * *

The regime installed by the Manchu invaders was unmistakably foreign, a fact underlined by an early imperial edict requiring all native Han Chinese men to shave their scalps and grow a pigtail, and by the maintenance of a purely Manchu military force of eight regiments of "bannermen." Manchu control, however, had to be balanced by Han Chinese harmony, and for that reason the new Qing Dynasty, as it was known, retained not just the culture and structure of the Ming government, but even the people who operated it. Thus in the mid-eighteenth century, most of the Qianlong emperor's senior Chinese mandarins in Beijing, as well as the leading officials in the rich Yangtze delta provinces such as Anhui, belonged to the families of the sixteenth-century upstart merchants.

To restrict the power of these increasingly aristocratic, provincial officials, the Qing Dynasty also re-created their predecessors' parallel administration. In its new form, the imperial staff was made up of Manchus rather than eunuchs, but they performed the same supervisory function and were armed with the same summary powers. Once established, however, the dynasty produced in succession three rulers of outstanding talent and energy, the Kangxi, Yongzhen, and Qianlong emperors, whose reigns lasted from 1661 to 1796. Their military and administrative genius extended the empire's boundaries to Taiwan, Tibet, Xingjiang, and Mongolia, creating the frontiers of modern China. The last of these mighty emperors was possibly the greatest in China's long history.

The artists who painted the Qianlong emperor found it easy to depict the variety of his interests. Sometimes he appeared as a warrior in armor, once as an incarnation of the Buddha, often as a scholar with a tasseled hat, and, most frequently, in the golden robes of an emperor. Over time their portraits showed his stern face becoming creased by age, and his Manchu mustache growing gray, but none of them succeeded in capturing the blazing energy that drove the engine of the empire with unremitting intensity for more than sixty years.

Most of the imperial city in Beijing is his work, a 180-acre-sized Chinese box of palaces within palaces, audience halls opening into pavilions that sit within parade-ground courtyards. But so too are the forty-two thousand poems he wrote, the mountainous encylopedias, dictionaries, and records of the language he commissioned, and the legendary art collection he amassed of almost twenty thousand paintings and seventy thousand pieces of porcelain and jade. Year after year, he toured his enormous country, making more than 150 progresses to the semitropical south, the prairie east, and mountainous north, accompanied by courtiers, concubines, administrators, and astronomers, drawing maps, examining accounts, measuring the position of stars in the sky. No detail escaped him.

It was a characteristic inherited from his grandfather, the Kangxi emperor who personally supervised every aspect of the empire's organization, once even sending an urgent message during a brief absence from Beijing to tell his son that "it should be about the season for the arrival of the songbirds in the capital, please let me know if you have seen them." His terrified son sent for some birders, and with their help was able to reply that he had been fortunate enough to see two songbirds, but, as he confessed, the command had caused him to "break out in a sweat all over his body."

In 1793, soon after the Qianlong emperor's eighty-third birthday, a delegation arrived in the magnificence of the imperial palace from an inconsequential island "cut off from the world by intervening wastes of sea," as the emperor's advisors put it. Its leader, Lord George Macartney, presented the emperor with gifts from King George III, intricately engineered astronomical instruments including a planetarium that mimicked the workings of the solar system. Brusquely, the emperor dismissed as unimportant both the delegation and the gifts. "I have but one aim in view," Qianlong wrote to the British king, "namely, to maintain a perfect governance and to fulfill the duties of the state . . . I set no value on objects strange or ingenious, and have no use for your country's manufactures."

To many modern historians, this failure to realize the significance of manufacturing marks the crucial element that would cripple China's standing as a world power. Less than half a century later, Britain, numerically one of the smallest of Europe's powers with a population of eighteen million, attacked China in what became known as the First Opium War. The superiority of British technology was made brutally apparent in 1841 when its steam-driven, iron-hulled ship, the *Nemesis*, powered upstream against wind and current past the imperial navy's wooden sailing junks and bombarded to rubble the forts protecting Canton, today's Guangzhou. Yet industrial incompetence does not by itself explain the mighty empire's failure to mount any worthwhile defense against this new power.

To Macartney, the British envoy, China's weakness went much deeper, and was obvious even under the Qianlong emperor's rule. The system of government was so divided it could only be made to work by a ruler of exceptional talent. "The Empire of China is an old, crazy, first rate man-of-war [a battleship carrying one hundred cannon]," he reported, "which a fortunate succession of able and vigilant officers has contrived to keep afloat for these one hundred and fifty years past, and to overawe their neighbors merely by her bulk and appearance, but whenever an insufficient man happens to have the command upon deck, adieu to the discipline and safety of the ship."

THE THREAT OF MUTINY that Macartney identified came from the Han Chinese scholar-bureaucrats and landlords who ran the provincial administration. Their jealousy of the Manchu officials who formed the parallel government provided a central theme in Cao Xuequin's classic bestselling novel of the Qianlong era, *A Dream of Red Mansions*. Raised as a Manchu, Cao's own grandfather had been directly appointed by the Kangxi emperor to the imperial post of commissioner of textiles in the southern city of Nanjing, located on the Yangtze delta in Jiangxi Province, next door to Anhui. Since the commissioner was in charge of the imperial silk factories and supervised cotton production in the region, the Cao family had become exceptionally wealthy by the early 1700s. But they were also expected to report directly to Beijing on the administration of the provincial aristocracy.

The novel is about the fortunes of just such a family, and it begins with their downfall, losers in a power struggle with local magnates. A messenger from Beijing counsels them, too late, to consult an imaginary advice book for imperial officials, known as *The Mandarin's Life-Preserver*, which "lists all the richest, most influential people in the area. There is one for every province. They list those families which are so powerful that if you were ever to run up against one of them unknowingly, not only your job, but perhaps even your life might be in danger. That's why they're called 'life-preservers.'"

Cao knew what he was writing about because that was the fate that befell his own family when confronted by four of Jiangxi's grandee families. Although it gave rise to one of the world's most enchanting, fantastical novels, the fall of the Cao family has a wider significance as an illustration of the challenge faced by imperial officials: how could control be reconciled with the preservation of harmony? Officials came and went, but landowners were there for generations. In the absence of the emperor's active support, the most powerful imperial officials frequently preferred to preserve harmony by turning a blind eye to the power of the provincial administrators. Some actively connived at the evasion of imperial supervision, but the majority were content simply to enforce existing levels of taxation, ignoring any new sources of income or wealth.

The difficulty that even the most energetic emperor faced in maintaining control was inadvertently revealed by the Qianlong emperor himself. At the height of his power in 1774, he boasted that during his reign imperial revenues had more than doubled, from thirty-four million silver taels to seventy-eight million. This may sound impressive, but was equivalent to just twenty-six million pounds raised from a population of 275 million. In that year, however, Britain's government raised seven million pounds in property and personal taxes from a population of 6.8 million. Either each British taxpayer was paying ten times as much as his Chinese equivalent in land tax and duties on expenditure, or the great bulk of Chinese taxes and levies never reached Beijing.

This was the weak link in the chain of government that Macartney had referred to. Much of Chinese territory was owned by the emperor and his officials, and more was administered by cities and their guilds, but the largest single block was owned by Cao's nemesis, the provincial landlords. Unlike the political cohesion that developed in other private property societies as magnates sought influence at the center, Chinese property owners only needed control of provincial government to protect their clan-based interests.

In the cold, cereal-growing north, property rights were usually vested in the most senior male in the extended family, while the junior and more distantly related members of the clan who worked the soil paid in duties and service. In the more productive south, where cotton and rice could be grown, land tended to be rented for profit, but was administered by a ruling elite from within the clan, and farms were largely tenanted by kin rather than strangers. Where disputes could not be settled internally, the codified rules of behavior that governed family obligations were arbitrated by local government officials, and a prudent landowner ensured that such people belonged to his immediate family.

This kinship-based network of villages and rural communities provided the base of the pyramid of government. Their produce served the estimated forty-five thousand market towns where taxes were levied and rents were paid. The market towns were in turn answerable to the county towns, home to the lowest level of provincial administrators, whose edicts were enforced by landowners backed by a local militia. Above them stood the provincial capitals where imperial and regional government competed ceaselessly for control of tax assessment, land registration, and the collection of revenues.

There could be little doubt about the winners in this competition. The opulence of the few surviving mansions built by eighteenth- and early nineteenth-century grandees in provincial cities such as Nanjing testifies to their wealth. Its foundation was laid during the century of agricultural improvement that followed the influx of money-minded merchant landowners. Farmers learned to increase yields by enriching the soil not just with manure but organic fertilizers made from crushed soybeans or oilseed. And in the eighteenth century, Qianlong's officials in the waterlogged Jianghan plain between the Yangtze and Han Rivers reported with admiration how the peasants adjusted their planting to flood conditions, experimenting with early or late-growing rice crops to avoid seasonal flooding, and, when catastrophe threatened, either put in sorghum that resisted immersion before the waters rose, or, the moment they began to recede, "quickly replanted buckwheat, beans, and vegetables. [In this way they] could still look forward to a harvest and avoid a famine."

The innovative methods of Chinese farmers led to an extraordinary growth of about 40 percent in cereal yields in the seventeenth and eighteenth centuries. With the increase of food came a second great explosion in the population, which tripled from one hundred million in 1650 to three hundred million by 1800. The pressure on land led to massive increase in the area taken under cultivation. Qianlong's boasted increase in tax revenues is evidence of his relative success in registering this new land for taxation. But between 1753 and 1910, it is estimated that the area of cultivated land in China grew by a further 30 percent, yet annual revenues barely rose during the period, and in 1890 still amounted to less than one hundred million taels, about 2 percent of GNP.

In the 1890s, when British colonial authorities in Hong Kong attempted to make a record of Han Chinese landholdings in Kowloon, formerly part of Guangdong Province, they found that much of the new land brought into cultivation since the sixteenth century had never been registered for taxation. Instead, when villagers began farming wasteland, they had put their new property under the protection of the head of the dominant clan or family group in the area. "The greater part of the land claimed by clans was never registered," British officials reported, "and, as a rule, it appears that no land tax was ever paid on this land to the Government." The farmers did pay an annual levy on their unregistered property, but, as the officials put it, to local "taxlords" rather than to the government. With just twenty thousand imperial administrators to supervise an army of provincial officials that had grown to more than 1.25 million in the nineteenth century, there was little risk of detection by Beijing.

Unable to exercise control over revenues from the land, the Qing Dynasty never possessed the resources to develop the major industrial projects of the nineteenth century—steel foundries and, above all, railway construction—or to finance the steam-driven navies, electric communications, and rifled artillery that Britain, the United States, and Japan, after the Meijis revolution of 1868, could boast. The frailty of the Qing government was underlined by the Taiping rebellion that broke out in 1853 and cost the lives of perhaps twenty-five million people before it was at last put down with foreign help in 1864.

Britain's success in opening up China to international trade, including the importation of opium, following the Opium War in 1842, encouraged other technologically advanced nations to impose their own will on the antiquated behemoth. The United States, France, Russia, Japan, and eventually Germany all carved out trading privileges by force and extracted financial indemnities from the Chinese government for its opposition. By the start of the twentieth century, these charges amounted to 40 percent of the government's vestigial revenues. "It is not China that is falling to pieces," declared one British official, "it is the [international] powers that are pulling her to pieces."

In effect, the Qing Dynasty had hijacked the land revolution, extinguishing any possibility that individual landowners might have created rural capital in their property. Yet even at its height, it could never exert enough dominance to establish its own rights over the land. And as the nineteenth-century emperors lost power to those who owned the earth, they were increasingly deprived of the income that a government needed to equip itself for the modern industrial age.

With little large-scale employment available in factories or cities, the mass of China's growing population—above four hundred million by the early twentieth century—was condemned to remain in the countryside. The pressure of numbers remorselessly depressed wages—a laborer's earnings that in 1600 would have supported four people barely fed two in 1750, and scarcely met his own needs in 1910—and created intense competition for land. Increasingly, landlords made their money from the bribes, rents, loans, duties, taxes, and labor dues they extracted from the people, often their own relatives, who tilled the soil. Their unrelenting efforts to squeeze more funds from peasants gave rise to a bitter rural saying, "A peasant always hangs himself in his landlord's doorway."

As the population grew and property was divided among sons, the average size of a farm shrank from just under three acres to less than one acre. In southern Guangdong, one tract of land that had supported a single wealthy family in the sixteenth century was split between more than seven hundred households by the end of the nineteenth century. For the landlords, the chief value of the land had come to lie in the number of people it would support rather than the return on the crops it produced. Profit-making farmers had become survivalist peasants.

Fundamentally, Mao's diagnosis of China's history was correct: the pattern of land ownership, exacerbated by foreign intervention, had condemned the Chinese to misery. But the form of communal ownership invented by the Cultural Revolution would prove just as effective in producing the same result.

Section Three

THE SOCIETY THAT PRIVATE PROPERTY CREATED

Chapter Ten

Land Becomes Mind

Compared to the electrifying pace with which Russia's serf ownership and China's Confucian family possession expanded in the course of the eighteenth century, the spread of private property was pedestrian. The Romanovs acquired perhaps one million square miles during that time, and the Qing Dynasty almost 1.5 million square miles, or, if the questionable claim to Tibet is accepted, 2.3 million square miles. In the same period, settlers who claimed land under common law took over fewer than two hundred square miles in North America, the Caribbean and, Bengal, or 450,000 square miles if all of the empty *taiga* of Quebec is included. Judged simply in terms of raw geography, private property could not compete with its two chief rivals.

Not until the nineteenth century would private ownership of land reveal a power that outweighed anything contained in the armies of either the Qing or Romanov Empires. Yet as early as the eighteenth century, there were clues to suggest how far a "natural" right to singular, exclusive possession might reach. The capacity of the common law to enclose more than the earth for an individual owner was made clear by its claim to create a quite new form of property in the amorphous realms of ideas.

In 1751, Walter Baker, a self-styled "professor of physic" in London who made a living from selling medicines, complained to the Privy Council that Dr. Robert James was marketing a patented powder guaranteed to cure fevers, catarrhs, coughs, and other respiratory maladies. The patent was invalid, Baker alleged, because the powder was no more than a copy of Baron Schwanberg's Universal Powder for Fevers whose recipe he,

Baker, had bought from the baron himself. Dr. James was a reputable chemist, and when his scientific colleagues testified to the originality of his fever powder, the Privy Council duly dismissed the complaint. That should have ended the matter. Patents were a royal privilege, supervised on the monarch's behalf by the Privy Council, and there was no appeal from a royal decision. But with terrier-like obstinacy, Baker refused to let go, and the entire body of modern patent law depends upon his tenacity.

He went to court accusing Dr. James of perjury, and called the secretary of the Privy Council as a witness. Affronted by his temerity, the council loftily declined to let its secretary attend. But the refusal awoke the big beasts of the law, and in particular, England's senior judge, Lord Chief Justice Mansfield. After a detailed look at Dr. James's specification of his powder—the ingredients had been left intentionally vague to prevent the recipe being copied—Mansfield decided privately that the patent should not have been given.

Until then, it had been accepted not just in Britain but throughout Europe that a patent could only be created by the crown. Giving a monopoly for a period of years to the inventor of a useful product or process served as a reward and an encouragement to others, but it necessarily prevented anyone else from using the invention to earn a living. That infringed the right to work, a right so fundamental that many jurists put it equal to life and liberty in importance. Both Sir Edward Coke, the preeminent spokesman for English common law, and the German jurist Samuel Pufendorf, chief exponent of a European theory of natural law, agreed that the word for monopolies was "odious." In Pufendorf's view, they offended "against the Law of Humanity" and in Coke's "against the liberty and freedom of the subject and the law of the land."

In 1623, the English Parliament had attempted to set bounds to the odious practice by passing the Statute of Monopolies. The statute emphasized the contractual nature of patents by limiting the length of time they could run, restricting them to new and useful inventions, and requiring a detailed description of the new idea so that society could benefit from it after the patent expired. Parliament's bid to seize control from the king failed, and the royal prerogative continued to be exercised through the Privy Council. Following Baker's appeal, however, Mansfield quickly persuaded the council that it was time the law assumed responsibility, and in 1753, the council formally relinquished the power of issuing and enforcing patents to the courts.

Through his own judgments in patent cases, Mansfield made it plain that he expected the courts to apply to a patent the sort of criteria that the crown ought to have applied under the Statute of Monopolies: the applicant for a patent had to show the invention to be new and useful and provide a specification so detailed that it would, in Mansfield's words, "teach an artist, when your [the applicant's] term is out, to make it—and to make it as well as you by your directions: for then at the end of the term [fourteen years], the public have the benefit of it."

Very clearly, Mansfield understood the patent to be a contract, offering a private monopoly now in return for the public use later. That was certainly how patents were regarded in France. The Marquis de Condorcet, a friend of Thomas Jefferson and a progressive thinker steeped in Locke's writing, declared roundly "there is no connection between ownership of an invention and that of a field which can only be cultivated by one person." A patent was a social arrangement created by society for its own good, and thus, "It is not a true right, it's a privilege." Once an invention was approved by the Académie des Sciences as beneficial to society, as in the case of the flying shuttle invented by the Englishman John Kaye, a cash prize and a limited monopoly or *privilège exclusif* would be awarded in exchange for training others to manufacture it. This system of state-sponsored innovation was clear cut and successful. In 1747, the French paid Kaye for his invention and awarded him a salary to teach its use to Normandy woollen weavers, while allowing him to retain for a short time a monopoly on its construction. A similar principle was applied to the introduction of silk weaving, and before the end of the century French textile production exceeded Britain's. Overall, the improvement in France's industrial capacity enabled it to mass-produce the artillery, uniforms, and weaponry needed to equip Napoleon's gigantic armies. Yet it was not in France that the Industrial Revolution began.

In the years immediately following Walter Baker's momentous challenge, England experienced a rush to patent technical inventions and improvements of every kind with almost as many patents being issued in the 1760s alone as in all five previous decades before. It marked the start of what became known as the Age of Inventions. Between 1750 and 1800, four hundred patents were approved and put into practice, eight times as many as in the first half of the century.

At first glance it is difficult to see why. Each inventor had to pay up to £350 for his patent, a sum beyond the means of all but the well-to-do, only to discover that it offered flimsy protection against infringements.

Attempts to sue competitors for infringing patents quickly revealed that the majority of judges remained hostile to monopolies not obviously for the public good. Indeed, without a watertight specification as backing, they were liable to strike down the original patent altogether rather than support its holder.

Their hostility was shared by Parliament when it passed the 1710 copyright law, the first to guarantee authors ownership in the books they had written. Terming it "an Act for the Encouragement of Learning," the lawmakers argued a monopoly was justified only because it would encourage "learned men to compose and write useful books," and in a patents case in 1769, Justice Joseph Yates applied the same reasoning, that public good was the payoff for private privilege, to inventions: "The whole claim that an *author* can *really* make, is on the public benevolence, by way of encouragement; but not as an absolute coercive right. His case is exactly similar to that of an inventor of a new mechanical machine."

On the other side of the Atlantic, the Constitution of the United States would make a similar contractual obligation the basis for the establishment of copyright and patent laws "to promote the Progress of Science and useful Arts, by securing for limited Times to Authors and Inventors the exclusive Right to their respective Writings and Discoveries." To ensure that the bargain of public usefulness was kept, American inventors were required to deposit a working model of their inventions before being issued with a patent.

This unfriendly atmosphere left inventors exposed to attack. The Reverend Edmund Cartwright shared the fate of many other inventors when he saw his 1790 patent for a wool-combing machine instantly stolen by textile operators, who tweaked it slightly so that they could escape being sued. Richard Arkwright, who in 1775 built and patented a water-powered frame for carding cotton and spinning it into long, tough thread, spent an estimated £2,200 in four years in unsuccessful attempts to defend his patent. Despite winning some cases, John Kaye found that every woollen manufacturer who pirated his patented flying shuttle had banded together to fight his claims for compensation, until the expense forced him to give up. Even James Watt, the canniest of patent holders, worried constantly about whether the risk of allowing competitors to build variants of his improved steam engine, outweighed the danger, if he went to court, of the judge removing his numerous patents altogether because of their inadequate specifications. "We had better bear with some inconvenience than lose all [in a lawsuit]," he told his partner, Matthew Boulton, "yet if we do not vindicate our rights we run a risk of losing all that way."

As a result, many inventors, including Samuel Crompton, who improved Arkwright's invention with his own machine or "mule" to make finer thread, did not bother to patent their innovations. By every rational standard, the French system of government direction and the American insistence on a working model to support patent applications were better ways of encouraging useful inventions.

Yet the messiness of the British process had one positive effect. The rampant piracy and furious lawsuits encouraged by British patent law helped spread information about new ideas. Every infringement generated paperwork that became available in court concerning the specification and potential applications. Reports of such cases and of the parliamentary debates they sometimes triggered were carried by the *Annual Register*, as well as by more practical periodicals such as *The Universal Magazine of Knowledge and Pleasure*, and even by general interest publications like *The Gentleman's Magazine*, whose publisher, Edmund Cave, took so close an interest in inventions that he bought the license to a water-powered spinning machine. News of discoveries that elsewhere might have been confined to specialists were available to anyone who was able to read.

Nevertheless, what chiefly drove the spread of British inventions was the influence of land ownership. Whatever Mansfield might argue, the sort of people who were rich enough to afford a patent fee believed that a patent conferred some form of exclusive property. Locke's thesis, that an individual established outright ownership of a parcel of ground by improving it, applied still more strongly to an invention that grew out of an individual's mental and manual labor. Lawyers, long accustomed to pleading common law cases, repeatedly used this reasoning to claim for their clients a natural right to ownership of their invention that bypassed any need to prove some social benefit. And to a layman like Adam Smith, it seemed obvious that "the property one has in a book he has written or a machine he has invented, which continues by patent in this country for fourteen years, is actually a *real right*."

In vain, Mansfield's senior colleagues on the bench objected that an idea could not be equated with land because it lacked "corporeal substance" and so was not containable within a boundary. Fighting their way through the battleground of competing claims to ownership of a technical innovation, ordinary common law judges increasingly made it plain that they no longer regarded the specification of the invention to be a contribution to the public good, but as the very boundary that surrounded the inventor's property. The law's only role was to adjudicate between rival assertions of ownership.

This interpretation made it as imperative for an eighteenth-century inventor to register his claim to possession as it was for a sixteenth-century encloser. No one with a significant idea, such as James Hargreaves with his bank of mechanically operated spinning-wheels, his "spinning jenny," could afford not to seek a patent. However fragile its protection, it provided legal evidence of a natural right to what both Boulton and Watt routinely called "our property." Without a patent, that natural right might pass to anyone who claimed it. With it, the property might become more profitable than land, and allow its owner, as Watt would show, to extend its brief life much longer than fourteen years.

The shift from contractual ownership of an idea to outright intellectual property became apparent in 1785 when Arkwright at last won a case of infringement against his patent. "Nothing could be more essentially mischievous," the judge, Lord Loughborough, declared in his summing up, "than that questions of property between A and B should ever be permitted to be decided upon considerations of public convenience or expediency." As late as 1806, an unsuccessful plea was made in court to regard a patent "not in the light of monopoly . . . but as a bargain with the public," but the argument no longer carried any weight. By the start of the nineteenth century, it was plain to lawyers and inventors, and even to pirates, that an idea detached from the uncharted wasteland of the mind belonged to the encloser, at least for a limited time, by the same natural right that made a plot of land the property of the improver. James Watt and Matthew Boulton's partnership in the Soho Works in Birmingham was built on that insubstantial concept. What they sold for the most part was the blueprint for a steam engine, not the machine itself, and the price was simply a portion of the savings that it produced for its new owner.

THE CREATION of this new kind of property was essential in determining the pattern of industrialization that began to transform the country during the eighteenth century. When it came later to other countries, industrialism was often imposed by government direction, as in Germany, or developed by bureaucratic intervention, as in France. But when it first appeared in Britain, the Industrial Revolution grew from the grassroots, driven by the ambitions of innumerable individuals who believed that by their own efforts they could own both the hardware of machinery and the software of ideas, and make money from them.

In 1701, Jethro Tull, a lawyer-turned-farmer and, evidently, an amateur musician, devised a machine for planting seed in rows based, as he explained, "upon a groove, tongue, and spring in the soundboard of the organ. With these a little altered and some parts of two other instruments, as foreign to the field as the organ is, added to them, I composed my machine." His drill, as he called it, allowed him to grow his crop in rows, and, with the use of a new horse-drawn plow to break down weeds between the rows, he was able to produce wheat profitably on the shallow, chalky soil of his farm, misleadingly called Prosperous, where every farmer before him had "either gone broke or quitted it before the end of his term." Although the laborers on his farm hated a machine that seemed to threaten their employment, and smashed up at least one early model, other landowners, keen to squeeze a better return from their investments, flocked to Prosperous to observe Tull's experiment.

The seed drill transformed farming—but not until the very end of the eighteenth century. During the intervening seventy years, lack of skill and lack of funds prevented the development of robust models of Tull's complicated device. When persistent farmers finally evolved a design tough enough for the job, they discovered that Tull had been right: sowing the seed in rows, rather than scattering them broadcast, and plowing the weeds in between, increased wheat yields by almost 25 percent, or four to five hushels per acre.

Tull's invention remains famous as the first of a succession of eighteenth-century innovations in crop and livestock production that were sometimes dubbed the "Agricultural Revolution." In reality, many supposed novelties, such as the selective breeding of livestock, four-year crop rotation, and the addition of lime or marl to increase wheat yields, had already been introduced in the sixteenth century. Mechanical developments like the horse-powered threshing machine that flailed and winnowed the ear from the wheat, suffered the same long development gap as the drill, with the first patent being issued in 1756, but no widespread use until the early nineteenth century.

This slow take-up of agricultural innovations and the need to return to old discoveries contradicts the conventional story that increased productivity on the land allowed the growth of an urban and industrial population, and thus provided the labor for the manufacturing revolution. In fact, agriculture, which had been the powerhouse of the British economy for almost two centuries, virtually ceased to expand during the eighteenth century. The reasons help to explain why industrial innovation was so eagerly embraced in Britain.

An explosive growth in the population, from about seven million inhabitants in 1700 to more than eleven million by the end of the century, should have pushed up agricultural prices and profits as the demand for food increased. Instead, prices for wheat and other cereals barely rose until the 1780s. Cheap food meant that Daniel Defoe did not exaggerate in 1726 when he claimed that "The working manufacturing people of England eat the fat, and drink the sweet, live better, and fare better, than the working poor of any other nation in Europe." Much of the demand was in fact met by imports of wheat from northern France, and some from an increase in the acreage worked by British farmers. But in the first seventy years of the century, the rising productivity of farming that had doubled wheat yields since the early 16th century began to flatten and almost level off.

By rights the price of land should have fallen, but instead it increased from about five pounds an acre for enclosed land in the early 1700s to more than thirty pounds in the 1760s. In other words, the value of the land was no longer dictated by its yield of crops and animals. What counted were the laws of supply and demand. More people wanted to buy land than there were owners prepared to sell. Anxious to protect their property, the descendants of the land revolution had used their political and legal muscle to keep it from being dispersed. By 1750 perhaps half of England's estates were protected from sale by entails and trusts of varying complexity set up to keep them within the family. And the widening application of the equity of redemption made it harder for lenders to foreclose on delinquent borrowers and force them to sell their land. Where sales did take place, almost half were between existing landowners anxious to increase or consolidate their holdings.

The rising price of land triggered a new surge in enclosure. Much of England's farmland had continued to be cultivated as "open fields" with some common rights of pasturing livestock, and almost a quarter remained communally owned and used. It was a measure of the landowners' influence in Parliament that more than four thousand "Inclosure Acts" were passed between 1700 and 1830, allowing their promoters to hedge and fence in most of this land as private, exclusive property. The legislation invariably extinguished other forms of property, such as traditional rights to grazing and use of the land, forcing their owners either to become paid workers or to leave the land.

By the end of the century, 40 percent of Britain's population lived in towns, compared with barely 4 percent in Russia, 7 percent in China, and 15 percent in France. An anonymous verse popular at the time conveys the reality of what had happened to England's well-managed, productive commons:

The law locks up the man or woman,
That steals the goose from off the common;
But lets the greater villain loose,
That steals the common from the goose.

Altogether some seven million acres were transferred into private ownership through the enclosure orders, brutal testimony to the political power now wielded by landowners. In many cases compensation was paid, but the total value of enclosed land represented the transfer of about £175 million of assets from communal possession to the lawyers, merchants, and wealthy landowners who controlled Parliament.

It is impossible to avoid the contrast between the eighteenth-century enclosers and their sixteenth-century predecessors. No longer the underdogs fighting for political influence, the descendants of the land revolution exploited their dominance for economic gain. Few large owners were interested in working the soil themselves. For the first time since the fifteenth century, it no longer made economic sense to invest in improving land. The obligation on landowners to pay land tax and parish contributions for relief of the poor made it difficult to earn as much as 3 percent from the produce of high-priced land. The government's Consolidated Fund, or Consols, paid the same interest for no effort, and the East India Company, twice as much with scarcely more risk. Even enclosure, sometimes thought to have been a surefire way of doubling profits, turned out to be so expensive that only the capital appreciation justified the cost.

Instead, property had become a source of political power, of capital, and, for some, of aesthetic enjoyment, enhanced by the deft touches of landscape artists like Capability Brown. Compared to Chinese or French peasant holdings, most farms were huge—two thirds were more than sixty acres in size—and their tenants unmistakably wealthy. Frequently, the largest estates consisted of little more than a small "home farm" surrounded by larger tenancies whose rents kept the owner's family in comfort. Shortly before emigrating to Illinois in 1817, Morris Birkbeck, a tenant who rented a fifteen-hundred-acre farm in the south of England, estimated his assets in terms of crops and livestock to be worth more then £8,000, enough to buy twenty-six thousand acres in the New World. Very often, the home estates were heavily mortgaged, with interest payments amply covered by the rising value of land, but rarely producing enough income to pay off the loan. By 1800 more than 85 percent of agricultural land in Britain was farmed by tenants. The social chasms that divided the three classes, landlords, tenants, and laborers, would persist with little alteration in rural Britain into the second half of the twentieth century.

What this picture concealed, however, was the political and economic crisis that eighteenth-century landowners had created. By removing most of their land from the marketplace, they had attempted to insulate the source of their power with its attendant privileges against outside threat. But, like Poland's sixteenth-century *szlachta*, they succeeded in creating an elite democracy, closed to all but the wealthiest or most determined newcomers. Politically, a once vigorous democracy had become aristocratic and corrupt. Not only did the landowners use their political dominance to loot communally owned land, but from the mid-eighteenth century they increasingly treated government posts as property that could be mortgaged and inherited: in 1762, the earl of Egmont secured the post of Registrar to the High Court of the Admiralty, a position that paid £12,000 a year and was later passed on to his elder son, Lord Arden. His younger and less fortunate son, the future prime minister Spencer Perceval, only got the job of Surveyor to the Meltings of the Mint, worth a paltry one hundred pounds a year.

Almost seamlessly, the three rural divisions passed into the classic structure of free-enterprise business—shareholders, managers, workers. The transition was made obvious in David Ricardo's *Principles of Political Economy and Taxation*, his pioneering work in 1817 on the laws of profit and value in a free-enterprise economy. In it he equated the providers of the three basic elements of industrial production—capital, machinery, and labor—with "the proprietor of the land, the owner of the stock or capital necessary for its cultivation, and the labourers by whose industry it is cultivated." His equation made sense since it was out of Britain's highly capitalized, stalled land market that the Industrial Revolution emerged.

* * *

Historians attempting to explain why the revolution should have happened in Britain rather than in China, the Netherlands, or France, all of which had access to cheap energy, inventive minds, and technical skills, have customarily picked one material ingredient, such as the availability of coal or the urbanization of society, and argued that it triggered a sequence of events that ended with industrialization. But neat cause-and-effect theories do not match the messy upsurge of development and experimentation in such vital but widely dispersed areas as the harnessing of steam power, the production of pig iron, and the mechanization of textile manufactures.

When the Society for the Encouragement of Arts, Manufactures, and Commerce was set up in 1753 to promote useful inventions, its first seven hundred members included many of Britain's largest landowners, as well as powerful government ministers with business addresses at the Treasury, the Admiralty, and the War Office. The majority of members were described as "not fashionable . . . with an income of under a thousand pounds a year," but since a schoolteacher or government clerk was paid only fifty pounds a year, even the unfashionable were far from poor.

Significantly the society's reports on its experiments and inventions were published initially in a magazine for landowners, the *Museum Rusticum et Commerciale*. The sheer range of subjects suggests the variety of opportunities that had opened up for those eager to find new ways of increasing the financial return from their properties. In the third issue of the *Museum*, the owner of "a small estate" described the geological conditions that convinced him to try mining it for coal. This prompted another correspondent, familiar with the availability of coal in northeast England, to claim, "I have known more than once, that from one single acre above thirty thousand pounds sterling, clear profit, has been made." In the absence of coal, he added, it might be possible to extract clay and start a pottery, as had been done in central England where Josiah Wedgwood would shortly establish his chinaware empire. Although the *Museum* liked to pretend that its readers were "plain, honest, well-meaning farmers," it also offered them papers on the production of chemicals for dyeing and bleaching, on experiments with making artificial fertilizer, on the construction of a hydrometer, and on the design of rails for "cast-iron railroads" in order to transport heavy loads of coal or iron ore.

Many disparate elements had to crystallize to produce the Industrial Revolution. It is easy to find most floating in solution in other economies. China especially had a market economy on the Yangtze and Pearl

River deltas, a tradition of inventiveness, an efficient transport system using canals and rivers, and abundant energy in the form of waterwheels, windmills, and, above all, human labor. Since water remained more important than coal as a source of nonhuman energy in British industry until the 1820s, the inaccessibility of China's inland coalfields is not relevant to its failure to industrialize. But two obstacles did make an industrial revolution there impossible. Ideas could only be communicated nationally through the medium of Mandarin, a language restricted to higher officials; and the land's value was measured not by its produce but by the population it could support.

The catalyst that crystallized all these elements in Britain was the nature of ownership. It had brought into existence a widely dispersed, politically powerful, highly capitalized class of property owners. It offered an incentive to obtain profit from the land and from innovation. And most amorphously but recognizably, it fostered a highly personalized, self-motivated outlook on the use to which possessions might be put.

When Samuel Garbett, cofounder of the Carron Ironworks, Britain's first mass-production armaments factory, wrote in 1782 to Matthew Boulton, partner of the inventor James Watt and owner of the Soho manufactory, about founding a bank to invest in new industrial ventures, he picked out two vital ingredients that only the descendants of the land revolution could supply. "Nothing but real and well known landed property joined with ministerial connections," he said, "can make a bank at Birmingham so lucrative as to be worth your or my notice as principals." Land represented capital, and influence with government ministers provided the political protection that every new property required.

The Duke of Bridgewater employed both in 1763 to build a canal, Britain's first entirely artificial waterway, so that he could transport coal from his huge estates to the city of Manchester forty miles away. He pledged part of his landed property to borrow £25,000, and used his political connections to have no fewer than four Acts of Parliament passed allowing the compulsory purchase of land along the canal's proposed route. The commercial success of the duke's enterprise unlocked a flood of capital for other canals, eventually creating a transport system that would allow manufacturers and miners to reach their markets cheaply.

Some of the investment needed for the myriad of early start-up industries came from the profits of Britain's mercantile trade with the colonies, and particularly the linked commerce in sugar and slaves, but recent research suggests that this amounted to less than 15 percent of what must have been needed. By one nineteenth-century economist's computation, two thirds of the capital available during this period before the spread of large private banks existed in the form of real estate rather than financial securities. As late as 1832, land still represented half of all the wealth in Britain, including stocks, cash, overseas earnings, buildings, and manufacturing stock. It was not just the wealthy Duke of Bridgewater who used his acres as security for capital investment.

Land was used by Thomas Baylies to finance the expansion of the pioneer ironworks, the Coalbrookdale Company; by landowner George Bowes, to develop his lead-mining and smelting works in the northeast of England; by textile manufacturer Robert Peel to construct his factories, and by innumerable textile machinery inventors, among them Jedediah Strutt, who raised loans against his farm to develop his own stocking-frame machine, the profits of which later helped finance the creation of Richard Arkwright's empire of water- and steam-powered textile factories. Matthew Boulton sold and mortgaged most of his land, then raised £28,000 from pledging his wife's property to finance his first large factory in Birmingham. Across Britain, property owners not only had the means but, as the eighteenth century progressed, the increasingly sharp incentive to find nonagricultural ways of exploiting both their old property in land and the new property in ideas.

A fully equipped textile factory capable of carding wool, spinning thread, and weaving cloth might cost as much as £50,000, but a basic spinning factory with fifty machines could be built and equipped for less than £3,000. The cost was far less than the price of an estate. The building was made from easily accessible wood, and, as John Fielden, himself an early industrialist, recorded, water costing nothing provided the power, so that most of the new factories were sited "on the sides of streams capable of turning the water-wheel."

Labor was cheaper still, if the human costs were overlooked. As Fielden confessed, the workers recruited to feed wool to the whirring spindles and thread to the flying looms were poorly paid children supplied by the workhouses of big cities, and required to work in alternating twelve-hours shifts. "In many of the manufacturing districts, but particularly, I am afraid, in the guilty county to which I belong [Lancashire]," he wrote, "cruelties the most heart-rending were practised upon the unoffending and friendless creatures who were thus consigned to the charge of master-manufacturers; they were harassed to the brink of death by excess of labour . . . [and] flogged, fettered and tortured in the most exquisite refinement of cruelty."

Unlike Fielden, however, most property owners were prepared to turn a blind eye to conditions in their rural factories for the sake of the phenomenal returns they could earn: in the late eighteenth century, a wool-to-cloth manufacturer could expect to return profits of 20 to 35 percent on the money invested, paying off the capital cost of its building and equipment in four to five years. In Nottinghamshire, George Robinson built no fewer than six mills on the river Leen in the 1790s and paid off the full cost from his profits in one year. By the early 1800s he had earned enough money to set up the Moore and Robinson's Bank that financed the textile industry in the area until the late nineteenth century.

Robinson's transformation into a financier was unusual only in being so successful. Until banks became commonplace in the mid-nineteenth century, manufacturers generally created the credit for their business by pledging the value of their property to their suppliers, and in turn would provide credit by carrying the debts of their customers. They became in effect their own bankers. But the basic foundation for their businesses was remorselessly laid bare in hard times when their profits could no longer meet the cost of their borrowing or of their lending. In the close-printed columns of the *London Gazette* and other authoritative newspapers where bankruptcies were announced, there was also a melancholy list of properties for sale: "a delightful villa," "a capital, large dwelling-house, pleasantly situated with extensive plantations, pleasure grounds and gardens," "a well-furnished gentleman's house of the first respectability."

Within a generation, the landed industrialists looking for extra income had either been transformed into businessmen or were displaced by practical, commercially minded manufacturers who were accustomed to handling the wool, cotton, or iron that was their raw material, who were ruthless in driving their child laborers harder, and who were ready to plow back their profits into this new kind of property.

The era of land as the prime source of wealth and income was ending, but the way the earth was owned had not only brought the industrial age into being, it had left an indelible mark on the way it would develop.

Chapter Eleven

The Independence of an Owner

Property alone might have paved the way to the independence of the thirteen United States of America in 1776. Self-evidently, as virtually every American patriot sensed, a free individual enjoyed three natural rights, to life, to liberty, and to the acquisition of property. All three came from the same centuries-old root-stock of English common law. Furthermore, almost two centuries of Puritan theology, backed by close to a century of Lockean philosophy, confirmed that they were innate and unalienable. Yet on the first Fourth of July, a new attribute of liberty, "the pursuit of happiness," was at the last moment grafted on to the existing root. Consequently, the republic came into being endowed with a quite exceptional commitment not to one, but two traditions of freedom, neither, as it turned out, wholly compatible with the other.

The formula that "the people of America . . . are entitled to life, liberty and property" appeared in the First Continental Congress's declaration of rights in 1774. Had it been incorporated into the United States's Declaration of Independence, it would not have weakened the new republic's argument that the assertion of these rights justified rebellion against an oppressive power. In the years that led from resistance to revolution, it had become normal to equate the defense of liberty with the defense of property.

Protesting the imposition of taxes in 1765 by a London parliament where Americans were not represented, the sickly, brilliant pamphleteer James Otis described the attempt as an attack on property and declared, "in a state of nature no man can take my property from me without my consent: if he does, he deprives me of my liberty and makes me a slave."

And his argument was echoed in Samuel Adams's rhetorical question, "Now what liberty can there be where property is taken away without consent?" Their case was implicitly endorsed by William Blackstone's magisterial *Commentaries on the Laws of England*. Natural rights gave rise to "civil immunities," wrote Blackstone, one of which protected the individual from being "constrained to pay any aids or taxes, even for the defence of the realm or the support of government, but such as are imposed by his own consent, or that of his representatives in parliament."

But the power of the property argument was more than legal, or even constitutional. Economically, the unfettered possession of land had unleashed an acceleration of wealth in the American colonies that brought to the surface tensions that made imperial control intolerable. A boom in land prices in the colonies transformed American society in the generation that grew up after 1740. It was driven by a rapid rise in population that Benjamin Franklin predicted provocatively would see the population of the American colonies double from just over one million in 1750 to 2.6 million by 1775, and that soon afterward, "the greatest number of Englishmen will be on this side of the water."

Attracted by the prospect of owning land outright, almost one hundred thousand immigrants from Ulster and Germany, augmented by 180,000 free individuals from Britain, together with sixty thousand indentured servants and criminals, came to America. But natural increase accounted for much of the growth, especially in New England, where large families—six to eight surviving children were common—pushed a population of twenty thousand inhabitants in the mid-seventeenth century to more than four hundred thousand by the 1750s.

Most of New England's immigrants moved southward through Dutch-owned New York to the more open markets of Pennsylvania, Maryland, and the southern colonies. The growing demand sparked the creation of more than a dozen land companies in the eighteenth century to exploit unoccupied land east of the Appalachians. The Connecticut Land Company claimed land on the New York–Pennsylvania border, and young George Washington was prominent among investors in the Dismal Swamp Company that intended to drain and reclaim nine hundred square miles of waterlogged land in southern Virginia. But as the main body of settlement moved from the coastline into the foothills of the Appalachians, the first scouts were exploring the fertile ground beyond the mountains. "Their vallies are of the richest soil, equal to manure itself, impossible in appearance ever to wear out," a South Carolina surveyor, John William de Brahm, reported in 1756 after traveling through what is now eastern Tennessee. "Should this country once come into the hands of the Europeans, they may with propriety call it the American Canaan, for it will fully answer their industry and all methods of European culture, and do as well for European produce." To would-be land speculators, the lure was irresistible.

Until 1763, however, they faced one insuperable obstacle. European maps showed the territory up to the Mississippi River to be French, although in reality it was occupied and owned by Creek, Choctaw, and Cherokee nations. But with the defeat of France in the Seven Years War, the maps changed to show the rich soil to be British. In the same year, the first combined campaign of resistance by Native Americans against the incomers, led by the Ojibwe chief, Pontiac, persuaded the government in London to issue a proclamation in King George III's name forbidding colonial governors "to grant Warrants of Survey, or pass Patents for any Lands" beyond the Appalachians, so that "the several Nations or Tribes of Indians with whom We are connected, and who live under our Protection, should not be molested or disturbed."

Since all of British America was technically held under feudal possession—the usual phrase employed in the colonial charters was that the king granted the land "in free and common soccage" to the proprietors—his legal power to prevent further occupation could not be questioned. The proclamation still has that force in the Canadian government's dealings today with the First Nations of Canada. But the response of American land speculators was typified by Washington's comment to his land-hunting associate, William Crawford, in 1767: "I can never look upon the Proclamation in any other light (but this I say between ourselves) than as a temporary expedient to quiet the minds of the Indians. It must fall, of course, in a few years."

His cool appraisal was well founded. With barely a pause, both individuals like Crawford and Washington and surveyors from a dozen land companies went back to work far to the west of the mountains. Astonishingly, the largest of them, the Vandalia Land Company, was backed by some of the most powerful figures in British politics, including the prime minister, Lord North. What the surveyors found beyond the Appalachians confirmed the discoveries of Thomas Hutchins, the most authoritative geographer of the region. On a celebrated map of modern Ohio, Kentucky, and Tennessee, published in 1778 but known long before, he had written lyrical descriptions, "A rich and level country," "Very large natural meadows; innumerable herds of Buffaloe, Elk, Deer, etc feed here," and along the Wabash River, "Here the country is level, rich and well timber'd and abounds in very extensive meadows and savannnahs . . . It yields Rye, Hemp, Pea Vine, Wild Indigo, Red & White clover etc."

In 1775, the Transylvania Land Company employed Daniel Boone to survey and acquire land in Kentucky, and the company's chief promoter, Judge Richard Henderson of North Carolina, put into words the aspiration that drove every land speculator into the western territory. "The country might invite a prince from his palace merely for the pleasure of contemplating its beauty and excellence," he wrote, "but only add the rapturous idea of property and what allurements can the world offer for the loss of so glorious a prospect?" The imperial government's attempt to curb that allurement, the iconic urge of every private property society, led directly to Virginia's uncompromising claim in 1776 that its citizens enjoyed among other inherent rights "the means of acquiring and possessing property."

WHAT ESCAPED most contemporary observers, with the notable exception of Benjamin Franklin, was how radically the land market was transforming the colonial economy. Very few companies aimed to buy land directly for their investors. Instead, most operated like modern mutual funds, using investors' money to purchase assets, in this case land, for sale at a profit. To make this possible, the necessary legal and financial instruments had to be imported from England, including laws of contract and partnership, good practice in accountancy, and more abstruse schemes of corporate governance such as the pure trust constructed in 1765 by Patrick Henry for Robert Morris's North American Land Company. Long before industrial production became the dominant way of earning money, the land market brought a capitalist structure into being. Driving the market was a spectacular growth in the supply of investment capital within the colonies.

Between 1730 and 1770, it increased at an annual rate of 1.6 percent, primarily as a result of the rising value of land. In 1600, the territory eventually covered by the thirteen original states would have been worthless in monetary terms, but in 1800 it was valued at about six hundred million dollars, including housing, with perhaps two thirds of that increase coming since 1720. Once war broke out, and gigantic loans had to be raised from the Dutch financial market to purchase arms, uniforms, and fodder, the security offered to the Amsterdam financiers was partly the estimated income streams from taxation, but more substantially the gigantic capital value of American land.

By 1776, the net worth of each American proprietor was growing twice as fast as that of his British equivalent. And since four out of five Americans lived on land they owned, the wealth was spread much more widely. "There is such an amount of good land yet uncultivated," commented the Swedish botanist Peter Kalm in 1750, "a newly married man can, without difficulty, get a spot of ground where he may comfortably subsist with his wife and children. The taxes are very low, and he need not be under any concern on their account. The liberties he enjoys are so great that he considers himself a prince in his possessions."

The evident prosperity of the American colonies intensified London's determination that they should pay their share of the costs of the Seven Years War from which they had so clearly benefited. The costs had fallen squarely on the shoulders of British taxpayers who were confronted by a national debt that had risen from £72 million in 1755 to £130 million in 1764. The proposed American taxes and duties on sugar, official documents, and imported goods, including tea, comprised the sort of indirect taxation that the British had become used to. To the colonists, however, they came as a shock, partly because internal taxation was light, and partly because after years of benign neglect, London's demands were a reminder of the realities of colonial rule.

But the Americans' explosive reaction when the 1765 Stamp Act was introduced pointed to the change of outlook that had taken place in the new, young generation of colonists. As poor, undermanned settlements, the colonies had had no choice but to accept London's rule—the restrictions on what could be manufactured, from hats to pig iron, the prohibition on New England shippers selling cod to French sugar planters, the duties on Virginian tobacco, and the impressment, or forcible enlistment, of sailors from American vessels; but in the previous thirty years they had grown into wealthy, populous societies that resented and resisted affronts by an outside power. And as they did so an authentically American note began to emerge.

When James Otis attacked the Stamp Act, he did so on the grounds that as a "British subject," he had the right not to be taxed without the consent of his representative in Parliament. His argument was repeated as the language of liberty became common in newspapers, pamphlets, and general meetings during the 1760s and early 1770s. But it sounded more like the protest of a disaffected British subject than an independent

American citizen. The deeper groundswell of dissatisfaction demanded something more.

In 1773, the New York Sons of Liberty declared that paying tax on imported tea would leave them with "no property that we may call our own," but concluded in a significant departure from the Otis argument that in such an event, "we may bid adieu to American liberty." What distinguished American from British liberty had still to be explained.

Many events served to transform British colonists into Americans—anger at London's punitive action against Massachusetts following the dumping of tea in Boston Harbor, suspicion of the Coercive Acts' threat to the independence of legislatures, resentment at the incorporation of western lands into Canada through the 1774 Quebec Act, and finally outrage at the killing of civilians by British troops—but they all fused into a single determination to assert independence from an oppressive power. And that entailed a definition of the liberty that oppression threatened to take from them.

THE FIRST APPEARANCE of a different argument had appeared in an influential series of articles, *Letters from a Farmer in Pennsylvania*, written in 1767 and 1768 by John Dickinson. Americans had to resist taxation, he argued, on the grounds "that we cannot be happy, without being free; that we cannot be free, without being secure in our property; that we cannot be secure in our property, if, without our consent, others may, as by right, take it away; that taxes imposed on us by parliament, do thus take it away." By the time George Mason came to write Virginia's Declaration of Rights in 1776, the association had become common enough for him to list among mankind's "inherent rights" to life, liberty, and property that of "pursuing and obtaining happiness."

The idea of happiness as a fundamental human goal was given birth in the 1730s by the founder of Scottish Enlightenment thinking, Francis Hutcheson. Before him, in his *Essay on Human Understanding*, Locke had speculated that one of the earliest impressions drawn on the tabula rasa of the human mind was a basic preference for pleasure and happiness over pain and suffering. But Hutcheson gave the impulse purpose. Brought up in the belief of reformed Calvinism that, far from being predestined to heaven or hell, the soul had simply been created with an instinct for goodness, Hutcheson translated goodness to its secular equivalent, happiness, and taught that the innately sociable nature of mankind led everyone to seek happiness as their goal. It was a moral impulse, inseparable from being human.

The optimistic teaching of the Scottish Enlightenment deeply influenced Hutcheson's fellow Calvinist, the Swiss law professor Jean-Jacques Burlamaqui. Lecturing on natural law at the University of Geneva, Burlamaqui defined the notoriously slippery word, *droit*, usually translated as "law," not as a requirement imposed from outside, but as an internal drive. His lectures, published in 1748 as *The Principles of Natural Law*, explained that *droit* was derived from the Latin word *dirigo*, "which implies, to conduct a person to some certain end by the shortest road." Following Hutcheson, he taught that happiness was the goal of every moral person. But in *The Principles* this was given a political and social context; it was an unconstrained moral right common to all people living in an ordered community.

Since he shared the same intellectual background as Adam Smith, it was perhaps not surprising that Burlamaqui should also have argued that the selfish pursuit of personal happiness would produce general happiness, and for the same psychological reasons that Smith advanced. Every moral individual would instinctively recognize that the welfare of others was the source of "all the knowledge, conveniency, and ease that form the security, pleasure, and happiness of life." This was the social contract. The shorthand description was "Do as you would be done by." So long as that awareness of others was in place, the social equivalent of the hidden hand's self-righting mechanism would do its work.

Thus, echoing the economic argument of the *physiocrates* that lifting taxes and duties would increase the national wealth, Burlamaqui insisted that the removal of social and political constraints would allow individuals to pursue their innate right to happiness and enable society to raise the general well-being of its citizens. Under eighteenth-century conditions, however, humanity was rendered miserable by laws, customs, and privileges that restricted its potential. In the ear-catching language that his fellow Swiss, Jean-Jacques Rousseau, would later use about human rights, "Man was born free, and everywhere is in chains."

Burlamaqui's universal right existed quite independently of English common law. And it was one with which Thomas Jefferson was entirely familiar. As a teenager, he had been taught and befriended by William Small, a Scottish teacher at William & Mary College, and developed a relationship that, as Jefferson testified, "fixed the destinies of my life." It etched into his mind the rationalism and unwavering confidence in social wisdom that ran through the teachings of Hutcheson and other followers of the Scottish Enlightenment. Their books, including Burlamaqui's *Principles*, crowded the shelves of his well-read library.

Jefferson's attitude to natural property rights, by contrast, remained consistently skeptical throughout his life. It was, he believed, "a moot question whether the origin of any kind of property is derived from nature at all" rather than being created by laws "flowing from the will of the people." But where the ownership of real estate was concerned, he had no doubts. "It is agreed by those who have seriously considered the subject," he wrote in old age, "that no individual has, of natural right, a separate property in an acre of land." In other words, Locke was wrong: No amount of mixing of labor created a natural right to own the soil. Property was simply a matter of civil law.

What the representatives of the United States gathered in Philadelphia drew from Locke was his belief that free citizens were justified in rebelling when their contract with government was broken. On that point, the young Jefferson concurred. But quite deliberately, when given the task of editing the draft of the Declaration of Independence, he chose to explain the birth of the United States not by referring to liberties created by the laws of an oppressive government, but to a universal freedom created by birth. This was the motive that shaped the declaration's defining phrase: "We hold these truths to be self-evident, that all men are created equal, that they are endowed by their Creator with certain unalienable Rights, that among these are Life, Liberty and the pursuit of Happiness."

With those imperishable words, the United States grafted on to its propertied roots an alien cutting that committed it to a perpetual struggle between the rights of property and the rights of people.

THE POTENTIAL CONFLICT was immediately clear to those fighting for their own freedom: slavery condemned one in six Americans to be treated as property and denied any rights to the pursuit of their happiness. "For shame," wrote Nathaniel Niles of Rhode Island, "let us either cease to enslave our fellow-man or else let us cease to complain of those that would enslave us." The contradiction led Pennsylvania to legislate in 1780 for the gradual abolition of slavery. "We rejoice that it is in our power to extend a portion of that freedom to others," ran the preamble, "which hath been extended to us; and a release from that state of thraldom to which we ourselves were tyrannically doomed."

Despite actively promoting the Atlantic slave trade themselves, the British also targeted the contradiction. "How is it that we hear the loudest yelps for liberty among the drivers of negroes?" demanded Dr. Samuel Johnson. In 1779, Sir Henry Clinton, in command of British forces, offered freedom "to every Negro that shall desert the rebel standard," and the following year the British switched their strategy from the original sources of rebellion in New England and Pennsylvania to focus on the South, with the same offer of liberty to the enslaved. As many as one hundred thousand slaves did find their freedom with the British, among them Titus Cornelius, known as Colonel Tye, who went on to conduct a fierce campaign of harassment against the rebels in New Jersey at the head of the Black Brigade guerillas.

Yet unmistakably, what brought tens of thousands of Americans to take up arms was the plain desire to defend their liberty against British military might. At the start, they provided the militia forces who fought at Bunker's Hill and successfully expelled British troops from Boston. And at the end, the most effective defense was mounted by General Nathanael Greene in the South who waged a genuine people's war that depended on civilian support and a popular commitment to what he himself described as "the defeat of oppression and diffusion of happiness." No one could doubt that it was for the freedom to pursue their own happiness that Americans fought and won their independence.

Even after the fighting ended, concerns for personal liberty still trumped those of property, leading Massachusetts to make the trade in slaves illegal in 1783, followed by all the New England states, and eventually New York and New Jersey. In the most important legislative act of its peacetime life, the Continental Congress made it a provision of the 1787 Ordinance governing the settlement of territory northwest of the Ohio River that "There shall be neither slavery nor involuntary servitude in the said territory, otherwise than in the punishment of crimes whereof the party shall have been duly convicted." That sentence preserved the entire band of states from Ohio to Minnesota, and perhaps the United States itself, from developing a slave economy.

The underlying conflict between human liberty and property rights came into the open when the delegates from twelve states, Rhode Island abstaining, met in Philadelphia in May 1787 to draw up a new constitution to replace the old Articles of Confederation that had united them through the fight for independence. The battle revolved around the poisoned concept of treating humans as property, and specifically whether a slave should count as a thing or a being when matters of taxation and representation in Congress were being discussed. Incomplete though the records of the debates are, they reveal how clearly those present understood the nature of the double standard being applied.

After tortuous discussion had ended with the compromise of treating a male slave as three fifths of a free man, James Wilson, soon to be a Supreme Court justice and author of a famous series of lectures on the natural rights of man, asked "on what principle the admission of blacks in the proportion of three fifths could be explained. Are they admitted as Citizens? then why are they not admitted on an equality with White Citizens? are they admitted as property? then why is not other property admitted into the computation?"

Equally damning were the clauses that postponed a ban on the slave trade for twenty years and required any slaves who escaped and reached a free state to be denied their freedom and returned to their masters. When they came to the wording of the Constitution, William Patterson of New Jersey pointed to the hypocrisy that prevented the framers even using the word "slave." Instead, slaves were referred to as "other Persons" where the three fifths rule was concerned, and the slave trade became the "Importation of such Persons as any of the States now existing shall think proper to admit." Luther Martin of Maryland, himself a slave owner, admitted that the reason the word could not be used was because "It is inconsistent with the principles of the Revolution, and dishonorable to the American character to have such a feature in the Constitution."

That was the crux of the problem. To the framers of the Constitution, a slave-owning society might be shameful, but it was possible. A society without property was inconceivable.

"The moment the idea is admitted into society that property is not as sacred as the laws of God, and that there is not a force of law and public justice to protect it," John Adams declared in his defense of the Constitution, "anarchy and tyranny commence. If 'Thou shalt not covet' and 'Thou shalt not steal' were not commandments of Heaven, they must be made inviolable precepts in every society before it can be civilized or made free."

It was this veneration of property, condemning millions of Americans to slavery, that led to the earliest portrayal of the Constitution by the anti-slavery movement as the product of a narrow class intent on protecting their own interests. In the early twentieth century, the economic historian Charles Beard produced an influential thesis based on exhaustive, though flawed, research on the financial wealth and real estate holdings of delegates that helped flesh out this charge. The rebuttal to his case led later historians to emphasize the inseparability of property rights from individual rights. The critical factor in the constitutional debates, they insisted, was the delegates' practical experience of representative government, and their consequent desire to safeguard a democratic spirit in any future United States government.

Yet what the Constitution achieved was rarer than either of those interpretations would suggest. Both its failure to appreciate the moral outrage of slavery and its achievement in creating a framework of democratic government sprang from the same source.

MOST DELEGATES to the Constitutional Convention expected merely to improve the existing Articles of Confederation that had united the states. The articles allocated control of foreign policy and military affairs to the central government but left it no powers to raise taxes or settle disputes between what were self-declared sovereign bodies. This omission had to be remedied, but that was the full extent of the convention's remit. When the fifty-five delegates met in the austere Georgian elegance of the Assembly Room in the Pennsylvania State House in early May, however, they were presented with a blueprint drawn up by the Virginia delegation for a federal government based on a national vote and exercising national executive powers. Although other designs were put forward, and many alterations were made in the next four months by a group that was exceptionally well grounded in law and the business of government, the agenda was effectively set by the Virginia plan. And that itself bore the unmistakable imprint of James Madison's thought.

To this day, the constrained, dogged character of Madison, widely regarded as "the father of the Constitution," remains enigmatic. Physically diminutive and handicapped by ill health, socially awkward, and a bachelor until, in his forties, he married the irrepressible Dolley Payne Todd, he compensated for those political shortcomings by an intellectual's capacity for prolonged research and logical argument that compelled his colleagues' admiration. "He perceives truth with great clearness," remarked his fellow congressman Fisher Ames in 1788, "and can trace it through the mazes of debate without losing it." And as even his rival, and later bitter enemy, Alexander Hamilton, freely admitted, "he is Uncorrupted and incorruptible." He had many followers but few close friends, with the one towering exception of Thomas Jefferson, whose appointment as ambassador to France, however, kept him absent from the Constitutional Convention's deliberations.

Madison's research on different types of governance ranged from Athenian democracy to sixteenth-century Poland's elected kingship and eighteenth-century Switzerland's federation of cantons. As he demonstrated in the notes he took during the convention and equally in the articles he contributed to *The Federalist Papers* in support of the new constitution, he had come to an understanding of democratic government that differed radically from anything that had occurred earlier in the European tradition.

The difference began with the primary goal of government, which he took to be the protection of "the rights both of property & of persons." But, as he explained to the convention, even at the basic stage of voting, the two rights were bound to be in competition: "Allow the right [of voting] exclusively to property, and the rights of persons may be oppressed. The feudal [system] alone sufficiently proves it. Extend it equally to all, and the rights of property or the claims of justice may be overruled by a majority without property, or interested in measures of injustice. Of this abundant proof is afforded by other popular Govts."

The assumption that private and public interests were irreconcilable was in the classic tradition of Western thought. Aristotle, as Madison knew from his own readings of the *Politics*, had declared that aristocratic government degenerates "when the few who are rich govern the state as best suits the interests of their avarice and ambition," and that republics are finished "when the many who are poor make the gratification of their own passions the only rule of their administration." And from the days of the Roman republic, praise for public virtue and condemnation of personal ambition were part of every orator's repertoire.

Individuals combining to promote their own selfish interests would create "parties" and "factions," two dirty words that explained to eighteenth-century politicians why democracy was unworkable. They produced the sort of vendetta politics in which, as George Washington put it, "the alternate domination of one faction over another, sharpened by the spirit of revenge . . . has perpetrated the most horrid enormities." To keep factions in check, a monarch or "chief Magistrate" was essential. A republic, as the influential Montesquieu had written in *The Spirit of the Laws* in 1748, could only survive if it were small and cohesive, otherwise it would be torn apart by dissension.

Montesquieu's diagnosis of democracy's future was bleak. Its survival in any form, even in a monarchy like Britain, must always be threatened by private factions. The only defense was a national policy to promote "a constant preference of public to private interest." Accordingly, every citizen had to be taught, almost brainwashed, to sacrifice selfish interests for the good of the country, "a self-renunciation, which is ever arduous and painful."

The outstanding accomplishment of those who met in Philadelphia in the summer of 1787 was the complete break they made with that long constitutional tradition. Madison was the unlikely architect of a constitution that destroyed two thousand years of European fearfulness about the poisonous effects of democracy.

MOST OF THE DEBATES at the convention were concerned with the immediate problem of deciding how much power should be given to the new federal government at the expense of the states, and whether the new system would allow Virginia, Massachusetts, and Pennsylvania, the three largest states, to ride roughshod over the remainder. But for Madison the challenge was deeper: to create a structure of government in which different interests could compete freely for power but without the risk of destroying their opponents' rights. "No free Country has ever been without parties, which are a natural offspring of Freedom," he remarked.

His research and his experience of Virginia politics convinced him that faction was inseparable from government. Human nature would always impel people with similar interests to band together. And other divisions lay beyond the basic split between propertied and unpropertied: "All civilized Societies would be divided into different Sects, Factions, & interests, as they happened to consist of rich & poor, debtors & creditors, the landed, the manufacturing, the commercial interests, the inhabitants of this district or that district, the followers of this political leader or that political leader—the disciples of this religious Sect or that religious Sect."

In every society, such groups naturally sought political power to protect their interests. As a result they inevitably came to associate themselves with their property, so that the shape of society itself in turn reflected those different interests. "From the protection of different and unequal faculties of acquiring property, the possession of different degrees and kinds of property immediately results," he wrote in *The Federalist Papers*; "and from the influence of these on the sentiments and views of the respective proprietors, ensues a division of society into different interests and parties."

This might not have sounded extreme to an eighteenth-century audience who naturally assumed "interests" to be the guiding light in people's social existence. Madison went further than that, however, with his assertion that people's relationship to what they owned affected their consciousness, and by extension helped mold the shape of society. Today that thesis has a radical ring because it also appeared in a more definite, Germanic style in Karl Marx's description of "property relations" or "relations of production" that shaped the outlook of the bourgeoisie and the proletariat. "The totality of these relations of production," Marx wrote in the 1859 preface to *A Contribution to the Critique of Political Economy,* "constitutes the economic structure of society, the real foundation, on which arises a legal and political superstructure and to which correspond definite forms of social consciousness."

As a political theorist, however, Madison possessed a quality lacking in either Marx or Montesquieu. Unlike them, he embraced the diversity of opinion as evidence of a free society. Madison did not deny that the instability of the thirteen states stemmed from the quarrels between different interests, and from the "factious spirit [that] has tainted our public administrations." But it was hopeless to expect education or even legal sanctions, as Montesquieu had urged, to stamp it out. Those remedies would only work "by destroying the liberty which is essential to . . . political life."

"The causes of faction cannot be removed," Madison concluded. The trick was to find "the means of controlling its effects." And by a stroke of genuinely creative imagination, he turned Montesquieu's theory on its head. Competition for power only became dangerous in a small republic where control could easily be seized by one group, Madison argued, but in a large republic there would be so many factions no single one could dominate all the others. "The smaller the society, the fewer probably will be the distinct parties and interests composing it; the fewer the distinct parties and interests, the more frequently will a majority be found of the same party . . . Extend the sphere, and you take in a greater variety of parties and interests; you make it less probable that a majority of the whole will have a common motive to invade the rights of other citizens."

It was akin to Adam Smith's thesis that free-enterprise capitalism worked automatically without a mercantile hand to guide it. No monarch was needed to keep control of Madison's government. With power diffused among the three branches of government, responsibilities divided between federal and state administrations, and popular passions expressed "through the medium of a chosen body of citizens" in Congress, no single-issue faction could take control. The system would be in essence self-regulating. "Society itself will be broken into so many parts, interests, and classes of citizens, that the rights of individuals, or of the minority, will be in little danger from interested combinations of the majority."

It is almost impossible to exaggerate the importance of the argument that Madison presented to the convention and amplified in *The Federalist Papers*. At a stroke, it undermined the almost sacred hold that political tradition and Montesquieu's dictum exerted on contemporary American thought. It certainly swayed delegates previously hostile to the sheer size of the proposed new federal state. Above all, it exorcized the specter of disorder that haunted all previous attempts to contemplate how democracy might work in government.

The inevitable growth of executive power and the Supreme Court's authority at the expense of legislative supremacy has blurred Madison's insight. But the Constitution and the experiment in democratic government that developed—the popularly elected House of Representatives, balanced until the twentieth century by a restricted selection of members of the Senate, the retention by the states of all powers not specifically allocated to the federal government, and the capacity of the judiciary to revise laws—created something unique, a political marketplace where different interests could compete safely for power.

As clearly as Adam Smith, Madison insisted that without a shared sense of justice—in constitutional terms, the confidence of each section of society that its rights would not be violated—the market would collapse. It was, however, this last condition that led him, and the delegates who crowded into the Assembly Room to hear his speech on the subject, into their fatal misjudgment concerning slavery.

Reflecting widespread unease in the convention about condoning slavery, Madison argued that its very unpopularity exemplified the danger of allowing the majority to have its way. "It is apprehended," he told his audience, "that if the power of the Commonwealth shall be in the hands of a majority, who have no interest in this species of property [i.e., slavery], that . . . injustice may be done to its owners." Precisely because they were a minority, therefore, the rights of slave owners had to be protected against abolitionists.

His logic, however twisted, was entirely consistent. When Madison endorsed the enslavement of black Americans, with only the saving compromise of regarding slaves as three fifths human, he did so in order to maintain the political balance that he regarded as essential for democracy. It was not an aberration.

Madison never deviated from his belief in the absolute necessity of maintaining equality in the political marketplace. It led him to advocate a form of government intervention apparently at odds with its role as protector of unfettered property rights. Looking to the future, he foresaw that as the population grew, the primarily rural economy of 1787 would give way to one dominated by "the great Capitalists in Manufactures & Commerce and the members employed by them." The political influence they could exert through their employees and their accumulated wealth posed a danger of distorting the political marketplace, but, Madison added, "it may be observed that the opportunities, may be diminished, and the permanency [of inherited wealth] defeated by the equalizing tendency of the laws."

Madison's expectation that government might need to pass "equalizing laws" was only part of his larger concern to establish "equality & fairness" between different interests. At times it almost seemed like an obsession: propertied had to be balanced against unpropertied, creditor against debtor, rich against poor, "landed interest" against "Commerce & Manufacture." The balance of interests was the one necessary condition for democratic government to operate freely.

To keep the scales level, Madison was prepared to alter voting rights, adjust the composition of Congress, and take whatever other steps were necessary. In the eyes of the father of the Constitution, freedom and political equality were indivisible.

Chapter Twelve

The Challenge to Private Property

At about four p.m. on March 3, 1792, Jacques-Guillaume Simonneau, the newly elected mayor of Étampes, a little town thirty miles south of Paris, went out to negotiate with a crowd that had assembled in the marketplace. Throughout the winter, there had been disturbances as a poor harvest and surging inflation sent the price of wheat soaring. Étampes lay between the productive, privately owned cereal farms around Orléans and the vast market of Paris, and daily convoys of grain passed through the town, or were warehoused nearby and sold in the marketplace. The owner of a large tannery that employed sixty workers, Simonneau was both wealthy and, like most businessmen, a strong supporter of the revolution, because it promised to provide what the ancien régime had failed to deliver, fairer taxation and freer trade within France.

Helping the Americans to independence at a cost of more than one billion livres was the factor that finally broke royalist France's rickety economy. Annual accounts showed that government revenues exceeded expenditure, but they did so only by ignoring the interest on the American debt that consumed 40 percent of the government's income. When the king reluctantly summoned the Three Estates to deal with the crisis, a wide confederation of interests—peasants, intellectuals, new landowners, and urban merchants or bourgeoisie—had welcomed the opportunity to reform the whole structure of the ancien régime. For the peasants, the great achievement was the abolition of aristocratic privileges on August 4, 1789, while the bourgeoisie and the landowners approved the National Assembly's efforts to modernize both the political and economic systems.

The apparent unity of their interests was reflected in the Declaration of the Rights of Man issued by the assembly later that month. Echoing the American Declaration of Independence, the first article stated that "All men are born free and equal in rights," while article 17 promised that "Property is an inviolable and sacred right. No one may be deprived of it unless public necessity, legally established, evidently requires it." When the new taxes failed to produce enough revenue, even the property owners and bourgeoisie had supported the assembly's decision to confiscate church land, about 10 percent of France's territory, and to issue paper money, known as *assignats*, against its value of about two billion livres.

Given this background, there was nothing incongruous in a businessman like Simonneau belonging to the Jacobins, the most radical wing in the National Assembly. That there might be a conflict between the declaration's two sets of rights, those of humans and of property, did not become apparent until the afternoon when he walked out to confront the demonstrators. Although armed with clubs, pitchforks, and scythes, the mob was not initially violent. For three hours, they argued with the mayor, demanding that the price of grain, 50 percent higher than the year before, be drastically reduced. For his part, the fifty-one-year-old Simonneau robustly defended the government's view that interfering in the market was counterproductive because "Liberty in commerce is the principal source of abundance."

By evening, tempers had begun to unravel. Feeling himself threatened, Simonneau ordered a detachment of National Guards with him to fire on the crowd. The soldiers refused, and the enraged crowd began to strike at the mayor with their weapons. He was clubbed and punched to the ground, then stabbed with scythes and pitchforks, and at last finished off, it was said, by a bullet from one of his own soldiers.

THE CONCEPT OF PRIVATE PROPERTY in land had only clearly emerged in France a generation earlier, but until the moment of Simonneau's murder there was nothing to suggest that it would not develop along English lines. As in England, the symptoms of the disease were easier to detect than the infection. Eighteenth-century France certainly seethed with peasant anger at the enclosure of common land and the elimination of traditional rights of access as wealthy merchants, motivated partly by a sustained period of high cereal prices, bought feudal estates for cash. But similar upheavals had occurred in earlier periods. From the 1750s, however, two new ingredients had become common, the employment of *géomètres*, or land surveyors, to measure out the properties exactly, and the preparation of *plans parcellaires*, or estate maps, drawn to scale to show precisely what a proprietor owned.

In place of the traditional variable units that indicated how much the earth would produce, the *géomètres* insisted on accurate measures that allowed one property to be compared in area to another in exactly defined *perches*, consisting of eighteen *pieds*, each 12.789 inches long, and invariable *arpents* measuring one-hundred square *perches* precisely. "We have put all these defective *arpents* in good order," surveyors in the Lyon area boasted, "so that in each district their content is regulated in either *perches*, *pas* or *pieds*." The significance of the new invariable measures was explained in an influential surveyor's encyclopedia, *Métrologie,* published in 1780: "They are the rule of justice and the guarantee of property which must be sacred."

By the 1760s, the bug had infected increasing numbers of existing *seigneurs* in Burgundy and eastern France, who engaged in a process of *renovation des terriers*, or renewal of traditional feudal dues, often accompanied by new, accurate plans of their estates. In the feudal west and sharecropping south, the old ways still held good, but even in La Vendée, the most conservative region of Brittany, richer peasants were enclosing communal fields and taking steps that might have led to private ownership.

From the 1780s, parts of Paris had become a building site as speculators, aristocratic and commercial, built northward toward Montmartre, and transformed the royal gardens beside the Champs Elysées into fashionable *hotels* for tenants such as the American minister Thomas Jefferson. An unofficial banking system run by the country's leading law firms channeled money and credit from savers to borrowers primarily for real estate deals. Access to credit enabled the same class to buy most of the land confiscated from the church, often paying with cheaply acquired devalued *assignats*, and later to snap up the estates of refugee aristocrats.

The new property owners enjoyed one other marked advantage. Unlike more than half of France's population and most of its patois-speaking peasants, they both spoke and read French, the language of their title deeds and of the royal law courts where, as a sudden spike in legal cases in the 1780s showed, they increasingly sought to enforce their rights. All this followed the English pattern, as did the eviction of peasants without written leases, the increase in rents, and the use of legislation to widen their claims to exclusive possession of the earth.

As late as 1792, their influence in the Legislative Assembly enabled the new proprietors to abolish communal grazing rights, known as *vaine pâture*, on arable land that had been harvested. "The right of *vaine pâture*," declared a sympathizer, "infringes on the rights of property. Any estate burdened with this right becomes common property when the proprietor has removed his crops." Depriving poorer peasants of the right to graze cattle on the stubble left after harvest must have hit particularly hard following a succession of bad harvests, and the proprietors' use of political power to protect their property offered unmistakable evidence that the French land revolution still had momentum.

In such circumstances, the news of Simonneau's murder created a wave of public revulsion. As the foreign minister, Pierre Lebrun, warned the assembly, the killing of the mayor showed that "all property, all authority is equally threatened." One of his audience proposed that the body be buried in the Panthéon as that of a national martyr. A memorial parade organized in Simonneau's honor attracted two hundred thousand spectators and included a procession of sixty regiments, bands playing funeral music, and a float bearing a model of the Bastille, the very icon of the revolution. Many in the parade carried banners with the words "*Liberté, Egalité, Proprieté*," while others simply said "*Indivisibles*." But Simonneau's killing revealed the opposite: between property rights and human rights existed a stark division.

THE ATTACK ON PROPERTY was launched by Pierre Dolivier, a priest in the parish next to Étampes. When entire families were starving, he said, "It is revolting that the rich man and all that surrounds him—men, dogs and horses—lack for nothing in their idleness, and that those who earn a living only by force of working succumb under the double burden of labor and undernourishment." The belief that anyone had a natural right to property beyond what they needed to support themselves and their families was wrong, he asserted. It was the law, not nature, that enabled an individual to claim property in the land. The state was entitled to curtail a proprietor's wealth in order to keep people fed. To the fury of the new landowners and the bourgeoisie, Dolivier roundly declared that "Only the Nation can really own its land. Natural property does not extend beyond the body of each individual."

No such claim had been made before. Under feudal conditions the king had been assumed to own the state, but that was a god-given property intrinsic to kingship itself. For the first time, it was supposed that the state actually owned the land, because it represented the people who lived there. In the early twentieth century the French Socialist leader

Jean-Jaurés praised Dolivier for having shifted "the Declaration of the Rights of Man towards the light of socialism." But at the time, even Maximilien Robespierre, leader of the most radical Jacobins, did not share such a view of property. However, Dolivier could and did claim powerful support from what was becoming the handbook of the revolution, Jean-Jacques Rousseau's *The Social Contract*.

In an earlier essay, *The Origin of Inequality*, published in 1754, Rousseau had given expression to the general unease in France as feudal possession gave way to private ownership. He pictured the very first property maker staking out some ground and claiming it as his own exclusive possession: "From how many crimes, wars, and murders, from how many horrors and misfortunes might not someone have saved mankind, by pulling up the stakes, or filling up the ditch, and crying to his fellows: Beware of listening to this impostor; you are undone if you once forget that the fruits of the earth belong to us all, and the earth itself to nobody." But once made, this claim to individual ownership of the earth inexorably brought into being laws to protect it—"property, once recognised, gave rise to the first rules of justice"—and eventually the beginnings of government. The problem was that governments also protected extremes of wealth and power. "It is manifestly against the Law of Nature," he concluded, "that a handful of men wallow in luxury, while the famished multitudes lack the necessities of life."

Virtually everything that Rousseau wrote, whether it concerned society, education, nature, or politics, became a best seller. He wrote dramatically and his passionate commitment to individual freedom was irresistible. In *The Social Contract*, published eight years later, he presented a solution not simply to the inequality problem but to the seeming impossibility of creating a government that would be strong enough to protect a person and yet would allow her to "remain as free as before."

Rousseau's ideal government was one that embodied "the general will" of the people. Reflecting his Calvinist background, he ascribed to the general will all the better qualities of human nature, those that naturally pursued happiness and cared for the welfare of others, leaving selfish ambition to the individual. While it would protect its citizens' absolute rights to life and liberty, the government would only guard such property as was needed for the individual's safety and subsistence—"Having his share, he ought to keep to it, and can have no further right against the community." Beyond that amount the importance of preserving equality might require the government to limit the property owner's rights. It clearly had the power to do so because "the right which each individual has to his own estate is always subordinate to the right which the community has over all."

With that sentence, Rousseau set his general will government, and any that followed his model, on a collision course with the solipsistic claim of private property that its individual rights came before any communal needs. When human rights struck property rights, the gutters would overflow with blood.

IN THE MONTHS after Simonneau's murder, the national mood changed. By the summer of 1792, the European monarchies had declared war on republican France, and the flood of *assignats* had driven the rate of inflation sharply higher. Resentment against cash-rich merchants and landowners grew bitter. In November, a petition, clearly influenced by Dolivier, was presented to the assembly, demanding an end to the free trade in corn, and a limit of 120 *arpents* (about one hundred acres) on the amount of land one person could own. That winter, the streets of Paris resounded to the violent attacks of Jacques Roux and his followers, nicknamed *les enragés*, against the rich. The Paris Commune, the city's local authority, pressed for price controls, and the Parisian poor, made desperate by hunger and deprivation, increased the pressure. Early in the New Year, a crowd of barelegged laundrywomen led the sansculottes of Paris to the assembly, demanding that it cap the price of wheat and put an end to the profits of speculators. On April 24, 1793, the explosion occurred. Robespierre, by then the most popular politician in France, told the Paris club of the Jacobins that the Declaration of Rights had been changed.

Robespierre's speeches were famous for their meandering length although, in the view of his critics, they "rarely culminated in any specific measure or legal provision." But they struck a confrontational tone that was increasingly in tune with the mood of ordinary Parisians driven desperate by hunger and deprivation. "Who are our enemies?" he would demand and in the next sentence supply the answer: "The vicious and the rich." His rhetorical device of eliding political and psychological hatred proved hugely effective. "All aristocrats are corrupt," he declared, "and every corrupt man is an aristocrat." Even delivered in a voice described as "dull, monotonous, and wearisome," these menacing, all-enveloping accusations drew wild applause from his followers in the public galleries. Thus it was in the knowledge that he was backed by popular opinion in Paris that Robespierre informed the senior Jacobins of the revised version of human rights. "The right of property is limited, and applies only to that portion which the law guarantees," he said. "Every ownership, any trade, which bears prejudicially on the existence of our fellow-creatures is necessarily illicit and immoral."

Across the country, Jacobin clubs persuaded local courts to block any moves by landowners that infringed on communal rights or peasant occupancy. New laws were passed giving local communes, the replacements of the old feudal parishes, the power to keep common land intact or allocate its use to the poor and propertyless. In June 1793, year one of the French Republic, its new constitution was ratified, giving the vote to all males and guaranteeing four rights to its citizens: "equality, liberty, security, and property." Ostensibly, France now shared with the United States the distinction of having both human and property rights written into its constitutional DNA, but in reality there was a crucial difference. Following Rousseau, the constitution deemed the government to be expressing the general will, and thus to be imbued with such moral authority it could "command only what is just and useful to society; it can forbid only what is injurious to it."

This was the antithesis of the United States Constitution, which created a marketplace of balanced competing interests. Armed with the absolute authority to determine what was useful and what was harmful to society, a government elected under the 1793 constitution would have been able to determine the extent of its citizens' rights. In the face of the worsening economic and military situation, however, the constitution was suspended in October 1793, and its sweeping power was invested in the nine members of the Committee of Public Safety.

Under the influence of Robespierre, the committee, whose remit was to "terrorize" France's foes, unleashed an official campaign of terror in the summer aimed at a new kind of enemy, hostile not to France, but to equality. "All the rich are vicious, in opposition to the Revolution," Robespierre told the Jacobins. An ever-widening circle of people fell within the definition, especially after a cap was set on the price of all essential goods. Shopkeepers whose prices were too high, peasants who hoarded wheat, lawyers who criticized the mock trials, all followed the aristocrats and wealthy and bared their necks to the blade of the guillotine. In his familiar contrapuntal rhetoric, Robespierre justified the use of fear to enforce loyalty to the revolution, praising "virtue without which terror is evil, [and] terror without which virtue is powerless."

Madison's nightmare of the propertyless seizing power from the propertied had become a reality. The blood that gushed down the gutters of

Lyon, one of the centers of resistance, and stained the waters of the Rhone for miles downstream was the more shocking because it was the outcome of deliberate violence by the government against its own citizens. Worse still, almost three-quarters of its victims were the very peasants and workers for whom equality was being sought.

"What signify a few lives lost in a century or two?" Jefferson had written in 1787, expressing sympathy with Shays's rebellion against the propertied interests of Massachusetts. "The tree of liberty must be refreshed from time to time with the blood of patriots and tyrants. It is its natural manure." The sansculottes would have applauded the sentiment. But the unravelling of society followed swiftly on the use of the guillotine. Unemployment soared as factory owners, shopkeepers, and landowners hid or emigrated. Abroad, France's conscript armies sustained themselves on their conquests, but at home an economic catastrophe spiraled out of control. By the time Robespierre was overthrown and guillotined in the Thermidor revolt of July 1794, bringing an end to the Terror, industrial production had collapsed, unemployed workers filled country lanes and city streets, and the state was in debt to the tune of over five billion livres.

THE IDEAS OF Father Dolivier did not disappear when Napoleon grandly announced in 1799 that the principles of the Revolution had been secured, and consequently "the Revolution is finished." A direct line of thought connected the radical clergyman's belief that the size of landed properties should be limited for the general good to the arguments put forward by the leader of the Society of Equals, François-Noel "Gracchus" Babeuf, the first person in modern times to be known as a "communist."

The lesson that Babeuf drew from the failure of the Terror was that it had not gone far enough. To create social equality, government must confiscate and redistribute any land above what was needed for survival and "eradicate within every last individual the hope that he might ever become richer, more powerful, or more distinguished because of his talents, than any of his equals." Government was justified in following this policy, because "whatever an individual hoards of the land and its fruits beyond what he needs for his own nourishment has been stolen from society."

From Babeuf by way of Pierre-Joseph Proudhon, who distilled this strand of French Socialism into the lambent phrase "Property is theft," the argument for the nationalization of private property was waiting for Karl Marx when he arrived in Paris in 1843. In *The Communist Manifesto* he began the task of applying a rural theory to the industrial age, showing how the goal of establishing an egalitarian state would come about through the proletarian revolution. Over the next thirty years, he would set the terms for the great war of the late twentieth century between capitalism and Communism.

THE POLITICAL FAILURE of the Revolution made it appear as though the two kinds of liberty could not coexist. If the freedom to acquire property existed independently of the state, it seemed that no government could legitimately restrict it; if the power of the state to enforce human rights was so overwhelming that its citizens could, in Rousseau's words, be "forced to be free" by the government, then property rights might, as Babeuf argued, lawfully be extinguished by the state.

As though to underline the divide, the English economist and cleric Reverend Thomas Malthus wrote an essay in 1800, *On the Present High Price of Provisions*, in which he explained in terms as uncompromising as Babeuf's why the unconstrained working of the free-market, even in times of famine, was the most efficient way of feeding a population. "The man who refuses to send his corn to market when it is at twenty pounds a load because he thinks that in two months time it will be at thirty [pounds]," Malthus argued, "if he be right in his judgment and succeed in his speculation, is a positive and decided benefactor to the state." The reason was that his load of grain would arrive when it was most needed rather than being put on sale when there was still a plentiful supply. And the higher price would encourage him and his fellow grain producers to plant more for the next season.

According to Malthus's rationale, a profit-driven system of land ownership had to operate without government interference, whatever the short-term pain, otherwise the producers would seek higher profits elsewhere, or, as happened in France, be driven out of production altogether. His thesis was warmly received by Britain's dominant political class, the "country gentlemen." They were determined to reduce the taxes they paid, and Malthusian economics offered a justification for cutting the welfare provisions of the Poor Law that had lasted since the land revolution.

From the outbreak of the Revolution, fear of French ideas of liberty had added to the already suffocating political influence of Britain's landowners. Their power so stifled party politics that just two increasingly reactionary Tory prime ministers, William Pitt the younger and the Earl of Liverpool, held office for thirty-three of the forty-four years between 1783 and 1827. Their long tenure testified to the ability of the government to keep the country gentlemen's support, even for the high level of taxation needed to pay for Britain's costly war against French ideas.

In exchange, the country gentlemen won a wave of "Inclosure Acts," a reduction in their contribution to the Poor Law, and a ferocious social program that prescribed capital punishment for any attack on property—the penalty for stealing a sheep or damaging farm machinery was hanging. With the outbreak of the French Revolution, Pitt pandered to their fear of equal rights by introducing bans on free speech and political meetings, by suspending habeas corpus, and by creating a gigantic army of informers and spies to report on any suspicious behavior. In 1793, the Scottish political reformer Thomas Muir was sentenced to fourteen years' exile in the prison colony of Australia simply for advocating universal suffrage. Thousands of others received lesser sentences for their participation in the Corresponding Societies that discussed the latest ideas from south of the English Channel.

From the repressive nature of Britain's response to the French Revolution, it was clear that a political system built purely on property rights had entered a blind alley. Having tamed their only real competitor, the monarchy, the landowners possessed a virtual monopoly of political power. They used it not merely to protect their property but to crush any calls for political reform that threatened their control. So long as they retained unchallenged power—and they would until a new kind of property manufactured by the Industrial Revolution came to challenge the old form—Britain's landed democracy seemed doomed to follow Poland's aristocratic version into political sterility.

Certainly to Thomas Jefferson, whose blueprint would globalize the idea of privately owned land during the nineteenth century, British politics and British property appeared equally moribund. What he dreamed of was a fairer, more democratic way of owning the earth.

JEFFERSON'S UNDERLYING SUSPICION about the scope of private property rights crystalized into outright hostility while he was minister, or ambassador, to France. The catalyst was an encounter in October 1785 with a poor woman on the outskirts of the royal hunting park at Fontainebleau. Although surrounded by unused but potentially productive land, the woman and her two sons had to survive on the few cents a day she could earn by casual labor, while the royal family and aristocrats with rental incomes of more than $2.5 million a year reserved for their own pleasure vast tracts of ground that could have provided a living for the poor.

"The consequences of this enormous inequality producing so much misery to the bulk of mankind, legislators cannot invent too many devices for subdividing property," Jefferson wrote indignantly to Madison. To break up large, inherited estates, he proposed legislation to outlaw entails and primogeniture that encouraged the concentration of land in a few hands. Liberty required government to intervene to prevent a minority accumulating too much wealth. Bluntly, he called for governments to "tax the higher portions of property in geometrical progression as they rise." Where privately owned ground was left uncultivated, and the poor were consequently denied land to work, "it is clear that the laws of property have been so far extended as to violate natural right." In other words, where the two conflicted, the natural right to happiness ought to have priority over property rights.

Shortly before he returned from Paris in 1789, Jefferson would propose to Madison a yet more radical plan based on the principle "that the earth belongs in usufruct to the living." By this, he meant that users of the land could naturally claim ownership of it during their lifetime, but that any further rights, such as passing it on to designated heirs, had to be created by laws "flowing from the will of society." The usufruct suggestion has generally been regarded as an aberration, largely because he linked it to a wider belief that all laws and contracts and even forms of government should be limited to nineteen years, after which period they would lapse and need to be renewed.

But the proposal that the territory of the new United States should have been owned by its citizens only as leasehold, rather than as outright property, was not unthinkable. By the Treaty of Paris that ended the war with Britain in 1783, all the ground between the Appalachians and the Mississippi passed to the United States. Consequently the land already belonged to the nation and could legally be distributed in any form the government chose.

In Britain, nineteen years was the usual term for a lease, and by retaining ownership, the government would benefit from any increase in the value of its new territory. In 1990, when President Mikhail Gorbachev started to introduce a market economy to the Soviet Union, thirty of America's most distinguished economists wrote an open letter strongly recommending him not to sell off the state's land, because in the long term it was more economically efficient to rent or lease it. Their argument was precisely the same as Jefferson's: leasing the land would allow future generations to enjoy a rising income from its growing value, while the sale of it would give a small gain but allow speculators to make the largest profit.

On his return to the United States, Jefferson dropped the usufruct proposal for owning land from public utterance, but it continued to appear in his private correspondence about other forms of ownership, such as that of inventions. Nor did he ever alter his belief that the right to individually owned land itself was simply a legal concept created by a long-established society, and that any idea of a natural right of private ownership was superficial nonsense.

A democratic government, consequently, had the right to legislate so that property was owned in the public interest, and he believed this to be especially true of a republican government that needed to safeguard the independence of its citizens by securing as wide a distribution of land as possible. To achieve that end, Jefferson argued, government intervention to restrict property rights and to redistribute wealth through increasing taxation was not only right but a duty.

Yet, by the sort of paradox that characterized his unsurpassedly creative political career, he, more than any other single person, laid the foundations for the greatest private property society in history.

THE FIRST STEPS were taken in 1784, just before Jefferson went to Paris. Three different Congressional committees under his chairmanship reported their recommendations for dealing with the formerly British territory lying between the Appalachians and the Mississippi River. The strategy they proposed was that it should become not merely American territory, but American property. The land had first to be bought from its native inhabitants, but not by individuals or states, only by the United States. Before the national government disposed of this territory, it should survey the land in squares—a shape simple to measure out, and easily checked for size by the would-be purchaser—with the lines running north-south and east-west.

Not only would the land be presurveyed, Jefferson's committee on the Western Lands proposed that it should be divided up into square territories—they were given exotic names like Cherronesus, Pelisipia, and Polypotamia—and when the population within any of them reached twenty thousand, the inhabitants could apply to join the Union as an independent state. Until then the territories were to be governed by officers appointed by Congress, and their admission would only be approved on certain conditions. The new states would "forever remain a part of the

United States of America"; their government had to be "republican in form," and "after the year 1800 of the Christian aera, there shall be neither slavery nor involuntary servitude in any of the said states."

What Jefferson had in mind when drawing up these proposals was a gigantic piece of social engineering. All Americans were to have at least "a little portion of land" because that would guarantee their republican independence of mind and freedom from outside pressure. "The small landholders are the most precious part of a state," he told Madison. In his ideal republic, these hardworking farmers would provide a bedrock of republican virtue. "Those who labour in the earth are the chosen people of God, if ever he had a chosen people," Jefferson wrote in *Notes on the State of Virginia* in 1782, "whose breasts he has made his peculiar deposit for substantial and genuine virtue." But the smallness of their holding was important. As his letters from Paris made clear, too great a size led to inequality and poverty, and thus threatened the republic's democratic structure.

Although some of his proposals were discarded in his absence, notably the names and a system of decimal measurement he had recommended, the acquisition of territory, its survey and sale as private property, and the power of Congress to supervise the entire process leading to statehood, were adopted into law. As much as his authorship of the Declaration of Independence and purchase of the Louisiana Territory, Jefferson's plan for the physical and political structure of the future United States earns him his place as the single most important influence in the nation's beginnings. That the Founding Father most hostile to the concept of private landed property should have been the architect of its greatest triumph must be reckoned as one of the stranger quirks of history.

Section Four

THE TRIUMPH OF INDIVIDUAL OWNERSHIP

Chapter Thirteen

The Evolution of Property

Just north of the decaying town of East Liverpool, Ohio, once the self-proclaimed "pottery capital of the world," a stone pillar stands as testimony to the first effects of Jefferson's blueprint. Half-hidden in the trees that grow along the banks of the Ohio River, the pillar carries a plaque that reads: "The Point of Beginning. 1112 feet south of this spot was the point of beginning for surveying the public lands of the United States. There on September 30 1785, Thomas Hutchins, first Geographer of the United States, began the Geographer's Line of the Seven Ranges."

What Hutchins began beside the Ohio was a grid, a checkerboard of straight lines running north-south as meridians and east-west as lines of latitude. Each square on the board measured thirty-six square miles. The process of making the pattern could hardly have been simpler. From the riverbank, Hutchins's first team of surveyors scrambled up a steep wooded hill heading directly westward. They were armed with two essential instruments, a magnetic compass and twenty-two yards of metal links known as a Gunter's chain. Originally invented to facilitate the transformation of feudal English land into private property, Gunter's chain was to become the instrument that tamed the West more effectively than any rifle. The compass gave the direction, marked physically by a blaze on a tall tree on the horizon; a small army of axmen then hewed a track through the woods and undergrowth, and finally the two chainmen began to measure out the distance toward the mark.

The rear man stood by the starting stake with one end of the chain and ensured that the front man carrying the other end was always in line with the blaze on the tree. At the end of twenty-two yards, a tally peg was inserted, the rear chainman came up, and the process was repeated. Thus they progressed through the wilderness like a caterpillar, hunching up and stretching out, drawing a straight line to the west. Eighty chains made 1,760 yards or a mile, and 480 chains made six miles or one side of a township. Later the surveyors would repeat the process, but this time traveling northward, and when the other sides of the square had been marked out, its area would be subdivided into thirty-six sections, each measuring one square mile.

In September 1787, the land surveyed by Hutchins's teams went on sale in New York City. John Martin bought a square mile identified as Lot 20, in Township 7, Range 4 (meaning that it was in the seventh square northward and fourth westward from the starting point), a tract now part of Belmont County, Ohio, and thus became the first owner of this new America that would eventually stretch to the Pacific. But the sale of the first seven ranges surveyed west of the Ohio was so disappointing—less than $120,000 was raised—that the public lands survey was set aside for eight years. Instead, Congress chose to privatize the process and sold millions of unsurveyed acres to land companies. Although the companies' surveys were conducted in hurried, often slapdash fashion, the properties covering most of Ohio were arranged in roughly the same pattern of squares as Hutchins had measured.

The ordinance enacted by the Continental Congress in 1787 "for the government of the Territory of the United States northwest of the River Ohio" also bore Jefferson's mark. The area covered all of present-day Ohio, Indiana, and Illinois and most of Michigan, and although neither the names of the states nor their shapes were those specified by the 1784 report, the ban on entails—specifying who among future generations might inherit the property—and on primogeniture were Jeffersonian measures, as was the provision making slavery illegal. His influence was apparent too in the phrase that justified the allocation of a square mile section at the center of each township to finance public education in the Northwestern Territory: it was, said the ordinance, "necessary to good government and the happiness of mankind." There was no suggestion, however, that the land would be sold as anything but private property as understood by common law.

The 1787 Ordinance was a remarkable document, not least because for the first time an American state was to grow up around an entirely American structure of government. In a striking sentence used by the Reverend Manasseh Cutler, one of the promoters of the Ohio Company, "there will be no *wrong* habits to combat, and no inveterate systems to overturn—there is no rubbish to remove before you can lay the foundation."

In 1796, the process of surveying the public lands was renationalized, and thereafter the gigantic task of converting what would amount to 1.8 billion acres of the United States landmass into federal property became a government enterprise. In the course of more than two centuries, a billion acres would be surveyed and sold as private property, the rest being retained as federal and state land. The lines drawn across the country would become the markers not only of individual properties, but of counties, cities, and states. Roads and streets still follow the original surveyors' lines, making it possible to peer down from an aircraft window and see below the physical evidence of the infrastructure of American society. In economic terms alone, it is a record of the greatest orderly transfer of public resources to the private sector in history.

The first effects of the survey could be seen in Ohio. The 1800 census found about forty-five thousand settlers in the state, but within twenty years the population had grown more than ten times, to 581,000. Significantly, almost nine million acres of federal land that had sold at between $1.25 and $2.25 an acre, raising more than seventeen million dollars for the U.S. Treasury, were by then worth five dollars an acre for unimproved lots, and almost twelve dollars for cleared land. That rapidly increasing capital value was already being translated into industrial and commercial wealth. A survey in 1819 showed that, driven by agriculture, Ohio boasted no fewer than twenty-seven banks, six furnaces, twenty wool and cotton mills, and three large factories, all this barely a generation after Hutchins's survey teams had first unrolled a Gunter's chain in the region.

Within the grid, land was at first measured out in parcels no smaller than the one square mile section, and sold for a minimum of $640, a sum that had to be paid in full. But legislation rapidly reduced the smallest area, to a half-section in 1800, a quarter-section or 160 acres in 1804, and eventually to a quarter-quarter section, or forty acres, in 1832. The minimum price was only fifty dollars with a down payment of no more than $12.50 and the remainder payable over three years.

Every variety of settler purchased these squares. Some came from Europe, others from already settled territory in the east. Most traveled westward as families, often as whole communities, and a few as individual adventurers. But whatever their background, the process of buying, settling, and improving the land brought each one of them into a process that was distinctively American. Even a pioneer family like the Pulliams, who had no use for authority, found themselves drawn into the system.

In 1796, John Pulliam, the head of the family, who had already squatted on farms in Virginia and Kentucky, chose to leapfrog far ahead of the survey, moving across the Ohio through what would become Ohio, Indiana, and Illinois as far west as the Mississippi River. Much of this was compacted prairie soil, where tall bluestem grass and wild rye grew taller than a horse's head, and their roots knotted into an unyielding mass that could not be broken up until John Deere's heavy, self-scouring steel ploughs were introduced in the 1840s. The Pulliam family was Scotch-Irish, and as stubborn and restless as its eighteenth-century forebears who had swarmed unchecked through the Virginia Piedmont in the 1730s. With their few goods piled in a cart, accompanied by long-legged hogs and some scrawny cattle, the Pulliams and their like settled for a year or two on land beside any creek where there was enough water to produce a stand of timber and slake the animals' thirst.

Even shallow-rooted elms and sycamores broke up the ground well enough for it to be ploughed and gave timber for making cabins. Along with maples, whose sweet sap in springtime could be boiled into sugar, there were oaks and beeches that produced acorns and mast for the hogs, and hickories like the pecan whose nuts could be pounded to flour or eaten whole, and fruit trees and wild vines carrying ripe cherries and sweet grapes. This produce ensured that the first prairie settlers were timber-dwellers rather than grassland farmers.

Thus far in the process, there was nothing distinctively American about the Pulliams. They shared the freebooting instincts of their equivalents on the Russian steppes a hundred years earlier, the *ornodvortsy*, and their self-reliant, muddy, bartering, lifestyle. Both were refugees from their own culture rather than its forerunners. But in 1823, when Robert Pulliam, the pioneer's son, was farming in what would form Sugar Creek, Illinois, 180 miles southwest of Chicago, the deputy surveyor for that district, Angus Langham, arrived with his chainmen and axmen, known in the woodless prairies as "moundmen" because they constructed mounds rather than blazing trees to mark section corners.

On the map Langham provided for the Public Land Survey, Robert Pulliam's farm was marked as being in Section 21, Township 14 North, Range 5 West, Third Principal Meridian. Beside it was written the letters "AP," meaning applied for, which showed that Robert was still squatting, as his father had done, but that he had claimed the right of preempting the land when the survey had been completed. Once the claim was entered on the definitive survey map, paid for, and patented, that parcel of prairie, amounting to 480 acres, became private property, whose ownership would be protected by the full force of the law. John Pulliam would have taken pride in defending his claim with a long rifle packed full of black powder and lead shot, but his son understood that a surveyor's plat carried far more firepower.

Nevertheless, the capital value of the land in Sugar Creek sucked Robert into a larger economy. Borrowing against the value of his original property, he bought another eighty acres on the far side of the creek and began to construct a dam to power a water mill for grinding flour. It might have been the classic transition from land to business, but in 1837 the land market collapsed, the banks called in the Pulliam loan, and his property evaporated.

It reappeared in the hands of people like the shrewd and careful farmer Philemon Stoute Jr., who in 1846 inherited 350 acres from his father, and by 1881 owned twenty-three hundred acres in Sangamon County. Unlike the first settlers, he employed laborers to work his land and invested the profits in quarter-sections that he rented out to tenant farmers. Most of his hired help and tenants were supplied by the families of settlers who had lost their farms following the 1837 slump. Jefferson's ideal of republican self-reliance was beginning to take on the classic appearance of private property capitalism.

DIVIDED UP INTO SQUARES, the America that reminded the earliest colonists of God and provoked a sensual hunger in later settlers could also be treated by speculators simply as a commodity defined by numbers. A uniform, invariable shape that took no account of springs or hills or swamps was an obstacle to efficient agriculture, but to a financier tracking the rise and fall in land values, it was a great convenience. The grid, designed by Thomas Jefferson to create republican farmers, also turned out to be ideal for buying, trading, and speculating. The consequence was what D. W. Meinig, doyen of twentieth-century American geographers, termed "the most basic feature of the settlement process: That it tended to be suffused in speculation." The paradox was that most of the speculators were not big-time financiers—though they were there in plenty—but small-time republican farmers.

The legal framework for this dynamic land market was established by two Supreme Court opinions delivered by Chief Justice John Marshall. In the case of *Fletcher v. Peck* in 1810, he had cleared the way for the owners of real estate to buy and sell their property according to the relatively clear-cut federal laws of contract rather than by the convoluted principles of common law that in England had become burdened with entails, reversions, jointures, indentures, and other legal defenses against the sale of land.

Thirteen years later, in the case of *Johnson v. M'Intosh*, Marshall confirmed what Jefferson had always asserted, that only the United States government had the right to buy the territory of "dependent nations," meaning Native Americans, within its frontier, and thereby ensured that a seemingly inexhaustible supply of nationalized land would be available for sale with clear title to new Americans. Taken together, Marshall's two judgments made it simple to treat a parcel of land as capital, meaning both as a reserve of past earnings and a resource to be exploited in the future.

The land market that was created by the survey and the law had an energy that astonished the young French nobleman Alexis de Tocqueville when he began to travel across the United States in 1831. "It is difficult to describe the rapacity with which the American rushes forward to secure the immense booty which fortune proffers to him," he wrote in wonder. "It seldom happens that an American farmer settles for good upon the land which he occupies: especially in the districts of the Far West he brings land into tillage in order to sell it again, and not to farm it: he builds a farmhouse on the speculation that, as the state of the country will soon be changed by the increase of population, a good price will be gotten for it."

Between May 1800 and June 1820 the United States sold over 13.6 million acres of public lands at an average price of less than $1.70. Once access to markets was established, the value of even "unimproved" land rose by more than five times that figure. The process of clearing trees or breaking the impacted soil of the prairie more than doubled the price of "unimproved" land, and it was this capital gain, estimated at more than two thirds of a farmer's total capital stock, that provided the economic impetus for the furious rush into newly released public lands. Adding the growth in value to revenue from the sale of crops and livestock, a farmer could expect an estimated 12 percent annual return on his investment in the mid-nineteenth century.

Adam Smith had pointed to the essential role that banks played in realizing the value in land, "by giving credit to the extent of a certain sum (two or three thousand pounds, for example), to any individual who could procure two persons of undoubted credit and good landed estate to become surety for him." In the United States, this process was accelerated by the speed with which banks opened up after the sale of public lands. The twenty-seven banks that operated in Ohio in 1819 were not exceptional. Altogether the number in the United States rose from 88 in 1811 to 392 in just seven years, with the new Western banks lending and issuing paper money far more aggressively than in the conservative East.

Banks were not the only means of releasing the capital value in land. Probates and inventories of valuables in rural Massachusetts showed that less than twenty years after the 1786 rebellion, when poverty drove desperate farmers to armed resistance, the rising value of their farms allowed them to borrow money to specialize in more profitable dairy farming, to invest in the region's cotton mills, and to buy shares in turnpikes, bridges, insurance companies, and even in the banks that lent them money. In 1839 the savings bank in Lowell, Massachusetts, revealed that a hundred working women each had more than $1,000 in her savings account. Farming capital was morphing into industrial and commercial investment.

What is striking about the birth of free-enterprise capitalism in the United States is how much it owed to government direction. The basic structure came from the fund of nationalized land released as private property, but the federal government also allocated millions of acres to encourage the spread of railroads, the mining of iron, the development of the lumber trade, and perhaps most interestingly, the growth of public education. The policy that began in Ohio, of reserving one square mile section in every range for education, would finance every kind of schooling from elementary schools through universities, and in particular the unrivalled system of 108 land-grant colleges and universities, stretching from Florida to California, that provided American industry with the largest well-educated workforce in the world. The whole thrust of government intervention was taken further during the crucial decades of the early nineteenth century, when rural capital was firing up the beginnings of the industrial revolution. Under the leadership of the two giants of Congress, Henry Clay and Daniel Webster, the federal government adopted a policy of planning that combined trade, tax, and spending measures to shape the development of the country's economy.

A wall of tariffs, imposing duties up to 40 percent on imported goods, was put in place to shield the fledgling American industries growing up around the Public Lands Survey from Britain's more developed, industrial production. To control the supply of money, a central bank, the Second Bank of the United States, was created in 1816 (the First Bank, set up by Alexander Hamilton in 1791 with a twenty-year charter had been dissolved in 1811); finally a federal investment program was put in place to create an infrastructure of roads, notably the Cumberland Road through the Alleghenies, and canals linking distant producers of wheat and hogs and cotton with their markets in the north and east.

The American System, as Clay named it, to distinguish it from "the British colonial system" of unregulated free trade, represented a new, government-directed form of capitalism. Its shortcomings, particularly the failure to control the cycle of boom and bust, were exploited by Andrew Jackson to bring about its demise in the 1830s, but for twenty years the system had a direct impact on the economic development of the United States by easing the transformation of rural capital into industrial investment. Indeed, its effectiveness created such an impression on one German visitor, the economist Friederich List, that he used the American System as the basis of his program for the hugely successful planned economy of nineteenth-century Prussia.

THE CONJOINED NATURE OF LAND and credit became obvious in 1819, when the engine of growth abruptly died. Confidence in the clouds of paper money issued by the banks, amounting to sixty-eight million dollars in 1816, suddenly faded. By chance, the public demand for cash coincided with the United States's need to make its last payment to European banks for the Louisiana Purchase. In an ill-judged move, the new central bank called in silver from its branches and from state banks just as customers were trying to change paper to cash. Unable to meet their obligations, many state banks crashed, causing more panic, the supply of paper money quickly contracted by a third, and sales of public lands collapsed from almost fourteen million dollars a year to little more than one million in 1821.

In its response, the Monroe administration conspicuously did not bail out the banks, but instead took significant steps to safeguard the capital investment of the purchasers of public lands, many of whom had bought on credit. Either the terms were eased, notably by extending the period of payment, or buyers were allowed to keep what land they had paid for and write off the rest. The engine soon fired again, and quickly became a boom producing a surge in sales that earned fourteen million dollars in 1835, almost half the revenues of the United States government. "Who ever heard of a man buying and selling a farm at the same or a lessened price?" an agricultural commentator observed in 1836. "It is so well understood that the seller is to have more than he gave, that it has almost become a settled principle in the purchase of real estate."

The next year the engine spectacularly blew up once more, before surging again in the 1840s. But despite its seemingly uncontrollable cycle of boom and bust, the power of rural capitalism continued to drive the nation's headlong expansion into the West. Inseparably attached to it was the relentless spread of government.

IN THE SUMMER OF 1836, at the height of the boom, Caleb Blodgett from Vermont built a log cabin with the help of his sons and some friends, and plowed a hundred acres on some grassy bluffs overlooking the Rock River that marked the western border of Illinois. With this evidence of "improvement," he and his helpers made squatters' preemptive claims to some seven thousand surrounding acres. The following spring, Dr. Horace White from Colebrook, New Hampshire, arrived and bought almost one third of Blodgett's claim, about two thousand acres, on behalf of the New England Emigrating Society for $2,500. As White explained fifty years later, "Purchasers of claims took their chances of being able to hold what they had bargained for. What was paid for in such a case was the chance that the government land office would eventually recognize the claim as valid under the pre-emption laws, and give a patent for it." Until then, the fourteen settler families had to rely on the unofficial rules of claimants' associations that based ownership not just on payment but on use and occupancy.

Squashed into three log cabins, they barely survived the first year. In winter the snow blew in through the crevices in the rough-hewn walls, and until the first crops were harvested, the community had to live on what they could hunt and fish, and on barrels of flour carted in on almost impassably muddy tracks. The married women suffered terribly. Worn down by childbirth and breast-feeding, with no respite from the need to farm and pickle, preserve and cook, several died in their thirties during the early years. Lack of food forced the settlers to slaughter an ox used for plowing and send an emergency team to buy a barrel of pork from a settlement downriver.

Yet, looking back over half a century, White could also remember the beauty of the untouched prairie. "Blackberries, strawberries, wild plums, wild grapes, hickory nuts, hazel nuts and black walnuts were to be had for the trouble of gathering them, and as for wild flowers I cannot begin to tell you how the prairies, the woods and the river banks glowed with them," he told a an audience of students in the 1880s.

During their first summer, the Public Lands Survey mapped Blodgett's Settlement, locating it inside Section 35, Township 1 North, Range 12 East, Fourth Principal Meridian. Despite their hunger, a delegate from the settlement was promptly sent to the General Land Office in Milwaukee to pay the federal government the purchase price for the land. According to a series of Pre-Emption Acts passed since 1831, the payment conferred a right of ownership until a formal patent could be issued. This was the classic squatter's progression, adding layer after layer of ownership from occupancy and improvement, through purchase and registration until with the issue of a patent for the land it became official property.

But what was most noticeable about the story of Blodgett's Settlement, and a thousand frontier communities like it, was the way the survey bound them into a system of democratic government. The surveyors had not only noted their claim but had placed it inside the newly designated Wisconsin Territory, whose federally appointed governor, Henry Dodge, nominated the chief justice, judges, and sheriffs to maintain order, including protection of land records. In 1836, the Blodgett Settlement pioneers registered with the territorial census, in order to be able to vote for a territorial legislature with the power to legislate for frontier needs. On the basis of the census, the territorial government divided the eastern half of the territory into four large counties. This placed the pioneer families of Blodgett's Settlement in Rock County, and made them eligible to vote for a Board of Commissioners with responsibility for law enforcement and administration of the county.

Thus even before the patent was issued confirming the settlers' ownership of the their land, and before they had completed the water-driven sawmill that would produce boards so that proper houses could be built to replace the log cabins, the settlement had three layers of government—county, territorial, and federal. By 1840, it also had a federally appointed postmaster, and a year later a county courthouse was being constructed in a place that now preferred to call itself Beloit City. It had taken less than five years for the frontier community of Blodgett's Settlement to transform itself into a city with a Board of Commissioners, a school district, a federal postmaster, a delegate to the territorial legislature, and a courthouse where prairie flowers and wild plums had grown just a few summers before.

★ ★ ★

THE IMPORTANCE OF THE SURVEY to the shape of capitalism and democracy was made vividly obvious by its absence from Kentucky, on the southern bank of the Ohio River. Instead of the simple squares of the Public Lands Survey, real estate there was delineated according to the old English system of "metes and bounds," that is by reference to natural objects such as streams, boulders, and mountain peaks, a method that gave rise to complex shapes beyond the ability of inadequately trained surveyors to measure accurately. Adding to the confusion, until 1792 the state had existed as a county of Virginia and the land had been used as backing for a mass of financial securities, including treasury bonds, military warrants, and paper money, creating multiple claimants to the same parcels of land. "The titles in Kentucky w[ill] be Disputed for a Century to Come yet, when it's an old Settled Country," predicted Uria Brown, a real estate lawyer, in 1816. The resultant turmoil of fraud and corruption prevented any but the wealthy establishing secure title to their property.

In 1820, land with uncertain title could be bought in Kentucky as cheaply as ¢12.5 an acre, and the population, five times that of Ohio in 1800, was now smaller than its neighbor's. Unable to establish their claims, a steady stream of poorer families, including that of Thomas Lincoln, father of Abraham, left the state. As Abraham Lincoln himself explained, their move to Indiana and then Illinois was "partly on account of slavery, but chiefly on account of the difficulty in land titles in Kentucky." By 1829, Supreme Court Justice Joseph Story concluded that Kentucky's system of land distribution had virtually broken down, forcing settlers to take land wherever they could, "without any previous survey under public authority, and without any such boundaries as were precise, permanent, and unquestionable."

For generations, Kentucky was taken as an awful warning of what could go wrong. When Stephen Austin secured Mexican agreement in 1821 to settle Texas, he specifically cited the state's problems as his reason for measuring out Texan land in rectangles before selling it to would-be settlers. But to some extent the South as a whole suffered the same distortions. From the colonial era, Virginia, the Carolinas, and Georgia had opted not just for metes and bounds surveys, but for a complicated system of registration and patenting ownership that rewarded those with political connections and deep pockets. With independence these characteristics spilled across the Appalachians, and, following the Louisiana Purchase, across the Mississippi. The consequences were far-reaching.

★ ★ ★

For obvious reasons, the conventional explanation for the particular nature of Southern society took slavery to be the critical factor. But only 384,000 of the Southern white population of 8,099,760 in 1860 actually owned slaves. And the great majority of owners held fewer than five slaves, not enough to be important economically, and socially significant only after color had come to define the difference between free and unfree. Because of the legal constraints imposed by a slave society, few in the South could escape the influence of the "peculiar institution." But to judge by editorials in Southern newspapers—almost uniformly hostile to slavery until the 1830s—the support of most Southerners was negligible until in the 1850s slavery started to become a test of Southern identity, and even then in the Appalachians, especially in west Virginia and eastern Tennessee, where slaves were virtually absent, anti-slavery feeling was widespread. At least as important in shaping Southern society was the pervasive economic and social effects of the uneven distribution of land.

By one modern estimate, up to 90 percent of Kentucky's agricultural land ended in the hands of an elite minority, while the least productive areas were left to mountain farmers, squatters, sharecroppers, and free people of color. When Kentucky's first historian, Humphrey Marshall, wrote of its foundation, he castigated the corruption that had enveloped its politics. The society that emerged from the chaos of its land distribution was not republican, he declared, but an oligarchy that proved that "those who hold and exercise the governing power . . . will take care of themselves—and by consequence will take care of those who possess a similarity of interest and of feelings."

When the new federal government attempted to introduce the Public Lands Survey in 1790 to the Southwestern Territory, roughly today's Tennessee, Alabama, and Mississippi, it proved impossible to measure out the North's neat squares. Surveyors encountered large swaths of land that had either been allocated under metes and bounds surveys to holders of military warrants and other financial securities, or been sold to state-sponsored land companies, such as the Yazoo Land Company, a consortium of investors who acquired forty million acres in the Yazoo valley from a bribed Georgia legislature. In addition to these frequently absent owners, the surveyors' plats had to register claims made under Spanish land law and individual deals arranged by speculators with Cherokee and Creek owners.

Despite such difficulties, the most important economic group of immigrants could always be sure of securing title to the property they wanted. When cotton prices doubled in the early years of the nineteenth century, growers in Virginia and the Carolinas started to move in increasing numbers from the exhausted soil in the east to find more productive plantations in Alabama and Mississippi. The cotton planters were accompanied by lines of slaves and long wagon trains carrying furniture and machinery in an undertaking on the scale of relocating an automobile factory today. Such buyers had to be sure beforehand that they had good legal title to the ground, and in 1818, a year after General John Coffee was appointed surveyor-general of Alabama, the Public Lands Office in Huntsville, Alabama, promised customers that it was prepared to "do business on commission . . . [and] give any information to people wishing to purchase an advantage" in return for "a liberal per centum" of the price. Whether the client wished to locate a suitable tract or to engross several different parcels, if necessary by removing squatters, the people in Coffee's office were prepared to "do business on commission, and receive in pay either a part of the land purchased; or money."

Unlike the North, with its broad-based access to rural capital, the antebellum South ended up with a vestigial middle-class—just 12 percent of the population owned plantations big enough to employ twenty or more slaves—and a minute elite of barely a thousand families owning gigantic spreads requiring more than one hundred slaves to work them. In 1850, this elite earned almost as much as the rest of the population, an income disparity that would not be repeated until the twenty-first century.

In 1803 the Louisiana Purchase added nine hundred thousand square miles of new territory to the four hundred thousand already in the public domain, giving fresh urgency to the work of the Public Lands Survey. Much of the territory around New Orleans was already measured out in French *arpents*; further north, on the banks of the Mississippi, more had been surveyed in *varas* by the Spanish Empire and sold to settlers, including a spread in Missouri to Daniel Boone. But as one outraged surveyor complained after examining land registry records in the Louisiana Territory, "There has been Leaves cut out of the Books and others pasted in . . . the dates have been evidently altered in a large proportion of the certificates. Plats have been altered from smaller to Larger. Names erased and others incerted . . ."

The need for greater authority in the work of the Public Lands Survey led to the appointment in 1803 of a new surveyor-general by the Jefferson administration, Professor Jared Mansfield, formerly head of mathematics at West Point Military Academy. Mansfield chose to align the survey's squares on a series of precisely drawn north-south lines known as the Principal Meridians, whose path was painstakingly established through celestial navigation, and crossed at right angles by an equally exact east-west baseline.

With these major lines acting as checks, any deviation in the lesser township and section lines run by grunt surveyors, such as those employed by Hutchins, could be easily corrected. The First Principal Meridian, calculated by Mansfield himself, was quite short, forming the state border between Ohio and Indiana, but the longest, the Fifth Principal Meridian, began in Arkansas, and was extended northwards as far as the Canadian border, acting as a control for the survey in Arkansas, Missouri, Iowa, South Dakota, North Dakota, and most of Minnesota.

Eventually the squares of the Public Land Survey would stretch west from the Appalachians as far as the Pacific Ocean, and from the Mexican border north to Canada. Painstakingly marked out yard by yard and chain by chain by teams of surveyors, they would cover more than three million square miles and represent what must be the largest, homogeneous, man-made structure in history.

During the three decades after the Louisiana Purchase, the history of the United States was marked by national events such as the War of 1812 that threw off the last British influence, the acquisition of Florida followed by the destruction of the Spanish Empire, the election of Andrew Jackson, and the development of a new kind of democracy. In a sense, however, these were merely superficial disturbances to the real history experienced by most Americans, the process that put three-quarters of them in possession of the land that fed, sheltered, and clothed them, and, quite extraordinarily, made many of them wealthy. Until about 1830, sales of public lands rarely amounted to more than a few million acres a year. But between 1830 and 1837, more than fifty-seven million acres were sold, proof of the effectiveness of Jared Mansfield's squares.

"The possession of land is the aim of all action, generally speaking and the cure for all social evils among men in the United States," wrote the visiting English writer Harriet Martineau in 1837. "If a man is disappointed in politics or love, he goes and buys land. If he disgraces himself,

Sir Humphrey Gilbert. PORTRAIT OF SIR HUMPHREY GILBERT (OIL ON BOARD), ENGLISH SCHOOL, (SIXTEENTH CENTURY)/COMPTON CASTLE, TORQUAY, DEVON, UK/NATIONAL TRUST PHOTOGRAPHIC LIBRARY/THE BRIDGEMAN ART LIBRARY.

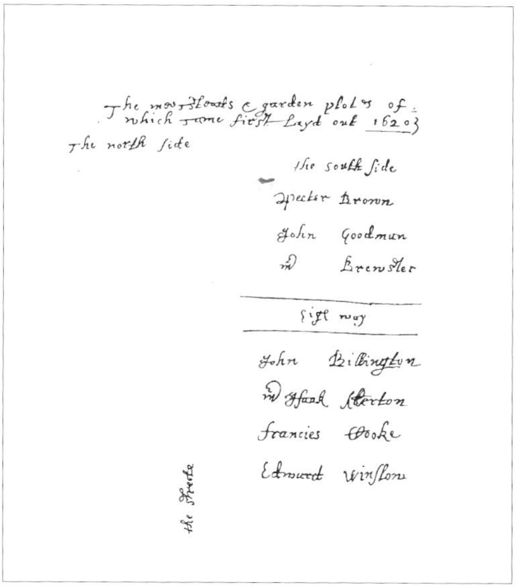
The meersteads & garden plots of which came first layd out 1620

The north side

the south side

Peeter Brown

John Goodman

mr Brewster

high way

John Billington

mr Isaak Alerton

Francies Cooke

Edward Winslow

the Streete

Facsimile of the first page of *Plimouths Great Book of Deeds*, in the handwriting of Governor William Bradford.

Thomas Hobbes. LIBRARY OF CONGRESS.

The cover of Thomas Hobbes's *Leviathan.* LIBRARY OF CONGRESS RARE BOOK & SPECIAL COLLECTIONS.

Sir William Petty. SIR WILLIAM PETTY, FROM *OLD ENGLAND'S WORTHIES* BY LORD BROUGHAM AND OTHERS, PUBLISHED LONDON, C. 1880S (LITHO), ENGLISH SCHOOL, (NINETEENTH CENTURY)/PRIVATE COLLECTION/KEN WELSH/THE BRIDGEMAN ART LIBRARY.

Adam Smith. LIBRARY OF CONGRESS.

John Locke. LIBRARY OF CONGRESS.

Jean-Jacques Burlamaqui. LIBRARY OF CONGRESS.

Karl Marx. LIBRARY OF CONGRESS.

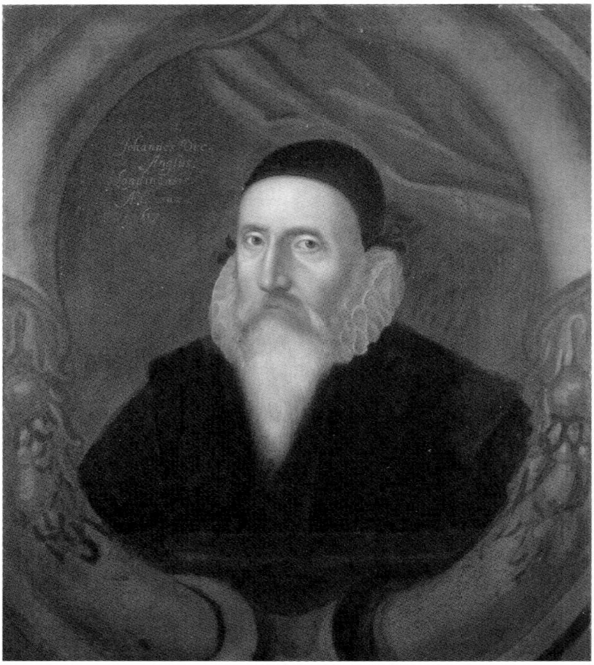

John Dee. PORTRAIT OF JOHN DEE (1547–1608) (OIL ON CANVAS), ENGLISH SCHOOL, (SEVENTEENTH CENTURY)/ASHMOLEAN MUSEUM, UNIVERSITY OF OXFORD, UK/THE BRIDGEMAN ART LIBRARY.

Sergei Eisenstein's vision of Ivan the Terrible, the founder of the Russian autocracy.

Peter the Great. PAINTING BY ALEKSEY ANTROPOV.

The Qianlong emperor. BEIJING PALACE MUSEUM.

Thomas Jefferson. LIBRARY OF CONGRESS.

Jean-Jacques Rousseau.
LIBRARY OF CONGRESS.

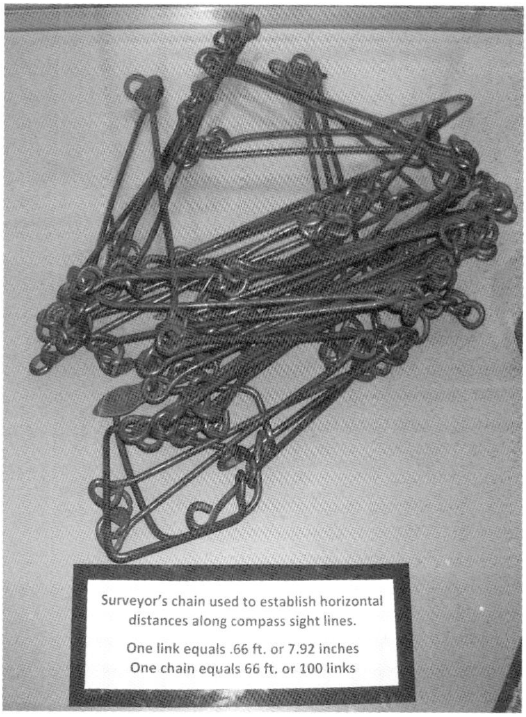
Surveyor's chain used to establish horizontal distances along compass sight lines.
One link equals .66 ft. or 7.92 inches
One chain equals 66 ft. or 100 links

Gunter's chain; twenty-two yards, one hundred links. The instrument that measured out the United States and the British Empire. COURTESY OF WIKIMEDIA COMMONS, PHOTO BY USER ROSEOHIORESIDENT.

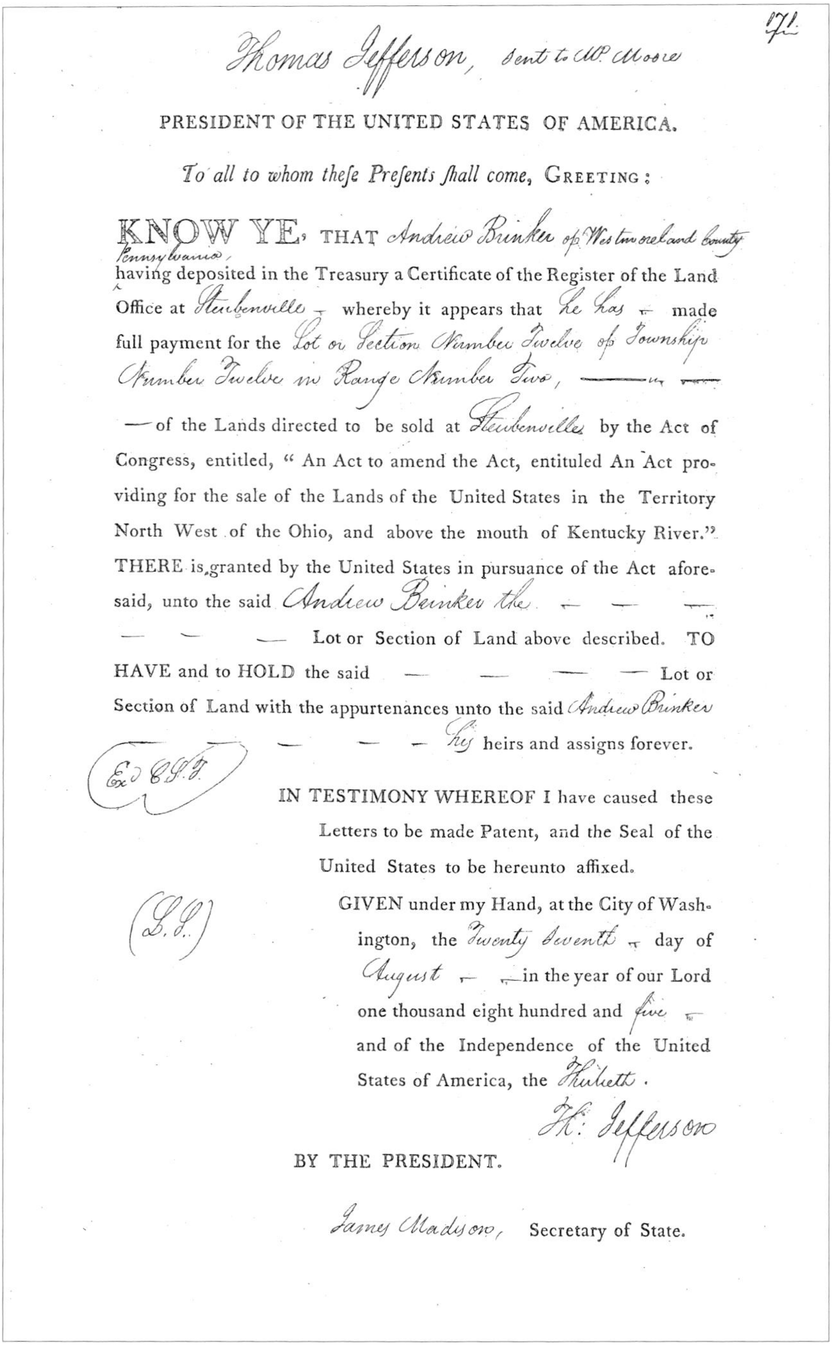

71

Thomas Jefferson, sent to Mr. Moore

PRESIDENT OF THE UNITED STATES OF AMERICA.

To all to whom these Presents shall come, GREETING:

KNOW YE, THAT Andrew Brinker of Westmoreland County Pennsylvania, having deposited in the Treasury a Certificate of the Register of the Land Office at Steubenville whereby it appears that he has made full payment for the Lot or Section Number Twelve of Township Number Twelve in Range Number Two, — of the Lands directed to be sold at Steubenville by the Act of Congress, entitled, "An Act to amend the Act, entituled An Act providing for the sale of the Lands of the United States in the Territory North West of the Ohio, and above the mouth of Kentucky River." THERE is granted by the United States in pursuance of the Act aforesaid, unto the said Andrew Brinker the — Lot or Section of Land above described. TO HAVE and to HOLD the said — Lot or Section of Land with the appurtenances unto the said Andrew Brinker his heirs and assigns forever.

Exd C.S.T.

IN TESTIMONY WHEREOF I have caused these Letters to be made Patent, and the Seal of the United States to be hereunto affixed.

(L.S.)

GIVEN under my Hand, at the City of Washington, the Twenty Seventh day of August in the year of our Lord one thousand eight hundred and five and of the Independence of the United States of America, the Thirtieth.

Th: Jefferson

BY THE PRESIDENT.

James Madison, Secretary of State.

Patent for land ownership in Ohio in 1805, signed by President Thomas Jefferson and Secretary of State James Madison. NATIONAL ARCHIVES AND RECORDS ADMINISTRATION.

A combine harvester in an Idaho wheat field. COURTESY OF THE UNITED STATES DEPARTMENT OF AGRICULTURE.

Edward Gibbon Wakefield. COURTESY OF THE WIKIMEDIA COMMONS AND THE NATIONAL LIBRARY OF AUSTRALIA.

Henry George. LIBRARY OF CONGRESS.

Like a European feudal knight, a samurai owed his standing to the peasants who worked his land. LIBRARY OF CONGRESS.

Che Guevara.

The brutal march of collectivization that laid the foundations for the cold war. LIBRARY OF CONGRESS.

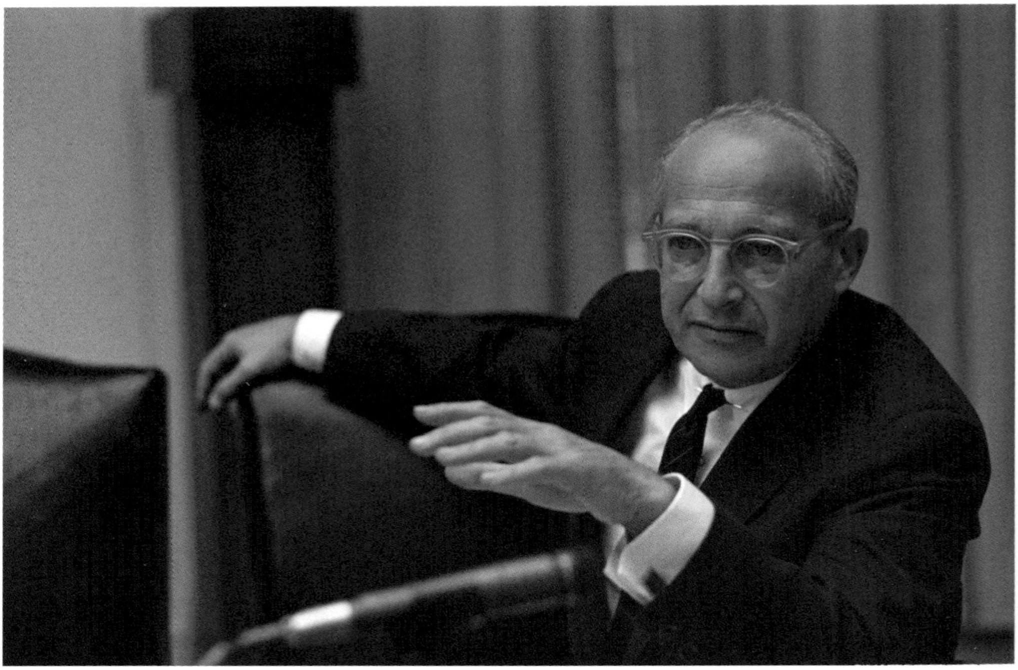

Walt Rostow. COURTESY OF THE LYNDON B. JOHNSON PRESIDENTIAL LIBRARY, PHOTO BY YOICHI R. OKAMOTO.

Norman Borlaug. COURTESY OF FLICKR USER CIMMYT, USED UNDER CREATIVE COMMONS 2.0 LICENSE.

Friederich von Hayek. LIBRARY OF CONGRESS.

Yang Wu's famous "nail house" in Chongqing. AP PHOTO/EYEPRESS.

he betakes himself to a lot in the west . . . If a citizen's neighbors rise above him in the towns, he betakes himself where he can be monarch of all he surveys."

It takes a small effort to appreciate how odd her words must have seemed to an English readership that expected the privilege of owning land freehold to be confined to the aristocrat, the squire, and the gentleman. Few Americans would have found anything remarkable in this pattern of land ownership, but to European visitors, used to hierarchical, agricultural societies, it was strikingly foreign.

In one earlier account, John Melish, a political radical who first traveled through the West in 1806, explained to his British readers that the way Americans owned land was the key to their independence of spirit. "Every industrious citizen of the United States has the power to become a freeholder, on paying the small sum of eighty dollars, being the first installment on the purchase of a quarter of a section of land," he wrote in *Travels in the United States*; "and though he should not have a shilling in the world, he can easily clear as much from the land, as will pay the remaining installments before they come due."

Even in the early days, this was optimistic. Not only were office records filled with entries of farmers who had failed to keep up their payments, many began their lives as tenants, renting land until they could afford their own. But Melish was quite clear about the social impact. "The land being purely his own, there is no setting limits to his prosperity. No proud tyrant can lord it over him—he has no rent to pay—no game laws—nor timber laws nor fishing laws to dread."

In his fascinated exploration of the phenomenon of democracy in America, Alexis de Tocqueville was drawn again and again to the same factor, the influence of this limitless source of unexploited property on the American character. Across the border, he found French Canadians "closely crowded on a narrow territory" where they held land under seigneurial conditions, and the contrast drove him to conclude, "Other peoples of America have the same physical conditions of prosperity as the Anglo-Americans, but without their laws and their manners; and these peoples are wretched. The laws and manners of the Anglo-Americans are therefore that efficient cause of their greatness which is the object of my inquiry."

In his experience, no one was immune to the psychological experience of owning land. "It is in America that one learns to understand the influence which physical prosperity exercises over political actions, and even over opinions which ought to acknowledge no sway but that of reason." As an example, he cited an old acquaintance from France, who in the 1790s had been "a great leveller and an ardent demagogue," but had undergone a complete change of heart on becoming a wealthy landowner in Pennsylvania, and, to de Tocqueville's astonishment, talked of "the rights of property as an economist or a landowner might have done."

Yet somehow in the United States, the unlimited freedom conferred by property rights had not resulted in inequality. The key to it, as de Tocqueville discovered in his exploration of the Midwest's rough and ready society, was the apparently inexhaustible supply of land. Frontier behavior repelled him, but it did not lessen his respect for the extraordinary nature of America's egalitarian society.

What the Public Lands survey created during the tumultuous early nineteenth century was the frontier, a propertied, free enterprise, egalitarian society based on individual ownership of the land. Its spiritual heart came from the Second Great Awakening of the early 1800s that gripped westerners in general and frontier people in particular.

The revivalist message of individual salvation they heard from wandering ministers in the backwoods cut across the deference that had been expected from them by Puritan and Presbyterian churches alike. The star preacher was Lorenzo Dow, whose sermons, enlivened by theatrical groans, tortured screams, and shouts of triumph, were anchored firmly in the American tradition of human rather than property rights. "But if all men are born equal," he cried out, "endowed with unalienable right by their Creator in the blessings of life, liberty, and the pursuit of happiness, then there can be no just reason, as a cause, why he may or should not think, and judge, and act for himself in matters of religion, opinion, and private judgment."

Like the Pilgrim Fathers, the camp meetings fused spiritual and material worlds. Neither faith nor property amounted to anything without individual effort and self-reliance. The personal commitment that Dow and other revivalists called for as the first step on the road to salvation was exactly what the survey's squares required if they were to become fruitful. Equality was guaranteed by the inexhaustibility of the reward. To win it demanded lifelong dedication, but no one was excluded, either from the endless spiritual bounty or from the unlimited supply of land.

This individualized, democratic form of Christianity was inseparable from the politics that came out of the West at the same time. While most Atlantic states continued to impose high property and wealth qualifications for voting so that the electorate was restricted to less than 10 percent of the white male population, the new Western states immediately admitted a much wider selection of voters. One third of Illinois's white males voted in 1820, and an electorate of more than one million sent Andrew Jackson to the White House in 1828. By the middle of the century a majority of states had done what would have been unthinkable to the Founding Fathers and removed voting restrictions for white males altogether.

Atlantic society still regarded frontier manners with a mixture of humor and amazement. In 1826, when Congressman Davy Crockett came to Washington from Tennessee, sophisticated journalists in the capital invented a coonskin cap for him and wrote a fake frontier autobiography in which he boasted that he was "fresh from the backwoods, half-horse, half-alligator, a little touched with the snapping-turtle." By the time Jackson stepped down from the presidency a decade later, frontier values had become the norm. Even the campaign managers of William Henry Harrison, the unmistakably aristocratic Whig candidate, found it an advantage to portray him on election posters in 1840 outside a log cabin with a pipe in his mouth and a jug of hard cider at hand.

Yet this unprecedented, astonishing, rumbustious democracy grew on territory that once belonged to other people. As early as 1789, Henry Knox, Washington's secretary of war, expressed his regret "that all the Indian Tribes once existing in those States, now the best cultivated and most populous, have become extinct." During the nineteenth century, that tragedy would be repeated around the globe with different degrees of severity wherever private property spread. Disease and warfare had cleared the Wampanaog and the Yamassee from colonial America. In the United States, Jefferson's constitutional advice and Marshall's legal judgments ensured that all federal land taken from Native Americans was acquired by treaty and purchase, but force, actual and threatened, unmistakably played its part. Innumerable wars and skirmishes persuaded Creeks, Seminoles, Blackfoot, Kickapoo, and others to cede their territory. When the federal government overrode legal opinion in 1838 to drive fifteen thousand peaceful, settled Cherokee out of Georgia to a new, unwanted home across the Mississippi in the tragedy known as the Trail of Tears, it underlined the lack of choice open to the original occupants.

For those most distant from the frontier, the astonishing expansion of the United States was seen as something unique—the working out, in the famous phrase coined by New Yorker John L. O'Sullivan of "our manifest destiny to overspread and to possess the whole of the continent"—but those closer to the action often used another term.

As early as 1783, General Rufus Putnam, a future surveyor-general of the United States, urged Congress to allow settlers to take up Iroquois land west of the Ohio River as a step "of lasting consequence to the American empire." In the 1820s, Missouri senator Thomas Hart Benton spoke of his dream that westward expansion would create an "American empire" stretching to the Pacific. His dream became a reality in 1848 when American troops encamped in Mexico City forced the Mexican government to surrender a territory that included present-day California, Nevada, Utah, most of Arizona, New Mexico, and Colorado and part of Wyoming under the terms of the Treaty of Guadalupe–Hidalgo. But in 1859, William Gilpin, the first governor of Colorado, demanded further expansion to north and south in order to encompass Canada and Mexico in "the Republican Empire of North America" and predicted that his state would soon become "the cardinal basis for the future empire now erecting itself upon the North American continent."

Such talk did not survive the outbreak of the Civil War. It was silenced in the Confederate states by the perception of the conflict as an imperial war directed at their subjugation, and in the North by the prime importance of saving the Union. But whether seen as manifest destiny or empire building, the future expansion of the United States could be easily visualized, so long as the Public Lands Survey continued to Americanize immigrants from every culture by making ownership of conquered territory available to all who wanted it.

The discovery of California gold in 1848 drew people to the far side of the continent, but it was the grid that enabled the country to be settled at such phenomenal speed. In 1854, Deputy Surveyor William Ives began to plot the most westerly of Mansfield's meridians, the Willamette Meridian that ran north from a point near Portland. Just sixty-six years after Thomas Hutchins's chainmen took their first westward steps on the banks of the Ohio River, the land survey had reached the Pacific, and in 1855 the land office of Oregon registered a claim from John Potter, married man of Linn County in Oregon Territory, for "320 acres of Land, known and designated in the Surveys and Plats of the United States as Part of Sections 22 & 27 T[ownship] 9 S[outh]. R[ange] 2 E[ast]." Most of the country from the Mississippi to the West Coast remained unsurveyed, but the squares now spanned the continent.

What had been measured out was unmistakably a democracy, and quite clearly a republic, but its foundation was undeniably imperial. And the structure that had made it possible was to be the model for the greatest territorial empire the world had ever seen.

CHAPTER FOURTEEN

THE EMPIRE OF LAND

THE ARCHITECT RESPONSIBLE for introducing Jefferson's blueprint to the British Empire was a jailbird. Edward Gibbon Wakefield began to write about land and empire in 1829 while serving three years in Newgate Prison for abducting a wealthy fifteen-year-old girl from school and marrying her in order to gain her fortune. Born into a prominent Quaker family but with a father who lived by his wits, Wakefield's character faithfully reflected his genetic inheritance. There was something of the evangelist about his boldness, conviction, and eloquence, and at least as much of the fraudster, yet his intelligence and the intensity of his self-belief, apparent in the stare of his pale blue eyes, swayed all but the most skeptical listeners. They, however, had much to be skeptical about.

Although the abduction was what most tarnished his name, the reason for it was equally disreputable. The thirty-two-year-old Wakefield was already wealthy, having eloped with and married another young heiress, but when her premature death left him short of the money he needed to win a seat in Parliament, he attempted to forge the will of her father in his favor. The failure of the forgery was what impelled him to kidnap the schoolgirl. Their unconsummated marriage was later annulled by act of Parliament, but Wakefield's reputation as a scoundrel remained indelible.

Nevertheless, the articles he wrote from Newgate had an immediate impact. Entitled *Letter from Sydney*, referring to the city in New South Wales, Australia, they purported to be from a colonist in Australia with plans for attracting more immigrants. But, when published in the liberal *Morning Chronicle* in 1829, they caused a sensation because they addressed a problem that weighed more heavily on Britain than the fate of any colony: what should be done with the rapidly growing numbers of workless poor who crowded the streets of every major city in the land?

In the past, the poor had often been sent as indentured servants or criminals to the colonies—North America, the West Indies, and, from 1787, Australia. Since 1815, more had gone voluntarily, often subsidized by charities, but, as one acerbic critic declared, the policy amounted to "little more than shoveling out your paupers to where they might die without shocking their betters with the sight or sound of their last agony." What Wakefield pictured was the creation of a new society in the colonies. He wanted middle-class emigrants, "merchants, clergymen, lawyers . . . If you can induce many of this class to settle in a colony, the other classes, whether capitalists or labourers, are sure to settle there in abundance."

Half a century had passed since there had been any policy for disposing of land in the colonies. In 1772, reflecting the opinions of British landowners, the Privy Council had declared, "Experience shows that the possession of property is the best security for a due obedience and submission to government." But putting the principle into practice had been a disaster. Legislation was passed in the 1770s and 1780s extending virtually the same rights as property-owning English squires to seigneurs in Quebec, Irish clan chiefs, and Bengali *zamindari*, or tax collectors. Nowhere did anything like English conditions develop: there had been rebellion in Ireland; the passage of the Quebec Act had helped propel the American colonies toward revolution, and the *zamindari* had turned into a type of upper class, moneylending official that was specifically Indian.

For want of any coherent plan, colonial authorities disposed of what was known as "waste land," meaning territory occupied by indigenous inhabitants, on a haphazard basis. The Canadian colonies had leased, sold, or granted ground to companies and individuals according to the influence they exercised on autocratic governments in Toronto, Quebec, and the Maritime Provinces. In Australia's penal colonies of New South Wales and Van Diemen's Land, shortly to be renamed Tasmania, a succession of governors had leased land on an equally random basis to cattle and sheep farmers, many of whom simply dispensed with formalities and squatted on gigantic spreads of twenty square miles or more without any authorization. The only official to try to impose order, William Bligh, already notorious for causing a mutiny on *H.M.S.Bounty*, provoked another revolt in New South Wales when as governor he ordered the destruction of squatters' cabins built on public land. His senior staff arrested him and had him sent back to Britain.

As had happened in colonial America, however, private land companies in Britain were beginning to take an interest in these distant sources of profit. In the 1820s, the Australian Agricultural Company, floated in Britain, had raised $2.5 million to invest in buying land in New South Wales, and the Van Diemen's Land Company put more than one million dollars into property and harbor-building in Tasmania.

In proposing an entirely new system, Wakefield, like Jefferson, was intending to create a society fashioned by the way land was distributed. His scheme was refined constantly over the next twenty years, but its essential features remained constant: colonial land should be sold at a price that was sufficiently high, firstly, to act as an incentive for the new owner to produce a profit and, secondly, to pay for the passage of poor immigrants to be employed as laborers on the new properties. Initially only the middle classes would be able to afford the "sufficient price," but because the colonies possessed more land than workers, wages would have to be high, enabling the immigrants to buy property for themselves within two or three years and employ laborers of their own. It was not an egalitarian society Wakefield proposed, but a capitalist economy with employers and employees, capitalists and workers.

When he came across Wakefield's writings later, Karl Marx regarded them with sidelong respect. "It is the great merit of E. G. Wakefield," he wrote in *Capital*, "to have discovered not anything new about the Colonies, but to have discovered in the Colonies the truth as to the condition of capitalist production in the mother-country." But for just that reason, free-market economists welcomed Wakefield's thinking because it offered a capitalist rationale for empire that had not existed before.

Seen through the eyes of eighteenth-century mercantilists, colonies were adjuncts of the mother country. Consequently their goods had to be sold to the mother country, and their imports could only come from the same source. Inevitably therefore, the British Empire was vilified by Adam Smith's free-market followers. Its monopoly trade kept prices higher than they needed to be, and it wasted good capital that would be more efficiently employed as investment in the free-market of industrial production at home. "Great Britain derives nothing but loss," Adam Smith declared unambiguously "from the dominion which she assumes over her colonies."

The particular bête noire of the free-marketeers was the West Indies sugar industry, whose planters knew that, in return for buying British goods, they had a guaranteed market of ten million dollars a year for their over-priced product in Britain. Discredited and increasingly flouted, the mercantilist orthodoxy nevertheless remained in place throughout the long, hidebound administrations of William Pitt and Lord Liverpool. Compared to that bleak, outdated pattern, Wakefield's optimistic, brightly colored vision of the colonies as new, capitalist Britains had the appeal of a vacation advertisement in winter.

WAKEFIELD EMERGED from the confines of Newgate in 1830, not redeemed but cautiously respected, with powerful allies among the reformers who were about to take power. To promote his ideas, he founded the National Colonization Society, whose influential members included the advocate of Utilitarianism Jeremy Bentham, the economist John Stuart Mill, the banker Sir Francis Baring, and a dozen members of Parliament. In 1832, a Whig government was at last voted into office, and their Reform Bill began a process of electoral change that would shift power from the dead hands of the landowners and reflect more accurately the weight of property possessed by the new industrial classes. The following year, the government's momentous decision to abolish slavery throughout the empire showed that it was ready to take a more active role in colonial affairs.

On the crest of the reforming wave, Wakefield published *England and America*, a book that made clear the debt he owed to the Public Lands Survey. He began with a comparison of the two countries' social and economic policies. Britain's overwhelming capital strength and its enormous investment in the infrastructure of factories, roads, canals, docks, and gaslit towns gave it the economic advantage. In almost every other way, however, he found American society to be preferable. It was more confident and open, and it was free of the divisions that split British society into upper, middle, and lower classes, or in Wakefield's terms, "the Spending class," "the Uneasy class," and "the Laboring class." But his chief concern was to answer one question: "What is the best way in which to dispose of waste land with a view to colonization?"

Deeply though Wakefield admired American society, it was nothing compared to his respect for the United States as "a colonizing power." The challenge it faced in incorporating the settlements in the territory of the Louisiana Purchase beyond the Mississippi were exactly the same as those that Britain encountered in administering colonies in Canada and Australia. "What is a new state formed in the western deserts of America," he demanded, "if it be not a new colony?"

The secret of the United States's wealth was not just the productivity of the soil, but its ability to dispose of it with secure title. While capital invested in the improvement of land in the Australian colonies had disappeared because neither the extent of the property nor the nature of the ownership could be known with certainty, Wakefield observed, the security of American titles had encouraged Dutch banks to lend money for the construction of the Erie Canal, enabling midwestern wheat to be transported cheaply to New York, and, even as he wrote, a British bank was arranging a $3.5 million loan to Alabama repayable over thirty years. From a capitalist point of view, everything that Britain had got wrong in its empire, America had got right. Above all it had obeyed the first rule in what he called "the art of colonization," and that was never to throw away the "power over waste land." This had enabled it to create a free-market economy that overcame the problem of under-capitalization by drawing in foreign investment in order to make full use of labor and land.

The uniform system of the Public Lands Survey, with its clear mapping, set prices, and secure titles, was, therefore, the model that Wakefield recommended for Britain's colonies. Two changes needed to be made. Slavery would not be permitted, and the price of land needed to be higher than in the United States in order to dissuade buyers from taking more ground than they could work. But with those exceptions, "their rule for the disposal of waste land would be quite perfect." Thus, by a supreme irony, the republican United States was made the model for the new British Empire.

As Wakefield's detractors, and most of his admirers, subsequently pointed out, his scheme never worked in the way he intended. The impossibility of trying to control property prices in order to regulate immigration was pointed out at the time and only became more obvious during his lifetime. Nor was the idea of paying for the passage of poor emigrants original, since many charities and hard-pressed parishes were already putting it into practice. But what made Wakefield's system so compelling was his unabashed appeal to free enterprise as the force that would make property-based colonization a success.

The vision of the colonies as new capitalist societies was coupled with a stirring appeal for international free trade, beginning with the repeal of the high tariffs that Britain's Corn Laws imposed on cereals imported into Britain. Once they were gone, Wakefield predicted that "the English will hunt over the world in search of cheap corn" to feed their industrial economy. There would be an enhanced two-way trade between the colonies and the home country, and where Australia was concerned, the chance of opening up a three-way network exporting cereals to China, Chinese tea to Britain, and British manufactures to Australia.

Wakefield's analysis of the colonies' economic potential was grounded in the theories of the era's two preeminent free-market economists, David Ricardo and Thomas Malthus. Ricardo's theories on profit made it clear that the high price of British property rendered its purchase an inefficient use of capital compared with investing it in cheaper, productive land elsewhere. Malthus's stark warning of overpopulation focused more closely on the wastage of labor in the unemployed poor: "Increase the demand for agricultural labour by promoting cultivation, and with it consequently increase the produce of the country, and ameliorate the condition of the labourer, and no apprehensions whatever need be entertained of the proportional increase of population."

Not only would Wakefield's system employ the mother country's excess of capital to maximum effect in a fresh, fluid market for land, it would reduce the "misery and vice" in its crowded cities that were the prime causes, in Malthus's opinion, of too much breeding. In these circumstances, Wakefield's theories of colonization were exciting enough to persuade many to overlook his abduction of the heiress.

THE OPENING EXPERIMENT was in South Australia, the first colony to be established on the continent without convicts as a source of cheap labor. Created by act of Parliament in 1834, it covered about three hundered thousand square miles, more than 10 percent bigger than Texas, but was inhabitable only along part of the coast and on the inland basin of the Murray and Darling Rivers. Wakefield's influence was obvious throughout the legislation. Land commissioners were to be appointed to survey and sell the territory, their funds were to be devoted to bringing in new immigrants, and the capital accrued would allow government loans to be paid off and any further investment to be covered by bonds. Finally, reflecting the Jeffersonian impulse, once the colony had fifty thousand inhabitants, it could elect its own representative council and move toward self-government. In short, the new colony was to be a self-financing example of free-enterprise capitalism.

Unlike the creation of a new territory in the United States, the act made no mention of buying the land from its indigenous inhabitants. A later amendment did refer to respect for Aboriginal rights of "occupation and enjoyment" of the land, but in the original colony of New South Wales, Australia had already been declared to be *terra nullius*, or empty land, effectively obliterating fifty thousand years of occupancy by about a half-million Aboriginal Australians. In practice, many farmers, such as John Stieglitz, running sheep into the outback in 1835, chose to bring "sundry articles for conciliating the natives" and to employ them as trackers and herdsmen, but none ever recognized their claims to ownership.

Within a decade almost every part of Wakefield's plan had to be adjusted: the emigration fund was applied to the survey itself, the London government had to write off its loan and reorganize the colonial administration, and the survey was haphazard. It used a combination of squares—in South Australia they were known as "parishes" and measured five miles by five—and metes and bounds that allowed ample scope for corruption, notably by the chief land commissioner, Robert Torrens, who acquired land worth more than £18,000, about $90,000, for himself. Beyond the coastal fringe and the inland region irrigated by rivers, the colony quickly became desert, and across the intermediate ground sheep and cattle had to range widely in search of meager pasture. Selling such variable soil at a uniform price of one pound, about five dollars, an acre was unrealistic, and even before the first boatload of colonists had sailed, the reluctance of buyers to commit themselves forced the commissioners to raise funds by selling off unsurveyed territory for twelve shillings, or three dollars, an acre to a land company.

Yet gradually the colony began to prosper. The process owed much to the discovery in 1845 of copper in the eastern mountains, and to the rising price of wool. But in the long run, wheat was the staple that was central to South Australia's economy—by the 1850s 160,000 acres had been sown—and cereal farmers depended on having secure title to their land. As agricultural prosperity took hold, Wakefield's virtuous circle of rising land prices and high wages at last appeared.

The letters home told of a society subtly different from the egalitarian one in the Jeffersonian experiment. There were similar references to the freedom and opportunities to be found in a new land, but the cost of travel raised the financial bar to ownership higher: immigrants had to find $250 for the price of a ticket to Australia, and it was reckoned to cost a minimum of $750 to buy and stock an eighty-acre parcel of land, about one third more than the investment needed to acquire a farm in Illinois. With 40 percent of the population living in Adelaide, it was also more urban and commercial than America, with skilled workers able to earn good wages: Thomas Newman, an apprentice carpenter from London, wrote his mother in 1838 that he was earning five dollars a week "with all my grub" and that he had already saved enough to buy an acre plot in the capital of Adelaide. He was the ideal Wakefield colonist, and his letter has a suspicious hint of boosterism, but his final sentence rings true: "nothing would give me greater joy than for you to come and bring Mary [his sweetheart] with you, for you really would think you was in Greenwich park."

Toward the end of his life, with South Australia moving rapidly toward self-government, Torrens used to boast that "The colony devised by Mr Wakefield was planted [settled] by me," but it was his son, Robert Torrens Jr., who solved the problems and corruption created by metes and bounds. He put in place the simple, almost foolproof "Torrens system" by which title to land depended on the registration document, a surveyor's plat, and a description of the property with the owner's name attached, which was held in the colonial land office. This clear evidence of ownership removed any confusion from competing claims, and cut through the complexities of common law deeds with their *Hamlet*-like history of entails, reversions, and covenants. Its simplicity quickly made the Torrens system the standard for the rest of the empire.

The South Australian model of surveying land and establishing title was immediately taken up by the next colony to be created, Victoria, and powerfully influenced subsequent settlement in New South Wales and Queensland. It received a further boost from the policies adopted by the legislative assembly of every Australian colony after it gained self-government, to use taxation and redistribution to break up the land claims of squatters.

The survey shaped both local government—its basis, the county, comprised sixty to seventy parishes—and the economy. Once land became an easily tradable property, banks rapidly followed, as in the new United States, giving owners access to credit. By midcentury, London investors had put fifty million dollars into Australian land, primarily backing ventures where a return could be expected from exports of wool and copper. In 1856, South Australia's 109,000 inhabitants became self-governing, with universal male suffrage exercised through secret ballot.

Long before then, Wakefield was engaged on his second experiment in colonization. It should have been in New Zealand. In 1837, he and the Earl of Durham, a maverick, landowning grandee, persuaded the Whig prime minister, Lord Melbourne, to let their land company, the New Zealand Company, acquire one millon acres and run a self-financing colony on Wakefieldian lines. Alarmed by the fate of Australia's Aborigines, however, missionaries and their political supporters protested that the new company would acquire "a sovereignty in New Zealand which would infallibly issue in the conquest and the extermination of the present inhabitants." Never enthusiastic about the new form of colonialism, Lord Melbourne withdrew support for the New Zealand project and presented Durham instead with the chance to rule another colony.

In British North America, a simultaneous rebellion of French and British Canadians had erupted against the corrupt and autocratic government of their two provinces, Lower and Upper Canada. The post offered to Durham was that of governor-general of all Canada, with complete power to put down the insurrection and establish a fairer form of government. Accepting the challenge, Durham appointed Wakefield as lands commissioner and a senior member of Wakefield's National Colonization Society, Charles Buller, as his secretary. It was a measure of how toxic Wakefield's reputation continued to be, that Melbourne immediately protested, "If you touch [Wakefield] with a pair of tongs, it is utter destruction, depend upon it." But Durham insisted on keeping him, promising only that his contribution would be anonymous.

The revolts had petered out before Durham arrived in May 1838, and less than five months later the irascible peer resigned and returned home. But during that time he and his team drew up an extensive plan for the government of Canada. For almost a century, the Durham Report, snidely described by critics as "thought by Wakefield, written by Buller and signed by Durham," occupied an iconic position in Canadian history. It presented for the first time a vision of a united Canada "with a representative government," beginning with a union of the two Canadas and looking forward to a confederation that included the Maritime Provinces of Newfoundland, Nova Scotia, Prince Edward Island, and New Brunswick. Modern historians are more inclined to give Durham the primary credit for his own report, but downplay its influence on the ground that a self-governing Canada did not arrive until 1867 and then largely as a result of internal political pressure aided by the cohesive effects of railroads and steamships. Yet Durham's recommendations had two direct consequences of lasting importance: politically the two Canadas were united in 1841, and the distribution of land took on a more methodical, Americanized shape.

Whatever contributions Durham made, Wakefield's thought and Buller's writing are most obvious in the section on land sales. This criticized British Canada for having made free grants of land amounting to almost six million acres, or half the surveyed area of the province, to loyalists escaping the American Revolution, veterans, and government officials, including 670,000 acres to "Protestant clergy." It noted that even when the ruling clique, known as "the Family Compact," began selling land in the 1820s, it was offered on favorable terms to friends, including three million acres sold cheaply to the crony-led Canada Company. The report excoriated French Canada for the same customs, and especially for the 1.5 million acres allocated at no cost to "township leaders."

Wakefield's hand could be seen in the section that directly compared the Canadian system of selling land—needlessly handicapped by "useless formality and consequent delay"—with the United States, where title to property was obtained "immediately and securely." Its shortcomings had already been exposed by the demands of a growing flood of immigrants: almost half a million would arrive in the Canadas during the late 1830s and early 1840s, virtually doubling the population. Despite the availability of vast tracts of ground, British purchasers had to pay bribes to officials or buy direct from surveyors to be sure of getting land, and a fourfold increase in the French population had only increased the area of settled land by a third. As a result, rates of settlement were beginning to slow as discouraged immigrants chose to move on to the United States. In language lifted straight from *England and America*, the report recommended more reliable surveys without which "there can be no security of property in land," public auction of lands on the American pattern to produce "large funds for emigration," encouragement for "the investment of surplus British capital," and the promotion of settlement "to add to the value of every man's property in land."

Politically, Durham's public exposure of government corruption led to reforms within Canada and an inexorable drive to transfer powers from the appointed Executive Council to the elected legislature. But what gave impetus to the domestic campaign for political reform was the land-based prosperity that surged through Canada in the decades after union.

The good times were powerfully affected by the United States land market as it recovered from the second great economic recession—the word was first used in that context in 1837—since independence. Attempting to cool the inflationary boom that saw thirty-seven million acres of public lands sold in the three years up to 1836, Andrew Jackson's administration had ordered land offices to accept only silver and gold in payment, rather than paper. The move prompted a catastrophic fall in land sales in 1837, followed by a panic run on the banks that was exaggerated in its effects by the withdrawal of British investment. About one quarter of the country's banks collapsed, reducing the money supply by an estimated 30 percent, and dragging down industrial and commercial business with it.

Fortuitously, the long recovery of United States land sales and the boom that followed began in 1841. As it spilled over the border, the first years of the united Canada were marked by widespread prosperity. Canada's own land market, just visible before the 1836 rebellion, took off, creating a widespread increase in private, tradable property. To meet the market's requirements, professional qualifications for land surveyors were introduced in the 1840s, and in 1847 the government of Ontario Province, formerly British Canada, introduced the American square township grid to survey public land before sale, beginning at the eastern end of Lake Huron.

THE SETTLEMENT OF BRUCE COUNTY, Ontario, carved out of the hunting territory of the Chippewas and Ojibwes on the shores of Lake Huron, illustrates the extraordinary speed with which some forested ground interspersed with hills, swamps, and lakes evolved into a private property society. The first sales, at two dollars an acre for parcels of fifty acres, occurred in 1849, with a bonus of fifty acres for owners who would clear a track through the trees. The 1851 census showed that twenty-seven hundred people were scattered across the county's sixteen hundred square miles. In 1854, the first bank, a branch of the Bank of Upper Canada, was established in the village of Southampton to accept deposits on land parcels. By then sufficient land had been cleared to grow wheat, and in the mid-1850s the Crimean War in Europe caused grain prices to double. Good farmland sold for $7.50 an acre, and more than double that in the villages. During the decade, bonds began to be issued for the construction of roads, and the building of schools, a county hall, a courthouse, and a jail. The 1861 census showed the population to have grown to twenty-seven thousand people owning land worth four million dollars. In that year, they returned a representative to the Legislative Assembly and were pushing to have complete control over the county laws that affected their property.

What happened in miniature in one county was replicated in various forms as settlement spread across Canada. A dramatic jump in the number of immigrants traveling westward cheaply in the empty holds of vessels that had carried timber east to the United Kingdom doubled the population to more than one million in the 1850s, and boosted land prices. The development of a land market promoted in turn the growth of banking. In 1835 there were only six banks in the two Canadas, but in step with the land boom, another twenty-five were chartered in the next twenty years, each with multiple branches. The availability of credit allowed farmers to invest not only in the improvement of land, but, as in New England and Ohio, also in industry and commerce. And as Wakefield had predicted, secure title to land also attracted foreign investment, with London banks such as Barings investing more than one million pounds during the 1850s in financial securities and real estate.

"In no spot within British territory could we find aggregated in so striking a manner the evidences of this startling change," the *Anglo-American Magazine* reported in 1852. "In none should we trace so strongly marked the imprint of national migration; in few discover such ripened fruits of successful colonization. The genius of Britain presides over the destiny of her offspring."

Nevertheless, Canada's frontier expansion never had the tigerish quality seen south of the border. In part, this was because George III's 1763 proclamation prohibiting settlement beyond the Appalachians still held good north of the border, offering First Nation inhabitants a legal protection against settlers that was lacking in the United States. But more immediately, a quirk of banking regulation reduced the incentive to improve, sell up, and move on. While American banks, restricted by statute to one state, had to lend locally, Canadian banks were centralized, with local branches remitting funds, as much as ninety-five cents in the dollar, to a head office in Toronto or Montreal. The result was a slower recycling of capital resources into frontier investment. In the financial centers of Toronto and Montreal, however, larger funds were available to buy government bonds and to back loans floated in Canada and Britain to fund infrastructure projects such as canals and railroads to link the Great Lakes to the Saint Lawrence.

That Canada's headlong economic surge during this period depended on the same factors as in the United States, the growth of rural capital and of a banking capacity to make use of its investment potential, is made clear by comparison with the slower agricultural development of Quebec, or French Canada. In the first half of the nineteenth century, Quebec's population tripled in size, a growth rate that lagged far behind the twenty-fold increase in the number of people living in Ontario.

Every study of French-Canadian farming shows it to have been less profitable than in British Canada, not because Quebec land was poorer or farmed less intensively—its wheat was a major Canadian export to Britain—but because the overhang of seigneurial dues, such as the *cens* or rent, and the *corvée* or forced labor, added 30 percent to a farmer's fixed costs, and because the province's legal framework, with its essentially seventeenth-century emphasis on shared land ownership, clashed with the concept of an individual monopoly of land. In the late 1850s, when the price of improved land in Bruce County was rising toward ten dollars an acre, seigneurial farms in Quebec were selling for $2.50 an acre. Although the last feudal dues were abolished in 1854, the continuing shape of French Canada's almost peasant system of agriculture, with its emphasis on family obligations and ownership, made banks reluctant to lend.

The Bank of Montreal, founded in 1817, was the oldest and largest bank in Canada, and its core deposits came from the province's agricultural and timber sectors. But in the 1860s, when it had 30 percent of Canada's banking business, two thirds of the bank's lending, two million dollars, was to government, channelling potential investment capital away from the region's producers. Consequently, the critical ingredient that lifted the profitability of Ontario farmers, the rising capital value of their land, played little part in Quebec's development.

As early as 1843, a government investigation suggested that the seigneurial system was responsible for creating a culture in which "all the generous emotions of the *habitant's* nature are stifled." Indirect confirmation came from a French priest questioned by de Tocqueville about the lack of individual ambition among French Canadians compared to that of farmers south of the border. The conservative Quebecois, the priest admitted, had "not got the spirit of adventure or the scorn of ties of birth and family which are characteristic of the Americans."

The Durham Report was read around the world, Wakefield bragged, "from Canada, through the West Indies & South Africa, to the Australias, & has everywhere been received with acclamation." Seen from the twenty-first century, its direct influence is now deemed to have been limited to concentrating minds on the political goal of representative government. But that ignores the context of its times. For the group of nineteenth-century reformers who backed Wakefield, including such key contemporaries as Bentham's social utilitarians and Mills's economic liberals, Durham's advocacy of free-market principles was taken as a decisive blow against the mercantile attitudes still entrenched in London. Karl Marx added his own backhanded compliment: "Wakefield discovered that in the Colonies, property in money, means of subsistence, machines, and other means of production, does not as yet stamp a man as a capitalist if there be wanting the correlative—the wage-worker, the other man who is compelled to sell himself of his own free-will. He discovered that capital is not a thing, but a social relation between persons, established by the instrumentality of things."

Apprehensive of the report's free-enterprise spirit, Melbourne tried to suppress it altogether, a move subverted by Wakefield leaking the document to the *Times* of London. Its argument for the creation of property in land, of waged labor, and of a responsive form of government had an impact not just in Bruce County, or Ontario, or even Canada itself, but across the entire farming area of the British Empire. Arguably its influence was felt even in South America, where Argentine and Brazilian governments both attempted to privatize native-held land, and in north Africa where the French, after experimenting with other forms of landholding, finally introduced surveys and individual titles to the territory they had conquered.

Lord Melbourne's hostility went beyond an aristocratic dislike of capitalism. Britain's painful colonial experience in North America had convinced his generation, and most of his successors as prime minister, with the notable exception of Lord Palmerston, that the acquisition of territory was a mistake. Until late in the century, the policy of the Colonial Office was to restrict new British settlements to armed trading posts like Hong Kong and Singapore, or coaling stations like Aden. The reluctance to acquire territory prompted the giant of late Victorian politics, William Gladstone, to warn against British ownership of the Suez Canal in 1877 on the grounds that "our first site in Egypt, be it by larceny or be it by emption [purchase], will be the almost certain egg of a North African empire."

Official opposition to Wakefield's plans continued to the day of his death, but the settlement of New Zealand demonstrated the unstoppable forces that led from individual land ownership, however brought about, to the creation of government.

In 1839, while Wakefield was still in Canada, the New Zealand Company on his advice sent out a ship to the islands with thirty-five colonists, including his brother, William, to buy land directly from the Maori inhabitants. Although not the first European settlers—whalers and sealers, and some adventurers from Australia had established permanent stations there—they were by far the most aggressive in acquiring land. Attempting to keep control of the situation, the British government dispatched its own representative, Lieutenant-Governor William Hobson, to negotiate an agreement with the Maori recognizing British sovereignty. In the Treaty of Waitangi, signed by some five hundred chieftains in 1840, sovereignty was acknowledged, and in exchange the British government guaranteed "to the Chiefs and Tribes of New Zealand the full exclusive and undisturbed possession of their Lands and Estates, Forests, Fisheries and other properties which they may collectively or individually possess."

Ignoring the treaty, William Wakefield concluded a series of purchase agreements with Maori chiefs for somewhere between three hundred thousand and twenty million acres—deliberately vague wording allowed for elastic interpretation—covering most of the South Island and the lower part of the North Island. Not only did this contravene the government's commitment at Waitangi but, as one of Hobson's team pointed out, "No Chief however high his rank could dispose of a single acre without the concurrence of his tribe."

Back in Britain, the government's fury was stoked further by the way the dubiously acquired property was being sold to investors "merely as means of carrying on gambling speculations by persons who never dream of becoming colonists," as a government report put it. More officials were sent out specifically to protect Maori interests, and the Colonial Office asserted the Jeffersonian principle that only the government had the right to buy directly from its indigenous owners. But nothing could stop the property engine.

The first New Zealand land was quickly sold in London, and in 1842 some thirty-two hundred emigrants, almost half of them children, arrived to farm the presurveyed land at Nelson in the South Island. Following Wakefield's blueprint, it had been planned that the first thousand lots, each of two hundred acres, would be sold for $7.50 an acre, with half the profits paying for the emigration of more buyers. The majority of immigrants, however, were laborers lacking the capital to create Wakefield's virtuous cycle, and with many of the lots unsold almost a quarter of Nelson's original inhabitants soon drifted away to squat on unsurveyed land. Harassed by the governor and short of money, the New Zealand Company attempted to seize more land in the South Island as assets to stave off bankruptcy. Angry Maori in the area resisted, and in a fight in 1843 William Wakefield and twenty-one settlers and surveyors were killed.

News of his brother's death caused Edward Wakefield to suffer a stroke. Once youthful and mesmerizing—in Toronto he managed to hypnotize a girl so deeply medical assistance was needed to resuscitate her—Wakefield had grown into a stout, pop-eyed, cigar-smoking speculator who had succeeded in creaming off $100,000 from a canal project in Canada. But his Machiavellian touch was undiminished. By involving the Church of England in the colonization of what would become the city of Canterbury on the South Island, he succeeded in making the company's program respectable, and by encouraging a press campaign to support British settlers farming land that had been lawfully purchased in Britain as private property, he made it popular.

However much the government disliked what a Colonial Secretary called the company's "petty trickery," it could not escape the overwhelming force of public opinion. With an ill grace, the Colonial Office arranged a loan to bail out the company, recognized the de facto validity of William Wakefield's purchase of much of the South Island, and dispatched an infantry regiment backed by artillery to protect the settlers.

By the time Edward Gibbon Wakefield went out to join them in 1852, there were more than twenty-seven thousand settlers occupying land across both islands of New Zealand, from Auckland in the north to Otago in the south. Their outlook was essentially that of Benjamin Ironsides who decided to emigrate from Sheffield to try his luck in a new land. "Dangers and fatigues I fear not," he told the company's agent, "I rather court them, I am in fact quite tired of working continually for [a wage] & never perceiving any future chance of bettering my condition."

The inevitable need to protect settler interests had by then brought into existence an elected legislature to represent their opinion alongside the executive power of the governor. Returned as a representative to the legislative assembly, Wakefield quickly gathered enough votes to push through the next constitutional step, to have the executive council answerable to the legislature rather than to the governor. The change decisively altered official policy toward New Zealand's colonization.

For the next twenty years, until the 1870s, governments in both Wellington, the colony's capital, and London supported the spread of colonists into the North Island, leading to a series of raids, retaliations, and occasional all-out battles, known collectively as the Maori Wars. In the course of them, most of the arable land in the island, home to the bulk of the Maori, passed into the ownership of settlers. The process was accelerated by the operation of the Native Lands Court set up in 1864 to combat the "communism" of tribal ownership. The court's legal decisions enabled individual Maori to register individual plots of tribal land as their own and sell them on to white buyers. An estimated eighteen million acres in the North Island, almost two thirds of the total area, was sold on in this way.

In 1862, the would-be architect of this haphazard expansion of the private property empire died. The program of social engineering that Wakefield planned had proved to be utterly impractical. Yet the ease of understanding how it might apparently solve social problems in Britain and create wealth in the colonies gave it political momentum. And, as the Public Lands Survey had already proved in the United States, the natural development of landed property into rural capital brought in economic forces that knocked aside the government's opposition.

In 1846, the voting strength of Britain's industrialists carried through what Wakefield had always wanted, the repeal of the Corn Laws that protected British cereal farmers with a high tariff on imported grain. From then on, the search for cheap corn to feed the workers employed in Britain's factories would suck farmers within its empire into a global trading network. The links that carried food and raw materials in one direction sent people and investment in the other, hastening the transition of imperial outposts from rural to industrial capitalism. It would be easy to suppose that such a pattern was inevitable. But without the colonizing example of the United States and the advocacy of Edward Gibbon Wakefield, the social and economic structure of the British Empire would have been very different.

ALMOST EVERYWHERE, however, the institution of individually owned title to land had devastating consequences for the existing inhabitants. In New Zealand, a population of perhaps one hundred thousand Maori in 1830 was reduced to about forty thousand by the early twentieth century, and, despite the Waitangi Treaty, they were left in possession of just 3 percent of the sixty-six million acres they had occupied a hundred years earlier. With the loss of land, the stories and histories associated with it almost disappeared, and a cultural identity built on owning the earth, not through the paper title recognized by the Torrens registration scheme, but through custom, use, and burial, was undermined. Despite the prominence of many Maori in the twentieth century, such as the reforming politician Apirana Ngata and the opera singer Kiri Te Kanawa, the symptoms of dislocation are still apparent in the twenty-first century in the poorer standards of housing and education and higher incidence of drug and alcohol abuse among indigenous New Zealanders.

A similar legacy of deracination afflicts to some degree the descendants of the hunter-gatherers who inhabited Australia for fifty thousand years and the First Nations of Canada. Amid the many attempts to restore a sense of identity, the most promising in each country seems to be the legal recognition of rights to land based on unwritten evidence of its central position in the community's cultural past. And in a private property society where the law has been built around single possession, it is still notoriously difficult to ascertain ownership even today among the multiple claimants to tribal land, a problem that paralyzes the potential value, cultural and commercial, of more than one million acres that remain in Maori possession.

To the first incomers, however, there could be no question of accommodating the ubiquitous tradition of communal possession. With genuine concern, Henry Knox, Washington's secretary of war, declared that if the Indians were not to be wiped out by the incoming settlers, they had to learn "a love for exclusive property." During the nineteenth century, the old justification of American settlers for taking Indian land, that their large hunting grounds could be used more efficiently for farming, was replaced by criticism of the social effects of tribal ownership. As Superintendent Elias Rector of the Southern Indian Agency put it in the 1850s, "the utter absence of individual title to particular lands . . . [removes] the chief incentive to labor and exertion, the very mainspring on which the prosperity of a people depends."

Because there was not the same conflict between settlers and government, and the law left no doubt that the United States government alone could acquire land legally from Native Americans, the formal process of transferring land was more orderly than in the British Empire, but the result was not very different. In the name of progress—as Indian agents assured their clients, "common ownership and civilization cannot co-exist"—up to one hundred thousand Native Americans, from Seminoles in the south to Wyandottes in the north, were removed from their territories east of the Mississippi to be transported, as the 1830 Indians Removal Act directed, to "Indian Territory" around present-day Oklahoma. Fewer than eight thousand remained between the river and the Appalachians, where they were confined to a few reservations, while a swath of territory from Florida to Illinois was made available for purchase.

The process of clearing the land was not confined to the private property empires, however. The most tragic single expulsion during Russia's expansion occurred in 1771 when more than 150,000 nomadic Kalmyks were driven off the Caspian steppe, and barely one third survived their migration to China's province of Xinjiang in central Asia. To this could be added the slower clearing of other ethnic minorities, such as Turkic nomads and Siberian Yakuts forced out by the arrival of Russian settlers, and the religious persecution in the nineteenth century that drove one hundred thousand Chechens from the Caucasus and two hundred thousand Muslim Tatars from Crimea to the Ottoman Empire. Many other native peoples were simply enveloped by the imperial command structure, and then at the end of the nineteenth century were assimilated by a conscious policy of Russification aimed at obliterating ethnic differences.

YET THE SUCCESS of the Afrikaaners of South Africa in fighting off every attempt to absorb them within the British Empire's propertied ethos, almost the only people to do so, also demonstrated that modernization had its benefits. What distinguished the Afrikaaner way of life after they were settled by the mighty Dutch East India Company around the Cape of Good Hope in the seventeenth century was a near-spiritual belief in living self-sufficiently from the land. Although united by devotion to the fiercely Protestant Dutch Reformed church and by membership of the *kommandos* or communal defense forces they formed to fight the Xhosa and other native inhabitants whose land they had taken, the Afrikaaners were authentic frontier people owing their possession of the soil to nothing but their self-reliant efforts to build homes and clear ground. Any insoluble disputes were settled by a *landdrost* or magistrate through whom they also supplied food and any other dues exacted by Company, but their requirement for outside government was minimal.

When farmers arrived from Britain in the early nineteenth century, following their country's seizure of the Cape in 1806, their need to measure out the ground and own it according to common law collided with the Afrikaaners' sprawling, barely marked circular tracts of ground measuring about six hundred acres where they raised livestock with slave labor. Faced by demands to pay land taxes and to have their properties properly registered, Afrikaaner frustration mounted and finally boiled over in 1833 when slavery was made illegal throughout the British Empire. To escape civilization and find new grazing, they moved north en masse, their long lines of ox-drawn wagons, scrawny sheep and cattle, and sullen slaves forming the central motif in Afrikaaner legends of the Great Trek.

In his poem "The Voortrekker," Rudyard Kipling, the British Empire's poet laureate, paid tribute to their stubborn refusal to be hemmed in by propertied living:

His neighbours' smoke shall vex his eyes, their voices break his rest.
He shall go forth till south is north, sullen and dispossessed.
He shall desire loneliness and his desire shall bring,
Hard on his heels, a thousand wheels, a People and a King.

To clear up the Cape Colony's haphazard development, the recommendations of the Durham Report for surveys of waste land, minimum prices, responsible government, and increased immigration were introduced in 1844. The prosperity that came in their wake ensured that the British and their hunger for property would continue to pursue the trekkers as they moved into modern Natal, then across the Vaal River into Transvaal. And when gold was found in Transvaal's Rand Mountains in 1886, the English-speaking *Uitlanders* and other foreigners who poured in to exploit the discovery were able to build on the existing financial institutions of rural capitalism to raise money for the expensive business of mining. By 1895 there were twenty-three British banks in Transvaal, but only one owned by Afrikaans-speakers. Tensions grew as the newcomers pressed their need for political control in Transvaal's legislative assembly, the *Volksraad*, dominated by stock-rearing Boers—the Afrikaans word for farmers. Mounting hostility between expansionist materialism and isolationist austerity led directly to the outbreak of the Boer War in 1899.

The eventual surrender of the Afrikaaners in 1902, after they had inflicted a series of humiliating defeats on the British, also demonstrated the seemingly limitless resources of men and arms commanded by the network of English-speaking, common law, exclusive land ownership societies. Australians, Canadians, and New Zealanders joined the South Africans, black and white, fighting to spread the propertied pattern of British imperialism.

It was never a world that the Afrikaaners wanted to join. They prided themselves on their white, Dutch, racial separateness, on *apartheid*. Despite defeat, that narrow certainty enabled them to adapt South Africa's political structures to their "whites only" form of owning the land, and to retain control of its security forces. Throughout the twentieth century they clung to the self-sufficient ethos of the Great Trek, guaranteeing that they would remain immune to outside ideas and broader values, and that their eventual end would be as isolated, anachronistic, bigoted upholders of *apartheid's* racist ideology. Like Britain's eigtheenth-century landlords before them, the Afrikaaners demonstrated not only that power followed property, but that without redistribution each led on to self-sterilized monopoly.

Chapter Fifteen

The End of Serfdom and Slavery

In the 1850s, a Russian aristocrat who owned an estate, Yasnaya Polyana, about 120 miles south of Moscow kept a detailed diary of what life was like for someone of his class in the last days of the serf empire. Situated in fertile country, Yasnaya Polyana had measured almost ten thousand acres worked by eight hundred serfs when the nobleman inherited it in 1847, but he had already had to sell two thousand acres together with two hundred serfs to pay gambling debts he incurred, first as a student and later as an artillery officer in Sevastopol during the Crimean War. Following Russia's defeat in 1857 by the combined armies of Britain, France, and the Ottoman Empire, the aristocrat returned to Yasnaya Polyana, and his diary records many of the concerns that were common to any landowner: the state of the harvest, the slaughter of hogs, the collection of timber. But other entries could only have come from an owner with total control, including sexual rights, over those on his estate.

"A wonderful day," he wrote for April 21, 1858. "Peasant women in the garden and by the well. I'm like a man possessed." And the following month, "Today, in the big old wood. I'm a fool, a brute. Her bronze flesh and her eyes. I'm in love as never before in my life. Have no other thought. [She is] clean and not bad-looking, with bright black eyes, a deep voice, a scent of something fresh and strong and full breasts that lifted the bib of her apron."

The one exceptional element in these encounters was the identity of the diarist, Count Leo Tolstoy; otherwise the sexual excitement of owning other people was as common to serfdom as to slavery. Thomas Jefferson was undoubtedly more discreet in his relationship with his slave

Sally Hemings, but he was also more insightful than Tolstoy about its nature. "The whole commerce between master and slave," he wrote in *Notes on the State of Virginia*, "is a perpetual exercise of the most boisterous passions, the most unremitting despotism on the one part, and degrading submissions on the other . . . The man must be a prodigy who can retain his manners and morals undepraved by such circumstances."

Tolstoy's reflections rarely went beyond paroxysms of self-loathing, mitigated by blaming the serf women for what had happened, but Jefferson was tormented by the injustice of the relationship and its corrosive effects, both personal and social—"can the liberties of a nation be thought secure when we have removed their only firm basis, a conviction in the minds of the people that these liberties are of the gift of God?"

The 1860s marked one of the great watersheds in the history of individual liberty when some forty-seven million serfs and four million slaves were set free, and the most powerful serf and slave economies in the world were destroyed. Each liberation was the outcome of war, but while the abolition of slavery in the United States was the direct consequence of the Civil War, the emancipation of Russian serfs occurred as a result of the shock of defeat in the Crimean War and the realization that the country needed to modernize.

The immediate outcome in both cases was to change the way the earth was owned. Once the labor needed to release the land's value had to be paid for, it was necessary to make a profit from its produce, and this gave the soil a capital value. In purely economic terms, abolition and emancipation proved that property in people was incompatible with free-enterprise capitalism. But the social consequences were more profound. Increasing the freedom of many people could only be achieved by curbing the extreme liberty enjoyed by a few others. Out of the change should have come a society that was not only more efficient but more just and therefore more stable.

In Russia, that process began with the emancipation manifesto issued by Tsar Alexander II in 1861. Defeat in Crimea had brought to a head a festering crisis in the serf economy. Criticism of Russia's feckless nobility was voiced not just by the tsar's bureaucrats but by writers of every description. It appeared even in Alexander Pushkin's 1833 verse epic, *Eugene Onegin*, where traditional aristocratic values were compared unfavorably to the system of "Adama Smit" or Adam Smith. An influential political analyst, Boris Chicherin, himself owner of some three thousand "souls," led the way in blaming the institution of serfdom. It was, he said, economically harmful because it encouraged owners to become "lazy, careless, extravagant, incapable of conducting serious business." The most pressing consequence was the rising debt they owed to the State Loans Banks that had reached 328 million rubles with no possibility of being paid off.

The tsar's emancipation of the serfs solved both problems at one stroke. While it freed serfs from their landlords' courts and the fear of the *knout,* the manifesto also required them to purchase the land they once had worked so that their owners' debts could be paid off.

On the face of it, the deal was all to the advantage of Russia's idle nobility. They kept their private, demesne land, usually the most fertile, and saw the cost of their borrowing from the State Loans Bank wiped out, while the twenty-two million impoverished peasants they had once owned were ultimately expected to pay for it all. The twenty-five million serfs owned by the tsar and the state later gained their freedom with more varied conditions, and generally at lower cost. Overall, the severity of the financial terms of emancipation meant three in four peasants could not afford more than twenty-five acres. Although the state lent them up to 80 percent of the purchase price at 5 percent interest, by 1881 the peasants' debt had reached 716 million rubles, worth, as a result of inflation, about $1.2 billion. Yet the effects of the tsar's March 3 manifesto set in motion social and economic forces that neither his government nor the aristocracy could control.

Despite emancipation, the Romanov goal remained autocratic government, only now in a modern context—"Genghiz Khan with an electric telegraph" in the jibe used by social reformers. But in legal terms freeing serfs transformed the private estates of the nobility into a form of landed property comparable with western Europe. It took time for the civil law to adjust, but broadly it was governed by Roman law that spread ownership among the family, while recognizing the contractual obligations of an individual so far as mortgages and sales were concerned. But, as anyone who had read *Oceana* might have predicted, the creation of landed property spawned a host of property owners' associations to lobby for their interests and to acquire political power.

To fill the gap in local government left by the abolition of aristocratic control over their serfs, Saint Petersburg was forced to create a more powerful form of provincial council, the *zemstvo,* still subordinate to the provincial governor appointed by the tsar, but with power to initiate schemes for roads, schools, and hospitals. Very quickly they became vehicles for reform-minded local landowners interested in making the system work better, or at least more responsively to what they wanted.

Among the torrent of petitions sent to the imperial government in Saint Petersburg was one from the *zemstvo* of Iaroslavl Province, 150 miles to the northeast of Moscow, demanding an overhaul of the legal and police system which was riddled with corruption and inefficiency—one million thefts had taken place in 1861 with only thirty thousand items recovered. To eliminate endemic bribery and intimidation of judges by the governor and other powerful officials, the assembly called for a wide range of changes that included a free press, an independent judiciary, and making officials subject to legal rules rather than to the lax supervision of Saint Petersburg. Until the 1860s, pressure for such reforms had been confined to exiled radicals like the Socialist Alexander Herzen, but now similar petitions came from other assemblies—Vladimir Province to the east of Moscow, for example, wanted trial by jury, a proper banking system, and equality before the law.

The most powerful case for presuming that a new society and economy grew out of the changed form of land ownership was made by its bitterest enemy, Vladimir I. Lenin. In his study *The Agrarian Question and the Forces of the Revolution*, published in 1908 and based on official statistics gathered from across European Russia by the *zemstvo* system, he warned his fellow revolutionaries that "Commercial farming is growing much more rapidly, the influence of exchange is wider, and capital is transforming agriculture much more profoundly than one might suppose from aggregate figures and abstract averages."

But his chief concern was with the huge peasant population that had been emancipated in 1861. In his view, ownership of the land was producing a bourgeois structure at alarming speed, with the richest 20 percent of peasants employing the poorest 40 percent to increase production, and either purchasing or renting additional land with their profits. "The richer that the peasants are in land," Lenin wrote, "the fainter are the traces of serfdom, the more rapidly economic development proceeds, the more energetic is this emancipation from allotment land [farmed before 1861], [and] the drawing of all land into the sphere of commerce."

Historians both then and since have questioned Lenin's analysis. The continuing logjam of peasant landholdings, whose use was still controlled by the *mir*, impelled two reforming chief ministers, Sergei Witte and Peter Stolypin, to initiate unpopular land reforms at the start of the twentieth century specifically to encourage the creation of privately owned smallholdings. And the two million peasant households in European Russia who asked between 1906 and 1915 to have their strips of land consolidated, surveyed, and registered as property showed how far the process still had to go at that late stage.

Yet other evidence also indicated that a land revolution was taking place across Russia. The creation of landed property was initially handicapped by a lack of capital except in the Baltic and Polish provinces, where a land registry system made lending easy. But nearly six hundred million rubles, almost nine hundred million dollars, allocated by the state in bonds and cash to new and aristocratic landowners, on top of the 328 million rubles in written-off debt, helped to fire up Russia's rural economy. Despite their slow start, a variety of banks and credit unions came into being, and by 1894 their mortgage lending had reached almost one billion rubles, including the notable sum of fifty-eight million rubles lent to former serfs by the Peasants' Bank since its foundation in 1883. That level of lending gave each landowner's property in European Russia, from peasant to Grand Duke, an average capital value of about ten rubles or fifteen dollars an acre. By chance, that was almost exactly the value of land in the United States according to the 1850 census, a period when its rural economy was beginning to turn on the afterburners of industrialization.

Writing at the same time as Lenin but with rather more humanity, Anton Chekhov gently lamented and laughed at the impact of this increasingly energetic, capitalist use of land on the Oblomovan outlook of old-fashioned aristocrats. In *The Cherry Orchard*, the past is represented by the charming fecklessness of the orchard's owner, Madame Ranevskaya, who is incapable of dealing with the fact that the land must be sold off to pay her debts; the future is the emotionally inept Lopahkin, the family's former serf, now a wealthy businessman, who buys the estate and chops down the cherry trees to build vacation homes. The scenario encapsulated Russia's social history. Unable to cope with the new conditions, the nobility who had owned 80 percent of European Russia in 1861 were forced to sell most of their land, and by 1912 two thirds of it belonged to Lopahkin-like newcomers. In the rush to make money, the Lopahkins created an ecological disaster, and by 1900 had cleared more than half the forests that once covered Russia as far south as the steppes in an orgy of wood-felling.

Perhaps the most telling example that a sea change had come over a large proportion of Russia's peasants was apparent in their sudden mobility.

Census returns recorded that until the end of the century well over 90 percent of peasants still lived in the place where they were born. But in the 1880s, out of relatively crowded and relatively capitalized European Russia came a surge of migration beyond the Urals into the vast expanse of Siberia. In the years up to the outbreak of war in 1914, more than ten million peasant migrants sold up and traveled east by steamship, riverboat, and, after the opening of the Trans-Siberian Railway in 1891, by train to find cheaper, more profitable land in the wild east. Many of the journeys were government aided, with an official allotment of forty acres at the end, but, as one pioneer boasted in a letter, "Here you can plough as much land as you want, and as much hay as you want! Life is possible!" Something akin to the kind of freebooting, individualized societies that had sprung up earlier in the century in the American Midwest, in Canada, Australia, and New Zealand, could be found in the former penal colony of Siberia.

The similarity struck foreign and Russian observers alike. "Instead of a gaunt, lone land inhabited only by convicts," wrote one British traveler, "I saw a country that reminded me from the first day to the last of Canada and the best parts of America." The Russian writer Nikolai Barsagin quoted a friend who had lived in the United States: "Siberians have many similarities with the Americans—in their manners, in their customs and even in their way of life." And an American agent selling agricultural machinery in the region said simply, "I tell you Siberia is going to be another America."

INFURIATED BY THE SELFISHNESS, the materialism, and, it must be added, the freedom encouraged by the new way of owning the earth, Tolstoy wrote a grim fable in his old age called "How Much Land Does a Man Need? " It concerned the peasant Pahom who is tempted by ambition and the devil to buy more ground than the parcel allocated to him by the *mir* in 1861. Moving eastward in search of larger, cheaper parcels of land, Pahom finally arrives beyond the frontier where a tribe of nomads offers him as much land as he can walk around in a day. Greed tempts him to run for miles, until, arriving back exhausted as the sun sets, he collapses and dies. The story ends: "His servant picked up the spade and dug a grave long enough for Pahom to lie in, and buried him in it. Six feet from his head to his heels was all he needed."

The popularity of Tolstoy's story was evidence of the growing backlash against the attitudes that went with private property. To a conservative brand of opinion that labeled itself Slavophile, the authentically Russian institution of the *mir* presented a far preferable model of owning the land. Instead of individual wants, its goals were set by the community's needs. "A *mir* is a union of the people who have renounced their egoism, their individuality, and who express their common accord," wrote one Slavophile, Konstantin Aksakov. "This is an act of love, a noble Christian act."

The *mir* had survived the abolition of serfdom, largely because of the onerous conditions of the emancipation decree. Unable to afford the cost of buying land, the majority of peasants had continued to live as laborers on the estate where they had once been serfs. Since the government made the *mir* liable for its members' taxes and public service, it wielded great power, not only assessing dues but sorting out village quarrels and supervising the periodic redistribution of common land so that growing families received strips of ground from those with fewer mouths to feed. And its members accepted its authority, even over redistribution, because the allocation of strips served as a form of social security. "Of course I want to keep the allotment I have got," one member of a *mir* told a foreign visitor in the 1890s. "But if the land is never again to be divided up, my grandchildren may be beggars. We must not sin against those who are to come after us."

There were, in consequence, special terms of abuse for peasants who shirked communal tasks or bought the land that had been held in common. The offenders were called *miroyedi*, meaning commune-eaters, and—referring to their tight-fisted selfishness—*kulaki*, or fists.

BUT HOWEVER HIGHLY Tolstoy esteemed the *mir*, it was a leftover from serfdom. In the early twentieth century, when Russia's private landowners were exporting ten million tons of wheat a year with a value of almost six hundred million rubles, the *mir* practiced subsistence farming. And while railroads and electricity were dragging Russia into the modern age, the *mir* continued to buttress the old subservient hierarchy that Slavophiles—and Tolstoy—remembered with fierce nostalgia. During the last years of the Romanov dynasty, Tsar Nicholas II's reforming minister, Stolypin, instituted a series of agrarian reforms aimed at turning the *mir's* communal peasants into private propertied smallholders, thereby creating a Russian version of the Jeffersonian yeoman or, in Stolypin's description, "an independent, prosperous husbandman, a stable citizen of the land."

His attempt to accelerate the land revolution persuaded another two million peasants to leave the *mir*, but it aroused ferocious opposition from both conservative Slavophiles and left-wing Socialist Revolutionaries, who regarded the *mir* as rural Socialism, and brought about Stolypin's assassination in 1911. Weakened by infighting between conservative supporters and loyal reformers, tsarist government was left fatally vulnerable to the social upheavals of the First World War.

The *mir's* survival—it was only eliminated by the collectivization of Soviet agriculture in the 1920s—symbolized Russia's failure to translate the individual freedom promised to the serfs in 1861 into political and economic power. Even as the tsarist government encouraged the spread of private ownership, its autocratic nature naturally led it to resist the pressure for political representation exerted by owners anxious to protect their property. The more obvious result of the contradiction was the proliferation of violent revolutionary movements aiming to overthrow tsarist rule, whose membership was heavy with university students and other children of the propertied middle-class, like Lenin himself. But the silent existence of the *mir* was more significant because it represented the majority of Russians who had been left outside the new system, and whose values and way of life were threatened by the reforming policies of the old autocratic government. Their rootlessness would make it possible for the urban leaders of the 1917 Bolshevik Revolution to capture the rural heartland of the Russian Empire.

In the year that the serfs were freed, the bloody struggle that would liberate American slaves engulfed the United States. The unparalleled savagery of the war saved the Union and defined modern America. But the majority of freed slaves, like the majority of freed serfs, were to find that without political power individual liberty was eroded as swiftly as it was won.

IN 1824, the elderly Thomas Jefferson, still wrestling with the problem of slavery, identified what seemed to him the insuperable difficulty that prevented its abolition. "For actual property has been lawfully vested in that form," he acknowledged, "and who can lawfully take it from the possessors?" In 1850, the value of a slave would reach $1,000, making the South's property in slaves worth four billion dollars—more than six times the capital value of Northern manufacturing—a sum too large either to redeem or confiscate. Yet there was nothing sacrosanct about the institution itself. Slaves had been owned since civilization began, but they had only been owned as private property since the late seventeenth century.

When Massachusetts' General Court issued its famous code of legislative principles known as the Body of Liberties in 1641, it still followed the traditional European principle, derived from Aristotle and Saint Thomas Aquinas, that people were naturally free, but that captivity or debt might allow them to be enslaved. Consequently the code banned "bond slaverie" except for "lawfull Captives taken in just warres, and such strangers as willingly selle themselves or are sold to us. And these shall have all the liberties and Christian usages which the law of god established in Israell concerning such persons doeth morally require."

In effect, the basis of slavery was contractual, a penalty imposed because of a military or financial failure to maintain one's freedom. The manumission laws on both sides of the Atlantic gave legal status to this moral outlook by enabling owners to return slaves to their naturally free state once the slave expiated the failure, either by paying off the debt or securing the owner's forgiveness. Since all British colonies in North America began by adhering to this concept of slavery as a mixture of servitude and freedom, there was initially little to distinguish between slaves and indentured servants. As Virginia's first historian, Robert Beverley, noted "the male servants and slaves of both sexes are employed together in tilling and manuring the ground [although] . . . some distinction indeed is made between them in their clothes and food." By the time his history was published in 1705, however, liberty was being squeezed out of the mixture for Africans in servitude, starting with those colonies where slave labor was essential to release the value in land.

In 1664, under pressure from tobacco planters, Maryland declared that slaves could never escape servitude, and that their children "shall be Slaves as their fathers were for the term of their lives." Five years later, Virginia decided that an owner who killed a rebellious slave could not be found guilty of murder because "it cannot be presumed that premeditated malice (which alone makes murder a felony) should induce any man to destroy his own estate [property]." In 1696, the Carolina slave code of 1696 defined slaves specifically as "chattel possessions," meaning they were totally owned, rather than constituting "real estate" as in the 1691 Virginia slave code, indicating that the owner possessed simply the right to their exploitation. Although the difference hardly affected everyday practice, the trend toward establishing unmixed property rights in a slave was beyond question.

As the reach of British ownership extended, the liberties that British slaves could claim retreated, until they were left with virtually no legal rights, unable to own property, to plead in court, or even to live with their families. What this might lead to emerges from the dispassionate account by Sir Hans Sloane of the punishments meted out in the West Indies sugar plantations to slaves in 1698. For rebellious behavior, they were pinned to the ground, he wrote, and burned "by degrees from the feet and hands, burning them gradually up to the head, whereby their pains are extravagant . . . For crimes of lesser nature Gelding [castration], or chopping off halve of the foot with an Ax . . . For Negligence, they are usually whipt by the overseer with Lance-wood Switches, till they be bloody, and several of the Switches broken, being first tied up by the hands in the Mill-Houses . . . After they are whip'd till they are Raw, some put on their Skins Pepper and Salt to make them smart; at other times their Masters will drop melted Wax on their skins and use several exquisite tortures."

The sadistic penalties inflicted on sugar plantations were notorious—in 1766 George Washington deliberately punished his runaway slave, Tom, by sending him for sale in the West Indies—but what makes this account truly shocking is its tone. Hans Sloane was the epitome of Enlightenment culture, a founder of the British Museum and president of the Royal Society, yet he noted these horrors with complete detachment. Even for such an intelligent, perceptive observer, it had become impossible to see the victims as human beings rather than recalcitrant property. His blindness, however, would be shared by many otherwise compassionate commentators for generations to come.

In the nineteenth century, states in the American South issued a succession of slave codes attempting to deal with the complex problem of identifying a human being as property. The legal characteristics were dryly listed in Louisiana's 1834 code: "The master may sell [a slave], dispose of his person, his industry, and his labour; [a slave] can do nothing, possess nothing, nor acquire anything, but what must belong to his master." What this meant in practice was spelled out by North Carolina's Judge Thomas Ruffin in 1830 when he explained why John Mann could not be guilty of harming a slave girl named Lydia whom he had shot and wounded after she ran away rather than be whipped by him. Whatever human feelings might be involved, Ruffin said, "We cannot allow the right of the master to be brought into discussion in the courts of justice . . . The power of the master must be absolute, to render the submission of the slave perfect . . . This discipline belongs to the state of slavery. It is inherent in the relation of master and slave."

His ruling made a striking contrast to the civil codes of France and Spain, where the mixed nature of slavery was retained. It was explicitly recognized in the article of France's 1685 *Code Noir* that required slaves to be baptized and instructed as Roman Catholics. For all the code's severity—penalties included flogging, branding, and slitting the hamstring of a persistently runaway slave—torture and murder were forbidden, and owners were required to provide for the marriage of younger slaves, for their clothing and shelter, and for the treatment of the sick and elderly. Although the legal restraints were widely ignored in France's West Indian colonies, especially Sainte Domingue, today's Dominican Republic and Haiti, where extremes of torture were commonplace, the underlying recognition of a free humanity within the slave condition had unmistakable consequences.

Manumission—the freeing of a slave—figured prominently in the *Code Noir*, with ample provisions made for owners to confer freedom and wealthy slaves to buy it. And because the *Code* recognized the child of a free woman to be born into liberty, free blacks enjoyed a social legitimacy rarely guaranteed in private property colonies. Even in the ferocious conditions of Sainte Domingue, there were almost as many free people of color as the thirty thousand whites, and they owned more than one hundred thousand slaves and one third of the plantations.

Paradoxically, since it was the home of the "Black Legend" of the supposedly unspeakable cruelty inflicted on their Indian captives, the Spanish Empire allowed more humanity into the slave mixture than either of the others. Slaves could marry, own their personal possessions, and testify in court—in a celebrated case in Spanish-ruled Baton Rouge in 1806, the testimony of slaves even secured the acquittal of two other slaves accused of attempting to poison their white overseer, an unthinkable scenario in a colonial common law court, and one that soon changed after Louisiana became an American state. Although in reality owners often ignored the legal provisions, even in sugar-producing Cuba where conditions were harshest, Spain's liberal policy of manumission resulted in almost 40 percent of African-Cubans being free in 1792, compared to just over 10 percent of black Virginians. In Havana, slaves enjoyed enough autonomy to run shops and, according to an eighteenth-century observer, become skilled craftsmen, "not only in the lowest [trades] such as shoemakers, tailors, masons, and carpenters, but also in those which require more ability and genius, such as silversmith's craft, sculpture, painting, and carving."

Once large-scale plantations took over Cuban sugar production in the early nineteenth century, many of these freedoms were swept away. But resourceful slaves there and elsewhere in Latin America continued to use Spanish law to improve their conditions. A significant minority still managed to buy their freedom during their lifetime, a right that the law recognized and that the Roman Catholic Church consistently encouraged owners to allow.

Perhaps the most interesting pointer to the effect of these legal differences was shown by the contrast in attitudes to sexual and social relations. In the Spanish Empire, the *mestizos*, or children of mixed race couples, faced discrimination and were ranked by color and parentage on a strict social hierarchy—the term for these classifications, *castas*, would be adopted by the British as "caste" to describe India's rigid social divisions—but the lowliest *mestizo* could claim, though perhaps no more than that, to be recognized by law as a full citizen. The most successful owned businesses and slaves, and they served in the militia. And by the late nineteenth century, *mestizos* constituted more than half the population of Latin America.

In the United States, where the common law allowed a slave to be treated as virtually complete property, sexual contact was always socially fraught, very often illegal, and, to many owners, close to irresistible. That illicit attraction gave rise to two centuries of legislation prohibiting sex between owners and slaves. They first appeared in the colonial era, beginning with Virginia's 1691 slave code prescribing banishment for anyone married to "a negroe or mulatto," whether slave or free. In 1705 Massachusetts also banned marriage to "any negro or mulatto," but now imposed the penalty of flogging on both man and woman. The wording made clear the increasingly racial hostility behind such legislation, and that it should have also accompanied the shift from servitude to slavery was not a coincidence.

Once black Africans were identified with slavery, part of the definition of freedom became whiteness. But that clear-cut opposite was blurred by the existence of both mulattoes and freed slaves. The sheer mass of legislation designed to prevent sex between bodies with black and white skins, and to regulate the activities of free people of color, revealed how difficult it was to keep the distinction clear. Racial prejudice culminated in the notorious "one drop rule" enacted in several states, defining as colored anyone with any black ancestor.

Legislation did not stop the sex—around one in five of Pennsylvania's slaves were defined as "mulatto" in the 1780s—but the importance of excluding blackness led to increasingly stringent restrictions being placed on free people of color to prevent them associating with either whites or enslaved blacks. Attempts were made to banish them, to make them live apart, to carry passes restraining their movement, and, in nineteenth-century Georgia, to deny that their freedom meant anything more than the absence of an owner: "to be civilly and politically free, to be the peer and equal of the white man," wrote Joseph Lumpkin, Georgia's chief justice, in 1853, "to enjoy the offices, trusts and privileges our institutions confer on the white man, is not now, never has been, and never will be, the condition of this degraded race."

THE DIFFICULTY IN THINKING past the property definition was demonstrated in 1833 when slavery was abolished throughout the British Empire, and the government paid twenty million pounds, about one hundred million dollars, in compensation not to the slaves but to their owners for their loss of assets. The same logical madness appeared in a famous speech by the dominant voice in Congress, Daniel Webster, in 1850 when he argued that the protection of property of every kind, including "property in persons," was "the great object of government." Aware that restive Northerners were opposed to a new Fugitive Slaves Act that required them to aid in the capture and return of an escaped slave, he bluntly demanded what right they had "as a question of morals and of conscience . . . to endeavor to get round this Constitution, or to embarrass the free exercise of the rights secured by the Constitution to the persons whose slaves escape from them?"

The purpose of his speech was to defend the Union, but it did so, as Ralph Waldo Emerson pointed out derisively, by treating "the Union as an estate, a large farm," in effect as a property. Instead of giving priority to the sense of justice that, as John Locke argued, provided the basis of private property, Webster proposed that property itself was so sacred that an individual's conscience should be sacrificed to the priority of protecting it. The very purpose of the Union was lost.

Yet that was what the upholders of slavery demanded. In Washington,

Southern representatives required Congress to observe the notorious "Gag rule" that banned any discussion of slavery for fear of inciting ideas of insurrection among slaves. In the world outside, free speech was punished brutally: prominent abolitionists invariably received threats of violence and often were physically assaulted; Elijah Lovejoy, an anti-slavery newspaperman in Illinois, was lynched, and in Saint Louis, Missouri, Francis McIntosh, a free black, was burned alive after being accused of abolitionist sympathies.

Throughout the South, slave codes regulated what white people could teach their slaves, when they could hire them out, and how they were to keep them disciplined. Pass laws restricted the movement of free blacks, and Southern ports routinely detained in prison black crew members of Northern ships. The regulations effectively taxed the whole of Southern society to safeguard the profits of an elite minority, and increasingly they were being spread throughout the United States.

Not only did the 1850 Fugitive Slaves Act require Northern abolitionists to assist in the arrest and return of people trying to win their freedom—as a result escaped slaves could only find genuine liberty in Canada—it also forced the new territories in the West to accept slavery and the slave codes' restrictions on the movement of free blacks. "We have a right of protection for our slave property in the Territories," declared Senator Albert G. Brown of Mississippi in 1858. "The Constitution as expounded by the Supreme Court awards it. We demand it, and we mean to have it."

The ruling of the Supreme Court ensured that federal law safeguarding slave property overturned any state legislation safeguarding individual liberty. The paradoxical result was that while the enslavement of humans was a matter of states' rights in the South, it became a federal concern sweeping aside state sovereignty in the North and West.

Yet the sheer size of the slave economy made it hard to argue for its abolition on purely rational grounds. By the 1850s, the value of cotton exports had soared above $120 million a year—more than half of all United States exports—and the multiplier effect spread commercial prosperity far beyond the deep South. Virginia, Maryland, and North Carolina grew rich supplying slaves for the cotton fields further south. The fisheries of New England depended on sales of salt cod to the plantations; shippers and financiers in Philadelphia, New York, and Boston took their cut from the cotton trade; and the cotton factories of England earned fortunes for their owners.

Unsurprisingly, therefore, the drive to abolish slavery in the private property societies had to step outside rationalism. "On this subject, I do not wish to think, or to speak, or write, with moderation," William L. Garrison declared in the first issue of his abolitionist newspaper, *The Liberator,* in 1831. In Britain, evangelical Protestants had started the campaign focusing simply on the evil of enslavement and presenting their case in the image of a chained black man with the slogan "Is he not a man and a brother?" Significantly, women, who provided much of the energy and finance for the abolition campaign, repeatedly chose to make justice a central theme in their appeals and speeches. And the final decision to put an end to American slavery depended on a stark moral choice: in Abraham Lincoln's iconic phrase, "If slavery is not wrong, nothing is wrong."

UNLIKE RUSSIA, whose society and economy were transformed by the sale of aristocratic estates following emancipation, most of the South's landowners retained their property after abolition. Cotton was too valuable to business interests in the North for any but the most heinous rebels to be deprived of their plantations. Existing growers resumed production, either with employed labor or under sharecropping arrangements with former slaves, and were joined by small farmers, black and white, either working their own fields or leasing them from larger owners. Freed from the restrictions of the slave codes on the employment and mobility of black workers, the cotton crop of 1870 was larger than any harvested before the war.

Massive changes were brought about in the South by Reconstruction—the construction of eight thousand miles of railroad track, reform of the tax system, the rebuilding of roads, the provision of free education in four thousand new schools, the foundation of black colleges like Fisk and Howard, and, backed by the presence of eight thousand federal troops, the participation of African Americans in government and law. Around twenty thousand Northern carpetbaggers came south to take part in these enterprises, and with the assistance of the Freedmen's Bureau, many former slaves were able to negotiate labor contracts and register to vote. Yet Southern society remained virtually unaltered.

"Political reconstruction is inevitable now," Mary Greenhow Lee, a wealthy Virginian widow, wrote in her diary in 1865, "but social reconstruction we have in our hands and we can prevent."

Social reconstruction failed because the old, hierarchical distribution of land remained untouched. The most important attempt to alter the pattern was swiftly ended. In January 1865 General William T. Sherman issued Special Field Order Number 15 confiscating four hundred thousand acres of Confederate territory along the coast from Charleston, South Carolina, to Jacksonville, Florida, and ordering its redistribution to freed slaves with the specification that "each family shall have a plot of not more than (40) forty acres of tillable ground."

As social engineering, the order had the potential for creating a Jeffersonian society of independent owners. In Congress, Thaddeus Stevens, the most radical exponent of Reconstruction, introduced a bill to spread the policy of land redistribution across the South, confiscating property from "traitors to the United States" and allocating it to those who had formerly been property themselves. Reconstruction on those lines would have led to the South being recolonized. But the program soon faltered. Following Lincoln's assassination, the new president, Andrew Johnson, canceled Sherman's order, and Stevens's death in 1868 dissipated the momentum for radical Reconstruction. The few African Americans who had taken up Sherman's offer lost their land, and the old structure was left largely untouched. Even politics soon turned out to bear a certain resemblance to what had existed before. "This is a white man's government," said the first postwar governor of South Carolina, "and intended for white men only."

Once the secessionist states had accepted the three new amendments to the Constitution outlawing slavery, extending citizenship to everyone born within the United States, and prohibiting racial or color restrictions on the right to vote, they could be readmitted to the Union. Any lingering enthusiasm in the North for intervention was killed by the economic crash of 1873. In the next presidential election, both Republican and Democratic candidates promised to bring an end to Reconstruction, and, as the high tide of equal rights began to ebb, a series of Jim Crow measures brought about segregation and the return of the old exclusive freedom that only whites could enjoy.

One by one, elected black representatives who had been admitted into state legislatures at the point of a federal bayonet were ejected. Then, in 1890 Mississippi Democrats, under the leadership of Senator James Z. George, introduced literacy tests that prevented 90 percent of African Americans from voting. Six years later the Supreme Court ruled in *Plessy v. Ferguson* that the provision of racially divided facilities, disguised as "separate but equal," did not conflict with the Fourteenth Amendment. Like the Polish *szlachta* and Britain's eighteenth-century aristocracy,

Southern whites had succeeded in creating a political monopoly for the exercise of their property rights. And like their predecessors, Southerners did so at the cost of ignoring the inner logic that every private property society had to follow: without a moral foundation, property had no standing except that of force. As a consequence, they too would find themselves stuck in a blind alley.

Chapter Sixteen

The Crisis of Capitalism

In December 1882, the four-masted sailing ship *Dunedin* docked in the sheltered harbor of Port Chalmers on the South Island of New Zealand and began to load a strange cargo. About five thousand calico parcels, each weighing almost as much as a human being and trailing a plume of condensation in the summer warmth, were carried into the ship's holds. Between the main masts protruded a small funnel, and the boiler below it, consuming three tons of coal a day, led many to believe that steam power was to help the *Dunedin* on her voyage to London. But wind alone drove the ship.

What the engine turned was the compressor of a refrigeration plant that kept the temperature of the hold and its cargo of chilled sheep carcases below freezing even during the long hot weeks as the ship drifted through the tropics. When this first delivery of frozen New Zealand lamb was put on sale in London in April, *The Times* of London hailed it as "such a triumph over physical difficulties, as would have been incredible, even unimaginable, a very few days ago." But the voyage of the *Dunedin* was not just a technical feat. It completed a network of food, and other landed produce, that had already spread east and west, and now tied the southern hemisphere to the north.

The east-west connection had been made possible by steam-power operating on land and sea. From the 1850s, more efficient marine engines that reduced coal consumption by two thirds made transatlantic crossings with predictable passage times instantly cheaper and more profitable. In the United States a web of 150,000 miles of railroad track, almost sixty-five thousand of them west of the Mississippi, carried the produce of wheat fields and cattle ranches to the eastern, increasingly industrialized states. As Jules Verne conjectured in his 1873 tale *Around the World in Eighty Days*, it took no longer than that to circle the globe simply using scheduled services operated by steamship lines and railroad companies in the United States, Europe, and across India's newly opened Bombay (Mumbai) to Calcutta (Kolkata) route.

The basic justification for this network was to carry the commodities of the earth. Almost twelve million bushels of wheat were shipped to Britain in 1880 from the United States alone, and another eight million from Russia, Canada, Australia, and India; about six hundred thousand "loads" of timber, each consisting of 1.5 million cubic meters, came from Canada every year along with perhaps two hundred thousand more from Russia and Sweden; and five million bales, or some three hundred million pounds, of American cotton a year, supplemented by another seventy million pounds from India and Egypt. And between the first sailing of the *Dunedin* and the outbreak of the First World War, 150 million frozen sheep arrived in Britain from New Zealand and Australia, and another seventy million from Argentina.

A similar pattern operated inside the territory of the United States. As the railroads provided swifter access to markets in the rapidly growing eastern and midwestern cities, the acreage under cereals in the Western states grew by a 100 percent between 1870 and 1890, and in turn wheat production doubled to half a billion bushels a year. The third transcontinental railroad in the United States, the Northern Pacific, was completed in the year of the *Dunedin's* pioneering voyage, adding cereals from the Dakotas as well as Pacific Coast lumber to the supply. Fanning out from Chicago, more railroads connected ranchers and livestock farmers to the Union stockyards where four hundred million animals were slaughtered between 1865 and 1900 to be redistributed as meat to the rest of the country. Before the end of the century, California fruit growers would be packing a quarter of a million tons of oranges, grapes, lettuces, and almonds into refrigerated railroad cars to add to the cascade of eastward-heading food. The flood of produce from the Midwest, railroaded into Chicago then shipped east in freight trains or by barge down the Erie Canal, prompted one New York observer to boast that the city "may call Ohio her kitchen garden, Michigan her pastures, and Indiana, Illinois and Iowa her harvest fields."

The opening up of the food network destroyed the basic Malthusian calculation that sex would always produce more than the earth could supply. Along the path covered by Verne's Phileas Fogg, it allowed explosive growth in a string of cities, London and Paris, Mumbai and Yokohama, Chicago and New York: from 1850 to 1880, the largest of them, London, doubled in size to 6.5 million, Paris to 2.7 million, and New York tripled to 1.5 million; Calcutta's population grew from perhaps 300,000 to 848,000 and the smallest, Yokohama, was transformed from a drowsy fishing village to a thriving port with more than four hundred thousand inhabitants.

Economic historians often focus on the revenues generated by the trade between what they usually term the core and the periphery—the mother-country and the colonies, developed economies and undeveloped, cities and their hinterland—and they point to the advantages enjoyed by the core exporting high value industrial goods that were paid for by importing low value earth produce from the periphery. But this limited perspective misses the unique capacity of the periphery in private property economies to benefit from the most important commodity that traveled down the network.

EVEN BEFORE THE RAILROADS, emigration societies and Wakefieldian land companies in both the United States and the British Empire encouraged large-scale migration. But once the railroads were built, the people network became so efficient that a company like the Kansas Pacific railroad employed permanent agents in Britain and Germany to help migrants buy combined steamer and railroad tickets straight through to Kansas and Nebraska. Carl B. Schmidt, an agent of the Atchison, Topeka, and Santa Fé railroad with three million acres of publicly surveyed land to sell, brought in twelve thousand Volga-based Mennonites in 1874, who not only spent $332,509.72 buying land from the company, but, as a local newspaper reported in September that year, "They are also purchasing horses, cattle, wagons and agricultural implements as well as household goods, and their purchases will aggregate a very handsome sum."

The Mennonites attracted attention for their foreign habits, but the 1850 census showed that 1.5 million immigrants to territories west of the Mississippi had come from eastern states, above all New England, the starting point for an entire swath of settlement reaching to Minnesota and beyond. Many arrived cash poor—unable to afford a wooden-frame house, the poorest in Nebraska dug dwellings in the ground, known as "sod houses"—but most had sold up and brought capital to invest in land and goods.

Similar networks operated internationally. Steamers carrying timber, cotton, wool, and wheat one way filled their holds with immigrants for the return voyage. Track that bore freight trains into the cities rattled to passenger trains heading out. By one recent estimate, the unprecedented churning of population in the late nineteenth and early twentieth centuries threw out an estimated twelve million migrants from Britain to the United States and the empire, about twelve million more from Germany and Ireland to North America and Australia, and a further twelve million from the long-settled U.S. Atlantic states to the newly settled territories and states in the west. Even compared to the imperial diasporas that scattered seven million Spaniards to Latin America, fifteen million Russians to Siberia and central Asia, and thirty million Chinese to Manchuria and along the Pacific rim, the dispersal of private property inhabitants was unparalleled.

EVERY MIGRANT ADDED TO THE CAPITAL of a new settlement. The estimated one million dollars spent by wealthy Mennonites in Kansas was at the top of migrant expenditure at roughly $8,300 per person, but even the landless laborers who paid twenty-five dollars for an assisted passage from Scotland to Tasmania in 1854 and came ashore with no more than their belongings had sufficient economic value to persuade the colonial government to pay the $120 outstanding on their fares.

But the migrants brought something more immediately valuable, the energy and optimism of the young. The 1860 census showed that only a thousand people in Kansas were over forty-four years old, and in 1845 a Melbourne reporter noted that on the streets, "there are no old people, and not many even who are advanced enough to come within the denomination of middle-aged." Their confidence and verve as well as the ease of acquiring property could only have added to the extremes of boom and bust that characterized landed economies during the nineteenth century. The pattern was most obvious in the United States, where five abrupt busts in 1819, 1837, 1857, 1873, and 1893 brought ends to periods of boom. Within each boom, there was a general upward rise in land prices over the period, at first gradual but then steepening as mortgage-lending accelerated to keep up, thereby fuelling an unsustainable burst of demand, and a final price explosion.

Similar cycles occurred in Australia, South Africa, and New Zealand, with similar symptoms of euphoric confidence. In Melbourne, a house boom in the 1830s enabled one speculator to buy a town lot for £150 in

1836 and sell it three years later for £9,280. But to make money systematically, rather than as a one-time speculation, it was necessary to think as John Jacob Astor did while amassing a fortune of twenty-five million dollars from the growth of Manhattan in the early nineteenth century. When a customer asked why he chose to sell a Wall Street location for $8,000 rather than hold on for a few years to get $12,000, Astor explained, "See what I intend doing with these $8,000. I shall buy eighty lots above Canal Street [the city limits at the time], and by the time your one lot is worth $12,000, my eighty lots will be worth $80,000."

During the twenty-year Australian boom that would bust spectacularly in 1867, this kind of thinking provoked what was generally termed "land mania" in Sydney, but the brash optimism of its rival, Melbourne, went further. "The Melbournians," wrote one commentator in 1855, "have shown themselves from the beginning of their brief history, a most mercurial race—the maddest speculators in the world."

Throughout the first three quarters of the century, the rhythm of boom and bust was unsynchronized. Each land market generated its own conditions, and although a boom would draw in immigrants and investment from outside, it did so in its own time. Thus, in 1842 Australia went bust as Canada was booming, and in 1865 non-Boer South Africa blew up spectacularly just as the United States production was beginning to boom after the Civil War.

The first coordinated global crash came in 1873. It was also the first where measures taken to deal with financial instability in one country—Germany's attempt to stave off inflation by tying its currency to gold rather than silver—rippled through others, destabilizing their booming, credit-swollen economies from Austria to Zanzibar. Silver-backed currencies like the dollar lost credibility, triggering runs on banks and a rolling wave of company failures. In the United States, bankruptcies totaled $775 million in four years, including that of the great tycoon Jay Cooke. American railroads defaulted on bonds worth $790 million, 65 percent of which were held by foreign investors, setting off crashes in Europe.

The "Great Depression," as it was known until displaced by the 1930s version, created a sense of gloom that lingered on into the 1880s, was briefly dispersed, then gathered again in 1893. The prolonged nature of the slump, with steadily falling prices that cut profits and inhibited investment, marked it out as different from earlier, more localized crashes. In fact the 1873 recession proved to be of critical importance to those parts of the earth occupied by private property economies. By the time its effects had cleared away, it was apparent that the theory of free-enterprise capitalism described by Adam Smith had a flaw.

RURAL CAPITALISM HAD OFFERED Smith a model of a free enterprise system based on a myriad of small producers competing on price and delivery in a market where overproduction of one product brought a fall in price and profit, leading either to more efficient production or to a switch to a more profitable item. In *The Wealth of Nations*, he noted that it was fully working in England, reasonably developed in Scotland, evolving in France, and well-grounded in colonial America. Although he did not predict the egalitarian nature of the societies that followed the expansion of private property, his theory did demand the absence of any artificial barriers hindering access to capital, credit, and productive capacity. Thus, he would presumably have welcomed the entrepreneurial enterprise, the freedom and equality that characterized the United States in the early nineteenth century, and the post-Wakefieldian British Empire. Nevertheless, inequality was intrinsic to his economic model and consequently, as his writing repeatedly made clear, he expected government to protect the property of the rich as effectively as it did the dignity of the poor.

In the United States, unlimited resources had allowed the intrinsically unequal mechanism of property rights and free-market capitalism to create an egalitarian society like none other in history. Once a limit on resources began to make itself felt, the conditions for this egalitarian state began to crumble. Those with land grew wealthier from its rising price, the poorest no longer found it possible to buy what had once been available to everyone. Wealth became concentrated in fewer hands, and the inequality inherent in private property rights made itself apparent. No one perceived this more clearly than the most influential critic of rural capitalism, the journalist and self-taught economist Henry George.

By the end of the 1870s, it was impossible to avoid seeing extremes of poverty—nothing shocked George more than the appearance after 1873 of children begging on the streets of New York and San Francisco—accompanied by the unparalleled opulence of the champagne-swilling Gilded Age. Central to the argument that he put forward in *Progress and Poverty*, published in 1879, was the assumption that the way the earth was owned provided the key to correcting what had gone wrong both socially and economically. "The ownership of land," he wrote, "is the great fundamental fact which ultimately determines the social, the political and consequently the intellectual and moral condition of a people."

Long before Frederick Jackson Turner's 1893 essay, Henry George identified the frontier as the critical agency in creating the old egalitarian America. Using the same arguments, and indeed the very phrases Turner would employ fourteen years later, he pointed to the impact of its limitless resources. "This great public domain is the key fact that has formed our national character and colored our thought," he wrote. "Whence comes our general intelligence, our comfort, our active invention, and our power of adaptation and assimilation? And further, our free, independent spirit, the energy and hopefulness that have marked our people? They are not causes—they are results. They have sprung from unfenced land. Our vast public domain has been the force that transforms unambitious European peasants into self-reliant Western farmers."

But with the filling up of the continent that era was ending. And just as the social equality of the early nineteenth century had come from the equal distribution of the land, so "the great cause of inequality in the distribution of wealth is inequality in the ownership of land." To eliminate poverty and revive the egalitarian nature of American society, George argued, it was necessary to redistribute land more fairly. The method was taxation.

In his analysis of rural capitalism, Henry George made a clear distinction between the increase in the value of land that was earned by labor, and the unearned rise in its price that came from growing demand created by a larger population. The latter, he argued, "represents a value created by the whole community . . . So it necessarily belongs to the whole community." To recover the value, this unearned profit should be taxed at 100 percent, leaving the owner only with the value of whatever improvements he had actually made. George estimated that the money raised would be enough to abolish all other taxes. And with the escalating ingredient of speculation removed, the price of land would drop to a level where anyone prepared to work hard could once more afford it.

Progress and Poverty sold more than three million copies on publication, and in the years since, a variety of state and provincial governments around the world have experimented with Georgist land taxes. Nowhere has society been transformed in the way he predicted, but the experiments have shown that it is notoriously difficult to arrive at a valuation system that can clearly separate earned from unearned capital appreciation. Georgists point out accurately enough that their beliefs have never been properly put into practice, but perhaps they cannot be.

George's analysis of rural capitalism was incisive, but it neglected one element that was taking shape even as he wrote. Landed values were gradually being displaced as the most powerful force shaping private property economies. The new engine was neither egalitarian nor subject to the sort of competitive pressure that determined price and profit in the marketplace described by Adam Smith.

THE THEORETICAL PROBLEM posed by the 1873 recession was that while prices of goods fell in the next five years and profit margins were squeezed pancake thin for a record sixty-five months, with unparalleled numbers of manufacturers, farmers, and producers driven to bankruptcy, the economies of major industrial states such as the United States, the British Empire, and Germany actually grew, albeit more slowly than before. Indeed, their economies enjoyed a short-lived land boom in the late 1880s before collapsing into recession again in 1893.

What became clear to later economists was that in the course of the long depression the rules of the marketplace had ceased to apply to the largest participants in an industrial economy. The scale of investment, the power of the financial industry, and the rewards of monopoly simply made Adam Smith's model unworkable. The crisis of capitalism predicted by Karl Marx had arrived. It did not come in the form of a proletarian revolution, however, but from the productive capacity of the system itself.

One of the first to appreciate what had happened was the outstanding American economist of the 1890s, David A. Wells. A severe academic with an obsessive interest in systems of production rather than grand theories, he believed firmly in free trade and free enterprise. Very early on he argued that capitalism's great strength lay in its capacity to modernize itself constantly through an inexorable process of destructive innovation. Just as powered looms had destroyed the usefulness of professional handloom weavers who had earlier displaced part-time cottage weavers, so railroads pushed aside the canals that had made wagon trains redundant. And deep-pocketed, publicly listed companies had bankrupted those private entrepreneurs who had only their own securities to fall back on.

But these new industries, the chemical factories and advanced steel manufacturers of the second industrial revolution, were different, Wells pointed out. "Those engaged in great industrial enterprises," he wrote, "whether they form joint-stock companies or are simply wealthy individuals, are invested with such economic powers that none of them can be easily pushed to the wall."

* * *

THE PROBLEM AROSE from the complexities of industrial production. At the end of the nineteenth century, a manufacturer of basic steel plate had to source iron ore with the right phosphorous content, coked coal with the right carbon content, alloys of copper and manganese in the right ratio, acquire land close to water and a railroad, build factories of the most efficient design, construct furnaces to withstand temperatures of 3,500 degrees fahrenheit, recruit and train scores of workers with skills ranging from accountancy to hammering, and find markets for the product. Above all, the manufacturers needed a bank with the right attitude. To fund such a project required a different sort of finance from the kind that had driven the undirected, helter-skelter spread of private property economies across the globe.

The need had first been made apparent in Britain by the exceptionally high and long-term cost of building railways. A term of twenty years might be needed to pay off investment on this scale but the rewards—up to 15 percent annually for rail companies in densely populated areas—were attractive. In response to the need to bring in more investment, two pieces of legislation, the 1855 Limited Liability Act and 1856 Joint Stock Companies Act, offered protection to investors by restricting their liabilities, should a company fail, to the loss of their investment. The birth of the modern financial industry may be said to have begun in that decade. Hundreds of limited liability companies were launched and financed their operation by issuing shares. But railway companies and other high borrowers with a monopoly of operations in a particular area also chose to raise money through bonds, a method of funding once largely confined to the payment of government debt, as a way of financing their capital needs.

Very quickly, British banks began to exploit their connections with property-owning communities overseas to create an international financial hub centered in London. Some of the earliest loans were made to the United States government, including the fifteen million dollars lent to the federal government to finance the Louisiana Purchase in 1803. But state governments also borrowed heavily with more than half the two hundred million dollars that was raised up to 1841 to pay for canals, roads, and early railroads coming from British investors. Between the end of the Civil War and the 1873 crash, almost two thirds of the $1.5 billion corporate borrowing for American railroad construction was raised in London. Russian government bonds and Argentine railway shares were issued there, and across the newly settled empire, investment in colonial land, railways, and construction came from the capital. By 1872 more than half of all the national debt in the world was quoted on the London Stock Exchange.

Backed by resources on this scale, the railroads, big steel plants, and chemical companies of the second Industrial Revolution were almost too big to fail. So much money was invested in them, it made more sense to continue trading at a loss rather than wipe out their entire capital worth by closing down. The result was uneconomic overproduction and a waste of both capital and labor. This was the crisis that bedevilled capitalism in the wake of the 1873 crash.

The solution, Wells suggested, was to abandon the basic competitive premise of free-market enterprise and to let "the great producers come to some understanding as to the prices they will ask; which in turn naturally implies agreements as to the extent to which they will produce."

IN THE UNITED STATES, a collection of big producers who fixed prices amongst themselves, and adjusted production accordingly was known as a trust. Most of the rest of the industrial world used the word "cartel," but the practice spread rapidly everywhere during the hard times after 1873, when large-scale manufacturers maximized production in order to service their debts. On razor-thin margins at best and chronic losses at worst, many were effectively owned by their banks and creditors. In order not to lose their investment, their financial backers seized at the opportunity offered by more powerful competitors, notably such industrial titans as Cornelius Vanderbilt, Andrew Carnegie, and John D. Rockefeller, to arrange price agreements, production targets, and trusts and so to be absorbed into existing webs of railroads, steel factories, and oil refineries. No one understood the new order of capitalism more clearly than J. P. Morgan, who used his influence as a banker to set up trusts in railroads, electricity generation, and steel manufacture—his creation, United States Steel, capitalized in 1901 at $1.2 billion, was the first billion-dollar industrial producer in the world, and had two thirds of the market.

This was the logic of Wells's analysis. Only a handful of manufacturers were making real profits in the last decades of the nineteenth century, but, benefiting from the failure of their overstretched competitors, those few produced spectacular results even in the midst of an economic depression. More than eight thousand miles of railroad were constructed each year during the 1880s, and in 1890 the value of the United States's industrial output reached $9.4 billion, outstripping Britain and Germany.

In the 1890s, coal production, the yardstick of every industrial economy, topped two hundred million tons a year in the United States, finally overtaking the total mined throughout the British Empire.

The same economic forces altered the way that land was owned in private property societies, effectively removing the advantage of rural capital from the person who tilled the soil. The change was seen most starkly on American farms. "The only possible future for agriculture," Wells concluded in 1895, "is to be found in large farms, worked with ample capital, especially in the form of machinery, and with labor organized somewhat after the factory system."

Increasing mechanization had been a fact of agricultural life throughout the nineteenth century, but what Wells identified was a step-change. Tracing its effect from "the great wheat fields of the state of Dakota," where machinery enabled one man to produce 5,500 bushels of wheat a year, to "the great mills of Minnesota," where another worker converted that wheat to a thousand barrels of flour, and perhaps two railroad employees were needed to transport the flour to the port of New York, "where the addition of a fraction of a cent a pound to the price will . . . deliver it . . . to any port in Europe," he demonstrated that labor, the ingredient that William Petty had identified as crucial for the creation of rural capital, had become "an insignificant factor in determining the market." As in industry, the real factor was the capital needed to buy machinery and power.

Amid tumbling prices—between 1870 and 1900, the price of American wheat slumped by half to approximately fifty cents a bushel, and cotton by the same amount to about seven cents a pound—farmers were forced to borrow. And despite the lean returns, the availability of credit attracted enough newcomers to double the number of farms to more than six million between 1870 and 1900. In South Dakota, mortgages accounted for 46 percent of the value of the state's farms, and other prairie states were not far behind, while nationwide 2.3 million farms, almost one third of the total in 1890, carried mortgages.

What underpinned the banks' lending was the steadily rising price of American farmland as demand exceeded supply. By 1900 it was worth more than twenty billion dollars. About 15 percent of it was owned by mortgage lenders, and beyond them by Wall Street. More agricultural credit, amounting to $2.2 billion, allowed farmers to purchase machines that combined harvesting and threshing, automatic milkers and cream separators. Rural capital had always financed American farming, but for most of the century mortgages had been short-term loans from local banks, and the return on a sold-up farm was easily reinvested in cheaper land to the west. These new loans were long-term, financed on small margins, and, if they were called in, there was no unimproved land on which to start again. Trapped on their capital-rich, income-poor farms, a growing proportion of those who worked the soil now shared its ownership, in practical and theoretical terms, with the banks.

The era of cheap food, signalled by the sailing of the *Dunedin,* was pushing American farmers into a dependency on financial institutions far beyond their own neighborhoods. They were equally reliant on the transport system described by Wells, the combination of railroads, grain elevators, and shipping lines that was needed to carry their crops to markets in the eastern states and beyond the distant Atlantic. And within that system were the pioneers of what would, in the twenty-first century, become the biggest industry in the world, the food business.

Among the grain merchants was a canny Scots-American, William Wallace Cargill, who not only built grain elevators in his home state of Minnesota and at the head of the Erie Canal in Buffalo, but offered farmers insurance against crop failure, a real estate service to newcomers, and a flour milling process directly plugged into the metropolitan retailers in Chicago and New York. George Archer and John Daniels of Illinois specialized in crushing linseed to make oils for animal feed, and in 1902 would team up to provide the same combination of food processing and finance that joined retailers to farmers. Agriculture had become a hybrid, still part of the template for free-market capitalism, but also part of a larger trading web that bore a closer resemblance to the old mercantile capitalism so derided by Adam Smith and all his followers.

The crisis of American farming was quickly exported around the world, and especially to Europe. To meet mortgage payments, financially constricted prairie farms poured out a flood of cheap grain, lifting exports of American cereals from forty-four million tons in 1877 to more than 184 million tons in 1890. Competitors in Russia and Australia found their profits cut to the bone, while Europe's cereal farmers reacted by throwing up tariff barriers in France and Germany, by switching to dairy farming in Denmark, and in Britain, relentlessly committed to free trade, by turning their faces to the wall and quietly giving up their bankrupt ghosts. Politically and economically, the descendants of Britain's eighteenth-century aristocracy had finally become irrelevant.

THE MOST SIGNIFICANT reaction to the influx of cheap cereals was Germany's. Its decision to protect its farmers by imposing duties of 40 percent on imported foreign grain flew in the face of Adam Smith orthodoxy on the importance of abolishing barriers to free trade. Indeed, its entire economic policy contradicted the ethos of free-enterprise capitalism, but results indicated that the German model provided the most effective solution to the problem of industrial overproduction.

In the years after 1873, Germany had developed more than three hundred cartels to control the production and pricing levels in every large industry from coal mines to the manufacture of ice skates. In 1913, nine Berlin banks commanded 83 percent of the nation's working capital; ten mining corporations were responsible for 60 percent of coal production; the five largest chemical companies produced 95 percent of all dyes; and two giants, Siemens and AEG, held half the electricals market.

Sheltered by high tariffs and knowing in advance their profit margins and product runs, the German iron and steel cartel produced 20 percent more pig iron between 1893 and 1907 at lower cost and higher profit than Britain's free-trade, free-market smelting plants as they attempted to upgrade old-fashioned technologies on paper-thin returns from oversupplied consumers.

In its most radical form, the policy of the country's largest political party, the left-wing Social Democrats, showed vividly how different the shape of the new cartelized capitalism was from the classic free-enterprise model. Financing the industrial power concentrated in the cartels had become so critical, according to the Marxist economist Rudolf Hilferding that the banks now exercised a controlling influence over the markets. To solve the crisis of overproduction and to arrive at a fully planned economy, he argued, a government only needed to nationalize the banks.

"Even today," he wrote in 1910, "taking possession of six large Berlin banks would mean taking possession of the most important spheres of large-scale industry . . . There is no need at all to extend the process of expropriation to the great bulk of peasant farms and small businesses, because as a result of the seizure of large-scale industry, upon which they have long been dependent, they would be indirectly socialized just as industry is directly socialized."

The ultimate sources of finance, however, were further away than

Berlin. In 1913, British financial institutions owned nine billion dollars of assets in the British empire; six billion in Africa, Latin America, Russia, and the Far East; and $3.8 billion in the United States. Until the First World War, the center of international finance was London, its dominance marked by the fact that American banks chose to locate more branches there than in New York. Acknowledging the financial reality in 1897, the *New York Times* confessed, "we are part, and a great part, of the Greater Britain which seems so plainly destined to dominate this planet."

The American response to the new age of cartels was to turn back the clock. Outraged by the excesses and corruption of the Gilded Age, the still influential farming electorate—at the end of the century, agriculture supplied 20 percent of GNP compared to industry's 30 percent—gave birth to the populist movement that pushed through the antitrust legislation known as the Sherman Act in 1890, and persuaded presidents Theodore Roosevelt and his successor, William Howard Taft, to use the act aggressively in the new century. The act might have helped break up some trusts, but it did nothing to solve the crisis of capitalism. And the most influential banker of the late twentieth century, Alan Greenspan, was scathing about the attempt to reintroduce the conditions of free-enterprise capitalism.

The Sherman Act, he wrote, "was a projection of the nineteenth century's fear and economic ignorance . . . it is utter nonsense in the context of today's economic knowledge." Monopolies and cartel agreements were necessary to control excessive production, he insisted, and as an example, he praised the monopolistic trust organized by Standard Oil in the 1890s, because it "yielded obvious gains in efficiency, through the integration of divergent refining, marketing, and pipeline operations; it also made the raising of capital easier and cheaper."

The deathblow to the nineteenth century's free-market ways came from the new, predominantly urban class that suddenly mushroomed in the service of these industrial behemoths. The salary-earning, white-collar employees who worked the interlocking processes that enabled a modern corporation to function were evidently wage slaves, by Marx's definition, but they tended to own or lease their own homes, suggesting they were members of the bourgeoisie. Even Madison's more straightforward categories of propertied and unpropertied did not really fit since their homes belonged in large part to the financial institutions funding their mortgages.

Reacting against corporate corruption and the self-rewarding greed of big business, many in this hybrid class appeared sympathetic to the claims of the unpropertied and to demands for redistribution and social justice. Some joined the rapidly growing membership of trade unions to protect their interests against corporate employers. Across Europe, they voted for parties that espoused such social-democratic policies as old-age pensions and sickness benefits. In Britain, the Liberal government that was elected in 1905 introduced similar measures with popular support, imposing an inheritance tax on wealth and dallying with the idea of a Georgist land tax. And progressives in the United States received enough support to reform corporate-corrupted government at state and city level, introduce a federal income tax, and push through the wider provision of public education.

YET AT THE VERY MOMENT when economists were in broad agreement that government or corporate planning of the markets was the only way to solve the crisis of capitalism, another, more acceptable solution began to emerge. It depended critically upon the new, hybrid way of owning the earth.

The solution was half-apparent in the phrase "conspicuous consumption" used by Thorstein Veblen in his *Theory of the Leisure Class* published in 1899. Veblen coined the term as a jibe against the bloated plutocrats who flaunted their wealth by their "unremitting demonstration of the ability to pay." But even at that date, the availability of credit was enabling white-collared, half-propertied wage slaves to do much the same, albeit on a reduced scale. As early as the 1880s, Boston furniture stores had allowed customers to buy expensive items, from beds to dining room tables, by paying in instalments. Sears Roebuck followed suit, and was copied by retailers of mass-produced sewing-machines. Most of the new automobile industry's products could be purchased in the same way, although not the bestselling Model T Ford. As electricity became more widely available, the practice spread to the acquisition of household goods such as refrigerators, washing machines, and radios.

By 1914, it was becoming apparent in private property economies that overconsumption might provide a way out of the crisis of overproduction. The property of most urban dwellers might not provide an income, but its value did provide security. And this value, together with assured salaries from large-scale industry and expanding government, was beginning to generate what would become known as the consumer economy. The inherent flaw in the model was not yet apparent. But evidently a system that allowed the consumer's buying power to be increased by the same financial markets that invested in the producer's factories was liable to abuse. It was equally easy to overlook the danger that the new kind of property created for democracy.

The problem lay in the nature of hybrid ownership. Its conflicting aims provides the starting point of John Steinbeck's tragedy of the Oklahoma dust bowl farmers, *The Grapes of Wrath*. To the human owner, possession of the earth is intimate and emotional: in Steinbeck's famous phrase "it's part of him . . . and in some way he's bigger because he owns it." But the business that owns his mortgage, and has now decided to foreclose, has no shape, no personality.

Desperate to defend his home, the farmer grabs a rifle and tells the tractor driver who is about to tear down the house that he is going to shoot the person responsible for taking his property away. "There's the president of the bank," the farmer says. "There's a board of directors. I'll fill up the magazine of the rifle and go into the bank."

To which the tractor driver replies laconically, "Fellow was telling me that the bank got orders from the east. The orders were, 'Make the land show profit or we'll close you up.' "

"But where does it stop?" the farmer exclaims in despair, "Who can we shoot?"

When the first great depression of the twentieth century struck in the 1930s, the government in every private property society, avowedly based on representing the interests of owners, needed to know whether it should listen to the house dweller, the mortgage lender, or Wall Street. And those owners who shared their properties with the financiers needed to know who to shoot. In short, the crisis of nineteenth-century free-market capitalism evolved in the twentieth century into a crisis of democracy.

Section Five

THE THREAT TO DEMOCRACY

Chapter Seventeen

State Capitalism

In Britain the birth of the industrial age had occurred messily behind a thousand privately owned hedgerows, but in Prussia it emerged as the direct result of government policy. And while private property societies experienced a land revolution before the industrial, in Prussia they developed side by side. The circumstances and the sequence of events combined powerfully to the making of a state that was both modern and denuded of democratic resources. Out of that background came regimes responsible for two world wars and a society that for twelve years represented the antithesis of civilization.

The impetus for change was created by catastrophe. At the battle of Jena in 1806 Prussia's iconic army whose professionalism had epitomized martial arts in the eighteenth century, and whose military ethos permeated Prussian society, was smashed by an invading force of French conscripts. The genius of Napoleon was not even necessary for France's victory. The decisive encounter in the battle, the one that destroyed the Prussian king's main force, was won by French citizen-soldiers under General Louis-Nicolas Davout without the presence of their great commander. Prussia's stunned survivors understood what it meant to face a nation capable of directing all its human resources onto the battlefield thanks to the efficiency of mass mobilization. To meet the challenge, reform was needed, root and branch.

The birth of the new Prussia began on October 9, 1807, with a royal edict issued by the king but formulated by his chief minister, Baron Karl von Stein. Entitled "Edict regarding Facilitated Ownership and Free Use of Real Estate, [and] Personal Conditions of the Rural Populace," its effect was to abolish serfdom and sweep aside a centuries-old tradition of restricting land ownership to the nobility, with the middle-classes confined to trade and the peasantry to land use. "Every inhabitant of our states," the edict declared, "is entitled without any limitations to possess immobile [landed] properties of any kind."

The law of entail, long used by the aristocracy to keep estates within the family, was abolished in order to create a larger land market and to make easier the granting of mortgages and other forms of credit. Like Jefferson and the eighteenth-century British Empire, Stein justified the change as a form of social engineering that would create property owners of the middle class and make them "the supporters of order, the strongest pillar of the existing monarchy and the class with the greatest obligation to the state."

The edict, later strengthened by Stein's successor, Karl von Hardenberg, also set the conditions for an industrial revolution by decreeing that every trade and occupation was "open to talent" whether noble or peasant, rather than being restricted to middle-class members of a guild or trade organization. The abolition of feudal restrictions theoretically created a marketplace where employers and workers were free to negotiate the value of labor. In law at least, Prussia's land and industrial revolutions began in the same year. Finally, the feudal administration based on manor courts in the countryside and the jurisdiction of trade guilds in the cities was to be replaced by elected provincial assemblies and town councils.

The philosopher Georg Wilhelm Friederich Hegel, who had heard the guns of Jena and recorded the celebrity-impact of seeing Napoleon riding by—"It is indeed a wonderful sensation to see such an individual who, concentrated here at a single point, astride a horse, reaches out over the world and masters it"—made it a central theme of his philosophy that history develops through the encounter between an ideal of perfect freedom and the reality of individual life. A Napoleonic hero, imbued with a totally self-realizing consciousness of freedom, could personally shift history onto a new level, but ordinary individuals had to accept "that all the worth which the human being possesses—all spiritual reality, he possesses only through the State."

It was in this sense that Stein and Hardenberg understood their reforms to be a step toward greater freedom, not by making the state more democratic, but by making it more effective. In practice, the Prussian state became one of the most efficient in the world, but whether it realized an accompanying degree of freedom was more open to question.

Eighteenth-century Prussia had been an eastern province, centered on Berlin, bordered by the Baltic and Poland. But during the war with France, it had absorbed much of Poland, and for its contribution to the defeat of Napoleon, it was rewarded in 1815 with a block of western states along the Rhine to act as a barrier against any future French aggression. The new Prussia was a strangely elongated, artificial country, stretching almost a thousand miles from France to Russia. In 1818, it was formally enclosed within a single customs union, the *Zollverein*, later extended in 1834 to include most of Germany. The first beneficiaries of reform were, therefore, the bourgeoisie, meaning the traders, small manufacturers, and commercial businesses, set free from the constriction of urban guilds and suddenly presented with a vastly expanded market cleared of tariff restrictions. The bourgeoisie flourished especially in the west, where urban prosperity spilled over into a countryside where French influence had ensured that peasant holdings were already held virtually as property.

Further east, in traditional Prussia's deeply conservative society, the changes caused widespread anxiety. Paradoxically the mood received its most eloquent expression in *The Communist Manifesto* in Karl Marx's famous paragraph raging against the bourgeoisie whose embrace of the profit motive had "put an end to all feudal, patriarchal, idyllic relations . . . it has substituted naked, shameless, direct, brutal exploitation . . . All that is solid melts into air, all that is holy is profaned, and man is at last compelled to face with sober senses, his real conditions of life."

Social upheaval exacerbated a need for national identity. The new enlarged Prussia was barely a generation old, and the idea of Germany existed only as myth and language. Most Prussians chose to look back to the smaller country of Frederick the Great, enlightened and militarily powerful, the power that with the eastern provinces of Brandenburg, Pomerania, and Brunswick had eventually brought about Napoleon's defeat at the battles of Leipzig in 1813 and Waterloo in 1815. This Prussia was exemplified not by the well-tended fields in the west but by the vast, sandy, European plain stretching eastward into what had once been Poland and disappearing without a boundary into the mist-shrouded marshlands around the Baltic. And the ideal Prussians were not its efficient bourgeois merchants but the sternly disciplined Junkers who possessed this land.

Like the hidalgos, the younger sons who colonized Latin America because they could find no land for themselves in Spain, Prussia's eastern states were originally occupied in the thirteenth and fourteenth centuries by land-hungry *junge Herren*, or young lords, a label that became shortened to Junker. Deeply influenced by the Sarmatian values and serf economy practiced by Poland's powerful aristocracy, the Junkers developed a caste mentality based on military discipline and total loyalty to the Prussian crown—the pejorative label to describe their unquestioning obedience was "corpse discipline"—and an absolute command over the peasant farmers on their estates, known as *Gutsherrschaft*, or judicial lordship.

In contrast to the small landholdings of west Prussia, four out of five Junker farms covered more than 250 acres, and many boasted additional forest and hunting grounds that extended across uncounted square miles. Much of the low-lying land beside the oozy rivers in the Oder basin and along the Baltic coast was virtually swamp, and Otto von Bismarck, himself a Junker lord, used to recall the importance of controlling the elaborate system of ditches and walls to save his cornfields from flooding. The great danger, he would say, was that "those who wish to operate with open pastures [peasant farmers with livestock] would win the upper hand from those who work with tilled, and water-free fields, and that all would be ruined by flood."

The distinctive feature of *Gutsherrschaft* was the social and economic power it conferred on the feudal lord over the peasants on his estate, not merely making them subject to his manorial court, but—in theory at least—acknowledging his near-parental degree of control over their lives. Discipline was routinely enforced by physical beatings, and even the peasants referred to themselves as *Untertanen*, or subjects. A reciprocal obligation of care was placed on the feudal lord, but since he determined its extent, the relationship was tilted in his favor.

As late as 1912, the decidedly conservative landlord Elard von Oldenburg-Januschau could still give a classic account of the *Gutsherrschaft* relationship. He had always made it his paternalist duty, he said, "to be available to my people at all times and concerning any matter. To be sure, I was not lenient; rather, I insisted that, on the estate, obedience was the highest principle." In fact, he added, "I had to enforce order and obedience with an iron fist." On the other hand, though poorly paid, his workers were warmly housed, and those who behaved well and accepted their landlord's guidance even in such personal matters as marital problems could expect to be "provided for during old age."

What made the iron fist necessary, however, was the long tradition of peasant resistance to landlord power, especially in defense of their rights to graze animals on common ground, and to run pigs and take wood from the forest. As Bismarck implicitly admitted in his allusion to their attempts to influence flood controls, they continued to do so after the 1807 reforms, exploiting the confusion as market forces and the law gradually dismantled the intricate system of duties and customs inherent in *Gutsherrschaft*. But those same forces brought an end to the peasants themselves. Widely separated strips of land and unenclosed meadows and fields were incorporated into compact, boundaried farms where the poorest among them now worked as employed laborers. But the most successful became prosperous farmers with enough money to buy estates from Junkers who could not adapt to the new conditions. By the end of the nineteenth century, no more than a third of eastern Prussia's land remained in traditional aristocratic hands.

For half a century, the new owners, both former peasants and wealthy outsiders, broadly prospered as they adjusted production to market demands, improving the breeds of cattle and sheep, and fertilizing their fields with nitrogen-fixing crops and manure from heavier, more numerous livestock. Under German's legal code, the land was owned by an individual male on behalf of his family, and the 1850 constitution gave a straightforward guarantee, "Property is inviolable," declaring it to be protected from seizure except by due process of law.

Working virtual prairies with low-waged labor and horse-drawn machinery, eastern Prussia's farmers grew fat on the demands of a growing population and improved transport to city centers, as canal barges replaced horse-drawn wagons, and were themselves overtaken by railroads. They found a growing market in Britain for their cheaply priced wheat, while Berliners bought their rye, the standby cereal that could be grown on the poorest soil. Agriculture was profitable enough for the area under cultivation to triple in size during the 1830s and 1840s.

Despite the number of newcomers, the Junker caste retained its old ethos, thanks to the *Landschaften*, the networks of landowners that provided both economic and social support for their members. Set up in the eighteenth century, the *Landschaften* offered a crucial source of investment through its credit unions, and politically they helped their members assert individual property rights against peasants defending communal rights to the use of forests and common land. The practical advantages of caste loyalty were obvious even to new recruits whose grandfathers might have fought to defend peasant rights.

Within months of the 1807 reform edict, the Junkers found that the old feudal remedies of manorial court decisions, backed up by physical beatings, were no longer effective. Faced by a rent and labor strike in 1808, the owners of the six-thousand-acre Stavenow estate in Brandeburg, together with seventeen other *Landschaft* members, turned instead to the untried system of local government created in 1807. In their petition to the district's freshly appointed commissioners, they admitted that their own courts could "offer no further help whatsoever" and asked for the assistance of the "local military" to enforce their demands for rent.

It was at this local level, and in the Pomeranian, Brandenburg, or Silesian state assemblies where land laws were administered and enforced by the increasingly effective state apparatus of police, judges, and prison, rather than in Berlin where legislation was enacted, that eastern Prussian property owners initially sought the political representation they needed to protect their interests.

However, the economic importance of agriculture in general—as late as the 1860s, two thirds of the population lived in the country and 30 percent of Prussian revenues came from taxes on land—ensured that the absolutist government of the Hohenzollern kings would heed the concerns of landowners. The geographical position of Berlin in Junker territory guaranteed that theirs would be the rural voice most clearly heard, and understandably the roughly nine thousand owners of the largest Junker estates took the lead in asserting property rights.

Their influence showed itself in privileges that allowed the Junkers to escape 90 percent of the land taxes levied on west Prussian farms. They also benefited from legislation that restricted the movement of labor, thus making it more difficult for underpaid laborers to leave their farms. Even the final abolition of manorial courts in 1848, ostensibly a setback for Junker power, saved them the expense of an institution they reckoned had become "far more costly than profitable" and was less efficient at protecting their interests than provincial courts and militia.

Seen in this perspective, the development of Prussian land ownership broadly resembled an early stage of the private property economies. Had the precedents of 1688 and 1776 been followed, at some point a clash would occur between the royal power and the landowners' drive for control over taxation, forcing the latter to seek allies and articulate ideas of rights and liberties that were immediate and practical rather than aspects of a remote Hegelian ideal.

That moment came in the convulsive year of 1861 when other societies across the Northern Hemisphere were about to be transformed by the freeing of serfs and the outbreak of civil war. At least as significant was the failure of Prussia to metamorphose into a democracy at the same time.

In 1861 the government of the new king, Wilhelm I, adopted a policy of raising taxes to fund a strengthened army and a more aggressive foreign policy. As a consequence the loopholes that had allowed Junkers to escape most of the tax paid by Rhineland farmers were eliminated. This warning that loyalty to the royal family of Hohenzollerns offered no guarantee of protection of their interests galvanized the Junkers into action.

A new political party, the Progressive Party, was formed in 1861 with the aim of making the executive arm of government answerable to the Prussian Landtag or legislature rather than to the king. Recognizing that royal power had hitherto been unconstrained by the Landtag, Heinrich von Sybel, the outstanding Prussian historian of the period and himself a member of the party, explicitly compared nineteenth-century Prussia to sixteenth-century England: "Today, the royal prerogative is stronger in Germany than in England; it maintains a position comparable in some ways to that of the Tudors."

Laboriously he explained that a parliamentary party should have "the right to approve state revenues on an annual basis" and that the royal government lacked any representative standing because it was responsible only to the king. The manifesto that he and his fellow Junkers drew up simply demanded that "government commits to the tax laws and the spending budgets approved by parliament; and that it does not pass any sort of laws without parliamentary assent."

Demonstrating their enthusiasm for a democratic goal that would serve their interests, large numbers of Junkers joined the Progressives, including the party's two leading figures, Leopold von Hoverbeck and Hans Victor von Unruh. Belatedly they started to seek political allies to challenge the power of royal government, especially among the rapidly growing industrial sector.

THE TIMING OF PRUSSIA'S INDUSTRIAL REVOLUTION, in tandem with the evolution of property in land, ensured that it could not follow the path of the private property economies where factories were financed through rural capital, and the recycled profits of colonial and slave-based trade. Although two Prussian businesses that would achieve iconic status, the Krupp steelworks and the Siemens electrical company, had begun in that way, by 1850 they employed barely fifty people between them. The largest textile and metal producers were some two million craftsmen and women—90 percent of weavers still used a handloom, thirty years after steam and water had wiped them out in Britain. Thirty years after reform, Prussian business still struggled to develop industrial plants or to build an efficient transport system. It found a solution across the Atlantic.

In 1841, after five years in Pennsylvania, Friederich List, by then a university professor, published the results of his observations in *The National System of Political Economy*. Prussia, he suggested, could benefit not from American democracy and liberty but from the American example of using the government's financial power to develop a managed industrialized economy. Although acknowledging that "It is bad policy . . . to promote everything by employing social [i.e., government] powers, where things may . . . be better promoted by private exertions," List was adamant that "it is no less bad policy to let those things alone which can only be promoted by interfering social power."

Railroads represented the perfect example of the advantages of public investment. Not only could government provide the finance, it was also able to see all the strategic considerations, rather than having to follow a purely commercial rationale, that determined where a line should be constructed. The national payoff from railroads was fourfold: they connected suppliers to markets, offered protection against famine, made defense easier, and, according to List's Hegelian conclusion, "The iron rails become a nerve system which, on the one hand, strengthens public opinion, and, on the other hand, strengthens the power of the state for police and governmental purposes."

Prussia's powerful bureaucracy, who were in charge of administration at every level of government, county, provincial, and state, and, like China's mandarins, were promoted through an examination system, adopted List's thesis as its economic bible. Every kind of manufacture, from steel mills to sugar beet refineries, came under officialdom's close supervision. Its powers were brought together in a far-reaching commercial code that Prussia's Trade Ministry enacted in 1849, allowing officials to manage each of the important components of manufacturing, from raising capital through the issue of bonds to the siting of factories and the movement of labor. The railroads found that routes, freight charges, and even timetables were all subject to government direction

Well financed and carefully nurtured, the textile industry grew by half from the early 1840s to 1860; mining and metal production tripled in value; and the newborn railroad companies increased their traffic by 20 percent a year. But by the late 1850s, manufacturers, and especially the railroads, were powerful enough to want to be rid of their government nannies. A lobbying campaign for greater freedom, orchestrated by chambers of commerce and trade organizations, was already underway when the Progressive Party was launched. Its call for constitutional reforms that would make government and civil servants answerable to the people rather than to the king drew an enthusiastic response from both business and industry.

The first opportunity for the new alliance of property owners to assert their rights came in 1862 when the royal government introduced a high-taxation military budget to the elected chamber of the Landtag. By a clear majority, the united representatives of landowners, industrialists, and businessmen rejected the budget. In retaliation, Wilhelm I appointed as his new *Minister-Präsident*, or Prime Minister, the Junker Otto von Bismarck.

A CLASSIC PHOTOGRAPH of Bismarck portrays him in gold-braided military uniform, standing as an equal with field marshals Helmuth von Moltke, the army's chief of staff, and Albrecht von Roon, the war minister, although his only army experience was as a reserve lieutenant. In his speeches, he harked back to his Junker origins as though he embodied their disciplined, rural qualities. But the Iron Chancellor's air of solidity, the drooping jowls, heavy mustache, and quilted eyelids, all were deceptive. It was with the wiliness of a coyote that he played upon the dreams and nightmares of Germans and non-Germans alike to herd them in the direction he wished them to go. "Bismarck's dodge," remarked Princess Victoria, the king's British daughter-in-law, "is always to make the Germans think they are going to be attacked, wronged, insulted, and their interests betrayed if he were not there to protect them."

The qualities were apparent in his first speech to the Landtag's budget committee in 1862, when he warned them of fearful dangers ahead, and Prussia's need for high military spending to defend itself. "The great questions of the time," he predicted, "will not be resolved by speeches and majority decisions . . . but by iron and blood." When the deputies still refused to vote for higher taxes, Bismarck bypassed them by declaring the previous year's budget to be still in effect.

This illegal move provoked nationwide opposition, and one protest meeting in Frankfurt attracted business owners with enterprises worth a total of three hundred million taler (approximately $250 million). But Bismarck countered with alarmist warnings of the threat to Prussia's northern and southern borders from Denmark and Austria. Out of a sense of patriotic duty some Junkers did succumb to his appeal to support the government, but it was Bismarck's wooing of industry that was most damaging to the campaign for representative government.

In the summer of 1862, the Trade Ministry announced a new commercial code that cut away a swath of government regulations on business, among them restrictions on the movement of labor, and allowed manufacturers to set their own economic agendas. Then in September, a series of large contracts were put out for military armaments, clothing, and victualling, the start of an extraordinary decade of government expenditure among steel manufacturers, coal miners, textile producers, and large farmers. Soon Progressives began to note that industrialists were no longer attending political gatherings in opposition to Bismarck.

In October 1864 Alfred Krupp, the steel magnate, gave a lead to his fellow manufacturers by advancing a two-million-taler credit to the War Ministry for the purchase of weapons. One after another, the mining, construction, and railroad industries followed with different schemes for underwriting the financial credibility of Bismarck's autocratic rule in return for government contracts that benefited their businesses. Their choice was brutally characterized by Marx and Engels as "a commercial and industrial class which is too weak and dependent to take power and rule in its own right . . . exchanging the right to rule for the right to make money."

The final dismantlement of the movement for political reform occurred when nationalist fervor swung Junker opinion solidly behind the government once it committed Prussia to war, first against neighboring Denmark in 1864 and, more crucially, against Austria in 1866. In an influential newspaper article written after the decisive battle of Konigrättz in 1866, Hermann Baumgarten, a founding member of the Progressives, confessed that the victory over the Austrians, gained at the cost of seven thousand Prussian casualties, had convinced him he had been wrong to oppose Bismarck's armaments program. "We have seen that these much-maligned Junkers know how to fight and die for the Fatherland," he wrote. "We will limit our bourgeois conceitedness a bit and be content with maintaining an honorable position beside the aristocracy."

Their reward and Bismarck's ultimate goal were gained in 1871 with Prussia's third great victory, this time over France, and the proclamation of Wilhelm I as emperor of a united Germany in the mirrored hall at Versailles. With a population of forty-nine million, an industrial base about to become the most productive in Europe, and an army that had no rival, a new world power had been born. But the political cost was high.

"The Bismarck System is developing terribly quickly in exactly the way I always feared," Max von Forckenberg, the mayor of Berlin, lamented to his Junker friend Franz von Stauffenberg in 1879. "Universal compulsory military service, unreasonable and exorbitant indirect taxes, a disciplined and humiliated *Reichstag*, and public opinion that is corrupted by the battle of material interests and thus helpless."

By then, it was too late. The new Germany was engulfed by the worldwide recession in 1873, and before its effects were over, the mechanization of North American grain lands began to flood Europe with cheap cereals. In response, after a decade of increasingly free trade in agricultural and industrial produce, Bismarck and his successors built a wall of tariffs and health regulations in the 1870s and 1880s to restrict imports of cheap foreign manufactured goods and food. The policy known as "the marriage of iron and rye" apparently protected agriculture as much as industry, and an elaborate system of subsidies to promote the export of Junker wheat seemed to show the political influence of Prussia's large landowners. A program of nationalization brought strategic industries such as railroads and telegraph companies into government ownership, while electrical and steel companies were the recipients of lucrative government contracts in the 1890s following the inception of a massive program of warship construction.

The final part of Bismarck's truly astonishing invention of the modern corporate state came as part of his battle with the rising appeal of Socialism. From its foundation in 1869, the Social Democratic party would grow to become the largest single political party in the Reichstag by 1913—because it promised a government responsive to the needs of the propertyless. To counter its popularity, Bismarck first banned all Socialist activity, then in 1879 pushed through three pieces of groundbreaking legislation designed to remove its chief attraction—the creation of a national health scheme, an accident insurance system, and an old-age pension for German workers.

What paid for this was Prussia's new model of managed capitalism. Unlike the first industrial revolution, the second that grew out of chemicals and electronics required systematic research and development, a complex production process, and large numbers of scientifically literate employees. To supply these needs, Germany's ministries of education and commerce worked closely with employers to match university research to industrial needs and improve an already highly developed system of science and technical education.

Even German agriculture benefited from their collaboration. In 1911 the work of Fritz Haber at the University of Karlsruhe, who developed a method of deriving ammonia from nitrogen, was allied to that of Carl Bosch at the chemicals company, BASF, to produce artificial fertilizer on an industrial scale. It is estimated that half the protein in each human today is made from chemically fixed nitrogen, and that a third of the world's population owe their lives to the process, a total that even outweighs the millions killed by the high explosives and poison gas that Haber also developed. The logic of Germany's new corporate capitalism was undeniable. The nature of its government was less clear.

Nearly every adult male could vote, and the lower houses of both the Prussian Landtag and the German Reichstag exercised increasing influence, although no power, over legislation. But the appetite for making the executive responsible to the legislature rather than to the king had gone. A supposedly representative system of government in fact left ultimate power concentrated entirely in the royal executive.

In the mid-twentieth century, German historians, led by Hans Rosenberg, argued that Bismarck's substitution of authoritarian for democratic government condemned Germany to follow a particular path of political development, the *Sonderweg,* that led to the imposition of Nazi rule in the 1930s. The lack of an ingrained tradition of democracy, it was argued, made it easy for thuggish bigots to seize the levers of power. Intrinsic to this argument was the role of the Junkers in promoting Prussian loyalty and discipline as national and social qualities rather than merely military virtues.

"If a manufacturing enterprise is to flourish," Carl Ferdinand von Stumm-Halberg, founder of the Neunkirch Steel Works, declared in the 1890s, "it must be organized in a military, not parliamentary, way . . . all take the field against a common enemy when their king calls them to arms, so the members of the Neunkirch Works stand united as one man when it comes to battling competition as well as the dark forces of revolution." Although not a Junker, Stumm-Halberg adopted their ethos, declaring that every aspect of his workers' lives was subject to his discipline—their behavior outside the factory, their political affiliations, and even their private lives, to the point of deciding whether an employee should get married: "If you don't follow my advice," he warned, "I will terminate your employment, obviously with notice."

As Rosenberg amply illustrated, similar values extolling the need for corpse discipline were transmitted by the brothers and sons of Junker estate owners, who provided a disproportionate number of officers in the all-powerful army, and senior officials in government ministries. Yet it was not the power of the Junkers that was toxic to democracy so much as their weakness. Despite their ingrained sense of social superiority—Bavarian farmers used to say that the typical Prussian Junker believed that "humanity begins at the rank of baron"—they failed to assert fundamental rights against the state that were claimed by the lowliest American and British property owner, and indeed by ordinary farmers in Bavaria.

The political impotence of the Junkers was exposed when Bismarck's successor, Count Leo von Caprivi, handpicked by the Emperor Wilhelm II, boasted in 1890 of his freedom from landowners' influence, declaring that, although a Prussian, he possessed "*Kein Ar und Halme*" not an acre or blade (of grass). Ignoring furious protests from the Junkers' Agrarian League, he signed free-trade deals with Russia and Romania to import their wheat at low prices in exchange for the export of German machinery. His policy reflected the sea change in Germany's economy. Agriculture, in 1871 the country's biggest employer with almost 49 percent of the workforce, and its biggest earner, supplying 40 percent of the country's gross domestic product (GDP), had been brushed aside by the growth of industry. By 1907, barely a third of German workers were still employed on the land; farming contributed 23 percent of GDP; and the accelerating exodus of country dwellers, either to cities or abroad, especially to the United States, had reduced the rural population by one fifth, with the sharpest falls occurring in the Junker homeland of eastern Prussia.

In *The Stechlin*, a book that encapsulated the atmosphere of the 1890s, the novelist Theodor Fontane used a telling metaphor to describe the growing futility of the Junkers. "They're no longer the pillars holding everything up," he wrote, "they're the old stone and moss roof that still goes on straining and pushing down on things, but can't offer protection against storms any longer."

THE FAILURE OF PRUSSIA'S LANDOWNERS to force property rights onto the political agenda of the united Germany when they had the power to do so was exacerbated by the simultaneous absence of any statement of innate human rights. In the 1871 constitution drawn up for the new empire, a German was declared to have the right "to have a fixed dwelling, to trade, to be appointed to public offices, to acquire property," but these were expressly "civic rights," created by law, and to be enjoyed only by Germans. Although the newly constituted Supreme Court did step in to sustain such rights in both civil and criminal cases, it also supported as a matter of course the government's greater right to override them in the interests of "national security."

The lack of any concept of natural rights for individuals, either through their possession of property or by being built into the constitutional foundation of the state, proved to be of fatal significance. During the later years of Bismarck's dominance, he deliberately chose to bolster his power by whipping up waves of nationalist hatred against Catholics, Poles, Danes, and Socialists. During these campaigns, the Supreme Court could be relied upon to uphold arbitrary arrests and confiscation of property by police and prosecutors whenever the executive argued that the safety of the empire required it. Not by chance, the most sustained resistance to Bismarck's fear-inducing tactics was voiced in the legislatures of former independent states, such as Bavaria and Saxony, where landed interests were most strongly established.

The weakness was incorporated into Germany's 1894 *Bürgerliches Gesetzbuch* (BGB), probably the most comprehensive and effective codification of civil law in existence. Its clarity and logic have led to its adoption as a model in one guise or another by countries around the world, from Japan in the nineteenth century to China in the twenty-first.

The five volumes cover the whole range of law, but the third volume, relating to ownership and its transfer, reveals a detail that points to a difference in its origin from codes based on common law. Both common law and the BGB separate the transfer of property in land into two phases that roughly speaking cover the exchange of payment and exchange of rights to the property. But through the morass of complications in the common law, it is possible to discern that the transfer conveys property rights that have been sustainable against the crown or state since the sixteenth century. The BGB conveys ownership guaranteed by the law of the land, but in extreme situations the code's guarantees cannot be defended against state intervention without one further safeguard—a constitutional commitment to innate human rights, an emblem of democracy since 1948.

★ ★ ★

LACKING EXECUTIVE AUTHORITY and any philosophy of individual rights to win broader popular appeal, the Junkers became increasingly isolated and so short of electoral support they routinely had to resort to ballot-box fraud in order to return sympathetic representatives to the Reichstag, even from their east Prussian stronghold. Nor could tariffs insulate them from the catastrophic drop in the worldwide price of cereals. While western and southern German farmers adapted by rearing livestock, growing beets for the sugar industry, and developing market gardens for city consumption, the east remained hamstrung by its dependence upon cereals. The introduction of a floor price for wheat in 1906 was less a reflection of Junker power than of Junker desperation.

It was not by chance that the Agrarian League founded in 1893 to represent Junker interests resorted to blaming their ills on a Jewish conspiracy incorporating free enterprise, free trade, and liberal opinion. Like Hitler's thugs in the 1920s, the aristocratic landowners of east Prussia had become political outsiders.

PRIVATE PROPERTY SOCIETIES in the last half of the twentieth century took the outcome of Germany's managed corporate society as a dreadful warning. The tragedy of the Holocaust seemed to flow directly from the country's culture of obedience to authority shaped by the Junkers and built into its political structure. But among the many strands that led to twelve years of Nazi tyranny, Junker influence was conspicuously absent. Germany's democracy failed because no system of individual rights was established before the country was industrialized.

Chapter Eighteen

The Cold War

During the twentieth century, many countries adopted different aspects of the Prussian experiment in building a corporate state. The example of Bismarck's welfare provisions carried particular weight in Scandinavian countries, and in the 1950s military governments in Latin America and the Middle East repeatedly tried to develop industry by government direction in a List-like manner. Most common of all, nearly every government, apart from those in Communist and private property societies, adopted its policy of taxing agriculture to finance industrialization. But nowhere was the Prussian example followed more slavishly than in nineteenth-century Japan.

The similarities of a militaristic society—samurai landlords in place of Junker nobles—shocked by the revelation of outside superiority—the arrival in 1854 of Commodore Matthew Perry's steam-powered fleet having the same effect as the defeat at Jena—might seem to have dictated Japan's adoption of the German model. And the outcome in the 1930s, when each country experienced terrorist assaults on fragile democratic structures that brought to power aggressive governments intent on war, offered a still more striking resemblance But the differences were more revealing. Above all, nothing could be less like the flat expanse of Prussian grassland than the rugged territory of Japan.

Roughly the size of California, almost three-quarters of the mountainous country tilts at more than fifteen degrees from the horizontal, and even with terraces cut into the slopes less than a fifth of it can be cultivated. Under the shogunate, the government of Japan was divided among almost three hundred lordships, or *daimyo*, who allocated the fragmented soil to their samurai warriors, the only class permitted to own it. The samurai in turn authorized peasants to work the tiny plots—three quarters of the farms measured less than three acres—in exchange for payment in rice and labor.

When an oligarchy of Japanese nobility expelled the shogunate in 1868 in the name of the Meiji emperor, they began their reforms with the dissolution of these feudal divisions. The daimyo were transformed into salaried governors of prefectures, soon reduced in number to fewer than fifty, and their samurai swordsmen either recruited into the imperial army or into other areas of government service. In effect the feudalism of the Tokugawa was nationalized by the Meiji emperor's new central government.

Like the Junkers, Japan's former landowning military caste was induced to identify its interests with those of the imperial government, partly through foreign wars in China and Korea and more insidiously through the creation of a nationalist ideology based on the *kokutai*, or "national community," that melded samurai values with either Shinto morality or the nationalist precepts of Nichiren Buddhism. The focus of the drive for communal unity was embodied in the person of the emperor.

This strategy was incorporated into the new constitution that took force in 1890. It prescribed an elected diet, or legislature, and an executive government headed by a prime minister that was responsible not to the Diet but to the emperor, or in practice to a group of aristocratic officials deemed to be expressing his will. Quite deliberately, the constitution was modeled on that of the German empire. Alternatives from private property societies, such as the American Constitution and the British parliamentary system, were rejected precisely because they vested too much power in the people. The Meiji economy was to be directed from the top.

For similar reasons, Japan's new code of civil laws was built round Germany's *Bürgerliches Gesetzbuch*. As in Germany, the rights of property owners were guaranteed by civil law, but the rights were restricted to Japanese, and in the name of the *kokutai*, courts consistently upheld the needs of government against personal claims and supported more powerful classes over someone of inferior rank.

With the uncertainties of samurai violence removed, the population of Japan, virtually static at around thirty million throughout the shogun period, grew by almost half to forty-three million between 1852 and 1900, and the number of peasants seeking land to farm soared in proportion.

Rice yields doubled under intensive cultivation, rents tripled, and owners grew wealthy, not by investing and increasing the value of their properties, but as moneylenders and sharecropping landlords to some six million hard-pressed tenants.

In the 1870s, when the samurai were deprived of their power, the Meiji government issued land certificates to peasants, giving them nominal ownership of the land they worked. This halfhearted attempt at social engineering on the Jeffersonian pattern quickly failed since landlords found it easy to use peasant indebtedness backed by legal bullying to force them to hand over the certificates. Almost half of Japan's farmland ended in the hands of village landlords, often enough descendants of the samurai.

The submissiveness of Japanese peasants was legendary, quite unlike the resentful, often violent resistance offered by their German equivalents to their landlords. Their behavior was prescribed by *Nihon-shugi*, the defining ideological statement of Shintoism, "agriculture is the base of the country and everyone should play his part according to his station for the good of the country." And the precept was routinely reinforced by physical beatings, a practice that continued when peasants became soldiers in the imperial army. Thus the effects of the Meiji land reforms were to tame the samurai landlords but to leave the pattern of land holding virtually unchanged.

In the absence of any movement by Japan's landed interests to assert claims to political power, the Meiji government deliberately taxed agriculture heavily in order to finance industrial development. Up to 80 percent of the revenues that kick-started Japanese industrial growth in the 1890s came from land taxes and were channeled either into military expenditure for Japan's successful wars with China and Russia, or into railroad construction and shipbuilding.

Yet for all their political impotence, the values of Japan's landowners, inherited from the samurai, became the standard for Japan's new industrialists, even though by the 1920s their manufactured products were three times as valuable as those grown on the land. Business pioneers such as Shibusawa Eiichi, founder of the First Bank of Japan and of some two hundred other commercial enterprises, constantly urged the once-despised merchant class not just to think of profits, but "to place the cloak of the public-spirited samurai on [their] shoulders." Giant conglomerates known as *zaibatsu*, such as Mitsui, Mitsubishi, or Nissan, which grouped the disparate activities of manufacturing, mining, and textiles under a single family ownership, expected from subsidiaries and workers alike a Shinto loyalty to the core company, and to the founding family, with each person contributing according to his or her particular position to the good of the whole.

PARADOXICAL THOUGH IT MIGHT SEEM, the basic difference between imperial Germany and imperial Japan after industrialization was determined by the shape of their land holdings. While Prussia's land revolution was still underway when industrialization took over, Japan's industrial power was constructed over what remained an unmistakably feudal pattern. When the onslaught of the 1930s economic depression struck, the response of each country was determined by that fundamental distinction.

In Japan, popular resentment at the failure of the government to deal with unemployment was centered in the countryside. Secret nationalist societies proliferated with the aim of reasserting the independence Japan once enjoyed from the outside pressures, and in the army, rival military societies, known collectively as the Young Officers, aimed at the restoration of military influence over government. These forces exploded into a campaign of terror in the 1930s that included the assassination of two prime ministers, two abortive military coups, and the murder of numerous lesser officials, and it led to the end of party politics in government.

In contrast to this rural-based terror, Germany's version came out of the cities. The dedication of *Mein Kampf* to the sixteen Nazis killed in the failed 1923 Munich uprising offers a snapshot of Hitler's followers at the time: six were junior employees, restaurant workers, or bank staff, six were self-employed, traders, craftsmen, and store owners, one was a student, one a retired soldier, and just two, a trained engineer and a senior civil servant, belonged to the white-collared middle class. Until the financial crash of 1929, the composition did not really change—most Nazis were young, about half were working class, and the rest were largely shopkeepers, artisans, and the unemployed. They stood outside Germany's directed economy that, despite the removal of the emperor, Wilhelm II, survived the First World War, and they evidently shared the rage against democratic society that permeates *Mein Kampf*.

So long as the Nazis remained outsiders, the immature democratic structure of the Weimar Republic coped more or less with the challenge of a party clearly intent on its destruction. It only became vulnerable following Hitler's crucial decision to alter one clause in the twenty-five-clause program that constituted the Nazi Party's bedrock of political beliefs.

Clause 17 called for the expropriation of landed property—a leftover from the party's Socialist origins—and, like the rest of the program, could not be altered. But in 1929 Hitler publicly gave it a different context, explaining that in fact it only referred to the confiscation of Jewish land.

Immediately, the party's struggle with the more powerful Social Democrats for the left-wing vote shifted in perspective. The street violence of brown-shirted Nazi thugs continued as before, but now the party portrayed it as necessary to preserve national order and the security of property against Socialists, Communists, and other agitators, usually portrayed as Jewish. Endorsed by funding from business leaders eager to quell labor unrest, the Nazis were brought inside Weimar's political structure and began to win respectable support. Small farmers were recruited through an amorphous reform program known as *Blut und Boden*, or blood and soil, that promised to free them from the exactions of Jewish-owned banks, and attacks on Junker superiority gave way to praise for Junker values.

Nevertheless, the surge in the party's popularity was short-lived, and its share of the vote was already declining by January 1933. The appointment of Hitler as chancellor in that month was anything but inevitable. A delay of several months, with the economy no longer deteriorating and criticism of Nazi tactics growing louder, might have made the transition to power infinitely more difficult.

In retrospect, the crucial element that the Weimar Republic lacked was an embedded tradition of individual rights. In 1931 a young lawyer, Hans Litten, used Weimar's twelve-year-old system of legal rights to force Hitler to appear in court in 1931, and crossexamined him mercilessly about his complicity in Nazi murders. That heroic achievement, for which Litten paid with his life in a concentration camp, showed what could have been done to expose the party's criminal underbelly had the courts inherited a robust ethos of individual entitlement to justice.

WHILE THE NAZIS' urban-based terrorism succeeded, Japan's rural version failed. The assassinations and attempted coups were certainly triggered by fury at a government incapable of dealing with the economic crisis, but the makeup of the secret societies, their constant reference to the past glories of Japan, and their choice of political targets demonstrated that this was more broadly a backlash by the grandchildren of the samurai against the Meiji rulers who had dethroned them. Consequently the campaign lost its impetus in 1937 when the government enlisted the army's support, with the agreement of zaibatsu and landlord interests, and allowed it to select its own prime minister. The cost of buying the generals' participation was a program of military spending that benefited the *zaibatsu* and a policy of expansion across the Pacific and into Indochina to secure strategic supplies of oil and rubber. By 1945, the price had risen to include the outbreak of war, the bombing of Hiroshima and Nagasaki, and unconditional surrender.

Given the close ties between Japan's feudal landlords and the army—a large majority of senior officers in the imperial army came from landowning families—American plans for introducing democracy to the conquered country in 1945 also required the elimination of Japan's existing pattern of land ownership. Reading from their own history, the officials of General Douglas Macarthur's administration aimed to replace feudalism with a society of owner occupiers.

In Europe, the U.S. War Department held an almost identical belief that government was shaped by the way land was owned, and in 1944 called for "the dissolution of the Junker holdings. Their continuation would constitute one of the most formidable obstacles to the establishment of a lasting democracy in Germany, for the holders of these estates have been consistent and active opponents of democratic government." But while this analysis misjudged Junker influence, the land reform program carried out under Macarthur in Japan was not only based on an accurate diagnosis but achieved a real cure. To a large extent this was due to the galvanizing influence of one man, Wolf Ladejinsky.

BORN IN 1899, the son of a wealthy flour miller, Ladejinsky had been raised in a shtetl in a part of western Ukraine that until the release of serfs in the nineteenth century had been owned by Russian-Polish landlords as *Gutsherrschaft* land. Within living memory, however, the region had been transformed into a private property, Junker-like society. In 1922, after five years of civil war that ended with the Bolsheviks nationalizing the land, Ladejinsky escaped to the United States. He took with him the profound certainty that, as he later said, "The foundations of the social structure must stand or fall in the countryside, and [so] the peasant and his interests and aspirations must be placed at the center of the piece." In the long, unwritten history of peasant farming, its concerns had never been taken so seriously.

In the 1950s, almost two thirds of the world's population and 70 percent of people in Asia were still living on the land, and this was where Ladejinsky's interest was directed. His enemies used to criticize his lack of direct farming experience, pointing out that his degree from Columbia University was in economics, but they overlooked his determination to learn directly from people on the ground. The plan for redistribution of feudal land in Japan was built on months of painstaking interviews with peasants, landlords, and village elders across the country. Even in old age and almost blind, he would insist on flying to a remote airstrip in Bengal, then being driven further in a jeep, so that he could finally stumble into the fields to talk to the people actually working there. As a young man, the practical experience he had acquired from peasant farmers in Asia led to his secondment from the Department of Agriculture in 1945 to work for General Douglas Macarthur's military government in Japan.

Referring back to the Meiji government's issue of land ownership certificates in the 1870s, Ladejinsky always insisted that "the reform idea was Japanese in origin" and the United States simply acted as "midwife" to its execution. The drastic measures recommended by his plan could, however, only have been put into effect by an occupying force that faced no opposition.

Under the land reform program, no absentee landlord could own more than about nine acres, or three *cho*. (In the forested northern island of Hokkaido, the limit was raised to thirty-six acres.) Every acre of ground above that maximum had to be sold to the government at a set price—one three hundredth of the market value in 1939—and, since the sum was paid in fixed interest bonds whose value was quickly destroyed by inflation, the compulsory purchase amounted to near confiscation. But in the course of little more than three years, about six million acres, one third of all the farmland in Japan, were taken from 2.3 million landlords and sold to the 4.7 million farmers who worked them. By 1950, 90 percent of Japan's farmland was owned by the people who cultivated it.

In typically extravagant style, Macarthur hailed the transformation of "several million tenant farmers, traditionally vassals of feudalistic landlords, into 'capitalistic' owners of the land they long have worked" as the most far-reaching act of social engineering that had been undertaken since the redistribution of land "in the days of the Roman empire." This was hyperbole—most farms were too small to act as rural capital—and missed the political significance of the change.

What struck the sociologist Ronald Dore, who visited scores of villages where committees decided whose land should be redistributed, was "the democratization of the villages." In place of the old paternalist order that regarded the gulf between landlord and submissive peasant "as a hallowed part of the order of nature," he detected a sense of empowerment as farmers once liable to be evicted for voicing their opinions learned to take charge of village affairs. As he noted on return trips, "redistribution of wealth [has] brought greater equality of opportunity to those who occupy positions of leadership." His subjective impression was confirmed by the results of an opinion poll in the early 1950s revealing that fewer than one in three of the new proprietors still believed in the deferential precepts of *Nihon-shugi*.

The abolition of "landlordism" is rarely seen as relevant to the phenomenal forces that within a generation catapulted Japan from nuclear-bombed defeat to the second largest economy in the world. But its role was essential at three different levels. The most fundamental was that the allocation of property to the peasants ensured their unwavering support for the constitution adopted in 1947 guaranteeing both property and human rights. More immediately, the change from tenancy to ownership brought an accompanying need to maximize profits rather than rents, leading to an exodus of rural inhabitants, as many as ten million in fifteen years, who might once have found some activity in the fields but who now left the countryside to find work in the cities. They went to swell an urban population that numbered just twenty-four million in 1945, about one in three of the population, but rose to more than sixty million by 1965. Finally, although this was not Ladejinsky's intention, an urban land market was created. Prominent in the balance sheets of postwar conglomerates and those of construction companies, banks, and other financial institutions, was a portfolio of office blocks and building land whose rising value helped boost their borrowing power.

AMAZINGLY, Wolf Ladejinsky achieved his goal of land redistribution in two other countries before he was reined in. Indeed, the most compelling evidence in the modern era that a more equitable pattern of land ownership was integral to social and economic revolution comes from his success in two other tiger economies in the region, Taiwan and South Korea. In both countries, the agenda was driven by Ladejinsky's single-minded belief that "land ownership . . . is the real vehicle of security and opportunity upon which a more resourceful economy can be built."

Undoubtedly the most violent change occurred in Taiwan. In 1949, Chiang Kai-shek's government arrived from mainland China with two million Kuomintang supporters and brutally established its rule over the indigenous Taiwanese inhabitants in a colonizing process known as the

White Terror. The island, a hundred miles from the mainland, had been a Japanese colony since 1895, and their expulsion left a power vacuum that the Kuomintang filled, but during more than four decades of martial law, up to four thousand people were executed and as many as 140,000 were exiled or imprisoned for opposing their rule. Some of the fiercest opposition flared up over the redistribution of land.

With the backing of the United States, a five-man Chinese-American Joint Commission on Rural Reconstruction that included Ladejinsky began the process of redistribution in 1950. The measures were as draconian as in Japan and bore Ladejinsky's unmistakable imprint: absentee owners limited to a maximum of three acres, compulsory purchase of all property above the limit, paid for with bonds backed by revenues from industry; and sale of these surplus lands at low prices to those who physically worked the soil.

Despite ferocious resistance—one Taiwanese peasant told the commission that getting land from a landlord was like "negotiating with a tiger for his fur"—the popularity of the program and the abandonment of large estates by their Japanese owners ensured that redistribution would be a success. By the time the process was complete in 1956, land had been taken from 106,490 landlords and transferred to one million new owner occupiers, representing almost 60 percent of Taiwan's farmland. The island's hierarchical, landlord-dominated society had been levelled to one where 90 percent of its near five million rural inhabitants lived on farms that they owned.

Millions of dollars of government and American aid were also directed to improve access to markets, make credit available for fertilizer and higher-yielding crops, and, since the average holding measured barely two acres, to set up cooperative purchasing and marketing organizations. The result was a striking increase of 50 percent in rice yields between 1949 and 1960, and a tripling of farmers' incomes with the abolition of oppressive rents. In 1960, farm produce, especially Taiwan's highly prized rice, made up 86 percent of the island's exports, a measure of how much its economy depended on rural prosperity.

Unlike Japan, where land rights and democracy had to be created within an existing industrial economy, Taiwan's industry grew out of the network of privately owned properties scattered across the countryside and supplying their own regional markets. More than two-thirds of farming families depended on a second job to supplement the earnings from their tiny plots of land, and banks reported that 80 percent of the start-up loans for new businesses in the 1960s used these same small fields as collateral. At the same time, almost 60 percent of the Kuomintang government's investment in large-scale manufacturing in 1960, especially electronics, was derived from taxes and forced savings levied on agriculture.

Although Ladejinky was not physically present in South Korea, his reforming zeal and the presence of experts who had worked with him allow this to be counted as his third success. In 1945, three-quarters of the population lived in the countryside, and almost 70 percent of them were peasants paying more than half the value of their crop to absentee landlords. Under the direction of the U.S. military governor, General John R. Hodge, the redistribution of land after thirty-five years of Japanese occupation followed Ladejinsky's formula for capping the maximum holding at about seven acres, expropriating the surplus and redistributing it at low cost "to the tiller of the soil." The result allowed for a direct comparison with North Korea, where the Soviet-backed government also confiscated all farms of more than seven acres, but redistributed them as collectives, a form of landholding that eventually applied to all land beyond a family's immediate vegetable plot.

After the Korean War, President Synghman Rhee's autocratic government in the South continued to apply the Ladejinsky policy in a manner that strongly resembled the Soviet pattern, by forcible purchase with the price being paid in bonds whose value diminished so rapidly that the majority of dispossessed landlords went bankrupt within five years. Neither in the North nor the South was the government democratic or its policy fair, but while the centralization of land rights laid the foundation for famine, the dispersal of rights led directly to individual autonomy and unprecedented wealth.

Within ten years, the bulk of South Korea's farms were privately owned, intensively worked smallholdings of less than five acres whose new owners supplemented their earnings from other village employment. Not only did rice yields more than double from just over one ton per acre in the next twenty years, so too did the area farmed to about 2.5 million acres. And among a population that remained predominantly rural until the 1980s, South Korea's often repressive government retained its legitimacy as the creator of a relatively egalitarian, property-owning economy.

In both countries, significant political change only occurred when the children of the original property holders, wealthier, more assertive, and above all better educated than their parents, came to maturity. In Taiwan, 96 percent of farmers' children attended school in 1959, a rise of almost one-fifth from the days before the land revolution. Chiang Kai-shek's death in 1975 marked the start of reform, with the development of civic independence at local level. Pressure from agriculture and industry alike brought an increasing degree of representative government that by the 1990s had developed into genuine democracy.

In South Korea dictatorial government lasted longer, until the 1980s, and change occurred more rapidly when the children of the original landowners took to the streets in massive numbers to demand political and civil liberties. The nature of the democratic government that emerged in the 1990s was expressed in a constitution that combined commitment to human rights and a distinctive Buddhist stress on social harmony.

In all three countries affected by Ladejinky's program, redistribution was manifestly unjust to the landlords. But the fundamental justification was still John Locke's argument that there was a moral basis for regarding the person whose labor improved the ground as its owner. It was not a complete defense, but the increase of personal liberty that it created, together with the impulse it gave toward economic prosperity and democratic government, made a compelling case. That achievement was the more striking when viewed within the wider context of the Cold War.

The prize in the competition between capitalism and Communism was the political loyalty of almost two billion people elsewhere in the world, known variously as *campesinos* in Latin America, *fellahin* in the Middle East, *ryot* in India, as well as a thousand other local terms, and generically in English as peasants. In order for them to become capitalist or communist, the land they cultivated had to be removed from a myriad different forms of ownership that were deemed "feudal" and transformed into private or communal possession.

In Japan, Taiwan, and South Korea, the west had for the first time a pattern of development to set against the gigantic system of communal ownership that was rolling across northern Asia, replacing the Romanov dynasty's post-serf economy in Russia and the Qing Dynasty's bureaucratic landlordism in China.

In the long and distinguished line of rulers stretching back at least to Tiberius Gracchus who attempted to shape people and society through the distribution of land, by far the most effective in terms of scale was Vladimir I. Lenin. Eventually his policy of collectivized ownership covered some three million square miles of arable ground, woodland, and steppes in the Soviet Union, and became the basis for similar systems affecting an area almost as great in China, Vietnam, Cuba, and eastern Europe.

Despite Marx's cautious endorsement of the *mir*, Lenin quickly dispensed with any thought of retaining small peasant strips. Learning from the mechanization of the American prairies, he argued in his 1899 text, *The Development of Capitalism*, for the creation of large farms that could be mechanized and fertilized on an industrial scale, and for communal ownership to give poor and landless peasants a share in the means of production. Middle peasants, those working their own small plots, might be allowed to keep them, but Lenin had an almost superstitious fear of the social impact of land ownership. "Small-scale production," he declared, "gives birth to capitalism and the bourgeoisie constantly, daily, hourly, with elemental force, and in vast proportions." Thus the wealthiest peasants, the *kulaki*, who employed waged labor on their farms, were to have their land confiscated by the state along with the emphatically capitalist estates of aristocrats.

Following their coup d'état in 1918, the Bolsheviks immediately began to put these plans into operation and "socialized" Russia's land, in effect asserting the claim of the Romanov tsars that the earth belonged to the rulers of the state. News that *kulak* farmers in Ukraine had responded by joining the White counterrevolution against the Soviet government drove Lenin to near-hysterical fury. The two million *kulaki*, he said, were "avaricious, bloated and bestial," they were "leeches," "spiders," and "vampires" who had to be exterminated. But rage could not save Muscovites from having to survive, as the writer Maxim Gorky remembered, on "bread that's half straw, on herring heads, cotton cakes and the like."

The threat of continuing starvation forced Lenin to conciliate the food producers. Reversing itself, the Soviet government announced its New Economic Policy, leaving in place privately owned property, and permitting marketplace pricing to continue, apart from a compulsory quota of grain to be sold at fixed prices. It was not until 1929 that Josef Stalin, as general secretary of the Communist Party, called for the elimination of *kulak* farmers by death or exile and the enforced collectivization of all farms—"the last, decisive battle," as Lenin had described it, in the war to establish Communism.

Over the next three years, the entire families of more than half a million farmers identified as *kulaki* were killed or expelled from their farms, but resistance to the collectivization of livestock and fields caused such disruption across the richest farmland in the Soviet Union that the harvests of cereals and potatoes dropped to half the level they had reached in 1914. International agencies fed as many as ten million more on imported food, but the famine was so extreme that the American Relief Agency reported many cases of cannibalism among the survivors. As many as seven million died from famine and disease during the early 1930s.

By 1936, however, 90 percent of the land was farmed by collectives, or *kolkhozi*, measuring on average about six thousand acres, whose workers were either paid by the state or out of the farm's earnings. The new face of the Soviet Union was displayed in the posters of the period depicting a strong-armed, golden-haired boy or girl riding a tractor through a grain field stretching to the horizon. The traditional image of rural life where gnarled peasants tilled pocket-sized strips of land by hand had been consigned to the graveyard.

The new Soviet method of possessing and working the land was untried. It had no other rationale for its existence than Lenin's belief that collective ownership must breed a collective mind-set in place of bourgeois individualism. But for almost forty years, there was good reason to think that collectivization might work, whatever the human cost of its creation.

Mechanization and irrigation enabled collectives to increase production of cereals above 1920s levels, although supplies of meat and milk lagged until after the Second World War, and improved transport put more calories on Soviet plates than had been available before the collectives. In the 1950s, as the Soviet Union recovered from the destruction of the Nazi invasion, Nikita Khruschev, the dynamic secretary of agriculture, launched the Virgin Lands program that brought into collective cultivation ninety million acres of steppe in Kazakhstan and on the Altai plateau beyond the Urals, and the size of farms rose to around fifteen thousand acres. By the early 1960s, the Soviet Union was exporting grain, more than three million tons a year, for the first time since before the First World War.

The profits made by the government from the difference between the low price paid to the collectives and the steadily rising price in the shops allowed it to invest heavily in industry and technology. Farming efficiency encouraged a migration of labor from the country where five out of six people lived in 1923 to the factories that surrounded the Soviet Union's new concrete towns where two-thirds of the population dwelled in 1970. As a result the Soviet economy grew more rapidly between the low point of 1928 and 1970 than any other except the Japanese, with personal incomes rising nearly five times from \$1,200 to \$5,900 a year. Its success, symbolized by the launch of the Sputnik satellite in 1957, was founded on collective farming. And the process had required no foreign investment or outside aid.

Thus, when Mao Zedong, Che Guevara, Ho Chi Minh, and others nationalized the land and collectivized its cultivation, they were following an apparently successful model. Indeed the effectiveness of collective ownership in delivering economic muscle and social justice left the West floundering in search of an alternative. The only capitalist solution that worked depended on the forcible expropriation of property and, to Ladejinsky's dismay, would soon be deemed politically unacceptable.

Chapter Nineteen

The End of Land Reform

For every person who has heard of Ladejinsky, there must be ten thousand who have worn a T-shirt bearing the image of his ideological opposite, Ernesto Che Guevara, the equally forceful prophet of land redistribution on behalf of Socialism. What made Che Guevara an icon was that he seemed to embody the ingredient that always threatened to be absent from individual ownership, the hunger for social justice. In the winter of 1958, when he and Fidel Castro with a few hundred guerillas finally burst out of the Sierra Maestra mountains that had been their fastness for two years and took control of the sugar plantations in the lowlands of Oriente Province, they came with a minimum of ideological baggage. They were not communist—Cuba's Communist Party dismissed Castro as "a petty bourgeois putschist"—and so far as they had a political philosophy, it was expounded by Guevara.

Born into a middle-class Argentine family, he showed little interest in politics until in 1954 a motorbike journey landed him in Guatemala. In one of the nodal moments of the Cold War, he was present when the CIA orchestrated the overthrow of President Jacobo Arbenz's elected government after its land redistribution policy threatened the assets of the United Fruit Company. Not only did the coup mark the beginning of the United States's abandonment of Ladejinsky's policy, it radicalized Guevara. The question of land ownership would form his entire revolutionary outlook. His later experience in the Sierra Maestra, where the guerillas were helped by peasants in conflict with the large sugar plantations in Oriente, confirmed his Guatemalan baptism.

"The peasants fought because they wanted land for themselves and their children, to manage and sell it and to enrich themselves through their labor," he explained in 1961. This motivation displayed their "petty-bourgeois spirit" but it also taught them that their interests clashed directly with those of "the imperialists, the large landholders and the sugar and cattle magnates" who could only be defeated with the help of the proletariat. Thus the happy ending was that "[t]he poor peasants, rewarded with ownership of land, loyally supported the revolutionary power."

In speeches, articles, and indeed throughout the rest of his life, Guevara repeatedly tried to work out the next stage that would lead to Communism. This was the opposite of Ladejinsky's efforts to realize peasant aspirations to own their land. Guevara wanted to replace their petty-bourgeois ideas with a sense of communal idealism. But however he worked the problem through, the solution always came out the same way: the leaders had to educate the people ruthlessly until "[t[he mass carries out with matchless enthusiasm and discipline the tasks set by the government."

In January 1959, Castro's guerillas marched into Havana, following the the withdrawal of U.S. support for former President Batista and the collapse of his corrupt regime. Days later, clad in military fatigues with a black beret crammed onto his tumbling hair, Guevara told a gigantic crowd what the revolution intended to do. Once the organized crime and gambling encouraged by Batista had been cleared out, he declared in his rasping, asthmatic voice, the immediate priority was to establish "the social justice that land redistribution brings about."

The creation of the National Institute of Agrarian Reform (INRA), the most powerful organ of government, headed by Castro himself, indicated the supreme importance that Guevara assigned to land ownership in the Cuban revolution. INRA not only organized agriculture, it built roads, harbors, and rural housing, oversaw the Department of Industry, and commanded a militia one hundred thousand strong that policed the countryside. At first it confiscated any estates measuring more than one thousand acres and redistributed the land to one hundred thousand peasants and to other owners loosely organized into cooperatives. But very soon, as American hostility increased and Soviet influence grew in response, the sugar plantations, tobacco farms, and cooperatives were collectivized into state farms, while private producers were required to sell their crops to INRA-regulated outlets at state-controlled prices.

The educational goal of INRA was to create a sense of "socialist emulation" and "fraternal competition" to take the place of "the possibilities of individual success," as Guevara explained. The failure to achieve this aim was underlined by the increasing harshness of INRA's policing of the farming community, and by Cuba's bleak record of human rights abuse leading to about twenty thousand executions up to 2010. The exodus of more than one million people, some 10 percent of the population, served as a popular vote on the policy. The economic goal of INRA was more practical, to generate enough profit from sugar, coffee, and tobacco to invest in the development of the island's mouthwatering deposits of nickel—as much as one fifth of the world's reserves. Guevara intended mining profits to kick-start the process of industrialization allowing Cuba to become a modern, but socially owned, economy. The United States economic blockade played a large part in INRA's failure to achieve this goal too. But falling sugar yields and Castro's repeated attacks on corruption, inequality, and materialism within the ranks of his own dictatorial administration, notably in the "rectification campaign" he launched at the end of the Cold War, made it clear that Guevara's system simply did not work.

MEASURED SIMPLY in terms of full bellies and happiness, Ladejinsky's program unmistakably delivered more in the long run than Guevara's, but before the full effects became obvious, it was abandoned. In 1954, at the height of the "Red scare" about Communist infiltration of the American government, Ladejinsky was denounced by the secretary of agriculture, Ezra Benson, as "a national security risk." The indictment was motivated by his Ukrainian upbringing, endemic anti-Semitism—the report of the Agricultural Department's security expert noted that "Jews who turned into Reds or fellow travelers were the worst kind of traitors"—and most damagingly by the charge in the *Chicago Tribune*, that Ladejinsky had pushed through a program "to take property from its owners and redistribute it in the name of social justice."

No doubt to Benson's surprise, his action provoked furious protests from an unexpected quarter, right-wing, anti-Communist Republicans, including the hawkish secretary of state, John Foster Dulles. A Congressional investigation excoriated Benson and his department's unconstitutional security procedures, and Eisenhower himself complained, "Why doesn't Benson just admit he made a mistake and apologize?"

Under pressure, the agriculture secretary withdrew the allegations, but they had exposed to public attention a contradiction at the heart of Ladejinky's program—redistribution betrayed the principle that a basic purpose of government was to protect property. In the 1950s, as the tensions of the Cold War mounted, the ideologists who believed property to be the sacred, untouchable bulwark of capitalist society, regardless of the social justice that brought it into existence, began to win the argument against the pragmatists.

In 1966, shortly before departing to Bolivia, where he would be killed, Che Guevara wrote a last appeal for worldwide revolution. In calling for "two, three or many Vietnams" to be fought in order to crush imperialism and to forward the cause of collectivization, he was, inadvertently, pointing to the greatest failure of his ideological rival. In South Vietnam, Wolf Ladejinsky discovered for the first time the difficulty of putting into practice a policy of land redistribution without the backing of draconian powers to enforce it. The mandate from the State Department to introduce land reform in South Vietnam required him to work through the existing political system run by President Ngo Dinh Diem, whose main source of support came from country's great landholding families.

Ladejinsky's new role reflected the sea change that was beginning to affect Cold War attitudes within Washington. In 1950, Dean Acheson, as secretary of state, had explicitly committed the United States to a policy of supporting "world-wide land reform" as the best way of "strengthening the system of free enterprise by diffusion of private property and reinforcing the economic foundation of the State." As late as 1961, the Kennedy administration's call at Punta del Este for "an equitable system of property" in Latin America showed that the old strategy was not entirely dead. But in the intervening years, its thrust had changed.

Although Ladejinsky was personally rehabilitated in 1954, his policy remained suspect. Later that same year came the CIA-engineered overthrow of Guatemala's freely elected president, Jacobo Arbenz Guzman, while he was undertaking a program of land redistribution in a country where 70 percent of the arable land was controlled by 2 percent of the population. The specific issue was Guatemala's expropriation of four hundred thousand acres of unused land from the United Fruit Company, but it was a pointer to the future. Land reform was becoming less important as a Cold War strategy.

When Ladejinsky was appointed personal advisor to President Diem in 1955, a post he would hold for the next six years, it was on the clear understanding that he would have to act with the agreement of the regime.

Nevertheless, in a country that was primarily divided between the basin of the Mekong River in the south, source of most of the region's rice, and the immense rubber plantations and mountainous, untouched forest in the north, the disparity of ownership was so gross that even Diem had promised land reform when he took power in 1954 following the collapse of French colonial rule.

One in three of South Vietnam's seven million peasants owned no land at all and most of the remainder worked plots of less than three acres that they did not own, while more than half the cultivated land belonged to an elite 3 percent of landlords with holdings that extended to thousands of acres containing several villages, each with twenty or thirty families paying as much as 60 percent of the value of their crops to rent the land. In the fertile Mekong delta, almost 75 percent of landlords, many owning fewer than twenty acres, were absentees choosing to live in cities, with Saigon the most popular residence. Yet, as Ladejinsky discovered from intensive research on the ground, a breathtaking opportunity for redistribution had opened up.

The exodus of French colonial owners following defeat by the Communist Viet Minh and the retreat to the cities of a large number of Vietnamese landlords left more than three million acres of farmland without clear ownership. The chief obstacle came understandably from the landlords, who also provided most forms of local government. "We have been robbed by the Viet Minh," one provincial administrator told Ladejinsky, "and we resent similar treatment from the national government." But Ladejinsky also discovered throughout South Vietnam an intense desire for the security that only ownership could create. "The village needs peace," one peasant told him, "and the landlord-tenant conflicts will never cease until the tenants own the land."

In North Vietnam, the Communists under Ho Chi Minh had embarked on a brutal program of land reform of their own that confiscated almost two million acres and redistributed them to collectivized peasant communes. The policy was carried out with such murderous violence, resulting in the execution of more than 170,000 supposed landlords, that it was condemned even by official histories that euphemistically ascribed its brutality to "leftist errors." Given that alternative, opposition to Ladejinsky might have been less than anticipated.

However, few of his proposals for creating a new generation of owner occupiers appeared in the plan of land reform that Diem announced in

1956. The maximum holding was to be capped at 100 hectares or 240 acres affecting barely two thousand landlords, and the excess land would only be available for rent. Nevertheless, as Ladejinsky reported to the U.S. State Department, by purchasing the excess and taking over other abandoned estates, the government could make available approximately 1.5 million acres for sale at low cost. Potentially, more than one third of South Vietnam's seven million peasants could become owner occupiers. The war that was eventually fought with North Vietnam for the hearts and minds of those peasants might have been won before it started.

Land reform, however, was no longer State Department policy.

CHE GUEVARA'S DEATH in 1967 left his reputation untainted by the dire consequences of his ideology. And the fact that he was killed while attempting to bring about revolution in Bolivia only enhanced his standing. Everyone, Communist and capitalist, agreed that social justice demanded a leveling of the vast inequalities of Latin America society, founded on sprawling estates, or *latifundias*, containing tens of thousands of acres, and sustained by the political oligarchies that served their interests. Of Latin America's 1.7 billion acres of farmland in the 1950s, almost two-thirds were owned by just over 1 percent of the population.

The owners of these gigantic *haciendas* rivaled the Russian aristocracy in their Oblomovan neglect not just of the peasants but of the land itself—their reluctance to invest in animal-drawn ploughs rather than human-held hoes was, one amazed observer claimed, "more primitive, less efficient, and more wasteful of human energy than those the Egyptians were using at the dawn of history." The T-shirts told the story—Guevara represented the raw appeal of social justice, while property rights were allied to inequality, corruption, and the grinding poverty of the *campesino*.

Fearful of seeing the Cuban revolution spread further, however, the United States gave a last declaration of its commitment to Ladejjinsky's vision of social reform through land redistribution. At a meeting of Latin American states at Punta del Este, Uruguay, in 1961, it called for *latifundias* to be replaced by "an equitable system of property" and for the introduction of a system of "integral agrarian reform leading to the effective transformation, where required, of unjust structures and systems of land tenure and use." This declaration not only exhibited the core values of the United States, it incorporated the sense of justice and ownership that, as Guevara himself had recognized, really motivated Latin America's *campesinos*. But its implementation faced a crucial obstacle.

LAND REFORM could be said to have been the one constant in all the political convulsions of Latin American politics. Whether elected or not, almost every new government repeatedly promised to bring it about. In Mexico, reform was integral to the program of the *Partido Revolucionario Institucional* (PRI) that governed from the 1930s to the twenty-first century, and more than fifty million hectares were nominally redistributed between 1934 and 1964. Yet control of the land, especially over the communally owned *ejidos* that had been reserved for Indian occupation, remained largely undisturbed in the hands of its traditional ruling families. In Brazil, reform had been advocated by both left and right throughout the twentieth century, but the north continued to be made up of gigantic ranches, while the large commercial farms in the dynamic south were mostly run by foreign owners.

Similar attempts to bring about land reform in the Middle East and India during the 1950s encountered the same problem. No government that represented the beneficiaries of an unfair distribution of land could be expected to push through measures for greater fairness. The dilemma forced the growing academic discipline of land reform to reconsider its principles. No one doubted the need for change—it was essential both to increase agricultural efficiency and to bring about social reform—and where it did take place there were clear gains. In Latin America, three countries—Uruguay, Argentina, and Chile—had gradually instituted a few genuine reforms in land holding, and overall their populations enjoyed better education, longer life expectancy, and more stable political systems. But the old Jeffersonian certainties, put into practice by Ladejinsky, that the wide dispersal of property gave rise to liberty and prosperity were dwindling.

In 1956, an influential paper entitled "The Take-Off into Self-Sustained Growth" by Walt W. Rostow, an economics professor at the Massachusetts Institute of Technology and later adviser on national security to President Lyndon B. Johnson, suggested another solution. A country with a traditional agricultural structure might quickly break through into industrialized growth, Rostow argued, in cases where there was a sudden shock to the existing system and an elite group of industrialists with "the will and the authority to install and diffuse new production techniques" exploited the opportunity to reap the economic rewards of innovation.

"Take-off" was achieved when a self-sustaining industry was in place, representing "a definitive social, political, and cultural victory of those who would modernize the economy over those who would . . . cling to the traditional society." In short, a small industrializing group could quickly achieve what land reform only hoped to do with difficulty over time. Jefferson's democratic distribution of land was irrelevant.

As would later become obvious, Rostow's thesis suffered from two debilitating flaws: it assumed that a modernized economy would, as he put it, "require movement towards democratic government," and its conclusions were narrowly based on the mechanics of "the take-off" at the expense of the preexisting state of society. Since he never had the opportunity to see how Russia and China could operate modern economies without democracy, Rostow might be forgiven the first mistake, but the second was his own choice and led to a deliberate distortion of the evidence from one part of the world in particular.

THE RAPID INDUSTRIALIZATION of Sweden in the late nineteenth century served as one of Rostow's chief examples, not least because the process appeared to be kick-started by the rapid growth of the timber industry in the 1890s, followed by the creation of a pulp and paper industry and the diffusion of its production techniques into other capitalist enterprises. To make his point, however, Rostow neglected to mention that at the beginning of the nineteenth century a surge of land enclosures had transformed Swedish agriculture in the populous south and central regions from peasant to capitalist production, that this was followed in the 1850s by the rapid spread of joint-stock banks with multiple branches issuing paper money, that compulsory education from the 1830s had made literacy virtually universal, and that from 1866 an elected parliament had represented farming, timber, and mining interests in government.

By choosing to omit these highly relevant events from his reading of Swedish history, Rostow managed to imply that Sweden was modernized purely as a result of its industrialization. This was not a solitary aberration. Rostow's reading of economic history consistently overlooked the role of land distribution and democratic government, enabling him to show that industry was always the central force in economic development.

In fact, nineteenth-century Scandinavia as a whole exhibited the classic sequence of a land market leading to banks and financial institutions, and eventually to representative government. The change was driven by a population explosion—the result "of peace, vaccination, and potatoes," in the mordant words of the Swedish poet Esaias Tegnér—that virtually doubled the number of inhabitants by 1850.

In Denmark, a comprehensive program of land distribution by the country's most influential aristocrat, Count Christian Reventlow, sped up the process so that by the 1820s a once feudal regime was transformed into one in which two-thirds of all Danish farmers had become owner occupiers. Unlike seventeenth-century England, Denmark's smaller farms and unproductive sandy soil, especially in the Jutland peninsula, forced the new rural capitalists to cooperate rather than compete. Working through farming associations, they marketed their grain in Britain, raised capital from Danish banks, and from the 1840s lobbied for their interests through the Friends of the Peasant political party. Although it played no part in Rostow's thesis, these circumstances gave Danish agriculture a unique character, at once capitalist and cooperative, committed to free trade even when flooded by cheap American cereals in the 1890s, yet taking communal action to switch to dairy farming with newly created pig farms at hand to consume waste milk products.

The rural poverty of Sweden, Norway, and, after independence in 1917, Finland ensured that their land revolutions took on a similar tendency toward cooperative capitalism. But, as in private property societies, they also enjoyed the incalculable advantage of developing a set of rights around rural ownership prior to industrialization. The modernization of Scandinavia was a long, slow process, with prosperity delayed until the last half of the twentieth century. The highly individual nature of the society that emerged owed little to industrialization but a great deal to the particular shape of its nineteenth-century agriculture.

Despite its flaws, Rostow's theory about modernization became economic and social orthodoxy in the 1960s. Consequently, it undermined the campaign for land reform at the very moment when the shortcomings of communism's collective ownership of the earth could no longer be concealed.

The most tragic failure was China's Great Leap Forward. For a decade following the nationalization of the land in 1949 and its redistribution from landlord to peasant, individual holdings had increasingly been brought into cooperative enterprises with as many as two or three hundred families farming in centrally directed units. But mechanization was slow, quotas were often not filled, especially in the hungry years of the early 1950s, and surplus income to the government was too small to allow the state to industrialize and thus match Russia's spectacular growth.

In 1958, Mao Zedong launched a new policy that abolished private property in farm produce and forced all farms into communes owned by the state. Within twelve months, as many as twenty-five thousand communes had been created, each the size of a small town containing about five thousand families. To bypass the slow accumulation of capital required to industrialize an economy, the communes were also given the responsibility of creating their own factories, symbolized by the construction of local furnaces where scrap metal was supposed to be smelted into high-grade steel. In the next two years, disastrous experiments in planting rice and wheat were compounded by drought and the diversion of labor into inefficient industrial production. Restricted by lack of fuel and the necessary technology, the backyard smelters produced nothing more valuable than pig iron before they were abandoned.

By 1962 the famine that resulted from the Great Leap Forward had exacted a death toll, now estimated at about forty-two million, or 7 percent of the population. In the attempt to reconcile the reality of falling grain production with the inflated requirements from Beijing, local party activists resorted to frenzied violence—as many as five million farmers were either driven to suicide by their demands or, according to one authority, "buried alive, clubbed to death or otherwise killed by party members and their militia."

Mao himself chose to ban the distribution of twenty-two million tons of wheat to starving peasants seemingly as a punishment for underproduction. "When there is not enough to eat, people starve to death," he said in 1959. "It is better to let half of the people die so that the other half can eat their fill." But, deprived of grain to sell, government revenues slumped by 82 percent in just three years, crippling any hopes of proper industrialization. Not until Deng Xiaopeng's introduction of individual family holdings under the *chengbao* scheme did agricultural production reach a scale sufficient to feed the cities and allow the accumulation of capital needed to unlock the country's industrial potential.

The failure of Soviet collectivization followed a decade later. It came with little warning. In 1969, the Soviet Union exported more than three million tons of wheat, but in 1971 it began to import American grain, forty million tons between 1970 and 1975, and more than one hundred million tons in the first five years of the 1980s. The reasons were complex—

although the virgin lands were rapidly exhausted, overall wheat production actually increased from 180 million tons to more than two hundred million tons a year—but the system was unable to meet the demands of Soviet consumers for a wider range of foods, for beef, chicken, fresh milk, and cheese. A structure geared toward increasing wheat production proved incapable of adjusting to meet the need for more fodder for livestock and poultry, or to produce anything other than basic foodstuffs. For visitors to the Soviet Union in its last years, the characteristic sight of long queues outside food shops and empty shelves inside was evidence of a systemic failure.

For thirty years, the collectives had been getting bigger, rising to an average of fifteen thousand acres. At the urging of both Khruschev and his successor, Leonid Brezhnev, the most powerful general secretary of the Communist Party since Stalin, almost 40 percent of collective farms had been converted to become state organizations, known as *sovkhozi*. Yet despite taking direct control of Soviet farming, the government found itself faced by an insuperable problem of wasteful, inefficient, and inflexible use of the land.

The failure of the collectives was underlined by the extraordinary productivity of the tiny privately owned plots, measuring less than two acres each, that every farming family was allowed to possess. Altogether they amounted to about 4 percent of Soviet farmland, but provided 30 percent of national agricultural production, and the quality of their poultry, vegetables, and fruit was far superior to that of the collectives. The contrast made it evident that the problems of Soviet agriculture were fundamentally a matter of ownership, a reality implicitly recognized by one of the beetle-browed Brezhnev's last decrees. In 1981, he ordered the maximum size of private plots to be increased by almost a quarter.

The failure of collective farming hamstrung the Soviet Union in the last years of the Cold War. The costs of the huge *sovkhozi* in terms of wages, machinery, and fertilizer absorbed more than a quarter of all government expenditure, equivalent to thirty-three billion dollars in 1981, and the purchase of American, Canadian, and Argentine wheat drained the Soviet treasury of almost eight hundred million dollars in 1972 and more than two billion in 1980. It was the reverse of the usual formula for economic development. Instead of rural revenues financing industrialization, the Soviet Union was using its industrial surplus to subsidize its agriculture. The result was what Mikhail Gorbachev would call "the era of stagnation" when the headlong growth of the socialist economy ground to a halt.

It was clear that the Marxist-Leninist solution had failed. Yet in the battle for the allegiance of the world's two billion peasants, the alternative was no longer Ladejinsky's redistribution of property to the tiller of the soil. The first quarter of the twenty-first century would be irredeemably marked by a shift in American policy in the 1950s away from the Jeffersonian impulse to spread ownership of the soil to as many people as possible.

Chapter Twenty

Rostow's Legacy

The shift in United States strategy for confronting Communism was not unconnected to a seismic change in American identity caused by an immense migration from country to city. Between 1920 and 1957, the farm population shrank by almost half, and by the 1960s, barely one in five Americans worked on the land. United States power, starkly demonstrated in the Second World War, grew unmistakably from its industrial strength. Cheap food could be taken for granted. In 1961, American farmers produced a super-abundance of wheat, 1.3 billion tons, an increase of 50 percent from the crop yielded by the same acreage in the 1920s. Corn, hogs, and cotton were also in surplus. The only problem was finding a market. Farmland itself was no longer significant to the general economy.

In step with this changed economic reality, United States foreign policy, and thus the West's strategy in the Cold War, gradually changed from promoting rural ownership to increasing rural production as a preparation for industrialization. Aid took the form of grandiose projects such as the construction of giant dams on the Indus River in India, the Nile in Egypt, and the Helmand River in Afghanistan. The buzzwords were "development" and "modernization" and industrial growth displaced agriculture at the heart of the new policy.

The godfather of the new theory of development was Walt W. Rostow. Industrialization remained his key marker for modernizing a state, but "the take-off" had been incorporated into a Darwinian, near-Marxist idea of economic evolution that led from peasant farming through five stages, including the take-off at number three, to the "high mass consumption" of the modern state. "The striking disparity between the standards of the inhabitants of the so-called developed or advanced nations of the mid-twentieth century and standards prevailing in today's underdeveloped countries," he wrote in *The Stages of Economic Growth* in 1960, "is essentially due to the fact that the former have industrialized and the latter have not."

In the new academic discipline of economic development, land simply served as a source of cheap labor as families left the countryside, a supply of "exogenous capital" to the industrial economy. The question of ownership that so exercised Ladejinsky was no longer important. Freed from their relatives' unproductive presence, the remaining rural inhabitants were expected to have sufficient earnings to invest and improve the land's fertility, enabling them to produce more food for industry. Industrialization would lead the state into the market economy which could be expected to provide the employment, wealth, and free-market outlook that would attach underdeveloped countries, soon to be dubbed the Third World, to the capitalist camp.

Development theorists often cited the startling growth of the Asian tigers as examples of how the model should work but ignored the role played by the wide distribution of land ownership. Only in 1991 did the World Bank acknowledge the vital importance of land reform in sustaining stable government during the upheaval of industrialization because it had served "to demonstrate the intent that all would have a share of future wealth." For Rostow's followers, however, the crucial factor in maintaining social order was the dictatorial power of the U.S. military government in Japan, of the Kuomintang in Taiwan, and of Presidents Synghman Rhee and Park Chung-hee in South Korea.

This emphasis was given its most persuasive expression by Samuel Huntington, the leading academic exponent of development theory in the late twentieth century, in his 1968 study, *Political Order in Changing Societies*. Huntington eloquently pleaded the necessity for strong rule during this period of "authoritarian transition" until legal and parliamentary institutions were sufficiently well-established to channel the new social forces into democratic forms. Underlying his hugely influential argument was Rostow's five-stage model that saw industrial development leading inevitably to a democratic form of government. In the words of Joseph Schumpeter, a seminal influence on Rostow's thinking, "modern democracy is a product of the capitalist process."

Thus in the belief that authority would lead to industry and so to liberty, the United States fostered an unholy spectrum of freedom-hating autocrats during the last three decades of the Cold War, from Diem to President Marcos in the Philippines and the Shah of Iran, by way of President Mobutu in Zaire, the Trujillo family in the Dominican Republic, a string of murderous generals in Guatemala, the Somoza dynasty in Nicaragua, and General Pinochet in Chile.

Events in Vietnam demonstrated what was lost by the change of policy. Diem's capacity to institute massive change in the countryside was demonstrated in 1961—the year that Ladejinsky finally resigned in despair—when he instituted the Strategic Hamlets Program that forcibly resettled as many as seven million rural inhabitants in more than seven thousand fortified villages, a huge logistical operation that swept aside the traditional rights of both peasant and landlord. And the effectiveness that redistribution might have had was demonstrated in 1970 when the Green Revolution persuaded American and Vietnamese agricultural experts to prepare the ground for the introduction of newly productive strains of rice. Their reform program saw title to almost half the farmland in the Mekong delta transferred in just three years from absentee landlord to on-the-ground farmer. By 1973, recruitment to the National Liberation Front and Vietcong in the area affected had dropped by 80 percent, and rice production had increased by 30 percent. But the withdrawal of United States troops in that year showed that the opportunity to change the course of history had been seized too late.

Defeat in Vietnam induced a mood of desperation that locked the West into its new policy of backing strong rulers despite the toxic contradiction it involved. Peasants who became property owners gave stability to government, however autocratic. Without that broad base, the autocrat had to be supported by Western democracies that consequently found themselves on the wrong side of the struggle for liberty. The poisonous outcome did not end with the Cold War.

Iran in the 1960s witnessed both the final flurry of Ladejinsky-inspired redistribution and, when it ran into the sand, its replacement by western-backed dictatorial rule. The effects of both policies were still visible in the twenty-first century.

ALTHOUGH IRAN IS VAST in extent, one fifth the size of the United States, its best-watered and therefore most productive land is confined to the northern and southwestern perimeters of a mountainous desert heartland that gives its geography an Australian emptiness. In both fertile rim and arid interior, once tribal holdings had morphed into feudal estates—equivalent to Latin American *latifundias*—each spread across thousands of acres containing several villages and ruled by an emir who also acted as judge, moneylender, and spiritual mentor. Services, rents, or crops amounting to more than half a year's production were demanded from the peasants in return for use of the land and, more importantly in the dry valleys, for use of the water. On their side of the feudal contract, the emirs were expected to provide both protection and the means of irrigation. For centuries, the hallmark of traditional Iranian agriculture had been the elaborate, Christmas-tree pattern of underground channels, known as a *qanat*, that took water from a central spring or aquifer controlled by the landlord to the fields farmed by his peasants.

Fearful that the feudal rule of the emirs was leading toward a Communist revolt, the U.S. State Department began to pressure Shah Mohammad Reza in the late 1950s to undertake social and land reform in the Ladejinsky mold—officials with experience of transforming South Korea were specifically posted to the Tehran embassy to help with its execution. The plan, incorporated into a series of reforms that the shah proudly announced as the White Revolution in 1963, was to be executed by the minister of agriculture, a fiery radical economist named Hassan Arsanjani. His program set a cap of 330 acres on the size of holdings, required the compulsory sale of property above that maximum with redistribution to the peasants who worked it, and nationalized common ground, such as forests and rough pasture, amounting to 12 percent of Iran's land surface.

Arsanjani's reforms began in the fertile northwest, in the province of Azerbayjan. Within eighteen months, more than 270,000 families representing well over a million people had acquired their own farms, and two thousand cooperatives had been set up to market their produce and purchase fertilizer. The social transformation of a feudalized population was unmistakable. "Our landlord is dead," one peasant reported triumphantly of the very much alive, but dispossessed, owner who had formerly subjected him to virtual servitude. The rapidity of change from deference to independence astonished foreign observers—one normally skeptical British land reformer dubbed it "a supersonic moment in history." Nor did the new attitudes disappear. Two generations later in 2009, when the Green Movement erupted in opposition to the corruption of President Mahmoud Ahmadinejad's government, its strongest support beyond the capital, Tehran, came from the areas where reform had taken deepest root, particularly in Azerbayjan.

However, the shah was less interested in creating property than in the intimidation of the country's powerful landed families. He had suspended the country's parliament, the Majlis, where their power rested, in order to push through the breakup of their estates. Once his power of confiscation had been made plain, he dismissed the increasingly popular Arsanjani, who died soon after, the victim, it was alleged, of Iran's secret service, Savak. Although the policy of redistribution continued, it now became a threat to terrify opponents, and the land was usually awarded not to the peasants but to the shah's cronies and his adherents in the army as a reward for their loyalty.

By the 1970s, the State Department was fully committed to the "development" strategy of backing strong rulers. Thus in 1986, on the department's advice, Vice-President George H. Bush greeted President Ferdinand Marcos of the Philippines, notorious for the imprisonment, torture, and murder of hundreds of political opponents, with the words, "We love your adherence to democratic principles and to democratic processes." Bush was being neither ironic nor foolish, only expressing the dogma that authoritarian rule led to democracy. In the same way, the shah's rule, however brutal, was judged to be creating the conditions for Rostow's elite group of modernizers to prepare the ground for capitalism and representative government.

During the last years of Mohammed Reza's reign, the combination of corruption and autocracy alienated all rural interest groups—aristocracy, tribal chiefs, and peasants—as well as religious and academic opinion in the cities. When his rule collapsed in 1979 and Ayatollah Ruhallah Khomeini returned as the flag bearer of Islamic fundamentalism, the adherents of western democracy had nothing to offer as an alternative.

From the perspective of the twenty-first century, the fundamental errors in "development" theory are glaringly obvious. The evidence offered by China, Russia, and Vietnam, among others, demonstrates beyond doubt that capitalism can in fact flourish very well without modern democracy. Nor did any of the despotic rulers backed by the West ever willingly give up power to a democratic assembly. What saved development strategy from its own contradictions was the spectacular success of the most effective weapon in the capitalist armory during the Cold War, the Green Revolution.

* * *

AWARDING THE 1970 NOBEL PEACE PRIZE to Iowa-born Norman Borlaug for his work on developing high-yielding strains of wheat, the nominating committee singled out the achievements of an "eclectic, pragmatic, goal-oriented scientist" who, as their citation put it, "can perform prodigies of manual labor in the fields, [and] brings to his work the body and competitive spirit of the trained athlete." The physicality of Borlaug's character—a typical image showed him knee-deep in wheat with a farmer's straw hat tilted on the back of his head—went with his utterly practical conviction that hunger in preindustrial countries had a chemical origin. "In all traditional agricultures throughout the world," he noted in the 1940s, "there is a deficiency of nitrogen."

Dramatic results came from introducing more nitrogen to a wheat plant that traditionally produced about fifty seeds from the tiny spikelets that make up each ear—in the New Testament parable of the sower and the seed, the total ranged from as low as thirty seeds to one hundred from the best ground. For centuries manure and clover had been used to increase yields by producing the ammonia that results from the breakdown of nitrogen. But following the 1909 work of Fritz Haber and Carl Bosch in Germany, the chemical industry began to produce almost unlimited quantities of ammonia-rich nitrogen.

With an abundance of fertilizer, the bottleneck then became the capacity of the wheat plant to absorb so much nutrient since the long stalk would collapse under the weight of the heavier seed head. In the 1930s, Japanese farmers and seed developers produced a dwarf species, Norin 10, that grew barely two feet tall, half the height of normal strains, and was thus able to bear the greater load. This strain became the basis of the electrifying increase in wheat yields after the Second World War in both temperate, developed economies and the hotter, less developed world. The number of stems per plant, of ears per stem, of spikelets per ear, and seeds per spikelet, were all multiplied, until a modern plant was producing in excess of 240 seeds, and up to ten short plants could be crammed into a square foot of soil.

In 1953, Borlaug, who was already working with Mexican growers on producing disease-resistant strains, began artificially pollinating scores of different kinds of hardy Mexican wheat with Norin 10 to produce a disease-resistant, nitrogen-absorbent new wheat that could be closely planted and grown in the country's hot regions. Within a decade, yields had increased by half to about 2.5 tons per acre, and Mexico had moved from being a wheat importer to being an exporter. But in 1965, Cold

War competition shifted both the Green Revolution and Borlaug to India.

FIVE CENTURIES of foreign domination by the Mogul Empire followed by the British in India had obscured the normal relationship between government and land ownership. As in China, the imperial administrations operated alongside the near-feudal rule of princes, maharajahs, and other native rulers, to ensure that taxes were paid and loyalty was maintained. Intent on introducing their own property-based legal system, the British went further than their Mogul predecessors by seeking to identify land as the property of the *zamindar,* the person who paid tax on it. This satisfied the common law's need for a single owner, but hardly fitted with the Indian reality that divided possession of more than fifty million tiny unregistered plots, averaging about two acres, between the tiller of the soil, the head of the extended family who permitted its use in return for rent or part of the crop, the village elders or tribal chief who controlled access to village or tribal land, the moneylender who held a more or less permanent mortgage on the crops and sometimes the plot, as well as the *zamindar* responsible to the government for paying the village or region's taxes.

Underpinning this mosaic of interests was the caste system that determined every rural dweller's activities and obligations. A broad, fourfold division of society into priest, warrior, trader, and farmer began to become more specialized under the pressure of population growth, especially in the Ganges valley, during the Mogul Empire. By the end of the nineteenth century, more than four thousand castes were attached to a myriad of different peasant occupations, from farming and weaving to butchery and silk production. Land was not an asset to be owned but the bedrock of a social and economic structure that spread work among the multiplying millions in the country. The system was sufficiently resilient to resist British pressure, and, following independence in 1947, the determination of Prime Minister Jawaharlal Nehru's government to reform and if possible to eradicate it. But while the caste system guaranteed employment, the inefficiencies of Indian agriculture condemned the country to a permanent food deficit.

India's Five Year Plans for the decade between 1955 and 1965 projected an annual demand for ninety million tons of grain, but a total production of only eighty milllion tons. The shortfall was even greater for wheat, with just twelve million tons of wheat being grown, while a further eight million tons had to be imported, mostly consisting of the United States's fabulously productive Gaines variety, derived from Norin 10. With the population of 500 million expected to grow to 750 million within twenty years, the need for increased production from the country's 328 million acres of farmland was overwhelming.

The Indian microbiologist Monkombu Swaminathan was already developing nitrogen-hungry rice in the Ganges valley by crossing Japanese varieties with Indian when he heard of Borlaug's results with Norin 10 and Mexican wheat. His invitation, together with funding from the Rockefeller Foundation, brought Borlaug to India in 1963, and Swaminathan's practical experience of dealing with the intricacies of Indian land ownership shaped the course of the wheat experiment. Their chosen test bed was Punjab, a traditional wheat–growing area straddling the border with Pakistan that was irrigated by five gigantic tributaries of the Indus River. In general, rural families there owned about five or six acres each, twice the Indian average, but Swaminathan and Borlaug restricted supplies of the new wheat to the richest farmers among them, those who owned at least two bullocks and enough irrigated land, eight to ten acres, to produce a commercial crop.

The policy of "betting on the strong," as Borlaug put it, offended the ruling Congress Party's belief in cooperative, peasant production, but in 1965 Nehru, a staunch upholder of communal values, died, and the following year the hovering threat of starvation became a reality. With startling speed, rising food prices spiralled uncontrollably and local markets were suddenly bare of wheat. Lal Shastri, Nehru's pragmatic successor, was quick to use the specter of famine as a reason for pressing forward with the new wheat. Eighteen thousand tons of the two most modern Mexican strains, Sonora 64 and Noreste 66, were distributed to wealthy farmers able to afford irrigation and purchase fertilizer. Aided by favorable growing conditions, the results were spectacular. The 1968 harvest was five times as large as the previous year, and in 1970 India produced twenty million tons of wheat, making itself virtually self-sufficient.

AROUND THE WORLD microbiology and nitrogen had the same striking impact. Using dwarf derivatives of Norin 10, Europe began to fill its warehouses with mountains of wheat, and in 1977 even Britain, a net importer of cereals for more than a century, produced a surplus, while traditional wheat exporters such as the United States, Canada, and Argentina scrabbled to supply the Soviet Union and other deficit countries with their unsold crops.

Rice production increased in even more dramatic fashion. Utilizing high-yielding Chinese and Filipino varieties, the International Rice Research Institute (IRRI) developed the miracle variety IR 8 in 1966 and transformed harvests around the tropics by lifting yields from less than a ton an acre to almost three tons, with maximum figures approaching five tons.

When an American aid official coined the phrase "Green Revolution" to describe what was happening, he explicitly contrasted it with the Red revolution promised by Communism that had left people hungry. But the analogy went further than he could have guessed. What the Green Revolution had introduced was a new, corporate way of owning the earth that made peasant farmers in the Catholic Philippines, Hindu India, Buddhist Thailand, and Muslim Pakistan and Indonesia part of the larger productive, capitalist economy.

Reviewing the results of the revolution, the Rockefeller Foundation, which had funded Borlaug's work from the 1940s and been intimately involved with the dissemination of the new strains of both wheat and rice, came to a startling conclusion—only part of the growth in yields was due to Borlaug's plants, the rest came from the changed attitude of the growers. "The real revolution," the foundation concluded, "is one that has happened not to farming but to farmers."

Quite simply, taking advantage of the Green Revolution was so expensive due to the cost of mechanization, fertilizers, pesticides, and irrigation, (unless a river could be diverted, access to piped water or a well was essential), a peasant had to think like a capitalist, aiming to maximize profits from a parcel of land whose use belonged to his family. A string of anti-Communist governments, including those of Thailand, Indonesia, and the Philippines, favored the Green Revolution for that very reason. "Even if it wasn't such a spectacular producer," said Rafael Salas, the minister in charge of introducing IR 8 to the Philippines, "one would advocate pushing the miracle rice culture if only to train the Filipino farmer into thinking in terms of techniques, machines, fertilizers, schedules and experiments."

The Green Revolution, however, offered an alternative to land redistribution. Increasing agricultural production would create capitalists out of peasants without the social upheaval of redistribution. It penalized the poorest—those with fewer than five acres or, in Ladejinsky's phrase, "the meek and humble among the farm owners"—who did not have the money to compete, a category that in India encompassed 80 percent of all farmers, but it gave the richest 20 percent the means to become owner producers, employing labor and using the land as capital.

The miraculous yields of the Green Revolution, almost tripling grain output worldwide between 1950 and the beginning of the twenty-first century, not only enabled the population to grow by more than double, to six billion, but fed it better than before. But less obviously, it paved the way for industrial globalization by promoting a form of agricultural production whose supply chains of seeds, chemicals, and finance and whose output of wheat, rice, and exotic fruits and vegetables spanned the world.

VIEWED FROM THE TWENTY-FIRST CENTURY, however, the least predictable impact of the Green Revolution was its effect on those countries in the Middle East that had once been part of the Ottoman Empire, where the land was still owned in a way that had been determined in 1858. In that year, the grand vizier, Mehmed Ali Pasha, in effect the sultan's chief executive officer, introduced the Ottoman Land Code, the centerpiece of a prolonged campaign, known as the *Tanzimat*, to westernize the empire. Designed to increase tax revenues by bringing order to the mosaic of different systems of ownership that had developed from Süleyman the Magnificent's edicts, it required all land in the empire to be registered, and, reflecting Ali's long experience as ambassador in London, each property was to have only one owner.

Although never completed, the registration revealed that about 40 percent of the empire's territory was owned by the state, and perhaps another third was held by religious organizations to pay for welfare services such as education and sustenance in times of famine, with the remainder in the communal possession of villages and tribes. Most of the state land in the northern parts of the empire, however, was settled semi-privately as *ciftliks*. The Land Code gave the holders paper title to their land and formal recognition that any unused ground they brought into cultivation could be regarded as their own, thereby creating a new landed aristocracy. Yet although this was privately owned land, legally defined as *mulk*, its use was determined by a web of Islamic rules, family ties, and local customs that still ultimately treated the holder as a trustee rather than a property owner.

The same constraints bounded the other great class of landowners, the tribal emirs in the southern, dryer regions of the empire. These leaders of extended families and clans were traditionally selected from the richest, most successful members of the tribe, and customarily depended for their position on their abilities as warrior, smuggler, judge, and negotiator. But, once designated as owner and taxpayer of the clan territory, the formal authority of an emir increased sharply because his tribesmen were now also his tenants. Their lands were held communally, but allocated to villages and families who paid in rent, services, and obedience to the emir's justice.

A century later, in the 1950s, 70 percent of Iraq's territory was still owned in large estates of more than 10,000 *donums*, or 6,250 acres, divided between *ciftliks* and tribal leaders. As late as 2003, after the invasion of Iraq, when a young British official, Rory Stewart, was appointed to be the civilian governor of a province near Basra in southern Iraq, he found that in the countryside outside the cities the government was still provided by two tribes, Aibu Muhammad and Beni Lam. His Sunni interpreter from Baghdad referred to them contemptuously as "uneducated people, tribal people, without reading and writing," but Saddam Hussein had not been able to tame them, and no one else was capable of maintaining order. In the western provinces of Anbar and Nineveh, the alliance that American forces made with other tribal leaders, many of them linked into federations commanding as many as 250,000 followers, proved to be the crucial strategy that turned the tide against sectarian insurgents in the last years of the Iraq war.

The Green Revolution had a particular appeal for these conservative, Islamic societies, whose rulers had no liking for godless Communism, but still less desire to upset existing power structures based on absentee landlordism. Iraq's ruling Ba'athist party learned its lesson in the 1960s when it flirted with a project for Leninist collectivization in the Tigris and Euphrates valleys where Ottoman land reforms had left more than 70 percent of the ancient farmland in the hands of an elite of emirs. The sheer ferocity of the opposition nullified the party's apparatus of military and police power forcing it to back down.

The alternative strategy, adopted by Saddam Hussein and other autocratic rulers in Pakistan, Iran, Indonesia, Turkey, and along the North African coast from Egypt to Tunisia, was to push forward the introduction of IR 8 and Noreste 66. The Green Revolution answered all their needs. It kept rural landlords prosperous, a rapidly rising urban population well-fed and peaceful, and it offered a way of rewarding the leadership's inner circle of generals and business cronies. As follow-up studies in India suggested, even richer farmers found that despite increased productivity, the high cost of seeds, fertilizer, and borrowing locked them into financial dependency on the banks and agribusiness corporations that senior military and political figures controlled.

In Egypt, even President Gamel Abdul Nasser, the untouchable hero of the country's struggle for independence from Britain, who had publicly committed himself to a revolution based on redistributing land from feudal landlords to the hard-worked *fellahin* tilling the Nile-enriched soil, failed in the attempt. After less than 15 percent of the designated land had been expropriated, ferocious resistance from power brokers within his own military and political supporters brought the program to a halt. But, as in Iraq, Egyptian autocracy went on to flourish on the back of the fertilized agriculture that fed Cairo's bursting slums, and filled the purses of the rural elite, many of them related to senior officers in the military.

The fix from the Green Revolution, however, revealed an awkward gap in Islamic thinking about how to deal with the capitalist intrusion into the Ottoman Empire's land system. Significantly, when the Ayatollah Khomeini returned from exile in 1979 to lead the Islamic revolution, he singled out Arsanjani's land reforms for particular vilification. Ostensibly, he blamed them for the dismemberment of large religious estates whose rents financed Shia colleges and clergy, but the real problem, that he never solved, was that a literal reading of the Koran offered no authority for dealing with the forces unleashed by individual ownership of land.

During the 1960s and 1970s, the need to relate a seventh-century text to twentieth-century conditions provoked lively debate in Islam, both in the Shi'ite crescent that circled from Bahrain through Iraq and Syria into Lebanon, and in the Sunni majority solidly quartered in Egypt, Iraq, and Saudi Arabia. Socialist Muslims, headed by the Shi'ite Ali Shariati at Tehran University, singled out the priority that the Koran attached to justice and called for the elimination of private property as a way of "fighting exploitation and capitalism." By contrast, the outstanding Sunni scholar Mohammad Baqir al-Sadr, resident in Iraq's holy city of Naja, asserted that Muslims could only support "a form of government which contains all the positive aspects of the democratic system." The most able of his followers, Murtaza Mutahhari, called for Islamic economists to come to a new accommodation with private property and modern capitalism, citing as his justification the Koranic text, "We have apportioned among [people] their livelihood in the life of the world, and raised some of them above others in rank that some of them may take labour from others."

The adventurous scope of these different interpretations of the Koran by distinguished scholars did not last. In Iraq, Mutahhari and al-Sadr fell victim to torture and execution by Saddam Hussein's sadistic henchmen. Throughout Sunni Islam, the literalist interpretation of the Koran spread by Wahabi Muslims under the sponsorship of Saudi oil billionaires soon snuffed out any intellectual exploration. And Khomeini's fundamentalism achieved the same result among Shi'ite scholars.

The ayatollah himself found it impossible to decide whether the Iranian economy was to be capitalist or Socialist. "Islam does not approve of an oppressive and unbridled capitalism," he declared in his last will. "Neither is Islam opposed to private property, as [are] communism, Marxism and Leninism. Islam provides for a balanced regime."

The consequences of Khomeini's inability to deal with privately owned property went beyond Iran. In effect it gave credence to a globalized agricultural economy draped over a corrupted Islamic version of feudal possession of the earth. The strongman governments, supported by the West's "development" strategy, that seized control across North Africa and the Middle East reflected that structural hollowness. Their legitimacy was based on their ability to provide security and feed their rapidly growing populations. But the absence of any moral or electoral underpinning left a void that would be filled by jihadists trying to hack back the modern world to the literal shape of society enjoined by the Koran. And it would leave the hopeful revolutionaries of 2011 with no Islamic economic model that incorporated both incentive and justice.

THE FALL OF THE STRONGMAN RULERS in the Arab Spring of 2011 was triggered by a failure in food supply, the one basic claim to legitimacy that a succession of increasingly corrupt regimes had to offer. Yet it was not hunger that brought about the Arab Spring so much as a demand for social justice.

There had been disturbances in Egyptian food markets in protest at the rise in the price of a bushel of wheat from $4.30 in June 2010 to $8 in December 2010, but the predominantly middle-class crowds who first demonstrated against President Hosni Mubarack's thirty-year-old government in Cairo's Tahrir Square in January 2011 were not starving. What motivated them, like the demonstrators in Tunisia who had earlier brought about the overthrow of President Zinelabidine Ben Ali, ruler for twenty-six years, was the discovery of their own entitlement to protest. Hunger had simply dissolved the regime's aura of authority. In Tunisia, the catalyst came from the desperate choice of the street-seller Mohammed Bouazizi to burn himself to death rather than tolerate more bureaucratic bullying from officials incapable even of maintaining adequate supplies of food. As the Tunisian poet Abolkacim Ashabi wrote, "If the people one day decide to live, fate must answer and the chains must break." The Tunisians themselves named the uprising that threw out Ben Ali's rule "The Dignity Revolution."

In Western societies, many commentators believed that this assertion of individual worth was the beginning of a social and political journey toward the values that they personally espoused. Certainly in the social media that played such a crucial role in coordinating the movements of the young, educated demonstrators, phrases demanding freedom, justice, and democracy were widely used. But the West's Cold War legacy had left no democratic institutions and no entitlements, only a Hobbesian capitalism whose inevitable corruption rendered it morally bankrupt. Nor could the Islamic movements that took up the call for justice and freedom offer any secular guarantees of human or property rights.

Section Six

THE EXPERIMENT THAT FAILED

Chapter Twenty-One

The Economics of the Industrial Home

With a prescience that evaded other, sharper intellects, President Warren Harding broached a truth about capitalism in 1922 that would dominate its development in the last half of the twentieth century. In a letter to the chairwoman of the Better Homes Campaign, he suggested that it was time to think of the place where Americans lived in a new light. Homes provided more than shelter. They were "absolutely elemental in the development of the best citizenship," the president asserted, and for "twenty millions of house-keepers," they served "as their industrial center as well as their place of abode."

Enthusiastically endorsed by his secretary of commerce, Herbert Hoover, the government's sudden concentration on the economic importance of the home was intended to attract the votes of newly enfranchized women. But its long-term importance emerged as the makers of automobiles, refrigerators, washing machines, and vacuum cleaners responded to the buying power of the home market. By 1929, the production of refrigerators had grown from 315,000 units in 1919 to 1.7 million; the number of radios in use multiplied fourteen times to seven million, and the automobile industry sold more than twenty-three million vehicles, employed 427,500 people, and sustained a distribution and service organization with sales of almost five billion dollars. Although muted by the 1930s depression, the economy that grew up around the home would galvanize the production of steel plants and plastic factories, transport and energy suppliers, and the provision of financial, marketing, and advertising services.

By the end of the century, the consumer economy, a sector in its infancy when Harding drew attention to it, was responsible for about 70 percent of the gross domestic product of the United States. In the opinion of a stream of economic commentators, from Thorstein Veblen at the beginning of the century to J. K. Galbraith near its end, it also provided one answer to industrial capitalism's crisis of overproduction.

"When a family buys a home, the ripple effect is enormous," President Clinton explained in 1995. "It means new homeowner consumers. They need more durable goods, like washers and dryers, refrigerators and water heaters. And if more families could buy new homes or older homes, more hammers will be pounding, more saws will be buzzing. Homebuilders and home fixers will be put to work. When we boost the number of homeowners in our country, we strengthen our economy, create jobs, build up the middle class, and build better citizens."

The new phase of land ownership was clothed in the same term, "property" and in declaring it to be elemental to citizenship both Harding and Clinton assumed that it conferred on the owner the old Jeffersonian attribute of republican independence. But the twentieth-century home differed in one radically different way from the nineteenth-century property whose relatively modest investment morphed readily into rural capital. Purchased with a mortgage, and equipped with labor-saving machinery paid for through bank loans and credit agencies, the new version came with a scale of debt that required most of a forty-year working life to pay off. Until it was, ownership was shared with the mortgage lender and credit issuer.

This dependency locked the new homeowners of the 1920s into the structure of modern mercantile capitalism. The mortgage corporations, banks, and other financial institutions from which they borrowed made their profits by borrowing in turn more cheaply than they lent. In the wake of the carnage and expense of the First World War that atomized London's financial dominance, Wall Street had become the international banking center of the world and the institutions' largest source of funds. The amount banks could raise and the price they paid for Wall Street's involvement were determined partly by the stock market—through the value of banking shares—but to a growing extent by the market's willingness to buy their bonds. To a degree unknown in the nineteenth century, property values in the new consumer societies were influenced by interest rates on Wall Street.

Not fully appreciated in the 1920s, however, was the Ponzi effect of allowing the same financial market to fund both industry's capacity to produce and homeowners' appetite to consume. From 1918, when fewer than one hundred thousand new homes were built, the dream of ownership drove housing construction to a spike of 550,000 units begun in 1927, and mortgage lending ballooned from about seven billion dollars to twenty-seven billion. On the back of this boom and the accompanying demand for automobiles and other machines to save time and labor, the American economy grew by 4.2 percent a year through the Roaring Twenties to more than one hundred billion dollars. In other words, the larger and more dynamic part of it was based on the construction, equipment, and servicing of the industrial home, and that in turn depended on the interest rates charged on Wall Street's bond market.

The first hint of the economic difference this made compared to the earlier economy primarily based on rural capitalism came when the stock market collapsed in the fall of 1929. Remembering the depression of 1873, when falling prices and wages cut the demand for goods, precipitating the downward spiral into depression, President Herbert Hoover's overriding priority was to prevent a recurrence.

The entire strategy of his administration, enthusiastically endorsed by business, industry, and labor leaders during a series of conferences in December 1929, was designed to maintain people's buying power and keep demand healthy. Until late in 1931, employers were pressed to maintain wages at pre-crash levels and corporations to keep dividend payments high, and the profits of both were protected against cheaper foreign goods by tariffs averaging 50 percent, introduced under the 1930 Smoot-Hawley Act.

Hoover's strategy was doomed to fail because it ignored the post-1873 economic climate. Wages and dividends played a small part in the consumer economy compared to credit. Unless the financial institutions could generate enough credit to stimulate overconsumption by the industrial home, overproduction would inevitably cut industrial profits. But when the banks lost confidence following the stock market crash, the engine went into reverse, sucking so much credit out of the system that the human owner of the industrial home, hit by a perfect storm of unemployment, high interest rates, and foreclosure, could not buy anything at all, leaving industry with a pile of goods it could not sell. The solution, according to Ben Bernanke, the twenty-first century's acknowledged expert on the depression, was for government to generate its own credit—quantitative easing as it became known following the 2008 crash—that could be channelled through the banks and finance houses restoring their readiness to lend once more, especially to the industrial home owner.

In the 1930s, governments groped blindly for a way out of the nightmare until in 1931 Britain decided to let the value of its currency fall by unpegging it from the gold standard. As Milton Friedman, the father of monetarist economics, would later explain, leaving the gold standard removed the need for high interest rates to prop up the currency, making credit easier and increasing the money supply, thus delivering a stimulus to kick-start demand in the consumer economy. The decision was forced on the British government, as in every other country that adopted the measure, by democratic pressure coming from the unemployed. "The deterioration of the conditions of millions of workers," declared Ernest Bevin, a senior British parliamentarian, "was too high a price to pay for the maintenance of a single industry [London's financial institutions]."

In the United States, the financial crash destroyed credit on a scale that dwarfed Hoover's attempts to keep cash flowing, and the deflationary effect was exacerbated by his decision to raise income tax. By the end of 1932, two fifths of the nation's 1929 wealth had evaporated, about ten thousand banks, more than a third of the total, had failed, and one in four workers was unemployed. Although the U.S. finally came off the gold standard in 1933, the extent of the devastation was not fully repaired until the gigantic managed economy of the Second World War, allied to the massive public works of the New Deal, had eliminated unemployment and restored demand.

THE ENTRAILS OF THE 1930s depression were picked over endlessly by economists of all kinds, but few did so more obsessively than those belonging to what became known as the Austrian School. Its general stance was articulated early by the most eclectic of its leaders, the abrasively inventive Joseph Schumpeter.

Among the host of fertile ideas that Schumpeter planted in the economic garden, two stood out: the belief that a capitalist economy was subject to uncontrollable cycles of expansion and contraction, and that these upheavals allowed innovative entrepreneurs to overthrow outmoded methods and technologies in a process Schumpeter termed "creative destruction." His 1930s Harvard economics class should not have been surprised, therefore, when the professor declared in his heavily accented English, "Chentlemen! A depression iss for capitalism like a good cold douche."

Not only was the 1929 financial crash a natural corrective to the inflationary decade before it, but the business cycle and entrepreneurial activity would in time naturally take advantage of the availability of cheaper goods and labor to bring about economic recovery. Thus, Schumpeter's advice during the Depression, backed by two fellow Austrian economists, the upper-class Ludwig von Mises and his protegé, Friederich Hayek, sounded uncannily like an eighteenth-century physiocrat counseling the heir to the French throne, "Do nothing."

In the late twentieth century, the politics of all private property societies would be profoundly influenced by Austrian economics, not least because at its heart lay a ferocious defense of property. But the theory that von Mises presented about the origin of property gave it a significantly different character. In *Socialism,* a coruscating attack on the political force that had supplanted imperialism in his native Austria after the First World War, von Mises imagined property emerging from a world as brutal and chaotic as anything Thomas Hobbes described, in which the strongest battled to win and keep as much as they could defend against their rivals. "All ownership," the Austrian declared bluntly, "derives from occupation and violence."

Over time, social order had spontaneously spread without any need for a Leviathan government, driven simply by people's recognition of the economic benefits of stability. "Out of violence emerges law," von Mises stated, adding that any further explanation about the origin of the law was meaningless. But the law had a power as irresistible as Leviathan's because it preserved peace, meaning that any who opposed it must want war. For that reason, the law's first priority was to defend property—"All violence is aimed at the property of others"—regardless of the circumstances by which it had been acquired. "Possession is protected even though it has, as the jurists say, no title. Not only honest but dishonest possessors, even robbers and thieves, may claim protection for their possession." In short, might became right, because it delivered the economic goods.

Von Mises swiped aside both John Locke's argument that there was moral authority based on a sense of natural justice involved in the creation of property, and the Enlightenment's theory that government emerged as a rational contract between individuals to preserve their property. Natural rights and natural justice did not exist—"all rights derive from violence," von Mises repeated, "all ownership from appropriation or robbery." Human nature had evolved from an animal state, he insisted, and this

Darwinian process made "the idea of a human nature which differs fundamentally from the nature of all other living creatures seem strange indeed; we no longer think of man as a being who has harbored an idea of justice from the beginning."

In his lifetime, the resolutely snobbish von Mises—he clung to the "von" for fifty years after Austria had abolished the rank—invested his philosophy with a Central European air of sophistication and realism. But reading *Socialism* without the persuasive charm of his Viennese accent and dapper presence, it is impossible not to be aware how restricted he was by his background.

The empire in which von Mises lived until he was almost forty years old had only recently emerged from being a serf society—nominally abolished in Austria in 1848 and in Hungary in 1861 while leaving the power of their aristocratic lords intact—and his understanding of democracy was based on the primitive, ramshackle structure that still answered to Emperor Franz-Josef II. Politically, the empire was virtually unworkable, consisting as it did of two autonomous kingdoms, Austria and Hungary, joined from 1861 in a union known as the Dual Monarchy, a semiautonomous state in Czechoslovakia with its own assembly and a dizzying number of provinces, each with its own legislative council, language, and culture.

Neither federated nor bound by a common set of laws, it was held together by three institutions: the emperor to whom the imperial army and executive governments of each monarchy were answerable; the aristocratic instincts shared by its nobility and reinforced by an overtly political and conservative Catholic hierarchy; and the dictatorial Austro-Hungarian National Bank, staffed by dazzlingly brilliant economists in Vienna and Budapest, whose independence from political constraints enabled them to control a single currency across a wildly heterogeneous empire, and in 1892 to impose a belt-tightening shift to the gold standard with barely a squeak of opposition.

The state of the Austro-Hungarian Empire confirmed von Mises's unwavering belief that economics came before democracy. But the idea originated with his mentor, Carl Menger, the founder of the Austrian School, who argued that in its "natural" state, an ordered economy would be self-generating and, over time, self-adjusting, with no need for government interference—the business cycle, elaborated later by his students, was one of Menger's original concepts. Even the crisis of overproduction would solve itself by the inevitable formation of cartels and price-fixing agreements within the different business sectors, independently of any official intervention.

One of the most powerful examples Menger presented of this spontaneous growth of order was the way that money, meaning paper and credit as well as cash, generated itself once traders agreed on a medium, such as bills of exchange and promissory notes, to take the place of barter. "The origin of money (as distinct from coin, which is only one variety of money) is, as we have seen, entirely natural," he concluded. "Money is not an invention of the state. It is not the product of a legislative act."

The golden era of Austrian finance ended in the shattering defeat of the First World War and the election of a social-democratic government in 1919 that was for the first time in the country's history responsive to the electorate. Among its most far-reaching actions was a program to redistribute aristocratic property. Thus the one article of faith that von Mises took with him into exile was a belief in economic freedom, a Menger-like absence of interference by government, epitomized by the unfettered possession of property. It was, therefore, incumbent on owners to be ready to defend rights that they alone had created by force, and any action by government must represent the first step toward a Socialist usurpation of their independence.

The most articulate of von Mises's students, Friederich von Hayek—in later life he dropped the "von"—wholeheartedly adopted his mentor's suspicion of government. His bestselling book, *The Road to Serfdom*, published in 1944, was a savage hymn to the belief that economic freedom could be equated to individual liberty.

There was no difference between Fascism and Communism, Hayek warned, or for that matter between Nazi Germany and the democratic governments who were attempting to defeat it by managing their economies to maximize wartime production. "Most of the people whose views influence development," he declared, "are in some measure socialists. Many who sincerely hate all of Nazism's manifestations are working for ideals whose realization would lead straight to the abhorred tyranny." Once embarked on the path of planning, Hayek predicted, any state would inevitably end up as a dictatorship. "Planning leads to dictatorship," he wrote, "because dictatorship is the most effective instrument of coercion and, as such, essential if central planning on a large scale is to be possible."

Hayek's followers attempted to soften the doomsday tone by explaining it as the consequence of his despair at the government-directed nature of wartime economies. But his diatribe had deeper roots in political ignorance.

Hayek had arrived in Britain in 1931 at the invitation of the London School of Economics, where his rigorous insistence on the unfettered working of market forces was welcomed as a corrective to Keynesian economics. But even after a decade of living in a parliamentary system, when he came to write his polemic, Hayek still did not appreciate that in a democracy, sovereignty lies in the electorate rather than in the government. What was government strategy, he took to be state policy, as would have been the case in Vienna where the imperial government was responsible to the aged emperor rather than to the voters.

By 1960, Hayek was well aware of the difference, and in that year he set out to describe from first principles how a capitalist democracy should work. In *The Constitution of Liberty*, he wrote one of the late twentieth century's most influential books on political economy. In 1979 Margaret Thatcher banged a copy on the table at a meeting with senior figures in Britain's Conservative Party soon after becoming leader and told them, "*This* is what we believe in." Its precepts formed the core of her policies, and jumped across the Atlantic to seed the low tax, government-light politics known generally as Reaganomics. Well into the twenty-first century its libertarian principles still informed much of the political debate on both sides of the Atlantic.

HAYEK STARTED with a bold statement that dismissed the possibility that a person might be born with inalienable natural rights. Even freedom was alienable and could be sold, he insisted—"a person may . . . contract himself into slavery." It followed, therefore, that "Freedom is not a state of nature, but an artefact of civilization." Removing the claim to inalienable rights to life, liberty, and the pursuit of happiness might still have left intact the fundamental tenet of common law that a craftsman had a natural right to property in his own work, but that too was excised. Having cleared out the central beliefs of a private property society, Hayek inserted in their place a model like that imagined by his teacher, von Mises, in which the creation of property, the conditions of a market economy, and the rule of law all arose spontaneously, as people recognized these ingredients to be essential to the efficient working of their communities.

The elimination of natural rights from Hayek's society, otherwise apparently identical to that of a private property society, also did away with the social fairness or natural justice that in John Locke's and Adam

Smith's theories had held society together and allowed the operation of the hidden hand to take place—Hayek in fact subtitled a later book *The Mirage of Social Justice*. Its place was occupied by the working of the marketplace that engaged everyone's efforts and rewarded everyone accordingly.

Hayek did not pretend that the rewards would be equitable, but argued they were just. In a flight of genuinely innovative thinking, he explained that the very imperfections of a free marketplace made it a more efficient means of rewarding effort than a centrally planned system. Because it involved many players, each forced to adjust to local conditions of supply and demand but equipped with only fragmentary knowledge of the wider world, the market would react more quickly and appropriately to the unpredictable complexities of life than would a centrally directed structure aiming at perfect knowledge and a rational response.

The substitution of the marketplace for any deliberate or government solution to social problems required the mechanism to work without interference. To create the necessary conditions, Hayek picked out the central importance of freedom, which he defined in its negative sense as "the absence of restraint and constraint"—any positive definition, he warned, would permit government to promote its own values. In practice, this meant that governments had to intervene as little as possible, because any intervention distorted the market, reduced freedom, and introduced inequality. Conspicuously, these threats were only posed by government, not by trusts, cartels, or monopolies, however large their budgets or extensive their operations. Nevertheless, he did allow that a government might provide for the poor "some minimum of food, shelter and clothing, sufficient to preserve health," although treating it as a charitable donation to keep them quiet rather than as a reciprocal to property rights.

This description of how society should work left it with no other collective purpose than to grow richer, and Libertarians in particular welcomed the lack of social values in its individualized, marketplace ethos. But Hayek himself rejected any association with libertarian thinking. His own values were, he said, those of Britain's nineteenth-century Whigs. It was a revealing admission. Throughout *The Constitution of Liberty* ran an implicit and sometimes explicit argument for the leadership of an elite, such as Hayek believed to have existed up to the 1880s.

By rewarding winners without limit, he believed, the marketplace would give rise to a "leadership of individuals or groups who can back their beliefs financially." This financial aristocracy was not only needed for "the preservation of competitive enterprise," but, according to Hayek, "is particularly essential in the field of cultural amenities, in the fine arts, in education and research, in the preservation of natural beauty and historic treasures, and above all in the propagation of new ideas in politics, morals and religion." The wealthy leaders of society might emerge by their own energies, but Hayek believed there were clear advantages to "selection through inheritance from parents," since those born with a silver spoon in their mouths would have been trained for the task.

To ensure that society could benefit from the wealth and ideas that came "filtering downward from the top of a pyramid," Hayek was adamant that taxation should not fall most heavily on the richest. Unlike Adam Smith who believed "It is not very unreasonable that the rich should contribute to the public expense, not only in proportion to their revenue, but something more than in that proportion," Hayek was certain that progressive taxation represented discrimination against the elite minority. Unlike the dull mass of people who simply did the jobs given to them without thought, the minority of "independents" as he dubbed them, were the enterprising creators of wealth whose freedom needed to be protected from the constraints of taxation, regulation, and intervention by a government representing the envious interests of the majority.

With its aristocratic agenda excised, however, Hayek's thesis looked like a return to eighteenth-century laissez-faire economics. The market was expected to take care of itself, and the crisis of overproduction would be sidelined by a combination of supply-side economics to stimulate consumption, an aggressive takeover culture to reduce competition, and the business cycle's creative destruction of weaklings. In effect, an Austrian cuckoo had laid its egg in the private property nest.

THE DIFFERENCE WAS NOT IMMEDIATELY APPARENT during the postwar years. Social democratic governments in Europe and Scandinavia developed more or less planned economies that nineteenth-century Prussian economists would have recognized, nationalizing strategic industries such as railroads and steel production, and providing universal health care systems, old-age pensions, and social care. In 1948, the British welfare state came into being with the creation of the National Health Service, free education to the age of fourteen, and a program of nationalization devoted to maintaining full employment.

Even in the United States, New Deal intervention and wartime planning spilled over into the postwar years. In the 1950s, the Eisenhower administration inaugurated the largest public works project in peacetime since the Public Lands Survey with the creation of the forty-six-thousand-miles Interstate Highway system, and was followed in the same decade by President Kennedy's launch of NASA and the moon landing project at a cost of up to twenty-five billion dollars, or 4 percent of the national budget. Both were dwarfed by federal and state expenditure on Medicaid for the elderly and Medicare for low-income families following President Lyndon B. Johnson's Great Society in 1965.

To pay for this, U.S. personal taxes on income rose up to 75 percent and and on dividends up to 95 percent, in theory although in practice the top rate was about 60 percent. The heavily taxed and regulated economy grew at 3.7 percent a year from 1950 to 1973, and Wall Street returned an annual rate of 9.58 percent to investors during the same period. In Britain similar figures—GDP growth of 3.1 percent annually from 1964 to 1973, and stock market returns of about 8 percent from 1950 to 1970—prompted the respected *Financial Times* economist Samuel Brittan to describe this period as "a Golden Age, which achieved far higher growth than experienced during any sustained period before or since."

Between 1950 and 1980 the population of the United States surged by 50 percent to 226,000,000. In the last ten years before the contraceptive pill was legalized in 1965, almost forty million babies were born, the most fertile decade in American history. The distinctive culture that these new Americans grew into was shaped by the force that Warren Harding had first identified in the 1920s, the industrial home.

Regulation of the hybrid consumer economy, notably through the 1933 Glass-Steagall Act that separated retail banking and mortgage lending from investment banking, kept house prices roughly in line with incomes from the 1940s to 1970s. But a notable change took place during the period. At the end of the Second World War, almost half of all Americans rented their homes; three decades later almost two thirds of them owned the place they lived in, either completely or with finance borrowed from one of more than three thousand savings and loans associations—cooperative financial institutions, equivalent to British building societies, that were dedicated to providing mortgages for their members. And most of these hybrid properties were located in the suburbs—by the 1980s, more American lived there than in cities or the countryside.

In the United States, the prototype was Levittown, Pennsylvania, created in 1951 by William Levitt, whose homogeneous, factory-assembled houses—he described his company as "the General Motors of the housing industry"—were lined up along curved streets and around a church, a school, and a leisure center in self-contained communities. The nature of suburbia's inhabitants was pored over by sociologists like Herbert Gans, sexologists led by Alfred Kinsey, and novelists among whom none surpassed John Updike, whose driven, promiscuous, selfish, idealistic creation, Harry Angstrom, known as Rabbit, embodied suburbia's conflicted yearning for social esteem and personal freedom, for admission to the country club and sex with the minister's wife.

DEBARRED FROM INFLUENCE until the 1970s, the political implications of Austrian economics were best explored not in fact but fiction. In *Atlas Shrugged*, published in 1957, the Russian-born, Hollywood scriptwriter Ayn Rand imagined how the potential giants of industry might escape the crippling effects of government regulation and social convention whose purpose was to spend their profits on "parasites" and "looters." According to her protagonist, John Galt, every attempt by government to regulate entrepreneurs or to tax them beyond what they wished to pay represented an assault on their fundamental right "to think, to work, and to keep the results—which means the right of property."

Recognizing that Austrian economic theory was being given popular form in her novel, Ludwig von Mises, by then in New York, sent Rand a fan letter soon after *Atlas Shrugged* was published, praising her "cogent analysis of the evils that plague our society." He added that he especially admired the unashamed elitism advocated by her book: "You have the courage to tell the masses what no politician told them: [that] you are inferior and all the improvements in your conditions which you simply take for granted you owe to the efforts of men who are better than you."

That the upper-class von Mises should hold "the masses" in contempt was understandable; all the Austrians, even the maverick Schumpeter, shared a nostalgia for the old imperial form of politics. But it was less easy to see why such sneering views should have been adopted most enthusiastically in the republic that most prided itself on being democratic. The best insight, however, would come from the career of Ayn Rand's leading disciple, Alan Greenspan.

In the early 1950s Greenspan had come upon Rand's Nietzschean philosophy which, because it equated self-realization with the discovery of an objective reality, she termed "Objectivism." As a brilliant, geeky young economist, devoted to mathematics but with few other interests—"intellectually limited" by his own admission—Greenspan adopted its tenets "with the fervor," he wrote in his autobiography, "of a young acolyte drawn to a whole new set of ideas." Out of his exposure to what he called "a remarkable course in logic and epistemology" came his conviction that postwar economic policies were not only inefficient, but, unless resisted, must lead to dictatorship. Government should control the money supply, he believed, but otherwise businesses could be left to pursue their own interests in the certainty that "unfettered market competition" would resolve its own problems, and that economic liberty was synonymous with individual liberty.

Greenspan's capitalism drew on von Mises's insistence that property existed as an absolute possession, founded on violence, and preserved on grounds of materialist self-interest. As a result, he and Rand took the Austrian view that government and property must forever be at one another's throats. It was erroneous to suppose, as James Madison had, that a democratic government should strike a balance between the interests of property and those of the propertyless. Any interference represented an attack on property.

By the early 1970s, the costs of the Vietnam War added to government expenditure on highways, the space race, and President Johnson's "Great Society" were creating an unsustainably inflationary effect. At the same time, the U.S. began to import oil for the first time, and when the OPEC oil cartel abruptly cut the supply in 1973, quadrupling its price, the American economy, followed by the rest of the industrial world, stalled in a stagflationary cycle of falling production and rising prices.

In its attempt to break the cycle, Britain became the first private property economy to hatch the Austrian egg. After her election in 1979, Prime Minister Margaret Thatcher began a crusade on behalf of Hayek's economics. Her privatization of Britain's airlines, telecommunications, energy suppliers, and even public housing were all inspired by his "crisp, clear analytical arguments against socialism." In 1986, her government endorsed the deregulation of the City of London's financial markets in a single measure, known as the Big Bang. Not only were the barriers between investment and commercial banking abolished, it became apparent that virtually any kind of institution of any nationality that borrowed and lent money could trade with the lightest supervision in London's financial markets. In the fallout, Wall Street's greater muscle allowed American investment banks such as Goldman Sachs and Lehman Brothers to prosper in London, providing an extra inducement to push for the same sort of freedom in the United States.

In 1986, President Ronald Reagan signaled his own conversion to the Austrian outlook in his much-quoted quip, "The nine most terrifying words in the English language are 'I'm from the government, and I'm here to help.'" But under his administration, Hayek's philosophy of deregulation was bundled up with the conceptually different monetarist theories of Milton Friedman and the Chicago School of Economics.

Monetarism, which aimed to control inflation by regulating the supply of money, both cash and credit, gave rise to the austere banking policies pursued by Paul Volcker, Greenspan's predecessor in charge of the Federal Reserve in the early 1980s. Volcker pushed interest rates to Himalayan heights in order to bring inflation under control. But this was accompanied by deregulation of a range of industries from airlines and telephones to natural gas and savings and loans associations until the finance industry, still regulated by the Glass-Steagall Act separating investment from commercial banking, was left as the last important holdout. The fate of the deregulated S&L associations, once famous as the safe "thrifts," now trying to operate as credit-generating banks, might have given pause for thought. Caught in a competitive spiral of risky loans, poor management, and inadequate funds, almost a third of them became bankrupt, and rescuing the industry cost almost nine billion dollars of taxpayers' money.

Nevertheless, encouraged by Greenspan, beginning his five-term tenure of the chairmanship of the Federal Reserve, American banks chipped away at the regulations until in 1997 Glass-Steagall was repealed. With the lifting of restrictions on derivatives dealing in 2000, the financial market had become unified. And the industrial home, driver of the consumer economy, became once more what it had been in the Roaring Twenties, a functional adjunct to Wall Street.

In evidence to Congress in 2008, Alan Greenspan would later admit there was "a flaw" in his faith that "unfettered market competition" would sort out its own distortions. The flaw was the one exposed by the bankruptcy of Lehman Brothers with six hundred billion dollars of assets—that a player might be so big its collapse would destroy the market itself. But his belief in Austrian economics blinded him to a more fundamental weakness, a contradiction within the theory of financial nonregulation that guaranteed its failure.

Integral to Carl Menger's innovative theory about the spontaneous creation of money was that it came about as an "entirely natural" agreement between self-interested traders and required no state intervention. From this observation, Greenspan, following Hayek, von Mises, and a rapidly growing band of like-minded bankers, drew the conclusion that government intervention had no place in the operation of financial markets. While the events following deregulation proved the truth of Menger's theory, they also exposed the mistake in his disciples' reasoning.

The most notorious example was to be the way that traders in investment banks took the mortgages held by commercial lenders and bundled them up for sale to other traders as interest-bearing bonds—"securitized" was the word for the process and "consolidated debt obligations" was the label pinned to the product. The minutiae of how consolidated debt obligations and other derivatives were created mattered less than the end result: by creating a market for them, a new form of money had been spontaneously generated. What had been a debt indirectly secured against the value of a property was now transformed into an asset that appeared as such in the bank's accounts, and against which it could borrow. Such was the traders' confidence in these invented assets, the level of borrowing quickly rose until it was leveraged at three or four times their supposed value.

Once a mortgage became not just an accountancy asset with an equivalent item on the debit column but a trading asset that increased the capital value of the lender, it became logical for the sales forces working for any kind of lending institution to create as much debt as possible. Even the notorious "Ninja" loans to borrowers with "no income, no job, and no assets" became valuable. By March 2007, the value of subprime mortgages was estimated to be $1.3 trillion. The same process converted credit default swaps, the insurance issued against such transactions going wrong, into capital assets, and the insurance on foreign exchange trades underwent the same process. So long as investment traders agreed, anything could become money.

This was the fundamental flaw in Austrian economic theory that Greenspan failed to see. No economy, and ultimately no government, could survive the convulsions in money supply created by the spontaneous generation of money on this scale. The consequences of Menger's theory were the opposite of what his twentieth-century followers had claimed—they made government regulation of financial markets absolutely essential.

Having stepped down in 2006, Greenspan was no longer personally involved when it became clear that the corollary of Menger's theory was equally true—that money could be degenerated just as spontaneously. As news spread of the rising default rates on risky mortgages, trade in derivative bundles dwindled, and then quite suddenly in the summer of 2008 their standing as capital assets evaporated.

At a stroke, the health of financial institutions that held them became poisoned. The roll call included the investment bank Bear Stearns, with eleven billion dollars in equity but almost four hundred billion in potentially worthless assets; the American International Group, the largest insurers in the world, notionally worth more than $110 billion but whose London office alone issued credit swap defaults valued at more than $440 billion; and the blue-blooded investment bank Lehman Brothers, broker to more than a hundred hedge funds, with equity of $639 billion but potential debts of $1.3 trillion.

When Lehman Brothers was allowed to go bankrupt in September 2008 as Austrian economics required, the Dow Jones index dropped five hundred points, stock markets around the world fell by close to 5 percent, and more significantly, banks stopped lending to each other. The realization that money could dissolve so quickly left every financial institution haunted by the same nightmare: any bank, however vibrant it appeared to be from its visible asset sheet, might turn out to be bankrupt when the real value of its untradable assets was revealed. The marketplace was filled with zombie banks, and it was impossible to tell the living from the living dead. Fear halted lending and brought the entire mercantile capitalist system close to gridlock.

In every country, the rescue plan involved government intervention on a massive scale. In the United States alone, government guaranteed more than one trillion dollars in direct rescue funds, followed by trillions more in federally invented money, the so-called quantitative easing, designed to take the place of traders' invented money and persuade the banks to start lending again.

The Austrian experiment had failed.

Chapter Twenty-Two

Undoing the Damage

On October 1, 2008, ninety-year-old Mrs. Addie Polk, living in a white clapboard house in southwest Akron, Ohio, shot herself with a handgun when the sheriff arrived to serve a foreclosure writ on her. Although Mrs. Polk and her late husband had paid off their mortgage on the once-handsome building in the 1970s, a succession of brokers later persuaded the frail widow she could pay for health care by taking out loans on the increasingly dilapidated property. The last of these, for $45,620, was repayable in 2034 when she would be 116 years old. For the financial institution backing the mortgage, this was an asset with a leveraged worth of about $150,000. But after just three years Addie Polk found herself unable to keep up the payments and, despairing at the arrival of the sheriff at the door, tried to kill herself. Although the attempt failed, she died some time later in hospital.

Mrs. Polk was not alone in her desperation. By then, hundreds of thousands, and around the world millions, of home owners faced the same threat of losing the roof over their heads. But there was a particularly bitter irony about the fate of an elderly widow who, with her blue-collar husband, a worker on the Firestone tire factory production line, had put every spare dollar aside to buy their home. She had fallen victim, not just to mortgage sharks, but to an economic policy that was both unjust in its exploitation of the poor, and systemically unworkable.

The policy depended not merely on deregulation but the spread of what both Margaret Thatcher in the 1980s and President Bill Clinton in the 1990s called "a property-owning democracy." In Britain, this was achieved through "right to buy" legislation passed in 1980, allowing public housing tenants to purchase their homes at a heavily discounted rate. During Mrs. Thatcher's government, 1.5 million publicly owned houses were privatized in what she described as "one of the most important social revolutions of the century." By the end of that century, the proportion in private ownership had risen from just over half to more than 70 percent of all homes in Britain.

The change was smaller in the United States, a 5 percent gain from 1990 to 2007 to just shy of 70 percent, but it too was politically driven and designed to effect social change. "You want to reinforce family values in America, encourage two-parent households, get people to stay home?" Bill Clinton demanded, when launching his National Homeownership strategy in 1995. "Make it easy for people to own their own homes and enjoy the rewards of family life and see their work rewarded . . . This is about the way we live as a people and what kind of society we're going to have."

When the bones of the 2008 crash came to be picked over, his political intervention would take on a baleful significance. Large mortgage lenders like Countrywide Financial were leaned on by the administration to take "proactive creative efforts" to make loans easier; Congress chastized officials at Fannie Mae (the Federal National Mortgage Association) who were responsible for insuring mortgages against default and thus acted as the first gatekeeper on the road to securitizing home loans, for not guaranteeing riskier borrowers; and Wall Street and Washington agreed that, with house prices rising five times as fast as incomes, the buoyant market would at last square the circle that had bedevilled private property economies since the sixteenth century—there need be no more losers, everyone with a property would win.

It vindicated the political beliefs of Ludwig von Mises, Ayn Rand, and others born into an imperial world, that there was no need to care for the poor: they would be lifted on the rising tide of prosperity created by the triumph of the entrepreneurs. But what it rested on was a worldwide Ponzi scheme.

THE QUESTION OF OWNERSHIP lay at the heart of the boom and of the crash. Once the regulatory barriers were removed in the private property economies, the investment strategies adopted on Wall Street and in the City of London meshed directly with the economy of the industrial home. The growth of lending, from $500 million in 1990 to $2.6 trillion in 2007, drove property values up, powering the phenomenal expansion of the consumer economy and creating an apparently unquenchable appetite for automobiles, electronics, toys, clothes, and furniture.

To meet its demand, trade routes spread outwards to suppliers around the world, but especially in the Far East. In reciprocal fashion, American debt was sold everywhere from Oslo to Sydney, but the most significant buyers turned out to be the city and provincial as well as central governments in the coastal crescent from Shanghai to Beijing. The collapse of Communism in the Soviet Union in 1989, and the growing strength of China's market economy, made it appear that one economic system now circled the world. Soaring on the wings of hubris, Thomas Friedman named his popular book on the globalized economy *The World is Flat*, while Francis Fukuyama updated Walt Rostow's development strategy and, in a scholarly article that assumed universal capitalism must lead to universal democracy, predicted "The End of History."

Absent from the writings of either author and from the published deliberations of the Federal Reserve and the Bank of England, of governments on either side of the Atlantic, of most of Wall Street and the City of London, and an array of international financial experts, was any suggestion that they understood that the phenomenon of globalization grew out of the disparity between two ways of owning the earth. While the apparent rise in the value of their properties enriched owners in the West, the lack of similar property rights in China drove as many as one hundred million peasants from the countryside to work in factories producing cheap consumer goods. They needed to earn the money for their retirement, but without property to invest in, their savings, amounting to two trillion dollars, had to be vested in the next safest location. This turned out to be U.S. treasury bonds.

The demand from Chinese and other foreign investors for American debt kept interest rates artificially low. Instead of being choked off by a rise in the cost of borrowing, mortgage lending remained buoyant, house values continued to climb, the consumer economy kept on expanding, and derivatives were still created, albeit with an ever-increasing proportion—it grew from 4 to 15 percent—of risky, or subprime, loans. In 2007, the accompanying exponential growth in derivative dealings, mortgage debt, foreign exchange, and insurance topped out at almost six hundred trillion dollars, and the sheer size of the financial colossus obscured the fact that most of it ultimately depended upon property. Only when the subprime mortgage market began to disintegrate in the summer of 2007 did the narrow basis of the boom become starkly apparent.

There were many penalties for failing to appreciate the pivotal role of the industrial home in the consumer economy—unemployment, tax rises, a decade of lost growth, a legacy of debt to later generations and, not least, the fate of Mrs. Polk and millions of property owners like her. But the damage that the Austrian experiment did to the democratic tradition that had grown up around private property dwarfed any harm it inflicted on the economy.

DURING THE THIRTY-YEAR EXPERIMENT, a transformation had taken place in other societies as they became linked to the globalized economy. In that period, the number of politically free countries, according to the index of democracy compiled by Freedom House, rose from forty-three to eighty-seven, home to three billion inhabitants or 43 percent of the global population. For "development" commentators, such as Professor Francis Fukuyama, this was cause and effect, the result of "an extraordinarily strong correlation between high levels of industrial development and stable democracy." But, as Fukuyama ought to have been aware, the 1992 paper he cited as evidence gave no more than the shakiest support for his belief that industrial development led to democracy.

Many of the countries offered as examples were from Eastern Europe and became democratic not because of industrialization but because they were liberated from the former Soviet Union by the end of the Cold War; others, such as Spain, Portugal, and Greece, were industrialized but then became dictatorships, and only later became democratic due to persistent pressure from western European neighbors; yet more, including South Korea, Taiwan, Uruguay, and Costa Rica, arrived at modernization through the prior redistribution of land as private property, while some at least of the remaining examples, such as Romania and Pakistan, were hardly shining examples of either industrialization or democracy. The author of the paper himself qualified the findings by saying that "economic development is not a prerequisite for democracy," a reservation amply confirmed by subsequent academic studies. Since then, Fukuyama's entire "development" thesis has been blown into oblivion by a series of Freedom House maps showing an entire swath of the globe from Moscow to Beijing and Hanoi occupied by some of the world's most vibrant industrial economies operating within repressive, undemocratic regimes.

In fact, the really striking feature of the new democracies, both in Europe and Latin America, was their near-unanimous rejection of the

Austrian-influenced private property model. In 1945, the common law democracies had served as a beacon to a war-torn world, demonstrating the freedom and equality that could be enjoyed by individuals in a stable private property society. Up to 1987, the influence of the United States Constitution so permeated aspirations to democracy that *Time* magazine claimed an analysis of 170 written constitutions showed all but ten to have borrowed "substantially" from the one drawn up in Philadelphia two centuries earlier. By 2012 that was no longer true.

IN HIS STATE of the Union address in 1941, Franklin D. Roosevelt, president of the largest, most privately propertied society in existence, put forward his vision of a future world "founded upon four essential freedoms." They comprised two positive freedoms, of speech and of worship, and two negative, freedom from want and from fear. All four were incorporated into the preamble to the Declaration on Human Rights adopted by the United Nations in 1948 as a flat statement that "the highest aspiration of the common people" was for "the advent of a world in which human beings shall enjoy freedom of speech and belief and freedom from fear and want."

To achieve that goal, a list of thirty human rights had been drawn up by an international committee chaired by Eleanor Roosevelt, the president's widow. The first article stated that "All human beings are born free and equal in dignity and rights," and the second that "Everyone is entitled to all the rights and freedoms set forth in this Declaration, without distinction of any kind, such as race, colour, sex, language, religion, political or other opinion, national or social origin, property, birth or other status." The right to own property "alone or in association with others" came in at number 17, with no indication that it was the source of a set of older and conflicting rights.

Although not binding on members of the United Nations, human rights had one immediate advantage: they solved what seemed to be an ineradicable weakness of property rights. It was manifested in the failure of two important groups of people, women and people of color, in the United States and the Commonwealth, as the British Empire had become since 1944, who, despite being property owners themselves, could not win social and political equality with white male owners. The web of sexual, social, and cultural prejudice that stood in their way was virtually immovable because masculinity and a pale skin were what defined a property owner.

The problem was exemplified by the educational program for African Americans instituted at the Tuskegee Institute in 1888 by Booker T. Washington, based on his assumption that African Americans could gain equality by showing that they possessed "industry, thrift, intelligence and property." But however wealthy the Tuskegee alumni became, the prejudice against their color remained, and those less privileged were subjected to oppression backed by the threat of murder and mutilation by a lynch mob. As one influential historian pointed out, Washington's strategy was doomed to failure, because at the time "Free black people were 'matter out of place.' Their emancipation was subversive of southern white freedom."

Washington's ideological opponent, W. E. B. DuBois, put equal rights of voting and education at the center of his campaign, and in the 1940s, before the United States endorsed the Declaration of Human Rights, the brilliant attorney Thurgood Marshall used the Bill of Rights to achieve a limited success. But it was after 1948, through landmark legal cases and the 1964 Civil Rights Act in particular enforcing equal rights in voting, education, jobs, and the provision of public services, that individual rights were seen to be the way around the prejudices of property.

American women were also included in the protection offered by Title VII of the 1964 act banning any discrimination in employment based on an "individual's race, color, religion, sex, or national origin," and by the Equal Employment Opportunities Commission set up to enforce the ban. When the Women's Movement gathered force in the 1960s, the statutory emphasis on individual rights provided the legal anvil against which its members hammered out cases of discrimination, both personal and professional.

In Britain, where racial discrimination sprang from 1950s immigration rather than nineteenth-century slavery, the resort to individual rights legislation and the creation of a Commission of Racial Equality in the 1970s came after the campaign for women's equality in education and employment had begun. Politically, women's rights traced their roots back to the suffragettes and the fight for votes in the early twentieth century, but socially it sprang into life with the invention of the contraceptive pill and the 1960s revolt against the remnants of the war's male-directed values. But the inability to shift attitudes of British white, masculine ownership without recourse to laws enforcing equal rights was equally fundamental to the movement to liberate women from the prejudices of a private property society.

Among the forty-four new democracies that were born between 1987 and 2008, there was a clear tendency to guarantee human rights above property rights. In the majority of their legal systems, generally derived at least in part from the German civil code, these individual rights were set in a context that stressed the importance of communal and family needs.

During the same period, as Austrian ideas sidelined the Lockean emphasis of property's reciprocal obligations, U.S. Supreme Court judgments, once frequently cited as pointers to desirable developments of law, were increasingly seen to be irrelevant outside North America. Even other private property societies, such as Canada, Australia, and New Zealand, shunned the narrowing focus of American legal developments, preferring instead to interpret private property law in the light of declarations of human rights. "Among the world's democracies," a recent study concluded in 2012, "constitutional similarity to the United States has clearly gone into free fall."

Quite evidently two forms of democracy had taken root in the free world. In fact the social democracies of Scandinavia and northern Europe that Hayek once warned would become Socialist dictatorships repeatedly came out ahead of most common law democracies when measured by such criteria as freedom of expression, lack of corruption, social equality and mobility, and ease of doing business. On a visit to Egypt soon after the fall of President Mubarak, Justice Ruth Bader Ginsburg of the Supreme Court acknowledged how remote American democratic values had become. To an audience desperate to establish constitutional guarantees of their new-won liberty, she advised, "I would not look to the United States Constitution if I were drafting a constitution in the year 2012."

One explanation is that the Constitution is old and inflexible, but it was just as inflexible and not very much younger in 1987 when it was still a democratic model. From a searching analysis of 729 constitutions adopted by 188 countries between 1946 and 2006, it is clear that sympathy for its values turned to antipathy during the 1980s and 1990s, the very years when the Austrian version of private property capitalism took over in the United States and Britain, and began to be exported around the world by globalization.

The more that supporters of the Austrian system insisted economic liberty was equivalent to personal freedom, the quicker they eroded the moral standing of the common law system with its guarantees of individual liberty based on a reciprocal responsibility of the propertied for the unpropertied. By the twenty-first century, it had become clear that in a private property society taken over by Austrian economics full and positive freedom had become a privilege confined, as in the Austro-Hungarian empire, to the financially favored few. To the rest of the world, the beacon of liberty had become a lighthouse warning of the greedy rocks beneath.

The loss of moral authority was evident enough in the rejection of the model of individual freedom evolved by private property societies. But even more damaging was their inability to offer any example to follow in the place where it was most urgently needed, the fastest growing propertied economy in the world.

In 2004, just about when Mrs. Polk's last mortgage was being issued, Yang Wu, an excitable, stubborn restaurant owner living in Chongqing, central China's megacity, began to build a redbrick house in the Hexing Road. It replaced the family's dilapidated wooden dwelling, and according to its owner was as smart as any in Shanghai or Beijing. Three years later, a semiofficial development company, Chongqing Shengbo Real Estate, with plans for a shopping mall, slapped a compulsory purchase order on Yang's house and demanded that he move out. The neighbors had all accepted compensation and left, but in March 2007 Yang refused to go, even when the company's diggers laid siege by gouging out a thirty-foot deep trench around his house.

The image of his redbrick home perched precariously on a pillar of earth was flashed up on the Internet and across the world, drawing widespread sympathy. But Yang Wu's demonstration had a specifically Chinese resonance.

Since *fanshen's* abolition of landlord property in 1949, China's land had belonged to the State Council, with its use divided between urban and rural occupants. In practice, control of urban land was exercised by planning bureaus under the local Communist Party, but in the countryside and the suburbs, decisions about how the earth would be used were made by the working brigades of thousands of agricultural collectives. This division was embodied in the *hukou*, an internal passport that defined each person as either "urban" or "rural" and restricted the holder to the area where she or he lived. Urban dwellers enjoyed privileges such as fixed rations and the right to move within the city, but peasants were expected to feed themselves as well as meeting food quotas, and they were confined to their particular collective in a manner not far from serf legislation.

Through all the upheavals of Mao's rule, the essential shape of rural organization had remained intact until 1978, when Deng Xiaopeng launched the economic revolution, known as "reform and opening." City dwellers like Yang then became eligible to buy thirty-year leases for their homes, while in the countryside individual households were allowed the right to use specific parcels of land for up to thirty years and sell the produce on the free market, so long as they first supplied the state with a fixed quota of rice or wheat at set prices. This contractual ownership, or *chengbao* arrangement, had ancient roots. It harked back to the fourth century BC when the Confucian scholar Mencius taught that farmers should be allowed exclusive use of their fields so long as they fed the nonfarmers in the community.

Unmistakably in the twenty years after Deng's reforms, Chinese farmers more than fulfilled the conditions of the *chengbao* system. Year on year, agriculture rivaled industry by increasing productivity by almost 8 percent annually. Not only were state quotas met, but farmers' markets opened up in every town and village in the country to sell off the surplus they had grown of rice and wheat, bean curd and salted plums, carp, catfish, almonds, and chillies. Farmers earned more than ever before, and their success increased the value they attached to the fields and fishponds they worked.

Chengbao rights, however, also provided developers with their opportunity. The rights were always allocated by "the collective," but despite its immense power as the embodiment of the state, the collective was never defined. Sometimes it was the village where the land lay, sometimes the collection of villages that administered the area, and sometimes the township or tax district. Since collectives were often represented by only a few village delegates and a party official, one collective might easily overrule another or in turn be overruled by a planning bureau backed by Communist cadres from a neighboring city.

With party backing, it was easy for speculators to hack free what land they wanted from *chengbao* possession. In less than three decades, the megacity of Zhenzhen had grown from a fishing village near Hong Kong to an urban empire of more than eight million inhabitants, and gobbled up close to two hundred square miles of homes, fields, and ponds. But Zhenzhen was only one of 160 cities with populations of more than one million that clawed into the countryside to provide housing and employment for their inhabitants. Their centers were usually planned, but much of the outer growth was uncontrolled. Typical was the random appropriation of a peasant commune to build a gas station outside the sprawling complex of Zidong in Sichuan Province, accomplished in a morning in 2007 with the help of several hundred militia to bulldoze houses and smash away protesting villagers.

The huge loss of agricultural land arbitrarily removed for industrial development—in 2000 a record fifteen million acres were taken, more than 5 percent of the total farmland in China—provoked increasingly fierce confrontations between farmers and developers. In 2005 alone, the country suffered an epidemic of riots and violence, with more than eighty-six thousand mass protests involving police and militia reported, not counting innumerable lesser confrontations. That same year, both China's administrative government, headed by Premier Wen Jiaobao, and its parallel, the Communist party, under General Secretary Hu Jintao, began to consider the hitherto unthinkable possibility of creating more clear-cut property entitlement to land in order to restore harmony to the countryside.

Land was not like industry. To the surprise of Deng Xiaopeng's hard-line Maoist critics, the capitalist system of privately owned factories and shops that developed under the formula "Socialism with Chinese characteristics" did not undermine the control of the Communist party. Security and harmony, it turned out, were as important to business as to government. Indeed, since industrialists and retailers needed the approval of Communist cadres at local, regional or national levels for major decisions, such as the location of a plant or the involvement of foreign investors, the existence of private ownership actually extended the party's influence, albeit with dramatically increased risk of corruption.

But where land was concerned, private ownership was a direct threat to party control. The very impetus behind the Communist revolution had been the use of private property rights by landlords to exploit vulnerable peasants. In 2005, when the question first began to be seriously considered, Professor Gong Xintian, a legal expert at the University of Beijing and an unrepentant Maoist, published an open letter to the People's National Congress condemning any move in that direction. "Recognition of the socialist public ownership system forms a most distinguishing feature of a socialist constitution, as opposed to a capitalist one," he asserted ponderously. "Therefore, 'the sanctity of public property under socialism' becomes one of the most defining characteristics of a socialist constitution . . . [It provides] the material basis for citizens' equal rights and for the Communist Party's own rule . . . If this basis is gone, what place remains for the Communist Party?"

Irritated by his article, the party hierarchy forbade Gong from publishing anything more on the subject. In 2007 the People's National Congress rubber-stamped a new property law that had been hammered out behind closed doors. But the professor's awkward point could not be so easily brushed aside—the sovereignty of the Communist Party, its moral authority, lay in its possession of the earth.

ONLY THE MOST POWERFUL INTERESTS could have persuaded China's two governments to remove such a vital plank from the party's claim to legitimacy. Peasant agitation might have put property rights on the agenda, but it counted for little within the People's National Congress and the party's Central Committee. There the strongest pressure for reform came from members of the State Organs committee and the Business Works committee—the representatives of China's booming industrial sector—anxious to boost domestic demand through growth in the housing market. Allied with them were representatives of the provinces and of municipalities, such as the megacity of Zhenzhen, well-known for advocating greater clarity in property law to facilitate its own acquisition of land for development.

Not surprisingly, their fingerprints were evident in the way the new property law favored corporate interests rather than those of individuals. It was modeled on the *Bürgerliches Gesetzbuch*, itself a product of German business and bureaucracy.

Nevertheless, the 2007 law unmistakably expanded the rights of property owners. In earlier legislation, such rights had been mentioned only in relation to the state, the one real owner of the land. The very term for property, *wu*, was not legally applied to land until 2002. By contrast, the new law used both the word *wu* in reference to property of all kinds, and, for the first time, with the added character *quan*, meaning "rights." Explicitly it declared that the *wuquan* of "private persons" should be protected as much as those of the state.

For city residents, the wording made it clear that they could buy, sell, and mortgage buildings almost as freely as in Hong Kong where British property regulations still applied. The consequences were immediate and direct. In 2009, the first full year of postrecession business, the value of the Chinese residential housing market grew by 80 percent to well over half a trillion dollars. Today the buying power of urban property owners has created a consumer economy that has almost doubled in value since 2005 to $2.1 trillion in 2012, the size of France's total GDP, and will account for almost 50 percent of China's GDP in 2015—in most private property economies it represents about three-quarters of GDP. In terms of economic policy, it commits China to following the Western model of using the value of the industrial home to mop up the overproduction of industrial capitalism.

Peasants were not given the same degree of freedom, but their *chengbao* agreements were no longer to be regarded as contracts that might be torn up for failure to meet their quota, but as something closer to leasehold property. Within limits, their holdings could be bought, sold to other farmers, and mortgaged. Even more significantly in the long-term, rural land was clearly stated to belong to "members of the collective," that is to people, rather than to a mere abstract "collective."

However, the 2007 law was not designed to meet the needs of either peasants or city dwellers. As events confirmed, its chief purpose was to make possible a more orderly transfer of land from land-rich collectives to urban developers, and to clarify the legality of corporate ownership. The land grab not only continued, but accelerated, leading to no fewer than 180,000 violent confrontations in 2011.

What drives the cities' growth is the gigantic migration from the countryside that has tilted the population from rural to urban—officially about half of all Chinese, almost seven hundred million, lived in cities in 2012; unofficially there might have been as many as 920 million. To meet their needs, city and provincial governments account for four fifths of all China's public expenditure, providing everything from housing and roads to electricity and water. They raise a substantial part of that money by selling to developers the land taken from peasants and pocketing the profit.

Like the Manchu government of the Qing Dynasty, the Communist Party needs to contain the divergent goals of regional and municipal governments on the one hand and on the other its own centralized control backed by its modern "bannermen," the increasingly powerful People's Liberation Army. This priority dictated the choice of Xi Jinping as General Secretary in succession to Hu Jintao. The son of one of the party's founders, Xi earned his spurs supervising the government of Shanghai, the least Communist, most independent-minded megacity in China. In a 2009 cable from the U.S. embassy in Beijing published by Wikileaks, Xi was described as "repulsed by the all-encompassing commercialization of Chinese society, with its attendant *nouveau riche*, official corruption, loss of values, dignity, and self-respect." His chief means of political management, other than by exercising the imperial power of the party, was through Beijing's control of finance—despite the sums raised from the sale of land, city and provincial governments must rely on central government subsidies for almost a third of their revenue. Kept on a short financial rein, Shanghai caused Beijing less trouble than most other provincial governments.

That this was the preferred policy for controlling regional government became clear from the spectacular fall from grace of Xi's chief rival, the more flamboyant Bo Xilai, who had been in charge of Chongqing. Adopting an overtly neo-Maoist policy, Bo had cracked down on behavior deemed to be excessively capitalist, but in a way that also boosted his personal standing. Corruption charges against Bo, and his wife's convenient conviction for murder, allowed the party's leadership to make known its disapproval of both parts of his strategy.

Nevertheless, in a potentially significant move in 2010, both Xi and Bo decided to place a small tax on mansions and second homes in their cities. A heavier tax on the property and rising wealth of the owners of urban land would solve the cities' chronic funding problems and give them greater independence. It would also give individual owners a direct interest in how government was conducted. At present, neither they nor the Communist party dare risk such an outcome.

The goal for the Communist party under Xi Jinping's leadership is therefore clear. It is to manage the cities so that they in turn can meet the aspirations of their property interests without granting any political rights.

The issue of property rights is not one that arouses much outside sympathy. Instead, visiting foreign leaders, including those of private property societies, repeatedly prefer to raise the question of China's dire record on human rights, for the excellent reason that these embody the universal aspiration for social justice. Nevertheless, for most of the time the defense of property interests through representation and consent is of wider and more practical concern for most Chinese.

The model of the consumer economy that China has adopted will only accentuate its citizens' need for political protection of their industrial homes. Denuded, however, of the tradition of individual and political rights founded on social justice that private property societies developed over centuries, no outside power has so far been able to give support to that basic drive that in the past always led on to democratic change.

THE TECTONIC PRESSURES at work in China operate with equal force in private property societies, but in almost mirror fashion. While China's system can only function by denying the political power that should go with individual ownership, the democratic marketplace in the United States and Britain requires equality of access to as many owners as possible. The concentration of wealth in a tiny percentage of the population of both countries during the last thirty years has clearly distorted the balance in favor of a small number of exceptionally powerful factions. If the goal for China's twin governments is to keep political power concentrated within the hands of the Communist Party, the task for a private property government is no less demanding—to redistribute it more widely.

In his obsessive calculations about what was needed to maintain equality in the political marketplace, James Madison sometimes seemed like a person pitching a tent in a gale, endlessly tweaking its supports, tightening the ropes here, slackening them there, lifting a flap on one side, hammering in a peg on the other. His goal was balance. To achieve it, the popular but potentially over-powerful commercial factions might have to be taxed heavily, while the unpopular faction that supported the cancerous institution of slavery might have to be protected. But without balance, the free competition for democratic power would be distorted.

In the late twentieth century, one faction did especially well in both the United States and Britain. In the United States, successive administrations brought down the 70 percent rate of personal tax for top earners in the 1970s to 35 percent in the 1990s, and capital gains tax from 40 percent to 15 percent; accompanied by changes in accountancy practices, the latter became especially beneficial to highly rewarded executives. The cuts left a gap that had to be filled by borrowing. Reagan increased the national debt by two hundred billion dollars, and George W. Bush by five trillion. As a result, the bond market that provided the loans became a more powerful influence on government policy than the electorate. But to service the interest and eventually pay back the principal, all taxpayers, including those unborn, inescapably became liable for a burden once shouldered immediately by the wealthiest.

Simultaneously, a policy of paying increased rewards to corporate executives saw the incomes of CEOs of Fortune 500 companies that had been forty-two times larger than that of the average worker in 1980 rise to become three hundred times greater in 2010. In Britain, salaries of FTSE 100 companies chief executives grew from 17 times average pay in 1980 to 220 times.

By 2007 there were 392,220 taxpayers in the United States with gross incomes of a million dollars or more, but the aggregate income, including capital gains, of the wealthiest four hundred Americans reached almost ninety-one billion dollars every year, meaning that on average each received an annual income of $227.4 million while paying tax at a rate of only 21.5 percent. Income eventually translates into capital wealth, and in 2007 the ultrarich four hundred owned as much wealth as the 150 million poorest Americans. Slightly below these peaks, the top 1 percent of Americans owned 34 percent of the nation's wealth while the bottom 90 percent owned just 29 percent. Hayek's goal of creating an aristocracy of wealth had been achieved.

Belatedly, even Alan Greenspan recognized that inequality on this scale "is not the type of thing which a democratic society—a capitalist democratic society—can really accept without addressing." James Harrington, author of *Oceana*, would have understood Greenspan's unease. Extremes of inequality in the distribution of property had to be accompanied by extremes of inequality in the distribution of power. And that would inevitably change the nature of government.

In the early twentieth century, the American commentator Vernon Parrington summarized in a sentence the dilemma that a century later gnawed at the heart of American politics: "We must have a political state strong enough to deal with corporate wealth," he wrote to a friend, "but how are we going to keep the state with its augmenting power from being captured by the force we want to control?"

In Britain, a similar tax regime left the top 3 percent of British taxpayers owning almost 80 percent of the country's personal wealth in 2008. That same year, a House of Commons committee was sufficiently alarmed to comment on the public's assumption that "there is an inside track, largely drawn from the corporate world, who wield privileged access and disproportionate influence." It singled out the influence wielded by "commercial corporations and organisations . . . which is related to the amount of money they are able to bring to bear on the political process."

Prominent among them were the financial chieftains of the City of London whose insistence on lax regulation helped make the City the most dynamic center in the globalized financial economy and home to more than 720 international banks and other financial institutions. By 2008, it contributed a fifth of Britain's GDP. In the wake of the crash, it also became clear that City practices had slithered beyond laxness to the borderline of corruption and malfeasance. Not only had three of Britain's largest banks engaged in dealings that would have bankrupted them but for a taxpayers' bailout—a fourth, Northern Rock, the smallest though hardly the most irresponsible, was allowed to go to the wall—but collectively London's major banks had mis-sold financial services worth almost three billion dollars to their customers, had routinely lied about lending rates between themselves, and persistently and deliberately misled the city's vestigial regulatory agencies about the way they conducted business. During this period their CEOs saw their salaries rise ten times over to ten million dollars a year, 230 times the average income of the taxpayers who were forced to save their bankrupt skins.

The reason why the traditional private property structure appealed to such a wide range of political reformers from eighteenth-century France to twentieth-century Japan was that it was seen to be fairer than the existing system. In the United States, fairness was generally taken to be a matter of equality of opportunity, while elsewhere it was measured more by equality of outcomes, but until the 1970s, private property societies could broadly claim to deliver on both counts. More individuals had the opportunity to succeed, and those societies also enjoyed greater wealth, better health and rising life expectancy than their competitors. All that had changed by 2008.

A slew of research by the Brookings Institution showed that social mobility had grown to be significantly higher in Scandinavia than in the United States and Britain. Meanwhile surveys by the Organization for Economic Co-operation and Development found that, measured by markers such as life expectancy and infant mortality, the health of Americans had dropped into the bottom half of the OECD's membership of forty nations. In Britain, the existence of the National Health Service softened the impact of inequality, but it too lagged behind major European competitors in terms of social mobility and public health.

More surprisingly, judged by the yardstick of wealth creation that Hayek preferred, his model fared worse than the system it replaced. During the twenty-five years from 1951 to 1976 when the United States labored under a business-deterring, high-taxation, heavily regulated regime, America launched no fewer than twenty-three of the largest companies in the world, three more than were created in the thirty-year Austrian period of low taxation, high rewards, and light regulation from 1976 to 2007. And after recording annual returns close to 10 percent from 1950 to 1970, Wall Street's returns dropped to a pallid reward of 5.58 percent for the two decades from 1988 to 2008. Far from equality being bought at the expense of economic efficiency, the economy expanded faster during the very years when, as the author Robert Putnam judged it, "America was . . . more egalitarian than it had been in more than a century."

In Madison's political marketplace, each faction was expected to fight for its own interests, the wealthiest as much as the poorest. The policy of cutting taxes and deregulating the markets had been publicly discussed and repeatedly voted for by the electorate and, until the crash, the outcome apparently benefited the entire nation. The richest had certainly done best from the boom, but it could be argued that inequality was inseparable from capitalism, and from their earnings the top 1 percent contributed up to a quarter of the government's revenue from income taxes. The process had been entirely democratic—yet it had ended by undermining the system that made it possible.

In eighteenth-century Britain, the landowners who spearheaded the first free-market capitalist system had behaved in the same way, using their political dominance to safeguard their own interests. With the backing of the law, they looted public land, insulated their property against moneylenders, and entailed their estates to keep them in the family. And to achieve these ends, they also corrupted the parliamentary system to the breaking point so that other groups could not gain access to the political marketplace. Yet none of this was intended, or even perceived, by a class that prided itself on its public-spirited patriotism.

When Warren Buffett called on Congress in 2011 to cease protecting millionaires "as if we were spotted owls or some other endangered species," it was precisely the corrosive effect on public opinion that he cited as the reason for taxing the very rich more heavily. "Americans are rapidly losing faith in the ability of Congress to deal with our country's fiscal problems," he wrote. "Only action that is immediate, real and very substantial will prevent that doubt from morphing into hopelessness."

Justice was not just a moral good, it was, as Adam Smith had always counseled, a practical necessity. Unless most people could be persuaded to believe that the market was fair, in both politics and the economy, it must wither and fail.

Chapter Twenty-Three

Feeding the Future

In one area of the world economy, resources remain infinite and the crisis of overproduction can never happen. Nevertheless, the phenomenon of intellectual property still bears the shape of its landed ancestor, especially in the assumption that the owner has a natural right to its exclusive possession that the law must protect. And because there appears to be no limit to the unknown world that might be divided up into patentable ideas, it seemed, until recently, as though a frontier territory were perpetually opening up ahead that might be settled, marked out, and turned into property simply by the efforts of the pioneer.

The tumultuous growth of intellectual property can be measured through the frequency of the term's use in U.S. federal courts—from an occasional reference up to the 1970s, it suddenly burgeoned to more than two hundred in the 1980s, then went through the roof, more than quadrupling in each of the next two decades—and in the figures conjectured for its economic value. In America, measuring the value of all industries heavily dependent on intellectual property in 2011, it was deemed to have created about 40 million jobs and to be worth five trillion dollars, or more than 34 percent of GDP. Using the narrower definition of direct investment, the British government estimated the value of intellectual property in 2011 at sixty-five billion pounds, more than one hundred billion dollars, or about 10 percent of GDP, and noted that during the previous decade investment in it had become greater than in business hardware.

All such figures are rendered suspect, however, by the vagueness of the term, and the constant extension of new claims to property rights in such unexpected areas as the lighting of the Eiffel Tower, the identification of a gene, and the shopping habits of a credit card user. One trend, however, is unmistakable—a corporate goal to make property out of anything that has required original mental activity. Without much thought, the trend has been backed by both courts and governments on the assumption that it will stimulate innovation with benefit to all. That assumption is loosely based on the phenomenal success of private property economies following the transformation in the eighteenth century of patents from royal monopoly into propertied ownership.

However, as the early industrialists understood, the connection between patent ownership and innovation was not direct. In reality, inventiveness was initially stimulated less by the law's defense than by the wide dispersal of information that resulted from the reluctance of judges to grant innovators a monopoly on the use of their ideas. A patent could only be justified, said England's Chief Justice Mansfield, if it was for something "substantially and essentially newly invented," and if "the specification [accompanying the claim for a patent] is such as instructs others to make it."

Even in the United States, where patents were more easily granted, the 1836 Patent Act made clear that such a monopoly could only be in the public interest if in return the inventor provided a model to show how the idea worked and a description written "in such full, clear and exact terms . . . as to enable any person skilled in the art or science to which it appertains . . . to make, construct, compound and use the same." As late as 1863, the German congress of economists questioned whether the innovation was worth the cost of the monopoly, and concluded "that patents of invention are injurious to the common welfare." Although every industrialized country adopted the 1886 Berne Convention on the protection of copyrights and its gradual extension to cover patents, well into the last quarter of the twentieth century the inadequacy of legal protection available to inventors and industrialists left many reluctant to file for patents for fear that a rival might copy the specification, modifying it sufficiently to avoid being sued for infringement.

A sea change occurred in the course of the 1980s and 1990s. Not only were defenses strengthened, they were extended from inventions and copyrights to cover trade secrets, distinctive designs, and trademarks. Between 1983 and 2010, the number of patents issued each year in the United States increased fourfold from 64,000 to 244,000, and in the United Kingdom from just over two thousand to more than ten thousand. Under pressure from the motion picture industry, the life of copyrights was extended from twenty-eight years after an author's death to seventy years, while other major corporate interest groups persuaded the courts that the appearance of a fast-food restaurant and the development of a surgical procedure should be judged to be a property exclusive to its creator. Any lingering belief that the public interest might be harmed by such monopolies disappeared.

During the Uruguay round of trade agreements concluded in 1994, the World Trade Organization brought into existence the concept of TRIPS or Trade-Related Aspects of Intellectual Property Rights. Every signatory nation was required to accept as intellectual property anything deemed to be so in another country "without discrimination as to the place of invention, the field of technology and whether products are imported or locally produced." Only where patents endangered public order or the environment could a national government modify the agreement.

Without public discussion, one particular kind of ownership was embodied in the TRIPS agreement and planted in the legal structure of every signatory nation of the WTO. Ignoring past concerns that monopolies constituted a restraint of trade, the TRIPS agreement asserted bluntly and fallaciously, "intellectual property rights are private rights" that had to be protected. Varieties of communal ownership of knowledge, such as the use of the periwinkle plant in traditional folk medicines in Madagascar, were deemed ineligible for protection, while the private, exclusive property that the pharmaceuticals company Eli Lilly claimed for its research into the plant after learning of its medical properties was instantly recognized, allowing the company to develop products from it worth two hundred million dollars worldwide. With TRIPS, the idea of private exclusive property that first appeared in relation to land in sixteenth-century England could be said to have conquered the world.

However, in the very year that the TRIPS agreement dispersed this system around the globe, the central edifice of intellectual rights threatened to evaporate through the even faster expansion of digitized information across the World Wide Web. In a prescient article written in 1994, John Perry Barlow, Grateful Dead lyricist and cofounder of the Electronic Frontier Foundation, warned of the impact of being able to express all information in binary form: "If our property can be infinitely reproduced and instantaneously distributed all over the planet without cost, without our knowledge, without its even leaving our possession, how can we protect it?"

Music, originally acoustic then electronic, proved to be especially vulnerable and attractive to copiers once it had been digitized, giving rise to a succession of file-sharing sites from Napster in 1999 to Megaupload and Pirate Bay in 2012 that arose to allow tracks and albums to be freely shared as MP3 files. Images removed from celluloid could be passed on almost as easily. Although lawyers for the artists and industries concerned sued for breach of copyright and succeeded in closing down the most prominent sites, their extension of property rights to digitized information was achieved at high cost to the public interest.

The problem was identified by Barlow, who pointed out that the nature of digitized property, in essence information about something in the physical world, rendered it so elusive that establishing ownership risked opening up an endless legacy chain as later information was discovered to have incorporated earlier information. Consequently, a successful claim to ownership of an early part of the chain had the potential to give ownership of all later information connected to it and of the inventions that stemmed from it—a nightmare scenario that gave rise to a series of billion-dollar court battles over smartphone technology in 2012.

There were notable exceptions to individually owned intellectual property—Wikipedia made its information freely available, propagating rather than possessing it, and Linus Torvalds, the Finnish inventor of the Linux operating system used in Android smartphones, developed it as an open source, cooperative venture—but their rarity seemed to prove the rule. The individualistic culture that had built up around the strange sixteenth-century way of owning the earth had become the norm by which other values were measured.

When Microsoft executives attacked Linux as "cancerous" and "un-American" in 2001, they were demonstrating not only how seriously they took the threat to their own privately owned operating system, but also their deep-seated, ideological reaction to an alternative built on different values. The same conceptual barrier had led Senator Henry Dawes in 1877 to dismiss the Cherokee tradition of owning the land in common because it did not encourage individualism. "There is no enterprise to make your home any better than that of your neighbor's," Dawes declared. "There is no selfishness, which is at the bottom of civilization."

Today, Dawes's failure to appreciate the value of any other principle, especially in respect to Native American culture, seems old-fashioned, but the owners of intellectual property who persuaded public opinion, law courts and legislatures, as well as the WTO, that greater protection of their individual rights would lead to greater innovation and more enterprise were thinking in exactly the same way.

Counterintuitive though it may seem, there is no independently sourced evidence to show stronger patent rights promote inventiveness. In fact the reverse is true. Research into innovation in sixty countries by Harvard's Professor Josh Lerner, covering a period of 150 years from the 1850s, showed that strengthening patents not only failed to encourage innovation, "the impact of patent protection-enhancing shifts on applications by residents was actually negative." Following a more detailed examination of the spread of protection since the 1980s, Lerner described its effects as an "innovation tax."

Despite the exponential rise in the number of patents, spending on research and development did not increase in either the United States or Britain, and the yields from each patent fell. The reason was simple. Every monopoly is a restraint of trade, and the more there are, the smaller the scope for new enterprises. Not only did the proliferation of patents and the spread of intellectual property hamper research in general, but the likelihood of expensive litigation deterred many firms from seeking to develop specific products. The effect on small and medium-sized enterprises was especially marked, since many decided to cut back on all research and development as a wasted expense. Among those firms that did continue to fund research, the budget for legal costs to defend their developments rose to at least 25 percent of what was spent on research. More insidiously, as even researchers in universities and government-funded institutions concede, what used to be a culture of sharing information on new discoveries has been replaced by one of secrecy for fear that a rival might patent results and so impede future development.

Digitization exaggerated the corrosive effect. In 1994, Barlow had warned that digitized property "would adhere to those who can muster the largest armies," and in 2010 Lerner discovered that indeed "an arms race" had developed as "the ability to litigate and expect to get substantial awards from litigation increased." In other words, the usefulness of any new idea had become of lesser importance than the chance of using the patent on it to pry damages from a rival or to knock the competition out of some potentially lucrative line of development. The damage done to the public domain by the extent of the monopolies never became an issue during these courtroom battles. Yet for all but the last few decades of inventive history, that had always ranked as a major concern.

Monopoly, by definition, damages competitiveness, but nowhere more destructively than in the realm of ideas. The consequences are already obvious in the pharmaceuticals industry. Using extensive political influence and the greater legal powers available to them since the early 1990s both domestically and internationally through TRIPS, pharmaceutical companies like Pfizer and Roche spent two decades successfuly defending wide-ranging patents on their products. But a whole generation of patents issued in the 1990s for blockbuster drugs, such as the acid reflux treatment Nexium and the antidepressant Abilify, with annual sales of $140 billion, have begun to expire—the industry terms it is a "patents cliff"—without any new breakthrough medicines to replace them.

Significantly, the serious work on most of these megaearners began in the 1980s, before the most draconian protection was in place, and was grounded often enough in still earlier research carried out in university laboratories where information was often freely shared. In other words, innovation flourished, as it did at the start of the Industrial Revolution, when patent support was weak, and the number of monopolies granted was small.

Nevertheless, it is easy to understand why the great barons of intellectual property should behave like their landed predecessors, the Polish *szlachta* and eighteenth-century British aristocracy, and use all their power to protect their estates against trespassers. The very nature of exclusive ownership rewards those who can best defend it. That is the prize that drives owners to seek political influence. But the efficiency of the marketplace, both political and economic, makes it vital that their defense should never succeed. No politician who believes in democracy or economist who supports free enterprise should back any extension of patent law.

IN THE FIVE CENTURIES since the first private property society began to emerge, the justification for this monstrous method of owning the earth has constantly veered between the arguments of Hobbes and Locke: either it is a creation of civil law enforced by the power of the state or it is the realization of a profound and inescapable sense of justice innate in humankind. The difference between the two remains implicit in John Locke's original formulation. The point at which there is no longer enough and as good left over is the point where those rights no longer have a basis in natural justice, but simply in the corrosive impact of expensive lawyers and skewed courts.

Where the enclosure of intellectual property is concerned, the loss to the public interest may be slow and difficult to see, but in the ownership of the earth, the matrix for the entire structure of property law, the outcome is unmistakable. And as the world approaches the choke point of 2050, when nine billion lives must be sustained and sheltered from its finite resources, the basis on which its ownership rests will become critical.

The countdown began in 2008. Around the world, the cost of grain doubled within nine months, and other products, such as oilseed and pork, rose by more than two thirds. Although prices fell back in the next two years, another jump in 2011 to levels in some cases higher than before signified the end of the era of cheap food that began in the nineteenth century with the sailing of the *Dunedin* from New Zealand. "Our mindset was surpluses," Dan Glickman, a former United States secretary of agriculture, remarked when the second surge occurred in 2011. "That has just changed overnight."

Some causes were temporary—drought in Russia and Australia reduced wheat sales, while disease and floods in Indonesia and Thailand hit rice production—but one was systemic, the creation of bioethanol fuels derived primarily from maize and sugarcane. In 2005, legislation in the United States made its use mandatory, and within five years approximately 40 percent of American maize was being used as a gasoline alternative. Together with a constant proportion of biomass in Europe and South America diverted to generating energy in machines rather than human, it was enough to upset the balance between supply and demand.

Demonstrating the efficiency of the free-market, existing farmers planted more cereals in 2009 to take advantage of higher prices. But the potential profits also encouraged an expansion of interest from a new kind of owner. In June 2009, George Soros, doyen of international financiers, alerted investors to opportunities opening up beyond the tainted world of derivatives and securitization. "I am convinced that farmland is going to be one of the best investments of our time," he declared. "Eventually prices will get high enough that the market probably will be flooded with supply either through development of new land or technology or both, and the bull market will end. But that's a long ways away yet." Putting his money where his mouth was, Soros backed a six hundred million dollar investment fund to buy more than six hundred thousand acres of land in Latin America.

Until 2008, large-scale land purchases averaged less than two million hectares, or 4.8 million acres, a year, but in 2009 alone almost 110 million acres of farmland, seventy million of them in Africa, were bought by corporate purchasers from the United States, Europe, the Middle East, and China. The area was greater than the total of agricultural land in Germany, France, Belgium, Denmark, the Netherlands, and Switzerland combined. In Liberia, where traditional family holdings of a few acres used to be the norm, the median size of privately owned farms in 2011 leaped to almost 130,000 acres. Although Sudan's corporate holdings were smaller—a relatively modest median area of eight thousand hectares, almost twenty thousand acres, each—they amounted in total to almost four million hectares, or about one fifth of the country's cultivated land.

In Russia, 45 percent of the cultivated area was corporately owned in 2012, with the thirty largest companies farming a total of 6.7 million hectares. The proportion was higher both in Kazakhstan at 60 percent, and in Ukraine at 55 percent, where just forty companies, many of them foreign, owned 13.5 percent of the country's farmland in 2011. In southern Brazil, the median size of corporately owned sugar plantations was thirteen thousand hectares, and in Argentina the thirty leading agribusinesses, including Soros's, owned on average eighty thousand hectares each of cattle, wheat, and oilseed land.

The most authoritative estimate of the amount spent—foreign landgrabbing is too sensitive a topic to be open to easy scrutiny—is that one hundred billion dollars have been invested up to 2012. Some of the money came from China, which signed about thirty agricultural cooperation treaties that gave food producing companies, such as New Hope, a giant producer of pork and poultry on an industrial scale, access to farmland in countries ranging from Kazakhstan and Mozambique to the Philippines and Queensland. Other major investors were Saudi and Middle Eastern sovereign funds, and commodity producers such as Brazil's JBS, the world's biggest meat company, and Malaysia's Sime Darby, the world's largest source of palm oil. And a growing proportion, up to fifteen billion dollars in 2012, came from institutional investors in Europe and the United States, such as the $650 million Altima One World Agriculture Fund, which boasted of its aspiration to be "the first Exxon Mobil of the farming sector."

Investors were offered bonanza returns of up to 20 percent as profits from food production, supplemented by the almost forgotten factor of farmland's growing capital value. "The first thing we're going to do is to make money off of the land itself," promised Susan Payne of Emergent Asset Management, a British investment fund targeting farmland in Africa, in 2009. "We could be moronic and not grow anything and we think we'd still make money over the next decade."

Unlike the Jeffersonian model of the yeoman capitalist, however, twenty-first century rural capital accrued not to the tiller of the soil, or even to a landlord in the same country, but to absentee international investors, including such powerful players as Japan's $1.3 trillion government fund, the California Teachers' $131 billion fund, and Canada's $122 billion state pension fund.

The free-trade argument for encouraging Ethiopia, a country dependent on food aid, to sell prime agricultural land to the Spanish group Jittu Horticulture, which used it to grow and export 180,000 vegetables a week to the Middle East, was that it attracted investment to parts of the world that had not received it in the past. "We bring foreign currency into the country, enabling the government to buy wheat for the hungry," Jittu's manager in Ethiopia explained. "It's the government's responsibility to feed people who are unable to buy anything for themselves."

However, as Winston Churchill had said, the nature of the commodity—its necessity for existence, its limited extent, and its immobility—set it apart from any other. Whether judged by Qianlong's need for the mandate of heaven or the gut necessity of keeping its citizens quiet, no responsible government could afford to allow its territory to be owned for the benefit of foreigners when its own people were undernourished. Consequently, it was precisely in those worst-governed countries with no clear property law, where land was occupied tribally and worked by families, but nominally owned by the state, that it was easiest for foreign buyers to operate. As even the World Bank recognized "investor interest is focused on countries with weak land governance."

The bank's criticism inadvertently pointed to a basic flaw in the financial calculations behind the land grab. The weakness of such corrupt governments left them vulnerable to the resentment of their rural population. Dispossession caused as much anguish to African farmers as it did to Steinbeck's dust bowl Oklahomans. And where the materialist goals of the investors sparked an upsurge in sectarian values, there was no certainty that any government at all would survive the explosion.

Curling through the arid, rock-ribbed landscape of the Sahara Desert, the clear flow of the river Niger that began as a cascade five hundred miles to the west in the mountains of Guinea slows to a swampy ooze in the northern regions of Mali, one of the world's poorest states. Across a flat expanse of red dust and grit, it spreads out into a gigantic inland delta where green fields of maize and rice grow around a web of ditches and canals that irrigate about half a million acres of land. Like many Islamic desert societies, ownership evolved a communal pattern, with tribes claiming use of particular areas and controlling access to unirrigated pasture and reserve land, while specific parcels of land, measuring around three acres, were recognized as belonging to individual families though liable to redistribution by village elders according to need and to rank. Under French colonial rule, ownership of the water, without which the land was useless, was vested in a shadowy government body, the *Office du Niger*. In 2009, however, this traditional shape was upset by forces from outside.

The first of the outside elements was a sovereign fund from Colonel Muammur Gaddafi's Libya that leased the water rights to a quarter of a million acres from the *Office du Niger*. It was followed by investors from the Saudi royal family, from China, and by the Millennium Challenge Corporation (the MCC) from the United States, who together secured leases covering about four hundred thousand acres. Some of this land was tribal pasture and some desert, but all had the promise of irrigation from the delta water. The leaseholders undertook to invest heavily in turning desert to productive arable land, and, with the exception of the MCC, all expected to export the maize, sorghum, and rice they grew there.

The MCC, created by the U.S. Congress in 2004, proposed to survey the almost four hundred thousand acres it leased, dividing it into parcels of twelve acres, twenty-five acres, and upward of seventy acres, for sale with individual title first to Mali's farmers and then to anyone prepared to invest. In effect, the Public Lands Survey was being introduced to the Niger delta. Put together, the different schemes would provide the irrigation canals, roads, and secure storage silos needed by modern agriculture, more than doubling both the area of arable land and its productivity.

Threatened with dispossession, however, the delta farmers protested fiercely against both the attempt to take their land and to modernize their society. Instead, they proposed the allocation of existing parcels of land to the families who worked them, but with secure leasehold title to give an incentive to improve the soil's fertility and conditions to prevent it being sold to outsiders. When the offer was ignored, the rebellious delta farmers promised Mali's distant, corrupt government in Bamako that foreigners would not be allowed to take their land.

The significance to the wider world of this remote, anonymous disturbance became clear in March 2012. Tuareg tribesmen mounted on pickup trucks armed with the machine guns and rocket launchers they had employed in the successful coup against Colonel Gaddafi invaded the delta region, encountering no resistance from a farming community that in the past had always opposed a nomadic people they regarded as natural enemies. The Tuareg in turn were swiftly displaced by militant Islamists who set up an al-Qaeda-friendly regime, attracting recruits from all over west Africa and creating links between the jihadist group Boko Haram in Nigeria and fundamentalists in Algeria, Libya, and Egypt. The drugs trade moved in to fund their activities, and when the French intervened militarily in 2013 the jihadists scattered into the mountains to the north of the country to continue their mission.

The pattern of dispossession leading to rural upheaval that created an opening for terrorist activity was not new. In the late 1950s, the adoption of Rostow's development strategy prompted a prolonged American attempt to modernize Afghan society through industrialization. At huge expense, a network of irrigation dams and canals were dug, and a hydroelectric power station was constructed in Helmand province to provide power for the entire region. It seemed such a model piece of development, the area was generally referred to as "Little America." Unfortunately, lack of drainage and water salinity left much of the soil unfit for growing anything but opium poppies, while the rush of incomers to Helmand and the neighboring province of Kandahar removed control of the land from the old hierarchy of clan chiefs and regional warlords. After the expulsion of the Soviet army in 1992, tribal patterns reasserted themselves elsewhere in Afghanistan. But in those two disturbed provinces the only structure awaiting the returning mujahideen resistance fighters was a form of Islam opposed to any form of modernism. It was no coincidence that Little America should have become the birthplace of the Taliban and eventually home to Osama bin Laden.

In the future, land ownership and government are liable to be undermined in similar fashion as the pressure from the world's rising population meets the growing buying power of corporate investors. The task of feeding nine billion people in the middle of the twenty-first century will create such a mass of urgent and seemingly insoluble problems, it might seem perverse to suggest that the most important is how the land is owned. But that will be the key to solving all the others.

In the twentieth century, the World Bank's research on the experience of Taiwan, South Korea, and elsewhere showed that equitable land distribution was fundamental to social stability and thus the key to economic growth. Even in the twenty-first century, it will continue to be a robust model. More than three billion people still live in rural areas, and the poorest 50 percent of them depend for survival on the produce of small plots of land that for various reasons they cannot clearly own.

Even in India, one of the world's fastest growing economies, two hundred million people still live undernourished, and a generation of children is growing up stunted and malformed for lack of food, because secure tenure of the land they work is almost impossible for "the meek and humble" small farmers who missed out on the Green Revolution. As a result, India actually produces less food than China despite possessing 40 percent more farmland.

Often security of possession is made impossible by the unwritten rules of tribal and clan possession requiring land to be redistributed according to need. But with perhaps one third of the world's food grown on small farms and supplied through local markets, the laborious process of enabling the family that tills the soil to establish tenure in a form suitable to local conditions is worth making for the double gain of improving the food supply and creating social stability.

The effectiveness of the model depends, as Wolf Ladejinsky insisted, on obtaining local consent. In Mali, MCC signed a contract with the government to promote "economic liberalism"—in the first seven years of its life, it expended almost nine billion dollars on twenty-six similar agreements—and undertook to lay the foundation of a private property society by stipulating that land should be measured out and registered, with secure title to individual owners. The disaffection of the delta farmers showed that the goal should have been security of tenure rather than social engineering.

DURING THE COLD WAR, the Green Revolution expanded the world's grain output by 270 percent, from 692 million tons in 1950 to 1.9 billion tons in 1999. To feed the anticipated growth in population might require a further increase of one billion tons, approximately 50 percent, by 2050. Part of this addition could come from higher yields—wheat harvests alone could increase by half in optimum conditions—but more land could also be brought into cultivation. The countries of the former Soviet Union hold 13 percent of the world's arable land, but are thought to produce just 6 percent of its grain and 3 percent of its meat. In 2008 less than half of Russia's potential farmland was being worked, and, according to a United Nations estimate, Brazil still farms less than one sixth of its potential arable land. Yet the greatest single source of extra food is to be found in the waste that presently occurs in its growth, transport, storage, and marketing. By some estimates, about a quarter of total production is lost in this way, and small gains in efficiency would produce large savings. Put together, the three ingredients make it very probable that the earth can sustain another two billion inhabitants—if the water holds out.

Agriculture already consumes up to 70 percent of the water used by the world's inhabitants, and irrigation needs will double existing requirements by 2050. More than 40 percent of global crops are grown on irrigated soil, but many sources are already under pressure from the demands of farmers. Great watercourses such as China's Yellow River and America's Colorado River are dry for much of the year in their lower reaches, and the largely invisible, underground supplies of water that are replenished over centuries have dropped by at least tens of meters, in some cases by up to a kilometer, since the Green Revolution. Shortages already affect cereal-rich areas in the North China plain, in the Punjab, known as India's breadbasket, and in the southern plains of the United States. Some two billion people presently depend on food grown on irrigated soil that, according to some estimates, will by 2030 be capable of supporting only one billion.

Drought and flood, unseasonable heat or cold, quickly produce shortages in a system finely balanced between supply and demand. And the earth itself may not be able to sustain the levels of intensive cultivation required. The soil's ecosystem becomes stressed in ways not wholly understood by excessive use of nitrogen-based fertilizers, depriving it of essential minerals and trace elements.

Each of these dangers exacerbates the global challenge of feeding the world's population, and increases the need for innovation to be released from the shackles of intellectual property law. But while the challenge is global, starvation is local. The severest famine rarely affects a whole country or even everyone within the area.

In 1943, the Nobel Prize–winning economist Amartya Sen was a schoolboy in Bengal when famine struck the province, now divided between India and Bangladesh, killing an estimated three million people. Yet Sen recalled that his wealthy family were untouched by the shortages, and "no one in my school or among my friends and relations had experienced the slightest problem during the entire famine; it was not a famine that afflicted even the lower middle classes." Nearly all who died were poor laborers without land to grow food or the ability to increase their wages to buy enough to keep themselves alive. Sen would later argue that famine was caused not by the shortage of food but by the inability of people to access it through the exchange of labor or money. Since supplies were always to be found somewhere in the world, famine represented a failure of government to make them available locally.

The imperative need for governments to respond to shortage and starvation is what puts the position of corporate landowners in the spotlight. Even the most corrupt administration would prefer to tear up its contract with a foreign owner rather than face hungry rioters in the streets. Nor would it be blamed in constitutional terms since the basic test of a government's legitimacy is to meet its citizens' entitlement to food. To force compliance, a corporate owner might in the past have turned to an international agency like the WTO, or to its own government, expecting to have sanctions applied to the defaulting government. But the potential for provoking insurrection and terrorism will bring into question the legitimacy of an absentee, foreign company's claim to exclusive possession of another country's vital and limited resource.

In other words, ownership based on a complex chain of international law cobbled together from civil, common, and commercial legal roots may be less substantial than it presently appears. But for centuries, another strategy has been adopted by landowners who needed to strengthen their claims to a scarce resource.

Disputes about water use date back at least to the growth of Babylonian civilization beside the Tigris and Euphrates Rivers in the third millennium BC. But so too do formal rules for resolving them. From the earliest times, excessive irrigation by an upriver farmer in a time of shortage has been seen to take place at the expense of another downriver, and the purpose of the rules has always been to regulate its use so that there is enough for both. In the arid southwest of the United States, agriculture and urban development continue to be governed by similar agreements, notably the 1922 Colorado River Compact specifying how much water should be released from the state of Colorado to users downriver in California, Arizona, and Nevada.

It is easy to suppose that rivalries, such as that between Turkey and Iraq about use of the Tigris and Euphrates Rivers, or between Vietnam and China about access to the headwaters of the Mekong River, must lead through intransigent demands to all-out war, but the evidence points the other way. Even three wars between India and Pakistan have not caused either of them to break the Indus Water Treaty they signed in 1960.

Underpinning these formal regulations for sharing water, as well as thousands of other informal arrangements, has been the understanding that it is worth limiting individual needs so that everyone benefits from a limited resource. However bitter the disputes, it is overshadowed by the realization that taking whatever one wants risks destroying the entire system and ruining everyone. Self-interest gives social awareness a sharp edge.

As domestic demand for land and its scarcity increase in the years ahead, foreign ownership will come under increasing pressure and ever closer scrutiny. From primarily selfish motives, most corporate investors will sooner or later realize that property based on state-enforced law looks less secure than the kind based on natural right. The basic Lockean premise is that such a right arises out of an innate sense of justice. On that basis a corporate owner's claim to property in land must ultimately depend on finding a way to make good the loss to those deprived of its use.

THE IRON LAW of private property turns out to be a paradox. Although it promotes individuality, it only works by giving equal weight to the public interest. That was the premise that Adam Smith specified for the working of the invisible hand, and James Madison for the operation of democracy. And most fundamentally, it is what involves everyone in a society that will reward a few more than the majority. The guardian of the public interest might be the press, the law, or the government, but ultimately it grows from humanity's simultaneous desire for individual fulfilment and for social justice.

Epilogue

A Final Trespass

Who possesses this landscape? –
The man who bought it or
I who am possessed by it?
False questions, for
this landscape is
masterless
and intractable in any terms
that are human.
A Man in Assynt by Norman MacCaig

I began work on this book in 2009 as an attempt to understand the circumstances of the economic crash. A tug at the broken banking thread pulled out the political failure of regulation, and that in turn led to the Austrian school of economics, and the particular meaning that Friederich Hayek and his colleagues gave to property and liberty. Thus step by step the focus of the book turned to ownership.

To 19th century Whig historians who took property to be the foundation-stone of democracy and to their Marxist successors who identified possession of the means of production as the central agent in shaping society and class consciousness, the impact of ownership across history was obvious. But that context is largely ignored by today's historians. Even those studying wills and inventories of possessions or specialists in consumer economies and gender politics, rarely examine their topics in the context of a need to assert possession. And in the realm of anglophone studies where property does attract attention, individually owned land is assumed unquestioningly to be the mark of an advanced society, not as a bizarre mutation alien to most of humanity.

Eventually ownership of the earth in every form became the focus of the book. I was aware that this might seem old-fashioned to the point of eccentricity. Nevertheless, I justified it to myself by arguing that the urge to possess land in one way or another had been the major driving-force in human society for most of its history. Although it had been displaced from that dominant position by industrialization, in some economies for almost two centuries but for no more than a few generations across the greater part of the world, the growing pressure from up to ten billion people on the earth's resources would, I felt, increasingly force its return to center-stage.

But the focus on land ownership yielded another advantage. It placed the emphasis on politics. Most attempts at a world view of history give the prioity to economics. To take two widely separated examples, in both Barrington Moore's 1966 *Social Origins of Dictatorship and Democracy: Lord and Peasant in the Making of the Modern World*, and Daron Acemoğlu's *Why Nations Fail: The Origins of Power, Prosperity and Poverty* published in 2012, the productive capacity of an industrial economy is assumed to be the foundation of democracy and international status. Not only does this analysis diminish the significance of pre-industrial institutions, it inevitably makes civilized society contingent on material prosperity; in Bill Clinton's encapsulation of political strategy, "It's the economy, stupid." But the success of an economy can only be measured by its growth. Since growth requires the accelerated consumption of limited natural resources, it is not a sustainable model in the long run.

If you concentrate on how a place is owned, however, the perspective changes. As this book demonstrates, matters of laws, of rights and of politics become crucial, taking precedence over economics. From that point of view, it is possible to arrive at a different distillation of what is important to humanity: "It's the neighborhood, stupid."

In other words, there is an alternative to the single, ultimately unviable measure of success imposed by economics. Around the world and throughout history, neighborhoods have succeeded in a million different ways. It all depends on how the earth is owned.

Acknowledgments

In the years since I began work on *Owning the Earth*, I have tried out my thoughts on the subject with almost everyone I have spoken to for more than five minutes. Almost all responses, including incomprehension and boredom, were useful, but among those to whom I owe most, I should like to thank the following particularly: Dr. Penry Williams and Professor Alan Ryan, both of New College, Oxford University; Professor Kevin Miles, Earlham College, Indiana; Professor Tom Schmiedeler, Lawrence University, Kansas; the late Professor Derick Thompson, Glasgow University; Robin Blackburn; the late John Roberts; Bernard Planterose; George Rouse; David Skinner; Chris Handley; Steve Thompson, Andy Wilkinson; Misha Smetana and Veronika Khokhlova.

I acknowledge with gratitude the professional assistance of the staff at the London Library, the British Library, the Library of Congress, the Massachusetts Historical Society, the American Philosophical Society, the New York Public Library, the National Archives and Records Administration in Washington D.C., and the National Institute of Standards and Technology in Gaithersburg, Maryland.

I would also like to record my thanks to my agent, Peter Robinson.

Closer to home, I must express how much it means in the solitude of writing to have the love and support of friends and family, especially of Clico and Gerald Kingsbury, Alan and the late Joanna Smith, Lyn Cole, Richard Morris, Paul Houlton and Charlotte Desorgher, and above all of my darling wife, Marielou.

Finally, I want to record the unpayable debt I owe to George Gibson, publishing director of Bloomsbury USA, who is the best of editors and the staunchest of friends.

Notes

Introduction: The Birth of a Revolution

1 *a storm of appalling violence*: The vivid firsthand account of the Newfoundland expedition comes from *Sir Humphrey Gilbert's Voyage to Newfoundland* by Edward Hayes, originally incorporated into Richard Hakluyt's *The Principall Navigations, Voiages and Discoveries of the English Nation* (London: George Bishop and Ralph Newberie, 1589), www.gutenberg.org/ebooks/3338. *Principall Navigations* also contains a portrait of Gilbert's character.

2 *crystal ball or scrying stone*: the British Museum has a crystal ball, and the Science Museum in London has a flat black disc known as a Claude stone, both of which belonged to Dr. Dee. Each was apparently used in his esoteric researches, especially after his association with Edward Kelley; see *John Dee's Conversations with Angels: Cabala, Alchemy, and the End of Nature* by Deborah E. Harkness (Cambridge and New York: Cambridge University Press, 1999).

2 *"5,000 akers of ye new conquest"*: July 3, 1582, entry in *The Private Diary of Dr. John Dee* (London: The Camden Society, 1841–42). The deal was made with Sir George Peckham, another of Gilbert's partners. But in 1580, Gilbert had promised Dee everything north of the fiftieth degree of latitude, a claim that would have given him most of Canada.

2 *"all the soyle of all such lands"*: "Letters Patent to Sir Humfrey Gylberte," available online at http://avalon.law.yale.edu/16th_century/humfrey.asp.

2 *"the elevation of the pole"*: Hayes, *Humphrey Gilbert's Voyage.*

3 *an adult must consume a minimum*: Calorie counting is as much assumption as science. The Food and Agriculture Organization of the United Nations's estimate is at www.fao.org/hunger/en.

3 *the challenge of caring for the nine billion inhabitants*: Figures for 2050 population from the United Nations Commission on Population and Development, 2011; for 2010 farmland, arable and pasture, Food and Agriculture Organization of the United Nations Statistical Yearbook 2012.

4 *intricate warren of dwellings*: Population of Dharavi is cited in Alex Perry, "Life in Dharavi, Inside Asia's Biggest Slum," *Time Asia*, June 19, 2006.

4 *"We feel and act about certain things"*: William James, "The Consciousness of Self,"in *The Principles of Psychology* (New York: Henry Holt, 1910). That this possessive impulse has a genetic basis is suggested by Jane Goodall's observation of ownership assertion by the wild chimpanzees of Gombe and the remarkable behavior of Lucy, a chimpanzee who had been taught American Sign Language. Noting Lucy's absorption in a glossy magazine, Goodall described how at the last page, she signed the comment, "'This Lucy's, this mine,' as she closed the magazine and laid it on her lap." In Jane Goddall, *Through a Window: My Thirty Years with the Chimpanzees of Gombe* (Boston, MA: Mariner Books, 2000).

5 *"This was the room I had to live in"*: Raymond Chandler, *The Big Sleep* (New York: Alfred A. Knopf, 1971), 97.

5 *"Every-single-one-of-them-is-right!"*: Rudyard Kipling, "In the Neolithic Age," in *The Works of Rudyard Kipling* (London: Wordsworth Poetry Library, 1994).

5 *much of the world's grassland*: The population of the United States was still largely contained between the Appalachian chain and the Atlantic; the Asian steppes and Siberia were still largely untouched by the Romanov empire; the rapidly disintegrating Hispanic empire was primarily urban; and Africa remained unexplored by Europeans.

6 *This book was devoted*: The reference to a "Brytish Impire" first appears in 1577, in Dee's claim to Gerald Mercator, "That all these Northern Iles and Septentrional Parts are lawfully appropriated to the Crown of this Brytish Impire"; it was published a year later in Dee's *General and Rare Memorials Pertayning to the Perfect Arte of Navigation*. See E. G. R. Taylor, "A Letter Dated 1577 from Mercator to John Dee,"*Imago Mundi*, vol. 13 (1956), 55–68.

6 *As night fell*: The fate of the *Squirrel* is recounted in *Sir Humphrey Gilbert's Voyage*.

Chapter One: The Concept

10 *"multitude of chimneys"*: William Harrison, "Of the Manner of Building and Furniture of Our Houses," in *Description of Britain and England*, originally published in 1578 as part of *Chronicles of England* by Raphael Hollinshed, http://www.fordham.edu/halsall/mod/1577harrison-england.asp.

11 *share the muddy space*: Description of French country house in Noël du Fail, *Propos rustiques* (1549). Modern edition edited by G.-A. Pérouse and R. Dubuis, *Propos rustiques de maistre Leon Ladulfi champenois* (Geneva: Droz, 1994).

11 *peasants in eastern Europe*: Jan Slomka, *From Serfdom to Self-Government: Memoirs of a Polish Village Mayor, 1842–1927*, trans. by William John Rose (London: Minerva Publishing Co., 1941); reprinted in *Documentary History of Eastern Europe*, eds. Alfred J. Bannan and Achilles Edelenyi (New York: Twayne Publishers, 1970), 210–216.

11 *on an island in Puget Sound*: William Yardley, "'Barefoot Bandit' Started Life on the Run Early," *New York Times*, July 21, 2010.

11 *I happened to be with dairy farmer*: I took this walk with Kristina Andersson in the summer of 2001. As well as upholding the right to own property, Sweden's 1994 Instrument of Government insists that "everyone shall have access to nature in accordance with *allemansrätten* [i.e., freedom to roam]."

11 *the planning committee of a kibbutz*: Private communication relating to Kibbutz Shomrat. Israel's nationalization of the land began with purchases made by the Jewish National Fund before 1949 and continued afterwards though the administrative body, the Israel Land Authority, set up by the Basic Land Law of 1960; in step with the rightward shift in Israeli politics, leases have in fact been routinely renewed, and as Joshua Weisman, professor of property law at Jerusalem's Hebrew University, has pointed out, leasehold over ninety-eight years becomes almost indistinguishable from outright ownership.

12 *mountainous jungle of Sarawak*: Andro Linklater, *Wild People: Travels with Borneo's Head-hunters* (New York: Atlantic Monthly Press, 1994).

12 *"If a man owns a little property"*: John Steinbeck, *The Grapes of Wrath* (London: Penguin, 2001).

12 *"when you enter my home"*: Bel Mooney, "My Home," *Good Housekeeping*, July 2001.

12 *"a necessity of all human existence"*: Winston Churchill, "Land and Income Taxes in the Budget" (speech, King's Theatre, Edinburgh, July 17, 1909).

13 *From about 1450*: Historians of the period give different emphases to the ingredients of the sixteenth-century revolution—silver inflation, population growth, the rise of the wool industry, the development of printing, Protestantism, and firearms: the classic positions are those of R. H. Tawney's emphasis on social and economic upheaval in *Religion and the Rise of Capitalism* (London: John Murray, 1926); Hugh Trevor-Roper on Calvinism in *The Crisis of the Seventeenth Century: Religion, the Reformation and Social Change*, (London: Macmillan, 1967); Christopher Hill on social upheaval in *The English Revolution* (London: Lawrence & Wishart, 1940), www.marxists.org/archive/hill-christopher/english-revolution; Robert Brenner stressing peasant tenure and agricultural production, "Agrarian Class Structure and Economic Development in Pre-industrial Europe," *Past and Present* 70 (1976): 30–74; Guy Bois picking out the impact of inflation on state revenues in *La Crise du féodalisme* (Paris: FNSP, 1974); Fernand Braudel weaving population growth into technological change in *Civilization and Capitalism 15th–18th Century: Volume 1, The Structures of Everyday Life: The Limits of the Possible* (London: Collins, 1981); Marc Bloch on rural change in *Land and Work in Medieval Europe: Selected Papers,* trans. by J. E. Anderson (Berkeley, CA: University of California Press, 1967). And for England in particular, Joan Thirsk giving prominence to rising agricultural production as editor of *Agricultural Change, Policy and Practice*, vol. 3 in *The Agrarian History of England and Wales* (Cambridge: Cambridge University Press, 1967); G. R. Elton emphasizing inflation and population growth in *England under the Tudors* (London: Methuen, 1974); Penry Williams selecting enclosure and farm practice in *Life in Tudor England* (London: Batsford, 1964); Eric Kerridge on rent returns in "The movement of rent, 1540–1640," *Economic History Review*, 2nd ser., VI (1953): 16–34. An important political and sociological substrate stressing private property as the source of individualism

appeared in C. B. McPerson's *The Political Theory of Possessive Individualism: From Hobbes to Locke* (Oxford: Clarendon, 1962) and Alan Macfarlane's *The Origins of English Individualism: The Family, Property and Social Transition* (Oxford: Blackwell, 1978). Later studies in rights, gender, and culture appear in subsequent chapters.

15 *"the landlord may perhaps have double the rent"*: Robert Thoroton, *The Antiquities of Nottinghamshire* (1677). Cited in Eric Kerridge, *Agrarian Problems in the Sixteenth Century and After* (London: Allen & Unwin, 1969).

15 *Close to William Harrison's parish*: Thomas Monnying's and Joan Payn's cases, entry for Monday, June 8, 1489 in "The Records of Earls colne," http://linux02.lib.cam.ac.uk/earlscolne/cprolls2.

16 *a landlord in the Mekong delta*: Robert L. Sansom, *The Economics of Insurgency in the Mekong Delta of Vietnam* (Boston: MIT Press, 1970), 29.

16 *"the tenants are the members"*: John Norden, *The Surveyor's Dialogue* (1618). Quoted in Kerridge, *Agrarian Problems*, 47.

16 *In a single day in 1567*: Ibid., 174.

17 *"The earth O Lord"*: The prayer appears in the 1553 revision to Archbishop Thomas Cranmer's 1549 *Book of Common Prayer.*

17 *"they plucke downe townes"*: Thomas More, *Utopia* (1516), bk I (Cambridge: Cambrige University Press, 1888), 32.

17 *"these ryche worldlynges"*: Thomas Becon, *Works* (1564), vol. ii, fols. xvi, xvii. Cited in R. H. Tawney, *The Agrarian Problem in the Sixteenth Century* (London: Longmans, Green and Co., 1912), 7.

18 *"Aftur my sympull reson"*: Letter from the Vicar of Quinton in Gloucestershire to the President of Magdalen College, Oxford. Cited in Lord Ernle, "English Farming," *Past and Present* (London: Longmans, 1922), 82.

18 *"the first year of king Henry the VII"*: Kett's plea quoted in J. Whittle, "Lords and Tenants in Kett's Rebellion 1549," *Past & Present* 207 (2010): 3.

19 *When Lord Dacre*: Andrew Buck, "Rhetoric and the Law of Inheritance," in *The Happy Couple: Law and Literature,* ed. by J. Neville Turner and Pamela Williams (London: Federation Press, 1994). See also E. W. Ives, "The Genesis of the Statute of Uses," *English Historical Review* 82, no. 325 (Oct. 1967): 673–697.

19 *more than two million acres of farmland*: F. A. Hibbert, *The Dissolution of the Monasteries* (London: Pitman, 1910), 2–3.

20 *Among them was the de Vere family*: Alan Macfarlane, "The Strife of Two Great Tides: The Harlakenden Case" (lecture, May 1990), www.alanmacfarlane.com/TEXTS/Strife.pdf.

20 *"When gentles go walking"*: from Thomas Tusser's *Hundreth Good Pointes of Husbandrie* (1557); quoted in Penry Williams, *Life in Tudor England* (London: Batsford, 1964), 87.

20 *The pattern was set*: Mary L. Robertson, "Profit and Purpose in the Development of Thomas Cromwell's Landed Estates," *The Journal of British Studies* 29, no. 4 (Oct. 1990): 317–346.

21 *"Merchant Adventurers"*: Petition to Henry VIII (1514), quoted in F. J. Furnivall, *Ballads from Manuscripts, Publications of the Ballad Society*, vol. 1 (1871): 101.

21 *"bie [buy] fermes"*: Thomas Lever's *Sermons* (1680); Arber's *Reprints*; quoted in Ernle, "English Farming," 94.

21 *a wealthy London cloth merchant*: Williams, *Life in Tudor England*, 103.

22 *Roger Harlakenden, the new owner*: Macfarlane, "The Strife of Two Great Tides."

22 *"there can be no better fodder devised for cattell"*: Barnaby Googe, *Foure Bookes of Husbandry* (1577). Cited in Ernle's "English Farming," 152.

22 *"the white rose redd"*: George Puttenham, *The Arte of English Poesie* (London: Field, 1589). Quoted in M. M. Slaughter, "Sacred Kingship and Antinomianism: Antirrhesis and the Order of Things," *Cardozo Studies in Law and Literature* 4, no. 2 (Autumn 1992): 227–235.

22 *"White meats"*: Harrison, *Description of Britain and England,* ch VI: "The food and diet of the English."

Chapter Two: The Rights and Politics of Owning the Earth

24 *"during which time"*: William Bradford, *History of Plimoth Plantation* (1620), 57. The description of the first months of the colony's life is from Bradford.

26 *"The land is our mother"*: No documentation exists to show this famous question attributed to Massasoit was uttered by him, but it is entirely consistent with the cultural dilemma he faced between his sworn friendship for the colonists after Edward Winslow helped cure him on his deathbed in 1623—"the English are my friends," he said, "and love me"—and their incessant desire to acquire Wampanaog land as private property.

26 *springing from Yahweh's commandment*: Leviticus 25:23.

26 *And the laws made it plain*: The Code of Hammurabi, online at http://avalon.law.yale.edu/ancient/hamframe.asp.

27 *"Plantations are for young men"*: Robert C. Winthrop, *Life and Letters of John Winthrop* (Boston: Ticknor & Fields, 1864), 329.

27 *"God has given"*: Ibid., 311.

27 *"Increase & multiply"*: Genesis 1:22.

27 *"appropriated certaine parcells"*: John Winthrop, "Reasons to be considered for justifying the undertakers of the intended Plantation in New England, and for encouraging such whose hearts God shall move to join with them in it"; *Winthrop Papers* (Boston: Massachusetts Historical Society, 1929–1992), 2:138–145. Online at http://www.winthropsociety.org/reasons.htm.

28 *Cotton's sermon*: John Cotton, "God's Promise to His Plantation," (1630), http://digitalcommons.unl.edu/etas/22/. The actual verses cited by John Cotton were from Genesis 21:30–31: "And [Abraham] said 'for these seven ewe lambs shalt thou take of my hand, that they may be a witness unto me, that I have digged this well.' Wherefore he called that place Beersheba because there they sware both of them."

28 *"a city upon a hill"*: John Winthrop, *A Model of Christian Charity* (sermon, printed 1630).

28 *Among the rest of Britain's burgeoning*: The seventeen colonies were Newfoundland (1583), Virginia (1607), Bermuda (1609), Nova Scotia (1621), New

Hampshire (1623), Barbados (1627), Massachusetts (1629; incorporating Plymouth in 1620 and Maine in 1622), Maryland (1632), Connecticut (1633), Rhode Island (1636), Jamaica (1655), New York (1664), New Jersey (1664), Carolina (1670), Leeward Islands (1674; incorporating Saint Kitts, Nevis, Antigua, and Montserrat), Pennsylvania (1681; incorporating Delaware in 1664).

29 *"Many good, religious, devout men"*: Captain John Smith, *Advertisements for the Inexperienced Planters of New England*, originally printed by John Haviland in London, 1631; http://www.winthropsociety.com/doc_adverts.php.

30 *in the words of its sixth-century codifier*: *The Institutes* were issued in AD 535 and remained the basis of Roman or civil law as understood in Europe in the sixteenth century. Apart from the emphasis on mutual obligation, the pattern of civil law tended to advance from abstract principles to practical cases, in distinction to the common law's testing of cases against precedent and statute.

31 *forcing King John to sign the great charter*: Although often taken to embody concepts of liberty as understood by later generations, the actual aims of the barons as delineated in the small number of clauses referring to individual rights are always made in the context of land ownership.

31 *"Day labourers, poor husbandmen"*: Sir Thomas Smith, *De Republica Anglorum* (1583), ch. 24, http://www.constitution.org/eng/repang.htm.

31 *"enslave and rule"*: Plato, *The Republic: Plato in Twelve Volumes*, vols. 5 & 6, trans. by Paul Shorey (London: Heinemann Ltd., 1969), bk. 4, sec. 442b.

31 *And the Hindu emphasis*: *Bhagavad-Gita*, ch. 16, verse 21, http://vedabase.net/bg/16/21.

32 *William Shakespeare paid William Combe*: Samuel Schoenbaum, *William Shakespeare: A Documentary Life* (Oxford: Oxford University Press, 1975), 185–86.

32 *measurements that varied*: Andro Linklater, *Measuring America* (New York: Walker Books, 2002), 17–18.

33 *The modern, definitive*: Sarah Bendall, *Dictionary of Land Surveyors and Local Mapmakers of Great Britain and Ireland* (London: British Library, 1997).

33 *the mathematical inventor*: Linklater, *Measuring America*, 23–25.

33 *a subtle change in mortgage law*: Thomas Lyttleton, *Tenures*, ed. by Eugene Wambaugh (Washington, DC.: Byrne, 1903), 157, http://archive.org/details/littletonstenure00littiala.

34 *"the equity of redemption"*: John Brewer and Susan Staves, *Early Modern Conceptions of Property* (London: Routledge, 1996), 115–116.

35 *"If you will not take"*: Sir John Baker, *The Oxford History of the Laws of England* (Oxford: Oxford University Press, 2003), 665.

35 *It was important to know what was happening*: Thomas Phayer, *The New Boke of Presidents*, originally published by E. Whytchurche, London, 1543. Cited in Amy Louise Erickson, *Women and Property in Early Modern England* (London: Taylor & Francis, 1993), 104.

35 *In the bleak words*: Sir William Blackstone, "Of Husband and Wife," in *Commentaries on the Laws of England* (Oxford: Clarendon, 1769), bk. 1, 430, http://avalon.law.yale.edu/subject_menus/blackstone.asp.

35 *Portia dresses the idea in more romantic guise*: *Merchant of Venice,* act 3, sc. 2, lines 157–71.

36 *But in disposing of his own property*: E. K. Chambers, *Shakespeare: A Study of Facts and Problems* (Oxford: Clarendon, 1989), 170.

36 *the twelve million acres of farmland in England*: Farmland in England is extrapolated from Thorold Rogers's classic, *A History of Agriculture and Prices in England from the Year After the Oxford Parliament (1259) to the Commencement of the Continental War,* vol. 1, giving an estimate of thirty-two million acres of arable and pasture, including rough pasture, for medieval England; the modern estimates of twelve to thirteen million acres of arable land in such sources as Stephen Broadberry, Bruce Campbell, and B. van Leeuwen, "Arable Acreage in England 1270–1871," in their long-term study "English Medieval Population: Reconciling Time Series and Cross Sectional Evidence"; and Gregory King, *A Scheme of the Income and Expence of the Several Families of England Calculated for the Year 1688*, quoted in André Vanoli, *A History of National Accounting* (Lansdale, PA: IOS Press, 2005), 6.

37 *declared that the selfish behavior of property speculators*: Becon, *Works*, 8.

38 *"superfluous appareling"*: François Egerton, *The Egerton Papers* (London: Bowson, 1840), 247.

38 *"insaciable gredyness of mynde"*: quoted in Tawney, *Agrarian Problem*, 7.

38 *"the rude son"*: *Troilus and Cressida,* act 1, sc. 3.

Chapter Three: The Rights of Private Property

39 *"[T]he earth was not made"*: Gerrard Winstanley, *The True Levellers* (1649); quoted in Christopher Hill, *The English Revolution* and online at http://www.marxists.org/reference/archive/winstanley/1649/levellers-standard.htm.

41 *the ruinous civil war that wracked*: Among numerous sources are Hill, *The English Revolution*; Trevor-Roper, *The Crisis of the Seventeenth Century; The Civil Wars: A Military History of England, Scotland, and Ireland, 1638–1660,* eds. J. Kenyon. and J. Ohlmeyer (Oxford: Oxford University Press, 1998); and Trevor Royle, *Civil War: The Wars of the Three Kingdoms, 1638–1660* (London: Little, Brown, 2004).

42 *"I can tell you, Sirs"*: Christopher Hill, *Oliver Cromwell, 1658–1958* (London: Taylor & Francis, 1973), 27.

44 *"An arrow against all tyrants"*: Richard Overton's pamphlet, "Printed at the backside of the Cyclopian Mountains, by Martin Claw-Clergy, printer to the reverend Assembly of Divines, to be sold at the sign of the Subject's Liberty, right opposite to Persecuting Court. 1646," http://oll.libertyfund.org/?option=com_staticxt&staticfile=show.php%3Ftitle=2252.

45 *The Putney debates broke up*: Sir William Clarke, *Puritanism and Liberty, being the Army Debates (1647–9) from the Clarke Manuscripts with Supplementary Documents*, ed. by A. S. P. Woodhouse (Chicago: University of Chicago Press, 1951), http://oll.libertyfund.org/index.php?option=com_content&task=view&id=1322&Itemid=264.

46 *One by one, their ringleaders*: R. H. Gretton, *The Burford Records: A Study in Minor Town Government* (Oxford: Oxford University Press, 1920), 251–252.

46 *Thomas Hobbes believed*: Thomas Hobbes, *Leviathan or the Matter, Form & Power of a Common-wealth, political and civill* (London: Penguin, 1968), http://www.gutenberg.org/files/3207/3207-h/3207-h.htm. *De Corpore* originally printed in London 1655, but composed in the late 1630s; trans. William Molesworth as *Elements of Philosophy* (London: Bohn, 1839), http://archive.org/stream/englishworkstho21hobbgoog#page/n8/mode/2up. Outline of Hobbes's life and thought at "Thomas Hobbes: Stanford Encyclopedia of Philosophy," http://plato.stanford.edu/entries/hobbes.

50 *In 1656, James Harrington published*: James Harrington, *The Commonwealth of Oceana* and *A System of Politics,* ed. J. G. A. Pocock (Cambridge: Cambridge University Press, 1992).

51 *"When you answer the question"*: George M. McBride, *The Land Systems of Mexico* (New York: American Geographical Society, 1923), 2.

51 "We believe in the family-size farm": Harry S. Truman (speech, War Memorial Opera House, San Francisco, October 17, 1950).

53 The earliest formulation of international law, usually credited to Hugo Grotius's groundbreaking work, in particular, *Mare Liberum* (1609) and *De Iure Belli ac Pacis* (1625), came as a response to the Treaty of Tordesillas (1494), which by papal authority divided the New World between Spain and Portugal. To justify Dutch incursions into the Portuguese half that included the East Indies, Grotius appealed to the prior authority of "natural law," derived from classical and biblical sources.

53 *"a turbulent state of affairs"*: Hugo Grotius, *De Iure Belli ac Pacis*, bk. 1, ch. 3, section 9, http://www.constitution.org/gro/djbp_103.htm

Chapter Four: The Two Capitalisms

55 The best accounts of Petty's life are to be found in Ted McCormick, *Willliam Petty and the Ambition of Political Arithmetic* (Oxford: Oxford University Press, 2009); Wilson Lloyd Bevan, *Sir William Petty: A Study in English Economic Literature* (New York: Guggenheimer, Weil & Co., 1894); John Aubrey, *Brief Lives,* ed. Andrew Clark (Oxford: Clarendon, 1898). Petty's writings are to be found in *The Collected Works of Sir William Petty* (London: Routledge, 1997). *Political Arithmetick* (1690) is also online: http://www.marxists.org/reference/subject/economics/petty.

61 *"a bad farmer"*: Lucius Junius Moderatus Columella, *On Agriculture*, trans. Harrison Boyd Ash (Cambridge, MA: Harvard University Press, 1941).

61 For the rising price of land in colonial America, see Andro Linklater *Measuring America* and A. M. Sakolski, *The Great American Land Bubble* (New York: Harper and Brother, 1932).

62 *"not minding anything but to be masters of great tracts of land"*: Robert Beverley, *History of Virginia in Four Parts* (Richmond, VA: Randolph, 1855), 45.

62 *"by taking up & purchasing"*: *The Writings of George Washington,* ed. by

Worthington Chauncey Ford (New York and London: G. P. Putnam's Sons, 1889), vol. II, http://oll.libertyfund.org/?option=com_staticxt&staticfile=show.php%3Ftitle=2377&chapter=225005&layout=html&Itemid=27.

63 For changes in the English economy in the late seventeenth and early eighteenth centuries, see *The Economic History of Britain since 1700: Vol. I: 1700–1860*, ed. Roderick Floud and D. N. McCloskey (Cambridge: Cambridge University Press, 1994) second edition; Julian Roche, *The International Wool Trade* (Cambridge: Woodhead, 1995); Robert C. Allen, "The Price of Freehold Land and the Interest Rate in the Seventeenth and Eighteenth Centuries," *The Economic History Review, New Series,* 41, no. 1 (Feb. 1988): 33–50; Robert C. Allen, "The High Wage Economy of Pre-Industrial Britain," www.helsinki.fi/iehc2006/papers2/Allen77.pdf.

64 *"the natural fertility of the soil"*: Adam Smith, *An Enquiry into the Nature and Causes of the Wealth of Nations* (New York: Random House, 1937), bk. 3, ch. IV, p. 133, http://www.marxists.org/reference/archive/smith-adam/works/wealth-of-nations/index.htm.

65 For the early development of mercantile capitalism, see Niall Ferguson, *The Ascent of Money: A Financial History of the World* (London and New York: Penguin, 2008).

65 *"This oligarchical power"*: Ibid., 71.

65 For the economy of the Netherlands in the seventeenth and eighteenth centuries, see Simon Schama, *An Embarrassment of Riches: An Interpretation of Dutch Culture in the Golden Period* (London: Collins, 1987); Jan de Vries, *The Dutch Rural Economy in the Golden Age, 1500–1700* (New Haven, CT: Yale University Press, 1974).

66 *"Will not only discourage us"*: M. F. Epstein, *The Early History of the English Levant Company* (London: Routledge, 1908), 271.

68 *"It is permitted to every man to enslave himself"*: *De Iure Belli ac Pacis,* bk. 3, sec. 8, http://www.constitution.org/gro/djbp.htm.

69 *"How selfish soever man"*: Adam Smith, *Theory of Moral Sentiments,* 6th edition (London: Millar, 1790). Part 1, sec. 1, ch. 1, para. 1, http://www.econlib.org/library/Smith/smMS1.html.

69 *"That action is best"*: Francis Hutcheson, *An Inquiry into the Original of Our Ideas of Beauty and Virtue,* first published 1725, modern edition ed. Wolfgang Leidhold (Indianapolis, IN: Liberty Fund, 2004), http://files.libertyfund.org/files/858/0449_LFeBk.pdf.

70 *"our own sentiments and motives"*: Smith, *Theory of Moral Sentiments,* part III, B, ch. 1b, para. c.

70 *"the vices and follies of mankind"*: Ibid., part I, sec. 2, ch. 3, para. 4.

70 *"Justice is the main pillar"*: Ibid., part II, sec. 2, ch. 3, para. 4.

70 *"two different systems of political economy"*: Smith, *Wealth of Nations.* bk. IV, "Of Systems of Political Economy," Introduction.

70 For the *Physiocrates* see Henry Higgs, *The Physiocrats: Six Lectures on the French Economistes of the 18th Century* (London: Macmillan and Co., 1897), http://oll.libertyfund.org/title/286; the basis of physiocratic economics was, in Quesnay's phrase, that "la terre est l'unique source des richesses," a concept that provides

the theme of of the first chapter in Richard Cantillon's *Essai sur la Nature du Commerce en Général*, and is fundamental to William Petty's *Political Arithmetick*.

70 For Richard Cantillon, see W. S. Jevons, "Richard Cantillon and the Nationality of Political Economy," *Contemporary Review* (January 1881), http://files.libertyfund.org/econtalk/CantillonNature/SingleChaps/Jevons.pdf.

72 *"It is not from the benevolence"*: *Wealth of Nations*, bk. 1, ch. 2, para. 2.

73 *"But the mean rapacity"*: Ibid., bk. IV, ch. III, part 2.

Chapter Five: The Morality of Property

75 *"millionous multitudes"*: George Alsop, "A Character of the Province of Maryland, 1666," in *Narratives of Early Maryland*, ed. Clayton C. Hall (New York: Scribner's Sons, 1910), 345.

75 *"Wild Turkies"*: Thomas Ashe, "Carolina, Or a Description of the Present State of that Country, 1682," in Alexander S. Salley Jr., *Narratives of Early Carolina: 1650–1708* (New York: Scribner's Sons, 1911), 150; "such infinite Herds of Deare," "innumerable of Pines, tall and good for boards or masts," and forests of oaks with "great Bodies tall and streight," "like to manure," Gerald Smith, "God and the Land: Natural Theology and Natural History in America" (lecture, at Sewanee, the University of the South, 1993), http://www.touroinstitute.com/Religion%20and%20Ecology.pdf.

75 *"we cannot sett downe"*: Father Andrew White, "Father White's Briefe Relation," (1634), quoted in *Narratives of Early Maryland*, ed. Clayton C. Hall (New York: Scribner's Sons, 1910), 45.

75 *"The mildnesse of the aire"*: Captain John Smith, *Description of Virginia and Proceedings of the Colonie*, printed in 1612, quoted in *Narratives of Early Virginia: 1606–1625*, ed. Lyon G. Tyler (New York: Scribner's Sons, 1907), 97–98.

76 *"a most fertile, gallant, rich soil"*: *Francis Yeardley's Narrative of Excursions into Carolina*, letter dated May 8, 1654, quoted in *Narratives of Early Carolina, 1650–1708.*

76 *"There is one square"*: "Second Letter of Hernando Cortés to Emperor Charles V," from *The Dispatches of Hernando Cortés, The Conqueror of Mexico, addressed to the Emperor Charles V, written during the conquest, and containing a narrative of its events.* (New York: Wiley and Putnam, 1843), http://mith.umd.edu/eada/html/display.php?docs=cortez_letter2.xml.

76 *"very fine woods and meadows"*: Samuel Champlain, *Voyages of Samuel de Champlain*, originally published in 1609; modern edition, trans. Charles Pomeroy Otis (Boston: Prince Society of Boston, 1878), http://www.usgennet.org/usa/topic/preservation/epochs/vol1/pg179.htm.

77 For the history of the Lords Proprietors, Sir John Yeamans and colonial South Carolina, see Walter B. Edgar, *South Carolina: A History* (Columbia, SC: University of South Carolina Press, 1998), 84–85; for correspondence sent by John Locke on behalf of the Lords Proprietors, see "America and West Indies: November 1670," *Calendar of State Papers Colonial, America and West Indies, Volume 7: 1669–1674* (1889): 122–140, www.british-history.ac.uk/report.aspx?compid=70201.

79 *"to chuse out of themselves"*: Penn's Charter of Liberties, April 25, 1682, http://avalon.law.yale.edu/17th_century/pa03.asp#1.

80 "In the beginning . . . all the world was America": *Two Treatises of Government*, ed. Thomas Hollis (London: A. Millar et al., 1764). ch. V, para. 49, oll.libertyfund.org/title/222/16269.

80 *"such a master of taciturnity and passion"*: Letter from the bishop of Oxford in 1684 quoted in H. R. Fox Bourne, *Life of John Locke* (Whitefish, MT: Kessinger Publishing, 2003), 484.

81 *"Consciousness always accompanies thinking"*: John Locke, *An Essay Concerning Human Understanding*, bk. 1, ch. XXVII, para. 9; "Self depends on consciousness," bk. 1, ch. XXVII, para. 17.

81 *"Though the earth"*: Locke, *Two Treatises of Government*, bk. 2, ch. V, "Of Property"; "the Turfs my Servant has cut," ch. V, ibid. "The great and *chief end*," bk. 2, ch. IX, "Of the Ends of Political Society and government."

82 *"like a Landlord to his Tenant"*: Daniel Defoe, *Party Tyranny, or an Occasional Bill in Miniature as now practiced in Carolina*, quoted in *Narrative of Early Carolina*, 221–264.

83 *three natural rights "which every man"*: *Commentaries on the Laws of England*, bk. 1, 125.

83 *"sole and despotic"*: Ibid., bk. 2, 2.

83 *"If taxes are laid upon"*: Samuel Adams's instructions to Boston's representatives on the Massachusetts Assembly in response to the 1764 Sugar Act, dated May 24, 1764.

83 *property "to which . . . people are entitled"*: Robert Nozick, *Anarchy, State, and Utopia* (New York: Basic Books, 1974), 235.

84 *"no one ought to harm another"*: *Two Treatises*, bk. 2, ch. II, "Of the State of Nature."

84 *"where there is enough"*: Ibid, bk. 2, ch. V, "Of Property."

84 *"As Justice gives every Man"*: Ibid, bk. 1, ch. IV, "Of Adams' title to sovereignty by donation Gen. I. 28."; "[N]o man could ever have," ibid.

85 *"From its birth in 16th century England"* : The element of social justice in the Poor Law, always in danger of being submerged by the element of self-interest, was made plain in the judgment delivered by Lord Chief Justice Ellenborough, a notoriously conservative judge, in *Rex v. Inhabitants of Eastbourne* 1803, concerning the reluctance of the inhabitants of a coastal town to fund poor relief for foreigners. "[T]he law of humanity which is anterior to all positive laws obliges us to afford them relief to save them from starving," Ellenborough stated; "and those laws (ie the laws of settlement) were only passed to fix the obligation more certainly, and point out distinctly in what manner it would be borne." George Nicholls, *A History of the English Poor Law in Connection with the State of the country and the condition of the people* (London: King & Son, 1904), 368.

86 *Sarah Brosnan, a young psychology professor*: Sarah F. Brosnan and Frans B. M. de Waal, "Animal behaviour: Fair refusal by capuchin monkeys," *Nature* 428, 140 (March 11, 2004).

87 *"the obvious and simple system"*: *Wealth of Nations*, bk. 4, ch. 9, para. 51.

88 For Cromwell's lifting of discriminatory laws against Jews, see Barbara

Coulton, "Cromwell and the 'readmission' of the Jews to England, 1656"; http://www.olivercromwell.org/jews.pdf.

89 *"One early example"*: The revolt of the South Carolina colonists against the Lords Proprietors' rule illustrated the difference between natural and civil rights of property. See Edgar, *History of South Carolina*, 113.

Chapter Six: What Came Before

Much of the material on traditional land use in Sarawak is based on my book *Wild People: Travels with Borneo's head-hunters* (London: John Murray, 1990). The radical transformation of the country since then has been described in Robert A. Cramb, *Land and Longhouse: Agrarian Transformation in the Uplands of Sarawak* (Honolulu, HI: University of Hawaii Press, 2007). The economic development is detailed through government publications, Sarawak as well as Malaysian, especially the latter's Department of Statistics. The deforestation is covered by two main sources, timber and paper and pulp industry publications, and conservation agencies such as WWF Malaysia, which together tell the same story. Many of the reports on the cultural and material impact are accessible through the website of BRIMAS, Borneo Resources Institute, http://brimas.www1.50megs.com.

94 *"Behold brains ooze out along with layers of fat"*: translation by Dr. James Masing, unpublished Ph.D. thesis (1984).

94 Aboriginal dreaming and the chanted myths associated with it have a literature of their own. Bruce Chatwin's *The Songlines* (London: Franklin Press, 1987) is unreliable, but conveys vividly to non-Aboriginals the reality of the songs.

95 *"The association between naming and owning"*: Patricia Lane, barrister, "Native Title—the End of Property as we know it?," paper for Australia's Property Law lecture series March 9, 1999.

95 *"In 2007, the Suprme Court of of British Columbia"*: Although the judgment given by Appeals Court Judge Justice Vickers, in the case *Tsilhqot'in Nation v. British Columbia,* 2007 BCSC 1700 (http://www.canlii.org/en/bc/bcsc/doc/2007/2007bcsc1700/2007bcsc1700.html), turned down their claim, it gave encouragement to the standard of evidence they presented, and the case is currently under appeal. It is also covered in Michael Barry, "Standards for Oral Tradition Evidence: Guidelines from First Nations Land Claims in Canada," University of Calgary, to the International Federation of Surveyors, October 1999, http://www.fig.net/pub/vietnam/papers/ts02a/ts02a_barry_3644.pdf.

95 *"Compiled in the twelfth century"*: Thomas Kinsella, *Taín Bó Cuaílnge—The Táin* (Oxford: Oxford University Press, 1969). All quotes are taken from this edition.

96 *"there was not ditch"*: Taken from the twelfth-century Irish source, *Lebor na Huidre,* quoted in Karl Marx's *Ethnographical Notebooks c.1881,* http://www.marxists.org/archive/marx/works/1881/ethnographical-notebooks/ch03.htm.

96 *"The colonists in Massachusetts Bay"*: Edward Winslow, *Good Newes from New England* (Carlisle MA: Applewood Books, 1996).

96 *"Where a Battel has been fought"*: *The Discoveries of John Lederer* (1672), http://rla.unc.edu/archives/accounts/lederer/ledererext.html.

97 *"And that Day Joshua"*: Book of Joshua 4:20.

97 *In his poem "The Gift Outright"*: Robert Frost, "The Gift Outright," *A Witness Tree* (New York: Henry Holt, 1942).

98 *"In the 1980s, the traditional Iban"*: Linklater, *Wild People*, 148–151.

99 *"The tracts show clearly"*: Engels to Marx, November 29, 1869, http://www.marxists.org/archive/marx/works/1869/letters/69_11_29a.htm. The records are largely contained within John Davies, *A Discovery of the True Cause Why Ireland Was Never Entirely Subdued Nor Brought Under Obedience of the Crown of England Until the Beginning of His Majesty's Happy Reign*, ed. Henry Morley (London: Routledge, 1890). Marx's own research was heavily based on the lectures of Henry Sumner Maine, on "The History of Institutions," delivered in 1875, and influenced by Lewis Morgan's *Ancient Society or Researches in the Lines of Human Progress from Savagery through Barbarism to Civilization* (New York: Henry Holt, 1877).

99 *"In the five previous centuries"*: *A Guide to Early Irish Law*, ed. Fergus Kelly (Dublin: Institute for Advanced Studies, 1988), ch 1. W. E. Montgomery, *The History of Land Tenure in Ireland* (Cambridge: Cambridge University Press, 1889), 26–41, http://archive.org/stream/historyoflandten00montrich#page/ii/mode/2up.

101 *"The land shall not be sold for ever"*: Leviticius 25:23.

101 *The jubilee fell out of favor*: Leviticus 25:10, 13. "A jubilee shall that fiftieth year be to you . . . in the year of this jubilee you shall return every man to his possession"; the idea of the land as a gift to his chosen people so that Israel could only be realized by returning to cultivate once more permeated nineteenth-century Zionist thought; thus Rabbi Zevi Hirsch Kalischer, writing in 1863: "there will be four redemptions. The first is redemption of the land itself, planting and raising the crops of the land and holy fruit . . ." *Documents on the History of Hibbat-Zion and the Settlement of Eretz Israel*, ed. Shulamit Laskov (Tel Aviv: Tel-Aviv University, 1982), 103–112.

102 *"The Russian empire"*: The continuing influence of the *mir* or *obschina* on peasant life worried other Russian Socialists, for example Victor Chernov of the Social Revolutionary Party, who wrote in the 1880s, "Everywhere the picture is the same. A full break with the mir is extremely rare. The overwhelming majority retain the household lot their *obschina* gave them [after the emancipation of the serfs in 1861], they run their livestock in a common herd, every year they distribute common meadows along with the whole *mir*, and they receive their due share in common woodlands and so on." In Judith Pallot and Denis J. B. Shaw, *Landscape and Settlement in Romanov Russia 1613–1917* (Oxford: Clarendon, 1990), 191.

103 *fuidhir, or landless workers*: Montgomery, *Land Tenure*, 41–47.

103 *"The utmost care was taken"*: J. Mill, "Tenants and Agriculture near Dublin in the Fourteenth Century"; *Proceedings, Royal Society of antiquaries of Ireland* I, 1, 57.

103 *"Every* Sachem *knoweth"*: Winslow, *Good Newes*, 62.

104 *"The Natives are very exact"*: Roger Williams, *A Key to the Languages of America* (Providence, RI: Rhode Island Historical Society, 1827), ch. XVI, 90.

105 *"The* sachims . . . *will not conclude":* Ibid., 121.

106 *"The effects were felt most acutely in the O'Neills' territory"* : A. T. Q. Stewart, *The Narrow Ground: The Roots of Conflict in Ulster* (London: Faber and Faber Ltd., 1989), 41–49.

106 *"not only looks like a desert"*: Charles Carlton, *Going to the Wars: The Experience of the British Civil Wars 1638–51* (London: Routledge, 1992), 213.

106 *"Ignatius Stacpole of Limerick"*: BBC, "A Short History of Ireland," http://www.bbc.co.uk/northernireland/ashorthistory/archive/intro100.shtml.

107 The figure of 2.1 million for the population of Ireland is given by M. Perceval-Maxwell in *The Outbreak of the Irish Rebellion of 1641* (Montreal: McGill-Queen's Press, 1994), 30.

107 *"a man might travel twenty or thirty miles"*: Carlton, *Going to the Wars*, 213.

107 *"And why should Men endeavour"*: Petty, *Collected Works*, 146.

109 *one of the most rapid land revolutions*: Sarawak timber statistics from the International Tropical Timber Organization (ITTO) Annual Review, 2011.

109 *"Taib translated political power into property"*: Yoolim Lee, "Getting Rich in Malaysia Cronyism Capital Means Dayak Lose Home," Bloomberg News, August 24, 2009; cites Transparency International's labelling of the Bakun Hydroelectric Dam on the Balui River in Sarawak as a "monument of corruption"; points to almost two hundred lawsuits pending in the Sarawak courts relating to claims by Dayak people on lands being used for oil palms and logging; quotes Sim Kwang Yang, former opposition MP, describing Sarawak's economy as "crony capitalism driven by greed without any regard for the people," and cites as examples the ownership by Taib's adult children and his late wife, Lejla, of more than 29.3 percent of Cahya Mata Sarawak Bhd., the state's largest industrial group, involved in construction, property development, and financial services.

Chapter Seven: The Peasants

The dramatic decline and disintegration of Poland's mighty kingdom is covered by *The Cambridge History of Poland,* eds. Oskar Halecki, W. F. Reddaway, J. H. Penson (Cambridge: Cambridge University Press, 1950); and Neal Ascherson, *The Struggles for Poland* (New York: Random House, 1991).

112 *"he was rowed by the Quene's men"*: May 1, 1583 entry in *The Private Diary of Dr. John Dee* (London: The Camden Society, 1841–42).

112 *seventy-five Muslim attacks*: Brian L. Davies, *Warfare, State and Society on the Black Sea Steppe: 1500–1700* (London: Routledge, 2001).

113 The 1505 constitution was known as the Nihil novi "constitution" because it forbade any new legislation unless the king consulted the Sejm, that is the senate (highest level officials), as well as the lower chamber of (regional) deputies, before enacting any changes.

114 *encapsulated in the gentlemanly code*: "Sarmatism" was as pervasive in seventeenth-century Poland as was the idea of the gentleman in eighteenth-century England.

At one level it represented gallantry, freedom, and knightly virtues, but at another shaded into an intolerant, narrow-minded defense of privilege.

114 *"shaken by the inrush of silver"*: Inflation—from a base of one hundred in the decade 1501–10, prices tripled in England, rose by 250 percent in the Netherlands, and by almost 200 percent in Spain by 1555. John Munro, "The Monetary Origins of the 'Price Revolution': South German silver mining, merchant banking and Venetian commerce, 1460–1540," a working paper, 2003.

114 *"portable firearms such as the arquebus"*: The price of firearms over hand-wielded weapons was calculated in detail in the Netherlands in the first half of the sixteenth century; pikes (long spears) cost about four *stuivers;* halberds (combined battle-ax and spear) cost about fourteen *stuivers*; a longbow, about fourteen *stuivers*; a crossbow about thirty *stuivers*; a harquebus (early musket) about thirty *stuivers*; but a wrought iron cannon weighing one thousand pounds cost at least 1,250 *stuivers*, and one in bronze, 2,500 *stuivers*, and ammunition was extra (in the sixteenth century there were about fifty *stuivers* in a *rijksdaalder*, that would become approximately equivalent to a silver dollar in the eighteenth century); James P. Ward, "Prices of Weapons and Munitions in Early Sixteenth Century Holland during the Guelders War," part of an unpublished doctoral thesis, "The Cities and States of Holland. A participative system of government under strain" (University of Leiden, 2001).

115 *A solid trade in cattle, wheat and rye*: Grain exports rose during the sixteenth century, from 10,000 tons of rye in 1500 to more than 150,000 tons by 1600, but most was consumed within Poland. Perry Anderson, *Passages from Antiquity to Feudalism* (London: Verso, 1996), 258–259.

116 *the Piotrków Privilege*: *Cambridge History*, 260.

116 *"Peasants . . . must not give"*: Witold Kula, "The Seigneury and the Peasant Family in Poland," in *Family and Society: Selections from the Annales, Economies, Scoietés, Civilisations*, eds. R. Foster and O. Ranum. (Baltimore, MD: Johns Hopkins Press, 1976), 192–198.

116 *"As the folk who knew this system"*: Jan Slomka, *From Serfdom to Self-Government: Memoirs of a Polish Village Mayor, 1842–1927*, trans. William John Rose (London: Minerva Publishing Co., 1941).

117 *"with a very small rod"*: Witold Kula, *Measures and Men*, trans. by R. Szreter (Princeton, NJ: Princeton University Press, 1986); cited by Linklater, *Measuring America*, 241.

117 *the historian Jan Dlugosz*: Quoted in Adam Zamojski, *The Polish Way* (London: John Murray, 1987), 52–53.

117 *"In order to encourage people"*: Kula, "The Seigneury," 196.

118 *It was the desperate need for money*: Dee, *Private Diary* and Charlotte Fell Smith, *John Dee 1527 to 1608* (London: Kessinger, 2004), ch. 7.

119 *The empire had its roots*: Marianne Yaldez, "Chinese Central Asia (Xinjiang): Its people and Its culture," in *Turks: Journey of a Thousand Years 600–1600,* ed. David J. Roxburgh (London: Royal Academy of Arts, 2005). Miriam Greenblatt, *Süleyman the Magnificent and the Ottoman Empire* (New York: Benchmark Books, 2003); Serpil Begci and Zeren Tanindi, "Art of the Ottoman Court," in Roxburgh, *Turks*.

119 *the* sipahis *shot arrows*: Jack A. Goldstone, "East and West in the Seventeenth Century: Political Crises in Stuart England, Ottoman Turkey, and Ming China," *Comparative Studies in Society and History* 30, no. 1 (Jan. 1988): 103–142.

120 *destructive effects of silver inflation*: Şevket Pamuk, "The Price Revolution in the Ottoman Empire Reconsidered," *International Journal of Middle East Studies* 33, no. 1 (Feb. 2001): 69–89.

120 *Süleyman's magnificence lay in his legal reforms*: Colin Imber, *Studies in Ottoman History and Law* (Oxford: Isis Press, 1996), 49–50.

120 *Measured by the crude but unforgiving test of war*: Mesut Uyar and Edward J. Erikson, *A Military History of the Ottomans* (Santa Barabara, CA: Greenwood, 2009); Jean de Thévenot, *Relation d'un voyage fait au Levant: dans laquelle il est curieusement traité des Estats sujets au Grand Seigneur*, originally published in Rouen, 1665, ch. LI.

121 *The eternal conflicts*: Goldstone, "East and West."

121 *"Most of the feudal lords today"*: Fernand Braudel, *The Mediterranean and the Mediterranean World in the Age of Philip II,* vol. II (Berkeley, CA: University of California Press, 1995), 723.

122 For the rise of the *szlachta, Cambridge History*, 333–346; monopolization of power by *szlachta,* Ascherson, *Struggles*, 19–21; *liberum veto,* Anna M Cienciala, "The Decline of Poland" (lectures, University of Kansas, 2002 and 2004), http://web.ku.edu/~eceurope/hist557/lect3-4.htm.

123 *In 1786 James Madison examined*: In *The Federalist 10,* Madison specifically ruled out Poland as a republican model; Poland's elected kingship was cited during the Constitutional Convention in 1787 as a reason not having an elected president, but Madison noted the objection by one delegate, James Wilson, that the Polish aristocratic example and proposed popular model for the United States were "totally dissimilar. The Polish nobles have resources & dependents which enable them to appear in force, and to threaten the Republic as well as each other" (July 17, 1787).

123 For the evolution of the *çiftlik*: Doreen Warriner, *Land Reform in Principle and Practice* (Oxford: Clarendon, 1969), 390.

124 *one third of the German-speaking population died*: Modern research focuses on the localized impact of the war, ranging from 50 percent of the population in the east to perhaps 15 percent in the west. See Geoffrey Parker, *The Thirty Years War* (London: Routledge, 1997), 177.

125 *Black Forest peasants in 1525*: From this meeting came a celebrated assertion of rights known as the Twelve Articles of the Black Forest. See *The German Peasants' War: A History in Documents,* ed. Tom Scott and Robert W. Scribner (Atlantic Heights, NJ: Humanities, 1991), 251–276.

125 *"Say, you wretched, shabby bag of worms";* Norman Cohn, *The Pursuit of the Millennium* (London: Mercury, 1972), 266–269.

125 *Usually the conflict was resolved*: Rouilliard's case is cited in Wolfgang Schmale, "Liberty Is an Inestimable Thing," in *The Individual in Political Theory and Practice,* ed. Janet Coleman (Oxford and New York: Oxford University Press, 1996).

126 The struggles of European peasants for control over their use of land is stud-

ied in Marcus J. Kurtz, "Understanding Peasant Revolution: From Concept to Theory and Case," *Theory and Society* 29, no. 1 (Feb. 2000): 93–124; E. J. Hobsbawm, "Peasant Land Occupations," *Past & Present*, no. 62 (Feb. 1974): 120–152; Edgar Melton, "Gutsherrschaft in East Elbian Germany and Livonia, 1500–1800: A Critique of the Model," *Central European History*, vol. 21, no. 4 (Dec. 1988): 315–349; Terence J. Byres, "The Landlord Class, Peasant Differentiation, Class Struggle and the Transition to Capitalism: England, France and Prussia Compared" (Paper for Land, Poverty, Social Justice & Development conference, Jan. 2006). For peasant economics more generally, see A. V. Chayanov, *The Theory of Peasant Economy*, trans. R. E. F. Smith and Christel Lane (Madison, WI: University of Wisconsin Press, 1986).

128 *land around Paris*: Robert Brenner, "The Agrarian Roots of European Capitalism," *Past & Present*, no. 97 (Nov. 1982): 77.

128 *Across western Europe, landowners reasserted their powers*: Fernand Braudel, *Civilization and Capitalism, 15th–18th Century, The Perspective of the World*, vol. III (Berkeley, CA: University of California Press, 1982), 394.

129 *raised only twenty-six million pounds*: The estimate of China's taxation is computed in the following way: in 1774, the Qianlong emperor boasted of raising seventy-eight million tael in taxes; with about 1.2 troy ounces of silver per tael this is roughly equal to 93.6 million ounces of silver; a George III silver crown coin contained about 0.85 troy ounce of silver, giving a value of approximately 3.4 ounce of silver to one pound; by this rough calculation, the sterling equivalent of seventy-eight million tael would be twenty-six million pounds, at a time when fortuitously, silver was worth about the same in Britain and China.

130 *"Having seen the extraordinary [taxes]"*: Braudel, *Civilization*, 394.

Chapter Eight: Autocratic Ownership

131 *the great film director Sergei Eisenstein*: The transcript of Eisenstein's remarkable meeting with Stalin was first published under the title *Kremlevskii Tsenzor [Kremlin censorship]* by G. Maryamov in Moscow, 1992; it first appeared in English in the Indian Communist journal *Revolutionary Democracy* III, no. 2, September 1997.

131 *It was in the spring of 1565*: Janet Martin, *Medieval Russia 980–1584* (Cambridge, Cambridge University Press, 1995), 345–347.

132 *one cavalryman "on a horse with complete equipment"*: V. O. Klyuchevsky, *A History of Russia*, vol. 2, trans. C. J. Hogarth (London: Dent, 1911), 280–281.

132 *a separate kingdom or* oprichnina: Ibid., and Heinrich von Staden, *The Land and Government of Muscovy: A Sixteenth Century Account*, ed. and trans. Thomas Esper (Stanford, CA: Stanford University Press, 1967).

133 *the tsar's decision to abdicate in 1565*: Matthew P. Romaniello, *The Elusive Empire: Kazan and the Creation of Russia, 1552–1671* (Madison, WI: University of Wisconsin Press, 2012), 170–173.

135 *"In those years"*: "Prologue" to *Requiem* by Anna Akhmatova in *Selected Poems*, trans. D. M. Thomas (London: Penguin Classics, 2006).

135 *None did so to more dramatic effect than Peter*: Orlando Figes, *Natasha's Dance: A Cultural History of Russia* (London and New York: Penguin, 2003), 15–18; Terence Emmons, *The Russian Landed Gentry and the Peasant Emancipation of 1861* (Cambridge: Cambridge University Press, 1968), 75–79.
136 *laws known as the* Ulozhenie: Law code of 1649, http://pages.uoregon.edu/kimball/1649-Ulj.htm.
136 *"Table of Ranks"*: Figes, *Natasha's Dance*, 18.
136 *Adam Weid was given an estate*: These and other examples of estates being clawed back appear in J. Paaskoski, "Noble Land-Holding and Serfdom in 'Old Finland,' from pomest'e to votchina," in *A Window on Russia,* ed. L. A. J. Hughes and M. di Salvo (Papers, Fifth International Conference on Eighteenth-Century Russia, Gargnano, 1994 and Rome, 1996), 83–91.
137 *almost thirty thousand square miles of new territory every year*: Computed by dividing the area in 1914, 8,803,129 square miles, by the 303 years from 1614 to 1917.
138 *"the fundamental factor"*:—Klyuchevsky, *History of Russia*, vol. 1, p. 2.
138 *"Nothing in nature could be finer"*: Nikolai Gogol, *Taras Bulba and Other Tales* (London: Floating Press, 2011), 36.
138 *"The tulips, roses, lilies of the valley"*: Peter Putnam, "John Perry: Engineer to the Great Tsar (1698–1712)," in *Seven Britons in Imperial Russia (1689–1812)* (Princeton, NJ: Princeton UniversityPress, 1952), 3–21.
139 For the *Ordnovortsy*, see Judith Pallot and Denis J. B. Shaw, *Landscape and Settlement in Romanov Russia 1613–1917* (Oxford: Clarendon, 1990), ch. 2, "The Ordnovortsy."
139 For the development of Voronezh, see Willard Sunderland, *Taming the Wild Field: Colonization and Empire on the Russian Steppe* (Ithaca, NY, and London: Cornell University Press, 2004); and Pallot and Shaw, *Landscape,* 58–63.
140 For the development of serfdom, see Terence Emmons, *The Russian Landed Gentry and the Peasant Emancipation of 1861* (Cambridge: Cambridge University Press, 1968), 17–24.
141 *criticize landowners for "beating and tormenting [serfs]"*: R. Nisbet Bain, *The Pupils of Peter the Great: A History of the Russian Court and Empire 1697–1740* (London: 1897); ukase of April 21, 1721, forbidding serfs to be sold separately, ibid., 533.
141 *Count Pyotr Sheremetev*: Figes, *Natasha's Dance*, 19–26.
142 *Obschina* or *mir*: Pallot and Shaw, *Landscape and Settlement*. See Ch. 6, "The Commune."
142 *Alexander Radischchev, an earnest*: Allen McConnell, "The Empress and Her Protégé: Catherine II and Radischev," *The Journal of Modern History*, vol. 36, no. 1 (Mar. 1964): 14–27.
143 *"The nobility is not identified"*: Anatole Leroy-Beaulieu, *The Empire of the Tsars and the Russians* (New York: G. P. Putnam's Sons, 1894), quoted in Seymour Becker, *Nobility and Privilege in Late Imperial Russia* (Dekalb, IL: Northern Illinois University Press, 1985), 29.
143 *the characteristics of the Asiatic temperament*: Figes, *Natasha's Dance*, 363–367.
143 *"indifference, naivety and cunning"*: Gogol, *Taras Bulba*. See introduction.

144 *the lassitude of the minor nobility was fictionalized*: Ivan A. Goncharov, *Oblomov*, trans. Marian Schwartz (New York: Seven Stories, 2011), 3.

144 *their "extreme immiseration"*: Sundarland, *Taming the Wild Field.*, *op. cit.*, 123–133.

144 *twenty-three thousand German Mennonites*: Having visited the Germans 1841, one official commented, "When you enter the Mennonite colonies, you feel as if you are entering another country . . . [everywhere else] there is laziness and neglect which together with a lack of education block evey path to progress." Sunderland, *Taming the Wild Field*, 117; Jeffrey Longhofer, "Specifying the Commons: Mennonites, Intensive Agriculture, and Landlessness in Nineteenth-Century Russia," *Ethnohistory* 40, no. 3 (Summer 1993): 384–409.

145 *"A German is like a willow tree, stick it anywhere and it will take"*: Alexander Solzhenitsyn, *The Gulag Archipelago, 1918–1956* (New York: Basic Books, 1997), 400.

145 *"the common people have but very little heart"*: Perry, *Seven Britons*, 57.

146 *families forcibly moved to Belgorod*: David Moon, "Peasant Migration and the Settlement of Russia's Frontiers, 1550–1897," *The Historical Journal* 40, no. 4 (Dec. 1997): 888–889; for families settled at Voronezh, see Pallot and Shaw, *Landscape and Settlement*, 26.

146 *"and after spending a short time on the Cossack settlements"*: Sunderland, *Taming the Wild Frontier*, 30.

146 1.7 million migrants moved to the steppes, see Ibid., 113.

147 *the state of New Russia*: Ibid., 128.

147 *When William Richardson*: "Extracts from *Anecdotes of the Russian Empire,"* in *Seven Britons*, 141–179.

148 *"eternal and hereditary disposition"*: J. Paaskoski, "Noble Land-Holding and Serfdom." Originally holdings were referred to as *zemlevladenie* or land possession, but in 1734 Count Petr Semenovich Saltykov received the former estate of Fedor Matveev in *vechnoe i potomstvennoe vladenie* or "eternal and hereditary possession."

148 *Mortgaging of serfs*: Ibid. "The first application [to the *Gosudarstvennyi Zaemnyi Bank*] was made in September 1786, when . . . General Fieldmarshal Count Ivan Petrovich Saltykov [son of Anna's favorite] and his wife Dar'ia Petrovna Saltykova applied for permission to mortgage their peasants.

Chapter Nine: The Equilibrium of Land Ownership

150 *an American farmer, William Hinton*: Hinton's experiences were described in his classic, *Fanshen: A Documentary of Revolution in a Chinese Village* (Berkeley, CA: University of California Press, 1966).

150 *Draft Land Law*: Ibid., 7.

151 *"This ancient lag"*: Ibid., 3.

152 *"Under the bondage of feudalism"*: Mao Zhedong et al., "The Chinese Revolution," in *Selected Works of Mao Tse-tung*, vol. II (Peking: Foreign Languages Press, No date).

152 *In the first house Hinton visited*: Hinton *Fanshen*, 253; home and social position of Sheng Ching-ho, ibid., 32–33.

153 *"China has long been one of the richest"*: Adam Smith, *Wealth of Nations*, vol. 1, ch. 8.

153 The argument about why China fell so far behind the West in economic and technical development—the "great divergence," to quote the title of Kenneth Pomeranz's *The Great Divergence: China, Europe, and the Making of the Modern World Economy* (Princeton, NJ: Princeton University Press, 2000), which largely set the grounds for the debate—has produced a large, enlightening literature exploring possible causes including availability of coal, efficiency of markets, level of farm production, and government competence, all of which are explored here. However, Pomeranz inadvertently obscured the most promising explanation, the particular nature of China's land ownership, by confusing it with the private property developed in common law societies. There is good reason for this mistake—Han Suyin, author of *A Many Splendored Thing*, who lived in China and whose husband was an expert in real estate, regarded Chinese land possession as personal possession. However, as will be clear by this stage, the common law ascribed a primacy to individual ownership that was unthinkable in China. Not only did it give rise to forms of personal behavior as well as social, economic, and political structures that were absent in China, its entire individualized ethos was completely at variance with the priority that Confucian principles accorded to the sustenance of the family.

153 China's agricultural productivity and market efficiency are the subjects of a series of studies influenced by the work of Robert Allen of Nuffield College, Oxford University, including Robert C. Allen, "Agricultural Productivity and Rural Incomes in England and the Yangtze Delta, c. 1620–c. 1820," *The Economic History Review* 62, issue 3 (August 2009): 525–550; R. C. Allen, J.-P. Bassino, D. Ma, C. Moll-Murata, and J. L. van Zanden, "Wages, Prices, and Living Standards in China, Japan, and Europe, 1738–1925," *LSE Research online* (2009), http://eprints.lse.ac.uk/27871/1/WP123.pdf; Robert C. Allen, "Involution, Revolution, or What? Agricultural Productivity, Income, and Chinese Economic Development," *Citeseer online*, http://citeseerx.ist.psu.edu/viewdoc/summary?doi=10.1.1.196.563.

153 *"a man standing permanently up to the neck in water"*: R. H. Tawney, *Land and Labour in China,* cited in Hinton, *Fanshen*, 45.

154 *warning not to "punish the people as thieves"*: Peter C. Perdue. *China Marches West* (Cambridge, MA: Belknap Press of Harvard University Press, 2005), 375.

154 *character for harmony*: The UCLA Confucius Institute explains, "The idea suggested in this character is that harmony is achieved when food and a hungry mouth come together," http://www.confucius.ucla.edu/think-qiu.

155 *needed only to memorize*: Perdue, *China Marches West*, 255.

155 On the impact of the silver trade, see Richard von Glahn, "Myth and Reality of China's Seventeenth-Century Monetary Crisis," *The Journal of Economic History* 56, no. 2 (June 1996): 429–454; Helen Dunstan, "Orders Go Forth in the Morning and Are Changed by Nightfall: A Monetary Policy Cycle in

Qing China, November 1744–June 1745," *T'oung Pao*, Second Series, vol. 82, fasc. 1/3 (1996): 66–136. Particularly interesting is the comparative study of the impact of silver on China to its effect on Britain and the Ottoman Empire by Jack Goldstone, "East and West in the Seventeenth Century: Political Crises in Stuart England, Ottoman Turkey, and Ming China," *Comparative Studies in Society and History* 30, no. 1 (Jan. 1988): 103–142.

156 *Chinese merchants, flush with silver, began to buy land*: Perdue, *China Marches West*, 375–380.

156 For the earnings of landless laborers, see Allen, "Agricultural Productivity," 6–15.

157 *Kuei Yu-kuang lamented the vulgarization*: Quoted in Jack A. Goldstone, *Revolution and Rebellion in the Early Modern World* (Berkeley, CA: University of California Press, 1991), 381.

158 *The most influential exponent of Confucian studies*: For Wang Yangming's teaching of Confucian precepts, essentially restoring their personal application in place of the mandarin's increasingly abstract interpretation, see Benjamin A. Elman, *On Their Own Terms: Science in China 1550–1900* (Cambridge, MA: Harvard University Press, 2005), 7–14.

158 For corruption in exams, see Goldstone, "East and West," 122–124 and Perdue, *China Marches West*, 249–255.

158 *"eight-legged essay"*: So-called because it came in eight parts and was widely citicized by nineteenth-century reform-minded Chinese and Western sinologists for rewarding abstruse details. See Elman, *On Their Own Terms*, 333–335.

158 *Yao Wen-jan, a descendant of merchants*: Hilary J. Beattie, *Land and Lineage in China: A Study of T'ung-ch'eng County, Anhwei, in the Ming and Ch'ing Dynasties* (Cambridge: Cambridge University Press, 1979), 68.

159 For the exploits of the Levelling Kings, see Mark Elvin, *The Pattern of the Chinese Past* (Stanford, CA: Stanford University Press, 1973), 245–246.

160 For the continued power of local merchant-descended families, see Beattie, *Land and Lineage*, ch. 4, 88–111.

160 For the artistic accomplishments of the Qianlong emperor, see "A Matter of Taste," by Harold Kahn in *The Elegant Brush, Chinese Painting under the Qianlong Emperor, 1735–1795*, ed. Ju-hsi Chou and Claudia Brown (Phoenix, AZ: Phoenix Art Museum, 1985).

161 *"it should be about the season"*: Quoted in Perdue, *China Marches West*, 417.

161 *"cut off from the world"*: This phrase appears in Qianlong's letter to George III, pointing out that Macartney's uncouth behaviour is supposing the emperor would be interested in his instruments, but excusing it because "I do not forget the lonely remoteness of your island, cut off from the world by intervening wastes of sea," http://www.fordham.edu/halsall/mod/1793qianlong.html.

161 *"The Empire of China is an old, crazy, first rate man-of-war"*: Macartney's comment in *An Embassy to China, Being the Journal Kept by Lord Macartney During His Embassy to the Emperor Ch'ien-lung, 1793–1794*, ed. J. L. Cranmer-Byng (London: Longmans, 1962), 212–213.

162 Cao Xuequin's classic novel is so huge, magical, and beguiling, any summary amounts to a travesty, but the danger faced by imperial officials and the Mandarin's Life-Preserver appears in chapter 4 in *The Story of the Stone,* vol. 1, trans. David Hawkes (London: Penguin Classics, 1973), 111.

163 For the calculation of the imperial taxes, see note to page 141.

163 For the power of the provincial gentry, see Beattie, *Land and Lineage* Ch 4; and Madeleine Zelin, *The Magistrate's Tael: Rationalizing Fiscal Reform in Eighteenth-Century Ch'ing China* (Berkeley, CA: University of California Press, 1985); *passim*; by the end of the eighteenth century, Zelin judged, "rational fiscal administration was dead," 301.

164 For China's enterprising farmers, see "Environment, Market, and Peasant Choice: The Ecological Relationships in the Jianghan Plain in the Qing and the Republic" by Jiayan Zhang. *Modern China* 32, no. 1 (Jan. 2006): 31–63.

164 *when British colonial authorities in Hong Kong.* A 1963 Hong Kong government report, "Chinese Customary Law in Hong Kong's New Territories: some legal premises" by Edwin Haydon, based its findings on an earlier report, entitled "Memorandum of Land," which formed an appendix to the Report of Mr. J. H. Stewart Lockhart, colonial secretary and registrar general of Hong Kong, dated February 7, 1900. Lockhart reported that although apparently measured by the *mu*, one sixth of an acre, the land was in practice measured by variable grain measures, pointing to an agricultural economy whose yardstick was family support rather than financial value. In addition, villages paid the equivalent of a land tax as protection money to the clan that offered them security against attack from outside.

165 *all carved out trading privileges*: Sir Robert Hart, British-appointed head of China's Customs service, pointed out that foreign countries were tearing China to pieces, because approximately 40 percent of the government's small revenue was allocated to them as reparations for supposed losses during wars with China. Stephen Thomas, *Foreign Intervention and China's Industrial Development, 1870–1911* (Boulder, CO: Westview Press, 1984) 11.

166 *split between more than seven hundred households*: Haydon, "Chinese Customary Law."

166 *the number of people it would support*: Allen, "Agricultural Productivity," 14.

Chapter Ten: Land Becomes Mind

169 *Walter Baker, a self-styled "professor of physic"*: For Walter Baker's struggle to break Dr. James's patent, see Adam Mossoff, "Rethinking the Development of Patents: An Intellectual History, 1550–1800," Occasional Papers in Intellectual Property and Communications Law, *Hastings Law Journal* 1255 (2001), 25–26.

170 *Sir Edward Coke, the preeminent spokesman*: Coke based his argument against monopolies on the grounds that "a mans trade is accounted his life, because it maintaineth his life; and therefore the monopolist that taketh away a mans trade, taketh away his life, and therefore is so much the more odious." Mossoff, ibid; while Samuel Pufendorf wrote in his 1672 treatise, *De Jure Naturae et Gentium*,

"Monopolies . . . tis an odious Name, and the Laws of many States brand it grievously," ibid., 23.

171 *"teach an artist"*: Mansfield's instructions to the jury in another patents case, *Liardent v. Johnson,* were printed in the *Morning Post*, Feb. 23, 1778, for everyone to read. Ibid., 30.

171 *"there is no connection between ownership"*: The Marquis de Condorcet's objection appears in *Oeuvres de Condorcet*, ed. A. Condorcet O'Connor and M. F. Arago, vol. 11 (Paris: Firmin Didot Frères, 1847), 308–309.

171 *This system of state-sponsored innovation*: Kaye's career in France is described in "Technological and legal transfers in the Age of Enlightenment" by Liliane Hilaire-Pérez. *La Revue de la Musée des Arts et des Métiers*, no. 12 (Sept. 1995). Granted a *privilège exclusif*, he was deemed to be "at the service of the State."

171 *At first glance*: The cost and dubious protection offered by a patent are explored in Christine MacLeod, "The Paradoxes of Patenting: Invention and Its Diffusion in 18th- and 19th-Century Britain, France, and North America." *Technology and Culture* 32, no. 4, Patents and Invention (Oct. 1991): 885–910; 891–901.

172 *"The whole claim"*: Justice Yates's objection in Mossoff, "Rethinking," 49.

172 *On the other side of the Atlantic*: Article 1, Section 8, Clause 8 of the United States Constitution, "the Copyright clause," empowers the Congress "to promote the Progress of Science and useful Arts by securing for limited Times to Authors and Inventors the exclusive Right to their respective Writigns and Discoveries."

172 *This unfriendly atmosphere*: The failure of Cartwright's and Arkwright's patents are studied in Trevor Griffiths, Philip A. Hunt, and Patrick K. O'Brien, "Inventive Activity in the British Textile Industry, 1700–1800," *Journal of Economic History* 52, no. 4 (Dec. 1992).

172 *"We had better bear with some inconvenience"* in Mossoff, "Rethinking," 33.

173 *Yet the messiness of the British process*: The counterintuitive consequence that weak patent law and hostile judges should have helped diffuse technical knowledge is explored in detail in Macleod, "The Paradoxes of Patenting," 885–910.

173 *"the property one has"*: Adam Smith's contention that a patent was a real right, in Christine MacLeod, *Inventing the Industrial Revolution: The English Patent System, 1660–1800* (Cambridge: Cambridge University Press, 2002), 198.

173 *Fighting their way*: The judicial struggle to decide whether patents were privileges or property is covered in Mossoff, "Rethinking," 43–50; Loughhborough's judgment, 46.

175 *Jethro Tull, a lawyer-turned-farmer*: For the background to Jethro Tull's inventions see Norman Hidden, "Jethro Tull I, II, and III." *Agricultural History Review* 37, pt. 1 (1989): 26–35.

176 *"The working manufacturing people"*: Daniel Defoe's opinion of the English diet appeared in *The Complete English Tradesman: In Familiar Letters; Directing Him in All the Several Parts and Progressions of Trade . . . Calculated for the Instruction of Our Inland Tradesmen; and Especially of Young Beginners*, vol. 1. London: Charles Rivington, 1726, 386.

176 *the price of land should have fallen* : For the price of land in the eighteenth century,

see Robert C. Allen, "The Price of Freehold Land and the Interest Rate in the Seventeenth and Eighteenth Centuries." *The Economic History Review, New Series* 41, no. 1 (Feb. 1988): 33–50; and John Habakkuk, "The Rise and Fall of English Landed Families, 1600–1800." *Transactions of the Royal Historical Society, Fifth Series* 29 (1979): 187–207.

177 *it no longer made economic sense*: Although rents for enclosed land in the eighteenth century rose considerably, Allen, in "The Price of Freehold Land," argued there was no gain in efficiency, while the economic returns were not much better than Consols according to Gregory Clark in "Commons Sense: Common Property Rights, Efficiency, and Institutional Change." *The Journal of Economic History* 58, no. 1 (March 1998): 73–102.

178 Shortly before emigrating, Morris Birkbeck, who rented Wanborough farm in Surrey, England, went on to found the anti-slavery center known as the English Settlement in Illinois. His reason for emigrating was primarily, he wrote in *Notes on a Journey in America*, "to escape the insolence of wealth and the servility of pauperism" that he had experienced in England.

178 *government posts as property*: Owning administrative posts as property did not end until the early nineteenth century. For the life and career of Spencer Perceval, see Andro Linklater, *Why Spencer Perceval Had to Die: The Assassination of a Prime Minister* (New York and London: Bloomsbury, 2012).

178 *The transition was made obvious in*: The far-reaching nature of David Ricardo's theory, most completely advanced in *The Principles of Political Economy, and Taxation* (1817), of the comparative advantage enjoyed by one means of production over another, where each employs equal quantities of capital and labor, tends to obscure its important context: Ricardian economics is grounded in rural, rather than mercantile, capitalism. His definition of rent as "that portion of the produce of the earth which is paid to the landlord [by the tenant] for the use of the original and indestructible powers of the soil" also applies to industrial production, as do his theories on taxation—that a tax on the economic rent, or unearned increase in value, of land cannot be passed on. But they do so only in certain conditions. Ricardian economics held good throughout the nineteenth century, and still do in many circumstances today, but become distorted by solutions to the crisis of overproduction.

178 The origins of the Industrial Revolution are endlessly debated, not least because they are multiple and interdependent. But the range of topics discussed by members of the Society for the Encouragement of Arts, Manufactures and Commerce and covered in its magazine indicate why Britain's rural capitalists should have morphed so easily into industrial capitalists.

180 When Samuel Garbett, described by Matthew Boulton to Benjamin Franklin in 1766 as "a Zealous Advocate for Truth & for the rights of your oppress'd Countrymen," combined roles as the founder of large scale chemical production (sulphuric acid) and armaments manufacture (Carron iron works) with political lobbying against taxation of industrial exports, and the promotion of Birmingham industry and finance. See J. M. Norris, "Samuel Garbett and the Early Development of Industrial Lobbying in Great Britain." *The Economic History Review, New Series* 10, no. 3 (1958): 450–460.

181 *two thirds of the capital available*: The significance of landed capital in the early nineteenth century appears from comparative tables from 1688 to 1863 produced by Robert Giffen in *The Growth of Capital (*1889) cited in Peter Mathias, *Industrial Economies: Capital Labour and Enterprise* 7, pt. 1, p. 33, in the *Cambridge Economic History of Europe*. The pattern is probably more reliable than the raw data:

date	**author**	**area**	**reproducible***	**land**	**plate/ cash**	**total**
1688	King/Davenant	England	112	180	28	320
1800	Beeke	UK	665	825	250	1740
1812	Colquhoun	"	837	1079	211	2127
1832	de Pebrer	"	1112	1438	293	2843
1863	Giffen	"	3749	1864	500	6113

Millions of £; * overseas assets, buildings, equipment, inventories

181 *A fully equipped textile factory*: For the cost of investment in factories, see Herbert Heaton, "Financing the Industrial Revolution." *Bulletin of the Business Historical Society* 11, no. 1 (Feb. 1937): 1–10.

181 *Labor was cheaper still*: John Fielden, manufacturer, social reformer, and member of Parliament, succeeded in passing the 1847 Ten Hours Act limiting the amount of time a child could be worked in a factory. His firsthand account of industrial conditions was published in *The Curse of the Factory System* (1836).

182 *George Robinson built no fewer than six mills*: George Robinson's career described in J. H. Beardmore, *The History of Hucknell Torkard* (1909), http://www.nottshistory.org.uk/hucknall1909/hucknall1.htm.

182 *pledging the value of their property*: Property as security, see Heaton, "Financing the Industrial Revolution."

Chapter Eleven: The Independence of an Owner

183 *described the attempt as an attack on property*: James Otis's claim to a natural right of property appeared in "Rights of the British Colonies Asserted and Proved" (1764). His argument was both constitutional, as a British subject his property rights were guaranteed, and grounded in the Puritan belief that freedom was the God-given liberty to exercise conscience freely and equally.

184 *And his argument was echoed*: Samuel Adams's instructions to Boston's representatives in the Massachusetts Assembly.

184 *"civil immunities"*: Blackstone, *Commentaries*.

184 *Franklin provocatively predicted*: Franklin's prediction that the population of the United States would double in twenty-five years turned out to be more accurate than his assumption that they would be English. "Observations Concerning the Increase of Mankind, Peopling of Countries, etc." (1751) in *The Papers of Benjamin*

Franklin. 35 vols. to date. eds. Leonard W. Labaree, et al. (New Haven, CT: Yale University Press, 1959–1999), 225–234.

184 *the creation of more than a dozen land companies*: For the proliferation of land companies see Sakolski, *The Great American Land Bubble*.

185 *the American Canaan*: in *De Brahm's report of the General Survey in the Southern District of North America*, ed. Louis de Vorsey Jr. (New York: Columbia, 1971), 105.

185 *"I can never look upon the Proclamation"*: George Washington to William Crawford, September 20, 1767. George Washington Papers, Manuscript Division, Library of Congress.

186 *"The country might invite a prince"*: For the early land explorations beyond the Appalachians, see Linklater, *Measuring America*, 44–51.

186 *it increased at an annual rate*: The figures on the growth of American capital are from Alvin Rabushka, "A Tax Revolt, First and Foremost." *Hoover Digest No. 4*. Hoover Institution on War, Revolution and Peace (Oct. 2008). Excerpted from Rabushka's book of the same name.

187 *"such an amount of good land"*: From *Travels in North America* by Peter Kalm, London (1771), quoted in *Readings in the Economic History of the United States* by Ernest L. Bogart and Charles M. Thompson (New York: Longmans, 1925), 110.

187 *confronted by a national debt*: The growth of the British national debt. Gary Nash, *The Unknown American Revolution: The Unruly Birth of Democracy and the Struggle to Create America* (New York: Viking, 2005), 45.

187 The change of tone is noted in Jeremy Waldron, *The Right to Private Property* (Oxford: Clarendon, 1988), 533–535.

188 *"We cannot be happy, without being free"*: Letter XII, by "A Farmer," i.e., John Dickinson, published *Pennsylvania Chronicle*, Philadelphia, PA, 1768.

188 *The idea of happiness*: That Calvinism should have been the cradle for the generous idea of an innate desire to seek happiness is less of a paradox than it might appear. The transmogrification of its bleak doctrine of predestined hell for the many and heaven for the elected few began with Jean Calvin himself, who pointed to a happy family life and concern for the welfare of others as a symptom of election. The emphasis had already shifted sufficiently in the reformed Calvinism that Francis Hutcheson imbibed in his youth for predestination to be regarded as close to an innate tendency to goodness in this world rather than a pre-stamped ticket for eternity.

189 *The optimistic teaching*: Jean-Jacques Burlamaqui, *The Principles of Natural Law*, trans. Thomas Nugent, 1752 (Cambridge, MA: University Press, 1807). http://www.constitution.org/burla/burla_1.htm. Part 1, chapter V contains the critical writing about *droit*, here translated as "rule," and about the desire for happiness as "the grand spring which sets us in motion."

190 *Jefferson's attitude to property rights*: Jefferson's doubts about natural rights in property were expressed in a letter to Isaac McPherson, Aug. 13, 1813.

190 *"For shame"*: The conflict appeared in a sermon preached by Nathaniel Niles in 1774; in the Pennsylvania Assembly's "An Act for the Gradual Abolition of Slavery, 1780"; in Dr. Johnson's pamphlet *Taxation no Tyranny* published in 1775; in the Philipsburg Proclamation issued by General Sir Henry Clinton on June 30, 1779.

191 *The underlying conflict*: Madison's notes on the constitutional convention are online: http://avalon.law.yale.edu/subject_menus/debcont.asp; and his thoughts appear in numbers 10, 14, 37–58, and 62–63 of *The Federalist Papers*; his notes form the basis of *The Constitution and America's Destiny* by David B. Robertson (Cambridge and New York: 2005). His views on the political marketplace are best found in *Federalist 10:* "The regulation of these various and interfering interests forms the principal task of modern legislation, and involves the spirit of party and faction in the necessary and ordinary operations of the government."

193 *"He perceives truth with great clearness"*: Fisher Ames made his comment in letter to George Minor, May 29, 1789; Alexander Hamilton's remark was made to George Beckwith in the same year, and is quoted in *The Age of Federalism: The Early American Republic, 1788–1800* by Stanley Elkins and Eric McKitrick (New York and Oxford: Oxford University Press, 1995), 125.

194 *"the alternate domination"*: George Washington's attack on faction was delivered in September 1796 in his "Letter to the People of the United States," better known as his Farewell Address.

Chapter Twelve: The Challenge to Private Property

199 *went out to negotiate*: For the background to the events at Étampes see David Hunt, "The People and Pierre Dolivier: Popular Uprisings in the Seine-et-Oise Department (1791–1792)." *French Historical Studies* 11, no. 2 (Autumn 1979), 184–214.

199 *Helping the Americans*: French involvement in the American War of Independence cost 1.3 billion *livres*, doubling the national debt. Interest payments produced an annual deficit of 112 million *livres*. William Doyle, *Origin of the French Revolution* (New York: Oxford University Press, 1999), ch 2.

200 *"Liberty in commerce"*: This argument had been put to the crowd with Simonneau present by two representatives from the National Assembly after a riot in Étampes the previous September. See Hunt, "Popular Uprisings," 189.

200 *seethed with peasant anger*: Rural discontent at the changes threatening an old way of life surfaced in the *cahiers de doléances*—the lists of complaints produced by each of the Three Estates, nobility, clergy, and others, in 1789—with a significant number from the Third Estate protesting the innovations of new *seigneurs*.

202 *the news of Simmoneau's murder*: For the response of the National Assembly, see Hunt, "Popular Uprisings," 26–29.

202 *"It is revolting":* Dolivier's response was contained in his pamphlet *L'Essai sur la Justice primitive, pour servir de principe générateur au seul ordre social qui peut assurer à l'homme tous ses droits et tous les moyens de bonheur*, published in July 1793 by the Commune d'Anvers.

203 *"From how many crimes"*: *The Origin of Inequality*, originally published in 1754, is best known for opposing Hobbes's picture of natural life as nasty, brutish, and short, with one of natural nobility and goodness. Inevitably, therefore, civilization must be corrupting.

203 *"the general will"*: Contmporary critics of the Revolution, such as Edmund

Burke in "Letter to a Member of the National Assembly" (1791) and Benjamin Constant in "On Ancient and Modern Liberty" (1819) held Rousseau responsible for the Revolution's attack on individual liberty.

204 *"dull, monotonous"*: For the monotony of Robespierre's voice but his electrifying effect on audiences, see Francois Furet and Mona Ozouf, *A Critical Dictionary of the French Revolution* (Cambridge, MA: Harvard University Press, 1989), 303–305.

205 *the influence of Robespierre*: For the pervasive influence of Rousseau on Robespierre's thought, see "The Fundamental Ideas of Robespierre" by Alfred Cobban. *The English Historical Review* 63, no. 246 (Jan. 1948), 29–51.

206 *A direct line of thought*: The linear connection between Dolivier and Marx was first made by Jean Jaurés in *Histoire socialiste de la Revolution française* (Paris, 1970), vol II, 460.

207 *On the Present High Price of Provisions*: The focus of Malthus's essay was the influence of the Poor Law in keeping the price of grain higher than it should have been. He was, apparently, unaware of the violence inflicted by the hungry poor on Simonneau.

208 *the Scottish political reformer Thomas Muir*: The judge delivered his sentence on Thomas Muir with a classic definition of prevailing opinion: "In this country, [the government] is made up of the landed interest which alone has a right to be represented; as for the rabble who have nothing but personal property, what hold has the nation of them? What security for the payment of their taxes? They may pack up all their property on their backs and leave the country in the twinkling of an eye, but landed property cannot be removed."

208 *The catalyst was an encounter*: Jefferson's encounter with the beggar woman outside Fontainebleau was described to Madison in a letter dated October 28, 1785.

209 *"that the earth belongs"*: The idea of usufruct ownership of the land or modified leasehold was put forward in a letter dated September 6, 1789; it reappeared at the foundation of the state of Israel in 1949 when nearly all its territory was vested in the state and was available only on a forty-nine-year, or sabbatical-length lease, and in the economists' public letter addressed to President Gorbachev November 7, 1990.

210 *Three different Congressional committees*: The reports of the committees on the acquisition, measuring, and disposition of the Western Lands were all made in March and April 1784, and appeared in conjunction with Jefferson's two other reports on decimalizing the currency and the weights and measures of the United States, an exceptional outpouring of constitutional creativity.

211 *"The small landholders"*: Jefferson, September 9, 1789, letter to Madison.

Chapter Thirteen: The Evolution of Property

215 The Public Lands Survey, the basic mechanics and the repeated changes and refinement of the process, are contained in the Bureau of Land Management's *Instruction for the Survey of Public Land*, Washington D.C., 1947; and in Linklater, *Measuring America*.

216 *In a striking sentence*: Cutler's remark, *Measuring America*, 82.

218 The Pulliam family's fortunes are recounted in John Mack Farragher's classic account of frontier life, *Sugar Creek: Life on the Illinois Prairie* (New Haven, CT: Yale University Press, 1986).

219 *"That it tended to be suffused in speculation"*: Donald W. Meinig, *The Shaping of America: A Geographical Perspective on 500 Years of History* (New Haven, CT: Yale University Press, 1995), 244.

220 For the influence of Marshall's two judgements see Stuart Banner, *How the Indians Lost Their Land: Law and Power on the Frontier* (Cambridge, MA; Harvard University Press, 2005), 170.

220 *"It is difficult to describe the rapacity"*: *Democracy in America*, vol. 1 by Alexis de Tocqueville, trans. John C. Spencer (New York: J. & H. G. Langley, 1841), 322.

220 *Between May 1800 and June 1820*: figures from "The Public Domain and Nineteenth Century Transfer Policy" by Gary M. Anderson and Dolores T. Martin. *Cato Journal* 6, no. 3 (Winter 1987).

220 *the value of even "unimproved" land*: See "Changes in Total U.S. Agricultural Factor Productivity in the Nineteenth Century" by Robert E. Gallman. *Agricultural History* 46, no. 1, American Agriculture, 1790–1840: A Symposium (Jan. 1972), for evidence that land improvement may have accounted for as much as 80 percent of American physical capital stock.

220 *the growth in value*: The estimate of 12 percent gains for farmers in the Midwest and Northeast comes in *To Their Own Soil: Agriculture in the Antebellum North* by Jeremy Atack and Fred Bateman (Ames, IA: Iowa State University Press, 1987), 252–262.

220 *"by giving credit"*: *Wealth of Nations*, bk. II, ch. 2.

221 *The twenty-seven banks*: For the structure of nineteenth-century banking, see "Comparing UK and US Financial Systems, 1790–1830" by Richard Scylla, in *The Evolution of Financial Markets and Institutions from the Seventeenth Century to the Present,* Jeremy Atack and Larry Neals, eds. (New York: Cambridge University Press, 2008).

221 *Banks were not the only means*: "The Emergence of a Capital Market in Rural Massachusetts, 1730–1838" by Winifred B. Rothenberg. *The Journal of Economic History* 45, no. 4 (Dec. 1985): 781–808.

221 *the rising value of their farms*: see Rothenberg, "Emergence of a Capital Market" for rural investment in industrial, financial, and other nonfarm activities.

222 *the American System*: described in "National Planning of Internal Improvements" by Carter Goodrich. *Political Science Quarterly* 63, no. 1 (March 1948): 16–44.

222 *"Who ever heard of a man"*: *The Cultivator* 1836, quoted in "Housing Bubbles Are Few and Far Between" by Robert J. Shiller. *New York Times,* Feb. 6, 2011.

223 *Horace White*: for his account of the settlement's foundation, see Beloit College archives published online at http://www.beloit.edu/~libhome/Archives/papers/beloitbegin.html.

225 *"The titles in Kentucky"*: See "Speculators and Settler Capitalists: unthinking the mythology about Appalachian landholdings 1790–1860" by Wilma A. Dunaway in *Appalachia in the Making: The Mountain South in the Nineteenth Century,*

Mary Beth Pudup, Dwight Billings, and Altina Waller, eds. (Chapel Hill, NC: University of North Carolina Press, 1995).

225 *"partly on account of slavery"*: David Herbert Donald, *Lincoln* (New York: Touchstone, 1996), 23.

225 *Judge Joseph Story*: his attribution of Kentucky's woes to the decision to allow settlers to appropriate land "by entries and descriptions of their own, without any previous survey under public authority, and without any such boundaries as were precise, permanent, and unquestionable" came in "An address delivered before Members of the Suffolk Bar" in *The American Jurist and Law Magazine* 1, ed. Charles Sumner (Boston: Freeman & Bolles, 1829), 1.

226 *the conventional explanation*: figures for slave ownership derived from the U.S. Census 1860.

226 *up to 90 percent*: for the the distribution of Kentucky land, see Dunaway, "Speculators and Settler Capitalists."

226 *"those who hold and exercise"*: in *The History of Kentucky, Exhibiting an Account of the Modern Discovery; Settlement; Progressive Improvement; Civil and Military Transactions; and the Present State of the Country*, vol. 1 by Humphrey Marshall (Kentucky: Robinson, 1824) 415.

227 *"do business on commission"*: Dunaway "Speculators and Settler Capitalists," 55.

227 *"Leaves cut out of the Books"*: Quoted in Linklater, *Measuring America*; description of the spread of the survey, ibid.

228 *"The possession of land is the aim"*: by Harriet Martineau, *Society in America* (Paris: Galignani, 1837), 292.

229 *"Every industrious citizen"*: John Melish, *A Geographical description of the United States . . . intended as an accompaniment to Melish's map"* (Philadelphia, 1818), 59.

229 *"Other peoples of America"*: In *Democracy in America*, vol. 1, by Alexis de Tocqueville, trans. Henry Reeve (New York: Dearborn, 1840), ch. XVII, part 4.

230 *Lorenzo Dow*: appears in *Appleton's Cyclopedia of American Biography,* vol. 2, James Grant Wilson and John Fiske, eds., 579.

231 *"fresh from the backwoods"*: No reliable source has been found for Davy Crockett's supposed self-description.

231 *"all the Indian Tribes once existing"*: Henry Knox comment, quoted in *Savagism and Civilization: A Study of the Indian and the American Mind* by Roy Harvey Pearce (Berkeley, CA: University of California Press, 1988), 56.

232 *American empire*: In his popular textbook, *American Geography* (Boston, 1789), Jedidiah Morse made clear the imperial nature of American expansion. "The Mississippi was never designed as the western boundary of the American empire . . . We cannot but anticipate the period, as not far distant, when the AMERICAN EMPIRE will comprehend millions of souls west of the Mississippi."

232 *a claim from John Potter*: Linklater, *Measuring America*, 209

Chapter Fourteen: The Empire of Land

234 *Edward Gibbon Wakefield*: see the generally admiring *Edward Gibbon Wakefield: Builder of the British Commonwealth* by Paul Bloomfield. London: Longmans,

1961; the generally critical *Edward Gibbon Wakefield and the Colonial Dream: A Reconsideration* (Wellington, NZ: Friends of the Turnbull Library, 1997); and the generally evenhanded *A sort of conscience: the Wakefields* by Philip Temple (Auckland, NZ: Auckland University Press, 2002).

235 *The Privy Council statement*: this appears to be the first official declaration that this was the policy of the British Empire. *Acts of the Privy Council: Colonial Series,* vol. 6, ed. W. L. Grant and J. Munro (Hereford, 1908–12), 491.

235 *William Bligh*: see *The Great Land Rush and the Making of the Modern World 1650–1900* by John C. Weaver (Montreal, London, Ithaca: McGill-Queen's University Press, 2003), 75.

236 *"It is the great merit of E. G. Wakefield"*: Marx paid his compliment in vol. I, ch. 33, of *Capital* (Moscow: Progress, 1972–76), http://www.marxists.org/archive/marx/works/1867-c1/ch33.htm.

236 *"Great Britain derives nothing but loss"*: *Wealth of Nations,* bk. IV, ch. 7, sec. 3, 2.

237 *a book that made clear the debt he owed*: Edward Gibbon Wakefield, *England and America: a comparison of the political and social states of both nations* (London: Bentley, 1837). "Their rule for the disposal of waste land," 175; "the English will hunt over the world," 88.

239 *The opening experiment was in South Australia*: Wakefield's own account appears in *A View on the Art of Colonization* (London, 1849). For a more dispassionate version, see Temple, *A Sort of Conscience*, 166–173.

241 *Thomas Newman*: His testimony appears in *A Description of South Australia with sketches of New South Wales, Port Lincoln, Port Philip and New Zealand* by Theodore Scott (Glasgow: Duncan Campbell, 1839), 29.

241 *London investors*: For early British investment in Australia, see ch. 3 of *Replenishing the Earth. The Settler Revolution and the Rise of the Anglo-World, 1783–1939* by James Belich (Oxford: Oxford University Press, 2009).

241 *Wakefield was engaged on his second experiment*: Wakefield's account of his Canadian activities appears throughout *The Art of Colonization*. Temple, *A Sort of Conscience*, pp. 209–21 is more reliable; Melbourne's warning not to touch him "with a pair of tongs," ibid., 210.

242 *an extensive plan for the government of Canada*: *Lord Durham's Report on the affairs of British North America*, 2 vols. by John Lambton Durham (Oxford: Clarendon, 1839). "useless and consequent delay," 210; "no security of property in land," 231.

244 *The development of Bruce County*: from *History of the County of Bruce* by Norman Robertson (Ontario, Canada: Briggs, 1906), http://www.electricscotland.com/history/canada/bruce/index.htm; the context comes from William L. Marr, "Nineteenth Century Tenancy Rates in Ontario's Counties, 1881 and 1891," *Journal of Social History* 21, no. 4 (Summer 1988): 753–764.

245 *"In no spot within British territory"*: quoted in Belich, *Replenishing the Earth,* 148.

245 *a quirk of banking regulation*: Canadian banking practices from "A history of banking in Canada" by B. E. Walker in vol. 2 of *A History of Banking in All the Leading Nations; Comprising the United States; Great Britain; Germany; Austro-Hungary;*

France; Italy; Belgium; Spain; Switzerland; Portugal; Roumania; Russia; Holland; The Scandinavian Nations; Canada; China; Japan (4 vols) ed. the Editor of the *Journal of Commerce and Commercial Bulletin* (New York: The Journal of Commerce and Commercial Bulletin, 1896).

246 *French-Canadian farming*: in "Land Tenure, Ethnicity, and the Condition of Agricultural Income and Productivity in Mid-Nineteenth-Century Quebec" by Morris Altman. *Agricultural History* 72, no. 4 (Autumn 1998): 708–762.

247 *"Wakefield discovered"*: Marx's comment on Wakefield, *Capital*, ch. 33.

247 *"Be it by larceny"*: Quoted in *Gladstone 1809–1898* by H. C. G. Matthews (Oxford: Oxford University Press, 2005), 276.

247 *the New Zealand Company on his advice*: Wakefield's activities in New Zealand comes from Temple, *A Sort of Conscience,* part 4, "A Suicide of the Affections"; William Wakefield's activities, ibid., ch. 22.

250 *With the loss of land*: The cultural alienation of Maori is addressed by numerous government and voluntary agency publications, among them *Suicide Prevention in New Zealand: A Contemporary Perspective* by S. Collings and A. Beautrais (Wellington: Ministry of Health, 2005). Similar sociological studies confirm the same dislocated pattern among the descendants of indigenous peoples in every private property society.

251 *"the utter absence of individual title"*: Elias Rector's comment is quoted in Alexandra Harmon, "American Indians and Land Monopolies in the Gilded Age." *The Journal of American History* 90, no. 1 (June 2003): 106–133.

252 *the success of the Afrikaaners*: The conflict between Afrikaaner farmers and British landowners is examined in "The Globalization of Property Rights: An Anglo and American Frontier Land Paradigm, 1700–1900" by John Weaver (*Working Paper 00/1* McMaster University, 2000).

253 *"His neighbours' smoke shall vex his eyes"*: "The Voortrekker" by Rudyard Kipling, *The Collected Poems of Rudyard Kipling* (London: Wordsworth, 1994), 581.

Chapter Fifteen: The End of Serfdom and Slavery

255 "I'm like a man possessed": Tolstoy's habitual raping of female serfs was detailed in his diary, which he forced his wife to read. "Peasant women in the garden," quoted Figes, *Natasha's Dance*, 265; "Today, in the big old wood," quoted in "In which we die on the altar of Leo Tolstoy" in *Intellectuals: From Marx and Tolstoy to Sartre and Chomsky,* Revised Edition, by Paul Johnson (New York: Harper Perennial, 2007).

256 *In Russia, that process began*: For the general impact of emancipation on landowners, see *The Russian Landed Gentry and the Peasant Emancipation of 1861* by Terence Emmons (Cambridge: Cambridge University Press, 1968). The Jarosval petition, ibid., 288.

256 *Boris Chicherin*: For his background and influence, see "Peasant Emancipation and Russian Social Thought: The Case of Boris N. Chicherin" by Gary M. Hamburg. *Slavic Review* 50, no. 4 (Winter 1991): 890–904.

258 *"Commercial farming is growing much more rapidly"*: Lenin's ambivalence about the consequences of emancipation—anxiety about the spread of "commercial farming" and relief that it signaled the bourgeois stage necessary for revolution—emerge clearly from *The Agrarian Question in Russia Towards the Close of the Nineteenth Century,* vol. 15 in *Lenin Collected Works* (Moscow: Progress, 1973), 69–147.

259 *mortgage lending had reached almost one billion rubles*: From "A History of Banking in the Russian Empire" by A. E.Horne, vol. 2 of *A History of Banking in All the Leading Nations.*

260 *The growing mobility of Russian peasants*: Researched in "Peasant Migration and the Settlement of Russia's Frontiers, 1550–1897" by David Moon. *The Historical Journal* 40, no. 4 (Dec. 1997): 859–893; the settlement of "American" Siberia comes from "Peasant Pioneering: Russian Peasant Settlers Describe Colonization and the Eastern Frontier, 1880s–1910" by Willard Sunderland. *Journal of Social History* 34, no. 4 (Summer 2001): 895–922.

260 *How Much Land Does a Man Need?"*: Tolstoy's story can be found online at http://www.online-literature.com/tolstoy/2738/.

261 *"A* mir *is a union of the people"*: Quoted in *Revolutionary Dreams: Utopian Vision and Experimental Life in the Russian Revolution* by Richard Stites (Oxford: Oxford University Press, 1988), 220.

261 *wielded great power*: The *mir's* redistribution of land as a source of welfare emerges clearly from a memoir based on extensive travel in the 1870s, *Russia* by Donald Mackenzie Wallace, originally published 1905, http://www.gutenberg.org/files/1349/1349-h/1349-h.htm.

262 *"For actual property"*: Jefferson's bleak conclusion in the last years of his life was written in a letter to Jared Sparks, February 4, 1824.

263 *"Body of Liberties"*: Digitized copy of *Old South Leaflets* (Boston, 1900), http://history.hanover.edu/texts/masslib.html. Definition of "bond slaverie," verse 91.

263 *"the male servants and slaves"*: In *The History and Present State of Virginia* (1705) by Robert Beverley, http://docsouth.unc.edu/southlit/beverley/beverley.html. ch IX, 235.

263 *"it cannot be presumed"*: Virginia's 1669 law, cited in *Statutes at Large; Being a Collection of All the Laws of Virginia* by William Waller Hening (Richmond, VA: Pleasants, 1809–1823).

264 *Hans Sloane*: His testimony is quoted in *The Making of New World Slavery: From the Baroque to the Modern, 1492–1800* by Robin Blackburn (London: Verso, 1995), 345.

264 *"The master may sell"*: From Louisiana Civil Code, Article 35, 1834.

264 *Judge Thomas Ruffin*: His verdict is quoted in *A Key to Uncle Tom's Cabin* by Harriet Beecher Stowe (Boston: John P. Jewett and Company, 1854), http://utc.iath.virginia.edu/uncletom/key/kyhp.html. Part 2, ch. II, "What is Slavery?"

265 *France's 1685* "Code Noir": Issued 1685, http://chnm.gmu.edu/revolution/d/335/.

265 *the Spanish Empire allowed more humanity*: Spanish law was derived from the thirteenth-century codification *Las Siete Partidas*, discussed especially in relation to Cuba in "Slave Law and Claims-Making in Cuba: The Tannenbaum Debate

Revisited" by Alejandro de la Fuente. *Law and History Review* 22, no. 2 (Summer 2004): 339–369.

266 *"a negroe or mulatto"*: The development of racial prejudice. The Massachusetts Act from *Massachusetts Acts and Resolves of 1705*, ch. 10, sec. 4, http://archives.lib.state.ma.us.

267 *Legislation did not stop the sex*: Advertisements for escaped slaves in the *Pennsylvania Chronicle* from 1767–73 and the slave register of Chester County, PA, 1780, both showed 20 percent of slaves were mulatto. Cited in *Slavery in the North* by Douglas Harper, http://www.slavenorth.com/slavenorth.htm.

267 *Chief Justice Joseph Lumpkin*: His opinion was delivered in *Bryan v. Walton*, 14 Georgia 185 (1853).

267 *"property in persons"*: Daniel Webster's much-quoted speech in defense of the Union was delivered in the Senate March 7, 1850. Emerson's response came in a lecture, "The Fugitive Slave Law," delivered in the Tabernacle, New York City, March 7, 1854. *The Works of Ralph Waldo Emerson, in 12 vols.* (*Fireside Edition.* Boston and New York: 1909), http://oll.libertyfund.org/?option=com_staticxt&staticfile=show.php%3Ftitle=1961&chapter=123098&layout=html&Itemid=27.

268 *"We have a right of protection"*: Senator Albert Brown's speech quoted in *A People & a Nation: A History of the United States* by Mary Beth Norton *et al.* (Stamford, CT: Cengage Learning, 2011), 381.

269 *Massive changes were brought about*: For Reconstruction, see *Forever Free: The Story of Emancipation and Reconstruction* by Eric Foner (New York: Knopf Doubleday, 2005).

269 *"Political reconstruction is inevitable now"*: Mary Greenhow Lee's entry in her nine-hundred-page diary is quoted in *Slavery in America* by Dorothy Schneider and Carl J. Schneider (New York: Infobase, 2005), 376–377.

Chapter Sixteen: The Crisis of Capitalism

272 *"such a triumph over physical difficulties"*: For the impact of the *Dunedin's* voyage, see *OECD Insights International Trade Free, Fair and Open?* by Patrick Love Patrick and Ralph Lattimore. (Paris: OECD), 116.

273 *Almost twelve million bushels of wheat*: For British and American commodity trade, see Belich *Replenishing the Earth,* ch. 14, "Urban carnivores"; "call Ohio her kitchen garden," ibid., 485.

274 *"They are also purchasing horses"*: For the impact of the Volga Mennonites, see "The Migration of the Russian-Germans to Kansas" by Norman E. Saul. *Kansas Historical Quarterly* 40, no. 1 (Spring 1974): 38–62.

275 *Similar networks operated internationally*: For nineteenth-century migration pattern, see Belich, *Replenishing the Earth*, ch. 3, "Exploding West," (267–268); 12 million migrants (ibid., 66); youthfulness of migrants (ibid., 205); "land mania" (ibid., 267); "most mercurial" (ibid., 187).

276 *"I shall buy eighty lots"*: Astor's advice, Linklater, *Measuring America*, 179.

277 *the freedom and equality that characterized the United States*: Even at its most

egalitarian, American society had its inequalities: as much as 25 percent of midwestern farms were rented before the Civil War, and the richest 1 percent owned 12 percent of the land. However, so long as the supply of land appeared inexhaustible, a statistical anomaly indicated that the society had achieved perfect equality. By entering infinity, representing open access to limitless resources, the Gini coefficient, the most informative equation for calculating income and wealth inequality, will give a result equivalent to zero, or perfect equality (where all the resources are owned by one person, the result is one).

277 *No one perceived this more clearly*: Henry George's *Progress and Poverty* is accessible online, http://www.henrygeorge.org/pcontents.htm.

279 *the rules of the marketplace had ceased to apply*: For the circumstances that led to the crisis of overproduction, see *Recent Economic Changes and Their Effect on Production and Distribution of Wealth and Well-Being of Society* by David A. Wells (New York: Appleton, 1891), "Those engaged in great industrial enterprises," 73.

280 *the need to bring in more investment*: Limited liability developed earlier in the United States, developing on a state by state basis, beginning with Massachusetts in 1808. It was especially beneficial to the spread of rural banking, with no fewer than 330 state banks in operation by 1825. See Scylla, "Comparing UK and US Financial Systems," 109–111. However American banks were limited to state operation, while British banks and other financial institutions operated internationally.

281 *"the great producers"*: Wells, *Recent Economic Changes*, 74.

281 *United States Steel*: For international steel production, see *The Rise and Fall of the Great Powers: Economic Change and Military Conflict from 1500 to 2000* by Paul Kennedy (New York: Vintage, 1989), 242–244; coal production, Henry Adams in "A Law of Acceleration" in *The Education of Henry Adams* (Boston: Massachusetts Historical Society, 1918).

282 *"the great wheat fields of the state of Dakota"*: Wells, *Recent Economic Changes*, 57–58.

282 *What underpinned the banks' lending*: For an explanation of the anomalous financial state of American farmers at the end of the 19th century, see "Economic Development and Competition for Land Use in the United States" by Philip M. Raup. *Journal of Farm Economics* 39, no. 5, Proceedings of the Annual Meeting of the American Farm Economic Association (Dec. 1957), 1,514–1,526; also "Corporate Farming in the United States" by Philip M. Raup. *The Journal of Economic History* 33, no. 1, "The Tasks of Economic History" (Mar. 1973), 274–290.

283 *Among the grain merchants*: Cargill, now the largest private owned corporation in the United States, and Archer and Daniels, have becomes two of the four giants known as ABCD—ADM, Bunge, Cargill and Dreyfus—that dominate the food industry.

284 *more than three hundred cartels*: For Germany's cartels, see *History of Germany 1780–1919: The Long Nineteenth Century* by David Blackbourn (Oxford: Blackwell, 2003), part 3, "The Age of Modernity," 311.

284 *"Even today," he wrote in 1910*: For his plan to take control of the economy

through the banks, see *Finance Capital* by Rudolf Hilferding (London: Routledge, 1981), 367–68.

285 *"part of the Greater Britain"*: quoted in Belchin, *Replenishing the Earth*, 481.

285 *"a projection of the nineteenth century's fear"*: Alan Greenspan's defense of monopolies appeared in a paper given at the Antitrust Seminar of the National Association of Business Economists, Cleveland, September 25, 1961.

286 *"conspicuous consumption"*: In *Theory of the Leisure Class* by Thorstein Veblen. Fairford, United Kindom: Echo, 2007, 33–36, and ch. 4 *passim*.

287 *"It's part of him. . . ."*: in *The Grapes of Wrath* by John Steinbeck. (New York: Barnes & Noble, 1997), 35.

Chapter Seventeen: State Capitalism

291 *The birth of the new Prussia*: German reform, see *History of Germany 1780–1919: The Long Nineteenth Century* by David Blackbourn (Oxford: Blackwell, 2003), 81–84.

292 *"The strongest pillar"*: Quoted in "Prussia in Transition: Society and Politics under the Stein Reform Ministry of 1808" by Marion W. Gray. *Transactions of the American Philosophical Society, New Series* 76, no. 1 (1986), 1–175, p. 128.

292 *"It is indeed a wonderful sensation"*: Hegel's encounter with Napoleon. *Hegel: A Biography* by Terry Pinkard (Cambridge: Cambridge University Press, 2001), 228.

292 *"all spiritual reality"*: in *The Philosophy of History* by G. W. F. Hegel, trans. J. Sibree (Kitchener, ON: Batoche, 1900). Introduction, "Classification of Historic Data," http://www.marxists.org/reference/archive/hegel/works/hi/lectures.htm.

293 *"put an end"*: *The Communist Manifesto in Marx/Engels Selected Works,* vol. 1 (Moscow: Progress, 1969), ch. 1, 98–137.

294 *land-hungry junge Herren*: For the *Junkers*, see *Ordinary Prussians. Brandenburg Junkers and Villagers, 1500–1840* by William Hagen (Cambridge: Cambridge University Press, 2002). Their origin p. 6.

294 *"those who wish to operate with open pastures"*: Bismarck's Speech in the North German Reichstag in Defense of his Draft Constitution (March 11, 1867), http://germanhistorydocs.ghi-dc.org/search/search.cfm.

294 *"to be available to my people"*: Elard von Oldenburg-Januschau, "The Rural Landlord and his people," c. 1883, from his *Erinnerung* [Memoirs], 1936, http://germanhistorydocs.ghi-dc.org/sub_document.cfm?document_id=487.

295 *Within months of the 1807 reform edict*: For the Junkers' classic move to seek political protection for their property, see Hagen, *Ordinary Prussians*, 606.

296 *Courts "far more costly than profitable"*: quoted in Gray, "Prussia in Transition," 97.

297 *"the right to approve state revenues"*: The Progressive party's goals according to von Sybel in *Vorträge und Aufsätze* [*Lectures and Essays*] by Heinrich von Sybel, 2nd ed. (Berlin, 1875) 322–327. English excerpt "Heinrich von Sybel Describes the Structure of the German Empire and the Prospects for Liberty" (January 1, 1871) in *German History in Documents and Images* (GHDI) (Washington, DC: German Institute).

297 *The timing of Prussia's industrial revolution*: For the persistence of handloom weavers and other preindutrial crafts see Blackbourn, *History of Germany*, 137–139.

298 *"It is bad policy"*: In "Outlines of American political economy," (1827) quoted in "Friedrich List and the political economy of the nation-state" by David Levi-Faur. *Review of International Political Economy* 4, no. 1 (Spring 1997), 154–157.

298 *"The iron rails become a nerve system"*: *The National System of Political Economy* (1841), quoted in *Cyclopædia of Political Science, Political Economy, and the Political History of the United States*, ed. John J. Lalor (New York: Maynard, 1899), vol. III, ch. 118, para. 35.

298 *Prussia's powerful bureaucracy*: For the ethos of the Prussian civil service, see "The Social Policies of Prussian Officials: The Bureaucracy in a New Light" by Hermann Beck. *The Journal of Modern History* 64, no. 2 (June 1992), 263–298.

299 *A lobbying campaign for greater freedom*: For the motives of German business 1861–63, see "*Salus publica suprema lex*: Prussian Businessmen in the New Era and Constitutional Conflict" by James M. Brophy. *Central European History* 28, no. 2 (1995), 122–151; the three hundred-million-taler meeting, 147; political withdrawal, 147–149.

299 *"Bismarck's dodge"*: quoted in *The Age of Bismarck: Documents and Interpretations* ed. Theodore S. Hamerow (New York: Harper & Row, 1973), 156–158.

300 *"these much-maligned Junkers"*: Baumgarten's self-criticism, "Der deutsche Liberalismus. Eine Selbstkritik" (1866) is quoted in "German Liberalism Recast: Hermann Baumgarten's *Self-Criticism*," GHDI.

301 *"The Bismarck System is developing terribly quickly"*: "Max von Forckenbeck to Franz von Stauffenberg on the need for National Liberal opposition (January 19, 1879) in GHDI, ibid.

301 *Bismarck's truly astonishing invention*: Bismarck's creation of the corporate state, see Blackbourn, *History of Germany*, 342–350.

302 *German historians, led by Hans Rosenberg*: Rosenberg's thesis that the roots of Nazism lay in Prussian absolutism has fallen out of favor for reasons explained in William W. Hagen, "Descent of the Sonderweg: Hans Rosenberg's History of Old-Regime." *Central European History* 24, no. 1 (1991), 24–50.

302 *"If a manufacturing enterprise is to flourish"*: In *Carl Ferdinand Freiherr Stumm-Halberg* (1936), quoted in "Carl Ferdinand von Stumm-Halberg, Address to his Employees (c. 1889), GHDI.

303 *brushed aside by the growth of industry*: For the decline in agricuture's share of GNP, see "Forging an Empire: Bismarckian Germany, 1866–1890," GHDI.

303 *"They're no longer the pillars"*: *The Stechlin by* Theodore Fontane, trans. William L. Zwiebel (Rochester, NY: Camden House, 1995), 228–229.

304 Bürgerliches Gesetzbuch (BGB): For an exceptionally lucid explanation of the intent of the BGB in property exchange, see the website http://www.dr-hoek.de/EN/beitrag.asp?t=German-Land-Law.

305 *they routinely had to resort to ballot-box fraud*: The evidence for ballot-box stuffing comes in "Shaping Democratic Practice and the Causes of Electoral Fraud: The Case of Germany Before 1914" by Daniel Ziblatt. *OCSID working paper 04*; Oxford Centre for the Study of Inequality and Democracy (2005).

305 *blaming their ills on a Jewish conspiracy*: For the Agrarian League's politics and embrace of anti-semitism, see "Anti-Semitism, Conservative Propaganda, and Regional Politics in Late Nineteenth CenturyGermany" by James Retallack, *German Studies Review* 11, no. 3 (Oct. 1988), 377–403.

Chapter Eighteen: The Cold War

306 *Roughly the size of California*: Japan's physical shape and fifteen-degree slope come from *Encyclopedia of World Geography* ed. Peter Haggett (New York: Marshall Cavendish, 2001), 3,062.

307 *the feudalism of the Tokugawa was nationalized*: For the impact of land reforms see *Land Reform in Japan* by R. P. Dore. (London: Athlone Press, 1984).

307 *ideology based on the* kokutai: The creation of the "national community" is explored in "The Japanese "Kokutai" (National Community) History and Myth" by Joseph M. Kitagawa. *History of Religions* 13, no. 3 (Feb. 1974), 209–226.

308 *"everyone should play his part"*: The rural context of *Nhon-shugi* and the transfer of samurai values to business come from *The rise of modern business: Great Britain, the United States, Germany, Japan and China (*3rd edition) by Mansel G. Blackford (Chapel Hill, NC: University of North Carolina Press, 2008), 125.

308 *the Meiji government deliberately taxed agriculture*: The Meiji government's policy of taxing agriculture to kick-start industry is a central theme in "The Role of Agriculture in Economic Development" by Bruce F. Johnston and John W. Mellor. *The American Economic Review* 51, no. 4 (Sept. 1961), 566–593.

309 *Secret nationalist societies proliferated*: For the Young Officers and 1930s violence, see Blackford, *The Rise of Modern Business*, 138.

309 *the basic difference between imperial Germany and imperial Japan*: Richard Sims explicitly contrasts the nature of fascism in Japan and Germany in "Japanese Fascism," *History Today* 32, issue 1, 1982.

309 *So long as the Nazis remained outsiders*: The change in Nazi fortunes from being outsiders to mainstream is customarily ascribed to the economic effects of the Depression, but Hitler's switch of emphasis on Clause 17 transformed popular perception of their street violence.

310 *That heroic achievement*: Appropriately, Litten is commemorated by the Hans Litten prize awarded for outstanding work in the defense of human rights.

311 For Wolf Ladejinsky's life and career, see "Wolf Ladejinsky, Tireless (and Frustrated) Advocate of Land Reform" by Ben Stavis, Temple University, PA (2004). http://astro.temple.edu/~bstavis/courses/215-ladejinsky.htm. And, *Agrarian Reform as Unfinished Business: The Selected Papers of Wolf Ladejinsky* ed. Louis Walinsky. (London: Oxford University Press, 1977); for reforms in Japans, ibid. 281–285; Ladejinsky noted that one "immediate result of the transfer of ownership was the sharp increase in the accumulation of rural capital," 285; and, looking back over a decade later, "Beyond the Land Reform: Japan's Agricultural Prospect" by R. P. Dore. *Pacific Affairs* 36, no. 3 (Autumn 1963), 265–276.

312 *"several million tenant farmers"*: Quoted in *Aftermath of War: Americans and the*

Remaking of Japan, 1945–52 by Howard B. Schonberger. (Kent, OH: Kent State University Press, 1989), 65.

312 *"the democratization of the villages"*: Dore's comments on change in social attitudes after land reform are in *Land Reform in Japan* by R. P. Dore (London: Oxford University Press, 1959), "end of hallowed hierarchy" (ibid., 161); "sense of equality" (ibid., 218); the number of peasants involved (ibid., 149).

313 Wider economic impact, see "Agricultural Land Reform in Postwar Japan" by Toshihiko Kawagoe. *Policy Research Working Paper 2111*; World Bank Development Research Group, 1999.

313 *its role was essential*: For the role of land reform in Taiwan's economic success, see "Agriculture as the Foundation for Development: the Taiwanese Story" by Tsu-tan and Shun-yi Shei, in *Taiwan's Development Experience: lessons on the roles of government and market*, eds. Erik Thorbecke and Henry Wan (Boston: Kluwer, 1999); for the increase in productivity, see "Economic Consequences of Land Reform in Taiwan" by Anthony Y. C. Koo. *Asian Survey* 6, no. 3 (March 1966): 150–157.

314 *"Negotatiating with a tiger"*: Quoted Ladejinsky, *Agrarian Reform*, 101.

315 *his third success*: Land reform in South Korea. "Outcome of Land Reform in the Republic of Korea" by Ki Hyuk Pak. *Journal of Farm Economics* 38, no. 4 (Nov. 1956), 1015–1023.

315 *a direct comparison with North Korea*: The differences between South Korea's development path and those of Japan and Taiwan are explored in "Contesting Models of East Asian Development and Financial Liberalization: A Case Study of South Korea" by Amiya Kumar Bagchi. *Social Scientist* 36, no. 9–10 (Sep.–Oct., 2008), 4–23.

316 *The prize in the competition*: Ladejinsky's supporters claimed his program was "the only successful anti-communist step we have taken in Asia," quoted in *The Hungry World: America's Cold War Battle Against Poverty in Asia* by Nick Cullather (Cambridge, MA: Harvard University Press, 2010), 95.

317 *"Small-scale production"*: Lenin's interest in agriculture surfaced in ch. 2 of *The Development of Capitalism in Russia* (1899), expressing his belief that rich peasants had become capitalist. The Bolshevik nationalization of land in 1918 was the necessary first step toward making agriculture socialist.

317 *"avaricious, bloated and bestial"*: Lenin's outburst was quoted in *The Pursuit of the Millennium* by Norman Cohn (Oxford: Oxford University Press, 1970), 312.

317 *families of more than half a million farmers*: The most commonly quoted figure for deaths from famine and government is twelve million. The figures for the growth of the Soviet economy are taken from "A reassessment of the Soviet industrial revolution" by Robert C. Allen in *Comparative Economic Studies* (Basingstoke: Palgrave Macmillan, 2005).

Chapter Nineteen: The End of Land Reform

320 *Castro as "a petty bourgeois putschist"*: quoted in "The Resurrections of Che Guevara" by Mike Gonzalez. *International Socialist* issue 77, 1997.

321 *"The mass carries out with matchless enthusiasm"*: taken from one of Guevara's last public pronouncements, "From Algiers, for Marcha: The Cuban Revolution Today," written March 1965 (*The Che Reader* [Sydney: Ocean Press, 2005]).

321 *the National Institute of Agrarian Reform*: The activities of INRA and Guevara's disillusionment with the growing power of the Communists are detailed in Gonzalez "Resurrections."

322 *"a national security risk"*: Ladejinsky's indictment, and the shift away from land reform. *Cold War Culture and Society: The Cold War* by Lori Lyn Bogle (New York: Routledge, 2001), 310–314.

323 *Ladejinsky's new role*: Ladejinsky's attempts to introduce land reform to Vietnam. Ladejinsky, *Agrarian Reform*, 246–258; "robbed by the Viet Min," 255; data on land distribution, 301–302.

325 *"more primitive, less efficient"*: *History of Latin American Civilization: Sources and Interpretations, the Colonial Experience*, vol. 1, ed. Lewis Hanke (New York: Taylor & Francis, 1969), ix.

326 *the one constant in all the political convulsions*: From the failed attempt in the 1930s by President Getualo Vargas in Brazil to redistribute land, to the twenty-first century Plan Zamora designed by the late President Hugo Chavez to put unused land into the hands of Venezuelan *campesinos,* plans for land reform in Latin America have remained as constant as the inequalities.

327 *"a definitive social, political, and cultural victory"*: "The Take-Off into Self-Sustained Growth" by W. W. Rostow. *The Economic Journal* 66, no. 261 (Mar. 1956), 25–48.

327 *Rostow neglected to mention*: For Sweden's land reforms, see "Towards Agrarian Capitalism: The Case of Southern Sweden during the 19th Century" by Jens Möller. *Geografiska Annaler. Series B, Human Geography* 72, no. 2–3 (1990), 59–72. For its financial development prior to "take-off," see "Sweden in 1850 as an 'Impoverished Sophisticate': Comment" by Charles P. Kindleberger. *The Journal of Economic History* 42, no. 4 (Dec. 1982): 918–920.

328 *Denmark's smaller farms and unproductive sandy soil*: For the cooperative development of Danish agriculture, see "Late 19th Century Denmark in an Irish Mirror: Land Tenure, Homogeneity and the Roots of Danish Success" by Kevin H. O'Rourke. *NBER Working Paper*, 2005.

328 *The most tragic failure*: For the failure of the Great Leap Forward, see *Mao's Great Famine: The History of China's Most Devastating Catastrophe, 1958–62* by Frank Dikötter (London: Bloomsbury, 2011).

329 For the failure of Soviet collectivization, see "The Former Soviet Union and the World Wheat Economy" by James R. Jones, Shuang L. Li, Stephen Devadoss, Charlotte Fedane. *American Journal of Agricultural Economics* 78, no. 4 (Nov. 1996), 869–878.

Chapter Twenty: Rostow's Legacy

332 *a seismic change in American identity*: The farm population in the 1920s was more than thirty-one million, but by 1960, it had shrunk to slightly more than than fifteen million.

333 *the former have industrialized*: "The Stages of Economic Growth" by W. W. Rostow. *The Economic History Review, New Series* 12, no. 1 (1959), 1–16.

333 *"all would have a share of future wealth"*: *World Development Report,* World Bank. 1991.

333 *Huntington eloquently pleaded*: *Political Order in Changing Societies* by Samuel P. Huntington (New Haven, CT: Yale University Press, 1968).

335 *the White Revolution*: For Arsanjani's reform, see *Land Reform in Principle and Practice* by Doreen Warriner (Oxford: Clarendon, 1969), 119–126.

336 *the Green Revolution*: For its weaving together of farming, science, and politics, see Cullather, *The Hungry World;* "there is a deficiency of nitrogen," 61; Norin 10 development, 190–200.

339 *"betting on the strong"*: Cullather, ibid., 189. So great was the extra demand for nitrogen associated with the Green Revolution, Bechtel of California offered to build five plants in India each producing 750 tons a day.

340 *the miracle variety*: The IR 8 variety of rice was dark green to absorb sunlight, short to minimize use of energy, pest and disease resistant, and stiff enough to be machine harvestable.

340 *"The real revolution"*: Cullather, *Hungry World*, 234; "Even if it wasn't such a spectacular producer," ibid., 171.

341 *"the meek and humble among the farm owners"*: Ladejinsky, *Agrarian Reform*, 535.

341 *the Ottoman Land Code*: The Tanzimat reforms produced a web of land ownership rules that were increasingly localized, although for tax purposes they gave an impression of regularity.

342 *70 percent of Iraq's territory*: For Iraq distribution of land, see Warriner, *Land Reform*, ch. 4, "Revolutions in Iraq," 77.

342 *"uneducated people, tribal people"*: Rory Stewart, *Occupational Hazards: My Time governing in Iraq* (London: Picador, 2006); "uneducated people," 31.

343 *lively debate in Islam*: Islamic responses to landed property are examined in "A Disputed Utopia: Islamic Economics in Revolutionary Iran" by Sohrab Behdad. *Comparative Studies in Society and History* 36, no. 4 (Oct. 1994), 775–813; "unbridled capitalism," 807.

344 *Khomeini's inability to deal with privately owned property*: For the intricate ownership of water and land in Iran, see "Robbing Yadullah's Water to Irrigate Saeid's Garden: Hydrology and Water Rights in a Village of Central Iran" by François Molle, Alireza Mamanpoush, and Mokhtar Miranzadeh (*International Water Management*, 2004).

345 *"If the people one day decide to live"*: quoted in a forum posting, "Tunisia: A Moment of Destiny for the Tunisian People and Beyond?" by Dyab Abou Jahjah on openDemocracy, Jan. 13, 2011.

Chapter Twenty-One: The Economics of the Industrial Home

349 *"absolutely elemental"*: Warren Harding to Mrs. Maloney, July 21, 1922.

349 *the production of refrigerators*: For the flood of consumer products, see *Business*

Cycles: A Theoretical, Historical and Statistical Analysis of the Capitalist Process by Joseph Schumpter (New York: McGraw Hill, 1939), 363.

350 *"When a family buys a home"*: President Clinton launching his National Homeownership Strategy, June 5, 1995.

350 *the new homeowners of the 1920s*: For the 1920s housing boom, see "Lessons from the Great American Real Estate Boom and Bust of the 1920s" by Eugene N. White, *NBER Working Paper No. 15573*, National Bureau of Economic Research, 2009.

351 *Hoover's overriding priority*: For Hoover's strategy, see *The Clash of Economic Ideas: Great Policy Debates and Experiments of the Last Hundred Years* by Lawrence White (New York: Cambridge University Press, 2012), ch. 3, "The Roaring Twenties and the Austrian Business Cycle Theory."

352 *"The deterioration of the conditions"*: *Ernest Bevin* by Peter Weiler (Manchester, UK: Manchester University Press, 1993), 54–55.

352 *"Chentlemen! A depression iss for capitalism like a good cold douche"*: remembered by Robert Heilbroner in "The Embarrassment of Economics" in *Challenge* 39, no. 6, 1996.

353 *the theory that von Mises presented*: Ludwig von Mises in *Socialism: An Economic and Sociological Analysis* (New Haven, CT: Yale University Press, 1951), http://mises.org/books/socialism/contents.aspx.

354 *the idea originated with his mentor*: For Carl Menger in particular and the context of the Austrian School, see *The Austrian Mind: An Intellectual and Social History, 1848–1938* by William M. Johnston (Berkeley, CA: University of California Press, 1995), 77–82.

355 *economic freedom could be equated to individual liberty*: *The Road to Serfdom* appeared in a shortened, best-selling *Reader's Digest* version, but the original is definitive (London: Routledge, 1944).

356: "This *is what we believe in.*": Story cited in *Margaret Thatcher: Portrait of the Iron Lady* by John Blundell (London: Algora, 2008), 41.

357 *It was a revealing admission*: *The Constitution of Liberty* by Friederich Hayek (Chicago: University of Chicago Press, 1960).

359 *The heavily taxed and regulated economy grew*: Economic growth 1950–70. U.S. GDP growth, "Historical trends 1950–92, and current uncertainties" by Ronald E. Kutscher. *Monthly Labor Review* Nov. 1993. Stock market returns, compound annual rates of return from S&P 500, figures from MoneyChimp. UK figures from "A backward glance: the reappraisal of the 1960s" lecture by Samuel Brittan to the Institute of Contemporary British history, April 1997.

359 *almost half of all Americans rented their homes*: U.S. housing figures, U.S. Census Bureau, Housing and Household Economic Statistics Division, 2011.

359 *"the General Motors of the housing industry"*: Quoted in *American Family Home, 1800–1960* by Clifford Edward Clark (Chapel Hill, NC: University of North Carolina Press, 1986), 221.

360 *you are inferior*: Von Mises to Rand, letter dated Jan. 23, 1958.

360 *"intellectually limited"*: Greenspan's remarks appear in his autobiography, *Age of Turbulence: Adventures in a New World* (New York: Penguin, 2008).

361 *the deregulation of the City of London*: Big Bang was the centerpiece of a wave of deregulation that included airlines, utilities, and communications.

362 *"unfettered market competition"*: Greenspan testified to Congress Oct. 23, 2008.

363 *the value of subprime mortgages*: $1.3 trillion of subprime mortgages, figure from "Move over prime," *The Economist*, February, 5, 2009.

Chapter Twenty-Two: Undoing the Damage

365 *shot herself with a handgun*: Mrs. Addie Polk's tragedy stood out because it happened quite early in the fallout from the crash, but as the tidal wave of foreclosures washed across private property economies, the loss of shelter, security, and even identity that a home represents brought millions more close to her despair.

365 *"a property-owning democracy"*: The flaw in this model of social engineering was that the banks owned the property, not the inhabitants. For the connection between a housing boom and an economic bust in 1929 and 2008, see "Household Cycles and Economic Cycles, 1920–2010" by Steven Gjerstad and Vernon L. Smith (Chapman University, CA, 2010).

366 *The growth of lending*: For the huge growth in mortgage lending, see "The Rise and Fall of the Mortgage and Credit Markets" by James R. Bart *et al.* (*Milken Institute*, 2009).

367 *almost six hundred trillion dollars*: The figure from the Bank for International Settlements for the last quarter of 2007, $596 trillion.

368 *the number of politically free countries*: Figures for 2007 from Freedom House, "Freedom in the World," 2008.

368 *the 1992 paper he cited*: Professor Fukuyama's assertion of a "strong correlation" between industrial development and democracy is made in "Reflections on the End of History, Five Years Later" by Francis Fukuyama, *History and Theory* 34, no. 2, Theme Issue 34: World Historians and Their Critics (May, 1995), 27–43. The paper he refers to is by Larry Diamond, "Economic Development and Democracy Reconsidered," *American Behavioral Scientist* 15 (March–June 1992), 450–499.

369 *"free and equal in dignity and rights"*: Compared to the painstaking arguments that backed the assertion to natural rights in property and to the pursuit of happiness, the United Nations' assertion of its human rights is strangely bare. But perhaps it was felt that the hideousness of Nazi ideology had made a case for human rights that was overwhelming.

371 *a recent study concluded*: The study was conducted by two law professors, David S. Law and Mila Versteeg, in "The Declining Influence of the United States Constitution," *New York University Law Review* 87, no. 3 (2012).

373 *eligible to buy thirty-year leases*: For the change in property law, see "The Law of Property and the Evolving System of Property Rights in China" by Albert H. Y. Chen (May 25, 2010).

374 *an open letter to the People's National Congress*: Professor Gong's lengthy letter pulled no punches. "[The proposed law's] essence and main agenda are to protect

the property rights of a small minority. The Draft seeks essentially to protect private property."

374 The "small minority," however, included city chieftains. Tensions between the Communist Party and the cities bear an obvious resemblance to ancient rivalries between imperial servants and provincial officials.

377 *a potentially significant move*: Significantly, the tentative move to tax mansions had a follow-up. In early 2013, the Party Congress announced a new wealth tax on the sale of houses.

378 *successive administrations brought down*: In practice, the cuts brought the average top rate down to under 29 percent.

378 *a gap that had to be filled by borrowing*: President Reagan's borrowing was partly to pay for his administration's hiring of an extra 324,000 employees, while President George W. Bush's borrowing included the costs of wars in Iraq and Afghanistan.

379 *the incomes of CEOs*: The 2007–8 United Nations Human Development Report showed that while the CEO of a major U.S. company drew a salary twenty-five times that of an average worker in 1965, the differential had grown to more than 250 times the average worker's in 2006.

379 *the top 1 percent of Americans*: Research by Thomas Piketty and Emmanuel Saez, "The Evolution of Top Incomes: A Historical and International Perspective" showed that the richest 1 percent earned 18.3 percent of national income, a figure not matched since 1929.

379 *"there is an inside track"*: Britain's finance industry used its muscle in the political marketplace to secure unprecedented freedom from regulation, and relief from bearing the cost of the consequences.

380 *the health of Americans had dropped*: Research by Harvard School of Public Health published by the *Harvard Magazine* July–August 2008 showed that while life expectancy is growing for most people, 4 percent of poor American men and 19 percent of poor American women would have shorter lives, or no longer, than their parents.

380 *the bottom half of the OECD's membership*: OECD report 2011 ranked the United States twenty-first among the OECD's forty nations in terms of life expectancy, and thirty-second in terms of infant mortality. The UK ranked eleventh and twenty-sixth, but behind France and all the Nordic nations.

381 *twenty-three of the largest companies in the world*: Start-up rates of S&P 500's largest companies, "The demographics of global corporate champions" by Luis Véron. *Bruegel*; Brussels, 2008

381 *a pallid reward*: Stock market returns 1988–2008, compound annual rates of return from S&P 500, figures from MoneyChimp.

Chapter Twenty-Three: Feeding the Future.

383 *it was deemed to have created*: U.S. figures from "Intellectual Property and the US economy," U.S. Patent and Trademark Office, April 2012. UK figures from Intellectual Property Office, July 2011.

384 *the German congress*: The German economists met at the *Kongress deutscher Volkswirthe* held in Dresden, September 1863.

384 *the number of patents*: The figures for U.S. patents issued came from "How Patent Laws Are Stifling American growth," *Bloomberg News,* February 24, 2013. UK figures from "British patent numbers (under the Patents Act 1977) 1979 to present day," Intellectual Property Office.

385 *the Uruguay round of trade agreements*: For the effect of TRIPS on communal and traditional medical knowledge, see "Native medicines—who should profit?," *New Scientist* 181, issue 2436 (February 28, 2004), 15.

385 *In a prescient article*: "The Economy of Ideas: A framework for patents and copyrights in the Digital Age" by John Perry Barlow. *Wired,* Mar. 1994.

386 *"cancerous" and "unAmerican"*: Microsoft's epithets are quoted in an interview with Linus Torvals in "Linux succeeded thanks to selfishness and trust," by Leo Kelion, *New York Times,* June 13, 2012.

386 *"There is no enterprise"*: Henry Dawes made his comment to the Senate in 1883.

387 *Research into innovation*: "The Patent System and Competition: A Statement to the Federal Trade Commission/Department of Justice Hearings on Competition and Intellectual Property Law and Policy in the Knowledge-Based Economy" by Josh Lerner, Harvard University and National Bureau of Economic Research. "Patent Protection and Innovation Over 150 Years" by Josh Lerner, Harvard University and NBER.

388 *"a patents cliff"*: appears in such quotes as "the pharmaceutical industry is about to fall off a patents cliff" in "Rebooting Industry" by Nick Clayton, *Wall Street Journal,* June 26, 2011.

389 *"Our mind-set was surpluses"*: Quoted in "A Warming Planet Struggles to Feed Itself" by Justin Gillis, *New York Times,* June 4, 2011.

389 *"farmland is going to be one of the best investments"*: Quoted in *The Great Food Robbery: How Corporations Control Food, Grab Land and Destroy the Climate* by GRAIN (Cape Town: Pambazuka, 2012).

389 *almost 110 million acres of farmland*: Land grab figures, ibid.

390 *"We could be moronic"*: Susan Payne, ibid., 123.

391 *"We bring foreign currency"*: Jittu's Ethiopian investment. "Speculating with Lives: How Global Investors Make Money Out of Hunger" by Horand Knaup *et al. Der Spiegel,* Sep. 1, 2011.

392 *this traditional shape was upset*: For the background to Mali's occupation by Tuareg and terrorists, see *Great Food Robbery,* 130–133. Subsequent developments in various media 2012–13 and ongoing.

392 *created by the U.S. Congress in 2004*: Millennium Challenge Corporation. www.mcc.gov.

393 *attempt to modernize Afghan society*: For Rostow-inspired development in Helmand province, Afghanistan, see *Little America: The War Within the War* by Rajiv Chandrasekaran (London: Bloomsbury, 2012).

393 *equitable land distribution was fundamental to social stability*: Typically government approaches to the challenge of feeding the future still deal with systems rather than the people who own the soil, the produce, or simply the labor. See,

for example, the British government's approach *The Future of Food and Farming: Challenges and Choices for Global Sustainability* (2011). For information, see Food Outlook reports twice yearly from"Global Information and Early Warning System" Food and Agricultural Organization.

395 *"the slightest problem during the entire famine"*: Amartya Sen's remarkable theory of food entitlement turns Malthus on his head, and placing the emphasis on accessing food rather than producing it. See *Poverty and Famines: An Essay on Entitlements and Deprivation* by Amartya Sen (Oxford: Clarendon, 1982).

Select Bibliography.

Books

Adams, Henry. *The Education of Henry Adams*. Boston: Massachusetts Historical Society, 1918.

Akhmatova, Anna. *Selected Poems*, trans. D. M. Thomas. London: Penguin Classics, 2006.

Allen, Robert C. *Comparative Economic Studies*. Basingstoke, United Kingdom: Palgrave Macmillan, 2005.

Anderson, Perry. *Passages from Antiquity to Feudalism*. London: Verso, 1996.

Ascherson, Neal. *The Struggles for Poland*. New York: Random House, 1991.

Atack, Jeremy and Larry Neals, eds. *The Evolution of Financial Markets and Institutions from the Seventeenth Century to the Present*. New York: Cambridge University Press, 2008.

Atack, Jeremy and Fred Bateman. *To Their Own Soil: Agriculture in the Antebellum North*. Ames, IA: Iowa State University Press, 1987.

Aubrey, John. *Brief Lives*, ed. Andrew Clark. Oxford: Clarendon, 1898.

Bain, R. Nisbet. *The Pupils of Peter the Great: A History of the Russian Court and Empire 1697–1740*. London: Constable, 1897.

Baker, John. *The Oxford History of the Laws of England*. Oxford: Oxford University Press, 2003.

Bannan, Alfred J. and Achilles Edelenyi. *Documentary History of Eastern Europe*. New York: Twayne, 1970.

Banner, Stuart. *How the Indians Lost Their Land: Law and Power on the Frontier*. Cambridge, MA: Harvard University Press, 2005.

Beardmore, J. H. *The History of Hucknell Torkard* (1909). http://www.nottshistory.org.uk/hucknall1909/hucknall1.htm.

Beattie, Hilary J. *Land and Lineage in China: A Study of T'ung-ch'eng County, Anhwei, in the Ming and Ch'ing Dynasties*. Cambridge: Cambridge University Press, 1979.

Becker, Seymour. *Nobility and Privilege in Late Imperial Russia*. Dekalb IL: Northern Illinois University Press, 1985.

Belich, James. *Replenishing the Earth: The Settler Revolution and the Rise of the Anglo-World, 1783–1939.* Oxford: Oxford University Press, 2009.

Bendall, Sarah. *Dictionary of Land Surveyors and Local Mapmakers of Great Britain and Ireland.* London: British Library, 1997.

Bevan, William Lloyd. *Sir William Petty: A Study in English Economic Literature.* New York: Guggenheimer, 1894.

Beverley, Robert. *History of Virginia in Four Parts.* Richmond, VA: Randolph, 1855. http://docsouth.unc.edu/southlit/beverley/beverley.html.

Blackbourn, David. *History of Germany 1780–1919: The Long Nineteenth Century.* Oxford: Blackwell, 2003.

Blackburn, Robin. *The Making of New World Slavery: From the Baroque to the Modern, 1492–1800.* London: Verso, 1995.

Blackford, Mansel G. *The Rise of Modern Business: Great Britain, the United States, Germany, Japan and China.* Chapel Hill, NC: University of North Carolina Press, 2008.

Blackstone, William. *Commentaries on the Laws of England.* Oxford: Clarendon, 1769. http://avalon.law.yale.edu/subject_menus/blackstone.asp.

Bloch, Marc. *Land and Work in Medieval Europe: Selected Papers,* trans. J. E. Anderson. Berkeley, CA: University of California Press, 1967.

Bloomfield, Paul. *Edward Gibbon Wakefield: Builder of the British Commonwealth.* London: Longmans, 1961.

Blundell, John. *Margaret Thatcher: Portrait of the Iron Lady.* London: Algora, 2008.

Bogart, Ernest L. and Charles M. Thompson. *Readings in the Economic History of the United States.* New York: Longmans, 1925.

Bogle, Lori Lyn. *Cold War Culture and Society.* New York: Routledge, 2001.

Bois, Guy. *La Crise du Féodalisme.* Paris: FNSP, 1974.

Bradford, William. *History of Plimoth Plantation.* Carlisle, MA: Applewoods, 1986.

Brahm, William de. *De Brahm's Report of the General Survey in the Southern District of North America,* ed. Louis de Vorsey Jr. New York: Columbia, 1971.

Braudel, Fernand. *Civilization and Capitalism 15th–18th Century: Volume 1, The Structures of Everyday Life: The Limits of the Possible.* London: Collins, 1981.

———. *Civilization and Capitalism, 15th–18th Century*: Vol. 3, *The Perspective of the World.* Berkeley, CA: University of California Press, 1982.

———. *The Mediterranean and the Mediterranean World in the Age of Philip II,* vol II. Berkeley, CA: University of California Press;. 1995.

Burlamaqui, J-J. *The Principles of Natural Law,* trans. Thomas Nugent. Cambridge, MA: Cambridge University Press, 1807. http://www.constitution.org/burla/burla_1.htm.

Calendar of State Papers Colonial, America and West Indies, Volume 7: 1669–1674, ed W. Noel Sainsbury. London, 1889. http://www.british-history.ac.uk/report.aspx?compid=70201.

The Cambridge History of Poland, ed. Oskar Halecki, W. F. Reddaway, J. H. Penson. Cambridge: Cambridge University Press, 1950.

Cao Xueqing. *The Story of the Stone,* Vol. 1, trans. David Hawkes. London: Penguin Classics, 1973.

Carlton, Charles. *Going to the Wars: The Experience of the British Civil Wars 1638–51.* London: Routledge, 1992.
Chambers, E. K. *Shakespeare: A Study of Facts and Problems.* Oxford: Clarendon, 1930.
Champlain, Samuel. *Voyages of Samuel de Champlain*, trans. Charles Pomeroy Otis. Boston: Prince Society, 1878. http://www.usgennet.org/usa/topic/preservation/epochs/vol1/pg179.htm.
Chandler, Raymond. *The Big Sleep.* New York: Alfred A. Knopf, 1939.
Chandrasekaran, Rajiv. *Little America: The War within the War.* London: Bloomsbury, 2012.
Chatwin, Bruce. *The Songlines.* London: Franklin Press, 1987.
Chayanov, A. V. *The Theory of Peasant Economy*, trans. R. E. F. Smith and Christel Lane. Madison, WI: University of Wisconsin Press, 1986.
Chou, Ju-his and Claudia Brown. *The Elegant Brush, Chinese Painting Under the Qianlong Emperor, 1735–1795.* Phoenix, AZ: Phoenix Art Museum, 1985.
Clark, Clifford E. *American Family Home, 1800–1960.* Chapel Hill, NC: University of North Carolina Press, 1986.
Clarke, William. *Puritanism and Liberty, Being the Army Debates (1647–49) from the Clarke Manuscripts with Supplementary Documents*, ed. A. S. P. Woodhouse. Chicago: University of Chicago Press, 1951. http://oll.libertyfund.org/index.php?option=com_content&task=view&id=1322&Itemid=264.
Cohn, Norman. *The Pursuit of the Millennium.* London: Mercury Books, 1972.
Coleman, Janet, ed. *The Individual in Political Theory and Practice.* Oxford and New York: Oxford University Press, 1996.
Collings, S. and A Beautrais. *Suicide Prevention in New Zealand: A Contemporary Perspective.* Wellington, Ministry of Health, 2005.
Columella, Lucius J. M. *On Agriculture,* trans. Harrison Boyd Ash. Cambridge, MA: Harvard University Press, 1941.
Cormack, Ted. *William Petty and the Ambition of Political Arithmetic.* Oxford: Oxford University Press, 2009.
Cortés, Hernando. *The Dispatches of Hernando Cortés, the Conqueror of Mexico, Addressed to the Emperor Charles V, Written During the Conquest, and Containing a Narrative of Its Events.* New York: Wiley and Putnam, 1843. http://mith.umd.edu/eada/html/display.php?docs=cortez_letter2.xml.
Cotton, John. *God's Promise to His Plantation* (1630). http://digitalcommons.unl.edu/etas/22/.
Cramb, Robert. *Land and Longhouse: Agrarian Transformation in the Uplands of Sarawak.* Honolulu, HI: University of Hawaii Press, 2007.
Cranmer-Byng, J. L., ed. *An Embassy to China, Being the Journal Kept by Lord Macartney During His Embassy to the Emperor Ch'ien-lung, 1793–1794.* London: Longmans, 1962.
Cullather, Nick.*The Hungry World: America's Cold War Battle Against Poverty in Asia.* Cambridge, MA: Harvard University Press, 2010.
Davies, Brian. *Warfare, State and Society on the Black Sea Steppe: 1500–1700.* London: Routledge, 2001.
Davies, John. *A Discovery of the True Cause Why Ireland Was Never Entirely Subdued*

Nor Brought Under Obedience of the Crown of England Until the Beginning of His Majesty's Happy Reign, ed. Henry Morley. London: Routledge, 1890.

Dee, John. *The Private Diary of Dr. John Dee.* London: Camden Society, 1841–42.

Defore, Daniel. *The Complete English Tradesman: In Familiar Letters; Directing Him in All the Several Parts and Progressions of Trade . . . Calculated for the Instruction of Our Inland Tradesmen; and Especially of Young Beginners,* vol. 1. London: Charles Rivington, 1726.

Dolivier, Pierre. *Essai sur la justice primitive: pour servir de principe générateur au seul ordre social qui peut assurer à l'homme tous ses droits et tous ses moyens de bonheur.* Paris: Éditions d'Histoire sociale, 1967.

Dore, R. P. *Land Reform in Japan.* London: Oxford University Press, 1959.

Doyle, William. *Origins of the French Revolution.* New York: Oxford University Press, 1999.

Durham, John Lambton. *Lord Durham's Report on the Affairs of British North America,* 2 vols. Oxford: Clarendon, 1839.

Edgar, Walter B. *South Carolina: A History.* Columbia, SC: University of South Carolina Press, 1998.

Editor of the *Journal of Commerce and Commercial Bulletin. A History of Banking in All the Leading Nations; Comprising the United States; Great Britain; Germany; Austro-Hungary; France; Italy; Belgium; Spain; Switzerland; Portugal; Roumania; Russia; Holland; the Scandinavian Nations; Canada; China; Japan* (4 vols). New York: The Journal of Commerce and Commercial Bulletin, 1896.

Egerton, François. *The Egerton Papers.* London: Bowson, 1840.

Elkins, Stanley and Eric McKitterick. *The Age of Federalism: The Early American Republic, 1788–1800.* New York and Oxford: Oxford University Press, 1995.

Elman, Benjamin A. *On Their Own Terms: Science in China 1550–1900.* Cambridge, MA: Harvard University Press, 2005.

Elton, G. R. *England Under the Tudors.* London: Methuen, 1974.

Elvin, Mark. *The Pattern of the Chinese Past.* Stanford, CA: Stanford University Press, 1973.

Emerson, Ralph Waldo. *The Works of Ralph Waldo Emerson, in 12 vols. Fireside Edition,* Vol XI. Boston and New York, 1909. http://oll.libertyfund.org/?option=com_staticxt&staticfile=show.php%3Ftitle=1961&chapter=123098&layout=html&Itemid=27.

Emmons, Terence. *The Russian Landed Gentry and the Peasant Emancipation of 1861.* Cambridge: Cambridge University Press, 1968.

Epstein, M. F. *The Early History of the English Levant Company.* London: Routledge, 1908.

Erickson, Amy Louise. *Women and Property in Early Modern England.* London: Taylor & Francis, 1993.

Ernle, Lord. *English Farming, Past and Present.* London: Longmans, 1922.

Farragher, John Mack. *Sugar Creek: Life on the Illinois Prairie.* New Haven, CT: Yale University Press, 1986.

Ferguson, Niall. *The Ascent of Money: A Financial History of the World.* London and New York: Penguin, 2008.

Fielden, John. *The Curse of the Factory System.* London: Routledge, 1836.

Figes, Orlando. *Natasha's Dance: A Cultural History of Russia*. London and New York: Penguin, 2003.

Foner, Eric. *Forever Free: The Story of Emancipation and Reconstruction*. New York: Knopf Doubleday, 2005.

Fontane, Theodore. *The Stechlin*, trans. William L. Zwiebel. Rochester, NY: Camden House, 1995.

Foster, R. and O. Ranum, eds. *Family and Society: Selections from the Annales, Economies, Societés, Civilisations*. Baltimore, MD: Johns Hopkins Press, 1976.

Fox Bourne, H. R. *Life of John Locke*. New York: Harper, 1876. http://archive.org/details/lifeofjohnlocke01bour.

Franklin, Benjamin. "Observations Concerning the Increase of Mankind, Peopling of Countries, etc." (1751) in *The Papers of Benjamin Franklin*, 35 vols. to date. Leonard W. Labaree, ed., et al. New Haven, CT: Yale University Press, 1959–1999.

Friends of the Turnbull Library. *Edward Gibbon Wakefield and the Colonial Dream: A Reconsideration*. Wellington, NZ: GP Publications, 1997.

Frost, Robert. *A Witness Tree*. New York: Henry Holt, 1942.

Furet, François and Mona Ozouf. *A Critical Dictionary of the French Revolution*. Cambridge, MA: Harvard University Press, 1989.

Furnivall, F. J. *Ballads from MSS.*, vol. 1. London: Publications of the Ballad Society, 1871.

George, Henry. *Progress and Poverty* (1879). http://www.henrygeorge.org/pcontents.htm.

Giffen, Robert. *The Growth of Capital*. London: Bell, 1889.

Gogol, Nikolai. *Taras Bulba and Other Tales* (1842). London: Floating Press, 2011.

Goldstone, Jack A. *Revolution and Rebellion in the Early Modern World*. Berkeley, CA: University of California Press, 1991.

Goncharaov, Ivan A. *Oblomov*, trans. Marian Schwartz. New York: Seven Stories Press, 2011.

Goodall, Jane. *Through a Window: My Thirty Years with the Chimpanzees of Gombe*. New York: Houghton, Mifflin, Harcourt, 2010.

GRAIN. *The Great Food Robbery: How Corporations Control Food, Grab Land and Destroy the Climate*. Cape Town: Pambazuka, 2012.

Grant, W. L. and J. Munro, eds. *Acts of the Privy Council: Colonial Series,* 6 vols. Hereford, 1908–12.

Greenblatt, Miriam. *Süleyman the Magnificent and the Ottoman Empire*. New York: Benchmark Books, 2003.

Greenspan, Alan. *Age of Turbulence: Adventures in a New World*. New York: Penguin, 2008.

Gretton, R. H. *The Burford Records: A Study in Minor Town Government*. Oxford: Oxford University Press, 1920.

Grotius, Hugo. *De Iure Belli ac Pacis* (1625). http://www.constitution.org/gro/djbp_103.htm.

Guevara, Ernesto "Che." *The Che Reader*. Sydney: Ocean Press, 2005.

Hagen, William. *Ordinary Prussians: Brandenburg Junkers and Villagers, 1500–1840*. Cambridge: Cambridge University Press, 2002.

Haggett, Peter, ed. *Encyclopedia of World Geography*. New York: Marshall Cavendish, 2001.

Hamerow, Theodore S., ed. *The Age of Bismarck: Documents and Interpretations*. New York: Harper & Row, 1973.

Hanke, Lewis, ed. *History of Latin American Civilization: Sources and Interpretations, the Colonial Experience,* vol. 1. New York: Taylor & Francis, 1969.

Harkness, Dorothy. *John Dee's Conversations with Angels: Cabala, Alchemy, and the End of Nature*. Cambridge and New York: Cambridge University Press, 1999.

Harrington, James. *The Commonwealth of Oceana* (1656) and *A System of Politics*, ed. J. G. A. Pocock. Cambridge: Cambridge University Press, 1992.

Harrison, Rev. William. *Description of Britain and England,* originally part of *Chronicles of England* by Raphael Hollinshed. 1578.

Hayek, Friederich. *The Constitution of Liberty*. Chicago: University of Chicago Press, 1960.

———. *The Road to Serfdom*. London: Routledge, 1944.

Hayes, Edward. *Sir Humphrey Gilbert's Voyage to Newfoundland* in Richard Hakluyt's *The Principall Navigations, Voiages and Discoveries of the English Nation*. London: George Bishop and Ralph Newberie, 1589. www.gutenberg.org/ebooks/3338.

Hening, William Waller. *Statutes at Large; Being a Collection of All the Laws of Virginia*. Richmond, VA: Pleasants, 1809–1823.

Hibbert, F. A. *The Dissolution of the Monasteries*. London: Pitman, 1910.

Higgs, Henry. *The Physiocrats: Six Lectures on the French Economistes of the 18th Century*. London: Macmillan, 1897. http://oll.libertyfund.org/title/286.

Hilferding, Rudolph. *Finance Capital*. London: Routledge, 1981.

Hill, Christopher. *The English Revolution*. London: Lawrence & Wishart, 1940.

———. *Oliver Cromwell 1658–1958*. London: Taylor & Francis, 1963.

Hinton, William. *Fanshen: A Documentary of Revolution in a Chinese Village*. Berkeley, CA: University of California Press, 1966.

Hobbes, Thomas. *De Corpore,* trans. William Molesworth as *Elements of Philosophy*. London: Bohn, 1839. http://archive.org/stream/englishworkstho21hobbgoog#page/n8/mode/2up.

Hobbes, Thomas. *Leviathan or the Matter, Form & Power of a Common-wealth, Political and Civill* (1651). London: Penguin, 1968.

Hughes, L. A. J. and M. di Salvo, eds. *A Window on Russia*, Papers from the 5th International Conference on Eighteenth-Century Russia, Gargnano 1994. Rome. 1996.

Huntington, Samuel P. *Political Order in Changing Societies*. New Haven, CT: Yale University Press, 1968.

Hutcheson, Francis. *An Inquiry into the Original of Our Ideas of Beauty and Virtue* (1725), ed. Wolfgang Leidhold. Indianapolis, IN: Liberty Fund, 2004. http://files.libertyfund.org/files/858/0449_LFeBk.pdf.

Imber, Colin. *Studies in Ottoman History and Law*. Oxford: Isis, 1996.

James, William. "The Consciousness of Self" in *The Principles of Psychology* (1890); reprinted *Journal of Cosmology*, vol. 14 (2011).

Johnson, Paul. *Intellectuals: From Marx and Tolstoy to Sartre and Chomsky*, revised edition. London and New York: Harper Perennial, 2007.

Johnston, William M. *The Austrian Mind: An Intellectual and Social History, 1848–1938*. Berkeley, CA: University of California Press, 1995.

Kelly, Fergus, ed. *A Guide to Early Irish Law*. Dublin: Institute for Advanced Studies, 1988.

Kennedy, Paul. *The Rise and Fall of the Great Powers: Economic Change and Military Conflict from 1500 to 2000*. New York: Vintage, 1989.

Kenyon, J. and J. Ohlmeyer, eds. *The Civil Wars: A Military History of England, Scotland and Ireland 1638–1660*. Oxford: Oxford University Press, 1998.

Kerridge, Eric. *Agrarian Problems in the Sixteenth Century and After*. London: Allen & Unwin, 1969.

Kinsella, Thomas. *The Táin*. Oxford: Oxford University Press, 1969.

Kipling, Rudyard. *The Works of Rudyard Kipling*. London: Wordsworth Poetry Library, 1994.

Klyuchevsky, V. O. *A History of Russia*, vol. 2, trans. C. J. Hogarth. London: Dent, 1911.

Kula, Witold. *Measures and Men*, trans. R. Szreter. Princeton, NJ: Princeton University Press, 1986.

Lalor, John J., ed. *Cyclopædia of Political Science, Political Economy, and the Political History of the United States*, vol. III. New York: Maynard, 1899.

Land Management, Bureau of. *Instruction for the Survey of Public Land*. Washington, DC: U.S. Government Printing Office, 1947.

Lederer, John. *The Discoveries of John Lederer* (1672). http://rla.unc.edu/archives/accounts/lederer/lederertext.html.

Lenin, Vladimir I. *Collected Works*. Progress: Moscow, 1973.

———. *The Development of Capitalism in Russia* (1899). http://www.marxists.org/archive/lenin/works/1899/devel/index.htm.

Linklater, Andro. *Measuring America*. New York: Walker Books, 2002.

———. *Why Spencer Perceval Had to Die: The Assassination of a Prime Minister*. New York and London: Bloomsbury, 2012.

———. *Wild People: Travels with Borneo's Head-hunters*. London: John Murray, 1994.

Locke, John. *An Essay Concerning Human Understanding, Book 1* (1690). http://oll.libertyfund.org/index.php?option=com_staticxt&staticfile=show.php%3Ftitle=761&Itemid=28.

———.—*Two Treatises of Government*, ed. Thomas Hollis. London: Millar, 1764. oll.libertyfund.org/title/222/16269.

Love, Patrick and Ralph Lattimore. *OECD Insights International Trade Free, Fair and Open?* Paris: OECD, 2009.

Lyttleton, Thomas. *Tenures*, ed. Eugene Wambaugh. Washington, DC: Byrne, 1903. http://archive.org/details/.

Macfarlane, Alan. *The Origins of English Individualism: The Family, Property and Social Transition*, Oxford: Blackwell, 1978.

MacLeod, Christine. *Inventing the Industrial Revolution: The English Patent System, 1660–1800*. Cambridge: Cambridge University Press, 2002.

Madison, James. "Notes on the Debates in the Federal Convention." http://avalon.law.yale.edu/subject_menus/debcont.asp.

——. *The Papers of James Madison*. Available in both hard copy and online through the University of Virginia, Charlottesville, VA. http://www.virginia.edu/pjm/.

Mao Zhedong. *Selected Works of Mao Tse-tung,* vol II. Peking: Foreign Languages Press, No date.

Marshall, Humphrey. *The History of Kentucky, Exhibiting an Account of the Modern Discovery; Settlement; Progressive Improvement; Civil and Military Transactions; and the Present State of the Country*, Vol 1. Kentucky: Robinson, 1824.

Martin, Janet. *Medieval Russia 980–1584*. Cambridge: Cambridge University Press, 1995.

Martineau, Harriet. *Society in America*. Paris: Galignani, 1837.

Marx, Karl. *Capital*, Vol 1. Moscow: Progress, 1972–76. http://www.marxists.org/archive/marx/works/1867-c1/ch33.htm.

———. *Ethnographical Notebooks* (c.1881). http://www.marxists.org/archive/marx/works/1881/ethnographical-notebooks/ch03.htm.

Matthews, H. C. G. *Gladstone 1809–1898*. Oxford: Oxford University Press, 2005.

Matthias, Peter and M. M. Postan, *Industrial Economies: Capital Labour and Enterprise*; Vol. 3 in the *Cambridge Economic History of Europe*. Cambridge: Cambridge University Press, 1978.

McBride, George M. *The Land Systems of Mexico*. New York: American Geographical Society, 1923.

McPherson, C. B. *The Political Theory of Possessive Individualism: From Hobbes to Locke*, Oxford: Clarendon, 1962.

Meinig, Donald. *The Shaping of America: A Geographical Perspective on 500 Years of History*. New Haven, CT: Yale University Press, 1995.

Melish, John. *A Geographical description of the United States . . . intended as an accompaniment to Melish's map*. Philadelphia, 1818. http://archive.org/details/geographicaldesc00mel.

Mises, Ludwig von. *Socialism: An Economic and Sociological Analysis*. New Haven, CT: Yale University Press, 1951. http://mises.org/books/socialism/contents.aspx.

Montgomery, W. E. *The History of Land Tenure in Ireland*. Cambridge: Cambridge University Press, 1889. http://archive.org/stream/historyoflandten00montrich#page/ii/mode/2up.

More, Thomas. *Utopia*, Book I. Cambridge: Cambridge University Press, 1888.

Morgan, Lewis. *Ancient Society or Researches in the Lines of Human Progress from Savagery through Barbarism to Civilization*. New York: Henry Holt, 1877.

Narratives of Early Carolina by Alexander S. Salley Jr. *Narratives of Early Carolina: 1650–1708*. New York: Scribner's Sons, 1911.

Narratives of Early Maryland, ed. Clayton C. Hall. New York: Scribner's Sons, 1910.

Narratives of Early Virginia: 1606–1625, ed. Lyon G. Tyler. New York: Scribner's Sons, 1907.

Nash, Gary. *The Unknown American Revolution: The Unruly Birth of Democracy and the Struggle to Create America*. New York: Viking, 2005.

Nicholl, George. *A History of the English Poor Law in Connection with the State of the Country and the Condition of the People*. London: King & Son, 1904.

Nozick, Robert. *Anarchy, State, and Utopia*. New York: Basic Books, 1974.

O'Connor, A. C. and M. F. Arago, eds. *Oeuvres de Condorcet*, vol. 11. Paris: Firmin Didot Frères, 1847.

Otis, James. "Rights of the British Colonies Asserted and Proved," (1764). http://oll.libertyfund.org/index.php?option=com_staticxt&staticfile=show.php%3Ftitle=2335.

Pallot, Judith and Denis J. B. Shaw, *Landscape and Settlement in Romanov Russia, 1613–1917*. Oxford: Clarendon, 1990.

Parker, Geoffrey. *The Thirty Years War*. London: Routledge, 1997.

Pearce, Roy Harvey. *Savagism and Civilization: A Study of the Indian and the American Mind*. Berkeley, CA: University of California Press, 1988.

Perceval-Maxwell, M. *The Outbreak of the Irish Rebellion of 1641*. Montreal: McGill-Queen's Press, 1994.

Perdue, Peter C. *China Marches West*. Cambridge, MA: Belknap Press of Harvard University Press, 2005.

Pérouse, G.-A. and Dubuis, R., eds. *Propos rustiques de maistre Leon Ladulfi champenois*. Geneva: Droz, 1994.

Petty, William. *Collected Works of Sir William Petty*. London: Routledge, 1997.

———. *Political Arithmetick* (1690). http://www.marxists.org/reference/subject/economics/petty/.

Pinkard, Terry. *Hegel: A Biography*. Cambridge: Cambridge University Press, 2001.

Plato. *The Republic: Plato in Twelve Volumes*, vols. 5 and 6, trans. Paul Shorey. London: Heinemann, 1969.

Pomerantz, Kenneth. *The Great Divergence: China, Europe, and the Making of the Modern World Economy*. Princeton, NJ: Princeton University Press, 2000.

Pudup, Mary Beth; Dwight Billings, and Altina Waller, eds. *Appalachia in the Making: The Mountain South in the Nineteenth Century*. Chapel Hill, NC: University of North Carolina Press, 1995.

Putnam, Peter, ed. *Seven Britons in Imperial Russia (1689–1812)*. Princeton, NJ: Princeton University Press, 1952.

Ricardo, David. *Principles of Political Economy, and Taxation* (1817). http://www.marxists.org/reference/subject/economics/ricardo/tax/.

Robertson, David B. *The Constitution and America's Destiny*. Cambridge and New York: Cambridge University Press, 2005.

Robertson, Norman. *History of the County of Bruce*. Ontario, Canada: Briggs, 1906. http://www.electricscotland.com/history/canada/bruce/index.htm.

Roche, Julian. *The International Wool Trade*. Cambridge: Woodhead, 1995.

Rogers, Thorold. *A History of Agriculture and Prices in England from the Year After the Oxford Parliament (1259) to the Commencement of the Continental War* (1793), Vol 1. Oxford: Clarendon, 1866–1902

Romaniello, Matthew P. *The Elusive Empire: Kazan and the Creation of Russia, 1552–1671*. University of Wisconsin Press, 2012.

Rousseau, Jean-Jacques. *Discourse on the Origin and Basis of Inequality Amongst Men* (1754), trans. G. D. H. Cole. London: Dent, 1923. http://www.constitution.org/jjr/ineq.htm.

Roxburgh, David J., ed. *Turks: Journey of a Thousand Years 600–1600.* London: Royal Academy of Arts, 2005.
Royle, Trevor. *Civil War: The Wars of the Three Kingdoms, 1638–1660.* London: Little, Brown, 2004.
Sakolski, A. M. *The Great American Land Bubble.* New York: Harper, 1932.
Sansom, Robert L. *The Economics of Insurgency in the Mekong Delta of Vietnam.* Cambridge: MIT Press, 1970.
Schama, Simon. *An Embarrassment of Riches: An Interpretation of Dutch Culture in the Golden Period.* London: Collins, 1987.
Schneider, Dorothy and J. Carl. *Slavery in America.* New York: Infobase, 2005.
Schoenbaum, Samuel. *William Shakespeare: A Documentary Life.* Oxford: Oxford University Press, 1975.
Schumpeter, Joseph. *Business Cycles: A Theoretical, Historical and Statistical Analysis of the Capitalist Process.* New York: McGraw Hill, 1939.
Scott, Theodore. *A Description of South Australia with Sketches of New South Wales, Port Lincoln, Port Philip and New Zealand.* Glasgow: Campbell, 1839.
Scott, Tom and Robert W. Scribner, eds. *The German Peasants' War: A History in Documents.* Atlantic Heights, NJ: Humanities Press, 1991).
Sen, Amartya. *Poverty and Famines: An Essay on Entitlements and Deprivation.* Oxford: Clarendon, 1982.
Slomka, Jan. *From Serfdom to Self-Government: Memoirs of a Polish Village Mayor, 1842–1927*, trans. William John Rose. London: Minerva Publishing Co., 1941.
Smith, Adam. *An Enquiry into the Nature and Causes of the Wealth of Nations* (1776). New York: Random House, 1937. http://www.marxists.org/reference/archive/smith-adam/works/wealth-of-nations/index.htm.
———. *Theory of Moral Sentiments (*1790). http://www.econlib.org/library/Smith/smMS1.html.
Smith, Captain John. *Advertisements for the Inexperienced Planters of New England.* Printed by John Haviland, London, 1631. http://www.winthropsociety.com/doc_adverts.php.
Smith, Charlotte Fell. *John Dee 1527 to 1608 (*1909). London: Kessinger, 2004.
Smith, Thomas. *De Republica Anglorum.* London: Midleton, 1583. http://www.constitution.org/eng/repang.htm.
Solzhenitsyn, Alexander. *The Gulag Archipelago, 1918–1956.* New York: Harper & Row, 1979.
Staden, Heinrich von. *The Land and Government of Muscovy: A Sixteenth-Century Account*, trans. Thomas Esper. Stanford, CA: Stanford University Press, 1967.
Steinbeck, John. *The Grapes of Wrath.* London: Penguin, 2001.
Stewart, A.T. Q. *The Narrow Ground: The Roots of Conflict in Ulster.* London: Faber, 1989.
Stewart, Rory. *Occupational Hazards: My Time Governing in Iraq.* London: Picador, 2006.
Stites, Richard. *Revolutionary Dreams: Utopian Vision and Experimental Life in the Russian Revolution.* Oxford: Oxford University Press, 1988.
Stowe, Harriet Beecher. *A Key to Uncle Tom's Cabin.* Boston: John P. Jewett, 1854. http://utc.iath.virginia.edu/uncletom/key/kyhp.html.

Sunderland, Willard. *Taming the Wild Field: Colonization and Empire on the Russian Steppe*. Ithaca and London: Cornell University Press, 2004.

Tawney, R. H. *The Agrarian Problem in the Sixteenth Century*. London: Longmans, Green and Co, 1912.

———. *Religion and the Rise of Capitalism*. London: John Murray, 1926.

Temple, Philip. *A Sort of Conscience: The Wakefields*. Auckland, NZ: Auckland University Press, 2002.

The Economic History of Britain since 1700, Vol. I: 1700–1860, Roderick Floud and D. N. McCloskey, eds. Cambridge: Cambridge University Press, 1994.

Thévenot, Jean de. *Relation d'un voyage fait au Levant: dans laquelle il est curieusement traité des Estats sujets au Grand Seigneur*. Rouen, 1665. http://gallica.bnf.fr/ark:/12148/bpt6k85317c.

Thirsk, Joan, ed. *Agricultural Change, Policy and Practice*, vol. 3 in *The Agrarian History of England and Wales*. Cambridge: Cambridge University Press, 1967.

Thomas, Stephen. *Foreign Intervention and China's Industrial Development, 1870–1911*. Boulder, CO: Westview Press, 1984.

Thorbecke, Erick and Henry Wan. *Taiwan's Development Experience: Lessons on the Roles of Government and Market*. Boston: Kluwer, 1999.

Tocqueville, Alexis de. *Democracy in America*, vol. 1, trans. Henry Reeve and John C. Spencer. New York: J. & H. G. Langley, 1841. http://archive.org/details/democracyiname01tocq.

Tolstoy, Leo. "How Much Land Does a Man Need?" http://www.online-literature.com/tolstoy/2738/.

Trevor-Roper, Hugh. *The Crisis of the Seventeenth Century: Religion, the Reformation and Social Change*. London: Macmillan, 1967.

Turner, J. Neville, and Pamela Williams, eds. *The Happy Couple: Law and Literature*. London: Federation Press, 1994. "Rhetoric and the Law of Inheritance" by Andrew Buck.

Uyar, Mesut and Edward J. Erikson. *A Military History of the Ottomans: From Osman to Atatürk*. Santa Barbara, CA: Greenwood, 2009.

Vanoli, André. *A History of National Accounting*. Lansdale, PA: IOS Press, 2005.

Veblen, Thorstein. *Theory of the Leisure Class*. Fairford, United Kingdom: Echo, 2007.

Vries, Jan de. *The Dutch Rural Economy in the Golden Age, 1500–1700*. New Haven, CT: Yale University Press, 1974.

Wakefield, Edward Gibbon. *A View on the Art of Colonization*. London: Parker, 1849.

Wakefield, Edward Gibbom [anon]. *England and America: A Comparison of the Political and Social States of Both Nations*. London: Bentley, 1837.

Waldron, Jeremy. *The Right to Private Property*. Oxford: Clarendon, 1988.

Walinsky, Louis, ed. *Agrarian Reform as Unfinished Business, the Selected Papers of Wolf Ladejinsky*. London: Oxford University Press, 1977.

Wallace, Donald Mackenzie. *Russia* (1905). http://www.gutenberg.org/files/1349/1349-h/1349-h.htm.

Warriner, Dorothy. *Land Reform in Principle and Practice*. Oxford: Clarendon, 1969.

Washington, George. *The Writings of George Washington,* ed. Worthington Chauncey Ford. New York and London: G. P. Putnam's Sons, 1889. http://oll.libertyfund.org/?option=com_staticxt&staticfile=show.php%3Ftitle=2377&chapter=225005&layout=html&Itemid=27.

Weaver, John C. *The Great Land Rush and the Making of the Modern World 1650–1900.* Montreal: McGill-Queen's University Press, 2003.

Weller, Peter. *Ernest Bevin.* Manchester: Manchester University Press, 1993.

Wells, David A. *Recent Economic Changes and Their Effect on Production and Distribution of Wealth and Well-Being of Society.* New York: Appleton, 1891.

White, Lawrence. *The Clash of Economic Ideas: The Great Policy Debates and Experiments of the Last Hundred Years.* New York: Cambridge University Press, 2012.

Williams, Penry. *Life in Tudor England.* London: Batsford, 1964.

Williams, Roger. *A Key to the Languages of America* (1643). Providence, RI: Rhode Island Historical Society, 1827.

Wilson, James Grand and John Fiske, eds. *Appleton's Cyclopedia of American Biography,* vol. 2. New York: Appleton, 1887.

Winslow, Edward. *Good Newes from New England* (1624). Carlisle, MA: Applewood Books, 1996.

Winthrop Papers. Boston: Massachusetts Historical Society, 1929–1992.

Winthrop, Robert C. *Life and Letters of John Winthrop.* Boston: Ticknor & Fields, 1864.

World Bank. *World Development Report 1991.* Oxford: World Bank and Oxford University Press, 1991.

Zamolski, Adam. *The Polish Way.* London: John Murray, 1987.

Zelin, Madeleine. *The Magistrate's Tael: Rationalizing Fiscal Reform in Eighteenth-Century Ch'ing China.* Berkeley, CA: University of California Press, 1985.

Journals

Allen, Robert C. "Agricultural Productivity and Rural Incomes in England and the Yangtze Delta, c. 1620–c. 1820." *The Economic History Review* 62, no. 3 (Aug. 2009): 525–550.

——. "Involution, Revolution, or What? Agricultural Productivity, Income, and Chinese Economic Development." *Citeseer online.* http://citeseerx.ist.psu.edu/viewdoc/summary?doi=10.1.1.196.563.

——. "The Price of Freehold Land and the Interest Rate in the Seventeenth and Eighteenth Centuries." *The Economic History Review, New Series* 41, no. 1 (Feb. 1988).

Allen, R. C., J.-P. Bassino, D. Ma, C. Moll-Murata, and J.-L. van Zanden-. "Wages, Prices, and Living Standards in China, Japan, and Europe, 1738–1925." *LSE Research online* (2009). http://eprints.lse.ac.uk/27871/1/WP123.pdf.

Altman, Morris. "Land Tenure, Ethnicity, and the Condition of Agricultural Income and Productivity in Mid-Nineteenth-Century Quebec." *Agricultural History* 72, no. 4 (Autumn 1998).

Anderson, Gary M. and Dorothy T. Martin.—"The Public Domain and Nineteenth Century Transfer Policy." *Cato Journal* 6, no. 3 (Winter 1987).

Bagchi, Amiya Kumar. "Contesting Models of East Asian Development and Financial Liberalization: A Case Study of South Korea." *Social Scientist* 36, no. 9/10 (Sep.–Oct. 2008).

Barlow, John Perry. "The Economy of Ideas: A Framework for Patents and Copyrights in the Digital Age." *Wired* (Mar. 1994).

Bart, James, *et al.* "The Rise and Fall of the Mortgage and Credit Markets." Milken Institute, 2009.

Beck, Hermann. "The Social Policies of Prussian Officials: The Bureaucracy in a New Light." *The Journal of Modern History* 64, no. 2 (June 1992).

Behdad, Sohrab. "A Disputed Utopia: Islamic Economics in Revolutionary Iran." *Comparative Studies in Society and History* 36, no. 4 (Oct. 1994).

Brenner, Robert. "Agrarian Class Structure and Economic Development in Pre-industrial Europe." *Past & Present* 70 (1976).

———."The Agrarian Roots of European Capitalism." *Past & Present* 97 (Nov. 1982).

Broadberry, Stephen, Bruce Campbell, and B. van Leeuwen. "Arable Acreage in England 1270–1871." *Reconstructing the National Income of Britain and Holland, c. 1270/1500 to 1850.* Leverhulme Trust, Ref f/100215AR.

Brophy, James M. "*Salus publica suprema lex*: Prussian Businessmen in the New Era and Constitutional Conflict." *Central European History* 28, no. 2 (1995).

Brosnan, Sarah and Frans B. M. de Waal, "Monkeys reject unequal pay." *Nature* 428, 140 (Mar. 2004).

Byres, Terence J. "The Landlord Class, Peasant Differentiation, Class Struggle and the Transition to Capitalism: England, France and Prussia Compared." School of Oriental and African Studies, University of London. Paper for Land, Poverty, Social Justice & Development conference, Jan. 2006.

Carter, Goodrich. "National Planning of Internal Improvements." *Political Science Quarterly* 63, no. 1 (Mar. 1948).

Chen, Albert H. Y. "The Law of Property and the Evolving System of Property Rights in China" (May 25, 2010).

Clark, Gregory. "Commons Sense: Common Property Rights, Efficiency, and Institutional Change." *The Journal of Economic History* 58, no. 1 (Mar. 1998).

Cobban, Alfred J. "The Fundamental Ideas of Robespierre." *The English Historical Review* 63, no. 246 (Jan. 1948).

Diamond, Larry. "Economic Development and Democracy Reconsidered." *American Behavioral Scientist* 15 (Mar–June 1992).

Dore, R. P. "Beyond the Land Reform: Japan's Agricultural Prospect." *Pacific Affairs* 36, no. 3 (Autumn 1963).

Dunstan, Helen. "Orders Go Forth in the Morning and Are Changed by Nightfall: A Monetary Policy Cycle in Qing China, November 1744–June 1745." *T'oung Pao,* Second Series, 82, Fasc. ⅓ (1996).

Fuente, Alejandro de la. "Slave Law and Claims-Making in Cuba: The Tannenbaum Debate Revisited." *Law and History Review* 22, no. 2 (Summer 2004).

Fukuyama, Francis. "Reflections on the End of History, Five Years Later." *History and Theory* 34, no. 2, Theme Issue 34: World Historians and Their Critics (May 1995).

Gallman, Robert E. "Changes in Total U.S. Agricultural Factor Productivity in the Nineteenth Century." *Agricultural History* 46, no. 1, American Agriculture, 1790–1840: A Symposium (Jan. 1972).

Gjerstad, Steven and Vernon L. Smith. "Household Cycles and Economic Cycles, 1920–2010." Economic Science Institute. Chapman University, CA. 2010.

Glahn, Richard von. "Myth and Reality of China's Seventeenth-Century Monetary Crisis." *The Journal of Economic History*, 56, no. 2 (June 1996).

Goldstone, Jack A. "East and West in the Seventeenth Century: Political Crises in Stuart England, Ottoman Turkey, and Ming China." *Comparative Studies in Society and History* 30, no. 1 (Jan. 1988).

Gonzalez, Mike. "The Resurrections of Che Guevara." *International Socialist* Issue 77 (1997).

Gray, Marion. "Prussia in Transition: Society and Politics under the Stein Reform Ministry of 1808." *Transactions of the American Philosophical Society, New Series* 76, no. 1 (1986).

Griffiths, Trevor, Philip A. Hunt, and Patrick K. O'Brien. "Inventive Activity in the British Textile Industry, 1700–1800." *Journal of Economic History* 52, no. 4 (Dec. 1992).

Gudrais, Elizabeth. "Unequal America." *Harvard Magazine* (July–August 2006).

Habakkuk, John. "The Rise and Fall of English Landed Families, 1600–1800." *Transactions of the Royal Historical Society, Fifth Series* 29 (1979).

Hagen, William. "Descent of the Sonderweg: Hans Rosenberg's History of Old-Regime." *Central European History* 24, no. 1 (1991).

Hamburg, Gary M. "Peasant Emancipation and Russian Social Thought: The Case of Boris N. Chicherin." *Slavic Review* 50, no. 4 (Winter 1991).

Harmon, Alexandra. "American Indians and Land Monopolies in the Gilded Age." *The Journal of American History* 90, no. 1 (June 2003).

Heaton, Herbet. "Financing the Industrial Revolution." *Bulletin of the Business Historical Society* 11, no. 1 (Feb. 1937).

Heilbroner, Robert. "The Embarrassment of Economics." *Challenge* 39, no. 6, 1996.

Hidden, Norman. "Jethro Tull I, II, and III." *Agricultural History Review* 37, pt. 1 (1989).

Hilaire-Perez, Liliane. Technological and Legal Transfers in the Age of Enlightenment." *La Revue de la Musée des Arts et des Métiers,* no. 12 (Sept. 1995).

Hobsbawm, E. J. "Peasant Land Occupations." *Past & Present,* no. 62 (Feb. 1974): 120–152.

Hunt, David. "The People and Pierre Dolivier: Popular Uprisings in the Seine-et-Oise Department (1791–1792)." *French Historical Studies* 11, no. 2 (Autumn 1979).

Ives, E. W. "The Genesis of the Statute of Uses." *English Historical Review* 82, no. 325 (Oct. 1967).

Jevons, W. S. "Richard Cantillon and the Nationality of Political Economy." *Contemporary Review* (January 1881). http://files.libertyfund.org/econtalk/Cantillon Nature/SingleChaps/Jevons.pdf.

Johnston, Bruce F. and John W. Mellor. "The Role of Agriculture in Economic Development." *The American Economic Review* 51, no. 4 (Sep. 1961).

Jones, James R.; Shuang L. Li, Stephen Devadoss, and Charlotte Fedane. "The Former Soviet Union and the World Wheat Economy." *American Journal of Agricultural Economics* 78, no. 4 (Nov. 1996).

Kawagoe, Toshihiko. "Agricultural Land Reform in Postwar Japan." *Policy Research Working Paper 2111*; World Bank Development Research Group, 1999.

Kerridge, Eric. "The Movement of Rent, 1540–1640." *Economic History Review*, 2nd ser., VI (1953).

Kindleberger, Charles P. "Sweden in 1850 as an 'Impoverished Sophisticate': Comment." *The Journal of Economic History* 42, no. 4 (Dec. 1982).

Kitagawa, Joseph M. "The Japanese 'Kokutai' (National Community) History and Myth." *History of Religions* 13, no. 3 (Feb. 1974).

Koo, Anthony Y. C. "Economic Consequences of Land Reform in Taiwan." *Asian Survey* 6, no. 3 (Mar. 1966): 150–157.

Kutscher, Robert. "Historical Trends 1950–92, and Current Uncertainties." *Monthly Labor Review* (Nov. 1993).

Kurtz, Marcus J. "Understanding Peasant Revolution: From Concept to Theory and Case." *Theory and Society* 29, no. 1 (Feb. 2000): 93–124.

Lane, P. "Native Title—the End of Property As We Know It?" *Australian Property Law Journal* 1 (2000).

Law, David S. and Mila Versteeg. "The Declining Influence of the United States Constitution." *New York University Law Review* 87, no. 3 (2012).

Lerner, Josh. "Patent Protection and Innovation Over 150 Years." *NBER Working Paper No. w8977* (June 2002).

Levi-Faur, David. "Friedrich List and the Political Economy of the Nation-state." *Review of International Political Economy* 4, no. 1 (Spring 1997).

Lipset, Martin Seymour. "Some Social Requisites of Democracy: Economic Development and Political Legitimacy." *The American Political Science Review* 53, no. 1 (Mar. 1959).

MacLeod, Christine. "The Paradoxes of Patenting: Invention and Its Diffusion in 18th- and 19th-Century Britain, France, and North America." *Technology and Culture* 32, no. 4, Patents and Invention (Oct. 1991).

Marr, William. "Nineteenth Century Tenancy Rates in Ontario's Counties, 1881 and 1891." *Journal of Social History* 21, no. 4 (Summer 1988).

Maryamov, G. "Kremlevskii Tsenzor." *Revolutionary Democracy* 3, no. 2 (Sep. 1997).

McConnell, Allen. "The Empress and Her Protégé: Catherine II and Radischev." *The Journal of Modern History* 36, no. 1 (Mar. 1964).

Mills, James. "Tenants and Agriculture near Dublin in the Fourteenth Century." *Journal of the Royal Society of Antiquaries of Ireland* 16 (1894).

Möller, Jens. "Towards Agrarian Capitalism: The Case of Southern Sweden during the 19th Century." *Geografiska Annaler. Series B, Human Geography*, 72, no. 2–3 (1990).

Moon, David. "Peasant Migration and the Settlement of Russia's Frontiers, 1550–1897." *The Historical Journal* 40, no. 4 (Dec. 1997).

Mossoff, Adam. "Rethinking the Development of Patents: An Intellectual History, 1550–1800." Occasional Papers in Intellectual Property and Communications Law, *Hastings Law Journal* 1255 (2001).

Norris, J. M. "Samuel Garbett and the Early Development of Industrial Lobbying in Great Britain." *Economic History Review, New Series* 10, no. 3 (1958).

O'Rourle, Kevin H. "Late 19th Century Denmark in an Irish Mirror: Land Tenure, Homogeneity and the Roots of Danish Success." *NBER Working Paper* (2005).

Pak, Ki Hyuk. "Outcome of Land Reform in the Republic of Korea." *Journal of Farm Economics* 38, no. 4 (Nov. 1956).

Pamuck, Sevket. "The Price Revolution in the Ottoman Empire Reconsidered." *International Journal of Middle East Studies* 33, no. 1 (Feb. 2001): 69–89.

Piketty, Tomas and Emmanuel Saez. "Income Inequality in the United States, 1913–1998." *Quarterly Journal of Economics* 118, no. 1 (2003).

Piketty, Thomas and Emmanuel Saez. "The Evolution of Top Incomes: A Historical and International Perspective." *NBER Working Paper No. 11955.*

Rabushka, Alvin. "A Tax Revolt, First and Foremost." *Hoover Digest No. 4.* Hoover Institution on War, Revolution and Peace (Oct. 2008).

Raup, Philip M. "Corporate Farming in the United States." *The Journal of Economic History* 33, no. 1, The Tasks of Economic History (Mar. 1973).

———. "Economic Development and Competition for Land Use in the United States." *Journal of Farm Economics* 39, no. 5, Proceedings of the Annual Meeting of the American Farm Economic Association (Dec. 1957).

Retallack, James. "Anti-Semitism, Conservative Propaganda, and Regional Politics in Late Nineteenth Century Germany." *German Studies Review* 11, no. 3 (Oct. 1988).

Robertson, Mary L. "Profit and Purpose in the Development of Thomas Cromwell's Landed Estates." *The Journal of British Studies* 29, no. 4, (Oct. 1990).

Rostow, Walt W. "The Stages of Economic Growth." *The Economic History Review, New Series* 12, no. 1 (1959).

———. "The Take-Off into Self-Sustained Growth." *The Economic Journal* 66, no. 261 (Mar. 1956).

Rothenberg, Winifred B. "The Emergence of a Capital Market in Rural Massachusetts, 1730–1838." *The Journal of Economic History* 45, no. 4 (Dec. 1985).

Saul, Norman E. "The Migration of the Russian-Germans to Kansas." *Kansas Historical Quarterly* 40, no. 1 (Spring 1974).

Shiller, Robert J. "Housing Bubbles Are Few and Far Between." *New York Times,* Feb. 6, 2011.

Sims, Richard. "Japanese Fascism." *History Today* 32, no. 1 (1982).

Slaughter, M. M. "Sacred Kingship and Antinomianism: Antirrhesis and the Order of Things." *Cardozo Studies in Law and Literature* 4, no. 2 (Autumn 1992).

Story, Judge Joseph. "An Address Delivered Before Members of the Suffolk Bar." *The American Jurist and Law Magazine* 1, ed. Charles Sumner. Boston: Freeman & Bolles, 1829.

Sundarland, Willard. "Peasant Pioneering: Russian Peasant Settlers Describe Col-

onization and the Eastern Frontier, 1880s–1910." *Journal of Social History* 34, no. 4 (Summer 2001).
Taylor, E. G. R. "A Letter from Mercator to John Dee." *Imago Mundi* 13 (1956).
Véron, Luis. "The Demographics of Global Corporate Champions." *Bruegel*; Brussels, 2008.
Weaver, John. "The Globalization of Property Rights: An Anglo and American Frontier Land Paradigm, 1700–1900." *Working Paper 00/1* McMaster University (2000).
White, Eugene N. "Lessons from the Great American Real Estate Boom and Bust of the 1920s." *NBER Working Paper No, 15573,* National Bureau of Economic Research (2009).
Whittle, J. "Lords and Tenants in Kett's Rebellion 1549." *Past & Present* 207, no. 1 (2010).
Zhang, Jiayan. "Environment, Market, and Peasant Choice: The Ecological Relationships in the Jianghan Plain in the Qing and the Republic." *Modern China* 32, no. 1 (Jan. 2006).
Ziblatt, Daniel. "Shaping Democratic Practice and the Causes of Electoral Fraud: The Case of Germany Before 1914." *OCSID Working Paper 04*; Oxford Centre for the Study of Inequality and Democracy (2005).

Online Sources

Allen, Robert C., "The High Wage Economy of Pre-Industrial Britain." http://www.helsinki.fi/iehc2006/papers2/Allen77.pdf.
Barry, Michael. "Standards for Oral Tradition Evidence: Guidelines From First Nations Land Claims in Canada" (Talk, University of Calgary, to the International Federation of Surveyors, October 1999). http://www.fig.net/pub/vietnam/papers/ts02a/ts02a_barry_3644.pdf.
BBC. "A Short History of Ireland." http://www.bbc.co.uk/northernireland/ashorthistory/archive/intro100.shtml.
Brittan, Samuel. "A Backward Glance: The Reappraisal of the 1960s" (lecture, Institute of Contemporary British History, April 1997). http://www.samuelbrittan.co.uk/spee4_p.html.
The Code of Hammurabi. http://avalon.law.yale.edu/ancient/hamframe.asp.
Coulton, Barbara. "Cromwell and the 'Readmission' of the Jews to England, 1656." http://www.olivercromwell.org/jews.pdf.
Harper, Douglas. "Slavery in the North." http://www.slavenorth.com/slavenorth.htm.
Haydon, Edwin. "Chinese Customary Law in Hong Kong's New Territories: some Legal Premises." http://hkjo.lib.hku.hk/exhibits/show/hkjo/browseArticle?book=b27720780&issue=440048.
Kenny, Charles. "How Patent Laws are Stifling American Growth.". *Bloomberg News,* February 24, 2013. http://www.businessweek.com/articles/2013-02-24/how-patent-laws-are-stifling-american-growth.

Lee, Yoolim. "Getting Rich in Malaysia, Cronyism Capital Means Dayak Lose Home." *Bloomberg News*, August 24, 2009. http://www.bloomberg.com/apps/news?pid=newsarchive&sid=aBC4ld4jmdV4.

Lerner, Josh. "The Patent System and Competition: A Statement to the Federal Trade Commission/Department of Justice Hearings on Competition and Intellectual Property Law and Policy in the Knowledge-Based Economy." Harvard University and National Bureau of Economic Research (2003).

Macfarlane, Alan. "The Strife of Two Great Tides: The Harlakenden Case." www.alanmacfarlane.com/TEXTS/Strife.pdf.

Munro, John. "The Monetary Origins of the 'Price Revolution': South German Silver Mining, Merchant Banking and Venetian Commerce, 1460–1540." Working paper, Dept. of Economics, University of Toronto (2003). http://ideas.repec.org/p/tor/tecipa/munro-99-02.html.

Overton, Richard. "An Arrow Against All Tyrants." http://oll.libertyfund.org/?option=com_staticxt&staticfile=show.php%3Ftitle=2252.

Penn, William. "Charter of Liberties," April 25, 1682. http://avalon.law.yale.edu/17th_century/pa03.asp#1.

The Qianlong emperor's letter to King George III. http://www.fordham.edu/halsall/mod/1793qianlong.html.

"The Records of Earls Colne." http://linux02.lib.cam.ac.uk/earlscolne/cprolls2/.

Smith, Gerald. "God and the Land: Natural Theology and Natural History in America" (lecture, Sewanee, the University of the South). http://www.touroinstitute.com/Religion%20and%20Ecology.pdf.

Stavis, Ben. "Wolf Ladejinsky, Tireless (and Frustrated) Advocate of Land Reform." Temple University, PA (2004). http://astro.temple.edu/~bstavis/courses/215-ladejinsky.htm.

Ulozhenie Law Code of 1649. http://pages.uoregon.edu/kimball/1649-Ulj.htm.Ward, James P. "Prices of Weapons and Munitions in Early Sixteenth Century Holland during the Guelders War." Unpublished doctoral thesis, "The Cities and States of Holland. A participative system of government under strain" (University of Leiden, 2001). https://docs.google.com/viewer?a=v&q=cache:zBNd3e85DFUJ:james.wardware.com/J-Europ-Econ-Hist.pdf+&hl=en&gl=uk&pid=bl&srcid=ADGEESgXKVrv—3v81gkVOOJ4k7aFQvurmS7VVkntcC9XjGQ6bIxUEU6AMhQduyJiEpDF4QtAIdTpw5QRvltSV9GBkuK_J8Z5QUzbK41T8G7WLvmg_9EB2qqixh0oZ1SB4i39q9D7S9I&sig=AHIEtbTBW2wr-MDg2CQCKB3oWuaOoMLn_g.

White, Horace. "The Foundation of Beloit City." http://www.beloit.edu/~libhome/Archives/papers/beloitbegin.html.

Index

A NOTE ON THE AUTHOR

Andro Linklater is the acclaimed author of *Measuring America, The Fabric of America, An Artist in Treason* and *Why Spencer Perceval Had to Die*. He lives in England.